DON'T COUNT ON IT!

DON'T COUNT ON IT!

Reflections on INVESTMENT ILLUSIONS,
CAPITALISM, "MUTUAL" FUNDS, INDEXING,
ENTREPRENEURSHIP, IDEALISM, *and* HEROES

JOHN C. BOGLE

WILEY

John Wiley & Sons, Inc.

Published by John Wiley & Sons, Inc., Hoboken, New Jersey.
Published simultaneously in Canada.

For general information on our other products and services or for technical support, please contact our Customer Care Department within the United States at (800) 762-2974, outside the United States at (317) 572-3993 or fax (317) 572-4002.

Wiley also publishes its books in a variety of electronic formats. Some content that appears in print may not be available in electronic books. For more information about Wiley products, visit our web site at www.wiley.com.

Library of Congress Cataloging-in-Publication Data:

Bogle, John C.
    Don't count on it! : reflections on investment illusions, capitalism, "mutual" funds, indexing, entrepreneurship, idealism, and heroes / John C. Bogle.
        p.   cm.
    Includes index.
    ISBN 978-0-470-64396-9 (cloth); ISBN 978-0-470-94900-9 (ebk);
    ISBN 978-0-470-94901-6 (ebk); ISBN 978-0-470-94902-3 (ebk)
        1. Investments.   2. Portfolio management.   3. Business mathematics.   I. Title.
HG4515.B64 2010
332.6—dc22
                                                                                2010033295

Printed in the United States of America

10 9 8 7 6 5 4 3 2 1

Dedicated to my family:
The generations that came before,
The generations that light up my life today,
The generations yet to come.

Contents

Foreword

Did someone say, *Don't count on it?* Or was it, don't count on *them?* As everybody knows, America's vaunted financial system let us down big-time during the raucous decade of the 2000s. The decade began with the spectacular stock market crash of 2000–2002, as corporate will-o'-the wisps, previously hyped by unscrupulous "analysts" who should have known (and did know!) better, collapsed before our eyes. That searing financial shock was followed in close order by the accounting scandals at Enron, WorldCom, and others in 2001–2002, the mutual fund scandals in 2003, and then, of course, the mother of all financial collapses: the stunning series of financial crises that started in the summer of 2007 and eventually brought the entire financial system to the brink of ruin and the world economy to its knees. With all this going on, you might have thought that America's leaders, both political and financial, would have been frequently out on the hustings giving both detailed explanations and copious apologies. But you would have been wrong. The silence has been deafening.

Enter Jack Bogle, the conscience of Wall Street, if that's not an oxymoron. More accurately, Bogle never left. His relentless voice, sharp pen, and indefatigable energy have been prodding the mutual fund industry in particular, and the financial industry more generally, to embrace higher business, fiduciary, and ethical standards for decades. Indeed, the essay that lends its name to this volume originated as a speech at Princeton University (Bogle's *alma mater* and mine) in 2002, and a few of the others are older than that. Our financial leaders and public officials had plenty of time to set things straight. Would that they had listened to Bogle more. But, too often, his was a lonely voice in the wilderness.

That fine voice is in ample evidence here, in this worthy collection of 35 essays, many of them short and pithy. The essays range widely over the usual Bogle themes: the unconscionably high costs of financial intermediation, the disgraceful failure to abide by what should have been normal fiduciary standards, the inefficient absorption of too much high-priced talent into financial manipulation rather than into useful productive activities, the dismaying triumph of emotion over cool-headed reason in so many investment decisions, and the related—and sometimes ruinous—triumph of speculation over investment. If you've heard these themes expounded by Bogle before, listen again because the lessons still haven't sunk in. If you haven't, you're in for a real treat, for Bogle writes not only with passion and conviction, but also with verve, wit, and literary flair. Where else, in a book on finance, will you find references to (in chronological order) Horace, Benjamin Franklin, Edgar Allan Poe, and Steven Colbert?

As a veteran of the mutual fund industry, and a father of low-cost index funds, it is no surprise that Bogle directs much of his ire at the high costs of financial intermediation. He never tires of reminding investors of this fundamental identity:

$$\text{Net returns to investors} = \text{Gross returns on the assets} \\ - \text{Costs of operating the financial system}$$

The identity implies, among other things, that an investment adviser, or broker, or mutual fund manager earns his keep only if the gross returns he *adds* by "beating the market" exceed the costs he *subtracts*. Armed with reams of evidence to the contrary, Bogle is skeptical that this happens often. In Chapter 4, for example, he estimates that, in 2007, the costs of intermediation in securities came to a staggering $528 billion. That was 3.8 percent of GDP and, by remarkable coincidence, almost exactly the amount of money that all businesses in America spent that year on new factories, offices, and stores. Were the benefits worth the brobding-nagian costs? Bogle thinks not and he's probably right. It will not surprise you to see the virtues of indexing—principally, the reduction of transactions costs—extolled by the man who brought us Vanguard. He should know—and he does.

The duties of a fiduciary have always commanded a central place in the Bogle pantheon of virtue and vice—and so it is here, in several essays that display both his strong moral sense and his limitless backbone. After all, as Bogle reminds us in the title of Chapter 19 (and elsewhere), "No man can serve two masters." (Too bad so many Wall Streeters served more than two.) According to St. Jack, as he is sometimes called, "Fiduciary duty is the highest duty known to the law." It requires, among other things, that the fiduciary "act at all times for the sole benefit and interests of the principal" and never "put personal interests before that duty" or "be placed in a situation where his fiduciary duty to clients conflicts with a fiduciary duty to any other entity." Can you imagine how much milder the financial crisis would have been if Wall Street had adhered to those simple precepts? If not, read Bogle's essays on the subject. You'll see.

I could go on, but you've picked up this book to read Bogle, not Blinder. Let me just close with a wistful thought that sticks in my mind after reading these essays.

Once the financial cataclysm of 2007–2009 had passed its nadir, in about March 2009, policymakers, financial market experts, scholars, and others could turn their attention away from the emergency measures needed to prevent a total meltdown, and start thinking about the long-lasting structural reforms needed to build a sturdier *and fairer* financial system. It was a great national debate, which has already produced the landmark Dodd-Frank Wall Street Reform and Consumer Protection Act of 2010. And it's not over. As the debate has progressed, I must confess to a mischievous and, frankly, somewhat undemocratic thought: Wouldn't it be better just to turn the whole thing over to a small group of wise heads like Jack Bogle? When you finish this book, you'll see why.

ALAN S. BLINDER
Gordon S. Rentschler Memorial Professor of
Economics at Princeton University
Co-Director of the Princeton Center for
Economic Policy Studies
Former Vice-Chairman, Federal Reserve Board

Princeton, NJ
May 2010

Introduction

Our society has put its trust in numbers without realizing how ephemeral they often are and how easy it is to manipulate them. We've taken the status quo for granted, blithely projecting yesterday's trends and today's circumstances into the future, even the distant future. These deceptions played a major role in our unwillingness to recognize the profound flaws that have developed in modern-day capitalism. But the global financial crisis and the stock market collapse of 2007–2009 have finally forced us to examine those flaws. As the past three years have demonstrated, ignoring reality comes with a cost. This book attempts to explain how our society got to the place it is today and how we can begin to repair the widespread damage we have suffered.

More broadly, *Don't Count on It!* is a book about how we deceive ourselves, and the consequences our society suffers when we fail to accept the realities of life. The purpose of the book is to present an anecdotal account of recent financial history, rife with examples of self-deception. *Don't Count on It!* also aims to encourage our citizens to better understand our complex financial system—to examine it, to debate it, to challenge it, and to fulfill our duty to ask simple questions and demand answers that are understandable, intelligent, and above all, wise.

Clearly, we deceived ourselves by ignoring the forces that would lead to the disastrous recession that began in 2008. While I didn't predict the housing meltdown that initiated the recession, I warned in October 2007 that such an unpredictable event had become a near certainty. The main clues were soaring debt; extreme market swings fostered by the triumph of speculation over investment; a shift from an economy focused on services to one dominated by finance; and a massive increase in financial complexity.

Well before disaster struck, I questioned what proved to be the catastrophic creation of credit default swaps (CDSs), collateralized debt obligations (CDOs), and structured investment vehicles (SIVs), which together played a starring role in the stock market crash and economic collapse of 2008–2009. In 2007, I worried about the impact of these "mind-bogglingly complex and expensive" products, and warned, "Now is the time to face up to these realities." The Dodd-Frank legislation that was signed into law by President Obama in July 2010 represents the first attempt to reform the financial system and prevent future speculative collapses. The new reform law cannot guarantee such an outcome, but it may have made a repeat of the recent era less likely.

Part One, "Investment Illusions," describes the folly of placing too much trust in numbers, and the catastrophic consequences that can follow. Among these illusions are the absurd notions that past returns on stocks foretell the future; that mutual funds as a group can earn the market's return; that fund investors actually earn the returns reported by the funds themselves; and that we can treat the financial reports of corporate managements—buttressed by the imprimatur of their "public" accountants—as reality.

I then discuss what went wrong in "The Failure of Capitalism" (Part Two), largely the consequences of our belief—now shattered—that self-interest and free markets alone can be trusted to guide our economy and our society to optimal effectiveness. I offer some solutions aimed at repairing the widespread damage from which our nation continues to suffer. Foremost among them is the establishment of a new fiduciary society, focused on requiring institutional money manager/agents—who now control corporate America—to put the interests of their client/principals as their highest priority. It's called *stewardship*.

Here's how Anatole Kaletsky, editor-at-large of the *Times of London*, sums up where we went wrong, buttressing my analysis in the first two parts of the book:

> Keynes never published an economic forecast, and neither did Hayek, Ricardo, or Adam Smith. What economics did claim

to offer was a set of analytical tools to explain reality and suggest sensible responses to unexpected events. . . . Substituting probability distributions for observable facts does not solve the problem of uncertainty. It merely covers up the true problem . . . ignoring the role of inherent unpredictability in finance. . . .

The propensity of modern economic theory for unjustified and over-simplified assumptions allowed politicians, regulators and bankers to create for themselves the imaginary world of market fundamentalist ideology, in which . . . efficient, omniscient markets can solve all economic problems, if only the government will stand aside. . . . [But] the self-serving assumptions of efficient, self-stabilizing markets have [now] been discredited.*

The mutual fund industry, in which I have spent my entire career, has proven a major exemplar of these flaws, as suggested by the quotation marks that I use in the title of Part Three—"What's Wrong with 'Mutual' Funds." (I know of only a single fund organization—Vanguard, the company that I founded 36 years ago—that meets the definition of *mutual*: owned by its participants). Capitalizing on the investor ebullience fostered by the greatest bull market in stocks in all history, conventional actively managed mutual funds became among the fastest growing financial "products" of all times, growth built on a record that could not—and did not—recur. By the time the market boom ended early in 2000, following two decades in which annual returns on stocks averaged an incredible 16 percent, $10,000 invested in the stock market in 1980 would have grown to $183,000. And that was the end of the boom. It would be followed, as always, by bust.

The growth in industry assets during that period—driven largely by equity funds—from $135 billion to $7.3 trillion belies the fact that few mutual funds succeeded in matching those gains. In fact, it has been passive ownership of stocks, not active equity management, that has proven to be the most effective means of capturing whatever returns are generated in the stock market. And the ability to do precisely that—by simply owning virtually the entire universe of publicly

---

*Anatole Kaletsky, "The Benefits of the Bust," *Wall Street Journal*, June 19, 2010.

owned U.S. corporations through a stock market index fund (or, in the U.S. bond market, through a bond index fund)—has now been available for more than three decades.

In recent years, index mutual funds have come into their own, a development that I discuss in "What's Right with Indexing" (Part Four). Simply because of the reality of humble arithmetic—gross market return, minus investment costs, equals the (much smaller) net return that investors receive—indexing is only at the beginning of its ascent. The intellectual foundation of indexing is based—not on some notion of "efficient markets"—but on low costs, wide diversification, and tax-efficiency. That's the reality. By contrast, the intellectual foundation of active management does not exist; the superiority of active managers as a group is an illusion.

In Part Five, I address the subject of "Entrepreneurship and Innovation," where the idea that a spirit of driving determination aimed at serving the greater good of society is far more important than simply the desire for self-serving monetary gain. After all, it was more than two centuries ago that in his *Theory of Moral Sentiments*, Adam Smith, whom many believe to be the patron saint of capitalism, asked more of our business leaders:

> The private man must . . . acquire superior knowledge in his profession, and superior industry in the exercise of it. He must be patient in labour, resolute in danger, and firm in distress. These talents he must bring into public view, by the difficulty, importance, and, at the same time, good judgment of his undertakings. . . . Probity and prudence, generosity and frankness, must characterize his behaviour upon all ordinary occasions; and he must, at the same time, be forward to engage in all those situations, in which it requires the greatest talents and virtues to act with propriety, but in which the greatest applause is to be acquired by those who can acquit themselves with honour.*

---

*Adam Smith, *The Theory of Moral Sentiments* (1759; Cambridge, England: Cambridge University Press, 2002).

In mid-2010, Adam Smith's view was echoed by the *Times of London's* Kaletsky, quoting (of all people) Machiavelli, who said that honor and the greater good drive the ambitions of leaders—presumably not only politicians but entrepreneurs as well. Machiavelli "described the accumulation of worldly 'glory' as the motivating principle that drives leaders to undertake 'great enterprises' and do 'great things' on behalf of their fellow citizens and not just themselves." In my discussion of entrepreneurship, I present 17 rules for success, including a final rule that echoes Adam Smith: "Our greatest rewards come when we help to build a better world." This part of the book also looks at innovation, a topic closely related to entrepreneurship. While recent financial innovations have created fabulous profits for Wall Street, most have hurt those who invested in them. But there are exceptions, including six innovations in the mutual fund arena that have met the important criterion of serving investors.

Lest we forget, idealism has always played a role in the American tradition, and the notion that we can count things that prove transitory and unimportant at the expense of priceless ideals and values that can't be quantified takes us far from that tradition. I tackle the subject of "Idealism and the New Generation" (Part Six) in the form of exhortations to our nation's students, as they undertake the callings of the various careers that lie before them, to heed the better angels of their nature. Included here is the speech "Enough," which I later expanded into a book. Many writers and leaders who have inspired me, including Rudyard Kipling, Kurt Vonnegut, Woodrow Wilson, Theodore Roosevelt, William Shakespeare, and Winston Churchill, find their way into this part of the book.

Even as I aspire to share my values with tomorrow's leaders, I pay homage to the great mentors of my career, who inculcated in me their own high values. In Part Seven, "Heroes and Mentors"—for the dear men whom I describe there have indeed been heroes to me—I pay tribute to an extensive roster of mentors who helped me to develop my character along the long road of my career, indeed the long road of my life. The roles played in my life by Walter Morgan—my boss at Wellington Fund for 23 years—author Peter Bernstein, economist Paul Samuelson, and cardiologist Bernard Lown each merit a chapter, but every one of the 29 remarkable mentors that I list have been not only my greatest friends and supporters, but credits to their professions. History will enshrine many of them as rare icons who stood on principle during the madness of capitalism's recent era.

How to Lie with Statistics

I haven't looked at Darrell Huff's classic 1954 book, *How to Lie with Statistics*, for years. But I haven't needed to. Every day I see numbers that, if not outright lies, are gross distortions of reality. For example, consider that during the three years, 2007–2009 inclusive, operating earnings for the companies in the Standard & Poor's 500 Stock Index totaled $1.67 trillion. But after write-offs of overvalued assets, high-priced acquisitions, and other stumbles by management, reported earnings totaled just $1.17 trillion. Nearly $500 billion of earnings had vanished into thin air. (Yes, I picked that period. But I can tell you that since 1970, in which the differences between these two methods of calculating earnings began to be reported, there has not been a single year when the gap between the illusion of operating earnings and the reality of reported earnings has not existed.) Yet with almost clock-like regularity, our Wall Street investment strategists rely on operating earnings, not reported earnings, as the basis for their market valuations. Given the number of tricks in the accounting trade, even reported earnings likely overstate the reality. As the late Robert Bartley, respected longtime editor of the *Wall Street Journal*, has observed: "True profits are represented by cash—a fact—rather than reported profit—an opinion."

Our government also contributes to the distortion of reality. David Einhorn, leader of Greenlight Capital, has observed that "over the last 35 years, the government has changed the way it calculates inflation several times. . . . Using the pre-1980-method, [inflation] would be over 9 percent, compared to about 2 percent in the official statistics." Another example: The Bureau of Labor Statistics reports that our mid-2010 unemployment rate is 9.7 percent. But the number we count as unemployed excludes workers too discouraged to look for a job; part-time workers looking for full-time jobs; those who want a job but aren't actively searching for one; and those who are living on Social

Security disability benefits. If we include these unemployed souls, the unemployment rate would likely double to nearly 20 percent—30 million human beings who aren't able to find useful work. The posted unemployment rate suggests that our economy is in recession; the real rate suggests something considerably worse.

Torturing the Mutual Fund Data

Even when the figures we rely on are sound and accurate, the deliberate distortion of data to prove one's point is all too easy. As I have often observed, when one controls both the metric and the time period, the data can be, as the saying goes, "tortured until they confess." The mutual fund industry is hardly an exception to that syndrome.

Every few years, for example, the Investment Company Institute is pleased to report that fund expenses are declining. Of course, the ICI is the lobbying organization for mutual fund managers (albeit paid, finally, by mutual fund shareholders). In the 2010 reincarnation of these data, ICI research reports that "mutual fund fees and expenses have declined by half since 1990." But the fact is that fees during that period actually soared from $12 billion to $69 billion, a fivefold increase.

When the ICI purports to talk about falling fees, it is confusing fee dollars with fee rates—a wholly different metric. By the latter standard (fees as a percentage of assets), the expense ratio of equity funds has dropped from 1.00 percent to 0.86 percent. When we include their calculation of annualized sales loads—which are said to have dropped from 0.99 percent to 0.13 percent (I doubt it)—the ICI calculates that the total cost (they really mean "total cost as a percentage of assets") of purchasing equity funds has fallen from 1.98 percent in 1990 to 0.99 percent in 2009.

When we consider another equally important metric—expenses as a percentage of dividend income—the picture also shows that fee rates are not declining, but rising. Fund expenses consumed a quite-healthy-enough 19.5 percent of equity fund dividend income in 1990; by 2009, that figure had nearly doubled to 38.5 percent. (In 2000, it reached an astonishing 51 percent.) Now think of that confiscation of dividend income in the context of the fact that dividend yields, as noted earlier, have accounted for one-half of the long-term return on stocks (4.5 percent out of 9 percent). Fund fees and costs, then, are now consuming almost 40 percent of that major contributor to stock returns. With that confiscation of income, combined with today's far lower stock market yields, the average equity fund currently delivers a dividend yield of a puny 1 percent to its shareowners.

Now let's change the period selected by ICI from the short term to the long term—here, the past half-century. Even using the conventional expense ratio standard shows not a decrease, but an astonishing increase of some 60 percent. The 1960 ratio, 0.54 percent of fund assets consumed by fund expenses; the 2009 ratio, 0.86 percent. The expense-to-dividend ratio is up by more than 100 percent, from 18.3 percent of fund dividend income to 38.5 percent. During that same half-century, total equity fund fees—obviously, it is dollars that are the ultimate metric—have risen 800-fold, from $50 million in 1960 to $40 billion in 2009. While equity fund assets also rose sharply, from $10 billion to $5 trillion, or 500-fold, that increase was dwarfed by the increase in costs. Are mutual fund fees really declining, as the ICI would have you believe? *Don't count on it!*

Conclusion: The huge and widely recognized economies of scale entailed in managing other peoples' money have been largely arrogated by fund managers to their own benefit, rather than to the benefit of their fund shareholders. The illusion of falling expenses that the ICI presents through its careful selection of both time period and metric is clearly punctured by the reality: The long-term drain of rising expenses—under all three metrics—has cost fund shareholders dearly.

"A Lantern on the Stern"

Sometimes numbers are accurate and complete, covering the entire period for which they are available. (Albeit even such a period—call it "inception date to current date"—is by definition a selected period.) Yet when we rely on the past to help us foretell the future, we are all-too-likely to reach invalid conclusions. One of my favorite targets here is the giving of a Gospel-based credulity to the historical record of long-term stock market returns. The list of distortions created by such a reliance on past returns as a reference point for future returns seems almost infinite.

First, these returns are measured in nominal terms (current dollars) rather than real terms (inflation-adjusted dollars). Thus the 9.4 percent average annual nominal return on stocks over the past 50 years has increased the value of a $10,000 initial investment to $893,000 in nominal terms (including reinvested dividends). But after accounting for the 4 percent inflation rate over that period, the resultant 5.4 percent real return would result in total wealth accumulation (say, for a retiree) of $138,700. Even that sum sounds handsome—but only until you realize that it ignores investment costs and taxes, which are inevitably deducted in nominal dollars, year after year. Those costs could easily total 3 percent per year, reducing that 5.4 percent return to 2.4 percent. The value of the retirement fund now tumbles to $32,700. That's the reality for investors, and it clearly (and sadly) trumps the illusion of $893,000.

Next, the past is not prologue, simply because while the sources of future stock market returns are the same as the sources of past returns (dividend yields, earnings growth, and changes in market valuations), the numbers themselves are rarely the same. Simply put, during the past 110 years, one-half of the 9 percent long-term investment return on stocks was generated by a 4.5 percent dividend yield. So with the mid-2010 dividend yield at about 2.25 percent, we ought to reduce our expectations for future stock market returns by two percentage points or so compared to historic norms.

Notably, "Monte Carlo simulations"—which are widely used by investment professionals to forecast a range of future returns on stocks—take no account of these changes in fundamentals. Such simulations, therefore, are fatally flawed. The general failure of the financial community to recognize this simple point—as well as to face the nominal-dollar versus real-dollar issue—is intellectually dishonest, to say nothing of self-serving on the part of Wall Street, striving to put the best possible face on the potential rewards of equity investing.

But even if we accept the illusion of historical market returns as the reality, don't count on its being repeated. As *Wall Street Journal* columnist Jason Zweig has observed, the earliest stock return data for most of the 19th century "isn't really valid . . . excluding 97 percent of all the stocks that then existed . . . and including only the bluest of blue-chip survivors." (In the early part of the century, it was bank and insurance stocks that dominated the data; in the latter part, it was railroads; neither is the case today.) Even when the data takes on a greater validity beginning in 1884, with the first calculation of the Dow Jones Average, it consisted solely of 11 transportation stocks. By 1896, when the Dow Jones Industrial Average appeared, the new index was more diversified by sector, but included only 12 stocks, including American Cotton Company, American Sugar, U.S. Leather Company, and Distilling and Cattle Feeding Company, along with stalwarts American Tobacco, National Lead, and General Electric, today's sole survivor of that early average.

In the modern era, where market returns have been more carefully refined, who is really to say that the data that we now accept as Holy Writ doesn't have serious problems? The Standard and Poor's data begins in 1926, for example, but today's redoubtable S&P 500 index consisted of only 90 stocks from that inception until 1948. The University of Chicago Center for Research in Securities Prices (CRSP) has produced data purported to reflect the entire U.S. stock market (also beginning in 1926) but it excluded "over-the-counter" (NASDAQ) stocks until 1972, when the number of stocks in its market universe leaped from some 2,000 to 5,000. When one stands back and looks at the entire 84-year period for which we have what are generally accepted as valid stock return data—including only about 50 years of solid evidence—it's obvious that we're considering a relatively short period, dominated (at least until 2007) by a powerful— perhaps a once-in-a-lifetime—bull market in the most prosperous nation in the world.

But even if we could develop data on stock market returns over the past two centuries that approached perfection (i.e., reality), the idea that future returns will center around past returns is an illusion. The world changes, in ways unimaginable and unpredictable. Nations rise and fall; war and peace reorder the global society; free-market competition disrupts the old order; technology changes once-reliable ground rules. So, the past simply cannot be a reliable prologue to the future. Samuel Taylor Coleridge uncovered an important kernel of truth when he warned that history is "a lantern on the stern, which shines only on the waves behind us."

The Wisdom of the Economists

Of course we need numbers to help us to understand the past, to manage the present, and to appraise the future. But there is so much more to capitalism than numbers. Two eminent economists and a poet confirm this view. Joseph Schumpeter (1883–1950) is said to be the first economist to recognize the entrepreneur as the moving force of economic development. Schumpeter focused not on the numbers that might validate his hypothesis, nor on the financial rewards of successful entrepreneurship, but on the character and motivation of the successful entrepreneur: "First, the dream and the will to found a kingdom. Second, the will to conquer, the impulse to fight, to succeed for the sake of success; not of the fruits of success, but of success itself. Third, the joy of creating, getting things done, of simply exercising one's energy and ingenuity." I can say from personal experience that these qualities—not mere money—have been the main drivers of my own long career.

John Maynard Keynes (1883–1946), the great British economist whose theories have returned to the fore in recent years, went even further in disassociating numbers from achievement. When he put forth "animal spirits" as the basis for successful investment, he gave us a phrase that remains in common use to this day:

> . . . a large proportion of our positive activities depend on spontaneous optimism rather than on a mathematical expectation . . . whether moral or hedonistic or economic. Most, probably, of our decisions to do something positive, the full consequences of which will be drawn out over many days to come, can only be taken as a result of animal spirits—of a spontaneous urge to action rather than inaction, and not as the outcome of a weighted average of quantitative benefits multiplied by quantitative probabilities.

> Enterprise only pretends to itself to be mainly actuated by the statements in its own prospectus, however candid and sincere. Only a little more than an expedition to the South Pole, is it based on an exact calculation of benefits to come. Thus if the animal spirits are dimmed and the spontaneous optimism

falters, leaving us to depend on nothing but a mathematical expectation, enterprise will fade and die.

It is safe to say that enterprise which depends on hopes stretching into the future benefits the community as a whole. But individual initiative will only be adequate when reasonable calculation is supplemented and supported by animal spirits. . . . Human decisions affecting the future, whether personal or political or economic, cannot depend on strict mathematical expectation, since the basis for making such calculations does not exist.*

While the English author and poet Rudyard Kipling was no economist (probably just as well!), his poem "The Gods of the Copybook Headings"† beautifully captures the thinking of Schumpeter and Keynes. Here are some excerpts:

As I pass through my incarnations in every age and race,
I make my proper prostrations to the Gods of the Market Place.
Peering through reverent fingers I watch them flourish and fall,
And the Gods of the Copybook Headings, I notice, outlast them all.

We moved as the Spirit listed. They never altered their pace,
Being neither cloud nor wind-borne like the Gods of the Market Place . . .
They denied that Wishes were Horses; they denied that a Pig had Wings;
So we worshipped the Gods of the Market Who promised these beautiful things.

---

*John Maynard Keynes, *The General Theory of Employment, Interest, and Money* (New York: Macmillan, 1936; Harcourt, Brace, 1964).
†"Copybook Headings," a phrase too rarely seen in this age of sophistication and complexity, is defined as "classic proverbs and wise quotes printed at the top of each page of blank school booklets (copybooks) used for essays and handwriting practice."

Then the Gods of the Market tumbled, and their smooth-tongued wizards withdrew
And the hearts of the meanest were humbled and began to believe it was true
That All is not Gold that Glitters, and Two and Two make Four
And the Gods of the Copybook Headings limped up to explain it once more.

What Kipling is telling us is that the reality of arithmetic—"that two and two make four"—ultimately trumps the illusion of the marketplace—the "beautiful things [promised by the] smooth-tongued wizards . . . the Gods of the Market." His oft-forgotten rhymes neatly summarize the central thesis that permeates this book: that the real market of intrinsic value ultimately triumphs over the illusory expectations market of speculation, hyperbole, and self-interest.

An Increasingly Fragile World

Even if we come to understand the value of simplicity in the things that we can count on, in a world where complexity seems to actualize only the things that can be counted, we have to do our best to deal with the challenges we face in the modern—and largely untested—global society in which we exist. The challenges include the interconnectivity and interdependence of our nations; the struggles that divide the world—often between the "haves" and "have-nots," and often based, paradoxically enough, on religion—and the soaring dependence on the role of technology in our lives. Together this combination has given us an increasingly fragile world. Since the beginning of history, totally unexpected events have suddenly erupted. But today these disruptions—now often man-made—impact vast swaths of human beings.

These kinds of events have come to be known as "Black Swans," events at the outermost edge of the probabilities by which we order our lives. But other disruptions can't be measured in terms of probability; they are uncertainties, often without historical precedent. But in either case, we human beings live our day-to-day existence as if they will never occur. But they do occur, and in this fragile modern age, they occur with seemingly increasing frequency. Consider:

- The 2010 explosion of an oil-drilling rig off the Louisiana coast, poisoning the vast Gulf of Mexico with hundreds of millions of gallons of oil, destroying marine life, birds, beaches, and the livelihoods of the local populace. It took our best engineers and scientists more than five months to close down the well.
- The explosion of the *Challenger* spacecraft in 1986, the result of a single flaw in an infinitely complex engineering project.
- The devastating obliteration of the Twin Towers of New York's majestic World Trade Center in 2001. Who could have predicted that in a matter of moments, two airplanes would fly into these monuments to American finance, setting the stage for our nation's decision to launch two wars, half-way 'round the world, both, nearly a decade later, still carrying huge costs in blood and treasure?
- The overwhelming force of Hurricane Katrina in 2005—an act of Nature—combined with the failure of the levees in New Orleans—an act of man—that left one of our nation's major cities devastated.
- Global warming that could change our very way of life—higher temperatures, rising sea levels, health challenges, along with many other potentially dire changes. This warming appears—to most objective scientists—to be largely man-made, as carbon from our factories and automobiles, and lots more, become increasingly omnipresent in our lives.
- The world financial crisis that began in 2007—continuing to this day—the result of, among many other contributing factors, cheap money, high leverage, a plunge in real estate prices, the stock market crash, and immensely complex financial instruments that involved risk that seemed to be measurable but wasn't.

Yes, things that we can't imagine happening actually happen, and things we ignore because we assume that the probabilities of their happening are too remote to bother with actually happen as well. When we contemplate the possibility of a catastrophic event, as *New York Times* journalist David Leonhardt has noted, "[where] nothing like that has ever happened before, even imagining it is difficult. It is much easier to hope that the odds of such an outcome are vanishingly small. In fact it's only natural to have this hope. But that doesn't make it wise."*

Challenging the validity of accepting numbers as reality, Temple University professor and author of *Beyond Numeracy*, John Allen Paulos struck just the right balance: "No method of measuring a societal phenomenon . . . exists that can't be second-guessed, deconstructed, cheated, rejected, or replaced. This doesn't mean we shouldn't be counting—but it does mean we should do so with as much care and wisdom as we can muster."†

Our financial system is both a measure of the kind of complicated society we have become and a major participant in its complexity. As recent financial history has taught us, complexity breeds deception. It is my prayer that my mission, my crusade (if those are not too-lofty characterizations of my career) will help the financial services industry to rethink its values and accordingly be of greater service to growing millions of investors all over the globe. If we do that, quoting Virgil, "through chances various, through all vicissitudes, we make our way. . . ."‡

JOHN C. BOGLE

Valley Forge, Pennsylvania
August 2010

---

*David Leonhardt, "Spillonomics: Underestimating Risk," *New York Times* magazine, June 6, 2010.
†John Allen Paulos, "Metric Mania," *New York Times*, May 10, 2010.
‡Benjamin Graham used this epigram from *The Aeneid* to begin the first edition of *The Intelligent Investor* (1949).

A Note to the Reader

In publishing this anthology of some of the major essays and speeches that I've prepared over the past decade—a sort of companion piece to *John Bogle on Investing: The First 50 Years*, published in 2000— I decided that each chapter should stand on its own, independent of the others. Thus, readers who are interested in a particular subject can move directly to the appropriate chapter, rather than reading the book as a continuum.

Readers who prefer to begin at the beginning and read through to the end of the book will note that a number of themes recur with some frequency. Among them are references to my Princeton senior thesis on the mutual fund industry (essentially the foundation of my long career); references to John Maynard Keynes and his insight that stock market returns arise from a combination of both enterprise and speculation (the historical centerpiece of my own investment analysis); and references to the dominance of today's institutional ownership of stocks over the earlier prevalence of individual ownership. (However rarely recognized, I believe that this change is the central investment issue of our era.)

Whichever type of reader you are, I hope that repeating these themes simply underscores their importance. My goal in writing *Don't Count on It!* is not only to make you a wiser and more successful investor, but to make you more aware of the chinks in the armor of today's financial system. That system is a critical part of our economy, and in the interest of investors and our society as a whole, it must be reformed.

* * *

In bringing this, my ninth book, to publication, I want to express my deep appreciation to Emily Snyder, Sara Hoffman, and Kevin Laughlin—my staff at Vanguard's Bogle Financial Markets Research Center—for their contributions, their professionalism, and (especially) their patience and understanding. Kevin took on the demanding task of working with me in compiling the material, laboring long and hard over the manuscript, verifying each piece of data, and making many helpful suggestions. I also want to thank Pamela van Giessen and Meg Freeborn of John Wiley & Sons for their support and their editorial expertise, and to extend a special salute to Leah Spiro, who also provided expert and comprehensive editorial assistance.

J.C.B.

DON'T COUNT ON IT!

Part One

INVESTMENT ILLUSIONS

Many of the themes in this book are captured in Chapter 1, one of my favorite efforts, and broad enough to provide the book's title: *Don't Count on It!* In this opening chapter, subtitled "The Perils of Numeracy," my keynote speech delivered at the Princeton Center for Economic Policy Studies in 2002, I challenge the growing trend in our society to give numbers a credence that they simply don't deserve, all the while assigning far less importance to the things that can't be expressed with numbers—qualities such as wisdom, integrity, ethics, and commitment.

The consequences of this misperception are damaging. They lead to expectations that past financial market returns are prologue to the future (they most certainly are not!); to our bias toward optimism, evidenced in the failure of investors to consider real (after-inflation) returns in their retirement planning; to creative accounting (or is it "financial engineering"?) that produces corporate earnings numbers that we accept as reality when they are often far closer to illusion; and to the damaging toll it inflicts upon the real world of real human beings, who ultimately produce the real goods and services that our society relies upon.

In Chapter 2, I explore another of my favorite themes, "The Relentless Rules of Humble Arithmetic," an essay published in the *Financial Analysts Journal* in 2005. In the long-run, the reality of the inescapable mathematics of investing trumps the illusion reflected in the performance numbers provided by fund managers. For example, during the

1

two-decade period 1983–2003, a fund emulating the S&P 500 index earned a cumulative return of 1,052 percent, and its investors earned a return of 1,012 percent. In remarkable contrast, the average equity fund reported a cumulative return of just 573 percent, and the investors in those very same funds averaged a gain of less than one-half that amount, only 239 percent. Surely using stock market returns as a proxy for equity fund returns—to say nothing of the returns actually earned by fund investors—ignores those relentless rules. The idea that fund investors in the aggregate can capture the stock market's return has proven to be yet another investment illusion.

In Chapter 3, I combat the investment illusion that the past is prologue, pointing out that the reality is far different. In "The Telltale Chart" (actually a series of 11 charts), I focus on the pervasive power of "reversion to the mean" in the financial markets—the strong tendency of both superior investment returns and inferior returns to revert to long-term norms. This pattern is documented over long historic periods among: (1) conventional sectors of the stock market, such as large versus small stocks and value versus growth stocks; (2) both past winners and past losers in the equity fund performance derby; and (3) stock market returns in general. I also show a powerful—and, I would argue, inevitable—tendency of the stock market's total return to revert to the mean of its *investment* return (dividend yields and earnings growth). *Speculative* return—generated by increases and decreases in price-to-earnings valuations—follows the same type of pattern. But since speculative return is bereft of any underlying fundamental value, it reverts to zero over the long term. Yes, the investment returns earned by our corporations over time represent reality; speculative booms and busts, however powerful in the short run, prove in the long run to be mere illusion.

Another investment illusion is that costs don't matter. The money managers who dominate our nation's investment system seem to ignore the reality that costs do indeed matter. That self-interested choice is smart, for those management fees and trading costs have resulted in soaring profitability for America's financial sector. Financial profits leaped from 8 percent of the total earnings of the firms in the S&P 500 index in 1980 to 27 percent in 2007—33 or more percent if the earnings from the financial activities of industrial companies (i.e., GE and GMAC) are included.

The enormous costs of our financial sectors represent, as the title of Chapter 4 puts it, "A Question So Important That It Should Be Hard to Think about Anything Else." Why? Because the field of money management subtracts value from investors in the amount of the costs incurred. Ironically, the financial sector seems to prosper in direct proportion to the volume of the devilishly convoluted instruments that it creates—immensely profitable to their creators, but destructive to the wealth of those who purchase them. This complexity is also destructive to the social fabric of our society, for in order to avoid financial panic, we taxpayers (a.k.a. "government") are then required to bail them out.

Finally comes the most devious investment illusion of all: confusing the creation of real corporate intrinsic value with the ephemeral illusion of value represented by stock prices. Chapter 5—"The Uncanny Ability to Recognize the Obvious"—focuses on how important it is to recognize the obvious, especially in this difficult-to-discern difference between illusion and reality. Part of that difference is the difference between the real market of business operations and the creation of value (essentially long-term cash flows) and the expectations market of trying to anticipate the future preferences of investors. Since they simply track the stock market, even index funds face the same challenges that all investment strategies face when stock prices lose touch with reality. In the recent era, it has been speculation on stock price movements that has dominated our markets, not the reality of intrinsic value. So I reiterate my long-standing conviction: When there is a gap between illusion and reality, it is only a matter of time until reality prevails.

Chapter 1

Don't Count on It!
The Perils of Numeracy[*]

Mysterious, seemingly random, events shape our lives, and it is no exaggeration to say that without Princeton University, Vanguard never would have come into existence. And had it not, it seems altogether possible that no one else would have invented it. I'm not saying that our existence matters, for in the grand scheme of human events Vanguard would not even be a footnote. But our contributions to the world of finance—not only our unique mutual structure, but the index mutual fund, the three-tier bond fund, our simple investment philosophy, and our overweening focus on low costs—have in fact made a difference to investors. And it all began when I took my first nervous steps on the Princeton campus back in September 1947.

My introduction to economics came in my sophomore year when I opened the first edition of Paul Samuelson's *Economics: An Introductory Analysis*. A year later, as an Economics major, I was considering a topic for my senior thesis, and stumbled upon an article in *Fortune* magazine on the "tiny but contentious" mutual fund industry. Intrigued, I immediately decided it would be the topic of my thesis. The thesis in turn

---

[*]Based on my keynote speech at the "Landmines in Finance" Forum of The Center for Economic Policy Studies at Princeton University on October 18, 2002.

5

proved the key to my graduation with high honors, which in turn led to a job offer from Walter L. Morgan, Class of 1920, an industry pioneer and founder of Wellington Fund in 1928. Now one of 100-plus mutual funds under the Vanguard aegis, that classic balanced fund has continued to flourish to this day, the largest balanced fund in the world.

In that ancient era, Economics was heavily conceptual and traditional. Our study included both the elements of economic theory and the worldly philosophers from the 18th century on—Adam Smith, John Stuart Mill, John Maynard Keynes, and the like. Quantitative analysis was, by today's standards, conspicuous by its absence. (My recollection is that Calculus was not even a department prerequisite.) I don't know whether to credit—or blame—the electronic calculator for inaugurating the sea change in the study of how economies and markets work, but with the coming of the personal computer and the onset of the Information Age, today numeracy is in the saddle and rides economics. If you can't count it, it seems, it doesn't matter.

I disagree, and align myself with Albert Einstein's view: "Not everything that counts can be counted, and not everything that can be counted counts." Indeed, as you'll hear again in another quotation I'll cite at the conclusion, "to presume that what cannot be measured is not very important is blindness." But before I get to the pitfalls of measurement, to say nothing of trying to measure the immeasurable—things like human character, ethical values, and the heart and soul that play a profound role in all economic activity—I will address the fallacies of some of the measurements we use, and, in keeping with the theme of this forum, the pitfalls they create for economists, financiers, and investors.

My thesis is that today, in our society, in economics, and in finance, we place too much trust in numbers. *Numbers are not reality.* At best, they're a pale reflection of reality. At worst, they're a gross distortion of the truths we seek to measure. So first, I'll show that we rely too heavily on historic economic and market data. Second, I'll discuss how our optimistic bias leads us to misinterpret the data and give them credence that they rarely merit. Third, to make matters worse, we worship hard numbers and accept (or *did* accept!) the momentary precision of stock prices rather than the eternal vagueness of intrinsic corporate value as the talisman of investment reality. Fourth, by failing to avoid these pitfalls of the *numeric* economy, we have in fact undermined the *real* economy. Finally, I conclude that our best defenses against numerical illusions of certainty are the immeasurable, but nonetheless invaluable, qualities of perspective, experience, common sense, and judgment.

Peril #1: Attributing Certitude to History

The notion that common stocks were acceptable as investments—rather than merely speculative instruments—can be said to have begun in 1924 with Edgar Lawrence Smith's *Common Stocks as Long-Term Investments.* Its most recent incarnation came in 1994, in Jeremy Siegel's *Stocks for the Long Run.* Both books unabashedly state the case for equities and, arguably, both helped fuel the great bull markets that ensued. Both, of course, were then followed by great bear markets. Both books, too, were replete with data, but the seemingly infinite data presented in the Siegel tome, a product of this age of computer-driven numeracy, puts its predecessor to shame.

But it's not the panoply of information imparted in *Stocks for the Long Run* that troubles me. Who can be against knowledge? After all, "knowledge is power." My concern is too many of us make the implicit assumption that stock market history repeats itself when we know, deep down, that the only certainty about the equity returns that lie ahead is their very uncertainty. We simply do not know what the future holds, and we must accept the self-evident fact that historic stock market returns have absolutely nothing in common with actuarial tables.

John Maynard Keynes identified this pitfall in a way that makes it obvious:* "It is dangerous to apply to the future inductive arguments based on past experience [that's the bad news] unless one can distinguish the broad reasons for what it was" (that's the good news). For there are just two broad reasons that explain equity returns, and it takes only elementary addition and subtraction to see how they shape investment experience. The too-often ignored reality is that stock returns are shaped by (1) economics and (2) emotions.

---

*John Maynard Keynes commenting on Edgar Lawrence Smith's book (1926).

Economics and Emotions

By *economics*, I mean *investment* return (what Keynes called *enterprise**), the initial dividend yield on stocks plus the subsequent earnings growth. By *emotions*, I mean *speculative* return (Keynes's *speculation*), the return generated by changes in the valuation or discount rate that investors place on that investment return. This valuation is simply measured by the earnings yield on stocks (or its reciprocal, the price-earnings ratio).[†] For example, if stocks begin a decade with a dividend yield of 4 percent and experience earnings growth of 5 percent, the *investment* return would be 9 percent. If the price-earnings ratio rises from 15 times to 20 times, that 33 percent increase would translate into an additional *speculative* return of about 3 percent per year. Simply add the two returns together: Total return on stocks = 12 percent.[‡]

So when we analyze the experience of the Great Bull Market of the 1980s and 1990s, we discern that in each of these remarkably similar decades for stock returns, dividend yields contributed about 4 percent to the return, the earnings growth about 6 percent (for a 10 percent *investment* return), and the average *annual* increase in the price-earnings ratio was a remarkable and unprecedented 7 percent. Result: Annual stock returns of 17 percent were at the highest levels, for the longest period, in the entire 200-year history of the U.S. stock market.

---

*John Maynard Keynes, *The General Theory of Employment, Interest, and Money* (New York: Macmillan, 1936; Harcourt, Brace, 1964), Chapter 12. This chapter makes as good reading today as when I first read it as a Princeton student in 1950. Interestingly, in the light of the thesis that I present in this essay, Keynes introduced these concepts with no quantification whatsoever. So I have taken the liberty of inserting the appropriate data.

[†] The earnings yield is also influenced by the risk-free bond yield. But because that relationship is so erratic, I have ignored it. For the record, however, the correlation between the earnings yield on stocks and the U.S. Treasury intermediate-term bond since 1926 has been 0.42. However, for the past 25 years it was 0.69, and for the past 10 years 0.53.

[‡] I recognize that one should actually multiply the two (i.e., $1.09 \times 1.03 = 1.123$), obviously a small difference. But such precision is hardly necessary in the uncertain world of investing, and when addressing the lay investor, simplicity is a virtue.

The Pension "Experts"

Who, you may wonder, would be so foolish as to project future returns at past historical rates? Surely many individuals, even those expert in investing, do exactly that. Even sophisticated corporate financial officers and their pension consultants follow the same course. Indeed, a typical corporate annual report expressly states, "Our asset return assumption is derived from a detailed study conducted by our actuaries and our asset management group, and *is based on long-term historical returns.*" Astonishingly, but naturally, this policy leads corporations to raise their future expectations with each increase in past returns. At the outset of the bull market in the early 1980s, for example, major corporations assumed a future return on pension assets of 7 percent. By the end of 2000, just before the great bear market took hold, most firms had sharply raised their assumptions, some to 10 percent or even more. Since pension portfolios are balanced between equities and bonds, they had implicitly raised the expected annual return on the *stocks* in the portfolio to as much as 15 percent. *Don't count on it!*

As the new decade began on January 1, 2000, two things should have been obvious: First, with dividend yields having tumbled to 1 percent, even if that earlier 6 percent earnings growth were to continue (no mean challenge!), the investment return in the subsequent 10 years would be not 10 percent, but 7 percent. Second, speculative returns cannot rise forever. (Now he tells us!) And if price-earnings ratios, then at 31 times, had simply followed their seemingly universal pattern of reversion to the mean of 15 times, the total investment return over the coming decade would be reduced by seven percentage points per year. As the year 2000 began, then, reasonable expectations suggested that annual stock returns might just be zero over the coming decade.*

If at the start of 2000 we were persuaded by history that the then-long-term annual return on stocks of 11.3 percent would continue, all would be well in the stock market. But if we listened to Keynes and simply thought about the broad reasons behind those prior returns on stock—investment versus speculation—we pretty much knew *what*

---

*Update: As it turned out, the annual return on stocks for the 1999–2009 decade came to −0.2 percent.

was going to happen: The bubble created by all of those emotions—optimism, exuberance, greed, all wrapped in the excitement of the turn of the millennium, the fantastic promise of the Information Age, and the "New Economy"—had to burst. While rational expectations can tell us *what* will happen, however, they can never tell us *when*. The day of reckoning came within three months, and in late March 2000 the bear market began. Clearly, investors would have been wise to set their expectations for future returns on the basis of current conditions, rather than fall into the trap of looking to the history of total stock market returns to set their course. Is it wise, or even reasonable, to rely on the stock market to deliver in the future the returns it has delivered in the past? *Don't count on it!*

Peril #2: The Bias toward Optimism

The peril of relying on stock market history rather than current circumstances to make investment policy decisions is apt to be costly. But that is hardly the only problem. Equally harmful is our bias toward optimism. *The fact is that the stock market returns I've just presented are themselves an illusion.* Whether investors are appraising the past or looking to the future, they are wearing rose-colored glasses. For by focusing on theoretical *market* returns rather than actual *investor* returns, we grossly overstate the returns that equity investing can provide.

First, of course, we usually do our counting in *nominal* dollars rather than *real* dollars—a difference that, compounded over time, creates a staggering dichotomy. Over the past 50 years, the return on stocks has averaged 11.3 percent per year, so $1,000 invested in stocks at the outset would today have a value of $212,000. But the 4.2 percent inflation rate for that era reduced the return to 7.1 percent and the value to just $31,000 in real terms—truly a staggering reduction. Then we compound the problem by in effect assuming that somewhere, somehow, investors as a group actually *earn* the returns the stock market provides. Nothing could be further from the truth. They *don't* because they *can't*. The reality inevitably always falls short of the illusion. Yes, if the stock market annual return is 10 percent, investors as a group obviously enjoy a *gross* return of 10 percent. But their *net* return is reduced by the *costs* of our system of financial intermediation—brokerage commissions, management fees, administrative expenses—and by the *taxes* on income and capital gains.

A reasonable assumption is that intermediation costs come to at least 2 percent per year, and for taxable investment accounts, taxes could *easily* take another 2 percent. Result: In a 10 percent market, the *net* return of investors would be no more than 8 percent before taxes, and 6 percent after taxes. Reality: Such costs would consume 40 percent of the market's nominal return. But there's more. Costs and taxes are taken out each year in *nominal* dollars, but final values reflect *real*, spendable dollars. In an environment of 3 percent annual inflation, a nominal stock return of 10 percent would be reduced to a real return of just 7 percent. When intermediation costs and taxes of 4 percent are deducted, the investor's real return tumbles to 3 percent per year. Costs and taxes have consumed, not 40 percent, but 57 percent of the market's real return.

Taken over the long-term, this bias toward optimism—presenting theoretical returns that are far higher than those available in the real world—creates staggering differences. Remember that $31,000 real 50-year return on a $1,000 investment? Well, when we take out assumed investment expenses of 2 percent, the final value drops to $11,600. And if we assume as little as 2 percent for taxes for taxable accounts, that initial $1,000 investment is worth, not that illusory nominal $212,000 we saw a few moments ago—the amazing productive power of compounding *returns*—but just $4,300 in real, after-cost terms—the amazing destructive power of compounding *costs*. *Some 98 percent of what we thought we would have has vanished into thin air.* Will you earn the market's return? *Don't count on it!*

Escaping Costs and Taxes

It goes without saying that few Wall Street stockbrokers, financial advisers, or mutual funds present this kind of real-world comparison. (In fairness, *Stocks for the Long Run* does show historic returns on both a real and nominal basis, although it ignores costs and taxes.) We not only pander to, but reinforce, the optimistic bias of investors. Yet while there's no escaping inflation, it is easily possible to reduce both investment costs and taxes almost to the vanishing point. With only the will to do so, equity investors can count on (virtually) matching the market's gross return: *owning the stock market through a low-cost, low-turnover index fund*—the ultimate strategy for earning nearly 100 percent rather than 60 percent of the market's nominal annual return. *You can count on it!*

The bias toward optimism also permeates the world of commerce. Corporate managers consistently place the most optimistic possible face on their firms' prospects for growth—and are usually proven wrong. With the earnings guidance from the corporations they cover, Wall Street security analysts have, over that past two decades, regularly estimated average future five-year earnings growth. On average, the projections were for growth at an annual rate of 11.5 percent. But as a group, these firms met their earnings targets in only 3 of the 20 five-year periods that followed. And the actual earnings growth of these corporations has averaged only about one-half of the original projection—just 6 percent.

But how could we be surprised by this gap between guidance and delivery? The fact is that the aggregate profits of our corporations are closely linked, indeed almost in lockstep, with the growth of our economy. It's been a rare year when after-tax corporate profits accounted for less than 4 percent of U.S. gross domestic product, and they rarely account for much more than 8 percent. Indeed, since 1929, after-tax profits have grown at 5.6 percent annually, actually lagging the 6.6 percent growth rate of the GDP. In a dog-eat-dog capitalistic economy where the competition is vigorous and largely unfettered and where the consumer is king—more than ever in this Information Age—how could the profits of corporate America *possibly* grow faster than our GDP? *Don't count on it!*

Earnings: Reported, Operating, **Pro Forma,** *or Restated*

Our optimistic bias has also led to another serious weakness. In a trend that has attracted too little notice, we've changed the very definition of earnings. While *reported* earnings had been the, well, standard since Standard & Poor's first began to collect the data all those years ago, in recent years the standard has changed to *operating* earnings. Operating earnings, essentially, are reported earnings bereft of all those messy charges like capital write-offs, often the result of unwise investments and mergers of earlier years. They're considered "non-recurring," though for corporations as a group they recur with remarkable consistency.

During the past 20 years, *operating* earnings of the companies in the S&P index totaled $567. After paying $229 in dividends, there should have been $338 remaining to reinvest in the business. But largely a result of the huge "non-recurring" write-offs of the era, cumulative reported earnings came to just $507. So in fact there was just $278 to invest—20 percent less—mostly because of those bad business decisions. But it is *reported* earnings, rather than *operating* earnings, that reflect the ultimate reality of corporate achievement.

Pro forma earnings—that ghastly formulation that makes new use (or abuse) of a once-respectable term—that report corporate results net of unpleasant developments, is simply a further step in the wrong direction. What is more, even auditor-certified earnings have come under doubt, as the number of corporate earnings restatements has soared. During the past four years, 632 corporations have restated their earnings, nearly *five times* the 139 restatements in the comparable period a decade earlier. Do you believe that corporate financial reporting is punctilious? *Don't count on it!*

"Creative" Accounting

Loose accounting standards have made it possible to create, out of thin air, what passes for earnings. One popular method is making an acquisition and then taking giant charges described as "non-recurring," only to be reversed in later years when needed to bolster sagging operating results. But the breakdown in our accounting standards goes far beyond that: cavalierly classifying large items as "immaterial"; hyping the assumed future returns of pension plans; counting as sales those made to customers who borrowed the money from the seller to make the purchases; making special deals to force out extra sales at quarter's end; and so on. If you can't merge your way into meeting the numbers, in effect, just change the numbers. But what we loosely describe as *creative* accounting is only a small step removed from *dishonest* accounting. Can a company make it work forever? *Don't count on it!*

That said, I suppose it does little harm to calculate the stock market's price-earnings ratio on the basis of anticipated *operating* earnings.

The net result of using the higher (albeit less realistic) number is to make price-earnings ratios appear more reasonable (i.e., to make stocks seem cheaper). By doing so, the present p/e ratio for the S&P 500 index (based on 2002 estimates) comes to a perhaps mildly reassuring 18 times based on *operating* earnings, rather than a far more concerning 25 times based on *reported* earnings. But our financial intermediation system has far too much optimism embedded in it to promulgate the higher p/e number.

Nonetheless, it is folly to rely on the higher earnings figure (and resultant lower p/e) without recognizing the reality that in the long run corporate value is determined, not only by the results of the firm's current operations, but by the entire amalgam of investment decisions and mergers and combinations it has made. *And they don't usually work.* A recent *BusinessWeek* study of the $4 trillion of mergers that took place amid the mania of the late bubble indicated that fully 61 percent of them destroyed shareholder wealth. It's high time to recognize the fallacy that these investment decisions, largely driven to improve the *numbers*, actually improve the *business. Don't count on it!*

Peril #3: The Worship of Hard Numbers

Our financial market system is a vital part of the process of investing, and of the task of raising the capital to fund the nation's economic growth. We require active, liquid markets and ask of them neither more nor less than to provide liquidity for stocks in return for the promise of future cash flows. In this way, investors are enabled to realize the present value of a future stream of income at any time. But in return for that advantage there is the disadvantage of the moment-by-moment valuation of corporate shares. We demand hard numbers to measure investment accomplishments. *And we want them now!* Markets being what they are, of course, we get them.

But the consequences are not necessarily good. Keynes saw this relationship clearly, noting that "the organization of the capital markets required for the holders of *quoted* equities requires much more nerve, patience, and fortitude than for the holders of wealth in other forms . . . some (investors) will buy without a tremor unmarketable investments which, if they had (continuous) quotations available, would turn their hair gray." Translation: It's easier on the psyche to own investments that don't often trade.

This wisdom has been often repeated. It is what Benjamin Graham meant when he warned about the hazard faced by investors when "Mr. Market" comes by every day and offers to buy your stocks at the current price. Heeding the importuning of Mr. Market allows the emotions of the moment to take precedence over the economics of the long term, as transitory shifts in prices get the investor thinking about the wrong things. As this wise investor pointed out, "In the short-run, the stock market is a *voting* machine; in the long-run it is a *weighing* machine."*

Momentary Precision versus Eternal Imprecision

Yet the Information Age that is part of this generation's lot in life has led us to the belief that the momentary *precision* reflected in the price of a stock is more important than the eternal *imprecision* in measuring the intrinsic value of a corporation. Put another way, investors seem to be perfectly happy to take the risk of being precisely wrong rather than roughly right. This triumph of perception over reality was reflected—and magnified!—in the recent bubble. The painful stock market decline that we are now enduring simply represents the return to reality. Is the price of a stock truly a consistent and reliable measure of the value of the corporation? *Don't count on it!*

Among the principal beneficiaries of the focus on stock prices were corporate chief executives. Holding huge numbers of stock options, they were eager to "make their numbers," by fair means or foul, or something in between. As the numbers materialized, their stock prices soared, and they sold their shares at the moment their options vested, as we know now, often in "cashless" transactions with bridge loans provided by the company. But unlike all other compensation, compensation from fixed-price options was not considered a corporate expense.

---

*Benjamin Graham and David Dodd, *Security Analysis* (1934, 1940; New York: McGraw-Hill, 2008), 70.

Such options came to be considered as "free," although, to avoid dilution, most corporations simply bought compensatory shares of stock (at prices far above the option prices) in the public market. It is not only that shares acquired through options were sold by executives almost as soon as they were exercised, nor that they were unencumbered by a capital charge nor indexed to the level of stock prices, that makes such options fundamentally flawed. It is that compensation based on raising the price of the stock rather than enhancing the value of the corporation flies in the face of common sense. Do stock options link the interests of management with the interests of long-term shareholders? *Don't count on it!*

Ignorant Individuals Lead Expert Professionals into Trouble

Years ago, Keynes worried about the implications for our society when "the conventional valuation of stocks is established [by] the mass psychology of a large number of ignorant individuals." The result, he suggested, would lead to violent changes in prices, a trend intensified as even expert professionals, who, one might have supposed, would correct these vagaries, follow the mass psychology, and try to foresee changes in the public valuation. As a result, he described the stock market as "a battle of wits to anticipate the basis of conventional values a few months hence rather than the prospective yield of an investment over a long term of years."*

A half-century ago, I cited those words in my senior thesis—and had the temerity to disagree. Portfolio managers in a far larger mutual fund industry, I suggested, would "supply the market with a demand for securities that is steady, sophisticated, enlightened, and analytic, a demand that is based essentially on the (intrinsic) performance of a corporation rather than the public appraisal of the value of a share, that is, its price." Well, 50 years later, it is fair to say that the worldly wise Keynes has won, and that the callowly idealistic Bogle has lost.

---

*John Maynard Keynes, *The General Theory of Employment, Interest, and Money* (New York: Macmillan, 1936; Harcourt, Brace, 1964), 155.

And the contest wasn't even close! Has the move of institutions from the wisdom of long-term investment to the folly of short-term specu-lation enhanced their performance? *Don't count on it!*

Economics Trumps Emotion—Finally

In those ancient days when I wrote my thesis, investment commit-tees (that's how the fund management game was then largely played) turned over their fund portfolios at about 15 percent per year. Today, portfolio managers (that's how the game is now played) turn over their fund portfolios at an annual rate exceeding 110 percent—for the average stock in the average fund, an average holding period of just 11 months. Using Keynes's formulation, "enterprise" (call it "investment funda-mentals") has become "a mere bubble on a whirlpool of speculation." It is the triumph of emotions over economics.

But it is an irrefutable fact that in the long run it is economics that triumphs over emotion. Since 1872, the average annual real stock market return (after inflation but before intermediation costs) has been 6.5 percent. The real investment return generated by dividends and earnings growth has come to 6.6 percent. Yes, speculative return slashed investment return by more than one-half during the 1970s and then tripled(!) it during the 1980s and 1990s. But measured today, after this year's staggering drop in stock prices, speculative return, with a net negative annual return of −0.1 percent during the entire 130-year period, on balance neither contributed to nor materially detracted from investment return. Is it wise to rely on future market returns to be enhanced by a healthy dollop of speculative return? *Don't count on it!*

The fact is that when perception—interim stock prices—vastly departs from reality—intrinsic corporate values—the gap can be rec-onciled only in favor of reality. It is simply impossible to raise reality to perception in any short timeframe; the tough and demanding task of building corporate value in a competitive world is a long-term propo-sition. Nonetheless, when stock prices lost touch with corporate values in the recent bubble, too many market participants seemed to anticipate that values would soon rise to justify prices. Investors learned, too late, the lesson: *Don't count on it!*

Peril #4: The Adverse Real-World Consequences of Counting

When we attribute certitude to history, when we constantly bias our numbers to the positive side, and when we worship the pleasing precision of momentary stock prices above the messy imprecision of intrinsic corporate values, the consequences go far beyond unfortunate numeric abstractions. These perils have societal implications, and most of them are negative.

For example, when investors accept stock market returns as being derived from a type of actuarial table, they won't be prepared for the risks that arise from the inevitable uncertainty of investment returns and the even greater uncertainty of speculative returns. As a result, they are apt to make unwise asset allocation decisions under the duress—or exuberance—of the moment. Pension plans that make this mistake will have to step up their funding when reality intervenes. And when investors base their retirement planning on actually achieving whatever returns the financial markets are generous enough to give us and tacitly ignore the staggering toll taken by intermediation costs and taxes, they save a pathetically small portion of what they ought to be saving in order to assure a comfortable retirement. Nonetheless, wise investors can totally avoid both the Scylla of costs and the Charybdis of taxes by educating themselves, by heeding the counsel of experienced professionals, or by attending the wisdom of academe.

An Ill-Done System of Capital Formation

But the peril of our preference for looking to stock prices—so easy to measure by the moment—rather than to corporate values—so hard to measure with precision—as our talisman is less easily overcome. Lord Keynes was surely right when he wrote, "when enterprise becomes a mere bubble on a whirlpool of speculation, the job [of capital formation] is likely to be ill-done." In the post-bubble environment, the job *has* been ill-done. But while some of the speculation has now been driven from the system and the day-trader may be conspicuous by his absence, the mutual fund industry still needs to get its high-wire act together and at last go back to the future by returning long-term investment policy to its earlier primacy over short-term speculation.

It is not just our capital markets that have been corrupted by the perils of relying so heavily on the apparent certitude of numbers. It is our whole society. The economic consequences of managing corporations by the numbers are both extensive and profound. Our financial system has, in substance, challenged our corporations to produce earnings growth that has not been and cannot be sustained. When corporations fail to meet their numeric targets the hard way—over the long-term, by raising productivity, improving old products and creating new ones, providing services on a more friendly, more timely, and more efficient basis, challenging the people of the organization to work more effectively together (and those are the ways that our best corporations achieve success)—they are compelled to do it in other ways.

One of these ways, of course, is the aggressive merger-and-acquisition strategy I've earlier noted. Even leaving aside the commonplace that most mergers fail to achieve their goals, the companies that followed these strategies were well-described in a recent *New York Times* op-ed essay as "serial acquirers [whose] dazzling number of deals makes an absence of long-term management success easy to hide."* Tyco International, for example, acquired 700(!) companies before the day of reckoning came. But the final outcome of the strategy, as the *Times* piece explained, was almost preordained: "Their empires of [numbers] hype can be undone very quickly by market discipline." Are such strategies a formula for long-run success? *Don't count on it!*

In this context, it's amazing how much of companies' returns today are based on financial factors rather than operating factors. The pension plan assets of the 30 companies in the Dow-Jones Industrial average now total $400 billion, not far from the corporations' collective book value of $700 billion. Off–balance sheet financial schemes proliferate (or *did!*). Selling put-options to reduce the cost of repurchasing shares and avoid the potential dilution of stock options helped prevent earnings penalties in the boom, but has come back to deplete corporate coffers in the bust. And lending by major corporations to enable consumers to buy their wares has skyrocketed. Perhaps unsurprisingly, it isn't looking so good in today's economic environment.

---

*Jeffrey Sonnenfeld, *New York Times*, June 5, 2002.

When Paper Covers Rock, What Comes Next?

Too many so-called industrial companies have become financial companies—companies that *count* rather than *make*. (Witness the fact that the senior aide to the CEO is almost invariably the chief financial officer, often viewed by the investment community as the *eminence gris*.) Such companies, again quoting the *New York Times* article, "base their strategies not on understanding the businesses they go into, but assume that by scavenging about for good deals, they can better allocate their financial resources than can existing financial markets." As we now observe the consequences of this strategy, we come to a painful realization. *Don't count on it!*

You may remember the children's game in which rock breaks scissors, scissors cut paper, and paper covers rock. In manias, as prices lose touch with values, paper indeed covers rock. "Paper" companies that *count* have acquired "rock" companies that *make*, and the results have been devastating. When I mention AOL/Time Warner, Qwest/U.S. West, and WorldCom/MCI, I don't have to tell you which is paper and which is rock. These are among the most poignant examples of a phenomenon in whose aftermath hundreds of thousands of loyal long-term employees have lost their jobs, and their retirement savings have been slashed unmercifully.

That the penalties for our financial mania are borne by our society was well-stated in a perceptive op-ed piece in the *Wall Street Journal*: "Stock prices are not simply abstract numbers. [They] affect the nature of the strategies the firm adopts and hence its prospects for success, the company's cost of capital, its borrowing ability, and its ability to make acquisitions. *A valuation unhinged by the underlying realities of the business can rob investors of savings, cost people far more innocent than senior management their jobs, and undermine the viability of suppliers and communities.*"* Yes, the human consequences of excessive reliance on numbers, as we now know, can be remarkably harsh.

---

*Joseph Fuller and Michael C. Jensen, *Wall Street Journal*, December 31, 2001.

Counting at the Firm Level

The perils of excessive numeracy don't end there. Even otherwise sound companies dwell too heavily on what can be measured—market share, productivity, efficiency, product quality, costs—and set internal goals to achieve them. But when *measures* become *objectives*, they are often counterproductive and self-defeating. Most measurements are inherently short-term in nature, but far more durable qualities drive a corporation's success over the long-term. While they cannot be measured, character, integrity, enthusiasm, conviction, and passion are every bit as important to a firm's success as precise measurements. (Call it the six-sigma syndrome.) It is *human beings* who are the prime instrument for implementing a corporation's strategy. If they are inspired, motivated, cooperative, diligent, and creative, the stockholders will be well served.

Yet recent years have shown us that when ambitious chief executives set aggressive financial objectives, they place the achievement of those objectives above all else—even above proper accounting principles and a sound balance sheet, even above their corporate character. Far too often, all means available—again, fair or foul—are harnessed to justify the ends. As good practices are driven out by bad, and the rule of the day becomes "everyone else is doing it, so I will too," a sort of Gresham's law comes to prevail in corporate standards.

"Management by measurement" is easily taken too far. I recently read of a chief executive who called for earnings growth from $6.15 per share in 2001 to a nice round $10 per share in 2005*—an earnings increase of almost 15 percent per year—but without a word about how it would be accomplished. I don't believe that the greater good of shareholders is served by such a precise yet abstract numeric goal. Indeed what *worries* me is not that it *won't* be achieved, but that it *will*. In an uncertain world, the company may get there only by manipulating the numbers or, even worse, relying on cutbacks and false economies, and shaping everything that moves (including the human beings who will have to bend to the task) to achieve the goal. *But at what cost?* The sooner companies cease their aggressive "guidance," the better.

---

*2010 update: Earnings topped the $10 per share target in 2009.

For I believe that a quarter-century from now the companies that will be leading the way in their industries will be those that make their earnings growth, not the *objective* of their strategy, but the *consequence* of their corporate performance. Will the numbers *counters* outpace the product *makers*? *Don't count on it!*

An Individual Perspective

Lest I be accused of innumeracy, however, please be clear that I'm not saying that numbers don't matter. Measurement standards—*counting*, if you will—is essential to the communication of financial goals and achievements. *I know that.* But for the past 28 years I've been engaged in building an enterprise—and a *financial* institution at that—based far more on the sound implementation of a few commonsense investment ideas and an enlightened sense of human values and ethical standards than on the search for quantitative goals and statistical achievements. Vanguard's market share, as I've said countless times, must be a *measure*, not an *objective*; it must be *earned*, not *bought*. Yet the fact is that our market share of fund industry assets has risen, without interruption, for the past 22 years. (We did benefit, greatly, by being a *mutual* company, with neither private nor public shareholders.)

Our strategy arose from a conviction that the best corporate growth comes from putting the horse of doing things for clients ahead of the cart of earnings targets. *Growth must be organic, rather than forced.* And I've believed it for a long time. Indeed, here is how I closed in my 1972 annual message to the employees of Wellington Management Company (which I then headed) about giving too much credence to the counting of numbers:*

> The first step is to measure what can be easily measured. This is okay as far as it goes. The second step is to disregard that which cannot be measured, or give it an arbitrary quantitative value. This is artificial and misleading. The third step is to presume that what cannot be measured really is not very

---

* Quoting pollster Daniel Yankelovich.

important. This is blindness. The fourth step is to say that what cannot be measured does not really exist. This is suicide.

There is, then, a futility in excessive reliance on numbers, and a perversity in trying to measure the immeasurable in our uncertain world. So when *counting* becomes the name of the game, our financial markets, our corporations, and our society pay the price. *So don't count on it!*

Numbers are a necessary tool and a vital one. But they are a *means* and not an end, a condition *necessary* to measure corporate success, but not a condition *sufficient*. To believe that numbers—in the absence of the more valuable albeit immeasurable qualities of experience, judgment, and character—are all that illuminate the truth is one of the great failings of our contemporary financial and economic system. Wise financial professionals and academics alike should be out there searching for a higher, more enlightened set of values. So, having begun this essay by describing how my career in the academy began, I'll close with a two-centuries-old quotation from the Roman poet Horace about the proper role of the academy:

> Good Athens gave my art another theme
> To sort what is from what is merely seen
> And search for truth in groves of academe.

Chapter 2

The Relentless Rules of
Humble Arithmetic*

W hen asked to reflect on the theme, "Bold Thinking on Invest-ment Management," I'm happy to leap into the fray, well aware of my reputation as a maverick in the world of invest-ing. But if it's iconoclastic to focus on the reality of investing rather than the illusions of investing, so be it. Most sophisticated investors already know, deep down, the elemental truth of my central message and accept it. But others—the majority, I suspect—either have kept it out of sight and out of mind, or haven't fully considered its implications.

Obvious as my message may be, the investment community, which has basked in the sunlight of the glorious financial excesses of the recent era, has a vested interest in ignoring the reality I'll soon describe. This is not a new problem. Two-and-one-half millennia ago, Demosthenes warned us that "what each man wishes, he also believes to be true." More recently, and certainly more pungently, Upton Sinclair marveled (I'm paraphrasing here) that "it's amazing how difficult it is for a man to understand something if he's paid a small fortune not to understand it."

---

*Based on an article published in the *Financial Analysts Journal* for November/ December 2005, republished in 2006 in the CFA Institute's anthology, *Bold Thinking on Investment Management.*

But my message today is one that we all jolly-well must understand, for it is central to the operation of our system of financial intermediation that underlies the accumulation of assets in our retirement systems and the collective wealth of our citizenry. In my book, *The Battle for the Soul of Capitalism*, I call it "investment America"; the current administration in Washington, D.C. calls it our "ownership society." But whatever words we use, the future of capitalism depends importantly on our understanding my message. That message is simple: Gross return in the financial markets, minus the costs of financial intermediation, equals the net return actually delivered to investors. While truly staggering amounts of investment literature have been devoted to the EMH (the Efficient Market Hypothesis), precious little has been devoted to what I call the CMH—the Cost Matters Hypothesis. However, to explain the dire odds that investors face in their quest to beat the market we don't need the EMH. We need only the CMH. Whether markets are efficient or inefficient, investors as a group must fall short of the market return by precisely the amount of the aggregate costs they incur. It is the central fact of investing.

Yet the pages of our financial journals are filled with statistical studies of rates of market returns that are neither achievable nor achieved. How can we talk about *creating positive Alpha* without realizing that after intermediation costs are deducted, the system as a whole has *negative Alpha*? Of what use is it to speculate on the amount of the equity risk premium when 100 percent of the return on the 10-year Treasury note (or bill, if that's what you prefer) is there for the taking, whereas as much as 50 percent or more of the real return on stocks can be consumed by the costs of our financial system? How can we ignore the fact that, as a group, unlike those kids out there in Lake Wobegon, we're all average before costs, and below average once our costs are deducted?

The fact is that the mathematical expectation of the short-term speculator in stocks and the long-term investor in stocks alike is *zero*. But it is only zero before the substantial costs of playing the game, which will produce a shortfall to the stock market's return that is precisely equal to the sum total of all those advisory fees, marketing expenditures, sales loads, brokerage commissions, legal and transaction costs, custody fees, and securities processing expenses. So often is this mathematical certainty overlooked that I'm delighted to have the opportunity to focus on it, and on its far-reaching implications.

"Trampling with Impunity on Laws Human and Divine"

With that background, let me now turn to the quotation that I've chosen as my title. In 1914, in *Other People's Money*, Louis D. Brandeis, later to become one of the most influential jurists in the history of the U.S. Supreme Court, railed against the oligarchs who a century ago controlled investment America and corporate America as well. He described their self-serving financial management and interlocking interests as "trampling with impunity on laws human and divine, obsessed with the delusion that two plus two make five."* He predicted (accurately, as it turned out) that the widespread speculation of the era would collapse, "a victim of the relentless rules of humble arithmetic." He then added this unattributed warning—I'm guessing it's from Sophocles—"Remember, O Stranger, arithmetic is the first of the sciences, and the mother of safety."†

As it is said, the more things change, the more they remain the same. Yet, paraphrasing Mark Twain, while the history of the era that Brandeis described is not repeating itself today, it rhymes. Our investment system—our government retirement programs, our private retirement programs, indeed, all of the securities owned by our stockowners as a group—is plagued by the same relentless rules. Since the returns investors receive come only *after* the deduction of the costs of our system of financial intermediation—even as a gambler's winnings come only from what remains after the croupier's rake descends—the relentless rules of that humble arithmetic devastate the long-term returns of investors. Using Brandeis's formulation, we seem obsessed with the delusion that a 7 percent market return, minus 3 percent for costs, still equals a 7 percent investor return (i.e., that costs are too trivial to be considered).

Of course, no one knows exactly what those intermediation costs amount to. It's high time that someone, maybe even the CFA Institute, conducts a careful study of the system and finds out. But we do have data for some of the major cost centers. During 2004, revenues of investment bankers and brokers came to an estimated $220 billion; direct

---

*Louis D. Brandeis, *Other People's Money and How the Bankers Use It* (1914; New York: Bedford Books, 1995), 45.
†It did collapse, a harbinger of the interaction of corporate America with investment America that would help foment the great financial collapse of 2007–2009.

mutual fund costs came to about $70 billion; pension management fees to $15 billion; annuity commissions to some $15 billion; hedge fund fees to about $25 billion; fees paid to personal financial advisers, maybe another $5 billion. Even without including the investment services provided by banks and insurance companies, these financial intermediation costs came to approximately $350 billion, all directly deducted from the returns that the financial markets generated for investors before those croupiers' costs were deducted.

The price of intermediation is going up. In 1985, these costs were in the $50 billion range. And my, how they add up! In the bubble and post-bubble eras (since 1996), the aggregate costs of financial intermediation may well have exceeded $2.5 trillion, all dutifully paid by our stockowners. Of course, some of these costs created value (for example, liquidity). But by definition, those costs not only cannot create *above-market* returns, they are the direct cause of *below-market* returns, a dead weight on the amount earned by investors as a group. *In investing, all of us together get precisely what we don't pay for.* So it's essential that we develop a more efficient way to provide investment services.

The Mutual Fund Industry

Perhaps obviously, this line of reasoning brings me to my essay in the January/February 2005 issue of the *Financial Analysts Journal* about the largest of all of America's financial intermediaries, the mutual fund industry. "The Mutual Fund Industry 60 Years Later: For Better or Worse?" examines the changes that have taken place in the industry in which I've now spent 56 years, for it was way back in 1949 that I began my research for my Princeton senior thesis, "The Economic Role of the Investment Company." That research has continued to this day. My long study of the field, I regret to report, has persuaded me that the answer to the question raised in the title of my *FAJ* article was, "for worse."

While I won't rehash the article here, I will summarize how the industry has changed.* We've created a mind-boggling number of new

---

*I recognize that there are fund organizations that are exceptions to these generalizations. However, the number is surprisingly small.

and often speculative funds; we've moved from investment committees focused on the wisdom of long-term investing to portfolio manager "stars" engaged in the folly of short-term speculation; we've enjoyed an enormous growth in our ownership position in corporate America along with a paradoxical and discouraging diminution of our willingness to exercise that ownership position responsibly, if at all; we've imposed soaring costs on our investors that belie the enormous economies of scale in money management; our reputation for integrity, sadly, has been tarred by the brush of scandal; in the larger management companies, we've moved away from private ownership in favor of public ownership, and then ownership by financial conglomerates; and we've changed from being a profession with aspects of a business to a business with aspects of a profession. As I put it in the article, mutual funds have moved "from stewardship to salesmanship."

That's all in the past, of course. As I look to the future, I would add a single thought to that essay, including this warning in my conclusion: "Unless we change, the mutual fund industry will falter and finally fail, a victim, yes, of the relentless rules of humble arithmetic." I love this industry too much to remain silent as I witness what's happening—call it, after Robert Frost, my "lover's quarrel" with the mutual fund industry.

Let's Look at the Record

When we examine the record of the past two decades, as I did in the *Financial Analysts Journal* article, the relentless rule that I described earlier has proven hazardous to the wealth of the families who have entrusted their hard-earned wealth to mutual funds. That humble arithmetic—*gross return, minus cost, equals net return*—has destroyed their wealth in almost precisely the measure in which our CMH suggests. Investors have learned the hard way that in mutual funds it's not that "you get what you pay for." It's that, almost tautologically, "you get what you *don't* pay for."

Let's look at the record. Over the past 20 years, a simple, low-cost, no-load stock market index fund based on the S&P 500 index delivered an annual return of 12.8 percent—just a hair short of the 13.0

percent return of the index itself. During the same period the average equity mutual fund delivered a return of just 10.0 percent, a shortfall to the index fund of 2.8 percentage points per year, and less than 80 percent of the market's return. Compounded over that period, each $1 invested in the index fund grew by $10.12—the *magic* of compounding *returns*—while each $1 in the average fund grew by just $5.73, not 80 percent of the market's return, but a shriveled-up 57 percent—a victim of the *tyranny* of compounding *costs*.

And that's before taxes. *After* taxes equal to 0.9 percentage points, the 500 index fund delivered a return of 11.9 percent; taxes for the average equity fund took a toll of 2.2 percentage points, producing an after-tax return of 7.8 percent, just 41 percent of the index's return. More relevant, the gap between the equity fund and the index fund rises from 2.8 to 4.1 percentage points per year. The average fund deferred almost *no* gains during this period; the index fund deferred *nearly all*. (Deferred taxes may be the ultimate example of how you get what you don't pay for.)

In fairness, the wealth accumulated in the index fund and the average equity fund should be measured not only in nominal dollars, but in real dollars. Now, the real annual return drops to 8.9 percent for the index fund and to 4.8 percent for the equity fund, obviously the same 4.1 percentage-point gap. But when we reduce both returns by an identical 3.0 percentage points a year for inflation, it will hardly surprise you who are in the mathematical "know" that the *compounding* of those lower annual returns further widens the cumulative gap. Over the past 20 years, the cumulative profit of each $1 initially invested in the equity fund comes to $1.55 in real terms, after taxes and costs, now only 34 percent of the real profit of $4.50 for the index fund. (Please don't forget that costs and taxes are deducted each year in *nominal* dollars, and thus take an ever-rising bite out of long-term *real* wealth.)

Fund Returns versus *Investor* Returns

What is more, when we look at the return earned, not by the average *fund*, but by the average fund *owner*, the shortfall to the market return gets even worse. As this industry came to focus more and more on marketing and less and less on management, we deluged investors with a plethora of enticing new funds. As the market's fads and fashions waxed and waned—most obviously in the "new economy" funds of the late market bubble—our marketing experts responded with alacrity. The fund industry aided and abetted the actions of fund investors, who not only poured hundreds of billions of dollars into equity funds as the stock market soared to its high, but chose the wrong funds as well. In addition to the wealth-depleting penalty of fund costs, then, fund investors paid a substantial penalty for the counterproductive *timing* of their investments, and another large penalty for their unfortunate *selection* of funds. (Not that investors are totally blameless for these errors.)

Intuition suggests that these costs were large. The data we have, while not precise, confirms that hypothesis. The *asset-weighted* returns of mutual funds—quite easy to calculate by examining each fund's quarterly cash flows—lag the standard *time-weighted* returns by fully 3.7 percentage points per year. Adding that shortfall to the 2.8 percentage point annual lag of time-weighted returns of the average equity fund relative to the 500 index fund over the past two decades, the *asset-weighted* returns of the average equity fund stockholder fell a total of 6.5 percentage points *per year* behind the index fund. Average annual return for period: equity fund, 6.3 percent; index fund, 12.8 percent in pre-tax nominal returns.

Applying the tyranny of compounding both to the costs of fund *operations* and to the costs of, well, fund *ownership*, each $1 invested at the outset grew by just $2.39 over the full period, compared to the $10.12 growth that was there for the taking, simply by owning the low-cost index fund—only 25 percent of the wealth that might easily have been accumulated simply by holding the stock market portfolio (see Table 2.1).

Much of this extra lag came from the specialized, usually speculative funds that the industry created and promoted. For example, during the bull market upsurge and subsequent bear market in 1998–2003, the asset-weighted returns of the industry's six largest broadly diversified funds lagged their time-weighted annual returns by an average of less than a single percentage point, while the six largest specialized funds lagged their time-weighted returns by an average of more than 11 percentage points. Compounded during the six-year bubble, the gap in returns

TABLE 2.1   DIVERSIFIED FUNDS VS. SECTOR FUNDS: DOLLAR-WTD. AND TIME-WTD. RETURNS

	1998–2000 Time-Wtd.	2001–2003 Time-Wtd.	1998–2003 Time-Wtd.	1998–2003 $-Wtd.	$-Wtd. minus Time-Wtd.
Diversified Funds					
Fidelity Magellan	14.4%	−5.6%	3.9%	3.7%	−0.2%
Vanguard 500	12.3	−4.2	3.7	2.4	−1.3
Inv. Co. of America	14.2	1.0	7.4	6.7	−0.7
Janus Fund	20.2	−11.0	3.4	0.9	−2.5
Fidelity Contrafund	15.2	0.4	7.5	7.9	0.4
Washington Mutual	9.6	2.8	6.2	5.5	−0.7
Average	**14.3%**	**−2.7%**	**5.4%**	**4.5%**	**−0.9%**
Sector Funds					
TRP Sci. & Tech.	23.5%	−19.1%	−0.1%	−8.8%	−8.7%
Seligman Comm. & Info.	13.5	−2.4	5.3	2.0	−3.3
AB Global Tech.	28.0	−15.7	3.9	−9.5	−13.4
Vanguard Healthcare	34.2	1.4	16.7	13.7	−3.0
Fidelity Sel. Electronics	37.0	−10.2	10.9	0.0	−10.9
Munder NetNet	35.7	−21.6	3.1	−25.7	−28.8
Average	**28.6%**	**−11.3%**	**6.6%**	**−4.7%**	**−11.4%**

was astonishing, with the specialized funds producing a positive time-weighted annual return of 6.6 percent, but losing a cumulative 25 percent of client wealth. On the other hand, despite a slightly lower annual return of 4.5 percent, client wealth in the broadly diversified large funds was enhanced by 30 percent. (That's a 55 percentage point difference!)

Two Costly and Counterproductive Trends

The stark pattern that illustrates the huge sacrifices of wealth incurred by fund investors brings me to two other subjects that I referred to in my earlier essay about the mutual fund industry. One is the "marketing-ization" of the mutual fund industry, in which most major firms have come to make whatever funds will sell; the other is the "conglomerati-zation" of the industry, in which giant international financial insti-tutions, eager to get a piece of the action for themselves—a share in the huge profits made in money management—have gone on a buying binge.

One reasonable proxy—obviously not a perfect one—for dif-ferentiating a marketing firm from a management firm is the number of funds it offers. Here, the data speak for themselves, thanks to a Fidelity study of the 54 largest firms, managing about 85 percent of the industry's long-term assets. The nine firms that operate fewer than 15 mutual funds clearly dominate the rankings, outpacing almost 80 percent of all their common rivals (i.e., their large-cap growth fund vs. other large-cap growth funds, their balanced fund vs. other bal-anced funds, etc.). On the other hand, the 45 firms with more than 15 funds (*averaging* 52 funds each!) outpaced only about 48 percent of their peers.* Marketing focus, apparently, comes at the expense of management results.

A similar pattern prevails when we compare the funds managed by the 13 private companies and the funds managed by the 41 compa-nies that are held directly by public investors (7 firms), or indirectly by publicly held financial conglomerates (34 firms). The funds managed by private companies—the industry's sole *modus operandi* until 1958— outpaced 71 percent of their peers, while the funds under the aegis of the conglomerates outperformed but 45 percent. (See Table 2.4 in the Appendix.)

It seems reasonable to assume that a publicly held firm, run by a far-removed management that may well have never looked a fund independent director in the eye, is in the fund business primarily to gather assets and to enhance its brand name, and is far more concerned about the return on *its* capital than the return on the capital entrusted to it by its *mutual fund owners.* (We saw something of that syndrome in

---

*The detailed data are put forth in Tables 2.4 and 2.5 in the appendix to this chapter.

the recent scandals.) While the conglomerate's management has a clear fiduciary duty both to its own owners and to the owners of its funds, however, the record suggests that, when fund fee schedules are considered, it resolves that dilemma in favor of its own public owners, ignoring the invocation in the Investment Company Act of 1940 that funds must be "organized, operated, and managed" in the interests of their shareholders, *rather than* in the interests of their managers.

Looking Ahead

Despite the problems I have described, fund investors (at least those investors who didn't jump on the bull market bandwagon late in the game) seem satisfied with earning the decidedly moderate positive returns achieved by the funds during the bull market of the past two decades. They seem willing to ignore the generally invisible costs of fund investing, willing to disregard the tax-inefficiency, happy to think in terms of nominal rather than real dollars, and perhaps willing to assume some responsibility for their own mistakes in fund timing and fund selection.

But let's look ahead to a likely era of lower returns, and measure what might be the typical experience in terms of the investment horizon of a young investor of today. Assume the investor has just joined the workforce and is looking forward to 45 years of employment until retirement and then to enjoying the next 20 years that the actuaries promise—a total time horizon of 65 years.

If the stock market is kind enough to favor us with a total return of 8 percent per year over that period and if annual mutual fund costs are held to 2.5 percent, the return of the fund investor will average 5.5 percent. By the end of the long period, a cost-free investment at 8 percent would carry an initial $1,000 investment to a final value of $148,800. However, the 5.5 percent net return for the investor would increase his cumulative wealth by only $31,500. In effect, the amount paid over to the financial system, also compounded, would come to $116,300.

The investor who put up 100 percent of the capital and assumed 100 percent of the risk, then, received just 21 percent of the return. The financial intermediaries, who put up zero percent of the capital and assumed zero percent of the risk, enjoyed a truly remarkable 79 percent of the return. Indeed, after only the 29th year, less than halfway through the 65-year period, the *cumulative* return of our young capitalist, saving for retirement, falls behind the cumulative return taken by the financial croupiers, never to return. Devastating as is this diversion of the spoils of investing, it is apparent that few investors today have either the awareness of the relentless rules of humble arithmetic that almost guarantee such a shortfall in their retirement savings, or the wisdom to understand the tyranny of compounding costs over the long-term.

The Wealth of the Nation

If our system of retirement savings were not the backbone of the wealth of the nation and our economic strength, perhaps this wealth-depleting arithmetic would not matter. But it *does* matter. Our corporate pension plans hold $1.8 trillion of stocks and bonds, our state and local pension plans another $2.0 trillion. Private noninsured pension reserves total $4.2 trillion, insured pension reserves $1.9 trillion, government pension reserves $3.1 trillion, life insurance reserves $1.0 trillion, for a total of $10.2 trillion, or nearly one-half of family assets (other than cash and savings deposits).

Since 1970, our national policy has been to increase private savings for retirement by providing tax-sheltered accounts such as individual retirement accounts (IRAs) and defined-contribution pension, thrift, and savings programs (usually 401(k) plans). The present administration in Washington seems determined to further extend the reach of these tax-advantaged vehicles, along with the amount that each family may invest in them each year. So let's delve a little further into how the relentless rules of arithmetic affect our "investment society," or, if you prefer, our "ownership society."

Certainly, it is clear from the data I've presented that the retirement savings of American families are too important to the wealth of our nation to be entrusted to the mutual fund industry. Whatever the case, we know that the system of the tax incentives provided to investors hasn't worked very well so far. Only about 22 percent of our workers are using 401(k) savings plans; only about 10 percent have IRAs, and about 9 percent have both. And even after three decades of experience with these tax-advantaged plans, the average 401(k) balance is now a modest $33,600, and the average IRA $26,900 — hardly the kind of capital with the potential to ultimately provide a comfortable retirement.

In addition, the massive shift that has taken place from defined-benefit plans to defined-contribution plans does not seem to be working well from an investment standpoint. Not only have defined-benefit plans produced higher returns than defined-contribution plans since 1990 (144 percent vs. 125 percent), they have done so with far less volatility, falling only about half as much (−12 percent vs. −22 percent) in the recent down-market years. Part of the shortfall, of course, can be laid to the higher costs that are imposed on investors in defined-contribution plans.

The Humble Arithmetic of Pension Plans

But if our foray into defined-contribution plans is not doing the job it should in terms of producing a solid base for retirement savings, our defined-benefit plans have surely done far worse—not because of the returns they have earned, but because of the excessive returns that they have projected. It is no secret that aggressive assumptions of future returns on pension plans are rife on the financial statements of America's corporations. Even as interest rates have tumbled and earnings yields have steadily declined, projections of future returns have soared. General Motors, for example, raised its assumption from 6 percent per year in 1975 to 10 percent in 2000. Why? Because it based its projection on "long-term historical returns." In effect, General Motors told us, "The more stocks have gone up in the past, the more they'll rise in the future." Amazingly, the higher the market rose, the higher the pension plans' expected returns rose, at least in the GM model.

To be fair, if mutual fund America has ignored the relentless rules of humble arithmetic, its peccadilloes have been vastly exceeded by those of corporate America in its projections of pension fund returns—in fact, a national scandal and an accident waiting to happen. Let's spend a moment on those relentless rules and analyze what might be reasonable for the future return of a pension plan today, one that assumes a future return of 8.5 percent, as General Motors now does. For the stock portfolio, based on realistic expectations using today's dividend yield and normal (say, 6 percent) earnings growth, we

**TABLE 2.2   REALISTIC RETURN ASSUMPTIONS:
CORPORATE PENSION PLAN**

Class	1. Allocation	2. Projected Return	3. (1 × 2) Return Impact	4. Gross Return	5. Expenses	6. (4 − 5) Net Return
Equities	60%	7.5%	4.5%	6.3%	1.5%	4.8%
Bonds	40	4.5	1.8			

might say that 7.5 percent is reasonable. Looking at the current yield on a conservative bond portfolio of Treasurys and corporates, we'd project bond returns at about 4.5 percent. Once we deduct estimated plan expenses (say 1.5 percent, including fees, turnover costs, etc.), the arithmetic takes us to a net return of 4.8 percent, a little more than half of 8.5 percent total. Here, I think, is a company either looking for trouble or trying to engineer upward the earnings it reports to its shareholders (see Table 2.2).

When I pursued the issue with General Motors, I was told that the old-policy portfolio (60 percent stocks, 40 percent bonds) is history; General Motors has added alternative investments such as venture capital, and "absolute return" investments like hedge funds. So let's make some reasonable assumptions about what these new-policy portfolios might hold:* 30 percent in equities, 40 percent in bonds, 10 percent in venture capital, and 20 percent in hedge funds. Now let's see what we need to do to reach that 8.5 percent total. If we leave our market returns unchanged, the equity managers will have to beat the stock market by 3 percent a year, and the bond managers beat the bond market by 0.25 percent. If we project venture capital at 12 percent, with smart managers who earn almost 18 percent, and hedge funds at 10 percent, with smart managers who earn 17 percent, and then deduct costs, *voila!* The pension fund reaches its goal of 8.5 percent per year! (See Table 2.3.)

Leave aside for the moment that equity managers who can beat the market by 3 percent a year are conspicuous by their absence. Leave aside,

---

*There are lots of variations on this theme. In the interest of space I've chosen just one.

**TABLE 2.3   EARNING AN 8.5 PERCENT RETURN:
A TEMPLATE FOR CORPORATE ANNUAL REPORTS**

Class	1. Allocation	2. Projected Return	3. Value Added*	4. Expenses	5. (2 + 3 − 4) Net Return	6. (1 × 5) Return Impact
Equities	30%	7.5%	3.0%	1.5%	9.0%	2.7%
Bonds	40	4.5	0.25	0.5	4.2	1.7
Venture Capital	10	12.0	5.5	3.0	14.5	1.4
Hedge Funds	20	10.0	6.5	3.0	13.5	2.7
					Total Return:	8.5%

*Required to produce expected rate of return.

too, the risks they'll have to take to do so. Then note that the assumed venture capital returns and hedge fund returns are far above even the historical norms inflated by the speculative boom in IPOs during the market madness of the late 1990s. Then ignore the obviously staggering odds against finding a *group* of "absolute return" managers who could consistently exceed those norms by six or seven percentage points per year over a decade. Surely most investment professionals would consider these Herculean assumptions absurd. But who really knows?

My point, however, is not that no one knows. Assumptions are, after all, only assumptions. Rather, my point is that each corporation's annual report should present to shareholders a simple table such as this one so that its owners can make a fair determination of the reasonableness of the arithmetic upon which the pension plan is relying to make its pension fund return assumptions. I'd put such a report high on my list of financial statement priorities, and I would hope that serious analysts would take this issue directly to corporate managements and challenge the assumptions that are being made. Corporate boards rarely touch this issue, but shareholders ought to force it.

Alas, dim as the outlook is for defined-contribution plans, the future for defined-benefit plans is fraught with challenges that can only be described as truly awesome. A recent report by Morgan Stanley's respected accounting expert, Trevor Harris (with Richard Berner), put it well:

Years of mispriced pension costs, underfunding, and overly opti-mistic assumptions about mortality and retirement have created economic mismatches between promises made and the resources required to keep them. Corporate defined-benefit plans as a whole are as much as $400 billion underfunded. State and local plans, moreover, may be underfunded by three times that amount. Those gaps will drain many plan sponsors' operating performance and threaten the defined-benefit system itself, especially if markets fail to deliver high returns, or if interest rates remain low.*

It's time to align both our private pension system and our govern-ment pension systems with the relentless rules of humble arithmetic, just as we must do with the retirement savings of our families, whether they are investing directly in mutual funds or in defined-contribution savings plans. (Those rules of arithmetic also apply to Social Security and the issues surrounding privatization, but these are topics for another day.)

Comparative Advantage versus Community Advantage

I want to close by making the fundamental point of my remarks today: the difference between "comparative advantage" and "community advantage." Much—sometimes I think almost *all*—of what I read in the learned journals of finance has to do with what I'll call com-parative advantage, such as capitalizing on a market inefficiency that improves performance relative to the total market, or gaining an edge in return over our professional rivals. But since we ply our trade in what is essentially a closed-market system, and can't change whatever the returns the markets are generous enough to bestow on us, each dollar of advantage we gain in the market comes only at the direct dis-advantage of other market participants as a group.

---

*Richard Berner and Trevor Harris, "Financial Market Implications of Pension Reform," Morgan Stanley Research, Global Economic Forum (January 18, 2005).

That's fine, as far as it goes. As a recent article in the *New Yorker* put it, however, "What if I turn out to be average? Yet, if the bell curve is a fact, then so is the reality that most [investors] are going to be average." The article continues, "There's no shame in being one of them, right? Except, of course, there is. Somehow, what troubles people isn't so much *being* average as settling for it. Averageness is, for most of us, our fate."* Alas, however, in the world of money management, we are average before costs and losers to the market after costs are deducted—that relentless rule of humble arithmetic that we want to deny, but cannot. Put another way, costs shift our entire bell curve to the left.

None of us wants to be average, and competition, up to a point at least, is healthy in terms of providing the transaction volumes that are required for liquidity and market efficiency. That market efficiency in turn moves us ever closer to a world in which the Efficient Market Hypothesis becomes a tautology. Of course, transaction costs also fatten the wallets of Wall Street's financial intermediaries. But if the strategy of a given fund remains undiscovered and sustained, that firm will attract more dollars under management, diverting fees into its pockets from the pockets of its rivals. Such success may even allow the firm to charge higher fees, thereby increasing (albeit only modestly, at least at first) its advisory fee revenues, by definition reducing the net returns of all investors as a group.

So it is probably vaguely painful to realize that if the upshot of all our feverish investment activity is designed to advantage Peter, that advantage comes only at the expense of Paul, a defiance of Immanuel Kant's categorical imperative that we must "act so that the consequences of our actions can be generalized without self-contradiction." Yet our best and brightest souls are competing in this zero-sum game that ultimately becomes a loser's game.

Warren Buffett's crusty but wise partner, Charlie Munger, is disturbed by the commitment of so many exceptional people to the field of investment management: "Most money-making activity contains profoundly antisocial effects. [As high-cost modalities become ever more popular], the activity exacerbates the current harmful trend in which ever more of the nation's ethical young brain-power is attracted into lucrative money-management and its attendant modern frictions, as distinguished from

---

*Atul Gawande, "The Bell Curve," *New Yorker*, December 6, 2004, 82–91.

work providing much more value to others."* As Mr. Munger recognizes, in the field of money-making, as far as the interests of clients go there can be no net value added, only value subtracted.

Adam Smith's invisible hand may give a minority of money managers a competitive edge. But it cannot improve the lot of investors as a group. Yet it is within our power to do exactly that, creating a *community* advantage that provides value to *all* investors. Enriching the returns of all investors as a group ought to be a vital goal for society itself, or at least for our ownership society. If capitalism is to flourish, we should be concerned about the recent triumph of managers' capitalism over owners' capitalism, not only in corporate America, but in investment America—the field of money management. So long as money-making activity simply shifts returns from the pedestrian to the brilliant, or from the unlucky to the lucky, or from those who naively trust the system to those who work at its margin, of course it has "profoundly anti-social effects." Wouldn't making capitalism work better for all stockowners, increasing their returns while holding risk constant, have, well, "profoundly *social* effects"?

Our Intermediation Society

There are two powerful forces that stand between the idealistic goal "to begin the world anew" in investment America and its realization. One of those forces is money. The field of investment management is so awesomely profitable to its participants that money has become a narcotic, and we are hopelessly addicted to those profits. But the second force may be even more powerful: the reliance of investors on financial intermediaries to protect their interests. While we may *think* we live in an "ownership society"—albeit one that has miles to go before it achieves its promise—with each passing day there are fewer actual owners of our wealth-generating corporations.

The fact is that we now live in an "intermediation society," in which the last-line owners—essentially, mutual fund shareholders and

---

*Charles Munger, speech before the Foundation Financial Officers Group, Santa Monica, California, on October 14, 1998.

beneficiaries of public and private pension plans—have to rely on their trustees to act as their faithful fiduciaries. There is too little evidence of this stewardship today, largely because of the dollar-for-dollar trade-off in which the more the managers *take*, the less the investors *make*. But if our 100-million-plus last-line owners and beneficiaries rise up and demand that their stewards provide them with, well, stewardship— how complicated is *that!*—then all will be well in investment America (or at least better).

So we need to change, not only the costs and the structure of our system of financial intermediation, but the philosophy of its trustees. Way back in 1928, New York's Chief Judge Benjamin Cardozo put it well:

> Many forms of conduct permissible in a workaday world for those acting at arm's-length, are forbidden to those bound by fiduciary ties. A trustee is held to something stricter than the morals of the marketplace. . . . As to this there has developed a tradition that is unbending and inveterate. . . . Not honesty alone, but punctilio of honor the most sensitive, is then the standard of behavior. . . . Only thus has the level of conduct for fiduciaries been kept at a level higher than that trodden by the crowd.

"The Next Frontier"

A final, poignant, note: As I began to wrap up the writing of these remarks, I glanced at the current issue of the *Financial Analysts Journal*, which includes my history of how the mutual fund industry has changed over the past 60 years. Of course, I was drawn to Keith Ambachtsheer's insightful essay, "Beyond Portfolio Theory: The Next Frontier."*

His perceptive thesis noted the conventional wisdom that the next frontier in investing is about "engineering systems to create better financial outcomes for investors. But is it really true?" he asked. He

---

*Keith Ambachtsheer, "Beyond Portfolio Theory: The Next Frontier," *Financial Analysts Journal* 61, no. 1 (January/ February 2005): 29–33.

doubted it, suggesting that we ought to be thinking more about information theory—knowledge about the costs of investing, for example—and agency theory—the conflicting economic interests that manager/agents confront when they make decisions on behalf of their investor/principals. He seeks "better outcomes" for investors by virtue of a material reduction in intermediation costs and a "value for money" philosophy in which the driving force is service to clients and beneficiaries. I can only express my deep appreciation for his willingness to stand up and be counted on these issues that are at the core of my message to you today.

It was Mr. Ambachtsheer's incredibly generous—and, I fear, not entirely deserved—appraisal of the role that I have been fortunate enough to play in articulating these issues over a full half-century that inspired me to provide the strong and perhaps argumentative, even strident, form of my hypothesis—in his words, "too little value at too high a cost"; in my words, after Churchill, "Never has so little been done for so many by so few." Creating Vanguard as a truly *mutual* mutual fund complex all those 30-plus years ago was an effort to pave the way for a new kind of financial intermediation that is designed to give investors their fair share of whatever returns our markets are kind enough to deliver. Had I not walked that walk ever since, I'd hardly be in a position to talk the talk I do today.

It has been a wonderful walk, enabling us to keep costs low and performance high, putting service to clients at the top of our priority list, with indexing and disciplined bond management—both focused on the broadest possible diversification—as the drivers of our remarkable growth. Our share of mutual fund assets has now risen for 23 consecutive years, from 1.8 percent in 1981 to 10.5 percent today. I hope you don't take those comments as bragging. They merely bring me full circle to where I began this commentary, proving, as Schumpeter told us, that "successful innovation is not an act of intellect, but of will." The fund industry has not yet emulated the innovation that is Vanguard, and it may be too much to ask that it will ever do so. But the message I bring you today is that the Relentless Rules of Humble Arithmetic—along with the attendant fiduciary concepts—will continue to resonate with investors, and they will accept no less. Forewarned is forearmed.

Appendix

**TABLE 2.4   MARKETING OR MANAGEMENT?:
RELATIVE RETURNS VERSUS NUMBER OF FUNDS**
(firms offering 15 or fewer funds are shaded)

Firm	Equal-Wtd. % Outperformance*	Number of Funds
Dodge & Cox	98	4
First Eagle	97	5
Calamos	91	8
So. Eastern/Longleaf	90	3
American Funds	79	26
Royce	79	14
Harris Associates	77	7
Vanguard	76	75
PIMCO	76	51
Franklin Templeton	71	100
T. Rowe Price	71	72
Janus	70	21
ING	69	60
Nuveen	65	36
American Century	64	54
WM Advisors	64	15
Davis	62	7
Fidelity	62	207
Waddell & Reed	61	45
USAA	61	31
Oppenheimer	60	48
MFS	59	61
Prudential	59	49
New York Life	58	22
US Bancorp	57	37
Columbia Mgmt	56	72
AllianceBernstein	55	57
Banc One	54	36
Neuberger Berman	54	14
Lord Abbett	53	27
Scudder	52	65

TABLE 2.4   (CONTINUED)

Firm	Equal-Wtd. % Outperformance*	Number of Funds
Van Kampen	52	43
Federated	52	37
Evergreen	51	57
Citigroup	50	57
Wells Fargo	50	39
Eaton Vance	49	73
Morgan Stanley Adv	49	50
Goldman Sachs	49	34
The Hartford	48	33
Putnam	47	54
John Hancock	47	35
Dreyfus	45	126
Delaware	44	56
Strong	44	42
Thrivent Fin'l	44	25
Trusco Cap	43	24
Merrill Lynch	40	58
Aim	39	62
Nations Funds	38	42
American Exp	37	60
BlackRock	36	32
Pioneer	33	24
JPMorgan	32	38

	15 Funds or Less		More Than 15 Funds	
Summary	Performance*	Number of Funds	Performance[†]	Number of Funds
(Average)	77%	8	48%	52

*Over 10 years.
[†]Outperformance data are adjusted because Fidelity study ignored initial sales charges and B-class shares.

**TABLE 2.5   PRIVATE OR CONGLOMERATE?:
RELATIVE RETURNS VERSUS ORGANIZATIONAL
STRUCTURE (private firms are shaded, publicly
held firms are in italics, and conglomerates are
in roman font)**

Firm	Equal-Wtd. % Outperformance
Dodge & Cox	98
First Eagle	97
Calamos	91
So. Eastern/Longleaf	90
Royce	79
American Funds	79
Harris Associates	77
PIMCO	76
Vanguard	76
T. Rowe Price	*71*
Franklin Templeton	*71*
Janus	*70*
ING	69
Nuveen	*65*
American Century	64
WM Advisors	64
Davis	62
Fidelity	62
Waddell & Reed	*61*
USAA	61
Oppenheimer	60
Prudential	59
MFS	59
New York Life	58
US Bancorp	57
Columbia Mgmt	56
AllianceBernstein	55
Banc One	54
Neuberger Berman	54
Lord Abbett	53
Van Kampen	52

TABLE 2.5   (CONTINUED)

Firm	Equal-Wtd. % Outperformance
Scudder	52
Federated	*52*
Evergreen	51
Wells Fargo	50
Citigroup	50
Goldman Sachs	49
Morgan Stan Adv.	49
Eaton Vance	*49*
The Hartford	48
John Hancock	47
Putnam	47
Dreyfus	45
Strong	44
Delaware	44
Thrivent Fin'l	44
Trusco Cap	43
Merrill Lynch	40
Aim	39
Nations Funds	38
American Express	37
BlackRock	36
Pioneer	33
JP Morgan	32

Summary

Financial Conglomerate				Publicly Held			
Perf.*	Firms	Avg. Funds	Assets (Tr.)	*Perf.**	*Firms*	*Avg. Funds*	*Assets (Tr.)*
45%	34	47	$1.6	*60%*	*7*	*55*	*$0.6*

Private			
Perf.*	Firms	Avg. Funds	Assets (Tr.)
71%	13	34	$1.3

*Outperformance data are adjusted because Fidelity study ignored initial sales charges and B-class shares.

Chapter 3

The Telltale Chart*

T he first sentence of Edgar Allan Poe's "The Telltale Heart" reads: "True!—nervous—very, very awfully nervous I have been and am . . . but will you say that I am mad?" And I confess to being a tad nervous in tackling a subject that I frankly wouldn't *dare* to tackle before most investors. The key to whatever success I may have enjoyed during my long investment career is that the Lord gave me enough common sense to recognize the majesty of simplicity. But I've learned that to discover the priceless jewels of simplicity, it's often necessary to cut through a swath of complexity. The complex subject I'll now address is *reversion to the mean (RTM)*; the jewel of simplicity is revealed in "The Telltale Chart," the title of this essay.

"The Telltale Heart," of course, is the story of a heart that doesn't seem to stop beating (sort of like mine, come to think of it!). Even after the death of its owner, its steady drumbeat ticks away like "a watch enveloped in cotton," as Poe described it, and becomes more and more distinct. RTM— the pervasive law of gravity that prevails in the financial markets—never stops. While its drumbeat is hardly regular, it never fails. For the returns of market sectors, of managed investment portfolios, and even of the market itself mysteriously return, over time, to norms of one kind or another.

---

*Based on a speech at the Morningstar Investment Forum in Chicago, Illinois, on June 26, 2002. Given the passage of time from its delivery to mid-2010, the charts have been updated, along with some of the data, all clearly identified in boldface type.

Six Manifestations of RTM

Today I'm going to talk about how RTM can help us to understand financial markets and thereby become more successful investors. I'll talk first about RTM in market sectors, focusing first on large-cap and small-cap stocks and second on growth and value stocks. Next, I'll turn to RTM in the returns of the recently beleaguered Standard & Poor's 500 Stock Index relative to total U.S. stock market. Third, I'll talk about the reversion of equity mutual fund returns to the market mean. Then—in part because the Bogleheads would be disappointed if I didn't—I'll turn to RTM as it is reflected in the results of what have become known as "slice-and-dice" portfolios, essentially diversified portions that seek to outpace the broad market index by systematically overweighting various sectors. Finally, I'll examine the question of whether stock market returns themselves revert to one kind of mean or another.

Giving you this copious stream of information requires me to present a total of no less than 11 charts. That's a tall order, but less so when we consider the remarkable similarity of each of the charts showing RTM—the irregular swings above and below the mean before returning to it—with which I summarize each of these six points; I think you'll understand my line of argument. For the telltale chart that demonstrates the tendency of investment phenomena to revert to the mean repeats itself in each example. When I'm finished, I hope you'll share my conclusion: *The most successful investors will respect the power of reversion to the mean.*

Let me begin by criticizing the vastly oversimplified but typical way we look at long-term results. We hear, for example, that "small-cap stocks outperform large-cap stocks by almost two percentage points a year," using as evidence the entire historical record we have available (from, as it happens, 1926 to 2002). Or that the, well, Magic Fund "has beaten the market by eight-and-a-half percentage points a year over its lifetime." Or that "stocks provide higher returns than bonds," in each case without acknowledging that each and every comparison we see is *period dependent*. Whether or not the period has been selected to prove a point, neither the starting date of a comparison nor its concluding date are random. Compilations of historical financial market returns are not actuarial tables, and, as you'll see, the past is *not* prologue. Indeed, it is usually *anti-prologue*. Each thesis, it turns out, tends to bear the seeds of its own antithesis.

RTM—Large-Cap Stocks versus Small-Cap Stocks

Few investment principles are as unchallenged as the perennial asser-tion that over the long-run small-cap stocks outperform large-cap stocks. The data we have available are unequivocal on this point: Since 1928, according to the University of Chicago Center for Research in Securities Prices (CRSP), small stocks have provided an annual return of 12.5 percent, versus 10.8 percent for large caps. And, over that 74-year period, the long-term compounding works its magic; each dol-lar in small-cap stocks grows to $6,000, while each dollar in large-cap stocks grows to just $2,000. Bear in mind, of course, small-caps carried a higher risk (standard deviation of 30 percent vs. 22 percent). But after adjustment to that higher risk level, the large-cap annual return rises to 12.9 percent, *higher* than for small-caps. So never ignore risk.

But that imposing chart—like the proverbial bikini—conceals more than it reveals. I would strongly urge you to not accept that con-clusion without transforming it into the telltale chart that is devised simply by dividing the *cumulative* returns of one data series into another, year after year—in this case dividing the cumulative large-cap stock return into the cumulative small-cap return. Then we see that the long period was punctuated by a whole series of reversions to the mean. Virtually the *entire* small-cap advantage took place during the first 18 years. Then large-cap (14.2 percent per year) dominates small-cap (11.7 percent) from 1945 through 1964; small-cap through 1968 (32.0 percent vs. 11.0 percent); large-cap through 1973 (2.5 percent vs. −10.8 percent); then small-cap through 1983, large through 1990, and so on. On balance, these to-and-fro reversions have canceled each other out, and since 1945 the returns of large-cap stocks and small-cap stocks have been virtually *identical* (12.7 percent vs. 13.3 percent). So ask yourself whether the evidence to justify the claim of small-cap superiority isn't too fragile a foundation on which to base a long-term strategy. **By the end of 2009, the respective returns were: large-cap 10.2 percent; small-cap 12.2 percent. The ratio rose to 4.2 in 2004 and ended 2009 at 4.4, a record high, but in fact about where it reposed three decades earlier (see Figure 3.1).**

Ask yourself, too, if the data are accurate. Reconstructing past returns of market segments is no mean task, especially among small-cap

FIGURE 3.1   RTM: SMALL VERSUS LARGE, 1928–2009

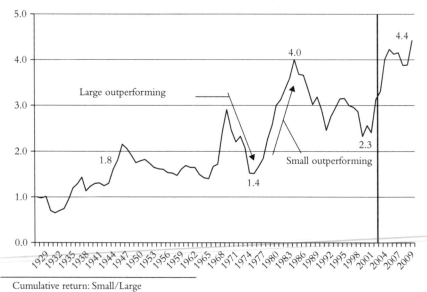

Cumulative return: Small/Large

stocks. Ask yourself whether transaction costs are accurately imputed (or even imputed at all), and whether survivor bias is present. Together, these issues raise questions about the validity of even the most responsibly conducted of academic studies. And then, even if they're valid, ask yourself whether the game is worth the 40 percent increase in investment risk.

Finally, ask yourself the extent to which any of the results of what are in effect indexes of market sectors can be replicated in the real world of investing. Investing costs money, and it is a truism—and increasingly a trite one—that all of the investors in the stock market (or in any discrete market sector) *earn* the market return *before* the costs of financial intermediation, but actually *receive* the return *after* those costs. If the cost of implementing a small stock strategy exceeds the costs of a large stock strategy by one percentage point a year or more, as seems to be the case, even if the alleged long-term advantage reflected in the data in fact materializes, the victory may be pyrrhic.

RTM—Value Stocks versus Growth Stocks

I won't belabor those important qualifications of data integrity, risk, and real-world costs. But each also comes into play in the next area that I'll consider, value stocks versus growth stocks.* Here, the long-term difference is even *more* dramatic than small versus large: The annual return since 1928 is reported as 12.2 percent for large-cap value stocks and 9.6 percent for large-cap growth stocks, a difference of fully 2.6 percentage points. The compounding of those returns results in a stunning chasm in the final value of an initial dollar: Value $5,100, Growth $900. Again, higher risk (standard deviation of value was 27 percent, vs. 20 percent for growth) accounts for much of the gap, but even the increased *risk-adjusted* return of 11.2 percent for growth stocks falls one percentage point short of the value outcome. The data are so impressive that one wants simply to say: *Case closed!* **Through 2009, large-cap growth's annual return was 9.1 percent, and large-cap value's was 11.2 percent. After an especially nasty 2008 for value stocks, the updated ratio had fallen to 5.0, well below the high of 7.2 reached in 2006 and the near-peak level of 6.5 achieved a full quarter-century earlier (see Figure 3.2).**

But now let's turn to our telltale chart and carefully examine the record. While the RTM is hardly as clear as its earlier counterpart, we can observe some significant things going on. Curiously, during the first 27 years(!), not much happens. Growth wins by a bit in the first 12 years, value in the next 11, after which both series deliver about the same annual returns through 1961 (16 percent). Value leads again through 1968, and after a four-year hiatus rises again through 1977, pauses for four years, and then surges through 1988. Then comes the heft of the great bull market, with growth leading value fairly consistently and by a wide margin (21 percent vs. 16 percent annually) through 1999. That sharp dichotomy was then followed by the sharpest mean reversion in market history, with growth toppling by −28 percent in 2000–2001, with value off less than 1 percent. RTM strikes again! But, perhaps

---

*The data for these charts are provided in the famously comprehensive studies undertaken by Professor Kenneth French of Dartmouth and Eugene Fama of the University of Chicago.

FIGURE 3.2   RTM: LARGE VALUE VERSUS LARGE GROWTH, 1928–2009

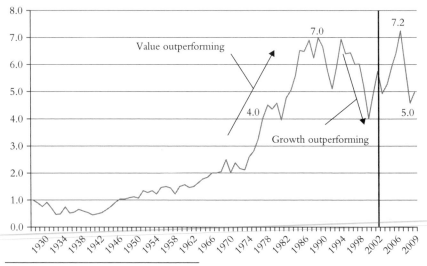

Cumulative return: LV/LG

surprisingly, over the entire period 1984-2001, growth (15.3 percent per year) retains a fragile grip on its leadership over value (14.4 percent).

The data I've shown you, of course, represent the statistical reconstruction of market sector returns. So, I'd like to examine not abstract portfolios, but growth and value *mutual funds* that operate in the real world. The data are available from 1937, and the general patterns parallel those of the French–Fama study, but with a curious dichotomy. While the average annual return of the *growth* mutual funds (11.6 percent) during this long period actually exceeded the French–Fama large-cap growth stocks (11.2 percent), the *value* mutual fund return of 11.0 percent fell far below that of French–Fama value return of 15.2 percent, perhaps because the French–Fama value *portfolio* has a risk fully 45 percent above the value *funds*. Nonetheless, the French–Fama combined growth and value returns exceed the combined fund returns by 1.9 percent per year, a pretty good approximation of the costs that mutual funds incur. So investors should not ignore the obvious costs of implementing a strategy that rises, pristinely, out of academic studies that cannot be precisely replicated in the real world.

The reason for the dichotomy between these markedly different sets of growth fund and value fund relative returns may rest on the fact that value managers invest less on the basis of the statistical criteria that sector indexes use to differentiate growth stocks from value stocks (usually price-to-book-value) and more on other factors. But in any event, the validity of the growth and value index statistics rests on the soundness of the indexes used in measuring the sectors they purport to represent. Consider, for example, the S&P/Barra Growth Index. Based on relative price-to-book ratios, this index categorizes 50 percent of the weight of the S&P 500 index as growth stocks. When their prices soared during the 1990s, the number of growth stocks in the index tumbled from 220 to 106 in 1999—114 erstwhile growth stocks were unceremoniously shoved into the Value Index. Then, when growth stocks stumbled, 51 "value" stocks returned to the Growth Index, bringing the present total to 157—and rising! With the huge asset write-downs we're currently seeing, many former growth stocks are now defined as value stocks. So differences in both management costs and index composition should make us extremely cautious about the application of abstract data to the real world.

In any event, place me squarely in the camp of the contrarians who don't accept the inherent superiority of value strategies over growth strategies. I've been excoriated for my views, but I'm comforted by this reported exchange between Dr. Fama and a participant at a recent investment conference: "What do you say to otherwise intelligent people like Jack Bogle who examine this same data and conclude that there is no size or value premium?" His response: "How far are they from the slide? If I get far enough away, *I don't see it either* . . . Whether you decide to tilt toward value depends on whether you are willing to bear *the associated risk.* . . . The market portfolio is always efficient. . . . For most people, the market portfolio is the most sensible decision."

RTM in the Market Portfolio

Like Dr. Fama, I believe that *the market portfolio is the most sensible decision.* It takes the need for judgment out of your decision making; it reduces cost; it increases tax-efficiency; it avoids the need to pore over past market data to figure out why the data are what they are. Then, if you accept the data, you have to decide whether the patterns they have revealed will persist during the span of years remaining on your investment horizon.

In a temporal sense, the all-market portfolio is consistent with the spiritual argument about the existence of God put forth by Pascal three centuries ago. If you bet God *is*, you live a moral life at puny cost of giving up a few temptations. But that's *all* you lose. If you bet God is *not* and give in to all your temptations, you're forever dammed. *Consequences*, Pascal concluded, must outweigh *possibilities*. Similarly in the stock market, if you bet the market is efficient and hold the market portfolio, you'll earn the market's return. But if you bet against it and are wrong, the consequences could be painful. Why would you run the risk of losing, perhaps badly, when the market return, earned by so few over the long-run, is there for the taking?

Still, we are faced with the question of how to *define* the market portfolio. When I started the first index mutual fund 27 years ago, the Standard & Poor's 500 Composite Stock Price Index was generally considered to be the appropriate market portfolio. Of course it represented only 80 percent of the market, but there were few other indexes from which to choose. (The Wilshire 5000 Total Market Index, dating to 1970, was little-known and untested.) Today, the Wilshire is readily available and widely accepted, its validity as a proxy for the total U.S. stock market confirmed by both CRSP and French-Fama, which take the data as far back as 1926. The three indexes share correlations of something like 0.999, so there can be little doubt about their validity. An all-market index fund is clearly the optimal way to hold the U.S. stock market.

But I must spring to the defense of index funds linked to the Standard & Poor's 500 index. Whereas the 500 index has been excoriated by Morningstar ("500 Index Funds Losing Their Allure?"), by *Money* magazine ("Is the S&P 500 Rigged?"), and by *Institutional Investor* ("Is Time Running Out for the S&P 500?"), I would answer those questions, "No," "No," and "No." The criticism has been greatly overdone. Yes, the 500 is heavily weighted by large stocks. But so is the U.S. stock market. Yes, during the great bubble, the 500 was dominated by overpriced technology stocks. But so was the U.S. stock market. Yes, many of the additions of large tech stocks in the 500 in recent years seem, in retrospect, absurd. But these companies were already major factors in the market itself. Yes, its composition changes substantially over the years, but so does the composition of investors' portfolios. And yes, the 500 didn't even *become* the 500 until 1955. From its inception in 1926, it had been comprised of just 90 stocks. In all of these respects, the S&P 500 is a flawed index. But for all of the criticism heaped on it, *the S&P 500 works.*

So now the most important "yes" of all: For all of its real and imagined failings, yes, the S&P 500 has provided a truly remarkable representation of what we now know to be the returns of the total U.S. stock market. What is more, with a 10.7 percent annual return since 1926, it has actually *outperformed* the broader market's 10.3 percent return. But yet another telltale chart warns us not to look to the 500 for excess returns. This entire excess arose during 1926–1932. Since then, the 12.2 percent annual return of the S&P 500 has been *exactly the same* as the return of the total stock market. But overall, the RTM has been remarkably small; almost trivial. Yes, when large-caps dominate, as in most of the 1982–2000 bull market, the S&P 500 will dominate. And yes, when small-caps dominate (as in 1975–1980), the S&P will lag. But since the S&P continues to represent more than 75 percent of the market's capitalization, it would seem a bit naïve to doubt that it will continue to revert to the market mean in the years ahead. One more valuable lesson from our telltale chart: Investors in 500 index funds need feel no compulsion to change horses and switch to a total market portfolio—especially if it would result in a taxable capital gain. Over the long haul, the S&P 500 will do the same job of matching the market that it has always done. **Through 2009, the annual returns were: S&P 500, 9.8 percent; total stock market, 9.5 percent. The ratio reverted sharply to the mean, falling from nearly 1.4 to 1.2, as small- and mid-cap stocks outpaced the S&P 500 (see Figure 3.3).**

RTM in Equity Mutual Funds

The telltale chart also helps us to observe the important role played by RTM in the returns of mutual funds. How much more we can learn if we look, rather than at a simple summary of a fund's long-term record,

FIGURE 3.3   RTM: S&P 500 VERSUS TOTAL STOCK MARKET, 1927–2009

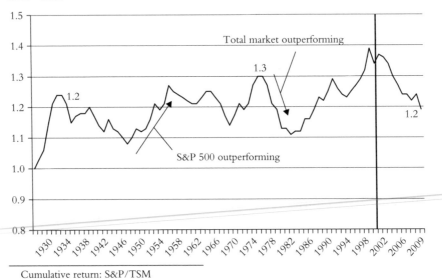

Cumulative return: S&P/TSM

at a chart showing its market-related returns over time! Consider the remarkable record of one of America's greatest mutual fund success stories. I'll call it the "Magic Fund," for its long-term record is probably as good a record as we can find. Formed in 1964, the annual return of Magic Fund averaged 19.7 percent per year, fully 8.5 percentage points ahead of the Standard & Poor's 500 index. Result: $10,000 invested at the outset, with all dividends reinvested, would have been worth $9.3 million(!) as 2002 began. The same investment in the index would have been valued at just $560,000. It sounds like a marvelous record. And it *is!*

But now let's convert those figures to an RTM chart. Like so many funds, the record was sensational in the early years when assets were small, and, in this case, before the fund ever became available to the public. From 1964 through 1981, Magic Fund's return averaged 22 percent a year, putting to shame the relatively dismal 9 percent return of the S&P 500. By the time it was first offered to the public in 1981, it had soared to *10 times* the market return. And in the first five years thereafter, it rose to almost 14 times the market's return. Even as assets grew into the billions, and the tens of billions, and then over the $30 billion mark, it continued to prosper, rising to nearly 19 times in 1993.

From such lofty heights, RTM becomes a virtual certainty, and accelerates as the fund gets larger and larger, its portfolio inevitably more and more marketlike. By 1993, the game was over. It lost one-sixth of its edge by 1997, and since then, it has been in lockstep with the S&P 500. As the telltale chart shows us (see Figure 3.4), Magic Fund's return has been virtually identical to that of the S&P index (14 percent). Indeed the chart suggests that it has now become a closet index fund, its old magic long gone. But the magic of the telltale *chart* remains, making obvious that the old order hath changeth, more than a dozen years ago. **Through 2009, the spread continued to shrink: the Magic Fund's return was 16 percent; the S&P 500's return was 9.5 percent. The reversion to the mean continued, as the ratio of the fund's return relative to the S&P 500 closed at 14.4, virtually the same as 1983, more than a full quarter-century ago.**

I'll offer up just two more RTM charts to reinforce the message that the telltale chart is virtually essential in appraising the records of individual funds (see Figures 3.5 and 3.6). In retrospect, such charts might have protected fund investors from the ghastly penalties they paid for adverse fund selection during the late bubble. One is a well-managed,

FIGURE 3.4 RTM: MAGIC FUND VERSUS S&P 500, 1964–2009

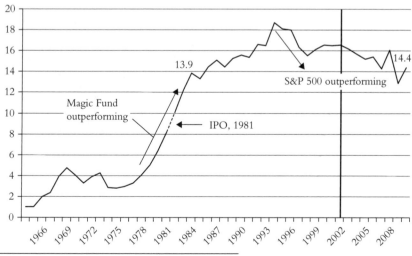

Cumulative return: Magic Fund/S&P 500

FIGURE 3.5   RTM: LARGE GROWTH FUND VERSUS S&P 500, 1986–2008*

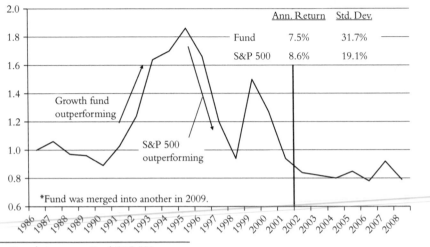

Cumulative return: Fund/S&P 500

FIGURE 3.6   RTM: LARGE VALUE FUND VERSUS S&P 500, 1986–2009

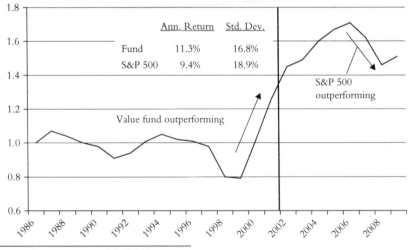

Cumulative return: Fund/S&P 500

low-cost, value-oriented equity fund. Despite its low-risk strategy, it tracked the bull market nicely in 1986–1997, only to fall back during the technology mania. But when the day of reckoning came, it showed its staunch character. The other pattern is just the reverse: An aggressive growth fund is not particularly impressive during the early part of the period, but then soars as its high-risk strategy pays off in 1991–1995. Attracting large assets, it falters badly during 1996–1998, only to make one last surge in 1999. Then comes the bust that always follows the boom, and the fund collapses again. No, higher risk doesn't necessarily equate to higher returns. **Such charts would have helped investors avoid the perils of the recent bubble. The large growth fund never recovered from its collapse from 1995 to 2002, and was merged out of existence in 2009. The large value fund's ratio, 1.3 in 2001, rose to 1.7 in 2006, only to fall back in 2009 to a level of about 1.5.**

Years ago, I suggested that Morningstar replace its traditional chart with one that included the RTM that is so clearly illustrated by these telltale charts. Alas, the editors decided against it. In fairness, however, by showing quarterly returns relative to peer funds, the revised charts Morningstar now provides *do* capture some of the spirit of the idea. But, ever the optimist, I still hold out hope that Morningstar will reconsider and decide to employ the telltale chart on its fund pages.

RTM and "Slice and Dice"

"Slice and dice"—S&D to the Bogleheads—is often talked about not only on the Morningstar web site, but among financial engineers, including those at (dare I admit it!) Princeton University. In its simplest form, the idea is to garner excess returns by holding a portfolio that (1) adds to the market portfolio those asset classes that are deemed likely to deliver superior returns; (2) introduces assets having a low correlation with the stock market; and (3) periodically rebalances each asset class to its original weight.

Let's quickly examine two such portfolios. First, a conventional one, one-quarter each in the S&P 500 index, large value stocks, small value stocks, and stocks in the smallest two deciles—that is, a portfolio that overweights value and small-cap shares. Over history, it has clearly delivered: an annual return of 12.9 percent vs. 10.3 percent for the S&P index, albeit with a 41 percent higher risk—a standard deviation of 28 percent, versus 20 percent for the S&P 500. When we bring the telltale Figure 3.7 into play, however, we see period-dependency and RTM at work. Note, for example, how much of its success came in the 1942–1945 bull market, when it rose by 410 percent(!), nearly three *times* the 150 percent return of the S&P index—doubtless a nonrecurring event. **Through 2009, the annual return on the first slice-and-dice portfolio declined to 12.1 percent, and the S&P 500 fell to 9.5 percent. The ratio rose to 7.1.**

Note, too, that the returns of the S&P index and S&D portfolios were virtually identical (13.8 percent and 14.0 percent annual return) for the next two decades, ending in 1964. Then the S&D portfolio surges intermittently through 1983, only to falter over the following 17(!) years (annual return of 13.9 percent, vs. 16.3 percent for the S&P)—meaning that there was virtually no gap for 32 years—a pretty

FIGURE 3.7 RTM: 4 × 25 PORTFOLIO VERSUS S&P 500, 1928–2009

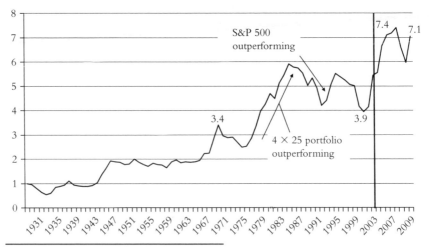

Cumulative return: Portfolio/S&P 500.

long horizon when you think about it. For the full period, of course, the S&D portfolio dominated, but if we simply levered the S&P 500 to equalize its risk with the S&D portfolio, its risk-adjusted return would have risen to 12.4 percent. Surely a shortfall of 0.5 percent is mere rounding error in a numerical exercise of this nature.

It is not insignificant, of course, that the value/small-cap tilted S&D portfolio we've examined was chosen largely in hindsight, reflecting the all-too-human temptation to rely on sectors that commend themselves by their past success. So, let's take a look at what an investor might have done 30 years ago. We'll hold a 25 percent S&P 500 position and then add three 25 percent allocations to alternative classes that might have been popular at the time: Small-cap, international, and, because it is the single asset class that most diversifies an equity portfolio (i.e., has the lowest correlation to the stock market of any asset class), gold (it didn't look silly *then!*). Now let's examine the record of this alternative portfolio. Obviously, this chart tells a different story. While the S&D portfolio again wins, it wins by only a modest amount—a 12.8 percent annual return for the 4 × 25 portfolio versus 12.3 percent for the S&P 500. Still, the value of $1 grew to $42 in the 4 × 25 portfolio, compared to $36 for the S&P index, a nice payoff for what proved to be, on balance, a smart selection of sectors.

But now see what the telltale chart reveals. First, the entire excess return—and then some!—appears in the first nine years, when gold boomed. Second, strength in the international sector pretty well maintained that gain through 1988, after which international stocks lagged the S&P 500, often by double-digit amounts, for 7 of the next 10 years. Yet, despite the recovery of this alternative 4 × 25 portfolio during the past two years, its cumulative average return of 10 percent since 1979 pales by comparison with the S&P 500 return of 15 percent. The telltale chart then, tells us two distinctly contradictory tales about this version of the S&D strategy: Yes, it wins during the first 8 years; no, it loses during the last 22. **Through 2009, the soaring price of gold has helped offset the below-average returns of the other components of the alternative slice-and-dice portfolio, which has provided an annual return for the full period of 12 percent. The S&P 500's return was 10 percent. The RTM**

ratio increased from 1.1 in 2001 to 2.0 in 2009, still far below its 2.9 peak reached back in 1979 (see Figure 3.8).

So slice and dice is what you make it. Like all other investment strategies ever devised by the mind of man, sometimes it works and sometimes it doesn't. Uncertainty rules. Even if the overall program appears to outpace the S&P index, over a long inevitably period-dependent span of years, don't forget how little(!) it costs to emulate the total stock market in the real world nor how much(!) it costs to use active funds to fill the S&D boxes, and even to use passive funds to do so. If we take the extra risk into account, there's a real question about whether the game is worth the candle. And even if you don't accept my challenge to S&D, I urge you, before you plunge into a 4 × 25 portfolio, to put more than 25 percent in the total market—say 55 percent. Then put just 15 percent in the three slices that you dice, thereby taking much of the risk out of your decision. Think then, about a *1 × 55 percent + 3 × 15 percent* portfolio. If it is true, as Dr. Fama (and most other academics, to say nothing of many, many

FIGURE 3.8   RTM: ALTERNATIVE 4 × 25 PORTFOLIO VERSUS S&P 500, 1971–2009

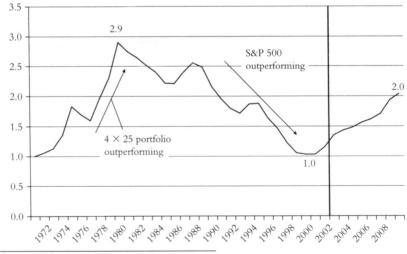

Cumulative return: Portfolio/S&P 500

practitioners) says, that "for most people, the market portfolio is the most sensible decision," you might as well make the most of it.

RTM and the Stock Market

And, yes, reversion to the mean is the rule, not only for stock sectors, for individual equity funds, and for investment strategies that mix asset classes, it is also the rule for the returns provided by the stock market itself. If we go back through a century of stock market history (using Jeremy Siegel's data), it's easy enough to chart it: The real (inflation-adjusted) return on stocks has *averaged* 6.6 percent per year, but with considerable extremes (see Figure 3.9). This powerful panorama shows that the highest 10-year annual returns have ranges around 15 percent, coming in the mid-1900s, the late 1920s, the early 1960s, and the late 1990s. Then, in the late 1910s, the late 1930s, and the late 1970s, returns tumbled to 2 percent or less, sometimes even negative.

FIGURE 3.9   ROLLING 10-YEAR STOCK MARKET REAL RETURNS, 1901–2009

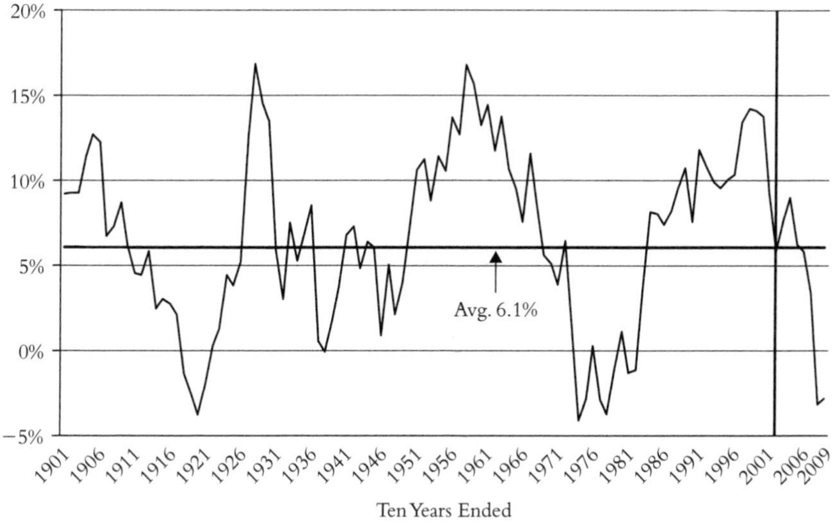

Ten Years Ended

Since the market's 15 percent return in the decade ended in 1998 was the third highest in all history, one can only hope that the full might of RTM does not strike again.* **Of course, RTM *did* strike again, and the real market return of −2.8 percent for the decade ended 2009 was close to the historical lows. Now let's hope RTM—upward this time—*will* strike again.**

Why do stocks provide such high returns in some periods and such low—even negative—returns in others? Part of the reason is that the course of our economy is not smooth. We have prosperity and recession, even boom and bust. Those are simply the *economics* of enterprise, and while they *may* be *tamer* than in the past, they are not *tamed*. But there is more: the *emotions* of investors, whose greed leads them to value stocks too dearly at one moment and whose fear leads them to value stocks too cheaply at another. It is this combination of economics—*reality*—and emotions—*illusion*—that shapes stock market returns.

Economics is reflected in *investment* return (earnings and dividends); emotions are reflected in the *speculative* return (the impact of changing price-to-earnings ratios). During the past century, the real investment return was 6.5 percent, accounting for the lion's share of the market's 6.6 percent real return, with speculative returns contributing just 0.1 percent. Clearly, the cumulative investment return is the piper that plays the tune, with earnings and dividends climbing year after year—sometimes faster, sometimes slower, sometimes even falling. Stock market returns dance assiduously to the investment tune, but periodically move above or below, seemingly independently. But the iron law of investing is apparent: *In the short run, speculative return drives the market. In the long run, investment return is all that matters.* **By the close of 2009, the annual long-term real return had dropped to 6.2 percent; the investment return had dropped to 6.0 percent; and the speculative return had risen to 0.2 percent (see Figure 3.10).**

---

*I've often addressed the issue of expected stock returns during the first decade of the 21st century—at length in the first edition (1999) of my *Common Sense on Mutual Funds* (especially in the appendix that compares 1999 with 1929), and in *John Bogle on Investing: The First 50 Years* (especially Chapter 4).

FIGURE 3.10 GROWTH OF $1: FUNDAMENTAL REAL RETURN VERSUS MARKET REAL RETURN, 1900–2009

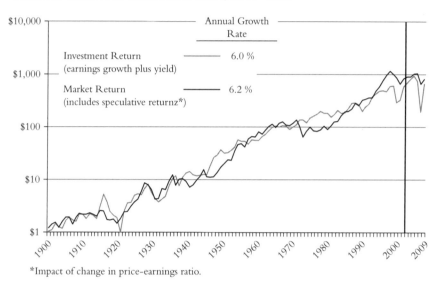

*Impact of change in price-earnings ratio.

While only our faith that our nation's capitalistic economy will continue to thrive can give us confidence in the long-term course of dividends and earnings, it is not faith but common sense that tells us when stock prices get substantially misaligned with corporate values. When the stock market's cumulative *total* return diverges significantly from the market's *investment* return, then it is only a matter of time until the two converge again. Here is where RTM comes into play. This final telltale chart reflects the division of the cumulative investment return into the actual market return at the end of each year. Result: These aberrations between investment return and market return are dramatically highlighted. Thus, the misalignment of prices with values at the 1929 peak was followed by the crash of the 1930s. On the other hand, the low valuations of the late 1940s and early 1950s laid the foundation for the go-go era of the mid-1960s and the "Favorite Fifty" craze of the early 1970s. The resulting bust set the stage for the Great Bull Market that began in August 1982 and ended abruptly in March 2000.

At that point as the chart shows, the disjunction between *market returns*—stock prices—and investment returns—enterprise values—only once before had been wider, so predicting a subsequent decline was no great challenge. But while we may know a lot about *what* will happen in the financial market, we never know *when* it will happen. Indeed the ratio was at 120—a clear warning sign—at the end of 1997. Yet the ratio continued to rise until it hit 150 at the end of 1999, and rose even further to 160 at what proved to be the 2000 peak. Yet despite the subsequent 40 percent market drop we have so far endured, the ratio remains at 110, still above the baseline. Where it goes next, *nobody* knows.

But history and the iron rule of RTM strongly suggest caution, since valuations remain high today. The future will depend on subsequent earnings growth. So we'd best hope American business turns its attention away from the ghastly financial manipulation of recent years—focused on hyping stock *prices* in the short-term—and toward its traditional character—focusing on building corporate *values* over the long term. That's a far harder job, for innovation, productivity, efficiency, economy—yes, and leadership and character, too—are tough standards to measure up to in a competitive global economy.

FIGURE 3.11   A CENTURY OF RTM IN THE STOCK MARKET: REAL MARKET VERSUS REAL INVESTMENT RETURN, 1900–2009

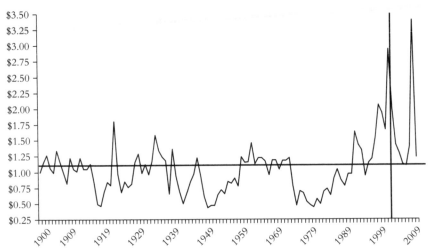

But it is what our society must demand of our corporate stewards. **"Caution" proved to be a good idea. The ratio fell from 2.9 in 2001 to 1.1 in 2006, soared to 2.4 in 2008, and collapsed, ending at 1.2 in 2009, reverting almost precisely to the long-term mean (see Figure 3.11).**

This, Too, Shall Pass Away

The message of the telltale chart is universal. Unlike the regular, louder, ever-more-distinct pulsations of the telltale heart in Poe's frightening story, however, reversion-to-the-mean in the financial markets is irregular and unpredictable—sometimes fast and sometimes slow, sometimes distinct and sometimes almost invisible. Just when we despair of its universality, it strikes again. And so there is always hope today for those who await the almost inevitable recovery in stock prices. But I remind you that while we may know *what* will happen, we never know *when*. So rather than relying on hope—never a particularly good idea in the stock market—rely on an asset allocation that focuses on not only the probability of reward, but the consequences of risk.

It occurs to me that the best advice I can leave with today's investors came in my first book, written way back in 1993. It was a *Caveat Emptor* entitled, "This Too Shall Pass Away":

An Eastern monarch asked his Wise Men to give him advice that would be "true and appropriate in all times and situations." Similarly, I sought such advice for investors in the financial markets, who "feel richer when the market rises and poorer when it declines . . . although the underlying value of the business enterprises that comprise the market may have changed not a whit." I cautioned investors not to give way to a bull market atmosphere and become infected with the enthusiasm and greed of the great public, any more than they should give way to a bear market atmosphere and become infected with the negativism and fear displayed by the great public.

Success in investing, I wrote, "will depend on your ability to realize, at the heights of ebullience and the depths of despair alike"—to answer the question asked by the monarch—that "this too shall pass away."*

In 2010, after the trials and tribulations of the past 17 years, I wouldn't change a word of this paragraph.

---

*John C. Bogle, *Bogle on Mutual Funds: New Perspectives for the Intelligent Investor* (New York: McGraw-Hill, 1993).

Chapter 4

A Question So Important That It Should Be Hard to Think about Anything Else*

During the past 60 years, the field of financial and securities analysis has undergone enormous growth and ever-increasing professionalization. Yet the investment principles upon which portfolio managers and investment advisers operate have in many respects remained unchanged.

Consider this advice regarding the responsibilities of the financial analyst:

It is my basic thesis—for the future as for the past—that an intelligent and well-trained financial analyst can do a useful

*Based on an essay published in the Winter 2008 edition of the *Journal of Portfolio Management*. The essay won the Bernstein Fabozzi/Jacobs Levy Award for Outstanding Article for 2008. Reprinted with permission from *Institutional Investor Journals*, copyright © 2010. For more information, please visit www.iijournals.com.

job as portfolio adviser for many different kinds of people, and thus amply justify his existence. Also I claim he can do this by adhering to relatively simple principles of sound investment; e.g., a proper balance between bonds and stocks; proper diversification; selection of a representative list; discouragement of speculative operations not suited for the client's financial position or temperament—and for this he does not need to be a wizard in picking winners from the stock list or in foretelling market movements.

While it might surprise those who may be familiar with the ideas I've advocated during my career, these words are not mine but are rather the words of the legendary Benjamin Graham, as they appeared in the *Financial Analysts Journal* of May/June 1963, celebrating the 25th anniversary of the New York Society of Security Analysts. To say that I passionately subscribe to these simple principles of balance, diversification, and focus on the long term—to say nothing of being skeptical that stockpickers and market forecasting wizards can, on balance and over time, add value—would be an understatement. Indeed, it's pretty much what I wrote in my college senior thesis in 1951.

I devote a chapter of my *Little Book of Common Sense Investing* to showing that, given the radical change in our investment environment since 1963, Graham would have gone even further; he would have endorsed the stock market index fund as the core strategy for the vast majority of investors. Warren Buffett, who worked closely with Graham, not only personally assured me of Graham's endorsement of indexing but put it in writing in his own endorsement of the *Little Book*.

When I entered the mutual fund industry 56 years ago—to work for fund pioneer Walter Morgan, whose Wellington Fund was and remains today the exemplar of these principles—the industry invested pretty much in the manner prescribed by Graham. The portfolios of the major equity funds consisted largely of a diversified list of blue-chip stocks, and their portfolio managers invested for the long term. They eschewed speculation; they operated their funds at costs that were (by today's standards) minuscule; and they delivered marketlike returns to their investors. What's more, as their long-term records clearly show, those fund managers were hardly "wizards in picking winners."

An Industry Changes

But if the conservative investment principles of the Wellington Fund have remained substantially unchanged to this day, the fund industry has become a vastly different creature from all those years ago. How different?—let me count the ways. Consider these seven changes in the industry that I entered in 1951 and the industry that I see today. I'm confining these remarks largely to equity funds, which now represent about 70 percent of mutual fund assets. While not all funds have succumbed to these pervasive trends, the exceptions are quite few.*

1. **Enormous growth.** In 1950, mutual fund assets totaled $2 billion. Today, assets total more than $12 trillion, an astonishing 17 percent rate of annual growth. Then, equity funds held about 1 percent of all U.S. stocks; today, they hold a stunning 30 percent.

2. **Investment focus.** In 1950, almost 80 percent of stock funds (60 of 75) were broadly diversified among investment-grade stocks. These funds pretty much tracked the movements of the stock market itself, and lagged its returns only by the amount of their then-modest operating costs. Today, such large-cap blend funds account for only 11 of all stock funds, although they account for about 16 percent of stock fund assets.† The Morningstar categories are based on nine style boxes, with three market cap categories (large, medium, and small) set on one axis of the matrix and three investment objectives (growth, value, and blend) on the other. These 500 market beta funds are now vastly outnumbered by 3,100 U.S. equity funds diversified in other styles, another 400 funds narrowly diversified in various market sectors, and 700 funds investing in international equities—some broadly diversified, some investing in specific countries. Some of these new fund categories (i.e., the global stock market)

---

* The Morningstar categories are based on nine boxes, with three market-cap categories (large, medium and small) set on one axis and three styles (growth, value, and blend) on the other.

† I'm confining these remarks largely to equity funds, which now represent about 70 percent of mutual fund assets. While not all funds have succumbed to these pervasive trends, the exceptions are quite few.

have served investors well; in others there have been disastrous consequences. In any event, the challenge to investors in picking funds has become almost equivalent to the challenge of picking individual stocks. (The stock market index fund, of course, provides a simple resolution to the fund selection challenge.)

3. **Investor behavior.** But fund investors no longer just select their funds and then hold them. They *trade* them. In 1951, the average fund investor held shares for about 16 years. Today, the holding period averages a fourth of that. To make matters worse, fund investors don't trade very successfully. Because they usually chase good performance, and then abandon ship after bad performance, the asset-weighted returns—those actually earned by fund *investors*—have trailed the time-weighted returns reported by the funds *themselves* by an astonishing amount—an average lag of more than 6 percentage points per year during the 10 years ended December 31, 2005.*

4. **Investment process.** In 1951, management by investment committee was the rule; today it is the exception.† This is the age of the portfolio manager; some 1,400 equity funds are managed by a single individual, and the remaining 2,500 are run by a team of about three managers, or (in a few cases) a whole series of "portfolio counselors." While committee management was hardly a guarantor of superior returns, the system served investors well. And while a system of individual portfolio managers is not bad in and of itself, this evolution—really a *revolution*—has led to costly discontinuities. A star system among mutual fund managers has evolved, with all the attendant hoopla, although most of these stars, alas, have turned out to be comets and hyperactive at that. The average portfolio manager serves a fund for but five years.

5. **Investment strategy.** In 1951, the typical mutual fund focused on the wisdom of long-term investing, holding the average stock in its portfolio for about six years. Today, the holding period for

---

*Cumulative 10-year return reported by the 200 equity funds with the largest cash inflows: 133 percent; return earned by their investors: 27 percent, for the years 1996–2005.

†Ironically, committee-managed Dodge and Cox is among the industry's most accomplished performers.

a stock in an actively managed equity fund is just one year. More charitably, on a dollar-weighted basis, the average holding period is about one-and-a-half years. Either way, the typical mutual fund of today is focused on the folly of short-term speculation.

6. **Industry mission.** Over the past half-century-plus, the mission of the fund business has turned from *managing* assets to *gathering* assets, from stewardship to salesmanship. We have become far less of a management industry and far more of a marketing industry, engaging in a furious orgy of product proliferation. Our apparent motto is: "If we can sell it, we will make it."

   During the 1950s and 1960s, some 240 new equity funds were formed, and during the 1970s and 1980s about 650. But in the 1990s alone, 1,600 new equity funds were created. Most of them, alas, were technology, Internet, and telecommunications funds, and aggressive growth funds focused on these areas, which then took the brunt of the 2000–2002 bear market. Such product proliferation has engendered the expected reaction. While 13 percent of all funds failed during the 1950s, the failure rate for this decade is running at near 60 percent.

7. **Costs.** Costs have soared. On an unweighted basis, the expense ratio of the average fund has doubled, from 0.77 percent in 1951 to 1.54 percent last year. (To be fair, when weighted by fund assets, the expense ratio has risen from 0.60 percent to 0.87 percent, a lower, but still staggering, increase of nearly 50 percent.)

However it is calculated, this rise in costs constitutes a major negative for drag on the returns earned by fund investors. Despite the quantum growth in industry assets since 1951, managers have arrogated to themselves the extraordinary economies of scale available in the field of money management, rather than sharing these economies with fund owners. Money managers—especially the giant financial conglomerates that dominate the industry (those conglomerates now own 40 of the 50 largest fund organizations)—seem to hold as their highest priority the return earned on their own capital, rather than the return earned on the capital they are investing for their fund shareholders.

This seven-way parlay of asset growth, truncated investment focus, counterproductive investor behavior, portfolio management process, hair-trigger investment strategies, product proliferation (inevitably followed by de-proliferation), and soaring costs has altogether constituted a serious disservice to fund investors.

Perhaps I shouldn't comment so bluntly, but I'm inspired by a sentence in the *New York Review of Books* review of *The Battle for the Soul of Capitalism*: "After a heart transplant eleven years ago, Bogle retired to a life of full-time hell-raising." That's not really the way I look at it. To paraphrase President Harry Truman: "I'm not giving 'em hell; I'm just telling 'em the truth, and they think it's hell."

The U.S. Financial System

The mutual fund industry is hardly unique in its soaring costs. In fact, it is a sort of poster child for the escalating costs that investors incur all across our nation's system of financial intermediation. The direct costs of the mutual fund system (largely management fees and operating and marketing expenses) are currently running at some $100 billion a year. In addition, funds are paying tens of billions of dollars in transaction fees to our brokerage firms and investment bankers and, indirectly, to their lawyers and all those other facilitators. Fund investors are also paying another estimated $10 billion of fees each year to financial advisers.

These mutual fund expenses, plus all those fees paid to hedge fund and pension fund managers, to trust companies and to insurance companies, plus their trading costs and investment banking fees and all the other costs of the system shown in Table 4.1, totaled about

TABLE 4.1   ESTIMATED COSTS OF SECURITIES INTERMEDIATION, 2007 (BILLIONS)

Investment Banking and Brokerage	$308
Mutual Fund Operating Expenses	100
Hedge Funds	45
Variable Annuities	30
Pension Fund Advisory Fees	15
Legal/Accounting Fees	15
Financial Advisers	10
Bank Trust Departments	5
Total	$528

$528 billion in 2007. But don't forget that these costs recur year after year. If the present level holds (I'm guessing that it will grow), aggregate intermediation costs would come to a staggering $5 trillion for the next decade. (Think about these cumulative costs relative to the $16 trillion value of the U.S. stock market and the $26 trillion value of the bond market.)

Does this explosion in intermediation costs create an opportunity for money managers? You better believe it does! Does it create a problem for investors? You'd better recognize that, too.

The argument that our financial system is costly because of the benefits it brings to investors belies the reality of our system, in that it does not operate under classic free market conditions. In fact, the system is a model of information asymmetry (which favors sellers over buyers), imperfect competition, and irrational choices driven by emotions rather than reason. Further, that argument defies the elemental arithmetic of investing: *Gross return in the financial markets, minus the costs of the system, equals the net return actually delivered to investors.*

To put it another way, as long as our financial system delivers to our investors in the aggregate whatever returns the stock and bond markets are generous enough to deliver, but only *after* the costs of financial intermediation are deducted (i.e., forever), these enormous costs seriously undermine the odds in favor of success for citizens who are accumulating savings for retirement. Alas, the investor feeds at the bottom of the costly food chain of investing.

This is not to say that our financial system creates only costs. It creates substantial value for our society. It facilitates the optimal allocation of capital among a variety of users; it enables buyers and sellers to meet efficiently; it provides remarkable liquidity; it enhances the ability of investors to capitalize on the discounted value of future cash flows and other investors to acquire the right to those cash flows; it creates financial instruments (so-called derivatives, if often of mind-boggling complexity) that enable investors to divest themselves of a variety of risks by transferring those risks to others.

No, it is not that the system fails to create benefits. The question is whether, on the whole, the costs of obtaining those benefits have reached a level that overwhelms them.

The Financial Sector and the Economy

Whatever the benefits, the tremendous drain on investment returns represented by the costs of our investment system raises serious questions about the efficient functioning not only of that investment system but also of our entire society. Over the past two centuries, our nation has shifted from an agricultural economy, to a manufacturing economy, to a service economy, and now to what is predominantly a financial economy. But the costs that we incur in our financial economy, by definition, subtract from the value created by our productive businesses.

Think about it. When investors—individual and institutional alike—engage in far more trading, inevitably with one another, than is necessary for market efficiency and ample liquidity, they become, collectively, their own worst enemies. While the owners of businesses enjoy the dividend yields and earnings growth that our capitalistic system creates, those who play in the financial markets capture those investment gains only *after* the costs of financial intermediation are deducted.

Thus, while investing in American business is a winner's game, beating the stock market before those costs—for all of us as a group—is a *zero-sum* game. And after intermediation costs are paid to the market's croupiers, beating the market becomes a loser's game.

The rise of the financial sector is one of the seldom-told tales of the recent era. Twenty-five years ago, financial corporations accounted for only about 5 percent of the earnings of the 500 giant corporations that compose the Standard & Poor's 500 Stock Index (Figure 4.1). Fifteen years ago, the financial sector share had risen to 10 percent, then to 20 percent in 1997, and to a near-peak level of 27 percent in 2007.

But that 27 percent figure substantially understates the importance of the financial sector, for it excludes the earnings of the financial affiliates of our giant manufacturers. (Think General Electric Capital, or the auto financing arms of General Motors and Ford.*) Including these earnings would likely bring the financial sector's share to more than one-third of the annual earnings of the S&P 500. But even without

---

*For the nine months ended September 30, 2007, financial services produced 42 percent—$52 billion—of General Electric's total revenues—$124 billion.

**FIGURE 4.1   FINANCIAL SECTOR'S SHARE OF S&P 500
EARNINGS, 1980–2007**

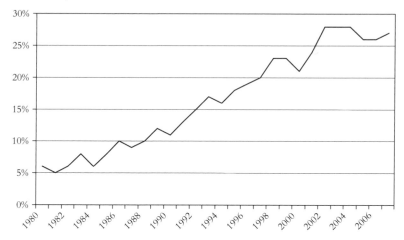

those earnings the financial sector is now by far our nation's largest
generator of corporate profits, larger even than the *combined* profits of
our huge energy and health-care sectors, and almost three times as big
as either industrials or information technology (Figure 4.2).

To some degree, of course, the growth of the financial sector not
only reflects the rise in demand for financial services. (The mutual

**FIGURE 4.2   SHARE OF THE S&P 500'S 2006 EARNINGS,
BY SECTOR**

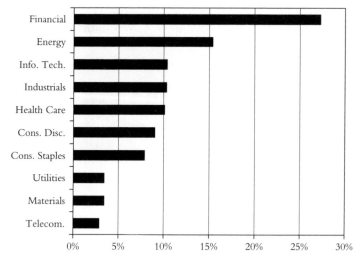

fund industry is a good example.) It also reflects the fact that many privately owned firms have become publicly owned, including investment banking firms, mutual fund managers, once-mutual insurance companies, and even our stock exchanges. In 1989, there were 56 stocks in the S&P financial sector, including 28 banks; today there are 92 stocks, but only 26 banks.

The combination of public ownership and earnings growth has been dramatic. For example, from 1981 to 2007 earnings of fund manager T. Rowe Price soared more than 150 times over—from $4 million to an estimated $650 million.

We're moving, or so it seems, toward becoming a country where we're no longer *making* anything. We're merely trading pieces of paper, swapping stocks and bonds back and forth with one another, and the house, to use a gambling casino metaphor, reaps a veritable fortune. We're also adding even more costs by creating ever-more complex financial derivatives that build huge and unfathomable risks into our financial system. Far too many financial innovations are profitable to their creators and marketers, but have proved to be hazardous and destructive to the wealth of those who purchase these devilishly convoluted products.

As evidenced by the growing crisis in mortgage-backed collateralized debt obligations, these risks are starting to come home to roost. In this context, it's worth considering the keen insight of the great British economist John Maynard Keynes, who some 70 years ago warned that "when enterprise becomes a mere bubble on a whirlpool of speculation," the consequences may be dire. "When the capital development of a country becomes a by-product of the activities of a casino, the job [of capitalism] is likely to be ill-done."*

Once a profession in which business was subservient, the field of money management has largely become a business in which the profession is subservient. Harvard Business School Professor Rakesh Khurana is right when he defines the standard of conduct for a true professional with these words: "I will create value for society, rather than extract

---

*John Maynard Keynes, *The General Theory of Employment, Interest, and Money* (New York: Macmillan, 1936; Harcourt, Brace, 1964), 159.

it."* And yet money management, by definition, extracts value from the returns earned by our business enterprises.

Warren Buffett's wise partner, Charles Munger, lays it on the line:

> Most money-making [i.e., money management] activity contains profoundly antisocial effects. . . . As high-cost modalities become ever more popular . . . the activity exacerbates the current harmful trend in which ever more of the nation's ethical young brainpower is attracted into lucrative money-management and its attendant modern frictions, as distinguished from work providing much more value to others.[†]

Yet even as I write this article, I read that this brainpower is pouring into financial services at a breath-taking rate. Today, the number of chartered financial analysts is at a record high of 78,000, and *Barron's* recently reported that "no fewer than 140,000 new applicants—also a record high—from every corner of the earth are queued up to take the exams that will confer on the lucky ones the coveted CFA imprimatur."[‡] In one sense this explosion is wonderful, suggesting that our professional designation is highly valued. But it also raises serious concerns that the field will become more and more crowded, pushing the costs of financial intermediation to even higher levels.

I don't dismiss out-of-hand the possibility that this influx of trained professional investment advisers might help individual investors make better choices than they have in the past. But the record of financial advisers is discouraging, suggesting that they subtract value from investor returns. A 2006 study by Bergstresser, Chalmers, and Tufano finds that adviser asset allocations were no better than allocations those investors made on their own, that advisers chased market trends, and that the investors whom they advised paid higher up-front charges. The study's conclusion: The weighted average return of equity funds held by investors who relied on advisers (excluding all charges paid up-front or at the

---

*Rakesh Khurana, "Q1," Yale School of Management (2007).
[†]Charles Munger, speech before Foundation Financial Officers Group, Santa Monica, California, on October 14, 1998.
[‡]Alan Abelson, "Swarm of Analysts," *Barron's*, May 28, 2007, 5.

time of redemption) averaged just 2.9 percent per year, compared with 6.6 percent earned by investors who took charge of their own affairs.

This is not to say that bright people in today's remarkable younger generation should not enter the profession of money management. Rather, it is to say that those who enter the field should do so with their eyes wide open, recognizing that any endeavor that extracts value from its clients may, in times more troubled than these, find that it has been hoist by its own petard.

While it is said on Wall Street that money has no conscience, the future leaders of this profession must not let that truism cause them to ignore their own consciences, or to alter their own conduct and character. Indeed, I expect that these future leaders will bring to the operation of our system of financial intermediation a level of honest introspection that I find too often lacking among today's leaders, as well as a return to our traditional focus on fiduciary duty, on service to others before service to self.

Lower Equity Returns in Prospect?

What's more, the burdensome costs of financial intermediation are all too likely to occur in an era of falling returns on equities. Briefly put, the 100-year return of 9.6 percent annually on stocks included a 4.5 percent dividend yield (Figure 4.3). Today's 2.0 percent yield represents a dead-weight loss of 2.5 percent points in future investment returns. By the same token, the glorious 12.5 percent return of the past 25 years included not only a 3.4 percent dividend yield and 6.4 percent earnings growth (well above the 5.0 percent long-term norm), but also a speculative return averaging 2.7 percent per year, borne of a price-earnings ratio that doubled from 9 times to 18 times.

The sharp drop in yields, and the likelihood (in my view) that today's price-earnings ratio of 18 will not only *not* redouble, but rather decline by a few points in the coming decade, means that we are likely to experience a future return on stocks of about 7 percent.*

---

*Please consider these numbers crude estimates. I've rounded the yield to 2.0 percent; earnings growth could easily revert to the long-term mean of 5.0 percent; and who can really be confident about the stock market's price-earnings multiple in 2018?

FIGURE 4.3   TOTAL RETURNS ON STOCKS, PAST AND FUTURE

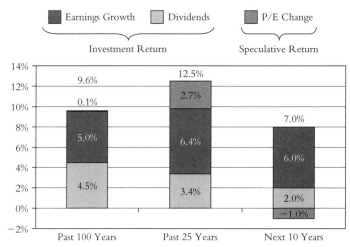

Annual fund costs—sales loads, expense ratios, and hidden turnover costs—now running at about 2.5 percent, would reduce a nominal 7.0 percent return on stocks to 4.5 percent for the average mutual fund. Shamelessly, I persist in reducing that likely *nominal* net annual return of 4.5 percent for the average fund by the expected 2.3 percent annual rate of inflation, slashing it to a humble *real* return of just 2.2 percent per year (Figure 4.4).* Clearly, reducing investment costs is at the crux of the ability of our nation's families—the very backbone of our savings base—to accumulate the wealth to which they properly aspire.

A Matter of Indifference

Yet most economists have been indifferent as to the issue of costs in our financial sector. One exception is Ronald H. Coase, who produced his seminal work on transaction costs, "The Nature of the Firm," in 1937.

---

*That may be a best-case scenario. While I've ignored taxes, most fund investors cannot ignore them. I've also ignored the likelihood, based on the past experience described earlier in this article, that the annual return of the fund investor will continue to fall far short of the net annual real return of 2.2 percent expected for the average fund.

FIGURE 4.4   EQUITY RETURNS OVER THE COMING DECADE

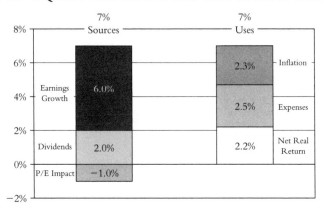

His paper postulates that the entrepreneur's choice between organizing activities within the firm versus relying on an exchange transaction in the marketplace depends on the level of transaction costs. But it was not until 1991—more than a half-century later—that Coase received the Nobel Prize in Economics.

In that same year, Murphy, Shleifer, and Vishny[*] argued that when excessive rewards go to rent-seekers whose returns come from the *redistribution* of wealth rather than the *creation* of wealth—the authors single out government, law, and financial services (including stock traders and money managers)—the economy suffers. The authors contrast these rent-seekers with wealth-creators such as engineers. But paradoxically, the fastest growth among college engineering majors is not in traditional engineering—aeronautical, electrical, mechanical, and the like—but in "financial engineering" for those seeking careers as hedge fund managers and Wall Street "quants."[†]

Grossman and Hart also explore the issue of transaction costs. They point out that transactions involving a principal and an agent affect the total amount of money that is available to be divided between the two

---

[*] "The Allocation of Talent." *Quarterly Journal of Economics* (May 1991).
[†] For example, in Princeton University's Class of 2000, there were 148 traditional engineering majors and 25 financial engineering majors. In the Class of 2009, there were 68 financial engineering majors (up 172 percent) and 122 traditional engineering majors (down 17 percent).

parties, and develop a method for analyzing the costs and benefits of different actions to the agent. They argue that the owner (the principal) rarely monitors the actions of the manager (the agent), but rather observes the outcome. Yet it is not clear to the owner whether the manager's results are the product of skill or luck—just as in the mutual fund industry. Management fees and transaction costs are at the heart of the issue in both instances.

More recently, in 2000, Obstfeld and Rogoff* discussed the issue of transaction costs in the context of international macroeconomic theory. They conclude that it is relative transaction costs that illuminate a wide range of puzzles, including why trading in goods and services is more national than international and why investors have a home bias in their portfolios (e.g., U.S. investors have 90 percent of their equity holdings in U.S. stocks). When trading costs are close to zero, these problems recede, but when they reach 25 percent of the value of trade, the negative dynamics are highly predictable. Surely an examination of the impact of the distinctly similar issue of financial intermediation costs (which are, broadly stated, simply trading costs) would illuminate the discussion of the gap between market returns and the returns that investors actually earn.

Despite the obvious importance of this issue, I know of not a single academic study that has systematically attempted to calculate the value extracted by our financial system from the returns earned by investors, nor (as far as I know) has a single article on the subject ever appeared in the professional journals—not the *Journal of Finance*, or the *Journal of Financial Economics*, or the *Journal of Portfolio Management*, or the *Financial Analysts Journal*. Perhaps the best way to honor the legacy of Benjamin Graham—and the value he created by his incisive view of our investment system—would be for our profession to join with academia and at long last tackle this vital issue of investment costs and how they relate to the benefits of an efficient system of capital formation. Only then can we begin to consider appropriate ways to improve the system, likely by some combination of education, disclosure, regulation, and structural and legal reform.

---

* "The Six Major Puzzles in International Finance: Is There a Common Cause?" *NBER Macroeconomics Annual*, 15 (2000).

In June 2007, Princeton's valedictorian, Economics major Glen Weyl, described his passion for intellectual inquiry this way (he attributes the words to Nobel Laureate Robert Lucas): *There are questions so important that it is, or should be, hard to think about anything else.*

The efficient functioning of our nation's system of financial intermediation is just such a question. It's high time not only to think about it, but also to study it in depth, to calculate its costs and its benefits, and ultimately to demand that it function far more effectively in the national public interest and in the interest of investors than it does today.

Chapter 5

The Uncanny Ability to Recognize the Obvious*

Coming as it does from a global organization renowned for its development and dissemination of knowledge and financial decision-making, it's a very special treat to be honored by receiving the 2005 Outstanding Financial Executive Award. Yet, confession being good for the soul, I'm also somewhat surprised to be your choice. While I have spent nearly five-and-one-half decades in this field—including more than three decades as the leader of two wonderful mutual fund management organizations (Wellington, 1965–1974; Vanguard, 1974–1996), I have never thought of myself as a particularly competent executive—an assessment that I imagine my long-suffering colleagues shared. But I was always surrounded by a crew—bless them *all*, not just the higher-ups—who knew how to get the things done that needed to be done.

I also confess that while I've been enlightened, indeed often transfixed, by the scores—no, hundreds—of articles I've read in the academic journals over the years (mostly the *Financial Analysts Journal* and the

---

*Based on remarks to the Financial Management Associates International (FMA) in Chicago, Illinois, on October 15, 2005, and to the Haas School of Business of the University of California, Berkeley, California, on October 27, 2006, where I was honored by receiving its award for "Distinguished Contribution to Financial Reporting."

Journal of Portfolio Management; much of your own *Financial Management* journal is well over my head) and even written a dozen or more myself, my intellectual credentials fall far short of those of most of you here today. Truth told, when I see a page that is filled only with formulas—Sigmas and Deltas and Lambdas—to the near exclusion of text, I move quickly on to the next article.

Indexing as the Ultimate Reality

Continuing my confessional litany, I have little knowledge of the convoluted intricacies of financial analysis and accounting standards, and have not done investment research on stocks and bonds since my early years as a rookie in this wonderful field. Worse—or, come to think of it, *better!*—I created a method of investing that deliberately and purposefully *ignored* analysis, accounting, and research. For in substance, the index mutual fund simply buys the entire stock market portfolio—blue-chips, blithe spirits, downtrodden dogs, and even bankruptcy candidates—and holds it for Warren Buffett's favorite holding period: *forever.*

I didn't invent the *idea* of indexing. (I'm not sure that any individual did.) But the founding of the world's first index mutual fund in 1975—initially "First Index Investment Trust" and now "Vanguard 500"—was, I think, a seminal moment in the history of indexing. Although nearly two decades were to pass before its position in the mutual fund firmament was largely accepted, we can now say that the original heresy that was indexing has at last become dogma. Do you want proof? Known as "Bogle's Folly" at the outset, it is now the largest mutual fund in the world. Including its sister "500" funds, its first cousin "5000" stock index funds, its brother bond index funds, and its brother-in-law index sector funds, investors at Vanguard have some $375 billion invested in passive strategies, one-half of the long-term assets we supervise.

Whatever the case, using the index mutual fund as the core—if not the entirety—of a diversified equity portfolio is now dogma in college and business school finance classes, and I thank the academic profession for that. It is advocated, as far as I can tell, by almost every American who has won the Nobel Prize in Economics. And most recently, even the leader of one of America's most successful endowment funds—Harvard—sang, indeed shouted, its praises. Here's what Jack Meyer said: "The investment business is a giant scam. Most people think they can find fund managers who can outperform, but most people are wrong. You should simply hold index funds. *No doubt about it.*"

The fact is that indexing is the ultimate reality of investing, guaranteed to capture for investors their fair share of whatever returns the stock market is generous enough to bestow upon us, or, in fairness, mean enough to inflict upon us. How good is that? Consider the alternative to this reality: investing based on the illusion that active fund managers as a group will be able to outpace this passive, low-cost, market-matching strategy.

Why must managers lose? Think about the reality: If the stock market is generous enough to reward equity investors a *nominal* annual return of 8 percent over the years ahead, and if our administration in the nation's capital and our central bankers have the guts and discipline to hold inflation to 3 percent, then the *real* return on stocks would be 5 percent. If actively managed funds persist in foisting high-cost "products" (as the industry is wont to call their mutual funds) on their investors, the real return on the average actively managed fund—after costs and after taxes—could come to as little as 1 percent per year, or even less.

Compounded over the long term (here I'm using 25 years), $1,000 simply invested in stocks at a real return of 5 percent produces a profit of $2,400; at 1 percent, the profit falls to just $280. Welcome to the *real* world, in which the relentless rules of humble arithmetic in the financial markets—essentially, *gross fund return*, minus costs and taxes, equals *net investor return*—doom actively managed funds as a group to an abysmal failure for their investor/owners. In the mutual fund business in the aggregate, you don't get what you pay for. You get precisely what you *don't* pay for.

That reality is why active management must be considered a failure. Yes, I realize that "failure" is a tough indictment. So don't take my word for it. In his recent book, *Unconventional Success*, the brilliant endowment fund manager, David Swensen of Yale University, describes "the colossal failure of the mutual fund industry; resulting from [its] systematic exploitation of individual investors . . . as funds extract enormous sums from investors in exchange for providing a shocking disservice." Mr. Swensen continues, "Thievery, even when dressed in the cloak of SEC-approved governance, remains thievery . . . as the powerful financial services industry exploits vulnerable individual investors."* These are strong words. But when challenged by the *Wall Street Journal* that his conclusions were "pretty harsh," Mr. Swensen simply replied: "The evidence is there." And so it is.

Reality and Illusion in the Stock Market

Even owning the stock market through an index fund has some of the attributes of illusion. Why? Because stock market returns merely reflect—and often powerfully magnify—the two vastly disparate elements of which they are a product. One element is the *real* market of intrinsic business value. The other element is the *expectations* market of momentary stock prices. In the *real* market of business, real companies spend real money and hire real people and invest in real capital equipment; they make real products and provide real services to real consumers who rely on those goods and services in their daily existence. If these real companies are highly efficient and compete with real skill, they earn real profits, out of which they pay real dividends. But to do so demands real strategy, real capital expenditures, and real research and development, to say nothing of real innovation, real foresight, and real determination.

Loosely linked to this real market is the *expectations* market. Here, market prices are set, not by the realities of business that I have just described, but by the expectations of investors. Crucially, these expectations are set by numbers, numbers that are to an important extent an illusion, the product of what corporate managements want them to be, too easily manipulated and defined in multiple ways. We have *pro-forma* earnings (reflecting the magical earnings growth that can be created by merging two firms, as well as a certain dissembling). We have *operating* earnings (absent all the write-offs of previous bad investment decisions, bad debts, and bad operations that were discontinued). And we have *reported* earnings, conforming to Generally Accepted Accounting Principles (GAAP) accounting, which itself is riddled with its own

---

*David Swensen, *Unconventional Success* (New York: Free Press, 2005).

substantial gaps in logic and implementation that permit all sorts of financial shenanigans by those who are so inclined (all under the eye of their supposedly independent certified public accountants).

As we entered the age of expectations investing several decades ago, growth in corporate earnings—especially earnings guidance and its achievement—became the watchword of investors. Corporate managers and corporate stockholders—now no longer true owners, but renters— came to accept that whatever earnings were reported were "true." In effect, as a corporate Humpty Dumpty might have told institutional investor Alice in Wonderland: "When I report my earnings it means just what I choose it to mean, neither more nor less . . . the question is who is to be the master—that's all." And Alice said, in effect, "Aye, aye, Sir."

Corporate managers became the master of the numbers, and our public accountants, too often, went along. In what I've called "the happy conspiracy" between corporate managers, directors, accountants, investment bankers, and institutional owners and renters of stocks, all kinds of bizarre financial engineering took place. The reported numbers sustained the illusions of the expectations market, but often had little to do with the real business market of intrinsic value. Loose accounting standards made it possible to create, out of thin air, what passes for earnings, even under GAAP standards. For example:

- Cavalierly classifying large charges against revenues as "immaterial."
- Hyping the assumed future returns of pension plans, even as rational expectations for future returns deteriorated.
- Counting as revenues sales made to customers by lending them the money needed to pay for their purchases.
- Merger adjustments involving huge write-offs of accounts receivable, only to collect them later on; and write-offs of perfectly good plant and equipment, eliminating future depreciation charges.
- Excluding the cost of stock option compensation from corporate expenses. (This practice is now, happily, prohibited.)
- And, lest I forget, timing differences between GAAP and tax accounting.

And I haven't even touched on the concealment of debt in special-purpose entities, abused most notably by Enron.

Under GAAP, these practices are all legal. Surely it can be said that the problem in such creative financial engineering isn't what's illegal. It's what's legal. Indeed, even when accounted for properly, the back-dating of options—the most recent example of the malfeasance of corporate managers—is legal. And so the management consultant's bromide—"If you can measure it, you can manage it"—became the mantra of the chief executive.

The Real Market versus the Expectations Market

I first encountered the compelling formulation of the distinction between the real market and the expectations market in the writings of Roger Martin, dean of the Rotman School of Business at the University of Toronto. I've been focused for a long time on the very same dichotomy, but with different words. My concern is that we place too much trust in numbers. But, as I wrote in Chapter 1 of this text, "*numbers are not reality*. At best, they're a pale reflection of reality. At worst, they're a gross distortion of the truths we seek to measure. . . . [As a result], we worship hard numbers and accept the momentary precision of stock prices as the talisman of investment reality rather than the eternal vagueness of intrinsic corporate value."

In the recent era, the triumph of illusion over reality has been reflected in the casino mentality of so many institutional investors, with harsh consequences. At every turn, the expectations market of prices has trumped the real market of business. Yet when perception—the precise but momentary price of the stock—vastly departs from reality—the imprecise and hard-to-measure but enduring intrinsic value of the corporation, essentially the discounted value of its future cash flow—the gap can be reconciled only in favor of reality. The fact is that it's relatively easy for a firm to raise the short-term price of its stock and meet the demands of the expectations market. But the job of building intrinsic value in the real business market over the long term is a tough, demanding task (I know something about that), accomplished only by the exceptional corporation.

When we have two vastly different markets, it is almost inevitable that major conflicts arise. Roger Martin sets up his challenge to the two-market concept using professional football as an analogy. There, the expectations market is reflected in the betting on the point spread between the scores of rival teams. When the game ends, the reality is revealed: the final score (i.e., the actual spread). In pro football, he notes, "No participant in the real market is permitted to participate in the expectations market." Star quarterbacks, as well as all of the other actors in those football dramas, are not allowed to bet on *any* games, even those in which they do not play. Surely few would argue that such a prohibition is not a sensible policy.

And then he drops the bomb.

> But there is an even bigger game in which players in the real market are not only allowed, but strongly encouraged, to play in the related expectations market: It is of course the price of a company's shares in the stock market. While the over-riding task of the CEO is (or should be) to build the real business, he spends a lot of his time playing in the expectations market, shaping investor expectations, controlling the numbers that will reflect whether or not they are met, and getting paid stagger-ing amounts of stock-based compensation on the theory that such compensation aligns the interest of executives with the interest of shareholders.*

Alas, stock-based compensation does nothing of the sort. It encourages chief executives—and their chief financial officers, too often with the tacit approval of their public accountants and their directors—to manipulate the expectations market to their own benefit. Even as it is banned in pro football, it shouldn't be allowed in executive compensa-tion. When we compensate executives based on illusion rather than reality, society pays the price.

"The Battle for the Soul of Capitalism"

This dichotomy between a market of reality and a market of illusion explains much of what went wrong in corporate America, in invest-ment America, and in mutual fund America. These are the themes in

---

*Roger Martin, "The Wrong Incentive: Executives Taking Stock Will Behave Like Athletes Placing Bets," *Barron's*, December 22, 2003.

my 2005 book, *The Battle for the Soul of Capitalism*, in which I examine (in each case) why it went wrong, and how to go about fixing it. My opening epigram is from St. Paul's letter to the Romans: "If the sound of the trumpet shall be uncertain, who shall prepare himself to the battle?" It is a book about the battle, and because I believe that the very soul of our capitalistic system is at stake, the trumpet that I sound is a certain one. Here are some of the major flaws that reflect this mutation in our capitalistic system, each described in some depth in my book.

In Corporate America

- The staggering increase in managers' corporations, with the pay of the five highest paid executives of public companies more than doubling, from 4.8 percent of profits in the early 1990s to 10.3 percent recently, a period in which earnings themselves—the measure our CEOs love to brag about—grew at a puny 1.9 percent annual rate.
- The rise of financial engineering—call it "manipulation"—in which earnings are managed to meet the "guidance" that these executives give to Wall Street, quarter by quarter. One of the prize tools: raising the assumptions for future returns on corporate pension plans even as prospective returns eroded. Just think of it: In 1981, when the long-term U.S. Treasury bond yielded 13.9 percent, the projective plan return was 7 percent. Currently, with bond yields at 4.7 percent, the projected return averages about 8.5 percent. It's not going to happen, and pension plan inadequacy will be our next financial scandal.
- The failure of our traditional gatekeepers—auditors (who became partners, if not co-conspirators, with managements through their provision of highly profitable consulting activities), regulators, legislators (who in 1993 forced the SEC to back down on requiring that option costs be treated as—of all things!—corporation expenses), and especially our corporate directors who, as I note in the book, "failed to provide adult supervision of the geniuses" who managed the firms.

In Investment America

- As our ownership society of direct holdings of stocks by individual investors nearly vanished—they held 92 percent of all stocks in

1950 but hold only 30 percent today—corporate control fell into the hands of giant financial institutions—largely pension funds and mutual funds—whose share rose commensurably, from 8 percent to 70 percent. But these agents, beset by conflicts of interest and their own agendas, failed to represent their principals.

- Part of this failure came because institutional investing moved from an *own-a-stock* industry (holding an average stock for six years during my first 15 years in this field) to being a *rent-a-stock* industry, now holding a typical stock for but a single year, or even less. Owners *must* give a damn about the rights and responsibilities of corporate governance. Renters could hardly care less.

- As our professional security analysts came to focus far more heavily on *illusion*—the monetary precision of the price of the stock—and increasingly ignoring the *reality*—what really matters is the inevitably vague, but eternally priceless, intrinsic value of the corporation. Using Oscar Wilde's wonderful description of the cynic, our money managers came "to know the price of *everything*, but the value of *nothing*."

In Mutual Fund America

- A once-noble industry that had been a profession with elements of a business became a business with elements of a profession. Our traditional guiding star of *stewardship* has been transmogrified into a new star—*salesmanship*. Once a business of management, we became largely a business in which marketing calls the tune, and our investors have paid a terrible price.

- Over the past two decades, the return of the average equity *fund* has lagged the return of the S&P 500 index by about three percentage points per year—10 percent versus 13 percent—largely because of costs. But largely because of poor timing and poor fund selection, the average fund *investor* has lagged by *another* 3 percentage points. Result: In this grand era for investing, the average investor has captured but 27 percent of the market's compounded return. Clearly, as Mr. Buffett has warned, the principal enemies of equity investors are *expenses* and *emotions*.

- When I entered this field all those years ago, virtually 100 percent of mutual fund management companies were relatively small, professionally managed, privately held firms. Since then, they have experienced their own pathological mutation. Today, 41 of the 50 largest firms are publicly held, including 35 that are owned by giant U.S. and global financial conglomerates. To state the obvious, these conglomerates are in business to earn a return on *their* capital, not a return on *your* (the fund investor's) capital. Remember: The more the managers *take*, the less the investors *make*.

Wrapping Up

Please don't be intimidated by this litany of flaws that have come to pervade today's debased version of capitalism. We can fix them. Our nation is moving, if haltingly, toward returning the system to its traditional roots of trusting and being trusted. Our *ownership* society is gone and will not return. Our *agency* society has failed to serve its principals, as corporate managers and fund managers alike have placed their own interests above the interests of their beneficiaries and owners. It is time to begin the world anew, and build a *fiduciary* society in which stewardship is our talisman. My *Battle* book is replete with recommendations to speed this metamorphosis.

If this mission is to succeed, investors everywhere—individual and institutional, large and small—must educate themselves as to what is real in investing, and what is illusory. We must understand the nature of traditional capitalism; the wisdom of long-term investing and the folly of short-term speculation; the productive power of compound interest to build returns and the confiscatory power of compound costs to slash those very same returns; and the relentless rules of humble arithmetic. If only we can stand back, take a moment for introspection, and finally recognize these obvious precepts.

Part Two

THE FAILURE OF
CAPITALISM

After the egregious financial speculation, the stock market crash, and the deep economic recession of 2007–2009, even the most articulate and powerful believers in the ability of free markets to regulate themselves came to recognize that modern-day capitalism has failed our society. In a stunning admission, Alan Greenspan, former chairman of the Federal Reserve Board, conceded that he had found "a flaw in the model that I perceived as the critical functioning structure that defines how the world works." An equally surprising concession came in a 2009 book from widely respected federal judge Richard Posner, a leader in the "Chicago School" of *laissez-faire* economics. Its title gets right to the point: *A Failure of Capitalism.*

I begin Part Two seeking to answer the question, "What Went Wrong in Corporate America?" In 2003, when I delivered this lecture at the Community Forum of the Bryn Mawr (PA) Presbyterian Church, the handwriting was on the wall: "stock market mania . . . the rise of the imperial chief executive officer . . . the failure of our (corporate) gatekeepers . . . the change in our financial institutions from being stock *owners* to stock *traders.* . . ." It turns out that the burst in the stock market bubble that I described in those remarks would, but five years later, be echoed in the burst of a real estate bubble that would lead to an even larger stock market collapse and the worst recession in the U.S. economy since the Great Depression. While I was belatedly aware of the mortgage mess, it was of a piece with the financial manipulation of corporate America that I describe toward the close of Chapter 6.

From the perspective of 2009, I examine the after-effects of the numerous failures in our system of free-market capitalism in Chapter 7, "Fixing a Broken Financial System." I illustrate my main points with three examples: Alan Greenspan and his apologia; Bernard Madoff and his Ponzi scheme; and President Barack Obama's articulate response to this failure in his inaugural speech, calling for "a new era of responsibility." Despite the awesome question facing our society—whether we have enough character, virtue, and courage to reform the system—I strike an optimistic note on the financial crisis that America has endured: "This, too, shall pass away."

The failure of capitalism is in large measure a failure of personal and professional values. When I was asked in 2007 to present a lecture at Princeton University on the subject of "vanishing treasures" in our society, I chose to illustrate the subject with the loss of "Business Values and Investment Values," which is the title of Chapter 8. The main points are: (1) Modern-day business standards have come to overwhelm traditional professional standards; and (2) our once-triumphant *ownership* society has been supplanted by a new *agency* society in which our institutional investor/agents have placed their own interests ahead of those of their principals, whom they are duty-bound to serve. Unless we build a new *fiduciary* society that demands virtuous conduct and a return to traditional values, I conclude that the treasures that made American business the dominant force in our nation's growth will indeed vanish. My 2009 op-ed essay in the *Wall Street Journal*—"A Crisis of Ethic Proportions"—concisely summarizes these views (Chapter 9).

In Chapter 10, I explain the failure of capitalism in part by the inevitable failure of the laws of probability when applied to the financial markets. As I examine the role of risk in the financial markets, I rely on the famous "Black Swan" formulation of the British philosopher Sir Karl Popper (1902–1994) to describe surprising events that are "outliers," beyond the realm of our regular expectations. In "Black Monday and Black Swans," published in the *Financial Analysts Journal* in early 2008, I draw the distinction between risk (an event with *measurable* distributions, such as a roll of the dice, even our mortality) and uncertainty (which is, simply put, *immeasurable*). The American economist Hyman Minsky (1919–1996) was right on the mark when he pointed out that rampant speculation in our financial sector inevitably flows over into our productive economy. In accord with his finding, I close by noting that "some surprising event . . . will surely come to pass . . . when it comes, [it] will be just one more Black Swan." That view was promptly validated by the market crash that followed.

That we cannot seem to learn from our historical experience in market crashes is illustrated in Chapter 11. In "The Go-Go Years," I go way back in time to describe the boom and bust in the wild and crazy era that began in the mid-1960s and essentially continued until the stock market collapse of 1973–1974. In this essay for a new edition of "Adam Smith's" *Supermoney* in 2006, I described my role as a witness to, and a participant in, this era. My own involvement with go-go investing proved to be a personal and professional disaster, but ultimately led to the creation of the Vanguard Group as an antidote to the insanity. While I paid a heavy price in terms of my career, I learned from it, and gained the perspective that helped me anticipate, first, the market crash of 2000–2003, and then the market crash of 2007–2009. Investors will, I pray, learn from these painful lessons of financial history that have recurred over and over again for centuries.

Chapter 6

What Went Wrong in Corporate America?*

A s so many of us have read in the gospel of Matthew: "A prophet is not without honor, save in his own country." Yet by your invitation to speak to you this evening you honor me, even as I stand here in my own country! I live right down the road from this great church, and for the better part of a half-century have regularly attended Sunday worship services in the thrall of such extraordinary preachers as David Watermulder and Eugene Bay, who have helped me beyond measure in gaining enlightenment, inspiration, and faith.

While my remarks center on what went wrong in corporate America, being in this sanctuary compels me to begin with some words from the teacher Joseph Campbell: "In medieval times, as you approached the city, your eye was taken by the Cathedral. Today, it's the towers of commerce. It's business, business, business."† We have become what Campbell calls "a bottom-line society." But our society, I think, is measuring the *wrong* bottom line: form over substance, prestige over virtue, money over achievement, charisma over character, the ephemeral over the enduring.

*Based on a lecture as part of the Community Forum Distinguished Speaker Series at the Bryn Mawr (PA) Presbyterian Church, February 24, 2003.
†Quoted in Warren G. Bennis, "Will the Legacy Live On?" *Harvard Business Review* (February 1, 2002), 95.

I'm sure it does not escape you that Joseph Campbell's analogy proved to be ominous. We have now witnessed the total destruction of the proudest of all America's towers of commerce, at New York's World Trade Center. We have seen a $7 trillion collapse of the aggregate market value of America's corporations—from $17 trillion to $10 trillion, in the worst stock market crash since 1929–1933. And we've seen the reputations of business leaders transmogrified from mighty lions of corporate success to self-serving and less-than-trustworthy executives, with several even doing "perp walks" for the television cameras.

Our bottom-line society has a good bit to answer for. As United Kingdom's Chief Rabbi Jonathan Sacks put it: "When everything that matters can be bought and sold, when commitments can be broken because they are no longer to our advantage, when shopping becomes salvation and advertising slogans become our litany, when our worth is measured by how much we earn and spend, then the market is destroying the very virtues on which in the long run it depends."*

So let's think about what went wrong in our capitalistic system, about what's now beginning to go right, and about what investors can do as a part-owner of corporate America. Whether you own a common stock or a share in a mutual fund, or participate in a private retirement plan, you have a personal interest in bringing about reform. Both as shareholders and as citizens, each of us must accept the responsibility to build a better corporate world.

Capitalism—A Brief Review

Capitalism, *Webster's Third International Dictionary* tells us, is "an economic system based on corporate ownership of capital goods, with investment determined by private decision, and with prices, production, and the distribution of goods and services determined mainly in a free market." Importantly, I would add, "a system founded on honesty, decency, and trust," for these attributes, too, have been clearly established in its history.

As the world moved from an agrarian society to an industrial society during the 18th and 19th centuries, capitalism came to flourish. Local

---

*Jonathan Sacks, "Markets and Morals," the 1998 Hayek Lecture (London: Institute of Economic Affairs, 1998).

communities became part of national (and then international) commerce, trading expanded, and large accumulations of capital were required to build the factories, transportation systems, and banks on which the new economy would depend. Surprising as it may seem, at the heart of this development, according to an article in *Forbes'* recent 85th Anniversary issue,* were the Quakers. In the 1700s and early 1800s, probably because their legendary simplicity and thrift endowed them with the capital to invest, they dominated the British economy, owners of more than half of the country's ironworks and key players in banking, consumer goods, and transatlantic trading. Their emphasis on reliability, absolute honesty, and rigorous record-keeping gave them trust as they dealt with one another, and other observant merchants came to see that being trustworthy went hand-in-hand with business success. Self-interest, in short, demanded virtue.

This evolution, of course, is exactly what the great Scottish economist/philosopher Adam Smith expected. Writing in *The Wealth of Nations* in 1776, he famously said, "The uniform and uninterrupted effort to better his condition, the principle from which (both) public and private opulence is originally derived, is frequently powerful enough to maintain the natural progress of things toward improvement. . . . Each individual neither intends to promote the public interest, nor knows how much he is promoting it . . . [but] by directing his industry in such a matter as its produce may be of the greatest value, *he is led by an invisible hand to promote an end which was no part of his intention.*"

And so it was to be, the *Forbes* essay continued, that "the evolution of capitalism has been in the direction of more trust and transparency and less self-serving behavior. Not coincidentally, this evolution has brought with it greater productivity and economic growth. Not because capitalists are naturally good people, [but] because, the benefits of trust—of being trusting and of being trustworthy—are potentially immense, and because a successful market system teaches people to recognize those benefits . . . a virtuous circle in which an everyday level of trustworthiness breeds an everyday level of trust." The system *works!*

Or at least it *did* work. And then something went wrong. The system changed—"a pathological mutation in capitalism," as an essay in

---

*James Surowiecki, *Forbes*, December 23, 2002.

the *International Herald Tribune** described it. The classic system—*owners'* capitalism—had been based on a dedication to serving the interests of the corporation's *owners* in maximizing the return on their capital investment. But a new system developed—*managers'* capitalism—in which "the corporation came to be run to profit its managers, in complicity if not conspiracy with accountants and the managers of other corporations." Why did it happen? "Because," the author says, "the markets had so diffused corporate ownership *that no responsible owner exists.* This is morally unacceptable, but also a corruption of capitalism itself."

The Broken Circle

What caused the mutation from virtuous circle to vicious circle? It's easy to call it a failure of character, a triumph of hubris and greed over honesty and integrity. And it's even easier to lay it all to "just a few bad apples." But while only a tiny minority of our business and financial leaders have been implicated in criminal behavior, I'm afraid that the barrel itself—the very structure that holds all those apples— is bad. While that may seem a harsh indictment, I believe it is a fair one. Consider that *Predators and Profits*, a 2003 book by Reuters editor Martin Howell, lists fully 176(!) "red flags," each of which describes a particular shortcoming in our recent business, financial, and investment practices, many of which I've witnessed with my own eyes.

It is now crystal-clear that our capitalistic system—as all systems sometimes do—has experienced a profound failure, a failure with a whole variety of root causes, each interacting and reinforcing the other: the stock market mania, driven by the idea that we were in a New Era; the notion that our corporations were trees that could grow not only to the sky but beyond; the rise of the imperial chief executive officer; the failure of our gatekeepers—those auditors, regulators, legislators, and boards of directors who forgot to whom they owed their loyalty—the change in our financial institutions from being stock *owners* to being stock *traders*; the hype of Wall Street's stock promoters;

---

*William Pfaff, September 9, 2002.

the frenzied excitement of the media; and, of course, the eager and sometimes greedy members of the investing public, reveling in the easy wealth that seemed like a cornucopia, at least while it lasted. There is plenty of blame to go around. But even as it drove stock prices *up*, this happy conspiracy among all of the interested parties drove business standards *down*. Yes, the victory of investors in the Great Bull Market had a thousand fathers. But the defeat in the Great Bear Market that followed seems to be an orphan.

If we had to name a *single* father of the bubble, we would hardly need a DNA test to do so. *That father is executive compensation, made manifest in the fixed-price stock option.* When executives are paid for raising the price of their company's stock rather than for increasing their company's value, they don't need to be told what to do: Achieve strong, steady earnings growth and tell Wall Street about it. Set "guidance" targets with public pronouncements of your expectations, and then meet your targets—and do it consistently, without fail. First, do it the old-fashioned way, by increasing volumes, cutting costs, raising productivity, bringing in technology, and developing new products and services. Then, when *making it and doing it* isn't enough, meet your goals by *counting it*, pushing accounting principles to their very edge. And when that isn't enough, *cheat.* As we now know, too many firms did exactly that.

The stated rationale for fixed-price stock options is that they "link the interests of management with the interest of shareholders." That turns out to be a falsehood. For managers don't *hold* the shares they acquire. They *sell* them, and promptly. Academic studies indicate that nearly *all* stock options are exercised as soon as they vest, and the stock is sold *immediately*. Indeed, the term "cashless exercise"—where the firm purchases the stock for the executive, sells it, and is repaid when the proceeds of the sale are delivered—became commonplace. (Happily, it is no longer legal.) We have rewarded our executives, not for long-term economic reality, but for short-term market perception.

Creating Wealth—for Management

Even if executives were required to hold their stock for an extended period, however, stock options are fundamentally flawed. They are not adjusted for the cost of capital, providing a free ride even for executives who produce only humdrum returns. They do not take into account dividends, so there is a perverse incentive to avoid paying them. Stock options reward the *absolute* performance of a stock rather than performance *relative* to peers or to a stock market index, so executive compensation tends to be like a lottery, creating unworthy centimillionaires in bull markets and eliminating rewards even for worthy performers in bear markets.

While these issues could be resolved by the use of restricted stock, or by raising the option price each year, or by linking the stock performance with a market index, such sensible programs were almost never used. Why? Because those alternative schemes require corporations to count the cost as an *expense*. (Heaven forbid!) The cost of fixed-price options alone is conspicuous by its absence on the company's expense statement. As the compensation consultants are wont to say, these stock options are "free."

The net result of the granting of huge options to corporate managers, all the while overstating earnings by ignoring them as an expense, is that total executive compensation went through the roof. In the early 1980s, the compensation of the average chief executive officer was 42 times that of the average worker; by the year 2000, the ratio had soared to 531(!) times. The rationale was that these executives had "created wealth" for their shareholders. But if we actually *measure* the success of corporate America, it's hard to see how that could be the case. During that two-decade period, while corporations had *projected* their earnings growth at an average annual rate of 11.5 percent, they actually *delivered* growth of 6 percent per year—only half of their goal, and even less than the 6.5 percent growth rate of our economy. How that lag can be the stuff to drive *average* CEO compensation to a cool $11 million in 2001 is one of the great anomalies of the age.

The fact is that the executives had "created wealth" for themselves, but not for their shareowners. And when the stock market values melted away, they had long since sold much of their stock. Let me give you a few examples:

- **AOL Time Warner.** In an extraordinary example of the delusions of grandeur that characterized the Information Age, the news of this marriage of the "New Economy" and the "Old Economy" as

2000 began sent the price of Time Warner soaring to a then-all-time high of $90 per share. But AOL's revenues began to tumble almost immediately, and the company recently reported losses totaling *$98 billion*(!). But in the first three years, the founder of AOL (and the chairman of the merged company) sold nearly *one-half-billion-dollars'* worth of his shares, mostly at boom-level prices. Today, the stock languishes at $10, down almost 90 percent from the high.

- **Sprint.** When they agreed to merge with WorldCom in October 1999, the directors accelerated the vesting of its executives' stock options. Although the merger scheme quickly fell apart, two senior executives quickly sold $290 million of their optioned shares at prices apparently in the $60 range. They also paid the firm's auditors $5.8 million(!) for a clever plan to circumvent the tax laws, and have paid not a penny of tax on these gains. (Yet! The IRS is now challenging the tax-evasion device.) Today, Sprint sells at about $13 per share, down 83 percent from its high.

- **General Electric.** While clearly a blue-chip company, the price of its shares has dropped from $60 to $23 per share since August 2000, a cool $370 billion reduction in its market value. Amid growing investor concern about its tendency to smooth its reported earnings by "creative accounting" practices, its once-legendary leader, Jack Welch, is not looking so good lately. Yet his total compensation from 1997 through 2000 came to nearly $550 million, plus another $200 million from the sale of option shares, some at prices of $55 or more. Now retired, he is still well-paid: a pension of $357,000, plus another $377,000 for consulting services, a total of $734,000 — *per month*! (He must enjoy an expensive lifestyle that leaves little to spare, for a recent report placed his monthly charitable giving at just $614.) Such is the world of executive compensation in corporate America today.

Clearly, *owners'* capitalism had been superseded by *managers'* capitalism, and managers' capitalism has created great distortions in our society. And chief executives, with all their fame, their jet planes, their perquisites, their pension plans, their club dues, and their Park Avenue apartments, seem to forget that they are employees of the corporation's owners, and the owners apparently have forgotten it, too. But their behavior has not gone unnoticed. They are now close to the bottom of the barrel in public trust. A recent survey showed that while 75 percent of the general public trust shopkeepers, 73 percent trust the military, and 60 percent trust doctors, only 25 percent trust corporate executives, slightly above the 23 percent that trust used-car dealers.

The Failure of the Gatekeepers

What happened? How did it all come to pass? Basically, we have had a failure of just about every gatekeeper we've traditionally relied on to make sure that corporations would be operated with honesty and integrity, and in the interests of their owners. Independent auditors became business partners of management. Government regulations were relaxed, and our elected officials not only didn't care, but actually aided and abetted the malfeasance. The elected representatives of the owners—the Boards of Directors—looked on the proceedings with benign neglect, apparently unmindful of the impending storm.

Let's begin with our public accountants. It would seem obvious that they should have constituted the first line of defense against pushing accounting standards to the edge and beyond, and, hard as it may be to discover, at least some defense against fraud. But the accounting standards themselves had gradually become debased. "Cookie jar" reserves were created after corporate mergers, and off–balance sheet special-purpose enterprises flourished, creating debt invisible to the public eye and giving "financial engineering" a whole new meaning. Of course the pressure has always been on accountants to agree with the corporate clients who pay them for their services. But over the past decade, to that seemingly unavoidable conflict of interest has been added the conflict of being business partners with their clients, providing management consulting services whose revenues often dwarf their audit fees. In the year 2000, for example, U.S. corporations paid their auditors nearly $3 billion for auditing services, only one-half of the $6 billion paid for consulting.

This added pressure on accountants to accede to management's demands, coming as managers promised quarterly earnings growth that was impossible to deliver, led to a company's *numbers* becoming more important than a company's *business*—a direct contradiction to the advice given to his colleagues by James Anyon, America's first accountant, way back in 1912: "Think and act upon facts, truths, and principles, and regard figures only as things to express them . . . so proceeding, [you will be] a credit to one of the truest and finest professions in the land."* The "creative accounting" of the recent era has taken us a long, long way from the wisdom of relying on figures to present facts.

On the regulatory and legislative front, our public servants were also pressed into relaxing existing regulations for accounting standards and disclosure. When proposals for reform came—for example, requiring that stock options *actually be counted* as a compensation expense, or prohibiting accountants from providing consulting services to the firms they audit—the outrage of our legislators, inspired (if that's the right word) both by political contributions and by the fierce lobbying efforts of both corporate America and the accounting profession, thwarted these long-overdue changes. Too many of our elected officials ought to be ashamed of themselves for their "play-for-pay" morality. Two centuries ago, Thomas Jefferson said, "I hope we shall crush in its birth the aristocracy of our monied corporations which dare already to challenge our government in a trial of strength, and bid defiance to the laws of our country." We didn't, of course, do so. But rather than defying our laws in this recent era of managers' capitalism, our monied corporations thwarted remedial legislation (it's a lot easier!), and compromised the highest interests of their investors.

The Role of the Board

That brings us to the board of directors. It is their job to be good stewards of the corporate property entrusted to them. In medieval England, the common use of the word "stewardship" meant the responsible use of a congregation's resources *in the faithful service of God*. In the corporate sense, the word has come to mean the use of the enterprise's resources in the faithful service of its owners. But somehow the system let us

---

*As quoted in David Boyle, *The Tyranny of Numbers* (London: Harpercollins, 2000), 8.

down. As boards of directors far too often turned over to the company's managers the virtually unfettered power to place their own interests first, both the word and the concept of stewardship became conspicuous by their absence from corporate America's values.

Serving as rubber-stamps for management, company directors have been responsible for approving option plans that are grossly excessive; audits in which the auditors are not independent appraisers of financial statements but partners of management; and mergers based on forcing the numbers rather than on improving the business. (As it turned out, according to *BusinessWeek*, 63 percent of all mergers have destroyed corporate value.) Directors also approved ethical codes in which words like "integrity," "trust," and "vision" were the order of the day, but corporate actions were another story. Some 60 percent of corporate employees, for example, report that they have observed violations of law or company policy at their firms, and 207 of 300 "whistleblowers" report they have lost their jobs as a result.

Yet our society has lionized our boards of directors nearly as much as our vaunted CEOs. Early in 2001, for example, *Chief Executive* magazine told us that "dramatic improvements in corporate governance have swept through the American economic system, [thanks to] enlightened CEOs and directors who voluntarily put through so many [changes] designed to make the operations of boards more effective." In particular, the magazine praised a certain "New Economy" company, "with a board that works hard to keep up with things . . . and working committees with functional responsibilities where disinterested oversight is required," a company whose four highest values were stated as, "Communication; Respect; Excellence; and Integrity—open, honest, and sincere. . . . We continue to raise the bar for everyone [because] the great fun here will be for all of us to discover just how good we can really be."* As it happens, we *do* now know just how good it could be: The company, so good that its board was named the third best among all of the thousands of boards in corporate America for 2000, is *bankrupt*. While its executives reaped billions in compensation, its employees are jobless, their retirement savings obliterated. Its reputation is shredded beyond repair. It was, of course, Enron.

---

*Robert W. Lear and Boris Yaritz, "Boards on Trial," *Chief Executive*, October 2000, 40.

The board of directors is the ultimate governing body of the corporation, and the directors are stewards charged with the responsibility of preserving and building the company over the long term. Yet the directors of corporate America couldn't have been unaware of the management's aggressive "earnings guidance"; nor of the focus on raising the price of the stock, never mind at what cost to the value of the corporation; nor of the fact that the lower the dividend the more capital the company retains; nor that it was management that hired the consultants who recommended to the compensation committee higher compensation for that very same management, year after year, even when its actual accomplishments in building the business were hardly out of the ordinary. Surely it is fair to say that it is our corporate directors who should bear the ultimate responsibility for what went wrong with corporate America.

Oh, No They Shouldn't!

Or should they? Why should the board bear the ultimate responsibility when it doesn't *have* the ultimate responsibility? Of course the directors' responsibility is large, indeed, but it is the stockholders themselves who bear the *ultimate* responsibility for corporate governance. And as investing has become institutionalized, stockholders have gained the *real*—as compared with the *theoretical*—power to exercise their will. Once owned largely by a diffuse and inchoate group of individual investors, each one with relatively modest holdings, today the ownership of stocks is concentrated—for better or worse—among a remarkably small group of institutions whose potential power is truly awesome. The 100 largest managers of pension funds and mutual funds alone now represent the ownership of one-half of all U.S. equities: *absolute control over corporate America.* Together, these 100 large institutional investors constitute the great 800-pound gorilla who can sit wherever he wants to sit at the board table.

But with all that power has come little interest in corporate governance. That amazing disconnection between the potential and the reality—awesome power, yet largely unexercised—reminds me of the original version of the motion picture *Mighty Joe Young.* In the film, the protagonist was a fierce gorilla who destroyed every object in his path. But whenever he heard the strains of "Beautiful Dreamer" he became serene and compliant. Not to push this analogy too far—especially for those who have not seen the film!—but I fear that, as institutional managers consider their responsibility for good corporate citizenship, they are hearing the sweet strains of "Beautiful Dreamer" playing in the background.

Yet mutual fund managers could hardly have been ignorant of what was going on in corporate America. Even before the stock market bubble burst, the industry's well-educated, highly trained, experienced professional analysts and portfolio managers *must* have been poring over company fiscal statements; evaluating corporate plans; and measuring the extent to which long-term corporate goals were being achieved, how cash flow compared with reported earnings, and the extent to which those ever-fallacious "pro-forma" earnings diverged from the reality. Yet few, if any, voices were raised. Somehow, our professional investors either didn't understand, or understood but ignored, the house of cards that the stock market had become. We have worshiped at the altar of the precise but ephemeral price of the stock, forgetting that the eternal sovereign is the intrinsic value of the corporation— simply the discounted value of its future cash flow.

We have yet to accept our responsibility for our abject failure, for the fact is that we have become, not an *own-a-stock* industry, but a *rent-a-stock* industry. During the past year, for example, the *average* equity fund turned over its portfolio at a 110 percent rate—meaning that the average stock was held for just *11 months*. When a company's stock may not even remain in a fund's portfolio by the time the company's next annual meeting rolls around, proxy voting and responsible corporate citizenship will rarely be found on the fund manager's agenda. What is more, money managers may avoid confrontation because even valid corporate activism could hurt the manager's ability to attract the assets of a corporation's pension account and 401(k) thrift plan, or limit its analysts' access to corporate information. Further, despite convincing information to the contrary, fund managers generally perceive only tenuous linkage between governance and stock price. But for whatever reason, the record clearly shows that the stockowners themselves—and especially the mutual fund industry—pay only sparse attention to corporate governance issues. "We have met the enemy, and he is us."

Actions and Reactions

As Sir Isaac Newton said, "for every action there is an equal and opposite reaction," and the reaction to the stock market boom and the mismanagement of so many of our corporations, to state the obvious, is already upon us. The first reaction to the bull market, of course, was the bear market that holds us in its throes to this day. The stock market, having quickly doubled from the start of 1997 to the high in March 2000, then dropped by half through mid-October 2002. That combination of percentages—plus 100 percent, then minus 50 percent—of course produces a net gain of *zero*. (Think about it!) But with the modest recovery that then ensued, stocks are just 10 percent higher than their levels were when 1997 began.

The sharp decline, it seems to me, has brought us "back to (or at least toward) normalcy" in valuation. And even *after* the Great Bear Market, the return on stocks during 1982 through 2002 averaged 13 percent per year, surely an attractive outcome for long-term stock owners. Through the miracle of compounding, those who owned stocks in 1982 and still held them in 2002 had multiplied that capital *10 times* over. So for all of the stock market's wild and wooly extremes, *owners* who bought and held common stocks have been well-compensated for the risks they assumed. For such investors, the coming of the bubble and then its going—the *boom* and then the *bust*—simply did not matter.

But that doesn't mean there weren't winners and losers during the mania—and lots of both. Simply put, the winners were those who *sold* their stocks in the throes of the halcyon era that is now history. The losers were those who bought them. Let's think first about the winners. A large proportion of these shares that were sold were those of corporate executives who had acquired vast holdings of their companies' stocks through options, and those of entrepreneurs whose companies had gone newly public as Wall Street investment banking firms underwrote huge volumes of initial stock offerings, many already defunct. *Fortune* magazine recently identified a group of executives in just 25 corporations in those categories, whose total share of sales came to $23 billion—nearly a billion dollars each.

Winners and Losers

Other winners included the financial intermediaries—investment bankers and brokers who sold the high-flying stocks to their clients, and mutual fund managers who sold more than *half a trillion*(!) dollars in speculative funds to the public. Why were they winners? Because the investment banking, brokerage, and management fees for their activities reached staggering levels. More than a few individual investment bankers saw their annual compensation reach well into the tens of millions, and at least a half-dozen owners of fund management companies accumulated personal wealth in the billion-dollar range, including one family said to be at the $30 billion level.

The losers, of course, were those who *bought* the stocks. "Greater fools?" Perhaps. But paradoxically, in order to avoid the dilution in their earnings that would otherwise have resulted from issuing those billions of optioned shares, the very corporations that issued those shares at dirt-cheap prices bought them back at the inflated prices of the day. But most of the buying came from the great American public—often in their personal accounts, and often through ever more popular 401(k) thrift plans—sometimes *directly*, by buying individual stocks; sometimes *indirectly*, through mutual funds. Greed, naiveté, the absence of common sense, and aggressive salesmanship all played a role in the rush to buy speculative stocks—technology, the Internet, telecommunications—that were part of the "new economy." During the peak two years of the bubble, $425 billion of investor capital flowed into mutual funds favoring those types of speculative growth stocks and $40 billion actually flowed *out* of those stodgy "old economy" value funds.

Clearly there was a massive transfer of wealth—a transfer, I believe, of as much as $2 trillion—during the late bubble, from public investors to corporate insiders and financial intermediaries. Such transfers, of course, are not without parallel all through human history. For whenever *speculation* takes precedence over *investment*, there is always a day of reckoning for the investors in the financial markets.

Fixing the Governance System

It's important to understand this history of what went wrong in corporate America and its impact on our financial markets, because only if we understand the root causes can we consider how to remedy them. So as I promised at the outset, I'm going to discuss the progress that is being made to right those wrongs. Newton's law holds here as well, for the reaction to the failures of our capitalistic system was swift in coming. Surprisingly, however, it was not the generalized problems of pushy earnings, faulty accounting, hyped expectations, imperial executives, loose governance, excessive speculation, and even the Great Bear Market that were the catalysts for reform. Rather, it was a handful of scandals—those few "bad apples," including Enron, Adelphia, WorldCom, Global Crossing—that galvanized the public's attention and generated the powerful reaction that, at long last, will help to bring the reform we need in our financial markets.

This pervasive reaction to the unacceptable actions of those we trusted to be our corporate stewards came swiftly.

- Last July, Congress passed the Sarbanes-Oxley bill, requiring senior corporate managers to attest to the validity of their companies' financial statements, providing for disgorgement of profits by executives who sell stocks and later restate earnings, and replacing self-regulation of accountants with a new federal Public Company Accounting Oversight Board, as well as other salutary provisions.
- In August, the New York Stock Exchange approved a powerful set of corporate governance rules for its listed companies—most of the major corporations in America—including substantially greater director independence, and new standards for audit committees and compensation committees. It even contemplated a "lead director" who is independent of corporate management. These changes should at long last lead to a separation of the powers of *governance* from the powers of *management*, and help us to return to a system of *owners'* capitalism.
- Just last month, The Conference Board Blue-Ribbon Commission on Public Trust and Private Enterprise—on which I was privileged to serve—completed its recommendations of a powerful set of "best practices" for public corporations. Our report on executive compensation included a recommendation that *all* types of stock options be treated as corporate expense, at last making it clear that fixed-price options are not "free." On corporate governance, we recommended an *independent* nominating/governance committee; the

establishment and enforcement of codes of ethics; and the separation of the chairman and CEO roles, making clear the distinction between ownership and management. On accounting standards, our Commission's recommendations include further strengthening of audit committees and auditor rotation, and a challenge to the remaining Big Four (also known as "the Final Four") accounting firms to focus on quality audits, and to eliminate *all* consulting and tax services that involve advocacy positions, including those grotesque tax-shelters designed so executives can circumvent the law.

Two centuries ago, James Madison said, "If men were angels, we wouldn't need *government*." Today, I say to our corporate leaders, "If chief executives were angels, we wouldn't need *corporate governance*." Through the reactions of Congress, the New York Stock Exchange, and the Conference Board Commission, to say nothing of the media, we're on our way to getting better governance right now.

Astonishingly, however, the reaction of institutional investors to the failings of our system has yet to occur. Even after the bear market that devastated the value of our clients' equity holdings, the only response we've heard from the mutual fund industry is the sound of silence. The reason for that silence seems to be that the overwhelming majority of mutual funds continue to engage, not in the process of long-term investing on the basis of intrinsic corporate *values*, but in the process of short-term speculation based on momentary stock *prices*. The typical fund manager has lots of interest in a company's price momentum—its quarterly earnings and whether or not they are meeting the guidance given to Wall Street. But when it comes to what a company is actually worth—its fundamental earning power, its balance sheet, its long-term strategy, its intrinsic value—there seems to be far less interest. When Oscar Wilde described the cynic as "a man who knows the price of everything but the value of nothing," he could have as easily been talking about fund managers.

Fixing the Investment System

It must be clear that we need not only good *managers* of corporate America, but good *owners*. That goal will *not* be easy to accomplish. For it will require shareholders—especially institutional shareholders—to abandon the focus on short-term speculation that has characterized the recent era and return at last to a focus on long-term investment. We need to return to behaving as *owners* rather than as *traders*, to return to principles of prudence and trusteeship rather than of speculation and salesmanship, and to return to acting as good stewards of the assets entrusted to our care. For example:

- Institutions and individual investors must begin to act as responsible corporate citizens, voting our proxies thoughtfully and communicating our views to corporate managements. We should be prepared to nominate directors and make business proposals in proxies, and regulators should facilitate these actions. The SEC's recent decision to require mutual funds to disclose how we vote our proxies is a long-overdue first step in this process.

- Shareowners must demand that corporations focus the information provided to the investment community on long-term financial goals, cash flows, intrinsic values, and strategic direction. Quarterly "earnings guidance," so omnipresent today, should be *eliminated*. So should efforts to meet financial targets through creative accounting techniques.

- Given the enormous latitude accorded by "Generally Accepted Accounting Principles," owners must demand full disclosure of the impact of significant accounting policy decisions. Indeed, we ought to consider requiring that corporations report earnings both on a "most aggressive" basis (presumably what they are reporting today), and on a "most conservative" basis as well.

- Mutual funds must report to their owners not only the *direct* costs of mutual fund investing (such as management fees and sales loads), but the *indirect* costs, including the costs of past and expected portfolio turnover and its attendant tax impact. Funds must also desist from advertising short-term investment performance (and perhaps from *any* performance advertising at all).

- Policymakers must develop differential tax strategies aimed at stemming excessive speculation. Some years ago, for example, Warren Buffett suggested a 100 percent tax on short-term capital gains, paid not only by taxable investors, *but also by tax-exempt pension funds*. While that tax rate *might* seem a tad extreme, perhaps a 50 percent tax on very short-term gains on trading stocks would force investors to come to their senses.

- Perhaps most important of all, investor/owners must demand that corporations step up their dividend payouts. Despite the absence of evidence that earnings retention leads to sound capital allocations, the payout rate has been declining for years. Yet history tells us that higher dividend payouts are actually associated with *higher* future returns on stocks. Investing for income is a *long-term* strategy, and investing for capital gains is a *short-term* strategy; the turnover of dividend-paying stocks is at but one-half of the rate for non-dividend-paying stocks.

Back to the Future

Calling for a return to the eternal principles of long-term investing is more than mere moralizing. Our very society depends on it, for our economic growth depends upon capital formation. Way back in 1936, Lord Keynes warned us, "When enterprise becomes a mere bubble on a whirlpool of speculation, the position is serious. *For when the capital development of a country becomes a by-product of the activities of a casino, the job is likely to be ill-done.*"* As a nation we can't afford to let that happen. The fact is that we need a whole new mindset for institutional investors, one in which *speculation* becomes a mere bubble on a whirlpool of *investment*. In the mutual fund industry, we need to go "back to the future," to return to our traditional focus on stewardship and abandon the focus on salesmanship that has dominated our recent history.

While the changes I have suggested will help return us to our roots, however, the fact remains that there is more profit potential for financial service firms in marketing (generating huge assets to manage) than in management. For, as both simple mathematics and the investment record of the past clearly indicate, beating the market is a loser's game, simply because of the staggering toll taken by the costs of financial intermediation. When fund investors realize that fact, they will

---

*John Maynard Keynes, *The General Theory of Employment, Interest, and Money* (New York: Macmillan, 1936; Harcourt, Brace, 1964), 159.

vote with their feet, and send their hard-earned dollars to funds that get the message. By doing so, using Adam Smith's metaphor, "it is the individual who acts in his own interests to better his financial condition who will promote the natural progress of things toward improvement." Similarly, when an investor puts his money into mutual funds that invest rather than speculate, he earns the highest possible proportion of whatever returns the financial markets are generous enough to provide (of course, we know them to be low-cost market index funds), promoting the public interest without intending to, or even knowing he is doing so.

That doesn't mean, however, that the trusted fiduciary, the honest businessman, or the good merchant should behave in an ethical way only because their clients have dragged them, kicking and screaming, into doing what's right. The fact is, as I noted at the outset, that in the long run *good ethics are good business, part of that virtuous circle that builds our society.* When in recent years our rule of conduct became "I can get away with it," or, more charitably, "I can do it because everyone else is doing it," integrity and ethics go out the window and the whole idea of capitalism is soured.

Man's Better Nature

If my appeal to man's better nature seems hopelessly out of tune with the discouraging era I've described this evening, I can only remind you that Adam Smith, that patron saint of capitalism, would be on my side. Even before *The Wealth of Nations*, he wrote *The Theory of Moral Sentiments*, reminding us of the better nature that

> has lighted up the human heart, capable of counteracting the strongest impulses of self-love. . . . It is reason, principle, conscience, the inhabitant of the breast, the man within, the great judge and arbitrator of our conduct who calls to us with a voice capable of astonishing the most presumptuous of our passions that we are of the multitude, in no respect better than any other in it . . . he who shows us the propriety of reining in the greatest interests of our own for the yet greater interests of others, the

love of what is honorable and noble, of the grandeur, and dignity, and superiority of our characters.*

At last we are beginning a wave of reform in corporate governance and are undertaking the task of turning America's capital development process away from speculation and toward enterprise. It will be no mean task. For there's even more at stake than improving the *practices* of governance and investing. We must also establish a higher set of *principles*. This nation's founding fathers believed in high moral standards, in a just society, and in the virtuous conduct of our affairs. Those beliefs shaped the very character of our nation. If *character counts*—and I have absolutely no doubt that character *does* count—the ethical failings of today's business and financial model, the financial manipulation of corporate America, the willingness of those of us in the field of investment management to accept practices that we know are wrong, the conformity that keeps us silent, the selfishness that lets our greed overwhelm our reason, all erode the character we'll require in the years ahead, more than ever in the wake of this Great Bear Market and the investor disenchantment it reflects. The motivations of those who seek the rewards earned by engaging in commerce and finance struck the imagination of no less a man than Adam Smith as "something grand and beautiful and noble, well worth the toil and anxiety." I can't imagine that the vast majority of our citizenry would use those words to describe what capitalism is about today. The sooner the better when we can again apply those words to our business and financial leaders—*and mean them.*

A Call for Virtue

So there is much work to be done. But it's about much more than assuring that the "bottom line" of business is not only stated with probity, but focused on investing based on long-term corporate value rather than speculating on short-term stock prices. It is the enduring reality of

---

*Adam Smith, *The Theory of Moral Sentiments* (1759; Cambridge, England: Cambridge University Press, 2002), 158.

intrinsic value—make no mistake, the worth of a corporation *is* neither more nor less than the discounted value of its future cash flows—*not* the ephemeral perception of the price of a stock that carries the day. And the enterprises that will endure are those that generate the most profits for their owners, something they do best when they take into account the interests of their customers, their employees, their communities, and indeed the interests of our society. *Please don't think of the ideals merely as foolish idealism.* They are the ideals that capitalism has depended upon from the very outset. Again, hear Adam Smith: "He is certainly not a good citizen who does not wish to promote, by every means of his power, the welfare of the whole society of his fellow citizens." So it's up to each one of us to speak up, to speak out, and to demand that our corporations and our fund managers represent our interests rather than their own—the owners first, not the managers. Please don't think that your voice doesn't matter. In the words of the motto I've tried to ingrain in the minds of our Vanguard crewmembers, "Even one person can make a difference."

While a call for virtue in the conduct of the affairs of corporate America—and investment America, too—may sound like a hollow "do-good" platitude, the fact is that in the long run the high road is the only possible road to national achievement and prosperity, to making the most of those priceless assets with which America has been endowed by her Creator. On this point, I am unable to find more compelling wisdom than some splendid words attributed, perhaps apocryphally, to Alexis de Tocqueville. I hope these words will resound far beyond the parochial issues I've addressed here into the larger world around us, troubled as it is:

> I sought for the greatness and genius of America in her harbors and her rivers, in her fertile fields and boundless forests, and it was not there.
>
> I sought for the greatness and genius of America in her rich mines and her vast world commerce, and in her institutions of learning, and it was not there.
>
> I sought for the greatness and genius of America in her democratic Congress and her matchless Constitution, and it was not there.

Not until I went into the churches of America and heard her pulpits flame with righteousness did I understand the secret of her genius and power.

America is great because America is good, and if America ever ceases to be good, America will cease to be great.

And so it is with corporate America and investment America, too. If we return to goodness, we can again strive for greatness. Let's all of us together make sure that happens.

Chapter 7

Fixing a Broken Financial System*

A merica's economic crisis continues to unfold, and only recently has the seemingly unrelenting bear market that began in October 2007 begun to recoup its lost ground. So of course the leaders of our financial community—as well as our business and legal communities—are deeply concerned by the present state of affairs. In many respects, my recent book, *Enough*, anticipated—some say, *predicted*—the crisis in our markets and our economy. But the book also sends a message about the decline in our society's character and values that we have witnessed over the past few decades.

Think about it. We live in wonderful and sad times—wonderful in that the blessings of democratic capitalism have never been more broadly distributed around the globe, sad in that the excesses of that same democratic capitalism have rarely been more on display. We see the excesses most starkly in the continuing crisis in our overleveraged, overly speculative banking and investment banking industries, creating the financial crisis that has been in turn the principal cause of the economic crisis we are facing, the worst since the Great Depression.

---

*Based on remarks at an assembly sponsored by Philadelphia law firm Stradley, Ronan, Stevens & Young on February 12, 2009.

Despite the economic and market meltdown, however, we witness the obscene (there is no other word for it) compensation paid to the chief executive officers of our nation's publicly held corporations—including failed CEOs, often even as they are being pushed out the door—compensation that, given the capital these institutions urgently require merely to survive, is being paid by the federal government, or, more accurately, the taxpayers, or, even more poignantly, *us*. Main Street bailing out Wall Street for its disgraceful conduct—it doesn't seem fair, does it? Well, it isn't!

But the rampant greed that has overwhelmed our financial system and corporate world runs deeper than money. Not knowing what *enough* is subverts our society's traditional values, as self-interest and greed replace community interest, professions behave as businesses (money versus service to the community), and service to self takes priority over service to others. This confusion about what is enough leads us astray in our larger lives, as we too often bow down at the altar of the transitory and finally meaningless; and we fail to cherish what is beyond calculation, indeed eternal. Unchecked, our failures ultimately result in the diminution of our national character and values. So in a broader sense, we all bear some of the responsibility for what has gone wrong in America, in important part because of our society's worship of wealth and the growing corruption of our ethics.

An Act of Faith

The failure of our financial system is reflected in its betrayal of the fundamental principles under which we invest, a betrayal of our faith. Paradoxically, just a decade ago, I wrote in the very first sentence of my 1999 book, *Common Sense on Mutual Funds: New Imperatives for the Intelligent Investor*, that "investing is an act of faith." I then amplified that short, simple declarative sentence in three areas: (1) faith that our corporate managers "will generate high rates of return on our investments"; (2) faith that the "success of the U.S. economy and the nation's financial markets will continue"; and (3) faith that our professional money managers "will be vigilant stewards of the assets we entrust to them."

As we now know, that faith, far too often, has been betrayed. Too many of our corporate managers—most recently those in the banking and investment banking industries, but earlier at Enron, WorldCom, and the like—have forfeited our trust by operating in their own financial interests and not in the interests of their shareholders/owners. Our economy is in the midst of the deepest recession since the Great Depression. Our stock markets have plunged to levels not seen since 1996, forfeiting nearly a dozen years of gains. (Leave aside that some of those gains reflected irrational exuberance and represented "phantom returns" destined to vanish.) And our professional money managers, rather than acting as long-term investors—serving as vigilant stewards of our assets and acting as prudent trustees for the mutual fund investors and the pension fund beneficiaries they were duty-bound to serve—have instead largely become short-term *speculators*, behaving as stock traders and placing their own interests ahead of the interests of their clients.

Fathers of the Crisis

There is plenty of responsibility to spread around for what went wrong. So while it is often said that "victory has a thousand fathers, but defeat is an orphan," the defeat suffered by investors in our devastating financial crisis seems to have, figuratively speaking, a thousand fathers: the Federal Reserve, keeping interest rates too low for too long after the 2000–2002 stock market crash, and failing to impose discipline on mortgage bankers; our banks and investment banks, which designed and sold trillions of dollars' worth of incredibly complex and risky mortgage-backed bonds and tens of trillions of dollars of derivatives (largely credit default swaps). They were also left holding the bag with many of these toxic derivatives, held in highly leveraged balance sheets—sometimes by as much as 33 to 1 or more. Just do the math: A mere 3 percent decline in asset value wipes out 100 percent of shareholder equity.

These institutions also brought us "securitization," selling off loans to untested financial instruments and severing the traditional link between lender and borrower. With that change, the incentive to demand creditworthiness on the part of those who borrow almost vanished as banks lent the money and then sold the loans to these new bond funds. In banking we've come a long, long way from community lending built on the financial probity and the character of the borrower, the kind of thing we saw in *It's a Wonderful Life*. (Remember Jimmy Stewart as George Bailey and Lionel Barrymore's crusty Mr. Potter?)

Our market regulators, too, have a lot to answer for: The Securities & Exchange Commission was almost apathetic in its failure to recognize what was happening in the capital markets. The Commodity Futures Trading Commission allowed the trading and valuation of derivatives to proceed opaquely, without transparency, without demanding the sunlight of full disclosure, and without concern for the ability of the counterparties to meet their financial obligations if their bets went sour.

And let's not forget Congress, which passed responsibility for regulation of the derivatives market to the CFTC almost as an afterthought. Congress allowed—indeed encouraged—risk-taking by our government-sponsored (now essentially government-owned) enterprises—Fannie Mae and Freddie Mac—allowing them to expand far beyond the capacity of their capital, and pushing them to lower their lending standards. Congress also gutted the Glass-Steagall Act of 1933, which had separated traditional banking and investment banking, a separation that for more than 60 years well-served our national interest.

Our professional security analysts also have much to answer for, especially in their almost-universal failure to recognize the huge credit risks assumed by the new breed of bankers and investment bankers who were far more interested in earnings growth for their institutions than in the sanctity of their balance sheets. So do our credit rating agencies, for bestowing AAA ratings on securitized loans in return for enormous fees—handsomely paid in return by the very issuers who demanded those ratings, which allowed what proved to be largely junk bonds to be sold in the marketplace. (It's called "conflict of interest.")

Yes, there's plenty of blame to go around, finally rooted in the American citizenry at large with our insatiable demand for "more" and our growing appetite for self-indulgence rather than the well-being of our system.

How Can We Fix Our Broken System?

So we have a real mess on our hands. How does it ever get resolved? The first thing to recognize is that it's *our* mess. In the economy, it will take considerable time to unwind the huge debt overload we have taken on in our mortgages, and our consumer debt, and considerable time for our banking system to re-liquefy its tattered balance sheets. The task will hardly be made easier when our hard-pressed families save more and spend less. We are living through "the paradox of thrift," economist John Maynard Keynes's formulation that described savings as good and necessary for the individual, even as those same savings are counterproductive for our consumer-driven economy, crying for the long-awaited upsurge in business activity.

How much time will it take? I'd guess—although I have neither great insight nor economic expertise—that it might take a year and a half to two years before the recession slows and business activity turns upward. It took a long time to create this economic crisis, and it will take a long time to fight our way out of it. But ultimately, given reforms in our system, the resilience of our American society and our American economy will reassert itself.

I should point out that while the tools we use to stimulate the economy are now being chosen by our president and our congress, these remedies are uncertain and untested. They can help us through the crisis, but what we need most of all are the clarity and consistency necessary to restore confidence. The $789 billion stimulus package that is now on the track to the president's desk is a long way from perfect, but it is largely doing the right things—increased unemployment benefits, tax cuts for those earning less than $200,000 per year, infrastructure improvements, help to mortgage holders. Imperfect as the bill surely will be, it's impossible to argue that the federal government should ignore this ghastly economic crisis.

In addition to the stimulus package, of course, we're dealing with a separate financial package designed to rescue our banking system—another $1 trillion (public and private) and counting, and $1 billion of federal loan backing. (We seem immune to shock over the nearly $3 trillion of federal commitment out there!) Treasury secretary Geithner's recent proposals seemed to fall on deaf ears, and the stock market—in its inevitably speculative unwisdom—immediately gave him a failing grade. But there is no miracle cure. Nonetheless, the essence of the Treasury plan is correct: We need to engage private capital as well as public capital in order to enable our banks—one by one—to clean up their balance sheets and resume normal lending practices. The secretary also promised "stress tests" designed to assess their financial health, again, bank by bank. (One might have thought this had been a long-standing practice of bank managers and bank regulators alike. But that was not the case.) And surely banks that don't pass the test—and there may be quite a few—will have to be liquidated, with their deposits largely guaranteed under existing federal law.

If the federal government pays the bank piper, of course, it has the right to call the tune. That's the right of ownership, and it brings up the issue of nationalization of our—let's face it—already partially nationalized system. My own view is that the government has not driven nearly a hard enough bargain with the institutions for which it has provided capital. Indeed, I suspect that, say, Dubai would have demanded a lot more equity for a $55 billion capital infusion into Citigroup than a low-yielding preferred stock and warrants that might entitle it to own less than 1 percent of the company. (For the record, the current market value of Citigroup is about $19 billion, down from $274 billion as recently as 2006. Citi also has some $500 billion of short- and long-term debt, which simple mathematics tells us must also be, to one degree or another, on the endangered species list.)

The Heart of the Matter

But little attention has been given to the broader systemic issues that have contributed to this crisis. Two overarching changes in capitalism have clearly played a major role. The heart of the matter goes to the very issue of the ownership of our giant publicly held corporations.

Only if its *managers* are focused on creating long-term value for its *owners* can corporate America be the prime engine of the nation's growth and prosperity and a major source of innovation and experimentation. To the extent that managers sit unchecked in the driver's seat, feathering their own nests at the expense of their owners, capitalism cannot flourish.

During the past half-century, the very nature of capitalism has undergone a pathological mutation. We have moved from an *ownership society* in which 92 percent of stocks were held by individual investors looking after their own interests and only 8 percent by financial institutions, to an *agency society* in which our institutions now hold some 70 percent of stocks and individuals hold but 30 percent.

These institutional agents have not only betrayed the interests of the *principals* to whom they owe a duty of trusteeship, but have also abandoned their traditional investment *principles*. For it is these agents who have been the driving force in changing the central characteristic of market participation from *long-term investment*—owning businesses that earn a return on their capital, creating value by reinvesting their earnings and distributing dividends to their owners—to *short-term speculation*, essentially trading stocks and betting on their future prices. It is not only hedge funds that are playing this game, but most mutual funds and many giant pension plans.

Today, we are witnessing an orgy of speculation the likes of which have never been seen before. Turnover in the U.S. stock market in 1929 was 140 percent; it fell to about 25 percent during my first few decades in this business. Last year, turnover was about 350 percent, speculators trading with other speculators, each with the idea of taking advantage of those on the other side of the trade, creating—to state the obvious—*zero* in economic value. It is the rise of speculation that explains why in a typical year the market *never* moved by daily increments of 3 percent or more (up or down) but has experienced 50 such days since the beginning of 2008.

Speculation Sits in the Driver's Seat

But Wall Street marketers and entrepreneurs loved this new system of speculation in complex products, quantification, innovation, and unconstrained risk, for it made them billions in profits. So it was easy for Wall Street insiders to wallow in the wealth it generated for themselves, and ignore its destruction of their clients' wealth. Revenues of our stock brokerage firms, money managers, and the other insiders soared from an estimated $60 billion in 1990 to some $600 billion in 2007.

So while trading back and forth with one another—foolish as it is—is by definition a zero-sum game, once the costs of our Wall Street croupiers are deducted it is a loser's game. (Think Las Vegas. Think the Atlantic City Race Track. Heck, think the Pennsylvania lottery.) So for investors as a group—who inevitably feed at the bottom of the food chain of investing, receiving whatever market returns remain after the croupiers' costs—trading is a loser's game, by the amount of these costs.

That $600 billion in 2007 plus many hundreds of billions in earlier years obviously represent a truly staggering hit to the gains investors earned in the bull market, and a financial slap in their face in the bear market that followed. Any confidence in Wall Street that our investors once may have had has largely vanished, just as it should have. The speculators among us, and those of us who have forgotten the distinction between investment and speculation—two groups that inevitably display a large amount of greed—must share a portion of the responsibility for the financial bubble and the ensuing crash.

When an own-a-stock industry becomes a rent-a-stock industry, concern about corporate governance is the first casualty—a harbinger that our capitalistic system is not working properly. Yet the ideal owner is a long-term stockholder, perhaps even a permanent owner, whose goals are closely aligned with those of the corporation. *The Economist* of London expressed it well:

> Everything now depends on financial institutions pressing even harder for reforms to make boards of directors behave more like overseers, and less like the chief executive's collection of puppets. . . . Financial institutions must also fight to restore their rights as shareholders and use their clout to elect directors, who would be obliged to represent only their collective interest as owners. Chief executives will still run their firms; but, like any other employee, they would also have a boss.*

The giant institutions of investment in America must take the lead in accomplishing these goals. Our money managers not only hold 75 percent of all shares, but they have the staff to pore over corporate financial statements and proxies; the professional expertise to evaluate CEO performance, pay, and perquisites; and, once full disclosure of all proxy votes (by pension funds as well as mutual funds) becomes mandatory, the incentive to vote in the manner that their beneficiaries have every right to expect. Their dereliction of duty in these areas also bears an important responsibility for what went wrong in our financial sector. (Who, for example, was analyzing those toxic balance sheets of our banks?)

---

*"Getting Rid of the Boss," *Economist*, February 6, 1993, 13.

When they return—as they must—to their traditional focus on long-term investing, these institutional owners must fight for the access to the levers of control over the corporations they own that are both appropriate for their dominant ownership position and a reflection of their willingness to accept both the rights and responsibilities of corporate citizenship. And if these institutions do not soon return to traditional standards of prudent investment, we'll have to institute a federal statute of fiduciary duty, under which the interests of those whose capital is at stake come first—a new ownership focus for our flawed agency-society. And this is one of the major reforms in the regulation we need in our emerging financial system.

The task of returning capitalism to its owners will take time, true enough. But the new reality—increasingly visible with each passing day—is that proper corporate governance is not merely an ideal to be debated. It is a vital necessity to be practiced. The role of the owners, I underscore, is to do no more than ensure that the interests of directors and management are aligned with those of the shareholders in a substantive way. When there is a conflict of interest, it is the shareholders who should make the decision. It is in the national public interest and in the interest of investors that the owners—represented largely by investment America—come to realize that enlightened corporate governance is not merely a right of business ownership. It is a responsibility to the nation.

In these days when we seem to like "stories" to explain complex issues, here are three short anecdotes centered on individuals whose names will be familiar to you—(1) Alan Greenspan, (2) Bernard Madoff, and (3) Barack Obama, an unlikely triumvirate of strange bedfellows if ever there were one—and their respective roles in: (1) how this financial crisis began, (2) how we fooled ourselves, and (3) what we must do to work our way through the incredibly intractable economic woes that now plague us.

Alan Greenspan and the Bubble

First, we'll consider former Federal Reserve Chairman Alan Greenspan. More than any other individual, he was central to the development of the financial bubble and the burst that inevitably followed. He successfully urged his fellow Fed governors to continue to make easy credit available when the time to tighten credit had long since arrived, and to ignore the perils created by a freewheeling mortgage banking business in which the necessary link between borrowers and lenders had been severed. His intellectual analysis and his market-moving power, it turns out, were based on a false premise.

To his credit, in his testimony before Congress last October, Greenspan admitted his mistake. He acknowledged that the crisis had been prompted by "a once-in-a-century credit tsunami," which had arisen from the collapse of a "whole intellectual edifice." "Those of us who have looked to the self-interest of lending institutions to protect shareholders' equity—myself especially—are in a state of shocked disbelief," he said. This failure of self-interest to provide self-regulation was, he said, "a flaw in the model that I perceived as the critical functioning structure that defines how the world works."

It's worth dwelling on that phrase: *the critical functioning structure that defines how the world works.* As *New Yorker* writer John Lanchester observed: "That's a hell of a big thing to find a flaw in." Here's another way of describing that flaw. Lanchester continues: "The people in power thought they knew more than they did. The bankers evidently knew too much math and not enough history—or maybe they didn't know enough of either."* To which I would add, *enough* indeed!

Bernard Madoff and How We Fool Ourselves

Next, let's turn to issue number two, how we fooled ourselves in the financial markets, where investors—individual and institutional alike—seemed to lose all perspective. Short-term speculation—more than at any time in the entire history of our nation—was the star of this show, and long-term investment barely played even a supporting role. Too many of us were too greedy, too willing to believe that there were managers who could roundly beat the returns generated in our markets; almost childlike in our eagerness to pay the substantial costs

---

*John Lanchester, "Heroes and Zeroes," *New Yorker*, February 2, 2009.

to capture these returns (which proved nonexistent); and more or less unaware of the powerful marketing system that greases the machinery of Wall Street. All of these baneful forces converged in the enormous Ponzi scheme directed by Bernard Madoff.

Unlike Greenspan, Madoff was only a marginal contributor to the present crisis, but he surely is its exemplar. Like so many of the complex innovations created by our nation's largest and most prominent financial institutions, Madoff's Ponzi scheme was indeed blown up by its own dynamite. While investors seemed surprised by the collapse of the Madoff fund and astounded by its magnitude, however, we should not have been.

In fact, the investment returns he claimed were preposterous. In my long career, I've seen some money managers who have earned *high* returns, and others who have succeeded in earning *consistent* returns—in each case, whether by skill or luck. But any seasoned investor knows that a pairing of returns that are *both* high *and* consistent is truly oxymoronic. Yet Madoff attracted wealthy investors who thought of themselves as part of the "smart money" crowd, or sought to join that crowd. Too often these investors entrusted their fortunes to managers who knew "the secret" of making lots of money, a secret that would enrich those who had, well, *enough*, but wanted still more. Alas, however, the secret of beating the markets is that there is no secret.

As his reputation for having the "smart money secret" was burnished by individual investors, institutional managers who should have known better also joined the "high-and-consistent-returns" throng. Madoff's scheme was fostered by marketers who recommended him to their own substantial clients—hedge-fund-of-hedge-funds managers who were taken in by Madoff's scam, even as they were grossly enriched by it. In just four years, for example, a single firm received $500 million of fees, simply by investing its clients' money in Madoff's fund. Apparently ignorant of the time-honored rule, "trust, but verify," these managers flunked the due-diligence test. Paid such huge revenues for so little effort, they are a vivid example of one of Upton Sinclair's timeless warnings, which I paraphrase here: "It's amazing how difficult it is for a man to understand something if he's paid a small fortune *not* to understand it."

President Obama, Leadership, and Confidence

My third and final subject is "Where do we go from here?" We are facing the worst economic crisis of my adult lifetime (I was born just before the Great Depression, so I don't remember it!), a financial mess that is enormous beyond imagination, and complex beyond the intellectual capacity of most (perhaps all!) of us. What's more, the solutions that we are considering are without precedent—and therefore uncertain of success. Resolving the crisis and reforming the system will take patience and sacrifice—two traits that at the moment seem far from being the defining elements of our national character.

Here is where Barack Obama comes in. For while resolution and reform will come neither easily nor quickly, both require strong leadership. And without strong leadership, we are lost. I speak not as a partisan but as a citizen when I express my belief that President Obama can—and will—give us the kind of leadership we urgently require. Clearly, he understands the challenge. Recall with me these words from his Inaugural Address:

> That we are in the midst of crisis is now well understood. . . .
> Our economy is badly weakened, a consequence of greed
> and irresponsibility on the part of some, but also our collective
> failure to make hard choices and prepare the nation for a new
> age. . . . The question before us [is not] whether the market
> is a force for good or ill. Its power to generate wealth and
> expand freedom is unmatched, but this crisis has reminded us
> that without a watchful eye, the market can spin out of control—
> and that a nation cannot prosper long when it favors only the
> prosperous. The success of our economy has always depended
> not just on the size of our gross domestic product, but on the
> reach of our prosperity; on our ability to extend opportunity to
> every willing heart . . . the surest route to our common good.

> Those values upon which our success depends—hard work
> and honesty, courage and fair play, tolerance and curiosity,
> loyalty and patriotism—these things are old. These things
> are true. What is demanded then is a return to these truths.
> What is required of us now is a new era of responsibility—a

recognition, on the part of every American, that we have duties to ourselves, our nation, and the world, duties that we do not grudgingly accept but rather seize gladly, firm in the knowledge that there is nothing so satisfying to the spirit, so defining of our character, than giving our all to a difficult task. This is the price and the promise of citizenship.

As I listened to the president's Inaugural Address, I was impressed with his obvious gift of oratory. And when I read the text in the next day's newspaper, I was even more struck by the power, the clarity, and the realism that resounded throughout his cadences. While he didn't use the phrase "America, we have had *enough*" (as he did—of course, to my delight—in his speech accepting his party's nomination), I was struck by how his words and values paralleled what I had written months earlier for my own *Enough*. In the section in which I ask, "Enough for America?," see if you don't find the echoes of my own ideals in the ideals of our new president:

> While we seem to have quite enough things in the United States, our traditional values seem to be eroding, and soon we'll not have nearly enough of them. So let's never forget that over the long term it is not things, nor power, nor money that form the heart of any nation. Rather, it is values, the very values, applied to our society that I have described here for us as individuals: the persistence, resilience, moral standards, and virtue that have made this nation great. The question, in short, is not whether the United States has enough money—enough productive wealth—to maintain and enhance its global presence and power, but whether we have enough character, values, and virtue to do so.

And that's really what *Enough* is all about. And that's surely *enough* words to inflict on you on this busy morning, during this long winter of our discontent. These are truly "the times that try men's souls," but please remember the eternal wisdom of these words: "This, too, shall pass away." And so today's crisis shall pass away, as time and the resilience of our system—and important changes in the way we manage American capitalism—heal our wounded economy. It can't pass away too soon for me!

Chapter 8

Vanishing Treasures: Business Values and Investment Values*

I must begin by telling you what a thrill it is to return again to the Princeton campus that has played such a definitive—even determinative—role in my life. Of course I'm honored to be asked by Andrew Gossen, associate director of the alumni education program, to participate in this year's Maclean House series. The theme "Vanishing Treasures" holds great appeal to me, for I'm deeply concerned about "cultures and values that are disappearing in the face of human activity."

When director Gossen wrote to me (by e-mail of course; letter writing seems to be yet another vanishing treasure), he suggested that I focus on corporate ethics. Since the decline of business values and investment values was one of the principal subjects of my fifth book, *The Battle for the Soul of Capitalism*, I promptly tendered my acceptance (yes, by e-mail). So I'm pleased to present my perspective.

---

*Based on remarks at the Maclean House 2007 Lecture Series at Princeton University on March 15, 2007.

The Battle for the Soul of Capitalism

Let me begin by discussing the deep concerns about the vanishing values of our nation that I expressed in *The Battle for the Soul of Capitalism*. *The Battle* begins with a remarkably modest rewriting of the opening paragraph of Edward Gibbon's *The Decline and Fall of the Roman Empire*, adapted to the present era. Compare the two first sentences. Gibbon: "In the second century of the Christian Era, the Empire of Rome comprehended the fairest part of the earth and the most civilized portion of mankind." *Battle*: "As the twentieth century of the Christian era ended, the United States of America comprehended the most powerful position on earth and the wealthiest portion of mankind."*

So when I add Gibbon's conclusion—"[Yet] the Roman Empire would decline and fall, a revolution which will be ever remembered and is still felt by the nations of the earth"—I'm confident that the thoughtful reader did not miss the point. But of course I hammer it home, anyway: "Gibbon's history reminds us that no nation can take its greatness for granted. There are no exceptions." As one of two reviews—both very generous—of *The Battle* that appeared in the *New York Times* noted, "Subtle Mr. Bogle is not."

No, I'm not writing off America. But I am warning that we'd best put our house in order.

> The example of the fall of the Roman Empire ought to be a strong wake-up call to all of those who share my respect and admiration for the vital role that capitalism has played in America's call to greatness. Thanks to our marvelous economic system, based on private ownership of productive facilities, on prices set in free markets, and on personal freedom, we are the most prosperous society in history, the most powerful nation on the face of the globe, and, most important of all, the highest exemplar of the values that, sooner or later, are shared by the

---

*Edward Gibbon, *The Decline and Fall of the Roman Empire* (1776–1788; New York: Random House, 2003); John C. Bogle, *The Battle for the Soul of Capitalism* (New Haven: Yale University Press, 2005).

human beings of all nations: "certain inalienable rights . . . to life, liberty, and the pursuit of happiness."

But something went wrong.

By the later years of the twentieth century, our business values had eroded to a remarkable extent—the greed, egoism, materialism and waste that seems almost endemic in today's version of capitalism; the huge and growing disparity between the "haves" and the "have-nots" of our nation; poverty and lack of education; our misuse of the world's natural resources; the corruption of our political system by corporate money—all are manifestations of a system gone awry.

And here's where the soul of capitalism comes in. The book reads, "The human soul, as Thomas Aquinas defined it, is the 'form of the body, the vital power animating, pervading, and shaping an individual from the moment of conception, drawing all the energies of life into a unity.' In our temporal world, the soul of capitalism is the vital power that has animated, pervaded, and shaped our economic system, drawing all of its energies into a unity. In this sense, it is no overstatement to describe the effort we must make to return the system to its proud roots with these words: *the battle to restore the soul of capitalism.*" (One reviewer thought that the title was, well, "inflated," but liked the book anyway.)

This idealism doesn't let up. The reader doesn't even finish the first page of the book's first chapter ("What Went Wrong in Corporate America?") before reading:

At the root of the problem, in the broadest sense, was a societal change aptly described by these words I've so often quoted from the teacher Joseph Campbell: "In medieval times, as you approached the city, your eye was taken by the Cathedral. Today, it's the towers of commerce. It's business, business, business." We had become what Campbell called a "bottom-line society." But our society came to measure the wrong bottom line: *form over substance, prestige over virtue, money over achievement, charisma over character, the ephemeral over the enduring, even mammon over God.*

Profession versus Business

Among the most obvious, and troubling, manifestations of the change from the stern traditional values of yore to the flexible values of our modern age, today's "bottom-line" society is reflected in the gradual mutation of our professional associations into business enterprises. According to a 2005 article in *Daedalus* by Howard Gardner, professor at the Harvard Graduate School of Education, and Lee S. Shulman, president of the Carnegie Foundation,* it was a mere 40 years ago that *Daedalus* proudly declared: "Everywhere in American life, the professions are triumphant." Since then, however, the professions have gradually "been subjected to a whole new set of pressures, from the growing reach of new technologies to the growing importance of making money."

Let's consider for a moment what we mean when we talk about professions and professionals. Messrs. Gardner and Shulman defined a profession as having six commonplace characteristics:

1. A commitment to the interest of clients in particular, and the welfare of society in general.
2. A body of theory or special knowledge.
3. A specialized set of professional skills, practices, and performances unique to the profession.
4. The developed capacity to render judgments with integrity under conditions of ethical uncertainty.
5. An organized approach to learning from experience, both individually and collectively, and thus of growing new knowledge from the context of practice.
6. The development of a professional community responsible for the oversight and monitoring of quality in both practice and professional educators.

They then add these wonderful words: "The primary feature of any profession [is] to serve responsibly, selflessly, and wisely . . . and to establish [an] inherently ethical relationship between the professional and the general society."

---

*"The Professions in America Today: Crucial but Fragile," *Daedalus*, Summer 2005, 13–18.

When we think of professionals, most of us would probably start with physicians, lawyers, teachers, engineers, architects, accountants, and clergy. I think we could also find agreement that both journalists and trustees of other people's money are—at least in the ideal— professionals as well. And yet, profession by profession, the old values are clearly being undermined. The driving force is our old friend (or enemy), the bottom-line society. Unchecked market forces not only constitute a strong challenge to our professions; in some cases, these forces have totally overwhelmed traditional standards of professional conduct, developed over centuries.

That legitimacy, in sad reality, has already been undermined in most of our professions.* Another article in the same issue of *Daedalus* asserts that the idea that "the market is self-regulating and morally self-sufficient" to assure the maintenance of professional standards has clearly proved inadequate. Indeed, that misguided idea lies at the heart of some of our major societal failures of recent years, examples that belie the idea that professionals must accomplish their good works with a commitment to use their mastery to fulfill a "mission that inspires passion, a mission that gives beyond the self." Of course we're all aware, as yet another *Daedalus* article expresses it, "that pursuing a noble mission is often painful . . . and that not letting the mission get out of hand is possible only for those who truly believe in the mission and have enough self-perspective to remain wary of dangers such as arrogance, megalomania, misguided beliefs, and distorted judgments."

These dangers have already come home to roost in some established professions, with incalculable harm to our society. Recent examples of the harsh consequences of this change are easy to come by. In public accounting, our once "Big Eight" (now "Final Four") firms gradually came to provide hugely profitable consulting services to their audit clients, making them business partners of management rather than independent and professional evaluators of generally accepted (if loose) accounting principles. The failure of Arthur Andersen, and the bankruptcy of its client Enron, was but one example of the consequences of this conflict-riddled relationship.

---

*The ideas in this paragraph have been inspired by other articles in the same issue of *Daedalus*, the journal of the American Academy of Arts & Sciences.

Think, too, about the increasing dominance of "state" (publishing) over "church" (editorial) in journalism, and the scandals that reached the most respected echelons of the press—the *New York Times*, the *Los Angeles Times*, the *Washington Post*. A similar transition has taken place in the medical profession, where the human concerns of the caregiver and the human needs of the patient have been overwhelmed by the financial interests of commerce, our giant medical care complex of hospitals, insurance companies, drug manufacturers and marketers, and health maintenance organizations (HMOs).

In all, professional relationships with clients have been increasingly recast as business relationships with customers. In a world where every user of services is seen as a customer, every provider of services becomes a seller. Put another way, when the provider becomes a hammer, the customer is seen as a nail. Please don't think me naive. I'm fully aware that every profession has elements of a business. Indeed, if revenues fail to exceed expenses, no organization—even the most noble of faith-based institutions—will long exist. But as so many of our nation's proudest professions—including accounting, journalism, medicine, law, architecture, and trusteeship—gradually shift their traditional balance away from that of trusted profession serving the interests of the community and toward that of commercial enterprises seeking competitive advantage, the human beings who rely on those services are the losers.

A few years ago, the author Roger Lowenstein made a similar observation, bemoaning the loss of the "Calvinist rectitude" that had its roots in "the very Old World notions of integrity, ethics, and unyielding loyalty to the customer."* "America's professions," he wrote, "have become crassly commercial . . . with accounting firms sponsoring golf tournaments" (and, he might have added, mutual fund managers not only doing the same thing but buying naming rights to stadiums as well). "The battle for independence," he concluded, "is never won." Put another way, we've moved from a concept that *there were certain things that one simply didn't do* (moral absolutism, I suppose) to the idea that *since everyone else is doing it, I can do it, too* (surely a form of moral relativism).

---

*Roger Lowenstein, "The Purist," *New York Times Magazine*, December 28, 2003, 44.

Business Values and Investment
Values Gone Awry

Now let's turn to the current state of our commercial enterprises—in particular, our giant publicly held corporations—and our investment institutions—now largely owned by giant publicly held financial conglomerates. Of course both represent a peculiar mix of business and profession, but they have moved a long way from the traditional values of capitalism. The origins of modern capitalism, beginning with the Industrial Revolution in Great Britain back in the late 18th century, had to do, yes, with entrepreneurship and risk-taking, with raising capital, with vigorous competition, with free markets, and with the returns on capital going to those who put up the capital. Central to these values of early capitalism was the fundamental principle of trusting and being trusted.

That is not to say that the long history of capitalism has not been punctuated by serious failings. Some were moral failings, such as the disgraceful treatment of laborers, often mere children, in the factories of an earlier era. Other failings included breaking the rules of fair and open competition, exemplified by the oil trusts and robber barons of yore. By the latter part of the 20th century, yet another failure fell upon us: the erosion of the very structure of capitalism. Not only had "trusting and being trusted" come to play a diminishing role, but the owners of our businesses were relegated to a secondary role in the functioning of the system.*

As I see it, there were two major forces behind this baneful change: First, the "ownership society"—in which the shares of our corporations were held almost entirely by direct stockholders—gradually lost its heft and its effectiveness. Since 1950, direct ownership of U.S. stocks by individual investors has plummeted from 92 percent to 30 percent, while indirect ownership by institutional investors has soared from 8 percent to 70 percent. Our old ownership society is now gone, and it is not going to return. In its place we have a new "agency

---

*Thanks to the comments of a discerning member of my Princeton audience, I added several of these criticisms to my text after delivering the speech.

society" in which our financial intermediaries now hold effective control of American business.

But these new *agents* haven't behaved as agents should. Our corporations, pension managers, and mutual fund managers have too often put their own financial interests ahead of the interests of the *principals* whom they are duty-bound to represent, those 100 million families who are the owners of our mutual funds and the beneficiaries of our pension plans. As Adam Smith wisely put it 200-plus years ago, "[M]anagers of other people's money [rarely] watch over it with the same anxious vigilance with which . . . they watch over their own . . . they very easily give themselves a dispensation. Negligence and profusion must always prevail." And so negligence and profusion among our corporate directors and money managers have prevailed in present-day America.

The second reason for the debasement of the values of our capitalistic system is that our new investor/agents not only seemed to ignore the interests of their *principals*, but also seemed to forget their own investment *principles*. In the latter part of the twentieth century, the predominant focus of institutional investment strategy turned from the wisdom of long-term investing to the folly of short-term speculation. During the recent era, we entered the age of expectations investing, where projected growth in corporate earnings—especially earnings guidance and its subsequent achievement, by fair means or foul—became the watchword of investors. Never mind that the reported earnings were too often a product of financial engineering that served the short-term interest of corporate managers and Wall Street security analysts alike.

But when long-term *owners* of stocks become short-term *renters* of stocks, and when the momentary precision of the price of the stock takes precedence over the eternal vagueness of the intrinsic value of the corporation itself, concern about corporate governance is the first casualty. The single most important job of the corporate director is to assure that management is creating value for shareholders; yet our new investors seemed not to care when that goal became secondary. While our institutional agents now hold absolute voting control of corporate America, all we hear from these money managers is the sound of silence. Not only because they are more likely to be short-term speculators than long-term investors, but also because they are managing the pension and thrift plans of the corporations whose stocks they hold, and thus face a serious conflict of interest when controversial proxy issues are concerned. This conflict is pervasive, for it is said that money managers have only two types of client they don't want to offend: *actual*, and *potential*.

And so in corporate America we have witnessed staggering increases in executive compensation not only unjustified by corporate performance but also grotesquely disproportionate to the pathetically small increase in real (inflation-adjusted) compensation of the average worker; financial engineering that dishonors the idea of financial statement integrity; and the failure of the traditional gatekeepers we rely on to oversee corporate management—our regulators, our legislators, our auditors, our attorneys, our directors.

"The Happy Conspiracy"

Way back in 1999, I described the shared focus on the price of a corporation's stock over all else as "the happy conspiracy" between our business sector and our investment sector, mutually reinforcing one another, in which traditional values and longstanding virtues were undermined. The web is wide, and includes corporate managers, CEOs and CFOs, directors, auditors, lawyers, Wall Street investment bankers, sell-side analysts, buy-side portfolio managers, and indeed institutional and individual investors as well. (Only short-sellers are on the outside looking in, and they are a small minority.) Their shared goal: to increase the price of a firm's stock, the better to please "the Street," to raise the value of its currency for acquisitions, to enhance the profits executives realize when they exercise their stock options, to entice employees to own stock in its thrift plan, and to make the shareholders happy. How to accomplish the objective? Aim for high long-term earnings growth, offer regular guidance to the financial community as to your short-term progress, and *never* fall short of the expectations you've established, whether by fair means or foul.

What's wrong with that? What's wrong, as I said in my 1999 remarks, is that when we "take for granted that fluctuating earnings are steady and ever growing . . . somewhere down the road there lies a day of reckoning that will not be pleasant." I was warning, of course, about the aftermath of the classic "new economy" bubble that had developed, where stock prices were wildly inflated by unrealistic expectations and irrational exuberance. Finally, the eternal truth reemerges: *The value of a corporation's stock is the discounted value of its future cash flow.* All over again, we learn that the purpose of the stock market is simply to provide liquidity for stocks in return for the promise of future cash flows, enabling investors to realize the present value of a future stream of income at any time.

Corporations, we again came to realize, must earn *real* money. Yet, going back to 1981, consensus estimates for future five-year annual earnings growth projected by corporate managers have averaged 11.6 percent, nearly *twice* the 6.3 percent *actual* annual growth actually achieved over the two decades. As a result of the happy conspiracy between business executives and financial institutions—relying on market expectations rather than business realities—we witnessed a bubble in stock market prices that inevitably burst, as all bubbles do, sooner or later. Then, the idea of *value* slowly returns to the stock market.

It is truly astonishing how pervasive have been the failures in our capitalistic system. While it's often alleged that these problems have been limited to just "a few bad apples," the evidence suggests that the barrel that holds all those apples, good and bad alike, has developed some serious problems. For example:

- Yes, there have been "only" a relatively few Enrons, WorldComs, Adelphias, and Tycos. But during the past five years, there have been 5,989 restatements of earnings by publicly held corporations, with stock market capitalizations aggregating more than $4 trillion, often reflecting overly aggressive accounting procedures.
- Yes, the investment banking scandals involved "only" 12 firms, but among them were 8 of the 9 largest firms in the field. As a result of the investigations by New York Attorney General Eliot Spitzer, they ultimately agreed to pay some $1.3 billion in penalties
- Yes, similarly, there were "only" a handful of insurance companies involved in the bid-rigging scandals, also uncovered by Mr. Spitzer. But, again, they included the largest companies in the field:

American International Group, Marsh & McClennan, ACE, Aon, and Zurich, all of which agreed to settle the litigation and paid billions of dollars in penalties.

• And yes, while a few of the largest mutual fund managers were not implicated in the disgraceful market-timing scandals unearthed by Mr. Spitzer and his staff, many of the 23 firms that *were* involved were giants, holding more than $1.5 trillion of investor assets, fully one-quarter of the fund industry's long-term asset base.

The Mutual Fund Industry Loses Its Way

With this background, I now turn to the very mutual fund industry where I've spent my entire career. So it is especially painful for me to acknowledge that the mutual fund industry is in many respects the poster child for the deterioration in business values and investment values that I've just described. I had been involved in this industry even before I began my career in 1951, and in fact spent well over a year researching the fund industry for my senior thesis in Economics, inspired by an article that I happened upon in *Fortune* magazine in December 1949. The thesis was entitled, "The Economic Role of the Investment Company."

When I wrote my thesis, assets of mutual funds totaled about $2 billion; today, assets *exceed $10 trillion*, a 17 percent annual rate of compound growth that was exceeded by few, if any, other enterprises. (Assets of life insurance companies, by way of contrast, grew from $53 billion to $4.7 trillion—from *25 times* fund assets in 1951 to less than one-half today.) The mutual fund industry has become America's largest financial institution.

Yet the record is clear that we have lost our way. Once a profession with elements of a business, we have become a business with elements of a profession—and too few elements at that. Once focused on management and investing, we are now focused on marketing and asset gathering. Once focused on stewardship, we are now focused on salesmanship. We have become an exemplar—alas, even a leader—in the new "bottom line" society that I earlier described. Lest you think that indictment is too strong, let me drive this point home with seven hard examples:

1. In 1951, mutual fund management companies were relatively small organizations, *privately held* by their principals, managed by investment professionals who were prudently investing to earn a sound return on the capital invested by their fund shareholders. Today, mutual fund management companies are behemoths, largely owned by giant *publicly held* financial conglomerates, run by businessmen whose highest priority is earning the maximum possible return on the capital invested by their firms in the management companies that they acquired.

2. In 1951, the vast majority of equity mutual funds were conservative, broadly diversified among blue-chip stocks, and offered returns that generally paralleled those of the stock market itself, making fund selection by investors fairly straightforward. Today, mutual funds come in a bewildering variety that would shame the mere 28 flavors of ice cream once offered by Howard Johnson's restaurants. The age-old middle-of-the-road equity funds now account for only about one-tenth of today's 4,300 such funds, including not only the standard nine-box Morningstar variety (large-, medium-, and small-cap; value and growth styles, and a blend of the two), but also a plethora of specialty funds (technology, Internet stocks, energy, gold, etc.) and foreign funds (Japan, Korea, Turkey, emerging markets, etc.), placing a staggering premium on selecting the "right" fund.

3. Conforming to the temper of the times, fund managers led the way in changing their focus, yes, again, from the wisdom of long-term investing to the folly of short-term speculation. In 1951 (and for nearly two decades thereafter), portfolio turnover averaged about 16 percent per year; during the past five years, portfolio turnover of the typical fund has averaged about 100 percent per year—*six times* as high. Yes, even my one-time "own-a-stock" industry has become a "rent-a-stock" industry.

4. Managed largely by prudent investment committees making painfully deliberate investment decisions in 1951, investment management in the fund industry today is handled largely by individual

portfolio managers with the ability to act immediately, indeed precipitately, in responding to fluctuations in the prices and valuations of specific stocks. In part for marketing reasons, we have developed a "star system" in which particular managers are portrayed, at least by implication, as having a durable talent for providing superior returns. Yet the fact is that nearly all of these one-time stars eventually prove to be insignificantly different from average. Indeed, they often turn out to be comets, losers who light up the sky for a moment and then flare out. There is no evidence that this sea change in investment approach has been advantageous for mutual fund shareholders. To the contrary.

5. In 1951, fund advertisements were limited to dull "tombstone ads" and funds were extremely limited in promoting their performance. For a time, they could not even present their total annual returns. Today, funds that have enjoyed strong returns (usually funds following extreme and/or risky strategies) freely hawk their own wares, bragging about their performance (when it's good!) in newspapers, magazines, and on television. (Alas, past performance is not only not predictive of the future, but, at least in speculative markets, predictive of quite the opposite.) Ultimately, of course, it is the fund shareholders who pay for all of this promotion.

6. As a result of all of this proliferation and promotion of funds, fund investors, eager to catch the next favorable market trend, move their money around at a frantic rate. Believe it or not, the average holding period of a mutual fund owner in 1951 was some 16 years. Today, it has shrunk but 4 years, admittedly, up from only 2 years in 2000, the peak of the illicit market-timing scandals. Then, too many fund managers—including, as I noted earlier, some of the industry's largest firms—conspired with favored hedge fund clients to allow rapid short-term trading in fund shares that diluted the returns of their long-term shareholders—a classic example of the change from the days "when there were some things one just didn't do," to "everyone else is doing it, so I can do it, too." And I've seen both, first-hand.

7. Importantly, fund costs have increased by staggering magnitudes since I joined the field all those years ago. In 1951, with fund assets at $2.5 billion, the average equity fund carried an expense ratio

(expenses relative to assets) of 0.77 percent. Last year, with equity fund assets at *$6.3 trillion*, the average fund carried an expense ratio of nearly double that amount: 1.43 percent. Result, expressed in dollars: Fund expenses rose from $15 million to *$51 billion—260 times* as large.* Not only have basic fee structures risen, but the staggering economies of scale in managing other people's money have been arrogated by fund managers to their own benefit. Exceptions to this pattern are rare: Among seven of the eight largest funds of 1951, the average expense ratio has actually increased from 0.60 percent to 1.10 percent. Only one fund actually reduced its costs to investors, from 0.60 percent to 0.32 percent. (That fund would be Vanguard's Wellington Fund.)

So, yes, it's fair to say that the idealistic principles I expressed in my ancient thesis—that funds "should be operated in the most honest, efficient, and economical way possible . . . that the industry should focus on reducing sales charges and expense ratios," and that "the principal role of the mutual fund should be to serve its shareholders"—not only have *not* been realized, but have been violated. Accordingly, the earlier business values and investment values of our industry became vanishing treasures.

Grounds for Hope

Had I not found agreement with this harsh indictment of the present-day capitalism from some of the most respected names in investing, I might be a little less certain of my ground. But leaders of great repute in the business community and the investment community have stood up and spoken out, making a positive difference. Consider, for example, the eminent financier, economist, and historian, Henry Kaufman. In his remarkable 2001 book, *On Money and Markets*, here's what he said:

> Unfettered financial entrepreneurship can become excessive—and damaging as well—leading to serious abuses and the trampling of the basic laws and morals of the financial system.

---

*Asset-weighted expense ratios of equity funds rose from 0.60 percent to 0.80 percent.

Such abuses weaken a nation's financial structure and undermine public confidence in the financial community. . . . Only by improving the balance between entrepreneurial innovation and more traditional values—prudence, stability, safety, soundness—can we improve the ratio of benefits to costs in our economic system. . . . When financial buccaneers and negligent executives step over the line, the damage is inflicted on all market participants . . . and the notion of financial trusteeship too frequently lost in the shuffle.*

Dr. Kaufman is not alone. Felix Rohatyn, the widely respected former managing director of Lazard Freres, is another of the wise men of Wall Street who have spoken out. Here's what he wrote in the *Wall Street Journal* a few years ago:

I am an American and a capitalist and believe that market capitalism is the best economic system ever invented. But it must be fair, it must be regulated, and it must be ethical. The last few years have shown that excesses can come about when finance capitalism and modern technology are abused in the service of naked greed. Only capitalists can kill capitalism, but our system cannot stand much more abuse of the type we have witnessed recently, nor can it stand much more of the financial and social polarization we are seeing today.†

The fact is that, in some important respects, the Invisible Hand of capitalism has failed us. Here are the familiar sentences that Adam Smith wrote in *The Wealth of Nations*.

It is not from the benevolence of the butcher, the baker, or the brewer that we expect our dinner, but from their regard to their own self-interest. By directing [our own] industry in such a manner as its produce may be of the greatest value, [we]

---

*Henry Kaufman, *On Money and Markets* (New York: McGraw-Hill, 2001).
†Felix Rohatyn, "Free, Wealthy and Fair," *Wall Street Journal*, November 11, 2003.

intend only our own gain, and [we are] led by *an invisible hand* to promote an end which was no part of [our] intention.

Writing in *Daedalus* in the summer of 2004, Nobel Laureate (in Economics) Joseph E. Stiglitz puts the Invisible Hand into perspective. Under the assumption of "perfect competition, perfect markets, and perfect information . . . selfishness is elevated to a moral virtue." But those assumptions are false. As Stiglitz's fellow Nobel Laureate Paul Samuelson observed in the first edition of his classic *Economics: An Introductory Analysis*—a textbook that I read at Princeton in 1948–1949—the problem with "perfect competition is what George Bernard Shaw once said of Christianity: 'the only trouble with it is that it's never been tried.'"* Nonetheless, Stiglitz continues, "societies in which there are high levels of trust, loyalty, and honesty actually perform better than those in which these virtues—*virtues*—are absent. Economists are just now beginning to discover how non-economic values—*values*—actually enhance economic performance."

So what's to be done? While the quest to restore these values and these virtues is hardly for the faint of heart, it's easy to conceptualize the path we need to follow. If each individual investor out there—not only those who hold their stocks directly, but those who hold their stocks through mutual funds—would only look after his or her own economic self-interest, then great progress would be made in restoring the vanishing treasures of capitalism. Here, I think, Adam Smith's Invisible Hand would be helpful.

For only if intelligent investors move away from the costly folly of short-term speculation to the priceless (and price-*less*!) wisdom of long-term investing—abandoning both the emotions that betray sound investment strategy and the expenses that turn beating the market into a loser's game—will they achieve their financial goals. When they do—and they will—our financial intermediaries will be forced to respond with a focus on long-term investing in *businesses*, not short-term speculation in *stocks*. (My latest book, published this month,

---

*Paul A. Samuelson, *Economics: An Introductory Analysis* (New York: McGraw-Hill, 1948).

drives this message home: *The Little Book of Common Sense Investing— The Only Way to Guarantee Your Fair Share of Stock Market Returns*.)

"The Impartial Spectator"

But we need more. Since our agency society has so diffused the beneficial ownership of stocks among 100 million or so mutual fund shareholders and pension beneficiaries, we also need to create, out of our disappearing ownership society and our failed agency society, a new "fiduciary society." Here, our agent/owners would be required by federal law to place the interest of their principals first—a consistently enforced public policy that places a clear requirement of fiduciary duty on our financial institutions to serve exclusively the interests of their beneficiaries. That duty would expressly require their effective and responsible participation in the governance of our publicly owned corporations, and demand the return of our institutional agents to the traditional values of professional stewardship that are long overdue.

We also need to raise our society's expectations of the proper conduct of the leaders of our businesses and financial institutions. So, in addition to Adam Smith's almost universally *known* Invisible Hand, we need to call on his almost universally *unknown* Impartial Spectator. This impartial spectator first appears in Smith's earlier *Theory of Moral Sentiments*—the force that arouses in us values that are so often generous and noble. It is the inner man shaped by the society in which he exists, even the soul, who gives us our highest calling. In Smith's words, "It is reason, principle, conscience, the inhabitant of the breast, the man within, the great judge and arbiter of our conduct."

This Impartial Spectator, Smith tells us,

> calls to us, with a voice capable of astonishing the most presumptuous of our passions, that we are but one of the multitude, in no respect better than any other in it; and that when we prefer ourselves so shamefully and so blindly to others, we become the proper objects of resentment, abhorrence, and execration. It is from him only that we learn the real littleness of ourselves. It is this impartial spectator . . . who shows us the propriety of generosity and the deformity of injustice; the

propriety of resigning the greatest interests of our own, for the yet greater interests of others . . . in order to obtain the greatest benefit to ourselves. It is not the love of our neighbour, it is not the love of mankind, which upon many occasions prompts us to the practice of those divine virtues. It is a stronger love, a more powerful affection, the love of what is honourable and noble, the grandeur, and dignity, and superiority of our own characters.

With these powerful words, Adam Smith—yes, Adam Smith—touches on nearly all of those traditional ethical principles of which I spoke at the outset. While our corporate values and investment values may be "vanishing treasures," those virtues have not entirely vanished. Indeed, there are scores of examples—although never nearly enough—of corporations and financial institutions that have held to their traditional bearings despite the powerful forces that are driving our society away from them.

As I express these thoughts this evening, I note a wonderful irony: The very same 1949 issue of *Fortune* that inspired my Princeton thesis included a feature essay entitled "The Moral History of U.S. Business." Alas, I have no recollection of reading it at that time. But I read it a few years ago, a full half-century later. As I reflect on the vanishing treasures of capitalism—the debasement of the values of businesses and investors—they seem to be related to the kind of moral responsibility of business that was expressed in that ancient *Fortune* essay. It began by noting that the profit motive is hardly the only motive that lies behind the labors of the American businessman. Other motives include "the love of power or prestige, altruism, pugnacity, patriotism, the hope of being remembered through a product or institution." Yes, it is all of the above.

As I have said in other forums, I also agree with *Fortune* on the appropriateness of the traditional tendency of American society to ask: "What are the moral credentials for the social power [the businessman] wields?" One answer came in the form of some comments written in 1844, words cited in the *Fortune* essay. William Parsons, "a merchant of probity," described the good merchant as "an enterprising man willing to run some risks, yet not willing to risk in hazardous enterprises the property of others entrusted to his keeping, careful to indulge no extravagance and to be simple in his manner and unostentatious in his habits, not merely a merchant, but a man, with a *mind* to improve, a *heart* to cultivate, and a *character* to form."

When I read those inspiring demands, uttered 163 years ago, they seemed directed right at me, and at the theme of my remarks this evening. As for the mind, I still strive every day—I really do!—to improve my own mind, reflecting on current events, reading history, and challenging even my own deep-seated beliefs. As for the heart, no one—no one!—could possibly revel in the opportunity to cultivate it more than I. Just three weeks ago, after all, I marked the 11th(!) anniversary of the amazing grace represented by the heart transplant that I received in 1996. And as for character, whatever moral standards I may have developed, I have tried to invest my own soul and spirit in my family, in my life's work, and in the character of the little firm I founded all those years ago, a firm focused on stewardship—a business, yes, but a business with strong elements of a profession.

While (as we say at Vanguard) "even one person can make a difference," the task of restoring the vanishing values of business and investing is far larger than one person can handle. We need wisdom and introspection from our business and investment leaders to learn from the lessons of history and to realize that, however profitable the operation of today's businesses and investment institutions may be to their managers, in the long run today's practices will be self-defeating. We need investors everywhere to join together to demand the development of that fiduciary society I have described, and we—all of us—need to awaken our fellow citizens to respect that Impartial Spectator who demands virtuous conduct and a return to traditional values by the leaders of our corporate businesses and our investment institutions. Without that, those treasures will indeed vanish.

Chapter 9

A Crisis of
Ethic Proportions*

I recently received a letter from a Vanguard shareholder who described the present global financial crisis as "a crisis of ethic proportions." Substituting *ethic* for *epic* is not only a fine turn of phrase; it accurately places a heavy responsibility for the meltdown on a broad deterioration in traditional ethical standards.

The fields of commerce, business, and finance have hardly been exempt from this trend. Relying on Adam Smith's "invisible hand," through which our own self-interest advances the interests of our communities, our society had come to rely on the marketplace and open competition to create prosperity and well-being.

But that self-interest got out of hand. It developed into a "bottom-line" society in which success is largely measured in monetary terms. Dollars became the coin of the new realm. Unchecked market forces totally overwhelmed traditional standards of professional conduct, developed over centuries.

The result has been a change in our society, from one in which "there are some things that one simply does not do," to one in which "if

---

*Based on an op-ed essay published in the *Wall Street Journal*, April 21, 2009.

everyone else is doing it, I can do it too"—a shift from moral absolutism to moral relativism. Business ethics has been a major casualty of that shift in our traditional societal values, and the idea of professional standards has been lost in the shuffle.

We seemed to forget that the driving force of any profession includes not only the special knowledge, skills, and standards that it demands, but the duty to serve responsibly, selflessly, and wisely, and to establish an inherently ethical relationship between professionals and the society they serve. The old notion of trusting and being trusted—which once was not only the accepted standard of business conduct but the key to success in the marketplace—came to be seen as a quaint anachronism, a relic of an era long gone.

The proximate causes of the instant crisis are usually laid to easy credit; the cavalier attitude toward risk of our bankers and investment bankers; "securitization," in which the traditional link between borrower and lender was severed; the extraordinary leverage built into the financial system by derivative securities of mindboggling complexity; and the failure of our regulators to do their job.

But the larger cause was our failure to recognize the sea-change in the nature of capitalism that was occurring right before our eyes. That change, simply put, was the growth of giant business corporations and giant financial institutions controlled not by their owners in the "ownership society" of yore, but by agents of the ultimate owners in today's "agency society."

The managers of our public corporations came to place their own interests ahead of the interests of their owners, and our money manager agents—who in the United States now hold some 70 percent of all shares of public companies—blithely accepted the change. Indeed, they fostered it by superficial security analysis and research, by ignoring corporate governance issues, and by trading stocks at an unprecedented rate, an orgy of speculation without historical precedent.

Adam Smith presciently described the characteristics of today's corporate and institutional managers (many of which are themselves controlled by giant financial conglomerates) with these words:

> Managers of other people's money [rarely] watch over it with
> the same anxious vigilance with which . . . they watch over

their own . . . they very easily give themselves a dispensation. Negligence and profusion must always prevail.

The malfeasance and misjudgments by our corporate, financial, and government leaders, declining ethical standards, and the failure of our new agency society reflect a failure of capitalism. Free-market champion (and former Federal Reserve chairman) Alan Greenspan shares my view. That failure, he said in testimony to Congress last October, "was a flaw in the model that I perceived as the critical functioning structure that defines how the world works." As one journalist observed, "That's a hell of a big thing to find a flaw in."

So what's to be done? We must set about establishing a "fiduciary society," one in which our manager/agents who are entrusted with the responsibility for other people's money are required—by federal statute—to place front and center the interests of the owner/principals whom they are duty-bound to serve, by focusing on long-term investment rather than short-term speculation, by providing appropriate due diligence in security selection, and by pressing corporations to govern in the interest of their owners, all reflecting their ethical responsibility to society at large. It will be no easy task.

Chapter 10

Black Monday and
Black Swans*

T he 20th anniversary of what came to be known as "Black Monday"—October 19, 1987—provides a memorable platform for considering, yet again, the role of risk in our financial markets. On that single day, the Dow Jones Industrial Average dropped from 2246 to 1738, an astonishing decline of 508 points or almost 25 percent. The drop was nearly twice the largest previous daily decline of 13 percent, which took place on October 24, 1929 (which became known as "Black Thursday"), a distant early warning that the Great Depression lay ahead.[†]

From its earlier high until the stock market at last closed on that fateful Black Monday of 1987, some one trillion dollars had been erased from the total value of U.S. stocks. The stunning decline seemed to shock nearly all market participants. But there were some veterans whom

---

*Based on a lecture for the Risk Management Association, October 11, 2007, and subsequently published as an essay in the *Financial Analysts Journal* (March/April 2008). The essay received the Graham & Dodd Perspective Article Award for 2008.
[†]From its September 1929 high of 381 to its July 1932 low of 41, the Dow would drop by an astonishing 90 percent.

it didn't surprise. Ace Greenberg, former chairman of Bear Stearns, was quoted in the newspapers as saying, "So markets fluctuate. What else is new?" And only a year before Black Monday, I observed to the Vanguard crew that even a 100-point decline in the Dow—something that had never before occurred—was possible. Why? Because, as I observed, "in the stock market, *anything can happen.*"

That truism remains, but I'd argue the point even more strongly today. Changes in the nature and structure of our financial markets—and a radical shift in its participants—are making shocking and unexpected market aberrations ever more probable. The amazing market swings we've witnessed in the past few months tend to confirm that likelihood. While the daily changes in the level of stock prices typically exceed 2 percent only three or four times per *year,* in just one recent *month* we've seen eight such moves. Ironically, four were up, and four were down. Based on past experience, the probability of that scenario was *zero.*

So the first—and most basic—point I wish to make today is that the application of the laws of probability to our financial markets is badly misguided. Truth told, the fact that an event has never before happened in the markets is no reason whatsoever to be confident that it can't happen in the future. Metaphorically speaking, *the fact that the only swans we humans have ever observed are white doesn't mean that no black swans exist.*

Black Monday, then, was a Black Swan. Unlike its 1929 antecedent, however, Black Monday was not a warning of dire days ahead. If anything, it was, totally counterintuitively, a harbinger of the greatest bull market in recorded history. *The Black Swan,* as most of you are likely aware, is also the title of a new book by Nassim Nicholas Taleb.* Here is his definition of the characteristics of a Black Swan, in our markets, and, for that matter, in our lives:

1. An outlier beyond the realm of our regular expectations. *(Rarity)*
2. An event that carries an extreme impact. *(Extremeness)*
3. A happening that, *after the fact,* our human nature enables us to accept by concocting explanations that make it seem predictable. *(Retrospective Predictability)*

---

*Nassim Nicholas Taleb, *The Black Swan* (New York: Random House, 2007).

So there it is: rarity; extremeness; and retrospective predictability. Together they define *the occurrence of an event that is regarded as impossible, or at least highly improbable.* What's more, as Taleb notes, a Black Swan is also the reverse of this definition: *the nonoccurrence of an event that is regarded as highly probable.* Life is full of them!

Today, I observe little concern about the ever-present possibility that what will occur in our financial markets in the coming months (or years) might in fact prove to be a nonoccurrence of what we expect. Indeed, despite the recent wild disturbances in both the stock market and the bond market, most market participants seem confident that future returns will resemble those of the past. Only time will tell whether yet another Black Swan, lurking out there beyond the horizon, will become part of stock market history.

Whatever the case, the fact that Black Swans can and do happen in our financial system holds important lessons for how we think about risk. While we look for corroboration of what we believe (*confirmation bias*), what we really ought to be looking for is the opposite—that observation that would prove us wrong. Sad to relate, we know what is wrong with a lot more confidence than what we know is right. Yet we continue to look ahead with apparent confidence that the past is prologue, based on our assumptions that the probabilities established by history will endure.

The idea of seeking out evidence that contradicts our belief goes far beyond the financial markets. It goes to the very nature of knowledge itself. For the eminent British philosopher Sir Karl Popper—well-known for his use of the Black Swan metaphor—the key question was "What if science didn't proceed from observation to theory? What if it was the other way around?" Writing in the *New Yorker,** journalist Adam Gopnik described Popper's reasoning: "No number of white swans could tell you that all swans were white, but a single black swan could tell you that they weren't. . . . Science, Popper proposed, didn't proceed through observations confirmed by verification; it proceeded through wild, overarching conjectures which generalized 'beyond the data,' but were always controlled and sharpened by falsification (i.e., proof that the theory was *wrong*)."

---

*April 1, 2002.

"It was the conscious, purposeful search for falsification by refutation, by the single decisive experiment" (or swan), Popper believed, "that allowed science to proceed and objective knowledge to grow." Yet most of us—in our investment ideas and political ideas alike—do quite the reverse: We search for facts that confirm our beliefs (*reinforcement bias*), not for the facts that would negate them.

The Light Shined by Frank Knight

In the markets, however, few theories are advanced with the search for falsification as the object, and we continue to speak of forecasts and probabilities. But *probability* is a slippery concept when applied to our financial markets. We use the term *risk* all too casually, and the term *uncertainty* all too rarely. This distinction was first made by the late University of Chicago economist Frank H. Knight, who spelled it out in his seminal work, *Risk, Uncertainty, and Profits,** in, well, no uncertain terms.

Here's what Knight wrote:

> . . . uncertainty must be taken in a sense radically distinct from the familiar notion of Risk, from which it has never been properly separated. The term "risk," as loosely used in everyday speech and in economic discussion, really covers two things which . . . are categorically different. The essential fact is that "risk" means in some cases *a quantity susceptible of measurement*, while at other times it is something distinctly not of this character. A *measurable* uncertainty, or "risk" proper, is so far different from an *immeasurable* one that it is not in effect an uncertainty at all.

Knight continues:

> The facts of life in this regard are in a superficial sense obtrusively obvious and are a matter of common observation. It is a world of change in which we live, and a world of uncertainty.

---

*Boston: Houghton Mifflin Company, 1921.

We live only by knowing something about the future; while the problems of life or of conduct at least, arise from the fact that we know so little . . . in business as in other spheres of activity. We act according to [our] opinion, of greater or less foundation and value, neither entire ignorance nor complete information, but partial knowledge. If we are to understand the workings of the economic system we must examine the meaning and significance of uncertainty; and to this end some inquiry into the nature and function of knowledge itself is necessary.

The [likelihood] of opinion or estimate to error must be radically distinguished from probability or chance, for there is no possibility of forming in any way groups of instances of sufficient homogeneity to make possible a quantitative determination of true probability [in which] any sort of statistical tabulation [provides] any value for guidance. *The conception of an objectively measurable probability or chance is simply inapplicable . . . there is much question as to how far the world is intelligible at all. . . . It is only in the very special and crucial cases that anything like a mathematical study can be made.* (Italics added.)

Mandelbrot on Risk, Ruin, and Reward

The abstract theories of Karl Popper and Frank Knight can be directly applied to the financial markets, which is exactly what Benoit Mandelbrot, the brilliant inventor of fractal geometry, has done with Richard Hudson in his book, *The (Mis)Behavior of Markets*, ominously subtitled "A Fractal View of Risk, Ruin, and Reward."*

Fractal geometry, simply put, is about patterns that repeat themselves continually, in nature and in geometry, scaling up or scaling down, sometimes defined by a determination rule, sometimes entirely by chance.

---

*Richard L. Hudson and Benoit B. Mandelbrot, *The (Mis)Behavior of Markets* (New York: Basic Books, 2004).

They often relate to power laws, where growth is not linear but logarithmic. The Fibonacci sequence, in which each successive number is the sum of the two previous numbers, $1 - 2 - 3 - 5 - 8 - 13 - 21 - 34 - 55 - 89 - 144$, and so on (well, you get the picture), is a soaring arc on a linear scale (Figure 10.1a), but a straight line on a logarithmic scale (Figure 10.1b). As it happens, each successive number is 1.6 times its predecessor, and after 144, 1.618, a ratio that our Greek ancestors called "the Golden Mean," appearing all through civilization, notably in nature, in architecture, and, more mundanely, in the size of book covers and playing cards.

FIGURE 10.1A   FIBONACCI SEQUENCE (LINEAR)

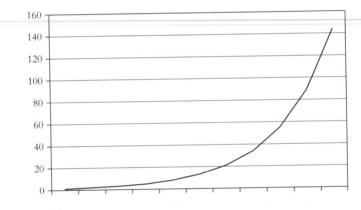

FIGURE 10.1B   FIBONACCI SEQUENCE (LOGARITHMIC)

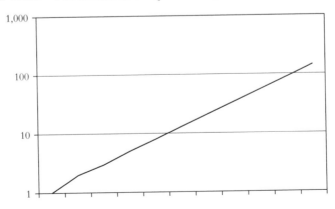

Mandelbrot applies this concept to the daily price movements of the Dow Jones Industrial Average. Nearly always (since 1915), the standard deviation (Sigma) of the daily change in the Dow has been about 0.89 percent (Figure 10.2), That is, two-thirds of the fluctuations were within 0.89 percentage points (plus or minus) of the average daily change of 0.74 percent. Nonetheless there are frequent occasions with standard deviations of 3 or 4, infrequent occasions when it exceeds 10, and just one 20-Sigma event. (The odds against such a happening are about 10 to the 50th power.) Black Monday, of course, was that 20-Sigma and Black Thursday was that 10-Sigma event. (The possible 100-point decline that I contemplated back in 1986 would have been a 6-Sigma event.)

While our markets are periodically defined by fractals and power laws (although we never know when), there are many areas in which they do not apply. The classic example is in the height of men, or the extremes of temperature, or the flipping of coins (Figure 10.3). These patterns lend themselves to Gaussian (standard-frequency) distribution curves, familiarly known as *bell curves*. Yes, when two dice are rolled 1,000 times, 7 will come up (roughly) 167 times; 6 or 8, 139 times each; 5 or 9, 111 times each; 4 or 10, 83 times; 3 or 11, 56 times; 2 or 12, just 28 times.

FIGURE 10.2   DAILY CHANGES IN THE DOW, NUMBER OF STANDARD DEVIATIONS

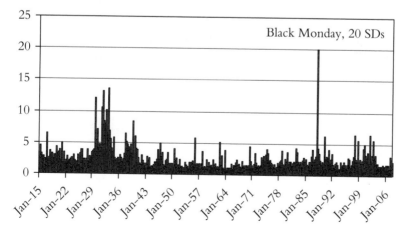

FIGURE 10.3   EXPECTED DISTRIBUTION OF 1,000 ROLLS OF TWO DICE

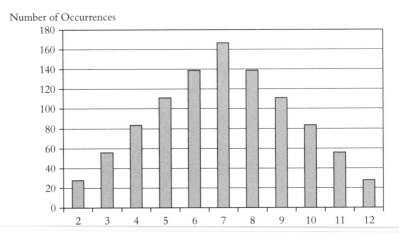

Number of Occurrences

But other areas surprise us. One classic fractal is the average wealth of our citizens. That figure follows a fairly neat distribution pattern, but only until we get to the very high figures. Bring a hedge fund manager with annual earnings of $200 million into a room with 100 persons earning an average of $50,000, and the average jumps to more than $2 million.

So as long as we look at past patterns of market repetition on a sort of Gaussian "bell curve," so long as we rely on Monte Carlo simulations in which past stock returns are thrown into a giant mixer that produces a million or more permutations and combinations, looking at probabilities in the stock market seems a fool's errand. Thus, we deceive ourselves when we believe that past stock market return patterns provide the bounds by which we can predict the future* (Figure 10.4). When we do so, we ignore the potential for future Black Swans.

The stock market has experienced relatively few of these extreme changes. And it is overwhelmed by the frequent—but

---

*The average annual return on stocks during this period was 10.4 percent. Curiously, in only two years of the 80 years examined did the returns realized fall between 9 percent and 11 percent. The "average" year, then, rarely occurs.

FIGURE 10.4   DISTRIBUTION OF THE S&P 500'S ANNUAL RETURNS, 1926–2006

Number of Occurrences

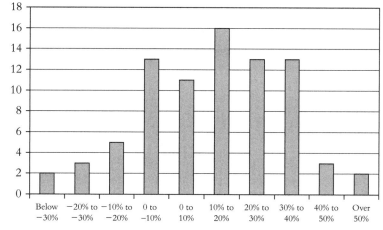

usually humdrum—fluctuations that take place each day within normal ranges. For example, the Standard & Poor's 500 Stock Index has risen from a level of 17 in 1950 to 1,540 at present. But deduct the returns achieved on the 40 days in which it had its highest percentage gains—only 40 out of 14,528 days!—and it would drop by some 70 percent, to 276. Or eliminate the 40 worst days; then, the S&P would be sitting at 11,235, more than *seven times* today's level. It is a good lesson, then, about "staying the course" rather than jumping in and jumping out.

Financial markets, then, are volatile and unpredictable. Importantly, the markets themselves are far more volatile than the underlying businesses that they represent, which collectively account for their aggregate market capitalization. Put another way, *investors* are more volatile than *investments*. Economic reality governs the returns earned by our *businesses*, and Black Swans are unlikely. But emotions and perceptions—the swings of hope, greed, and fear among the participants in our financial system—govern the returns earned in our *markets*. Emotional factors magnify or minimize this central core of economic reality, and Black Swans can appear at any time.

The Wisdom of John Maynard Keynes

More than 80 years ago, the great British economist John Maynard Keynes recognized this critical distinction between economics and emotions. Observing the predilection of investors to implicitly assume that the future will resemble the past, Keynes warned: "It is dangerous to apply to the future inductive arguments based on past experience unless we can distinguish the broad reasons for what it [the past] was."*

A decade later, in 1936, in his amazing *The General Theory of Employment, Interest, and Money*, Keynes focused on the two broad reasons that explain the returns on stocks. The first was what he called *enterprise*—"forecasting the prospective yield of an asset over its entire life."† The second was *speculation*—"forecasting the psychology of the market." Together, these two factors explain "The State of Long-Term Expectation" for an investment, the title of Chapter 12 of *The General Theory*.

From his vantage point in London, Keynes observed that "in one of the greatest investment markets in the world, namely, New York, the influence of speculation is enormous. . . . It is rare for an American to 'invest for income,' and he will not readily purchase an investment except in the hope of capital appreciation. This is only another way of saying that he is attaching his hopes to a favorable change in the conventional basis of valuation, i.e., that he is a speculator." Today, 70 years after Keynes wrote those words, the same situation prevails, only far more strongly.

Lord Keynes's confidence that speculation would dominate enterprise was based on the then-dominant ownership of stock by individuals, largely ignorant of business operations or valuations, leading to excessive, even absurd short-term market fluctuations based on events of an ephemeral and insignificant character. Short-term fluctuations in the earnings of existing investments, he argued (correctly), would lead to unreasoning waves of optimistic and pessimistic sentiment.

---

*John Maynard Keynes, *Review of Common Stocks as Long Term Investments* (Edgar Lawrence Smith, 1925).
†John Maynard Keynes, *The General Theory of Employment, Interest, and Money* (New York: Macmillan, 1936; Harcourt, Brace 1964).

While competition between expert professionals, possessing judgment and knowledge beyond that of the average private investor, Keynes added, should correct the vagaries caused by ignorant individuals, the energies and skill of the professional investor would come to be largely concerned, not with making superior long-term forecasts of the probable yield of an investment over its whole life, but with foreseeing changes in the conventional basis of valuation a short time ahead of the general public. He therefore described the market as "a battle of wits to anticipate the basis of conventional valuation a few months hence rather than the prospective yield of an investment over a long term of years."

In my 1951 Princeton senior thesis on the mutual fund industry, I cited Keynes's conclusions. And I had the temerity to disagree with the great man, arguing that he was wrong. Rather than professional investors succumbing to the speculative psychology of ignorant market participants, I argued, these pros would focus on enterprise. In what I predicted—accurately—would become a far larger mutual fund industry, our portfolio managers would "supply the market with a demand for securities that is *steady, sophisticated, enlightened, and analytic* [italics added], a demand that is based essentially on the [intrinsic] performance of the corporation rather than the public appraisal reflected in the price of its shares." Alas, the sophisticated and analytic focus on enterprise that I had predicted from the industry's expert professional investors has failed to materialize; rather, the emphasis on speculation by mutual funds has actually increased manyfold. Call the score, Keynes 1, Bogle 0.

Interestingly, Keynes was well aware of the fallibility of forecasting stock returns, noting that "it would be foolish in forming our expectations to attach great weight to matters which are very uncertain." He added (shades of Frank Knight!) that "by very uncertain I do not mean the same thing as 'improbable.'" While Keynes made no attempt to quantify the relationship between enterprise and speculation in shaping stock market returns, however, it occurred to me, decades later, to do exactly that.

Putting Numbers on Keynes's Distinction

By the late 1980s, based my own first-hand experience and my research on the financial markets, I concluded that the two essential

Speculative return is, well, speculative, and has alternated from positive to negative over the decade. But over the long run speculation hasn't produced any Black Swans, either. In fact, if p/e ratios are historically low (say, below 10 times), they have been likely to rise over the subsequent decade. And if they are historically high (say, above 20 times), they have been likely to decline (though in neither case do we know *when* the change is coming). Nonetheless, certainty about the future never exists, nor are probabilities always borne out. But applying reasonable expectations to investment return and speculative return and then combining them has been a sensible and effective approach to projecting the total return on stocks over the decades.

The point is this: Over the very long run, it is the *economics* of investing—enterprise—that has determined total return; the evanescent *emotions* of investing—speculation—so important over the short run, have ultimately proven to be virtually meaningless. In the past century, for example, the 9.6 percent average annual return on U.S. stocks has been composed of 9.5 percentage points of investment return (an average dividend yield of 4.5 percent plus average annual earnings growth of 5 percent), and only 0.1 percent of speculative return, borne of an inevitably period-dependent increase in the price-earnings ratio from 10 times to 18 times, amortized over the century. Despite the Black Swans of market history, ownership of American business has been a winner's game.

Hyman Minsky Adds the Crucial Ingredient

While my simple insight provides a solid framework for understanding stock market returns, however, I failed to consider the extent to which speculation in the financial economy (emotions) might influence changes in the business economy (enterprise). But when I learned of the work of the great American economist, Hyman Minsky (1919–1996), who dedicated his career largely to what he described as the "financial instability hypothesis," I recognized that yet another element of risk— here, clearly, meaning *uncertainty*—existed.*

---

*In the following four paragraphs, I quote investment adviser Frank K. Martin, CFA, writing in the 2006 annual report of his firm, Martin Capital Management (*Martin Capital Management Annual Report*, 2006).

"In 1974, Minsky observed a fundamental characteristic of our economy that linked finance and economics: 'The financial system swings between robustness and fragility, and these swings are an integral part of the process that generates business cycles.' Moreover, according to Minsky, the prevailing financial structure is a central determinant of the behavior of the capitalist economy. Likewise, the dynamism of profit-driven motives influence economic activity within the context of a given institutional structure in that the structure itself changes in response to profit seeking. Resonating with the ideas of economist Joseph A. Schumpeter, Minsky emphasized that:

> Financial markets will not only respond to profit-driven demands of business leaders and individual investors but also as a result of the profit-seeking entrepreneurialism of financial firms. Nowhere are evolution, change, and Schumpeterian entrepreneurship more evident than in banking and finance, and nowhere is the drive for profits more clearly the factor making for change.

"The financial system takes on special significance in Minsky's theory, not only because finance exerts a strong influence on business activity, but also because this system is particularly open—or, as some might claim, prone—to innovation, as is abundantly evident today. Continues Minsky: 'Since finance and industrial development are in a symbiotic relationship, financial evolution plays a crucial role in the dynamic patterns of the economy.'

"In addition to emphasizing the relations between finance and business, Minsky identified progression through at least five distinct stages of capitalism. The five stages can be labeled as follows: merchant capitalism (1607–1813), industrial capitalism (1813–1890), banker capitalism (1890–1933), managerial capitalism (1933–1982), and money-manager capitalism (1982–present). But the broad historical framework that Minsky developed in the last years of his life has gone almost unnoticed. According to Minsky, money-manager capitalism 'became a reality in the 1980s as institutional investors, by then the largest repositories of savings in the country, began to exert their influence on financial markets and business enterprises.'

"The *raison d'être* for money managers, and basis by which they are held accountable, is the maximization of the value of the investments made by their clients. Not surprisingly, therefore, business executives became increasingly attuned to short-term profits and the stock-market valuation of their firm. The growing role of institutional investors fostered continued financial-system evolution by providing a ready pool of buyers of securitized loans, structured finance products, and myriad other exotic innovations."

I've written a book about these issues,* and I express my conclusion bluntly. Using words remarkably close to those of Minsky, I describe how capitalism has changed for the worse. In a half-century we've moved from an *ownership* society, where individual shareholders owned 92 percent of all stocks and financial institutions owned only 8 percent, to an *agency* society, in which institutional shareholders now own some 70 percent of all stocks. But we haven't changed the rules. These mutual fund and pension fund managers have largely ignored the interests of their principals—fund shareholders and pension beneficiaries. To restore balance to the system, we need a new *fiduciary* society in which the interests of these 100 million principals—the last-line investors of America—come first.

The Rise of the Financial Economy

I've taken you on this long trip through risk and uncertainty, not only because I find these ideas both important and intellectually stimulating, but because they set the stage for my discussion of the concerns I hold today regarding our financial system and our society. I recognize that some of these ideas are complex, so let's summarize the ground we've covered so far:

1. Black Swans—extreme and unexpected outcomes—are part of investing, and can't be predicted in advance.

---

*John C. Bogle, *The Battle for the Soul of Capitalism* (New Haven: Yale University Press, 2005).

2. As Karl Popper recognized, not only our market, but science itself, depends not on observations confirmed by verification, but on wild conjectures sharpened by falsification (proof that the theory is wrong).

3. Frank Knight focused on a critical distinction between *risk*—which is subject to measurement—and *uncertainty*—which is not.

4. Stock market returns, in the short-term, are not normally distributed, but are explained by the fractal patterns discovered by Mandelbrot. We can't ignore the possibility—indeed, the virtual certainty—that such extreme patterns will persist, and we never know *when*.

5. Keynes's insight was to separate stock returns into two elements: *enterprise*, subject to a reasoned financial analysis, and *speculation*—the madness of crowds—which, he argued, would become increasingly dominant.

6. Bogle (if you will) applied numbers to Keynes's insight, showing that future *investment* returns were subject to reasonable expectations, and that even *speculative* returns tended, over time, to move toward zero.

7. Minsky added a sobering note: The financial economy, focused on speculation, was not separate and distinct from the productive economy, focused on enterprise. Rather, the former would come to overwhelm the latter.

Was Minsky right? Has a new element of uncertainty been introduced into our economy? I'm inclined to agree. Indeed, I express the secular changes in the economy in a way quite similar to Minsky. Over the past two centuries, our nation has moved from being an agricultural economy, to a manufacturing economy, to a service economy, and to what is now predominantly a financial economy, and a global one at that. But the costs that we incur in our financial economy, by definition, subtract from the value created by our productive businesses.

Think about it. When investors—individual and institutional alike—engage in far more trading—inevitably with one another—than is necessary for market efficiency and ample liquidity, they become, collectively, their own worst enemies. While the owners of business enjoy the dividend yields and earnings growth that our capitalistic system creates, those who play in the financial markets capture those investment gains only *after* the costs of financial intermediation are deducted.

Thus, while investing in American business is a *winner's* game, beating the stock market—for all of us as a group—is a *zero-sum* game before those costs are deducted. After intermediation costs are deducted, beating the market becomes, by definition, a *loser's game.*

The rise of the financial sector to preeminence is one of the seldom-told tales of the recent era. Twenty-five years ago, financials accounted for only about 5 percent of the earnings of the 500 giant corporations that compose the Standard & Poor's 500 Stock Index, rising to 10 percent 20 years ago, then to 20 percent in 1997, and to a near-peak level of 27 percent in 2007. If we add to this total the earnings of the financial affiliates of our giant manufacturers (think General Electric Capital, for example, or the auto-financing arms of General Motors and Ford), financial earnings now likely exceed one-third of the annual earnings of the S&P 500. In fact, the finance sector is now by far our nation's largest generator of corporate profits, larger even than the *combined* profits of our huge energy and health-care sectors, and almost three *times* as much as either the industrial sector or the information technology sector.

The Soaring Costs of Our Financial System

The growth of the financial sector has been spurred by the costs of our system of financial intermediation, which have soared to staggering proportions. Led by Wall Street bankers and brokers and mutual funds, followed by hedge funds and pension fund managers, adviser fees and all the other costs incurred by financial market participants have risen from an estimated $2.5 billion as recently as 1988 to something like $528 billion this year, or some *20 times* over. But don't forget that these costs recur year after year. If the present level holds for the next decade (I'm guessing that it will grow), total intermediation costs would come to a staggering $5 trillion. Then think about these cumulative costs relative to the $16 trillion value of the U.S. stock market and the $12 trillion value of our bond market. Those costs would represent an astonishing 18 percent of that value.

Does this explosion in intermediation costs create an opportunity for money managers? You'd better believe it does! Does it create a problem for investors? You'd better recognize that, too. For as long as our financial system delivers to our investors in the aggregate whatever returns our stock and bond markets are generous enough to deliver, but only *after* the costs of financial intermediation are deducted, these enormous costs seriously undermine the odds in favor of success for our citizens who are accumulating savings for retirement. Alas, as we all know, the investor feeds at the bottom of the costly food chain of investing.

This is not to say that our financial system creates only costs. It creates substantial value for our society. It facilitates the optimal allocation of capital among a variety of users; it enables buyers and sellers to meet efficiently; it provides remarkable liquidity; it enhances the ability of investors who wish to capitalize on the discounted value of future cash flows (stock sellers), and other investors who wish to acquire the right to those cash flows (stock buyers); it creates financial instruments (so-called "derivatives," albeit often of mindboggling complexity) that enable investors to divest themselves of a variety of risks by transferring those risks to others. No, it is not that the system fails to create benefits. The question is whether, on the whole, the costs of obtaining those benefits have reached a level that overwhelms them. But I believe the financial extraction of value represented by the costs assessed by money managers, brokers, marketers, and administrators has come to overwhelm the benefits provided by the financial system.

The Dominance of Finance over Business

I now turn to the rise to dominance of our financial economy over our production economy, just as Minsky predicted. I earlier noted that the earnings of the financial sector of the S&P 500 have risen to preeminence, and so has the capitalization of the stock market risen to exceed our Gross Domestic Product, the value of the goods and services that we as a nation produce each year (Figure 10.6). In 1975, the stock market had an aggregate market capitalization of $800 billion, about 50 percent of our $1.6 trillion GDP. But while GDP has risen eight times since then, stock valuations have risen nearly 20 times over. Today the $15.7 trillion aggregate value of stocks is actually equal to about 120 percent of our $13 trillion GDP.

FIGURE 10.6   MARKET CAP/GDP, 1929–2009 (UPDATED)

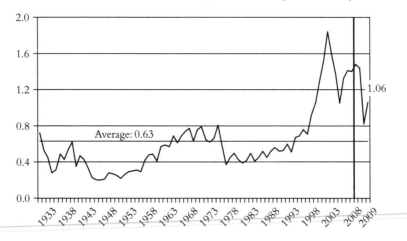

Even more striking is the truly staggering increase in financial trans-actions, a global phenomenon whose implications are far from clear. While the world's GDP is about $60 trillion, the aggregate nominal value of worldwide financial derivatives is said to be $600 trillion, fully *10 times* as large as all of the net goods and services produced by our entire world.

A simple comparison, based solely on U.S. financial centers, makes the point. In 1957, the market value of stocks in the S&P 500 index was $220 billion, and futures and options markets on the S&P index didn't even exist. By 1982, the value of the S&P 500 had soared to $1.2 trillion and the newly created S&P futures outstanding were valued at $206 billion and S&P options at $232 million. But by the close of 2006, with the S&P 500 valued at $12 trillion, futures contracts on the S&P index had reached $5 trillion and options contracts had soared to $15 trillion, together an "expectations market" valued at almost *double* the value of the "real market" itself.

If that 160-fold increase in instruments based on ownership of the S&P index over the past half-century—two-and-one-half times the 60-fold increase in the production of goods and services in the U.S. economy—doesn't show that our financial system has come to dominate our productive economy, I'm not sure what would. Minsky's concerns seem to have been realized in full.

Risk and Ruin—A Reprise

Even as the volume of financial transactions has soared, so has their mind-numbing complexity. The most recent case in point, of course, was the boom in mortgage-backed debt obligation, part of the secular trend in the "securitization" of assets of all kinds. Two trends were at work here: One was the disintermediation of mortgages, once held largely by community banks for local citizens. (The Jimmy Stewart movie, *It's a Wonderful Life,* comes quickly to mind.) It hardly offends one's common sense to learn that lenders, once they pool their loans and send them off to Wall Street, never to be seen by them again, pay far less attention to loan quality. (Nor is it surprising that the creators of these mortgage-backed bonds have little interest or incentive to help mortgagees in distress to work through their financial difficulties and retain their homes.)

The second trend was the growing complexity of these "new products." Given Wall Street's ever-pressing need to have something, anything, to sell in the way of "new product," it is hardly surprising that these instruments became ever more complex, with risk even more deeply concealed. In league with SEC-registered rating agencies (which were paid, as I understand it, some $300,000 for placing their imprimatur on each issue), some new issues of bonds were created entirely out of subprime mortgages. Nonetheless, in one typical example, 75 percent of the value of the bonds was in "tranches" (series) rated AAA, another 15 percent rated at least A, and 5 percent rated BBB. Only the remaining 5 percent carried a rating of BB. One might call this the *new alchemy*—turning lead to gold. But that was an illusion. (I've seen a lot of financial legerdemain in my day, but none to equal that.) Early this year, when the first wave of mortgage defaults began to snowball, the financial crisis in mortgages was upon us, at a great and growing cost to our citizens and our society, a classic example of the impact of the financial economy on the real economy.

Given the nature of our financial system, few of our giant investment banking firms had the courage to summon the discipline to jump off (or even not to jump on) the mortgage-backed bond bandwagon. The issuance of such bonds in the past five years totaled $2 trillion (including both prime and subprime mortgages), likely generating some $80 billion of revenues to "the Street," its investment bankers, its brokers, its rating agencies, its attorneys, and its securities processors. The only thing the banks could not resist was, of course, temptation, and even the biggest and most savvy firms reveled in the party, its rocking music, and its joyous dancing.

Charles Prince, chairman of the giant Citigroup, said it as well as any friend—or foe—of the situation could have: "As long as the music is playing, you've got to get up and dance. We're still dancing."* (Epilogue: Just last week, Citigroup slashed the value of its mortgage-backed portfolio by more than $3 billion. Not to be outdone, Merrill Lynch followed suit with a $5 billion writedown; UBS wrote down $3.4 billion, and Deutsche Bank has written down a mere $3.1 billion. Following a long age of rife credit availability, and borrowers with high confidence and low collateral, then, we are beginning to pay the price, even as we face a whole plethora of other risks created by our financial system. Stay tuned.)

Looking Ahead

But if systemic risks are increasing, how can it be that risk premiums on stocks are at less than one-half the historic average? Today's projected equity premium, for one example, is just 2 percent, some 60 percent below the century-long average of 5.2 percent (Figure 10.7). Bonds, based on the current yield on investment-grade issues, should return about 5 percent over this period. The stock return over the coming decade is projected at 7 percent, based on today's dividend yield of about 2 percent and prospective nominal earnings growth of about 6 percent, with a shading for the slightly lower price-earnings ratio that I expect a decade hence. And while the spread of high-yield bonds relative to U.S. Treasury bonds has risen from 3 percent to about 4 percent after the recent unpleasantness in the mortgage market, it remains below its long-term average of 5 percent (Figure 10.8).

---

*Michiyo Nakamoto and David Wighton, "First Section: Bullish Citigroup Is 'Still Dancing' to the Beat of the Buy-Out Boom," *Financial Times*, July 10, 2007.

FIGURE 10.7   EQUITY RISK PREMIUM FOR TRAILING TEN-YEAR PERIODS

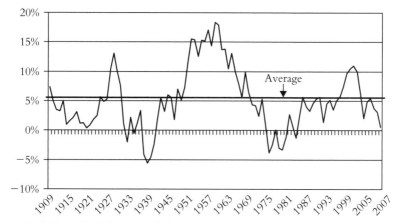

SOURCE: Bogle Financial Markets Research Center.

FIGURE 10.8   SPREAD BETWEEN YIELD OF HIGH-YIELD CORPORATE BONDS AND IT TREASURYS

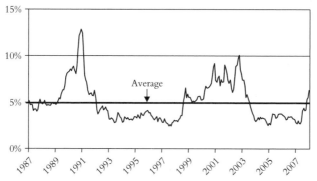

SOURCE: Lehman Brothers and Federal Reserve.

Our markets, then, seem to be ignoring the warning issued by then–Federal Reserve Chairman Alan Greenspan in 2005: "History has not dealt kindly with the aftermath of protracted periods of low risk premiums."* When participants in the financial services field ignore the lessons of history, yet another series of risks are created.

---

*Alan Greenspan, remarks at a symposium sponsored by the Federal Reserve Bank of Kansas City, Jackson Hole, Wyoming, August 26, 2005.

Other Risks

There are, I regret to say, other huge, seemingly unacknowledged risks beyond the financial sector, out there in our society—the risks presented by the Social Security and Medicare payments committed to by our national government, and, for that matter, the staggering string of huge (and in fact *understated*) deficits in our federal budget; our enormous (soon to reach $1 trillion) expenditures on war in Iraq and Afghanistan (with more to come, perhaps in Iran), bleeding the resources of our empire; terrorism; and the threat of global warming and the cost of dealing with it.

You all know about these risks, of course, but there are other, more subtle risks, too: a political system dominated by money and vested interests; a congress and an administration seemingly focused entirely on the short-term, the long-term consequences be damned; the vast chasm between the very wealthiest among us (the top 1 percent of our citizenry holds more than a third of our total wealth) and those at the bottom of the economic ladder (did you know that 20 percent of New York City residents earn less than $8,300 per year?); the implications of our enormous trade deficit and unfettered global competition; our self-centered "bottom-line" society, focused on money over achievement, charisma over character, and the ephemeral over the eternal; and finally, the paucity of leaders who are willing to, well, lead, to defy the conventional wisdom of the day, and to stand up for what is right and noble and true.

So the risks are high, the uncertainties rife. Yet perhaps we'll all muddle through. After all, America has always done just that, all through our 230-year history. Perhaps, too, our society and our economy will continue to reflect the resilience that they have demonstrated in the past, often against all odds. And perhaps we'll come to our collective senses and develop the courage to take arms against this sea of troubles and by opposing, end them. The stock market, indeed, seems to be saying just those things, and I hope it's right.

But we'd best not forget Lord Keynes's warning of 70 years ago: "When enterprise becomes a mere bubble on a whirlpool of speculation the consequences may be dire. . . . When the capital development of a country becomes a by-product of the activities of a casino, the job [of capitalism] is likely to be ill-done." Whatever the case, some surprising event out there, far beyond our expectations, will surely come to pass, an event that may carry an extreme impact, and one for which, once it happens, we'll quickly concoct an explanation as to why it was so predictable after all. That event, if—perhaps I should say *when*—it comes, will be just one more Black Swan.

Chapter 11

The Go-Go Years*

S upermoney, along with its predecessor, *The Money Game*, told the story of what came to be known as the "Go-Go Years" in the U.S. stock market. It is the book that introduced Warren Buffett to the world, long before he became the paradigm of investment success and homespun financial wisdom and who is now the world's most noted investor. In *Supermoney*, author "Adam Smith" travels to Omaha to meet this Will Rogers character, and later brings him on his television show, *Adam Smith's Money World*. Buffett's distinction in the Go-Go era was that he was one of the few who divined it correctly, quietly dropping out and closing the investment fund he managed. His remaining interest, in a thinly traded New England textile company, Berkshire Hathaway, would later become the vehicle for what may well be the most successful investment program of all time.

The era of speculation described in the *Money Game*—and in *Supermoney*—began in the early 1960s and was pretty much over by 1968, only to be succeeded by yet another wave of speculation—albeit starkly different in its derivation—that drove the stock market ever higher through early 1973. Then the bubble of that era burst. By the autumn of 1974, the market had fallen by 50 percent from its high, taking it back below the level it had reached in 1959, 15 years earlier.

---

*The foreword to a new edition of *Supermoney*, by "Adam Smith," published in 2006. Reprinted with permission of John Wiley & Sons.

Both books reached large, eager, and well-informed audiences, deservedly earning "bestseller" status. In them, author "Adam Smith" recounted perceptive, bouncing, often-hilarious anecdotes about the *dramatis personae* of the stage-show that investing had become. While *The Money Game* was essentially a study in the behavior of individual investors, *Supermoney*, as its book jacket reminded us, was about the social behavior of institutional investors, focusing on the use of "supercurrency"—income garnered through market appreciation and stock options—which became the coin of the realm during the Go-Go years.

These two books quickly became part of the lore of investing in that wild-and-crazy era. In retrospect, however, they provided Cassandra-like warnings about the *next* wild-and-crazy era, which would come, as it happens, some three decades later. The "New Economy" bubble of the late 1990s, followed by, yes, another 50 percent collapse in stock prices, had truly remarkable parallels with its earlier counterpart. Surely Santayana was right when he warned that "those who cannot remember the past are condemned to repeat it."

In the aftermath of that second great crash, as investors again struggle to find their bearings, the timing of this new edition of *Supermoney* is inspired. It is a thoroughly enchanting history, laced with wit and wisdom that provides useful lessons for those investors who didn't live through the Go-Go years. It also provides poignant reminiscences for those who *did* live through them. Using the insightful (but probably apocryphal) words attributed to Yogi Berra, it is "déjà vu all over again."

I consider myself fortunate to have learned the lessons of the super-money bubble, albeit the hard way. While I was among those who lived and lost, both personally and professionally, in that era, I summoned the strength to return and fight again. Hardened in the crucible of that experience, I reshaped my ideas about sound investing. So as the New Economy bubble inflated to the bursting point in the years before the recent turn of the century, I was one of a handful of Cassandras, urging investors to avoid concentration in the high-tech stocks of the day, to diversify to the *n*th degree, and to allocate significant assets to, yes, bonds.

I also consider myself fortunate to have known and worked with Jerry Goodman (the present-day Adam Smith) during this long span, periodically interviewed for the *Institutional Investor* maga-zine (of which he was founding editor) and for his popular Public

Broadcasting Network television show, *Adam Smith's Money World*. We served together on the Advisory Council of the Economics Department of Princeton University during the 1970s, where his strong and well-founded opinions were a highlight of our annual roundtable discussions. While I have no hesitation in acknowledging Jerry's superior mind and writing skill—a nice combination!—I console myself with our parity on the fields of combat. (*Exact* parity: Years ago, on a Princeton squash court, we were tied at 2–2 in the match and at 7–7 in the deciding game when the lights went out and the match ended.)

As one of a very few participants who have been part of the march of the financial markets during a period that has now reached 55 years—including both the Go-Go bubble of yore and the New Economy bubble of recent memory—I'm honored and delighted to contribute the foreword to this 2006 reissue of a remarkable book. I'll first discuss the excesses of the supermoney era; next, the relentless retribution that came in its aftermath; and finally, the coming and going of yet the most recent example of the "extraordinarily popular delusions and the madness of crowds" that has punctuated the financial markets all through history. Of course if tomorrow's investors actually learn from the hard-won experience of their elders and the lessons of history chronicled in this wonderful volume, there will never be another bubble. But I wouldn't count on it!

Part One: The Supermoney Era

The Goodman books chronicled an era that verged on—and sometimes even crossed the line into—financial insanity: the triumph of perception over reality, of the transitory illusion of earnings (to say nothing of earnings calculations and earnings expectations) over the ultimate fundamentals of balance sheets and discounted cash flows. It was an era in which investors considered "concepts" and "trends" as the touchstones of investing, easily able to rationalize them since they were backed by numbers, however dubious their provenance. As Goodman writes in his introduction to this new edition: ". . . people viewed financial matters as rational, because the game was measured in numbers, and numbers are finite and definitive."

During the *Money Game/Supermoney* era, perception was able to overwhelm reality in large measure because of financial trickery that made reality appear much better than it was. "Adam Smith" described how easy it was to inflate corporate earnings: "Decrease depreciation charges by changing from accelerated to straight line . . . change the valuation of your inventories . . . adjust the charges made for your pension fund . . . capitalize research instead of expensing it . . . defer the costs of a project until it brings in revenues . . . play with pooling and purchase (accounting) . . . all done with an eye on the stock, not on what might be considered economic reality." And the public accountants, sitting by in silence, let the game go on. The most respected accountant of the generation, Leonard Spacek, chairman emeritus of Arthur Andersen, was almost alone in speaking out against the financial engineering that had become commonplace: "How my profession can tolerate such fiction and look the public in the eye is beyond my understanding . . . financial statements are a roulette wheel." His warning was not heeded.

The acceptance of this foolishness by the investment community was broad and deep. Writing in *Institutional Investor* in January 1968, no less an industry guru than Charles D. Ellis, then an analyst at institutional research broker Donaldson Lufkin and Jenrette, concluded that "short-term investing may actually be safer than long-term investing sometimes, and the price action of the stocks may be more important than the 'fundamentals' on which most research is based . . . portfolio managers buy stocks, they do not 'invest' in corporations."

Yet reality, finally, took over. When it did, the stocks that were in the forefront of the bubble collapsed, fallen idols that proved to have feet of clay. Consider this table from *Supermoney*:

	High	Subsequent Low
National Student Marketing	36	1½
Four Seasons Nursing Homes	91	0
Parvin Dohrmann	142	14
Commonwealth United	25	1
Susquehanna	80	7
Management Assistance	46	2

Stocks like these were among the favorites of mutual fund managers, and those that played the money game the hardest had the greatest near-term success. In its 1966 edition, the *Investment Companies* manual, published annually by Arthur Wiesenberger & Co. since the early 1940s, even created a special category for such funds. "Maximum Capital Gain" (MCG) funds were separated from the traditional "Long-Term Growth, Income Secondary" (LTG) funds, with remaining equity funds in the staid "Growth and Current Income" (GCI) funds category. During the Go-Go era (1963–1968 inclusive), the disparities in returns were stunning: GCI funds plus 116 percent; LTG funds plus 151 percent; MCG funds plus a remarkable 285 percent.

At the beginning of the Go-Go era, there were 22 MCG funds, at the peak 143. Amazingly, after its initial offering in 1966, Gerald Tsai's Manhattan Fund—a *hot* IPO in an industry that had never before had even a *warm* IPO—was placed in the LTG category. The offering attracted $250 million, nearly 15 percent of the total cash flow into equity funds for the year, and its assets would soar to $560 million within two years. Tsai was the inscrutable manager who had turned in a remarkable record in running Fidelity Capital Fund—+296 percent in 1958–1965 compared to a gain of 166 percent for the average conservative equity fund. *Newsweek* epitomized Tsai's lionization: "radiates total cool . . . dazzling rewards . . . no man wields greater influence . . . king of the mutual funds." Tsai, no mean marketer, described himself as "really very conservative," and even denied that there was "such a thing as a Go-Go (fund)."

During the bubble of 1963–1968, equally remarkable gains were achieved by other Go-Go funds. With the S&P 500 up some 99 percent, Fidelity Trend Fund rose 245 percent; Winfield Fund leaped 285 percent, and Enterprise Fund a remarkable 643 percent. But after the 1968 peak, these funds earned unexceptional—indeed subpar—returns during 1969–1971. Nonetheless, with their extraordinary performance during the boom years (however achieved), their lifetime records through 1971 continued to appear extraordinary.

It was not only mutual funds that joined in the market madness. While the cupidity of fund managers could at least be understood, it was not obvious why major not-for-profit institutions also succumbed. Even the Ford Foundation added fuel to the fire, warning that, "over the long run, caution has cost our universities more than imprudence or excessive risk-taking." The poster-child for imprudence was the University of Rochester's endowment fund. *Supermoney* describes its approach: "to buy the so-called great companies and not sell them," a portfolio dominated by holdings in IBM, Xerox, and Eastman Kodak. The unit value of its portfolio (presented as an appendix in *Supermoney*) soared from $2.26 in 1962 to $4.95 in 1967, and to $5.60 in 1971—an aggregate gain of 150 percent. Could it really be that easy?

Alas, if only I knew then what I know now. Lured by the siren song of the Go-Go years, I too mindlessly jumped on the bandwagon. In 1965, I was directed by Wellington Management Company chairman and founder Walter L. Morgan to "do whatever is necessary" to bring the firm that I had joined in 1951, right out of college, into the new era. I quickly engineered a merger with Boston money manager Thorndike, Doran, Paine, and Lewis, whose Ivest Fund was one of the top-performing Go-Go funds of the era. The merger was completed in 1966. In 1967 I callowly announced to our staff that "We're #1," for during the five years ended December 31, 1966, the fund had delivered the highest total return of any mutual fund in the entire industry. So far, so good.

The story of that merger was chronicled in the lead article in the January 1968 issue of the *Institutional Investor*, whose editor was none other than George J. W. Goodman. "The Whiz Kids Take Over at Wellington" described how the new partners had moved Wellington off the traditional "balanced" investment course to a new "contemporary" course. In Wellington Fund's 1967 annual report, it was described as "dynamic conservatism" by the fund's new portfolio manager, Walter M. Cabot:

> Times change. We decided we too should change to bring the portfolio more into line with modern concepts and opportunities. We have chosen "dynamic conservatism" as our philosophy, with emphasis on companies that demonstrate the ability to meet, shape and profit from change. [We have] increased our common stock position from 64 percent of resources to 72 percent, with a definite emphasis on growth stocks and a reduction in traditional basic industries. A conservative investment

fund is one that aggressively seeks rewards, and therefore has a substantial exposure to capital growth, potential profits and rising dividends . . . [one that] demands imagination, creativity, and flexibility. We will be invested in many of the great growth companies of our society. Dynamic and conservative investing is not, then, a contradiction in terms. A strong offense is the best defense.

When one of the most conservative funds in the entire mutual fund industry begins to "aggressively seek rewards," it should have been obvious that the Go-Go era was over. And it *was* over. Sadly, in the market carnage that would soon follow, the fund's strong offense, however unsurprisingly, turned out to be the *worst* defense.

Part Two: Retribution Comes

When there is a gap between perception and reality, it is only a matter of time until the gap is reconciled. But since reality is so stubborn and tolerates no gamesmanship, it is impossible for reality to rise to meet perception. So it follows that perception must decline to meet reality. *Après moi le déluge.*

The ending of the Go-Go era in 1968 was followed by a 5 percent market decline in the stock market during 1969 and 1970. Even larger losses (averaging 30 percent) were incurred by the new breed of aggressive investors. But that decline was quickly offset by a 14 percent market recovery in 1971 (just as Jerry Goodman was writing *Supermoney*). In 1972, with another 19 percent gain, the market's snapback continued. For the two years combined, both the market and the MCG funds produced a total return of about 35 percent.

Those final two years of the bubble reflected a subtle shift from the Go-Go era to the Favorite Fifty era. But that metamorphosis didn't help the other, more conservative, equity funds. Why? Because as the bubble mutated from generally smaller concept stocks to large, established companies—"the great companies" epitomized in the Rochester portfolio, sometimes called the "Favorite Fifty," sometimes the "Vestal Virgins"—the stock prices of these companies too lost touch with the underlying economic reality, trading at price-earnings multiples that, as it was said, "discounted not only the *future*, but the *hereafter*."

But as 1973 began, the game ended. During the next two calendar years, the aggressive funds tumbled by almost 50 percent on average, with Fidelity Trend off 47 percent and Enterprise Fund off 44 percent. (Winfield Fund, off 50 percent 1969–1970, was no longer around for the final carnage.) Tsai's Manhattan Fund, remarkably, did even *worse*, tumbling by 55 percent. By the end of December 31, 1974, Manhattan Fund had provided the worst—the *worst*—eight-year record in the entire mutual fund industry—a cumulative loss of 70 percent of its shareholders' capital. In the meanwhile, Tsai, the failed investor but still the brilliant entrepreneur, had sold his company to CNA Insurance in 1968. By 1974, Manhattan Fund's assets had dwindled by a mere 90 percent to $54 million, a shell of its former self, a name that virtually vanished in the dustbin of market history.

And at Rochester University, the value of the endowment fund—for all the noble intentions of its managers—also plummeted. The coming of the Go-Go bubble followed by the Favorite Fifty bubble had carried its unit value from $3.17 in 1964 to $7.20 in 1972, but their going had carried it right back to $3.13 in 1974—even below where it began a decade earlier. *Après moi le deluge*, indeed! (Reflecting the embarrassment of the Rochester managers, the cover of the endowment fund's annual report for 1974 was red, "the deepest shade we could find.")

My face was red, too. I can hardly find words to describe first my regret and then my anger at myself for having made so many bad choices: associating myself—and the firm with whose leadership I had been entrusted—with a group of Go-Go managers; the stupid belief that outsized rewards could be achieved without assuming outsized risks; the naive conviction that I was smart enough to defy the clear lessons of history and select money managers who could *consistently* provide superior returns; putting on an ill-fitting marketing hat to expand Wellington's "product line" (a phrase I have come to detest when applied to the field of money *management*, accurate today only because the fund field is now one of money *marketing*, and, *ugh!*, product development). I too had become one of the mad crowd that harbored the extraordinary popular delusions of the day.

Ultimately, alas, the merger that I had sought and accomplished not only failed to solve Wellington's problems, it exacerbated them. Despite the early glitter of success for the firm during the Go-Go years, the substance proved illusory. As a business matter, the merger worked beautifully for the first five years, but both I and the aggressive investment managers whom I had too opportunistically sought as my new partners let our fund shareholders down badly. In the Great Bear Market of 1973–1974, stock prices declined by a devastating 50 percent from high to low. Even for the full two-year period, the S&P 500 index provided a total return (including dividends) of *minus* 37 percent.

Most of our equity funds did even worse. During the same period, for example, Ivest lost a shocking 55 percent of its value. In my annual Chairman's letter to shareholders for 1974, I bluntly reported that, "the fund's net asset value declined by 44 percent for the August 31 fiscal year. . . . Comparing this with a decline of 31 percent for the S&P 500 . . . we regard the Fund's performance as unsatisfactory." (One of the fund's directors was appalled by my recognition of this seemingly self-evident fact. He soon resigned from the board.) We had also started other aggressive funds during this ebullient era. When the day of reckoning came, they too plummeted far more than the S&P 500: Explorer minus 52 percent; Morgan Growth Fund minus 47 percent; and Trustees'(!) Equity Fund minus 47 percent. The latter fund folded in 1978; and a speculative fund—Technivest—that we designed to "take advantage of technical market analysis" (I'm not kidding!) folded even earlier.

Even our crown jewel Wellington Fund, with that earlier increase in its equity ratio and a portfolio laden with "the great growth companies of our society," suffered a 26 percent loss in 1973–1974. Its record since the 1966 merger was near the bottom of the balanced fund barrel. With the average balanced fund up 23 percent for the decade, Wellington's cumulative total return *for the entire period* (including dividends) was close to *zero*—a mere 2 percent. (In 1975, portfolio manager Cabot left the firm to become manager of the Harvard Endowment Fund.)

In a business environment that was falling apart almost week by week, this terrible performance put enormous strains on the once-cooperative partnership, strains that were soon exacerbated by personal differences, conflicting ambitions and egos, and the desire to hold the reins of power. Not surprisingly, my new partners and I had a falling out.

But they had more votes on the Board, and it was *they* who fired *me* from what I had considered "my" company.

I had failed our shareholders and I had failed in my career—not in getting fired, but in jumping on the speculative bandwagon of aggressive investing in the first place. Life was fair, however: I had made a big error and I paid a high price.* I was heartbroken, my career in shambles. But I wasn't defeated. I had always been told that when a door closed (this one had slammed!) a window would open. I decided that I would open that window myself, resume my career, and change the very structure under which mutual funds operated, which was importantly responsible for the industry's abject failure during the Go-Go era. I would make the mutual fund industry a better place to invest.

But how could that goal be accomplished? With the essence of simplicity. Why should mutual funds retain an *outside company* to manage their affairs—then, and now, the *modus operandi* of our industry—when, once they reach a critical asset mass, funds are perfectly capable of managing *themselves* and saving a small fortune in fees? Why not create a structure in which mutual funds would, uniquely, be truly *mutual*? They would be run, *not* in the interest of an external adviser—a business whose goal is to earn the highest possible profit for its own separate set of owners—but in the interest of their own shareholder/ owners, at the lowest possible cost. The firm would not be run on the basis of product marketing. The funds would focus, not on hot sectors of the market, but on the total market itself. The core investment philosophy would eschew the fallacy of short-term speculation and trumpet the wisdom of long-term investing. And so, on September 24, 1974, out of all of the hyperbole and madness of the Go-Go era and the Favorite Fifty era, and the travail of the great crash that followed, came the creation of the Vanguard Group of Investment Companies.

---

*Ironically, the original partners who fired me—those who were directly responsible for the performance problems—paid no price at all. They took full control of Wellington Management and earned enormous rewards in the Great Bull Market that would begin in 1982. Nonetheless, they too apparently learned from their experience in the crash and ultimately restored Wellington to its earlier incarnation as a sound, respected, and conservative money manager.

Part Three: Another Bubble

One of the most engaging anecdotes in *Supermoney* is the tale of an annual investment conference in New York City that attracted some 1,500 trust officers and mutual fund managers (presumably the 1970 Conference held by the *Institutional Investor* magazine). Jerry Goodman was the moderator, and as he writes, he "thought it would be a nice psychological purge after the [then] worst year of the Big Bear, if some of the previous winners could get up and confess their big sins." However good for the soul that might have been, few confessions were forthcoming. But the crowd was reminded of its sins by crusty New Englander David Babson, who described the stock market of the day as "a national crap game." His philosophy as an investment manager revolved around hard work and common sense, "virtues that would triumph in the long run."

He lashed into the assembled crowd, describing how professional investors had "gotten sucked into speculation," reading off a list, name by name, of once-vaunted stocks that had plummeted in price (from 80 to 7, 68 to 4, 46 to 2, 68 to 3, and so on), and suggesting that some of the assembled managers should leave the business. Despite Goodman's warning ("David, you have passed the pain threshold of the audience"), Babson singled out "the new breed of investment managers who bought and churned the worst collection of new issues and other junk in history, and the underwriters who made a fortune in bringing them out . . . and elements of the financial press which promoted into new investment geniuses a group of neophytes who had . . . no sense of responsibility for managing other people's money." Babson concluded that "no greater period of skullduggery in American financial history exists than 1967 to 1969. It has burned this generation like 1929 did another one, and it will be a long, long time before it happens again."

As one might imagine, Mr. Babson's remarks were not well-received by the audience of money managers. But while he failed to foresee a second leg of the bubble (the Favorite Fifty era) that would quickly follow, he was right. Just as some 35 years had elapsed from 1929 until the start of the Go-Go era in 1965, so some 33 years would elapse before the next bubble emerged. Once again, a new generation would forget the lessons learned by its predecessors.

Some of the causes of the new bubble were the same. (They may be eternal.) David Babson had listed them: "Accountants who played footsie with stock-promoting managements by classifying earnings that weren't earnings at all. 'Modern' corporate treasurers who looked upon their company pension funds as new-found profit centers . . . mutual fund managers who tried to become millionaires overnight by using every gimmick imaginable to manufacture their own paper perform- ance . . . security analysts who forgot about their professional ethics to become storytellers and let their institutions be taken in by a whole parade of confidence men." Charles Ellis's 1968 insight that "portfolio managers buy stocks, they do not 'invest' in corporations" also came back to haunt us. (With a twist, of course: Managers didn't merely *buy* stocks; they *traded* them with unprecedented ferocity.)

If you conclude that *the more things change, the more they remain the same,* you get my point. But each bubble has its own characteristics, too, and the bubble of the late 1990s added a host of new elements to the eternal equation. Part of the bullish thesis underlying that bubble (as it was described by *Wired* magazine) was based on a heavy dose of rose-colored vision: "the triumph of the United States, the end of major wars, waves of new technology, soaring productivity, a truly glo- bal market, and corporate restructuring—a virtuous circle . . . driven by an open society in an integrated world." And there was more: the excitement accompanying the turn of the millennium that would begin in 2001 (even though most people celebrated it on January 1, 2000); the "Information Age" and the technology revolution; the (once-capitalized) "New Economy." Together, these powerful changes seemed to hold the prospects of extraordinary opportunity. And so, once again, investors lost their perspective.

Why should that surprise us? After all, way back in the second century B.C. the Roman orator Cato warned us:

> There must certainly be a vast Fund of Stupidity in Human Nature, else Men would not be caught as they are, a thou- sand times over, by the same Snare, and while they yet remem- ber their past Misfortunes, go on to court and encourage the Causes to which they were owing, and which will again pro- duce them.

After my experience in the earlier bubble, I hardly needed Cato's warning. Late in March of 2000—within days of the stock market's hyper-inflated peak—I was writing a speech that would soon warn a gathering of institutional investors in Boston that we could well be "caught in one of those periodic snares set by the limitless supply of stupidity in human nature. . . . Professional investors who ignore today's rife signs of market madness—of a bubble, if you will—are abrogating their fiduciary duty, and dishonoring their responsibility for the stewardship of their clients' assets."

"How should that responsibility be honored?" I asked.

> By recognizing that, for all of the projections and assumptions we make (and almost take for granted) . . . stock market returns are completely unpredictable in the short-run and—unless we know more about the world 25 years from now than we do about the world today—may prove even less predictable over the long-run. The problem is that future expectations often lose touch with future reality. Sometimes hope rides in the saddle, sometimes greed, sometimes fear. No, there is no "new paradigm." Hope, greed, and fear make up the market's *eternal* paradigm.

In the speech, I also noted that, "by almost any conventional measure of stock valuation, stocks have never been riskier than they are today," pointing out that major market highs were almost invariably signaled when the dividend yield on stocks fell below 3 percent, when the price-earnings ratio rose much above 20 times earnings, and when the aggregate market value of U.S. equities reached 80 percent of our nation's gross domestic product (GDP). "Yet today," I warned, "dividend yields have fallen to just over 1 percent . . . stocks are now selling at something like 32 times last year's earnings . . . and the equity market value has almost reached 200 percent of GDP. (Just be patient!) Clearly, if past data mean anything, risk is the forgotten man of this Great Bull Market."

The disquieting similarities between the Go-Go era and the recent technology-driven market also caught my attention. In the course of my remarks, I presented the exhibit in Table 11.1 to show the striking

TABLE 11.1   DÉJÀ VU? COMPARISON OF GO-GO ERA TO TECH-BOOM ERA

5 Large Go-Go Funds			5 Large Tech Funds
1963–1968		**1997–2000**	
Fund return	344%	Fund return	403%
S&P return	99	S&P return	92
Ratio	3.4×	Ratio	4.3×
1963 assets	$200M	1997 assets	$5.6 B
1968 assets	3.4B	2000 assets	40 B
Increase	17×	Increase	7×
1969–1974		**2000–2002 (updated)**	
Fund return	−45%	Fund return	−71%
S&P return	−19	S&P return	−38%
Ratio	2.4×	Ratio	1.9×

parallels between the huge upside returns of the aggressive funds of each era and the enormous capital inflows that they enjoyed when investors—as always, late to the game—chased those returns. (I've taken the liberty of filling in the subsequent performance for the tech funds and the S&P 500.)

My conclusion:

So, let me be clear: You can place me firmly in the camp of those who are deeply concerned that the stock market is all too likely to be riding for a painful fall—indeed a fall that may well have begun as I began to write this speech ten days ago. From Milton Friedman to Robert Shiller (author of the newly published *Irrational Exuberance*), to John Cassidy of the *New Yorker*, and Steven Leuthold, Jeremy Grantham, Jeremy Siegel, Julian Robertson (who just threw in the towel), Gary Brinson (whose convictions may have cost him his job), and Alan Greenspan (whose convictions haven't). Viewed a decade hence, today's stock market may just be one more chapter in *Extraordinary Popular Delusions and the Madness of Crowds.*

As it turned out, the painful fall *had* begun, on March 10, 2000, just as I began to write that speech. (There's luck in that; while we often know *what* will happen in the stock market, we never know *when*.) But what about those three question marks about *future* returns that I posted in the lower right corner of the exhibit? Again, the similarities to the earlier bubble were to prove stunning. While the S&P 500 was off 38 percent in 2000–2002, the total return of the average large technology fund was a staggering *minus* 71 percent. "History may not repeat itself," in Mark Twain's wise formulation, "but it rhymes."

So, dear reader, learn from the past, from a wild-and-crazy era, the kind of an era that, as Cato warned us, repeats itself over and over again. Profit, too, if you will, from my own personal and professional failures, and learn from them the easy way rather than the hard way that was my lot. (Not that, after a long and character-building struggle, it didn't have a wonderful outcome!) Above all, heed the idealistic goal set out by John Maynard Keynes 70 years ago, quoted at length in *Supermoney*:

> [While] the actual private object of most skilled investors today . . . is a battle of wits to anticipate the basis of conventional valuation a few months hence . . . the social object of investment should be to defeat the dark forces of time and ignorance which envelop our future.

Part Three

WHAT'S WRONG WITH "MUTUAL" FUNDS

art Three of *Don't Count on It!* includes five chapters that trace the historical development of the mutual fund industry's peculiar structure and how that structure shaped the industry's development. As the late, great economist and author Peter Bernstein has written, "[W]hat happens to the wealth of individual investors cannot be separated from the structure of the industry that manages those assets." These chapters include colorful anecdotes regarding industry leaders and regulators during the industry's formative years, which provide a powerful contrast between the structure of America's first mutual fund and the very different structure that the industry subsequently adopted. Since the now-prevailing structure has failed to adequately serve fund shareholders, I offer a set of sound, long-term-oriented principles of stewardship to which I urge the industry to promptly return.

Chapter 12—"The Alpha and the Omega"—analyzes those changes in industry structure starting with America's first mutual fund, which was created in 1924. As I explain in this essay, that original mutual fund used the *Alpha* model—under which trustees were employed by the fund itself, without the need to retain a separate investment advisory company to manage its affairs, and with share distribution provided by a separate and independent sales organization. This original Alpha model was almost immediately supplanted by a new, now-dominant *Omega* model, in which a separate advisory company, now usually publicly held, essentially controls the fund's affairs and distributes its shares.

This chapter also contrasts the faltering investment returns and diminishing growth that occurred when, in 1969, the managers of that first fund abandoned its original "mutual" Alpha model based on stewardship. Instead, it adopted the prevailing industry model focused on salesmanship. The result: deteriorating fund performance and plummeting market share. Just a few years later, in 1974, another firm (which happened to be the newly created Vanguard) revived the original Alpha model in an innovative and unique manner. That bold step was accompanied by, yes, improved fund performance and soaring growth in market share. In 2010, it ranked as the largest mutual fund firm in the world, holding an unprecedented market share of 16 percent of the assets of all U.S. stock and bond mutual funds. Yet despite that accomplishment, this truly mutual structure has yet to be adopted by a single other firm.

"A New Order of Things—Bringing Mutuality to the 'Mutual' Fund," is presented in Chapter 13. That essay was inspired by a 1968 speech by then–SEC Chairman Manuel Cohen. His speech, entitled "The 'Mutual' Fund," was prescient to a fault—especially the quotation marks he placed around the word "mutual." However, his warnings fell upon deaf ears. As he feared, the legal floodgates that had prevented fund management companies from "going public" or selling out to financial conglomerates had been thrown wide open by a California appellate court in 1958. As a result, fund managers, in Chairman Cohen's words, "may be obligated to serve the business interests of the very companies in which they invest." And that is what has happened.

In Chapter 14—"The Fiduciary Principle: No Man Can Serve Two Masters"—I discuss the cataclysmic stock market crash and economic crisis that began in 2007, and the role played by institutional investors in that failure. I cite 10 striking examples of how fund managers have violated their fiduciary duty to mutual fund investors. The principles that I advocate are age-old, clearly echoing the principles so beautifully enunciated by Supreme Court Justice Harlan Fiske Stone in 1934, in the wake of the stock market crash in 1929 and the Great Depression that followed. To reduce the chances of yet another crash, I recommend the establishment of a federal standard of fiduciary duty, a simple concept that would require fund managers to place the interest of their fund shareholders first, just as the preamble to the Investment Company Act of 1940 demands.

Chapters 15 and 16 also reflect my mission to return the mutual fund industry to its founding values. In "Fund Directors and Fund Myths," I urge that fund independent directors stand up for the rights of the shareholders who elected them—an idea, alas, that has yet to gain much traction. To guide directors along the way, I offer Ten Commandments and a Golden Rule. The final chapter focuses on "Fair Dealing with Investors." Here, I call for far better disclosure of relevant information to fund shareholders and prospective shareholders, so that the mutual fund industry can truly operate with "high standards of commercial honor and just equitable principles of trade." We have a long way to go.

Chapter 12

Re-Mutualizing the Mutual Fund Industry: The Alpha and the Omega*

M arch 21, 2004, two months from now, will mark the 80th anniversary of America's first mutual fund. Organized in Boston, Massachusetts Investors Trust (MIT) was a Massachusetts trust managed by its own trustees, who held the power "in their absolute and uncontrolled discretion" to invest its assets. The trustees were to be compensated at "the current bank rate for trustees," then 6 percent of the investment income earned by the trust.

Our industry began, then, with the formation of a truly *mutual* mutual fund, one organized, operated, and managed, not by a separate management company with its own commercial interests, but by its

---

*Based on an essay published in the *Boston College Law Review* in 2004 (vol. 45, no. 2), which in turn was based on a speech delivered at Boston College Law School on January 21, 2004.

own trustees; compensated not on the basis of the trust's *principal*, but, under traditional fiduciary standards, its *income*.

We use the word *Alpha* to describe the first event in a series, and the word *Omega* to describe the last event, the end of the series or its final development. To state what must be obvious, however, MIT's Alpha was followed by the development of a very different mode of fund organization. Today, the industry's almost-universal *modus operandi* is not individual *funds* but fund *complexes*; they are managed not by their own trustees but by external corporations; they encompass not only investment management but also administration, operations, distribution, and marketing. The model of the 1924 Alpha *mutual fund*, then, has been replaced by the 2004 Omega mutual fund *complex*—a term that, all those years ago, would have somehow seemed jarring or inappropriate.

But "the national public interest and the interest of investors"— the focus of our industry's guiding statute, the Investment Company Act of 1940—precludes our acceptance of today's almost universally accepted industry structure—today's Omega model—as the end of mutual fund development. Why? Because the reality is that this structure has been shaped, increasingly and almost unremittingly, to *serve* the interest of fund managers, a *disservice to* the public interest and the interest of fund shareholders.

Sharply rising fund costs have widened the shortfall by which fund returns have lagged the returns earned in the financial markets; the age-old wisdom of long-term investing has been importantly crowded out by the folly of short-term speculation; and "product marketing" has superseded investment management as our highest value. The recent fund scandals provide tangible evidence of the triumph of *managers capitalism* over *owners capitalism* in mutual fund America, an unhappy parallel to what we have observed in corporate America itself.

These developments are indisputable, and they fly in the face of the very language of the Investment Company Act: Mutual funds must be "organized, operated, and managed" in the interests of their shareowners rather than in the interests of their "investment advisers and underwriters (distributors)"—a policy now honored more in the breach than in the observance. It is high time for a *new* Omega, an industry structure that would, paradoxically enough, parallel the Alpha structure under which MIT was created nearly 80 years ago.

The Development of MIT

Almost from its inception, MIT was a remarkable success. While in its first few years the going was slow, assets had soared to $3.3 million by the end of 1926. As the boom of the late 1920s continued, it flourished. It earned a return of 88 percent for its investors in 1926– 1928, only to lose 63 percent of their capital in the bust that followed in 1929–1932. But as the market recovered, its assets grew apace— to $128 million by 1936, and to $277 million by 1949, the largest stock fund in the industry throughout that entire period. MIT would maintain that rank until 1975, when its assets reached a total of *$1.15 billion*—a truly amazing half-century of preeminence.

To its enviable status as both the oldest and largest mutual fund, MIT added the luster of consistently ranking as the lowest-cost fund. Its trustees soon reduced that original 6 percent fee to 5 percent of income, and then, in 1949, to 3.5 percent. Measuring its costs as a percentage of fund assets (now the conventional way we report expenses), the Trust's expense ratio fell from 0.50 percent in the early years to 0.39 percent in 1949, to a fairly steady 0.19 percent during 1960– 1969. During that entire period, MIT was publicly offered through stock brokers by an underwriter originally named Learoyd-Foster, later to become Vance, Sanders & Co. Managed by its own trustees and unaffiliated with its distributor, the truly mutual structure of Massachusetts Investors Trust played a major role in its sustained leadership of the industry.

As 1969 began, then, MIT was an industry maverick. It stood for trusteeship, and did not engage in salesmanship. It kept its costs at rock-bottom levels. Its portfolio was broadly diversified and had little turnover. It invested for the long-term, and so did the shareholders who purchased its shares. And while virtually every other fund in the industry operated under the conventional structure with an external "management company" assuming full responsibility for its operations, investment advice, and share distribution in return for an *asset-related*—not *income*-related—fee paid by existing investors and a share of the sales loads paid by its new investors, MIT held to its own high standards and prospered—a success story, in its own way, for the idea that mutuality worked.

MIT—From Alpha to Omega

During 1969, however, the structure changed. The trustees solicited proxies from the shareholders of MIT (and its sister fund, Massachusetts Investors Growth Stock Fund—originally named "Massachusetts Investors Second Fund") for the approval to "demutualize" and adopt the conventional external management structure. When the shareholders approved the proposal, the Trust became a member of a fund family that adopted the name "Massachusetts Financial Services" (MFS). If MIT was a fund that for nearly a half-century had stood for something unique, in 1969 it became one of the crowd.

Was that change from Alpha to Omega good or bad? We can say unequivocally that, in terms of the fees it generated for its managers, it was *good*. We can also say unequivocally that in terms of the costs borne by its shareholders, it was *bad*. That 0.19 percent expense ratio in 1968 doubled to 0.39 percent in 1976, and doubled again to 0.75 percent in 1994, continuing to rise to 0.97 percent in 1998 and to 1.20 percent in 2003 (Figure 12.1). And that old limit of 3.5 percent of income the trustees put into place in 1949? It was long gone. In 2002, in fact, MIT's expenses consumed precisely 80.4 percent of the trust's income.

But these ratios greatly *understate* the increase in the Trusts' costs. For even as its assets were growing, so were its fee *rates*, resulting in

FIGURE 12.1   CHANGING FROM ALPHA TO OMEGA: THE MIT EXPERIENCE

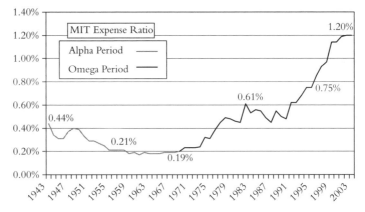

FIGURE 12.2   MIT FEE GROWTH, 1969–2003

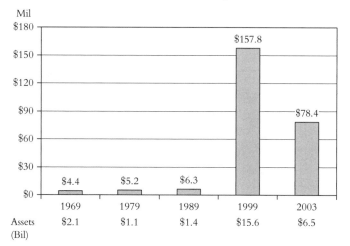

enormous increases in the *dollar amounts* of fees paid. With assets of $2.2 billion in 1969, MIT's management fees (including some relatively small operating expenses) totaled $4.4 million (Figure 12.2). Even a decade later in 1979, although the Trust's assets had *declined* by 50 percent to $1.1 billion after the 1973–1974 market crash and the troubled times faced by the fund industry, fees had actually *risen* to $5.2 million. In 1989, with assets at $1.4 billion, fees continued to rise, to $6.3 million. And in 1999, when assets soared to $15.6 billion, fees totaled $158 million. While the Trust's assets had grown *sevenfold* since MIT demutualized in 1969, its fees had increased *36 times* over. (Assets slumped to $6.5 billion last year, with fees totaling nearly $80 million.)

MIT's Long-Term Investment Record

What effect did the new structure have on MIT's shareholders? It is not difficult to measure. For MIT was the prototypical mutual fund, widely diversified among about 100 blue-chip stocks, and, unsurprisingly, provided returns that closely paralleled those of the Standard & Poor's 500 Stock Index (a 90-stock index until 1957), with an average correlation (R^2) of 0.94 that has remained remarkably steady over its entire 80-year history. Given the tautology that the gross return of the

FIGURE 12.3   AVERAGE ANNUAL RETURNS:
MIT AND S&P 500 INDEX

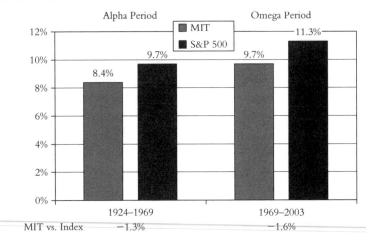

stock market, minus the costs of financial intermediation, equals the net return earned by market participants, it would be surprising if the rising costs that followed MIT's demutualization were not accompanied by a deterioration in the returns enjoyed by its shareowners.

No surprise, then. The Trust's relative returns declined. During its mutual era (1925–1969), the Trust's average annual return of 8.4 percent lagged the S&P 500 index return of 9.7 percent, by 1.3 percent per year (Figure 12.3). (Because the S&P 500 index return ignores the real-world costs of investing, of course, that shortfall may not be surprising.) But *after* demutualization (1969–2003), its average annual return of 9.7 percent lagged the S&P 500 index return of 11.3 percent by 1.6 percent per year—a 0.3 percent reduction that exactly matches the increase in its average expense ratio from 0.3 percent in the 1925–1969 period to 0.6 percent in 1969–2003. (The ratio has risen to an estimated 1.2 percent in 2003, suggesting a much wider lag in the years ahead.)

This increase in the shortfall in MIT annual returns during the Trust's 34-year Omega period may seem trivial. But it is not (Figure 12.4). Thanks to the miracle of compounding *returns*, each $1 initially invested in the Standard & Poor's 500 index at the end of 1969 would have been valued at $38 at the end of 2003. Confronted by the tyranny of

FIGURE 12.4   PERFORMANCE OF MIT AND S&P 500, 1969–2003

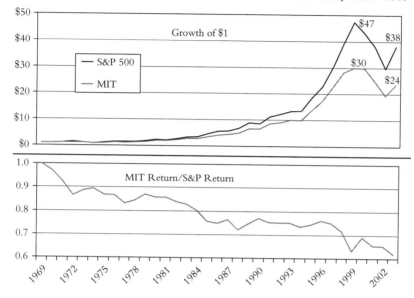

compounding *costs* over that long period, however, each $1 invested in Massachusetts Investors Trust would have had a final value of just $23.60 — a 38 percent loss of principal in relative terms.

The Wellington Group—From Omega to Alpha

Even as MIT was abandoning its Alpha mutual structure in favor of an externally managed Omega structure in 1969, the stage was being set for another firm to take precisely the opposite action. Philadelphia's Wellington Group—11 associated mutual funds with assets of some $2.4 billion (over $1 billion behind the then-combined total of $3.5 billion for MIT and its sister growth fund)—was operated by Wellington Management Company, then largely owned by its executives but with public shareholders as well. Its stock had recently sold at an all-time high of $50 per share, nearly three times its initial public offering price of $18 in 1960. Despite the travail that followed the demise of the Go-Go years, the stock market was again rallying, on the way to its then-all-time high early in 1973, and the company was prospering.

With the so-called "currency" that its public stock had made available, Wellington Management had merged with the Boston investment counsel firm of Thorndike, Doran, Paine and Lewis, Inc., in 1967. TDP&L was also the manager of Ivest Fund, a "Go-Go" fund that was one of the industry's premier performers during that era of speculation, and it soon became a major generator of the Wellington Group's capital inflows. And yet, even as MIT had just gone in the opposite direction, the Wellington CEO (and also the chairman and president of Wellington *funds*)* was pondering whether this Omega structure was the optimal one for the funds' shareholders, and whether a change to the recently vanished Alpha structure would improve both the lot of its fund shareholders as well as the firm's competitive position in the industry.

In September 1971, he went public with his concerns. Speaking at the annual meeting of the firm's partners, he talked about the possibility of mutualization, beginning his remarks with a 1934 quotation from Justice Harlan Fiske Stone:

> Most of the mistakes and major faults of the financial era that has just drawn to a close will be ascribed to the failure to observe the fiduciary principle, the precept as old as holy writ, that "a man cannot serve two masters". . . . Those who serve nominally as trustees but consider only last the interests of those whose funds they command suggest how far we have ignored the necessary implications of that principle.[†]

The Wellington CEO endorsed that point of view, and revealed what he described as

---

* It was I who served in these positions, but I feel more comfortable using the third-person format. This combination of seemingly conflicting roles was then, and remains now, the industry norm.

† Harlan F. Stone, "The Public Influence of the Bar," *Harvard Law Review* 48, no. 1 (1934): 8–9.

an ancient prejudice of mine: *All things considered, it is undesirable for professional enterprises to have public shareholders.* Indeed it is possible to envision circumstances in which the pressure for earnings growth engendered by public ownership is antithetical to the responsible operation of a professional organization. Although the field of money management has elements of both a business and a profession, any conflicts between the two must, finally, be reconciled in favor of the client. [Emphasis added.]

He then tranced on some ideas about how such a reconciliation might be achieved: (1) "a mutualization, whereby the funds acquire the management company"; (2) "internalization, whereby the active executives own the management company, with contracts negotiated on a 'cost-plus' basis, with incentives for both performance and efficiency, but without the ability to capitalize earnings through public sale"; and (3) limited internalization, with funds "made self-sustaining with respect to administration and distribution, but with external investment managers."

Omega to Alpha

Within three years, the CEO was put in a position in which he would not only *talk the talk* about mutualization, but would *walk the walk.* Even before the 1973–1974 bear market began, Wellington's business had begun to deteriorate and the cash *inflows* of the Wellington funds, $280 million in 1967, had by 1973 turned to cash *outflows* of $300 million. The speculative funds created by the firm were suffering serious capital erosion, and most would be merged out of existence before the decade was out. Assets of the conservative Wellington Fund flagship had tumbled from $2 billion in 1965 to less than $1 billion, on the way to $480 million in 1980. Earnings of $2.52 per share in 1968 would drop to $1.14 in 1974, and the stock price had fallen to $9.75 per share, on its way to a low of $4.87 (Figure 12.5). This concatenation of dire events was enough to cause the happy partnership formed by the 1967 merger to fall apart, and Wellington Management

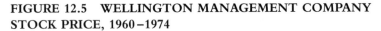

FIGURE 12.5   WELLINGTON MANAGEMENT COMPANY
STOCK PRICE, 1960–1974

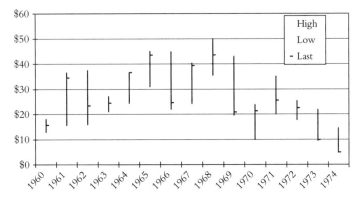

Company's CEO got the axe on January 23, 1974. But he remained as chairman of the funds, with their largely separate (and independent) board of directors.

Shortly before the firing, the handwriting was on the wall, as it were, suggesting the nature of the change that might be in store. On January 12, 1974, the CEO had submitted a proposal to the *mutual fund* board of directors to mutualize the funds and operate under an internally managed structure:

> I propose to have the Wellington Group of mutual funds acquire Wellington Management Company and its business assets. . . . The Funds would pay an estimated $6 million [the adjusted market capitalization of the company's stock*] and would receive liquid and fixed assets of $4 million, with the remaining $2 million representing the "going concern" value [or goodwill] of the enterprise. . . . Wellington Management would become a wholly owned subsidiary of the funds and would serve as investment adviser and distributor on an "at-cost" basis, resulting in estimated savings of $2 to $3 million per year.

---

*Under the proposal, the Funds would acquire only Wellington's mutual fund business. Its counseling business would have been returned to the pre-merger partners.

One need only understand the stunningly high profit margins of the investment management business in order to imagine a *less-than-one-year*(!) payback of the net acquisition cost of $2 million. While Wellington's stock price had tumbled, and its fee revenues had declined, the firm's pre-tax profit margin nonetheless remained at a healthy 33 percent (revenues $9.6 million, expenses $6.4 million, profits $3.2 million). While the fund chairman openly acknowledged that such a conversion to mutual status was "unprecedented in the mutual fund industry," the cautious fund board was interested enough to ask him to expand the scope of his proposal and undertake "a comprehensive review of the best means by which the funds could obtain advisory, management, and administrative services at the lowest reasonable costs to the fund shareholders."* The board also asked Wellington Management Company to produce a similar study.

By March 11, the chairman's first report was completed. Entitled "The Future Structure of the Wellington Group of Investment Companies," the report offered seven structural options, of which the board decided to focus on these four:

1. Status Quo—the continuation of the existing relationships.
2. Internal Administration—administration by the funds themselves; distribution and investment advice from Wellington Management.
3. Internal Administration and Distribution—with only investment advice from Wellington.
4. Mutualization—acquisition by the funds of all of Wellington's fund-related activities.

The Future Structure study spelled out the ultimate objective: *independence.* The goal was "to give the funds an appropriate amount of corporate, business, and economic independence," the chairman wrote, noting that such a structure was clearly contemplated by the Investment Company Act of 1940. But such independence, his study added, had proved to be an illusion in the industry, with "funds being little more than corporate shells . . . with no ability to conduct their

---

*John C. Bogle, "The Future Structure of the Wellington Group of Investment Companies," Part I (March 11, 1974).

own affairs. . . . . This structure has been the accepted norm for the mutual fund industry for more than fifty years."

"The issue we face," he bluntly concluded, "is whether a structure so traditional, so long accepted, so satisfactory for our infant industry as it grew during a time of less stringent ethical and legal standards, is really the optimal structure for these times and for the future—or whether the funds should seek the greater control over their own destiny so clearly implied by the word *independence*." While the fund chairman clearly preferred his original proposal of mutualization, he was prepared to begin with less, concluding the study with these words: "[P]erhaps, then, the issue is not *whether*, but only *when* the Wellington Group will become completely independent."

As it would soon turn out, he would have to be content with less than full mutualization. After much study, even more contention, and debate that sometimes seemed to be endless, the board made its decision on June 11, 1974. It chose the least disruptive option, #2, establishing the funds' own administrative staff under the direction of its operating officers, who would also be responsible, as the board's counsel, former SEC Commissioner Richard B. Smith, wrote, "for monitoring and evaluating the external (investment advisory and distributors) services provided" by Wellington Management. The decision, the counselor added, "was *not* envisaged as a 'first step' to internalize additional functions, but as a structure that . . . can be expected to be continued into the future."

Enter Vanguard

Late in the summer, to the chairman's amazement and disappointment, the board agreed that Wellington Management Company would retain its name. While Wellington Fund would also retain *its* name, a new name would have to be found for the administrative company. In September, he proposed to call the new company "Vanguard" and, after more contention, the board approved the name. The Vanguard Group, Inc. was incorporated on September 24, 1974. Early in 1975, the SEC cleared, without apparent difficulty, the funds' proxy statements proposing the change; the fund shareholders approved it; and

Vanguard, a wholly owned subsidiary of the funds operating on an at-cost basis, began operations on May 1, 1975.

But no sooner than the ink was dry on the various agreements, things began to change. With the funds controlling only one leg— and, arguably, the least important leg—of the operations/investment management/distribution tripod on which any fund complex rests, the chairman began to have second thoughts. As he would later write,

> It was a victory of sorts, but, I feared, a Pyrrhic victory. . . .
> I had realized all along that the narrow mandate that pre-cluded our engaging in portfolio management and distri-bution services would give Vanguard insufficient power to control its destiny. . . . Why? Because success in the fund field is *not* driven by how well the funds are administered. Though their affairs must be supervised and controlled with dedication, skill, and precision, success is determined by what kinds of funds are created, by how they are managed, by whether superior investment returns are attained, and by how—and how effectively—the funds are marketed and distributed. We had been given one-third of the fund loaf, as it were, but it was the least important third. It was the other two-thirds that would make us or break us.*

The next one-third of the loaf was seized quickly. The newly named Vanguard Group's entry into the investment management arena came in a groundbreaking way. Only a few short months after the firm began operations, the board of the funds approved the creation of an index fund, modeled on the Standard & Poor's 500 Stock Index. It was incorporated late in 1975. When its initial public offering was completed in August 1976, it had raised a disappointing $11 million. But the world's first index mutual fund had come into existence. It is now the largest mutual fund in the world.

Only five years after that halting entry into what was, arguably, equity investment management, the firm assumed full responsibility

---

*John C. Bogle, *Character Counts: The Creation and Building of the Vanguard Group* (New York: McGraw-Hill, 2002), 5, 6.

for the management of Vanguard's bond and money market funds. A decade later, Vanguard began to also manage equity funds that relied on quantitative techniques rather than fundamental analysis. A variety of external advisers continue to manage Vanguard's actively managed equity and balanced funds, now constituting some $180 billion of the Group's $700 billion of assets. (Wellington Management continues to manage Wellington Fund, as it has throughout the fund's now-75-year history.)

Improved Returns in a Full-Fledged Alpha Complex

The final one-third of the mutual fund loaf was acquired only five months after the index fund IPO had brought investment management under Vanguard's aegis. On February 9, 1977, yet another unprecedented decision brought share distribution into the fold. After yet another contentious debate in a politically charged environment, and by the narrowest of margins, the fund board accepted the chairman's recommendation that the funds terminate their distribution agreements with Wellington Management, eliminate all sales charges, and abandon the broker-dealer distribution system that had distributed Wellington shares for nearly a half-century. Overnight, Vanguard had eliminated its entire distribution system, and moved from the seller-driven, load-fund channel to the buyer-driven, no-load channel. Narrow as the mandate was, it set the fledgling organization on a new and unprecedented course.

What would the flourishing of Vanguard into a full-fledged Alpha complex—its full mutualization—mean to its fund investors? First, it would mean far lower fund operating expenses, with the group's weighted expense ratio tumbling from an average of 0.67 percent in 1975 to 0.26 percent in 2002—a reduction of more than 60 percent. Second, it would mean that the earlier 8.5 percent front-end load—and the performance drag on shareholder returns inevitably entailed by that initial sales charge—would be forever removed. And since gross returns in the financial markets, minus costs, equal the net returns earned by investors, this slashing of costs was virtually certain to enhance shareholder returns.

And that's just what Vanguard's change from Omega to Alpha did. What followed over the subsequent 29 years was a major enhancement in the *absolute* returns (sheer good luck!) and the *relative* returns earned by Wellington Fund. Specifically, this balanced fund provided an annual return of 12.9 percent from 1974–2003, actually *outpacing* the 12.3 percent annual return of its unmanaged (and cost-free) benchmark—35 percent Lehman Aggregate Bond Index, 65 percent Standard & Poor's 500 Stock Index, an allocation comparable to Wellington's—and by a wider margin, the 11.1 percent rate of return earned by the average balanced fund (Figure 12.6). During the comparable prior period (1945–1974) under the Omega structure, the Fund's return of just 5.7 percent had actually *lagged* the benchmark return of 7.6 percent by a full 1.9 percentage points per year.

Part of that near-miraculous 2.5 percentage point *annual* improvement in relative returns—a staggering margin—was related to lower costs. The Fund's average expense ratio, low enough in the earlier period at 0.56 percent, fell 20 percent to 0.45 percent, and the sales charge drag was eliminated. But the largest part of the improvement arose from a 1978 change in the Fund's investment strategy, in

FIGURE 12.6   AVERAGE ANNUAL RETURNS: WELLINGTON FUND VERSUS BENCHMARK

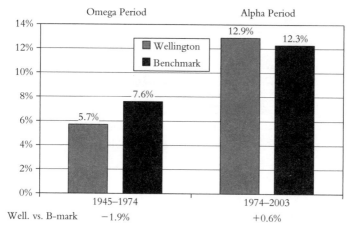

which the *Fund's* management directed its reluctant adviser to return Wellington to its traditional conservative, income-oriented policies from which it had strayed during the late 1960s and 1970s. Result: By the end of 2003, each $1 invested in Wellington Fund in 1974 would have grown to $33.60 (Figure 12.7). The same investment in the balanced index benchmark, on the other hand, would have grown to just $28.90. (A similar investment in the average balanced fund would have grown to just $20.96—about 40 percent *below* Wellington's value.) The lower chart in Figure 12.7 presents a stunning contrast with the lower chart in Figure 12.4.

Other than the direct impact of costs, it is not easy to characterize "cause and effect" in the attribution of investment performance. While Wellington Fund's return to its conservative investment tradition was a major benefit, the new Alpha structure itself, under which Wellington Management became an external investment adviser that *had* to perform in order to retain its independent client, could well have itself provided a major benefit. While we can't be certain, the development of the arm's-length relationship that is part of the Alpha model clearly did no harm.

FIGURE 12.7   PERFORMANCE OF WELLINGTON FUND AND BENCHMARK, 1974–2003

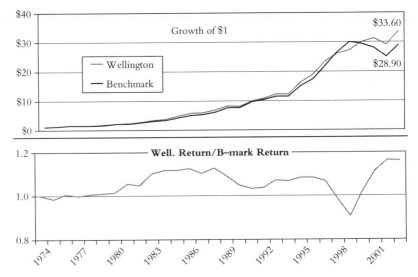

Alpha versus Omega: Lower Costs and Higher Market Share

Whatever the case, we do know that there is a powerful and pervasive relationship between expense ratios and fund net returns. We know, for example, that the correlation coefficient of the 10-year returns of individual equity funds and their costs is a remarkably impressive *negative 0.60*. We also know that during *each* of the past two decades the returns of the equity funds in the *low-cost* quartile have consistently outpaced the returns of funds in the *high-cost* quartile by an enormous margin of about 2.5 percent per year. *The higher the cost, the lower the return.* And it is crystal clear that the Alpha model of fund operations is, well, cheap, while the Omega model is dear.

The contrast in costs could hardly be sharper than in the two fund complexes we have just considered. Both were dominated by a single mutual fund until the 1960s, before becoming more and more diversified fund complexes thereafter. Both had roughly comparable assets under management up until the 1980s—in the hundreds of millions in the 1950s, then the billions in the 1960s and 1970s, growing to the tens of billions in the 1980s. Then their paths diverged. While Massachusetts Financial Services enjoyed solid asset growth to some $94 billion at the market's peak in 2000, Vanguard grew even faster, then overseeing some $560 billion of assets.

Late in their Alpha period, the asset-weighted expense ratio of the MFS funds averaged less than 0.25 percent. Under its new Omega model, the MFS ratio jumped to 0.67 percent in 1984, to 0.92 percent in 1988, to 1.20 percent in 1993, and to 1.25 percent in 2002, an *increase* of 421 percent for the full period (Figure 12.8). By way of contrast, late in their Omega period the Vanguard funds' ratio averaged about 0.60 percent. Under its new Alpha structure, the Vanguard ratio tumbled to 0.54 percent in 1984, to 0.40 percent in 1988, and to 0.30 percent in 1993, continuing to drop in 2002 to just 0.26 percent, a *reduction* of 61 percent from the pre-Alpha rate.

These ratios may seem diminutive and trivial, but they are not. They entail hundreds of millions, even billions, of dollars. In 2003, the assets of the Omega MFS funds totaled $78 billion, and their 1.25 percent expense ratios, including management fees, 12b-1 fees, and

FIGURE 12.8   THE ALPHA AND OMEGA: VANGUARD AND MFS EXPENSE RATIOS

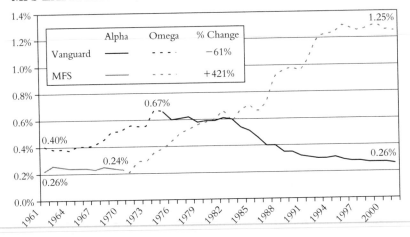

operating costs, totaled $975 million. Had their earlier 0.25 percent ratio prevailed, those costs would have been just $195 million, a remarkable *$780 million*(!) savings (Table 12.1). Again by way of contrast, assets of the Alpha Vanguard funds totaled $667 billion in 2003; with expenses of $1.7 billion, the expense ratio was 0.26 percent. Had the earlier 0.60 percent ratio under its Omega structure prevailed, Vanguard's expenses would otherwise have been $4.0 billion, representing *$2.3 billion* of additional costs that would have been incurred by its fund shareholders.

Even as Vanguard, under its Alpha structure, did *good* in building value for its fund shareholders, it did *well* in implementing its business

TABLE 12.1   THE MANIFESTATION OF THE ALPHA BENEFIT

	MFS	Vanguard
2003 Assets	$78B	$667B
Omega Expense Ratio	1.25%	0.60%
Fees Generated	$975M	$4,000M
Alpha Expense Ratio	0.25%	0.26%
Fees Generated	$195M	$1,700M
Savings Under	$780M	$2,300M
Alpha Structure	(projected)	(actual)

strategy. Assets under management have grown from $1.4 billion in 1974 to nearly $700 billion currently, and its share of mutual fund industry assets has soared. While a late entry into the money market business resulted in a plunge in its market share from 3.5 percent in 1974 to 1.7 percent in 1981, the rise since then has been unremitting, consistent, and powerful (Figure 12.9). As 2004 begins, Vanguard's share of industry assets stands at 9.2 percent—by far the largest market share increase achieved by any mutual fund firm.

The growth of MFS assets, too, has been awesome—from $3.3 billion in 1969, when it abandoned its original Alpha structure, to $78 billion currently. But its original 7.0 percent market share began to shrink within a few years after the change, falling to just 1.1 percent in 1982, where it remains today. To the extent that we can measure it, then, under the Omega strategy—which is of course the strategy that is pervasive in the industry—the MFS transition from its original roots has not only resulted in increased costs and reduced returns for its fund shareholders, but proved to be a losing strategy in the highly competitive mutual fund marketplace.

Nonetheless, the Omega strategy does have something very important going for it: It is immensely profitable for the funds' *managers*. Immediately after its demutualization in 1969, MFS remained a private

FIGURE 12.9 THE ALPHA AND OMEGA: VANGUARD AND MFS MARKET SHARE

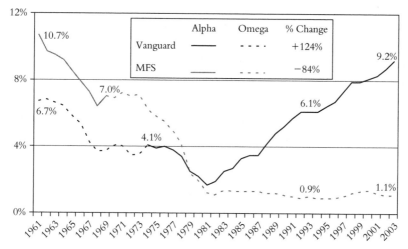

company, with its profits divided among its own executives and employees. But in 1981, in a curious twist, the firm sold itself to Sun Life of Canada, which remains its owner today (MFS executives now hold about 8 percent of its stock). According to Sun Life's financial statements, the pre-tax earnings of MFS during the five-year period 1998–2002 totaled $1,924,000,000, certainly a splendid return on their initial (but undisclosed) capital investment—a near–$2 billion goldmine for the Sun Life shareholders.

Tested in the Crucible

Both the Alpha fund model and the Omega fund model have been tested over almost the entire 80-year history of the industry (1970–1974 was the only period in which no Alpha model existed). The 45-year preeminence that MIT achieved from 1924 to 1969, to say nothing of the flourishing of Vanguard almost from the day it was created, hardly suggest major flaws in the Alpha model. Yet the economics of the business remain a major stumbling block to the creation of new Alpha organizations. If funds are run at cost, after all, there are no profits for the management company owners. It is hardly surprising, then, that Vanguard's structure has yet to be copied, or even imitated.

It is a curious paradox that the transformation of MFS from the Alpha model to the Omega model was accomplished with apparent ease. Vanguard's conversion from Omega to Alpha, however, was fraught not only with contention and debate, but with regulatory opposition. While the internalization of the *administration* of the Wellington funds was straightforward, and even the internalization of the *management* of the index fund raised no regulatory eyebrows, the decision to internalize *distribution* was a bombshell. It was opposed by a Wellington Fund shareholder, who called for—and received—a formal SEC administrative hearing, which was said to be the longest hearing in the history of the Investment Company Act, lasting, if memory serves, something like 10 full days in court, and a long period of examination by the regulators. Finally, in July 1978, after considering the issues, the Administrative Law Judge who presided at the hearing made his decision on our application for the Vanguard funds to jointly assume financial and administrative responsibility for the promotion and distribution of our shares: *rejection!* We were back to square one.

At issue was a long history during which the SEC had successfully argued that funds could not spend their own assets on distribution. (Clearly all major fund complexes were making such expenditures, but it was successfully, if problematically, argued that the managers were paying the distribution costs out of their own profits.) Shortly after we made the no-load decision in February 1977, we had asked for an exemption that would allow the funds to spend a limited amount (a maximum of 0.20 percent of net assets) on distribution. While our argument in favor of this plan was somewhat technical, it came down to the fact that while we would spend $1.3 million on distribution, we would simultaneously slash by $2.1 million the annual advisory fees paid to Wellington Management for that purpose: Assuming responsibility for distribution would result, not in a cost to the funds' shareholders, but in a net *savings* of $800,000 per year.

Happily, the SEC had allowed us to temporarily pursue our distribution plan pending Commission and fund shareholder approval. So Vanguard had in fact been running the distribution system since 1977. Despite his rejection of our plan, the judge gave us the opportunity to amend it, and after making a few technical changes, we resubmitted it early in 1980. With this sword of Damocles suspended above us during this long period, we blithely pursued our distribution activities. The threatening sword was finally removed on February 25, 1981, when the Commission at last rendered its decision.

The decision was a home run for Vanguard! Far better than any characterization I could use to describe the decision, the Commission's words speak for themselves:

> The Vanguard plan is consistent with the provisions, policies, and purposes of the Act. It actually furthers the Act's objectives by ensuring that the Funds' directors, with more specific information at their disposal concerning the cost and performance of each service rendered to the Funds, are better able to evaluate the quality of those services.

The plan will foster improved disclosure to shareholders, enabling them to make a more informed judgment as to the Funds' operations. In addition, the plan clearly enhances the Funds' independence, permitting them to change investment advisers more readily as conditions may dictate. The plan also benefits each fund within a reasonable range of fairness.

Specifically, the Vanguard plan promotes a healthy and viable mutual fund complex within which each fund can better prosper; enables the Funds to realize substantial savings from advisory fee reductions; promotes savings from economies of scale; and provides the Funds with direct and conflict-free control over distribution functions.

Accordingly, we deem it appropriate to grant the application before us.

The decision was unanimous. We had at last formally completed our move from the Omega model under which we had operated for nearly a half-century, to a full-fledged Alpha mutual fund model. Our joy was profound and unrestrained, and our optimism about the future was boundless.

An Elementary Principle, Too Often Ignored

The Commission's decision, in its own blunt words, was based on "one of the 1940 Act's basic policies: that funds should be managed and operated in the best interest of their shareholders, rather than in the interests of advisers, underwriters, or others." And that would also seem to be the most elementary principle of the common law as it relates to fiduciary duty and trusteeship. And yet it must have been obvious to the Commissioners that while they had just approved our Alpha model, the entire rest of the industry was operating under an Omega model in which the advisers and underwriters—the funds' management companies—were in the driver's seat.

Fully 15 years earlier, in fact, the SEC had vigorously recommended legislative changes that were designed to restore a better balance of interest between shareholders and managers. In *Public Policy Implications of Investment Company Growth*, a report to the House Committee on Interstate and Foreign Commerce dated December 2, 1966, the Commission pointedly noted that "internally managed companies which had their own staff had significantly lower management costs than externally managed funds compensated by fees based on a fixed percentage of the fund's assets."

After considering the level of fund fees ($130 million a year seemed large in 1966; but by 2003, fees had soared to *$32 billion*), the far lower fee rates paid by pension plans and internally managed funds, the then-average 48 percent(!) pre-tax profit margin earned by publicly held management companies, and the effective control advisers held over their funds, as well as "the absence of competitive pressures, the limitations of disclosure, the ineffectiveness of shareholder voting rights, and the obstacles to more effective action by the independent directors," the SEC recommended the adoption of a "statutory standard of reasonableness," which it described as a "basic fiduciary standard that would make clear that those who derive benefits from their fiduciary relationships with investment companies cannot charge more for services than if they were dealing with them at arm's length."

The SEC described reasonableness as "a clearly expressed and readily enforceable standard that would measure the fairness of compensation paid for services furnished by those who occupy a fiduciary relationship" to the mutual funds they manage. This standard

> would *not* be measured merely by the cost of comparable services to individual investors or by the fees charged by other externally managed investment companies . . . [but by] the costs of management services to internally managed funds and to pension funds and other non-fund clients . . . [and] their benefit to fund shareholders . . . [including] sustained investment performance.

"The Commission is not prepared to recommend at this time the more drastic statutory requirement of compulsory internalization and the performance of services at cost," the SEC report added, for it "might be more costly for smaller funds . . . or could be insufficient to provide an adequate full time staff . . . [and] might prove a determent to the promotion of new investment companies." Accordingly, the Commission believed that, "an alternative to the more drastic solution of compulsory internalization should be given a fair trial." If the standard of reasonableness does not "resolve the problems in management compensation that exist . . . *then more sweeping steps might deserve to be considered*" (emphasis added).

Alas, the Commission's "reasonableness" proposal was never put to the test. The industry fought hard, and lobbied the Congress vigorously. Finally, five years later, in the Investment Company Amendments Act of 1970, the Commission had to settle for a weak provision in which the investment adviser was charged with "a fiduciary duty with respect to the compensation for services," with damages limited to the actual compensation received, and with no definition of what might constitute reasonableness. And even 33 years later, "more sweeping steps" have yet to be considered.

In its 1966 report, the SEC had also expressed concerns about the growing trend of sales of management companies to other firms at prices far above book value, transfers the Commission opined, that have "some elements of the sale of a fiduciary office, [which is] *strictly prohibited under Common Law*" (emphasis added). It also expressed a concern about earlier "widespread 'trafficking' in advisory contracts." The Commission recommended that the sale of a management company could not take place if it came with "any expense or implied understanding . . . likely to impose *additional* burdens on the fund." The implication that funds were *already* bearing heavy burdens would have been lost on few observers, and even that protection was diluted in the subsequent legislation.

Had the initial SEC recommendations prevailed, they may well have aborted the accelerating trend toward higher fund expense ratios that today seems endemic in the fund industry. The *unweighted* expense ratio of 0.87 percent for the average equity fund that concerned the Commission in 1965 has risen by 86 percent, to 1.62 percent. (For those who think that *asset-weighted* expense ratios are a better test, the increase was from 0.51 percent to 0.95 percent—the same 86 percent increase!)

But we deceive ourselves when we look at fee *rates* instead of fee *dollars*. When applied to the burgeoning assets of equity funds (*$26.3 billion* in 1965 and *$3.36 trillion* in 2003), equity fund expenses have leaped from $134 million in 1965 to an estimated $31.9 billion in 2003

(Table 12.2). That fund expenses have risen 238-fold(!) since 1965, nearly double the 128-fold increase in equity fund assets, in a field in which, as today's lone Alpha fund complex demonstrates, the economies of scale in fund operations are truly staggering, is a truly astonishing anomaly.

Further, the SEC's 1966 concern about trafficking in advisory contracts could hardly have been more prescient. Although a number of fund management firms had gone public with IPOs by then, the large majority remained privately held. Today, only 6(!) privately held firms remain (7 if we include Vanguard) among the largest 50 fund managers. Another 7 are publicly held, and fully 36 are owned by giant financial conglomerates, from Sun Life and Marsh and McLennan, to Deutsche Bank and AXA, to Citicorp and J. P. Morgan. With these consummate *business* firms in control, it is small wonder that the idea of fund management as a *profession* is gradually receding. Using the words I used in my 1971 speech, these firms are "the financial heirs of the [original mutual fund] entrepreneurs . . . if it is a burden to [fund shareholders] to be served by a public enterprise, should this burden exist in perpetuity?"

Apparently the burden *should*. For such trafficking takes place with the tacit consent of fund directors, who seem all too willing to ignore the burdens imposed on funds that are part of giant conglomerates—firms whose overriding goal is a return on *their* capital, even at the expense of the returns on the *fund shareholders'* capital. When such transfers are proposed, fund directors could easily insist on fee reductions—or even mutualization—but they have *never* done so. In a recent sale (for $3.2 billion!) of a large fund manager to Lehman

TABLE 12.2   WHERE ARE THE ECONOMIES OF SCALE?

	1965	2003	Change
Total Equity Assets	$26.3B	$3,361B	+128×
Average Expense Ratio	0.87%	1.62%	+86%
Weighted* Expense Ratio	0.51%	0.95%	+86%
Fees Generated	$134M	$31,900M	+238×

*Weighted by fund assets.
Fees generated uses weighted average.

Brothers, the earlier fee structure remained intact. So far, at least, the directors seem disinclined to act even when a scandal-ridden firm is on the auction block (Strong Management) or is already part of a conglomerate (Putnam, which has delivered nearly $4 billion of pre-tax profits to Marsh and McLennan over the past five years). The idea that "the burdens of public ownership *should* exist in perpetuity" has yet to be challenged.

It Is Time for Change

It is time for change in the mutual fund industry. We need to rebalance the scale on which the respective interests of fund managers and fund shareholders are weighed. Despite the express language of the 1940 Act that arguably calls for *all* of the weight to be on the side of fund shareholders, it is the managers' side of the scale that is virtually touching the ground. To get a preponderance of the weight on the shareholders' side, we need Congress to mandate: (1) an independent fund board chairman; (2) no more than a single management company director; (3) a fund staff or independent consultant that provides objective information to the board; and (4) a federal standard that, using the Act's present formulation, provides that *directors have a fiduciary duty to assure that* "funds are organized, operated, and managed in the interests of their shareholders" rather than in the interests of "their advisers and distributors." (The italicized language would be added to the statute.)

As I wrote five years ago in *Common Sense on Mutual Funds*, changes such as these would at long last allow independent directors "to become ferocious advocates for the rights and interests of the mutual fund shareholders they represent . . . they would negotiate aggressively with the fund adviser . . . they would demand performance-related fees that enrich managers only as fund investors are themselves enriched. . . . They would challenge the use of 12b-1 distribution fees . . . and no longer rubber-stamp gimmick funds cooked-up by marketing executives . . . becoming the fiduciaries they are supposed to be under the law."

Alternatively, and perhaps even more desirably, I then argued, the industry may require "a radical restructuring—the mutualization of at least part of the mutual fund industry. . . . Funds—or at least large fund families—would run themselves; and the huge profits now earned by external managers would be diverted to the shareholders . . . they wouldn't waste money on costly marketing companies designed to bring in new investors at the expense of existing investors. With lower costs, they would produce higher returns and/or assume lower risks. But regardless of the exact structure—(a new) conventional form or a truly mutual form—an arrangement in which fund shareholders and their directors are in working control of a fund will lead . . . to an industry that will enhance economic value for fund shareholders." And it is in that direction that this industry must at last move.

How to Get from Omega to Alpha

During its 45 years of existence, the Alpha operating model instituted by MIT nearly 80 years ago worked well for its shareholders. Similarly, during Vanguard's soon-to-be 30 years of existence, our Alpha model has resulted in amazingly low costs for shareholders, and generally superior returns compared to peer funds, to say nothing of a spectacular (and unmatched) record of asset growth and enhanced market share. As an illustration of a demonstrably winning strategy for fund shareholders, our Alpha model has met the test of time.

Of course, we have enjoyed an advantage some of our rivals have described as "unfair." Since the fund shareholders own Vanguard—lock, stock, and barrel—*none* of their investment returns have had to be diverted to the owners of a management company—private, public, or financial conglomerate, whatever the case may be. Put another way, our structure has been an essential element in the returns that our shareholders have enjoyed. It shouldn't surprise anyone, for as the economist Peter Bernstein has observed, "[W]hat happens to the wealth of individual investors cannot be separated from the structure of the industry that manages those assets."

With MIT long since having abandoned the Alpha model, Vanguard alone has remained to test it. With this single exception, it is the Omega model that prevails. *But I simply cannot accept that today's model can be, as the word "Omega" suggests, the final stage of the mutual fund industry's development.* That this model has ill-served fund investors could hardly be more obvious. This industry's present high levels of operating and transaction costs have led—as they must—to a lag in the returns of the average equity fund of some three percentage points per year behind the stock market itself over the past two decades, with similar cost-related lags for the industry's bond funds and money market funds. And our focus on asset-gathering and marketing has helped to create an even larger lag—at least *another* six or eight percentage points behind the returns of the stock market itself, there for the taking—for the average equity fund *shareholder*.

I have no illusions that a return of industry to its original Alpha model will be easy—not in the face of the powerful forces that are entrenched in this industry and whose economic interests are at stake. But I believe that this is the direction in which shareholders, competition, regulation, and legislation will move. While we won't get all the way to that goal in my lifetime, and maybe not even in the lifetimes of most of my readers, I'm certain that investors will not ignore their own economic interests *forever*.

However, if Congress acts to impose on fund directors the responsibilities that so many of us believe they have always held but rarely exercised, I see no reason that full mutualization should be mandated by law. As long as advisory firms are owned by managers who act responsibly and put the interests of their fund shareholders first, and who make manifest their dedication to that proposition in their actions—self-imposed limits on fees and on marketing activities, focus on long-term investment strategies, and superior service to their shareholders—mutualization hardly need be considered. On the other hand, when a fund complex reaches a certain size or age—when it has become more *business* than *profession*—it is high time to demand that mutualization—the Alpha model—be placed on the board agenda, and honestly and objectively considered. It won't be easily done, of course, and literally *no one* in this industry knows as well as I do the obstacles that may be faced in reaching that goal. But if there is a will, there will be a way.

Structure, Strategy, and Spirit

Yet please understand me: While the Omega structure has caused many of the mutual fund industry's serious shortcomings in serving our shareholders, the Alpha structure is hardly a panacea that will cure them. For a mutualization *structure* in which interests of fund share-holders are placed front and center is, in and of itself, not enough. Without the proper *strategy*, such a structure will lead nowhere. In the ideal, the strategy of mutualization would emphasize low operating costs and more spartan operations, a minimization of the dead weight of marketing costs, and investment policies for stock, bond, and money market funds alike that focus on the wisdom of long-term investing rather than on the folly of short-term speculation.

Strategy, alas, does not necessarily follow structure. One need only look at the life insurance field to see how its sensible mutual struc-ture, finally, came to fail. With their heavy emphasis on sales and their apparent lack of concern about costs, nearly all of the giant mutual life insurance companies relinquished the *strategy* of service to policyhold-ers long before they abandoned their original Alpha *structure*, and this dominant industry of a half-century ago has lost much of its earlier appeal to American families.

But it will take even more than *structure* and *strategy* to get today's Omega mutual fund industry back to its Alpha origins. We need the *spirit* of mutuality—a spirit of trusteeship, a spirit of fiduciary duty, an all-encompassing spirit of *stewardship*—a spirit of service to the 90 mil-lion shareholders who have entrusted the mutual fund industry with their hard-earned dollars. As the recent scandals show, we need regu-lation to curb our avarice. As our record since the publication of the SEC's 1966 report has made clear, we need legislation to improve our governance structure, a major step toward the ideal Alpha structure whose development I have described in this essay. But no regulation, no legislation, can mandate a spirit of trusting and being trusted. Trust must come from within the character of the organization—whether Omega or Alpha—and those firms that evince the spirit of trust will ultimately dominate the mutual fund field. Our industry's future depends on the simple recognition that the management of Other People's Money is a loyal duty and solemn trust.

Chapter 13

A New Order of Things: Bringing Mutuality to the "Mutual" Fund[*]

I'm profoundly honored by the privilege of delivering the Manuel F. Cohen Memorial Lecture for 2008 here at the National Law Center of the George Washington University. Part of my pleasure comes from the fact that, during the latter time of his 27-year tenure at the Securities and Exchange Commission, I came to know Chairman Cohen (universally known as "Manny"). He had served on the staff from 1942 until 1961 and as a member of the Commission from 1961 until 1969, serving as its chairman during the final five years of his tenure. I remember him as being wise, smart, blunt, tough, intolerant of beating around the bush, and a pillar of personal rectitude and professional integrity. It should go without saying that I had the highest admiration for this consummate public servant.

---

*Based on an essay in the Winter 2008 *Wake Forest Law Review*, which in turn was based on the 27th Annual Manuel F. Cohen Memorial Lecture that I delivered at the George Washington University Law School in Washington, D.C., on February 19, 2008.

He left the Commission in 1969 to enter the private practice of law at Wilmer, Cutler and Pickering, but continued to speak out on issues affecting the securities field, lecturing here at the George Washington School of Law. One of his speeches, given when he was SEC Chairman, sets the theme for my own lecture this afternoon. That speech, delivered at the 1968 Federal Bar Conference on Mutual Funds, was entitled simply "The 'Mutual' Fund."* And, yes, he put quotation marks around the word *mutual*. The title—and the theme—of my remarks today follows that same formulation: "A New Order of Things—Bringing Mutuality to the 'Mutual' Fund." Please note that the word *mutual* is again bracketed by quotation marks.

The fact is that "mutual" remains an inappropriate adjective to apply to our business. The operation of virtually all mutual funds is about as far from the concept of mutuality as one can possibly imagine. Hear Chairman Cohen on this point in that 1968 speech: "The basic idea of a 'mutual' fund is deceptively simple," he said, "[but its] salient characteristics raise a serious question whether the word 'mutual' is an appropriate description." While the policyholders of mutual insurance companies and the depositors in mutual savings banks were at least puta-tively sharing in the profit of their institutions, mutual funds, he said, were different, noting that fund shareholders paid fees to their external managers, corporations in business to earn profits for their own share-holders, with a completely different, and often opposed, set of interests.

Chairman Cohen pointedly observed that "the [external] fee struc-ture has provided a real opportunity for the exercise of the ingenuity for which fund managers have established an enviable reputation. After all," he said in his speech, "that is where the money is, and despite the common use of the word 'mutual,' the principal reason these funds are created and sold is to make money for the people who sell them and those who manage them."

Of course he was right. Virtually all mutual funds are organized, operated, and managed, *not* in the interests of their shareholders, but in the interest of their managers and distributors. Is there something improper, or wrong, or unethical about having funds operated with

---

*"The 'Mutual' Fund," an address by Manuel F. Cohen before the 1968 Conference on Mutual Funds, Palm Springs, California, March 1, 1968.

this purpose? Perhaps not. But if this structure is not illegal *per se*, there seems to be something about the way in which the industry has evolved that flies directly in the face of the provisions in the Investment Company Act of 1940 that require that investment companies be "organized, operated, and managed"[*] in the interests of their shareholders, "rather than in the interest of their managers and distributors."[†] (Interestingly, the phrase *mutual funds* does not appear in the statute.)

A Lone Exception to the Conventional Structure

Now, when I said that *virtually* all funds operate under this external management structure, please note that I did not say *all*. The creation of Vanguard in 1974 marked my attempt to create a family of mutual funds that was truly mutual, doing away with the conflict of interest that exists between funds and their advisers, by returning the enormous profits that accrue to external managers directly to the fund shareholders themselves. The now-150 funds in our group actually *own* our manager, The Vanguard Group, Inc., roughly in proportion to their share of the Group's aggregate assets, and share in the total expenses incurred by the funds in their operations in approximately the same proportion. (That is, if a given Vanguard fund represents 1 percent of our assets, it would own 1 percent of Vanguard's shares and assume 1 percent of Vanguard's operating expenses.)

The directors of the funds and their management company are identical. Eight of our nine directors are otherwise unaffiliated with the company, and only one (the chief executive) serves as an officer. No director is permitted to be affiliated with any of the funds' external advisors.[‡] Our funds essentially operate and manage themselves on an

---

[*]Investment Company Act of 1940, 15 U.S.C. § 80a-1(b)(2) (2000), available at www.sec.gov/aboutlaws/ica40.pdf.

[†]*In re: The Vanguard Group, Inc.*, Investment Company Act Release No. 11,645, 22 SEC Docket 238 (Feb. 25, 1981).

[‡]The investment advice for approximately 70 percent of Vanguard's fund assets—largely index, bond, and money market funds—is provided internally by Vanguard itself. The remaining 30 percent is advised under contracts held by a score of external advisers.

"at-cost" basis, enabling our shareowners to garner the extraordinary economies of scale that characterize investment management (i.e., the costs of managing $10 billion of assets is nowhere near 10 times the cost of managing $1 billion). It is fair to describe Vanguard as the only truly "mutual" mutual fund complex.

This shareholder-first structure has produced enormous savings for investors in the Vanguard funds. For example, in 2007, our composite expense ratio of 0.21 percent (21 "basis points") was 76 basis points below the 0.97 percent (97-basis-point) composite weighted average expense ratio of our largest competitors. That saving, applied to our average assets of $1.2 trillion during the year, came to almost $10 billion for 2007 alone. By 2009, cumulative savings for our mutual fund owners will have crossed the $100 billion mark.

Whence "Mutual"?

The Vanguard structure is unique in industry annals. While the first mutual fund (Massachusetts Investors Trust, formed in 1924) was managed by its own trustees rather than by an external company—a structure it abandoned in favor of the external structure in 1969—its shares were marketed and financed by a separately owned distribution company. And while the funds in the Tri-Continental (now Seligman) group were for many years operated at cost by their management company, the manager reaped substantial (if undisclosed) profits by serving as the broker-dealer for the funds' portfolio transactions.* In 1978, this structure, too, was converted into an external manager structure.

Since the word "mutual" did not appear in the Investment Company Act of 1940, whence did it arise? I've looked through those old *Investment Companies* manuals published by Arthur Weisenberger & Company

---

*While the funds operated by TIAA-CREF and USAA have a shareholder-oriented structure that is similar in philosophy to Vanguard's, they differ by being managed, in effect, by insurance/annuity providers that are themselves mutual, owned by their policyholders. While the funds pay fees to the manager in the same way as in the conventional external model, those fees are far below industry norms.

all the way back to the 1945 edition, and it is not until that 1949 edition, a quarter-century after the industry began, that I find the first mention of *mutual* funds. But while the derivation of the term remains a mystery, the paradoxical fact is that it first appears only a short time before the industry began to abandon its early mutual values.

History confirms that from the inception of the first U.S. mutual fund in 1924 until the late 1940s, the predominant focus of mutual fund management was on portfolio selection and investment advice, rather than on distribution and marketing. In fact, the managers who founded not only Massachusetts Investors Trust, but State Street Investment Corporation and Incorporated Investors, the original "Big Three" of the fund industry, put themselves forth as "the twentieth-century embodiment of the old Boston trustee."*

During the industry's early years, sales of fund shares were often the responsibility of separate underwriting firms financed by distribution revenues from sales loads, and predominately unaffiliated with fund managers. For example, "the primary concern of the State Street [Research and Management Company] partners was that they not be distracted by the sales effort. As they wrote to investors in 1933, 'it is our intention to turn over the active selling and the commissions to dealers . . . thereby leaving us free to devote . . . our entire time and effort to research and the study of the problems of investment.'" (The partners were even better than their word; in 1944 the fund entirely ceased the sale of its shares.)

The same spirit was echoed by Judge Robert F. Healy, the SEC Commissioner primarily responsible for the development of the legislation leading to the Investment Company Act of 1940. Here's how he opened his testimony at the hearings for the Act in 1939: "The solution (to the industry's) shocking record of malfeasance . . . was a group of expert trust managers who do not make their profits . . . distributing trust securities, styled principally for their sales appeal, but from wise, careful management of the funds entrusted to them." The SEC Commissioners, Judge Healy said, "were anxious to protect the fund

---

*This and the quotations that follow over the next three pages are from Michael Yogg's fine book, *Passion for Reality* (Xlibris, 2006).

investor from the distorting impact of sales. *Products* [Italics added] designed for their appeal to the market did not, and do not, necessarily make the best investments."

Legendary industry pioneer Paul Cabot, one of State Street's founders and a major force in the drafting of the 1940 Act, agreed with the SEC on this point. Earlier, in 1928, he had described the abuses in the investment-trust movement of the day as "(1) dishonesty; (2) inattention and inability; (3) greed, by which he meant simply charging too much for the services rendered. 'Even if a fund is honestly and ably run, it may be inadvisable to own it simply because there is nothing in it for you. *All the profits go to the promoters and managers*'" (emphasis added).

While the derivation of the term *mutual* remains obscure, the prudent idealism that undergirded the spirit of the industry when the 1940 Act was drafted arguably justified the use of the term. Yet *mutual fund* actually came into being just as the industry began to turn away from its original spirit of mutuality, from its early mission of stewardship of investor assets to its modern-day mission of salesmanship, a mission, as Chairman Cohen seemed to be suggesting, that would make the use of the term "mutual" something of a joke.

The Straw That Broke the Camel's Back

As with any transformation, multiple, doubtless innumerable, factors were responsible for the sea change that gradually subverted the fund industry's mission. Operating for decades as an industry composed of a group of small firms, entirely privately owned by the professional managers who were actually providing the advisory services, and focused on earning a return on the capital that investors had entrusted to them, the industry gradually morphed into a group of giant firms, largely publicly owned and controlled by corporate executives whose mission was asset gathering, and focused on earning a return on the capital of the owners of the management company. But the proverbial "straw that broke the camel's back" of the traditional industry was when the owners of privately held management companies gained the right to sell their ownership positions to outsiders, and then to the public, and finally to giant financial conglomerates.

Paul Cabot did not approve of that change. For him, the private ownership of fund managers was essential. Indeed it represented a moral imperative for him, and he sharply criticized firms that would sell out to insurance companies and other financial institutions. In 1971, he recalled the negotiations over the Investment Company Act of 1940: "Both the SEC and our industry committee agreed that the management contract between the fund and the management group was something that belonged . . . to the fund . . . and therefore the management group had no right to hypothecate it, to sell it, to transfer it, or to make money on the disposition of this contract . . . the fiduciary does not have the right to sell his job to somebody else at a profit."

Yet, ironically, in 1982, Paul Cabot's successors did exactly that: The partners of State Street Research and Management Company sold the firm to the (paradoxically, then-mutual) Metropolitan Life Insurance Company for an astonishing (in those ancient days) profit of $100 million. The stated reasoning of the Fund's board: "[T]he affiliation of State Street with an organization having the financial and marketing resources of Metropolitan Life will result in the development of new products and services which the fund may determine would be beneficial to its [the fund's] shareholders." (Mr. Cabot, still a partner, was apparently enriched to the tune of $20 million, in 1982 dollars.)

It is hard to imagine how such "new products and services would be beneficial" to the *fund's* shareholders, even as they would likely benefit the *management company*, which became a subsidiary of the insurance behemoth. In fact, the merger hurt the fund shareholders. "Performance lagged, and the manager's position in the industry declined from tops to average." By 2002, Metropolitan Life abandoned the fund business, selling State Street Management and Research Company to Blackrock Financial for an estimated $375 million. Among Blackrock's first moves was to put State Street Investment Corporation out of its misery, merging the industry's third-oldest fund into another Blackrock fund. I still refer to this event as "a death in the family."

The Floodgates Open

The sale and resale of State Street exemplified what might be called the "trafficking" in fund advisory contacts that greatly concerned the Commission during the drafting of the 1940 Act. But while the SEC and the industry agreed that the management contract was an asset of the fund, the 1940 Act failed explicitly to articulate this sound principle. It would be only a matter of time until a sale would take place. That sale opened the floodgates to public ownership of fund management companies.

The date was April 7, 1958, when the United States Court of Appeals for the Ninth Circuit ruled that the 1956 sale of shares in Insurance Securities, Incorporated (ISI), at a price equal to nearly 15 times its book value, did not constitute "gross misconduct" or "gross abuse of trust" under Section 36 of the 1940 Act. The SEC had gone to court to oppose the sale, on the grounds that the excess price represented a payment for succession to the adviser's fiduciary office.

The Court agreed with the Commission that "the well-established principles of equity barred a trustee standing in a fiduciary relationship with another from either transfer of the office or exploiting such a relationship for personal gain." But it weighed even more heavily the fact that the value of the contract, rather than representing an asset of the trust fund, represented the reality that the manager receives a profit for rendering its services in return for stipulated fees that the fund had contracted to pay.

Well-decided or ill-decided by the Ninth Circuit (I believe the latter*), the U.S. Supreme Court refused *certiorari*. And that was that. That narrow legal decision, now almost exactly a half-century ago, played a definitive role in setting the industry on a new course

---

*A note in the *Harvard Law Review* of April 1959 (vol. 72, no. 6) agreed with me, taking issue with the Ninth Circuit's decision: "If [the Act] is construed to incorporate the basic principle that a fiduciary owes individual loyalty to the beneficiary and must avoid any conflict of interest, then a seller should not be allowed to transfer his fiduciary office for personal gain. . . ." (p. 180).

in which manager entrepreneurship in the search for personal profit would supersede manager stewardship in the search for prudent investment returns for fund shareholders.

Within a decade, many of the major firms in the fund industry joined the public ownership bandwagon, including Vance Sanders (now Eaton Vance), Dreyfus, Franklin, Putnam, and even Wellington (the firm I had joined in 1951, right out of college). Over the next decade, T. Rowe Price and Keystone (now Evergreen) also went public. In the era that followed, financial conglomerates acquired industry giants such as Massachusetts Financial Services (adviser to the fund complex of which MIT had become a part), Putnam, State Street, American Century, Oppenheimer, Alliance, AIM, Delaware, and many others. The trickle became a river, and then an ocean.

Today (continuing that somewhat stretched analogy), the tide of public ownership of fund management companies has come in, and the tide of private ownership is at an all-time low. Among the 50 largest mutual fund management complexes, only 8 have maintained their original private structure—including Fidelity, Capital Group (American Funds), Dodge & Cox, and TIAA-CREF, plus Vanguard, owned by its fund shareholders. Of the remaining 41 firms on the list, 9 are publicly held (including T. Rowe Price, Eaton Vance, Franklin, and Janus) and 32 are owned by banks, giant brokerage firms, and U.S. and international conglomerates. As we shall soon see, this seemingly irresistible tide of public—largely conglomerate—ownership has ill-served mutual fund shareholders.

Vanguard Goes the Other Way

Only a single firm resisted this epic tide. In the context of my theme this evening, the story of its creation is a story worth telling. As you may recall, in 1960, my employer, Wellington Management Company, was among the firms to ride that early wave of industry IPOs. In 1965, when I was given the responsibility of leading the firm, I recognized the challenge involved in serving those two demanding masters whose interests were so often in direct conflict. To state the obvious, we had a fiduciary duty *both* to our fund shareholders *and* to our management company shareholders as well. However, when a privately held management company becomes publicly held, this conflict is exacerbated.

In September 1971, I went public with my concerns. Speaking at the annual meeting of my Wellington partners, I began my remarks with a 1934 quotation from Justice Harlan Fiske Stone: "Most of the mistakes and major faults of the financial era that has just drawn to a close will be ascribed to the failure to observe the fiduciary principle, the precept as old as holy writ, that 'a man cannot serve two masters.' . . . Those who serve nominally as trustees but consider only last the interests of those who funds they command suggest how far we have ignored the necessary implications of that principle." It is high time, I added, that any conflicts between the profession of finance and the business of finance must be reconciled in favor of the client. It is a matter of fiduciary principle.

I then explored some ideas about how such a reconciliation might be achieved, including, "a mutualization, whereby the funds acquire the management company . . . or internalization, whereby the active executives own the management company, with contracts negotiated on a 'cost-plus' basis, with incentives for both performance and efficiency, but without the ability to capitalize earnings through public sale."

Within three years, a situation developed in which I was put in a position whereby I would not only *talk the talk* about mutualization, but would *walk the walk*.* Even before the 1973–1974 bear market began, the investment returns of the Wellington funds had begun to deteriorate (both on an absolute and on a relative basis) and the large cash *inflows* they had enjoyed had turned to huge cash *outflows*. Assets of our flagship, the conservative Wellington Fund, had tumbled from $2 billion in 1965 to less than $1 billion, on the way to a low of $480 million. Wellington Management Company's earnings plummeted, and its stock price followed suit. This concatenation of dire events was enough to destroy the happy partnership formed by an unfortunate

---

*An expanded version of this transaction can be found in Chapter 12.

merger I implemented in 1966, and I got the axe as Wellington Management Company's CEO on January 23, 1974. But—here's the catch—I remained as chairman of the mutual funds, with their largely separate (and largely independent) board of directors.

Shortly before the firing, seeing the handwriting on the wall, I submitted a proposal to the *mutual fund* board of directors under which the Wellington Group of mutual funds would acquire Wellington Management Company and its business assets. The company would become a wholly owned subsidiary of the funds and serve as investment adviser and distributor on an "at-cost" basis. I openly acknowledged that my mutualization proposal was "unprecedented in the mutual fund industry." The cautious fund board nonetheless asked me to expand the scope of my proposal and undertake "a comprehensive review of the best means by which the funds could obtain advisory, management, and administrative services at the lowest reasonable costs to the fund shareholders."

My first report, completed on March 11, 1974, was entitled "The Future Structure of the Wellington Group of Investment Companies." It spelled out the ultimate objective for the fund shareholders: *independence*. The goal was "to give the funds an appropriate amount of corporate, business, and economic independence," under a mutual structure that was clearly contemplated by the Investment Company Act of 1940. But, I added, such independence had proved to be an illusion in the industry, with "funds being little more than corporate shells . . . with no ability to conduct their own affairs. . . . This structure has been the accepted norm for the mutual fund industry for more than fifty years."

On June 11, 1974, perhaps unsurprisingly, the board rejected my proposal to have the funds acquire the manager, and chose a different option, the least disruptive of the seven options that I had offered. We established the funds' own administrative staff under the direction of its operating officers, with my continuing as their chairman and president. We would also be responsible, as the board's counsel, former SEC Commissioner Richard B. Smith wrote, "for monitoring and evaluating the external (investment advisory and distribution) services provided" by Wellington Management. The decision, the counselor added, "was *not* envisaged as a 'first step' to internalize additional functions, but as a structure that . . . can be expected to be continued into the future."

Since the Board agreed that Wellington Management Company would retain its name (and Wellington Fund would also retain *its* name), a new name would have to be found for the administrative company. I proposed to name the new company "Vanguard" and the Board approved, albeit somewhat reluctantly. The Vanguard Group, Inc. was incorporated on September 24, 1974. Without apparent difficulty, the SEC soon cleared the funds' proxy statements proposing the change, which the fund shareholders promptly approved. Vanguard began operations on May 1, 1975.

No sooner than the ink was dry on the various agreements, the situation began to change. The creation of Vanguard, as I've written, "was a victory of sorts, but, I feared, a Pyrrhic victory . . . and the narrow mandate that precluded our engaging in portfolio management and distribution services would give Vanguard insufficient power to control its destiny. Why? Because success in the fund field was not then, and is not now, driven by how well the funds are *administered*. Though their affairs must be supervised and controlled with dedication, skill, and precision, success [will be] determined by what kinds of funds are created, by how they are managed, by whether superior investment returns are attained, and by how—and how effectively— the funds are marketed and distributed."

We first determined to start a new fund that we would manage internally. Paradoxically (if not disingenuously), it would be a fund that arguably didn't conflict with our limited mandate, for, technically speaking, it wasn't *managed*. It was the world's first index mutual fund, modeled on the Standard & Poor's 500 Stock Index. Incorporated late in 1975, its initial public offering was completed in August 1976. While the offering raised a puny $11 million, despite that unhappy start, Vanguard 500 Index Fund is now among the largest mutual funds in the world.

Our control over fund marketing came only shortly thereafter. On February 9, 1977, after yet another contentious debate, the fund board accepted my recommendation that the funds terminate their distribution agreements with Wellington Management, eliminate all sales charges, and abandon the broker-dealer network that had distributed

Wellington shares since its inception in 1929. (I argued that we weren't violating the memorandum of understanding by *internalizing* distribution. Rather we were *eliminating* distribution.) While the board approval was by the narrowest of margins, Vanguard moved, literally overnight, from a seller-driven, load-fund channel we had relied upon for almost a half-century to the buyer-driven, no-load channel we maintain to this day. Only 21 months after Vanguard began operations, the fledgling organization had become a fully functioning fund complex. What we called "the Vanguard Experiment" in fund governance was about to begin in earnest.

Let's See How It All Worked Out

It will soon be 34 years since Vanguard began operating under its unique mutual structure, and almost exactly 50 years since that ghastly Ninth Circuit decision opened the door of public ownership to fund managers and led to the age of conglomeration that has now overwhelmed the industry. Surely it must occur to you that the philosophies underlying these two events are diametrically opposite. Outside ownership, in effect, demands that investment funds be viewed as *products* of their management companies, manufactured (in the current grotesque parlance) and distributed to earn a profit for the company. Mutual ownership, on the other hand, views mutual funds—yes, *mutual* funds—as trust accounts, managed under the direction of prudent fiduciaries.* It's high time to look at the record, and compare the results achieved by the firms following these opposing philosophies.

As I'm fond of saying, over our three-plus decades of our existence, Vanguard has proven to be both a *commercial* success and an *artistic* success—a commercial success, because our structure has been proven to be a superb business model. The assets we manage for investors have grown from $1.4 billion at our 1974 founding to some *$1.2 trillion* today. At this moment, in fact, we may well be the largest firm in our industry. (In fairness, Vanguard, American Funds, and Fidelity have

---

*I intensely dislike the use of the word "product" to describe an investment company, and, early in Vanguard's history, banned its use at the firm.

gone back and forth in the lead position for several years now. Each of these giants manages about *three times* the fund assets of the next largest firms, Franklin Templeton and Barclays Global.)

Of course, the stock market boomed during that period (at least through early 2000), and the fund industry could hardly help but flourish. Nonetheless, Vanguard's market share of industry assets has soared from a mere 1.8 percent in 1980 to 10.6 percent currently, *without a single year of decline.* Let me illustrate the impact of that rise in share: If it had remained at 1.8 percent, assets of the Vanguard funds today would be $220 billion. Thus, fully $1 trillion of our growth—80 percent of it—has come from our increased market share; that is, out of the pockets of our competitors. (Not bad, dare I say, for a firm in which I consistently drummed home this philosophy: "Market share is a measure, *not* an objective; market share must be earned, *not* bought.")

How did we earn that commercial success? By our artistic success, which I define as providing superior investment returns to our shareholders. The data indicate that the performance of the Vanguard funds was indeed superior. To the contrary, the financial conglomerates that now dominate this industry generally produced performance returns that were distinctly inferior.

There are, of course, lots of ways to measure fund performance. I'll use one of the more sensible methodologies, relying largely on the Morningstar system, in which the risk-adjusted returns of each fund are compared with the risk-adjusted returns of its peers over a full decade (albeit with a heavier weighting on the recent years of the decade). For example, a given manager's large-cap growth fund is compared with other large-cap growth funds; its investment-grade intermediate-term corporate bond fund with other peers, and so on. Under this system, 10 percent of funds receive five stars (the top rating) and 10 percent one star (the bottom rating); 2.5 percent receive four stars and 2.5 percent receive two stars; the middle 35 percent receive the average grade of three stars.*

---

*By weighting the analysis by number of funds rather than by assets, this procedure has one strength not in evidence in other methodologies, which almost invariably ignore the impact of sales loads. My methodology captures the returns of "B" and "C" shares, usually smaller in assets but which have sales loads built into their expense ratios. This method gives a more realistic picture of the net returns actually delivered to fund shareholders in all share classes.

My deceptively simple methodology is to calculate, for each fund complex, the percentage of its funds in the four- and five-star categories, and subtract from that total the percentage of funds in the one- and two-star categories. The result: the balance between funds that provided distinctly superior returns and those that provided distinctly inferior returns. While I've never seen this done before (although there's lots of promotional bluster for funds that get four or five stars), my own view is that staying out of the one- and two-star categories is at least an equally important benefit for shareholders.

We measured the returns achieved by the 50 largest fund complexes, defined as the firms managing at least 40 individual funds, excluding money market funds. (The complex with the largest number of funds, Fidelity, includes 471 long-term funds.) Only one of these firms managed less than about $25 billion. This remarkably representative list includes more than 8,800 funds with some $7 trillion in fund assets, 80 percent of the industry's long-term asset base.

The full study is clearly too extensive to inflict on this audience, but I've presented it in the appendix of this essay (see Table 13.4). What I'll now present to you (Table 13.1) is a summary showing the scores of six of the top firms, the bottom six firms, and six fairly well-known firms that achieved roughly average performance records for their funds. The top-ranking fund complex, in terms of providing superior returns to its investors, was Vanguard. With 59 percent of our funds in the top group and less than 5 percent in the bottom group, the firm's performance rating is +54.*

Joining Vanguard among the top three are DFA and TIAA-CREF, both at +50. (More than coincidentally, all three firms are focused largely on index-like strategies.) At number four is T. Rowe Price (+44), followed by Janus (+38) and American Funds (+26). Honestly, I think most objective observers would agree that over the past decade, at least five of these six firms have been conspicuous in delivering superior risk-adjusted returns, a judgment that confirms the methodology. Again more

---

*Full disclosure: Two much smaller firms have higher ratings. Dodge & Cox, with 4 funds, is at +100; Royce and Associates, with 31 funds, has a score of +65.

TABLE 13.1   MAJOR MUTUAL FUND MANAGERS:
FUND PERFORMANCE*

| | | Manager | Percent of Funds Ranked | | |
			Highest 4 or 5 Stars	Lowest 1 or 2 Stars	Highest Minus Lowest
	1	Vanguard	59%	5%	54%
	2	DFA	57	7	50
Highest	3	TIAA-CREF	54	4	50
Returns	4	T Rowe Price	53	9	44
	5	Janus	54	16	38
	6	American Funds	46	20	26
	7	Franklin Temp.	31	22	9
	8	Morgan Stanley	32	30	2
Average	9	Fidelity	31	34	−3
Returns	10	Barclays Global	27	31	−4
	11	AIM Inv.	20	34	−14
	12	Columbia Funds	23	38	−14
	13	Goldman Sachs	15	55	−40
	14	Dreyfus	12	53	−40
Lowest	15	MainStay Funds	20	60	−40
Returns	16	John Hancock	17	60	−43
	17	ING Investments	9	64	−55
	18	Putnam	4	62	−58

*Morningstar ratings as of 12/2007 (long-term funds only).

than coincidentally, this six-firm list is dominated by four management companies that are not publicly owned—Vanguard, DFA, TIAA-CREF, and American—and none are controlled by conglomerates.

On the other hand, each of the bottom six firms are units of giant brokerage firms or financial conglomerates. Their ratings range from −40 for Goldman Sachs to an astonishing −58 for Putnam, with only 4 percent of its funds in the top category and 62 percent ranking in the bottom category. Strikingly, every one of the 17 lowest-ranking firms on the 50-firm list is conglomerate-held, while only one of the firms among the top 10 can be similarly characterized.*

---

* The success of Neuberger Berman, ranking #8 with a score of +19, was largely achieved before its 2003 sale to Lehman Brothers.

The middle group—all producing more or less average scores (mostly less) for their funds—includes one publicly held firm (Franklin, +9), one owned by a giant investment banker (Morgan Stanley, +2), one privately held (Fidelity, −3), and three owned by conglomerates (all below par, at −4, −14, and −14). Putting the three groups—high-performing, average-performing, and low-performing—together, it seems patently obvious that the truly mutual structure (which has only a single entrant) and the other three privately held structures that dominate the top group have provided consistently superior returns for their shareholders, with an average score of plus 48—54 percent in the top group and only 6 percent at the bottom. This positive score stands in sharp contrast with the inferior scores that characterize the financial conglomerates at the bottom, with an average score of minus 46—13 percent in the top group and 59 percent in the one- and two-star categories.

Performance Evaluations from a Higher Authority

While the performance methodology I have chosen is inevitably imperfect, I believe that it is not only entirely reasonable, but a significant enhancement over most other methodologies. But, let's not rely only on the statistics to evaluate fund performance. Let's find out how the fund shareholders themselves regard the funds they actually own. Happily, thanks to a survey done in 2007 by Cogent Research LLC, we have measures of how fund shareholders feel about the mutual fund firms that manage their money. (The study focused on shareholders who have mutual fund investments of at least $100,000.)

The Cogent study, reported by the *Wall Street Journal,** measured client loyalty, presenting investors with a scale representing the extent of their trust in their managers—10 the highest rating ("definitely recommend" to other investors), 1 the lowest ("definitely *not* recommended"). Each firm was scored by subtracting the percentage of

---

* The *Journal* published the ratings for only eight of the firms in the survey. The other ratings were made available for this paper. Many of the firms in the performance survey were not included in the loyalty survey.

shareholders who rated the firms at 5 or below ("detractors") from the percentage who rated the firms at 9 or 10 ("supporters"). Only 11 of the 38 firms evaluated had positive loyalty scores. The average score was −12, a message about investor confidence in the fund industry that would not seem to be much of a tribute.

Simply put, fund shareholders seem to "get it." When we juxtapose these loyalty scores for each firm with its performance scores, we see a remarkable, if by no means exact, correlation (Table 13.2). In fact, Vanguard's performance score (+54) and its loyalty score (+44), both the highest in the field, were quite similar. Putnam's scores, also similar (−58 and −54, respectively), were the lowest in the field. Of course there is a relationship between how well one has served investors and how loyal they are!

TABLE 13.2   MAJOR MUTUAL FUND MANAGERS: FUND PERFORMANCE AND SHAREHOLDER LOYALTY

		Manager	Percent of Funds Ranked Highest Minus Lowest	Client Loyalty Score
	1	Vanguard	54%	44%
	2	DFA	50	n/a
Highest	3	TIAA-CREF	50	n/a
Returns	4	T Rowe Price	44	21
	5	Janus	38	−30
	6	American Funds	26	12
	7	Franklin Temp.	9	1
	8	Morgan Stanley	2	−18
Average	9	Fidelity	−3	12
Returns	10	Barclays Global	−4	n/a
	11	AIM Inv.	−14	−48
	12	Columbia Funds	−14	−47
	13	Goldman Sachs	−40	−32
	14	Dreyfus	−40	−45
Lowest	15	MainStay Funds	−40	n/a
Returns	16	John Hancock	−43	−10
	17	ING Investments	−55	−11
	18	Putnam	−58	−54

There were also numerous significant disparities between the two scores. Most of them were explained, I think, because the performance ratings that I presented reflect the returns *reported* by mutual funds. But such reporting has a major failing. To be blunt about it, fund investors could hardly care less about reported returns when they vastly overstate the returns that they've actually earned. That's often the case in this business, for fund marketers have a seemingly irresistible impulse to promote shares of a fund only *after* the fund has achieved sterling performance, an impulse, alas, that also seems irresistible to fund investors. Following such superior performance, however, such funds seem to have an almost equally irresistible impulse to revert not only to the market mean, but even below it. What goes up, it seems, must go down.

The most glaring gap between performance rating (+38) and loyalty rating (−30) appears for the Janus funds. Let's examine their records. During the 10 years ended December 31, 2007, the five largest Janus funds turned in an average annual return of 9.3 percent, a solid margin over the annual return of 5.9 percent for the S&P 500 index. During the first three years of that period, however, the Janus returns soared far above the S&P 500 index return, and as the market soared to new heights some $50 billion of investor capital flowed into the funds. In the bear market that followed, the funds collapsed. Result: Most Janus investors actually experienced dismal returns.

To summarize the math: For the decade, these Janus funds reported *time-weighted* returns averaging 9.3 percent per year, a compound 10-year return of 157 percent. The Janus fund investors, on the other hand, earned *dollar-weighted* returns averaging but 2.7 percent per year on the money they actually invested, a compound return of only 38 percent. That is, the returns actually earned by Janus shareholders for the decade fell fully 119 percentage points behind the returns that the Janus funds reported. That truly remarkable lag doubtless accounts for the gross disparity between the funds' high scores in reported performance and their low loyalty scores based on what Janus shareholders actually experienced. Such experience also likely characterizes the lack of shareholder loyalty at Morgan Stanley, AIM, and Columbia (Bank of America).

Costs Rear Their (Ugly) Head

The data are clear, then, that truly mutual investing has not only reaped rewards for its clients but has also earned their loyalty. Equally clearly, the financial conglomerates have not only failed their investors, but have earned (if that's the right word) their opprobrium. How do we account for these differences in return? Obviously, there's a certain amount of luck, skill, and timing in performance ratings, even though much of the impact of those variations evens out over a period as long as a decade, and even more of the disparity is mitigated when the management firms run a hundred funds or more.

It turns out, however, that there is one factor that plays a major role in the relative returns of peer funds. Happily, it is a factor that persists over time: *the costs that funds incurred in delivering their returns to investors.* It must be obvious that funds with similar objectives, managed by competent and experienced professionals, and compared over an extended period of time are more likely to achieve similar (and inevitably market-like) returns—but only before the costs of investing come into play.

Fund costs come in many guises. The major costs are: (1) the expense ratio (annual percentage of asset value consumed by management fees and operating expenses); (2) sales loads, representing the cost to acquire fund shares; and (3) transaction costs, the real—but hidden—expenses incurred in the execution of the investment decisions made by the fund's portfolio managers. Since transaction costs are not publicly available, the "all-in" expense ratios I'm using—including sales loads built into the B and C share classes—are the most satisfactory measure of fund costs.

Now let's add to our previous chart a column showing the expense ratios for the equity funds in each group* (Table 13.3). The three firms with the highest performance ratings are the very same firms—in the very same order—that have the lowest annual expense ratios, averaging

---

*Since the largest variations in fund expense ratios come in equity funds, I have excluded bond fund expense ratios—which are generally lower—from this comparison. This practice also eliminates the distortion that would be created when firms manage different proportions of bond funds to stock funds.

**TABLE 13.3   MAJOR MUTUAL FUND MANAGERS: FUND
PERFORMANCE, SHAREHOLDER LOYALTY, AND COSTS**

		Manager	Funds Ranked Highest Minus Lowest	Client Loyalty Score	Avg. Eq. Fund Exp. Ratio
	1	Vanguard	54%	44%	0.23%
	2	DFA	50	n/a	0.33
Highest	3	TIAA-CREF	50	n/a	0.37
Returns	4	T. Rowe Price	44	21	0.93
	5	Janus	38	−30	1.21
	6	American Funds	26	12	1.06
	7	Franklin Temp.	9	1	1.48
	8	Morgan Stanley	2	−18	1.23
Average	9	Fidelity	−3	12	1.31
Returns	10	Barclays Global	−4	n/a	0.41
	11	AIM Inv.	−14	−48	1.59
	12	Columbia Funds	−14	−47	1.41
	13	Goldman Sachs	−40	−32	1.59
	14	Dreyfus	−40	−45	1.65
Lowest	15	MainStay Funds	−40	n/a	1.49
Returns	16	John Hancock	−43	−10	1.40
	17	ING Investments	−55	−11	1.72
	18	Putnam	−58	−54	1.56

0.31 percent. For the top-performing group in total, the average ratio is 0.69 percent. Expense ratios for the middle group average 1.24 percent, fully 80 percent higher.* The bottom group of performers, on the other hand, have the highest expense ratios, averaging 1.57 percent per year, 127 percent above the top-performing group. Together, these data tell us that, when looking to the sources of mutual fund returns, yes, *costs matter.*

But please don't take my word for it. In fact, these data merely confirm what industry experts and academics have been saying for decades. Morningstar puts in unequivocally: "[E]xpense ratios are the fund

---

*The funds managed by Barclays, with a ratio of 0.41 percent, largely follow lower-cost index or index-like strategies.

world's best predictor" of performance, adding that "*all* studies show that expenses are the most powerful indicator of a fund's performance" (Italics added). Nobel laureate (in Economics) William F. Sharpe is equally unequivocal: "The smaller a fund's expense ratio, the better the results obtained by its shareholders."* He wrote those words in 1966(!), and confirmed them in 1996. "If you had to look at one thing only [in selecting a fund], I'd pick expense ratio."†

Sharpe's observations have met the test of time, nicely confirmed by the data that I have just presented. Crude data showing the relationship between expense ratios and Morningstar ratings suggests that an extra percentage point of cost means one *less* star in ratings; a percentage point reduction in cost means one *more* star. That is, if a three-star fund had an expense ratio one percentage point lower, it would be transformed into a four-star fund; if the same fund had a ratio one percent higher, it would become a two-star fund. Despite this powerful data, however, despite the opinion of experts, and despite the common sense that tells us that investment costs are the central element in determining the relative returns of mutual funds within their peer groups, price competition remains conspicuous by its absence from the mutual fund industry.

Price Competition?

Investors seem to be largely unaware of the direct and causal relationship between fund costs and fund returns. The industry's only three *very-low-cost* firms dominate the performance statistics, yet together they constitute a mere 14 percent of industry assets. How can the industry continue to maintain expense ratios that average 1.5 percent per year, *five times* as high? (Yes, along with Vanguard, T. Rowe Price, American Funds, and Fidelity—with costs that average 1.1 percent, somewhat

---

*"Mutual Fund Performance," *Journal of Business* (January 1966): 119.
†"In the Vanguard" (Summer 1996).

below industry norms, but many times Vanguard's costs—accounted for about one-third of all industry cash flow last year. But that still leaves two-thirds of the cash flowing largely into high-cost funds.)

The fact is that there are many "signs the mutual fund marketplace may not be performing in a way one would expect in a satisfactorily functioning competitive market." That is the opinion of the general counsel of the U.S. Securities and Exchange Commission.* One sign, he adds, is "the law of one price," the principle that, in an efficient, competitive market, nearly identical goods will sell at nearly identical prices. That's obviously because with full information "no rational buyer would pay more." Yet without such price convergence in the fund field, "American investors may be being deprived of the long-term returns they deserve."

Put another way, as a University of Washington professor† wrote, "as the information about a commodity improves, its price variability will decline." He quotes the great English economist Alfred Marshall, "[T]he more nearly perfect a market is, the stronger the tendency for the same price to be paid for the same thing at the same time in the market." Price variability, then, is a measure of our ignorance about what the makeup of a commodity is, dividing goods into what the author calls "brand-name commodities" and "caveat emptor commodities."

The fact is that some kinds of funds—money market funds, for example—are clearly commodities. So are index funds. Investment-grade bond funds and U.S. Treasury bond funds (with comparable maturities) are at least commodity-like. What about managed equity funds? When sorted by objectives (i.e., compared to their peers, as in, for example, large-cap value funds), they are also commodity-like in the short run, even more so in the long run. (And since the various equity investment styles tend to revert to the mean over time, all—or

---

*Speech by Brian G. Cartwright before the 2006 Securities Development Conference, December 4, 2006.
†Dr. Yoran Barzel, "Replacing the Law of One Price with the Price Convergence Law" (University of Washington Department of Economics Working Paper No. UWEC-2005-10, March 28, 2005).

nearly all—equity funds tend to be commodity-like in nature in the *very* long term.) When *brand-name* commodities have different prices, then, they quickly become *caveat emptor* commodities, a lesson fund investors have yet to learn.

Clearly, price ought to be the talisman that drives investor choice, forcing fund managers to reduce costs. But that is simply not happening. Yes, money flows (as I have noted) are increasingly directed toward the lower-cost funds, and Vanguard has been a beneficiary of, indeed a creator of, that structure. But other fund complexes are not following the lead.* In short, *if price competition is defined, not by the action of consumers, but by the actions of producers, then price competition is conspicuous by its absence in the mutual fund industry.* Why don't fund managers compete on costs? Because to do so would be antithetical to their vested financial interests.

The fund industry, of course, argues that it is characterized by vigorous competition. To a point that is true: There is competition in the marketplace. Witness the incentives offered to brokers to sell shares and the hundreds of millions spent each year on print and television advertising. There is performance competition. Witness the ongoing advertising of funds that have had superior past records, or are investing in hot market sectors. But there is little evidence to suggest that there is price competition. While the most vigorous industry advocates find "evidence of price competition clear,"† the data presented by these advocates show that while there were 1,240 fee decreases during 1998–2004, there were even more fee *increases*—1,469 per year on average. Even these advocates do not dispute "the empirical fact that mutual fund boards of directors rarely 'fire' advisers and do not put advisory contracts up for bids among advisers." Without such competition, mutual fund managers are hardly likely to reduce their fees, and hence their own profitability.

---

* I'm often told that Vanguard's demonstrably low costs—increasingly recognized in the marketplace—are responsible for setting an upper limit on prices among our competitors. But that level is still far too high for my taste.

† John C. Coates IV and R. Glenn Hubbard, "Competition in the Mutual Fund Industry," *Journal of Corporation Law* 33, no. 1, University of Iowa (Autumn 2007): 173–174.

Recap of the Issues

Let me summarize here the arguments I've made so far: In its early years, the investment company industry had many characteristics that well-served fund investors. The focus was largely on private trusteeship; prudence and diversification were the watchwords of investment policy; fund trustees often were a step removed from fund distribution; expense ratios were moderate, and far below today's levels. Today, public ownership—largely by giant conglomerates—overwhelmingly dominates the fund industry, and it has ill-served fund investors. By way of contrast, the results of that "Vanguard Experiment" in mutual fund governance are now clear. It has been both a remarkable commercial success for the firm itself, and an artistic success for its shareholder/owners.

Our central idea was to create a firm honoring the industry's original values. I expected that becoming the low-cost provider in any industry where low cost (by definition) is the key to superior returns, would force our competitors to emulate our structure. Indeed, I chose the name "vanguard" in part because of its meaning: "leadership in a new trend." But I was wrong. After more than three decades—during which at least one of our industry peers has described us as "the organization against which others must measure themselves"—we have yet to find our first follower.* We remain unique.

Of course, not everyone shares my view of the positive power of the mutual structure. Hear the American Enterprise Institute (AEI), in a recent book entitled *Competitive Equity: A Better Way to Organize*

---

*I had hoped that when Marsh & McClennan decided to sell its Putnam Management Company subsidiary—obviously a deeply troubled firm whose previous management ill-served its investors in so many ways—it would mutualize and internalize its organization. However, my attempts to persuade three directors of the funds (including its then-independent chairman) fell on deaf ears. The fund board approved the sale of the management to a Canadian conglomerate for $4.9 billion. For a further explanation of why and how such a conversion might have taken place, see my speech, "Corporate Governance and Mutual Fund Governance—Reflections at a Time of Crisis," November 21, 2003.

*Mutual Funds** (Hint: It doesn't consider the Vanguard way "a better way.") The authors are skeptical of our claim that we operate on an "at-cost basis," albeit without identifying the basis of that skepticism. They allege that our managers do not accept compensation substantially lower than that paid to other fund advisers, apparently unaware that we fully disclose the rates and fees we pay to the unaffiliated external advisers that manage many of our actively managed funds. For the record, the average fee paid to the advisers to Windsor Fund is 0.12 percent of fund assets; the fee paid to the adviser to our GNMA Fund is 0.01 percent. (Yes, that's one basis point.)

Despite these shortcomings in their argument, their conclusion is unequivocal: "[T]he idea that the mutual form of organization is inherently superior to the external form . . . is something of an overstatement." They also allege that conversion to a mutual form would require buying out the existing shareholders (of the management company), ignoring the fact that Vanguard, as noted earlier, did no such thing. In fact, the fund directors have the awesome power to simply terminate the manager's contract and either manage the funds internally or hire new external advisers. (I note that while this never happens in the fund field, it happens with considerable frequency among corporate pension funds.)

The Triumph of Conglomeration

In any event, the mutual model remains stuck, still used by only a single firm, and the conglomerate model has triumphed. Early on, and presciently, Chairman Cohen recognized the serious problems that would be created by this conglomeration. In a 1966 speech, he spoke of the "new and more complex relationships . . . [between] institutional managers and their beneficiaries," and sought "a more adequate scheme of regulation that ultimately will protect beneficiaries from unwarranted action by their managers, and will realize the fullest benefits of their participation" in their funds. He then noted, prophetically,

---

*By Peter J. Wallison and Robert E. Litan (Washington, DC: AEI Press, 2007).

his concern about "public ownership of investment advisers . . . and the beginning of a trend toward [their] acquisition by industrial companies," which makes it "increasingly difficult to define the responsibilities of institutional managers," who may "be obligated to serve the business interests of the very companies in which they invest."

The snowball that began to roll with the onset of public ownership of management companies in 1958 took a while to gather speed. But during the 1980s and 1990s it came into full flower and, as noted earlier, among the 50 largest firms in the industry only 9 remain privately held. This massive wave of conglomeration by what are essentially giant marketing firms led to a wave of, yes, "product proliferation" that carried the number of mutual funds from 560 in 1980 to 12,039 today.

It's Time for a Change

Only two weeks after that 1966 speech by Chairman Cohen, the Commission sent to Congress a massive report by its staff entitled *Public Policy Implications of Investment Company Growth* (PPI).* In that report, the SEC noted the burgeoning level of fund fees (then at an annual level of a mere $134 million vs. more than *$100 billion* today). The Commission also called attention to the effective control advisers held over their funds, and "the absence of competitive pressures, the limitations of disclosure, the ineffectiveness of shareholder voting rights, and the obstacles to more effective action by the independent directors."

The Commission also noted "the adviser-underwriter permeation of investment company activities to an extent that makes rupture of existing relationships a difficult and complex step . . . [rendering] arm's length bargaining between the fund's board and the managers . . . a wholly unrealistic alternative." Yet the Commission was "not prepared to recommend at this time the more drastic statutory requirement of compulsory internalization of management [i.e., mutualization]."

---

*U.S. Government Printing Office (December 3, 1966).

Rather, the SEC recommended the adoption of a "statutory standard of reasonableness . . . *a basic standard that would make clear that those who derive benefits from their fiduciary relationships with investment companies cannot charge more for services than if they were dealing with them at arm's length*" (emphasis added).

The SEC described *reasonableness* as a "clearly expressed and readily enforceable standard [that] would not be measured merely by the cost of comparable services to individual investors or by the fees charged by other externally managed investment companies . . . [but by] the costs of management services *to internally-managed funds* and to pension funds and other non-fund clients." If the standard of reasonableness does not "resolve the problems in management compensation that exist . . . *then more sweeping steps might deserve to be considered.*"

With vigorous lobbying by the Investment Company Institute, the self-anointed representative of fund shareholders but in fact the powerful voice of fund managers, that reasonableness standard was never adopted. Yet, even as fund fees soared and conglomeration gradually took over, transaction after transaction, unchallenged (and, arguably, unchallengeable) after that ghastly 1958 decision by the Ninth Circuit, even as Chairman Cohen's worst fears were being realized, even after PPI's warning 42 long years ago, more sweeping steps have yet to be considered by the SEC.

But some baby steps have been considered. In 2004, the Commission recommended a significant strengthening of fund boards, only to be reconsidered and likely watered down by a differently led Commission in 2008. Of course I'd prefer more sweeping steps. Indeed, as I wrote in my book *Common Sense** nearly a decade ago, "[T]he industry's further evolution must take one of two critical turns: [One is] a radical restructuring, a change in the status quo, a change that places more power in the hands of shareholders. The radical restructuring would be the mutualization of at least part of the American mutual fund industry. Rather than contracting with

---

*Paraphrased from my book, *Common Sense on Mutual Funds: New Imperatives for the Intelligent Investor* (Hoboken, NJ: John Wiley & Sons, 2009).

external management companies to operate and manage the portfolios, funds—or at least large fund families—would run themselves. Mutual fund shareholders would, in effect, own the management companies that oversee the fund.

"They would have their own officers and staff, and the huge profits now earned by external managers would be diverted to the shareholders. Under such a structure, the character of the industry would return to its traditional roots. Funds wouldn't waste their shareholders' money on costly marketing campaigns designed to bring in new investors at the expense of existing investors. With markedly lower costs, they would produce markedly higher returns and/or assume commensurately lower risks. They would provide full and candid disclosure to their shareholder-owners. They'd have no need to organize and market 'fund-of-the-moment' funds, and they might even see the merit of market index funds.

"The other choice would be the rise of more activist independent mutual fund directors. Independent board members would become ferocious advocates for the rights and interests of the mutual fund shareholders they represent. They would negotiate aggressively with the mutual fund adviser, allowing the management company to earn a fair profit, but recognize that the interests of the mutual fund shareholders must always come first. Independent directors would approve only portfolios that are based on sound investment principles and meet a reasonable investment need. The independent directors would at last become the fiduciaries they are supposed to be under the law. And if the creation and encouragement of activist independent directors is a more practicable solution than the wholesale mutualization of the American mutual fund industry, then perhaps it is an objective deserving of our energies and effort. And who knows? As the values of such a refocused organization move toward the values of the mutual organization, full mutualization for some firms may be only a step further away.

"Regardless of the exact structure, mutual or conventional, an arrangement in which fund shareholders and their directors are in working control of a fund—as distinct from one in which fund managers are in control—will lead to funds that truly serve the needs of their shareholders, meeting the crying need to return this industry to the traditional role of trusteeship that largely characterized its *modus operandi* through its first three decades. Under either structure, the industry will enhance economic value for fund shareholders."

What's to Be Done?

Given the industry's growth; its sharp turn from stewardship to salesmanship; the army of conglomerates that has swept across it, leaving only a handful of survivors; its failure to produce anything like satisfactory returns to the investors who have entrusted funds with their hard-earned dollars; and, dare I say, the success of the singular, still unique, firm that has, for nearly 34 years now, almost unequivocally demonstrated the value of that internalization that the SEC was unprepared to mandate all those years ago, not a single additional moment should elapse before those long-justified, long awaited "more sweeping steps" are not only considered, but enacted into the law.

My idealism tells me to fight for compulsory internalization,* at long last making it possible to delete those quotation marks around "mutual" fund that reflected the prescient concerns expressed by Chairman Cohen in the speech he delivered in 1968. But my pragmatism disagrees. Powerful and well-financed lobbyists—led by the Investment Company Institute, the fabulously profitable management companies and their conglomerate owners, and the U.S. Chamber of Commerce (of course!)—would take up arms against such a seemingly radical proposal. The campaign would come with unbridled enthusiasm and virtually unlimited financial firepower, K Street's dreams come true. Given the state of our nation's governance, such opposition, self-interested as it obviously is, would defeat "the national public interest and the interest of investors," the very interests that the 1940 Act was designed to protect.

But hope is not lost. There is a way—not, of course, an easy way—to honor the spirit and letter of the Act so that investment companies are organized, operated, and managed in the interests of

---

*But not for all fund complexes, only for complexes that exceed certain thresholds; for example, fund complexes that manage over $25 billion in assets and more than 30 mutual funds.

their shareholders rather than their managers and distributors. It would take a series of logical steps to achieve this goal, some already in the works, some proposed by an earlier Commission and now seemingly abandoned; new steps that take us even further toward that goal; one simple—if dramatic—organizational change that would create enormous momentum toward fund operational independence from their advisers; and a change in federal law.

Here's the plan I propose:

1. Require that 100 percent of fund directors be unaffiliated with the management company. There is simply no point in any longer subjecting management company officers to the profound conflicts of interest that they face when they also serve as fund directors. It's time to honor the principle that "no man can serve two masters." (As noted earlier, since the firm's inception, the Vanguard funds have prohibited representatives of any external adviser from serving on their boards. It hasn't seemed to impair the returns we earn for investors.)

2. Require that the chairman of the fund board be independent of the management company, even if, as under the Commission's 2004 proposal, only 75 percent of the board is required to be independent. Such a separation of powers, ordained for our federal government in the Constitution, is not only a fundamental principle of governance, but simple common sense.

3. Require the retention by the funds of legal counsel independent of the adviser and a chief compliance officer. Both are already mandated by the Commission, but we must require them to be responsible to the fund board, reporting to the independent fund chairman.

4. Importantly, require that the fund boards retain advisers and experts necessary to carry out their duties, in order to provide truly objective and independent information to the board. (I'm guessing that few fund boards have seen the kind of comparative performance, loyalty, and cost data that I've presented in these remarks.) The SEC recommended language "authorizing" such a staff (or consultants) in its 2004 recommendations, which now seem to have gone aborning. As I see it, this requirement would apply only to

fund complexes of a certain (large) size and scope.* It's time to face up to the fact that directors who are overseeing 100 funds or more can't do so without staff support.

5. A specific regulatory authorization that enables funds to assume responsibility for their own operations, including administration, accounting, compliance, shareholder record-keeping, etc. Such a structure would cut the Gordian knot that gives fund managers de facto control over the funds they manage.† It is this very step that was central to the creation of Vanguard, which (as noted earlier) soon enabled the fledgling firm to extend its reach to investment management and then to distribution.

6. Enact a federal standard of fiduciary duty for fund directors. The fact is that mutual fund managers, indeed pension fund managers, public and private alike, face serious conflicts of interest in carrying out their duties. In today's relatively new *agency* society, in which financial institutions control more than 70 percent of stock ownership, there has been a serious failure to serve their *principals*—largely fund shareholders and pension beneficiaries. As the Honorable Leo E. Strine, Jr., Vice Chancellor of the Delaware Court of Chancery, has noted, it would be "passing strange if professional money managers would, as a class, be less likely to exploit their agency than the managers of corporations that make products and deliver services."‡ Yes, the world has changed, and we need to redress that imbalance in favor of the principals.

---

*For example, complexes meeting the standards outlined in the note on page 266. But in my darker moments, I'd consider applying this requirement only to fund complexes in which a majority of the directors are unable to actually name all of the funds on whose boards they serve. If that requirement is too demanding, then only when directors are unable to specify the exact number of funds on whose boards they serve.

†It is a curious fact that the operational function was ignored in the 1940 Act. It refers solely to the other two functions of fund management, investment advice and share distribution (underwriting).

‡"Toward Common Sense and Common Ground," *Journal of Corporation Law (Iowa)* 33, no. 1 (Fall 2007): 1.

Two Powerful Endorsements

Once again, this critical analysis of the mutual fund industry is not mine alone. Listen to Warren Buffett: "Fund independent directors . . . have been absolutely pathetic. They follow a zombie-like process that makes a mockery of stewardship. 'Independent' directors, over more than six decades, have failed miserably." Then, hear this from another investor, one who has not only produced one of the most impressive investment records of the modern era but who has an impeccable reputation for his character and intellectual integrity, David F. Swensen, Chief Investment Officer of Yale University:

> The fundamental market failure in the mutual-fund industry involves the interaction between sophisticated, profit-seeking providers of financial services and naïve, return-seeking consumers of investment products. The drive for profits by Wall Street and the mutual-fund industry overwhelms the concept of fiduciary responsibility, leading to an all too predictable outcome . . . the powerful financial services industry exploits vulnerable individual investors. . . .
>
> The ownership structure of a fund management company plays a role in determining the likelihood of investor success. Mutual-fund investors face the greatest challenge with investment management companies that provide returns to public shareholders or that funnel profits to a corporate parent—situations that place the conflict between profit generation and fiduciary responsibility in high relief. When a fund's management subsidiary reports to a multi-line financial services company, the scope for abuse of investor capital broadens dramatically. . . .
>
> *Investors fare best with funds managed by not-for-profit organizations*, because the management firm focuses exclusively on serving investor interests. No profit motive conflicts with the manager's fiduciary responsibility. No profit margin interferes with investor returns. No outside corporate interest clashes with portfolio management choices. Not-for-profit firms place investor interest front and center. Ultimately, a passive index fund managed by a not-for-profit investment management

organization represents the combination most likely to satisfy investor aspirations. [Emphasis added.]

I regard these two powerful endorsements of the positions that I hold as a clarion call for action. Yes, it's time to make fund directors aware of their duty to serve the fund shareowners rather than the entrenched fund managers, and to bring independent leadership—*real* leadership—to fund boards. That is the purpose of the six changes I've delineated. And yes, I'm well aware that, for some firms, these changes may lead to the full mutualization that, in the only case study that exists, has served shareholders so well. Yes, it's also time to overturn the ghastly legacy of the Ninth Circuit's erroneous decision in 1958 that opened the floodgates first to public ownership and then to conglomerate ownership.* It's also high time for firms that now place asset-gathering at the heart of their mission to return to the industry's professional roots and again act as true fiduciaries.

So, yes, it's time for a new order of things. It's time to facilitate the development of mutualization in the mutual fund industry. It's time to go back to the future and honor the vision of trusteeship held by Paul Cabot, and the vision of SEC Commissioner Healy to protect investors from the distorting impact of fund sales. And, especially on the occasion of this 27th annual Manuel F. Cohen Memorial Lecture, it's time to honor Manny Cohen's legacy, his implicit demand that we build an industry worthy of deleting those darned quotation marks that he placed around the word "mutual," at last bringing mutuality back to the mutual fund industry. Only then will we honor the crystal-clear spirit of the 1940 Act, and protect the national public interest and the interests of investors.

---

*Interestingly in light of my recommendations here, the note in the *Harvard Law Review* cited in the note on page 244 concludes with this caveat: "However, the sellers might be allowed to sell control for any consideration if the fund had an independent board of directors . . . with control of the proxy machinery and the power to select another adviser."

Appendix

TABLE 13.4 MAJOR MUTUAL FUND MANAGERS: FULL STUDY

Manager Name	Total Assets $MM (as of 11/07)	Number of Funds Rated						4/5 Star Share	1/2 Star Share	5/4 Minus 1/2	Loyalty Score
		5 Stars	4 Stars	3 Stars	2 Stars	1 Star	Total				
1 Vanguard	1,089,489	31	78	67	5	4	185	58.9%	4.9%	54.1%	44
2 DFA	108,655	2	22	15	3		42	57.1%	7.1%	50.0%	
3 TIAA–CREF	17,788	3	22	19	2		46	54.3%	4.3%	50.0%	21
4 T Rowe Price	230,424	7	47	38	9		101	53.5%	8.9%	44.6%	
5 Janus	97,181	14	27	23	9	3	76	53.9%	15.8%	38.2%	-30
6 Schwab	54,203	3	16	32	2	1	54	35.2%	5.6%	29.6%	26
7 American Funds	1,157,019	63	80	106	47	16	312	45.8%	20.2%	25.6%	12
8 Neuberger Berman	26,589	4	10	15	4	3	36	38.9%	19.4%	19.4%	-1
9 PIM CO/Allianz Gbl	244,039	40	71	114	56	15	296	37.5%	24.0%	13.5%	-27
10 Franklin Templeton	331,866	20	66	131	45	17	279	30.8%	22.2%	8.6%	1
11 Oppenheimer Funds	165,845	15	61	61	42	18	197	38.6%	30.5%	8.1%	-6
12 Waddell & Reed	46,146	27	40	57	34	19	177	37.9%	29.9%	7.9%	
13 Prudential Finl	34,645	28	34	62	48	2	174	35.6%	28.7%	6.9%	
14 BlackRock	146,125	34	80	138	65	31	348	32.8%	27.6%	5.2%	-18
15 American Century	76,854	13	44	65	41	8	171	33.3%	28.7%	4.7%	-21
16 Morgan Stanley	69,075	8	61	84	60	5	218	31.7%	29.8%	1.8%	-18
17 Russell Invst Grp	36,242		11	34	6	4	55	20.0%	18.2%	1.8%	
18 Fidelity	928,528	44	102	165	116	44	471	31.0%	34.0%	-3.0%	12
19 Barclays Global	321,630	4	23	41	20	11	99	27.3%	31.3%	-4.0%	
20 Alliance Bernstein	95,286	7	37	96	38	17	194	22.7%	28.4%	-5.7%	
21 Principal Funds	54,435	10	50	154	72	13	299	20.1%	28.4%	-8.4%	-33
22 Nuveen	72,537	16	21	57	30	19	143	25.9%	34.3%	-8.4%	-7
23 GE Asset Mgmt	19,666	4	11	24	16	4	59	25.4%	33.9%	-8.5%	
24 The Hartford	49,878	10	25	52	42	8	137	25.5%	36.5%	-10.9%	-11

(Continued)

TABLE 13.4 (CONTINUED)

Manager Name	Total Assets $MM (as of 11/07)	Number of Funds Rated						4/5 Star Share	1/2 Star Share	5/4 Minus 1/2	Loyalty Score
		5 Stars	4 Stars	3 Stars	2 Stars	1 Star	Total				
25 Northern Trust	21,035		6	39	13	7	58	10.3%	22.4%	-12.1%	
26 AIM Investments	63,308	5	37	94	62	7	205	20.5%	33.7%	-13.2%	-48
27 Columbia Funds	118,967	19	50	115	73	38	295	23.4%	37.6%	-14.2%	-47
28 Federated	42,731	8	25	59	46	11	149	22.1%	38.3%	-16.1%	
29 Wells Fargo	45,270	16	52	79	82	29	258	26.4%	43.0%	-16.7%	-20
30 FAF Advisors	20,994	4	20	76	39	11	150	16.0%	33.3%	-17.3%	
31 Eaton Vance	98,196	11	27	87	63	16	204	18.6%	38.7%	-20.1%	-47
32 JPMorgan Funds	76,723	4	46	93	77	26	246	20.3%	41.9%	-21.5%	10
33 Lord Abbett	58,698	7	19	46	44	10	126	20.6%	42.9%	-22.2%	-5
34 MFS	84,708	12	36	111	88	20	267	18.0%	40.4%	-22.5%	-9
35 MassMutual Finl	23,373	3	25	67	48	18	161	17.4%	41.0%	-23.6%	
36 Delaware	27,285	7	29	71	74	8	189	19.0%	43.4%	-24.3%	
37 Evergreen Inv Mgmt	55,444	8	38	59	68	28	201	22.9%	47.8%	-24.9%	-48
38 Pioneer	38,732	8	19	35	47	13	122	22.1%	49.2%	-27.0%	
39 DWS Scudder	65,492	9	31	73	68	31	212	18.9%	46.7%	-27.8%	-41
40 Legg Mason Funds	90,049	3	30	67	59	28	187	17.6%	46.5%	-28.9%	4
41 Van Kampen	93,901	3	17	45	45	10	120	16.7%	45.8%	-29.2%	-12
42 RiverSource	56,223	12	34	63	86	34	229	20.1%	52.4%	-32.3%	2
43 State Street Glbl	42,831		5	16	8	11	40	12.5%	47.5%	-35.0%	
44 UBS Glbl Asset Mgt	23,951		15	37	38	15	105	14.3%	50.5%	-36.2%	
45 Goldman Sachs	60,131	4	21	49	79	11	164	15.2%	54.9%	-39.6%	-32
46 Dreyfus	62,997	5	37	120	133	47	342	12.3%	52.6%	-40.4%	-45
47 MainStay Funds	24,470	3	18	21	41	23	106	19.8%	60.4%	-40.6%	
48 John Hancock	59,228	8	9	24	43	18	102	16.7%	59.8%	-43.1%	-10
49 ING Investments	29,746	4	12	48	70	44	178	9.0%	64.0%	-55.1%	-11
50 Putnam	89,318	1	9	92	121	48	271	3.7%	62.4%	-58.7%	-54
Total	6,947,135	571	1,706	3,335	2,427	817	8,856	25.7%	33.6%	-7.9%	

272

Chapter 14

The Fiduciary Principle: No Man Can Serve Two Masters*

I write at a time of financial and economic crisis in our nation and around the globe. I venture to assert that when the history of the financial era which has just drawn to a close comes to be written, most of its mistakes and its major faults will be ascribed to the failure to observe the fiduciary principle, the precept as old as holy writ, that "a man cannot serve two masters." No thinking man can believe that an economy built upon a business foundation can permanently endure without some loyalty to that principle. The separation of ownership from management, the development of the corporate structure so as to vest in small groups control over the resources of great numbers of small and uninformed investors,

---

*Based on an essay published in the *Journal of Portfolio Management* (Fall 2009), which in turn was based on a lecture on business ethics delivered at Columbia University School of Business on April 1, 2009.

273

make imperative a fresh and active devotion to that principle if the modern world of business is to perform its proper function.

Yet those who serve nominally as trustees, but relieved, by clever legal devices, from the obligation to protect those whose interests they purport to represent, corporate officers and directors whose award to themselves huge bonuses from corporate funds without the assent or even the knowledge of their stockholders . . . financial institutions which, in the infinite variety of their operations, consider only last, if at all, the interests of those whose funds they command, suggest how far we have ignored the necessary implications of that principle. The loss and suffering inflicted on individuals, the harm done to a social order founded upon business and dependent upon its integrity, are incalculable.*

Alas, except for the first sentence, the preceding words are not mine. Rather they are the words of Harlan Fiske Stone, excerpted from his 1934—yes, 1934—address at the University of Michigan Law School, reprinted in the *Harvard Law Review* later that year.†

But his words are equally relevant—perhaps even more relevant— at this moment in history. They could hardly present a more appropriate analysis of the causes of the present-day collapse of our financial markets and the economic crisis now facing our nation and our world.

One could easily react to Justice Stone's words by falling back on the ancient aphorism, "the more things change, the more they remain the same," and move on to a new subject. But I hope financial

---

*H. F. Stone, address to the University of Michigan School of Law on June 15, 1934, reprinted in the *Harvard Law Review* (1934).

†Harlan Fiske Stone (1872–1946) received his law degree at Columbia in 1898, and served as dean of Columbia Law School from 1910 to 1923. In 1925, President Calvin Coolidge appointed Stone as Associate Justice of the United States Supreme Court. In 1941, President Roosevelt appointed him as Chief Justice of the United States, and he served in that position until his death in 1946. A curious coincidence is that Justice Stone appeared on the cover of *Time* magazine on May 6, 1929, just two days before my own birth on May 8. In its profile story, *Time* accurately speculated that one day Stone would become the Chief Justice, in part because (in those backward sentences that distinguished the early style of the magazine), "Well he has always tackled the public interest."

professionals will react differently, and share my reaction: In the aftermath of that Great Depression and the stock market crash that accompanied it, we failed to take advantage of the opportunity to demand that those who lead our giant business and financial organizations—the stewards of so much of our nation's wealth—measure up to the stern and unyielding principles of fiduciary duty described by Justice Stone. So, 75 years later, for heaven's sake, let's not make the same mistake again. Justice Stone's stern words force us to fasten on ethical dilemmas faced by today's business leaders. Included among these leaders are the chiefs who manage our nation's publicly held corporations—today valued in the stock market at some $12 trillion—and the professional managers of "other people's money" who oversee equity investments valued at some $9 trillion of that total, owning 75 percent of all shares and therefore holding absolute voting control over those corporations. Like their counterparts in business, those powerful managers have not only an *ethical responsibility*, but a *fiduciary duty*, to those whose capital has been entrusted to their care.

Fiduciary Duty

The concept of fiduciary duty has a long history, going back more or less eight centuries under English common law. Fiduciary duty is essentially a legal relationship of confidence or trust between two or more parties, most commonly a *fiduciary* or *trustee* and a *principal* or *beneficiary*, who justifiably reposes confidence, good faith, and reliance on his trustee. The fiduciary is expected to act at all times for the sole benefit and interests of the principal, with loyalty to those interests. A fiduciary must not put personal interests before that duty, and, importantly, must not be placed in a situation where his fiduciary duty to clients conflicts with a fiduciary duty to any other entity.

Way back in 1928, New York's Chief Justice Benjamin N. Cardozo put it well:

> Many forms of conduct permissible in a workaday world for those acting at arm's length are forbidden to those bound by fiduciary ties. A trustee is held to something stricter than the morals of the marketplace. . . . As to this there has developed a tradition that is unbending and inveterate. . . . Not honesty

alone, but the punctilio of an honor the most sensitive, is then the standard of behavior. . . . Only thus has the level of conduct for fiduciaries been kept at a level higher than that trodden by the crowd.*

It has been said, I think, accurately, that fiduciary duty is the highest duty known to the law.

It is less ironic than it is tragic that the concept of fiduciary duty seems far *less* imbedded in our society today than it was when Stone and Cardozo expressed their profound convictions. As ought to be obvious to all educated citizens, over the past few decades the balance between ethics and law, on the one hand, and the markets on the other has heavily shifted in favor of the markets. As I have often put it: We have moved from a society in which *there are some things that one simply does not do,* to one in which *if everyone else is doing it, I can do it, too.* I've described this change as a shift from moral absolutism to moral relativism. Business ethics, it seems to me, has been a major casualty of that shift in our traditional societal values. You will hardly be surprised to learn that I do not regard that change as progress.

At least a few others share this view. In her book *Trust and Honesty,* published in 2006, Boston University Law School professor Tamar Frankel provides worthy insights on the diminishing role of fiduciary duty in our society. She is concerned—a concern that I suspect many investment professionals would share—that American culture has been moving toward dishonesty, deception, and abuse of trust, all of which have come to the fore in the present crisis. What we need, she argues, is "an effective way to increase trust [by] establishing trustworthy institutions and reliable systems," even as she despairs that the pressures brought out by the stock market and real estate bubbles have led to "deteriorating public morals . . . and burst into abuse of trust" (p. 99).†

In Professor Frankel's view, "we reduced the power of morality in law . . . emasculated the regulation of trusted persons [that is, fiduciaries] . . . abused the laws that govern fiduciaries' honesty . . . and

---

*Meinhard v. Salmon, 164 N.E. 545 (N.Y. 1928).
†Tamar Frankel, *Trust and Honesty: America's Business Culture at a Crossroad* (Oxford, England: Oxford University Press, 2006).

opened the door to enormous losses to the public and the economic system" (p. 119). We also came to ignore the critical distinction between fiduciary law itself and a fiduciary relationship subject to contract law. What's more, she writes, "the movement from professions to businesses was accompanied by changes in the way the law was interpreted" (p. 146). We forgot the fundamental principle expressed by the apostles Matthew and Luke,* and repeated by Justice Stone: "No man can serve two masters."

My principal objection to moral relativism is that it obfuscates and mitigates the obligations that we owe to society, and shifts the focus to the benefits accruing to the individual. Self-interest, unchecked, is a powerful force, but a force that, if it is to protect the interests of the community of all of our citizens, must ultimately be checked by society. The recent crisis—which I have described as "a crisis of *ethic* proportions"—makes it clear how serious that damage can become.

Causes of the Recent Crisis

The causes of the recent crisis are manifold. Metaphorically speaking, the collapse in our financial system has 1,000 fathers: the cavalier attitude toward risk of our bankers and investment bankers in holding a toxic mix of low-quality securities on enormously leveraged balance sheets; the *laissez-faire* attitude of our federal regulators, reflected in their faith that "free competitive markets" would protect our society against excesses; the Congress, which rolled back legislative reforms dating back to the Depression years; "securitization" in which the traditional link between borrower and lender—under which lenders demanded evidence of the borrowers' ability to meet their financial obligations—was severed; and reckless financial innovation in which literally tens of trillions of dollars of derivative financial instruments (such as credit default swaps) were created, usually carrying stupefying levels of risk and unfathomable levels of complexity.

The radical increase in the power and position of the leaders of corporate America and the leaders of investment America has

---

* See Luke 16:13 and Matthew 6:34 of the King James Version of the New Testament.

been a major contributor to these failures. Today's dominant institutional ownership position of 75 percent of the shares of our (largely giant) public corporations compares with only about 8 percent a half-century ago. This remarkable increase in ownership has placed these managers—largely of mutual funds (holding 25% of all shares); private pension funds (12%); government retirement funds (9%); insurance companies (8%); and hedge funds and endowment funds—in a position to exercise great power and influence over corporate America.

But they have failed to exercise their power. In fact, the agents of investment in America have failed to honor the responsibilities that they owe to their principals—the last-line individuals who have much of their capital wealth committed to stock ownership, including mutual fund share-owners and pension beneficiaries. The record is clear that, despite their controlling position, most institutions have failed to play an active role in board structure and governance, director elections, executive compensation, stock options, proxy proposals, dividend policy, and so on.

Given their forbearance as corporate citizens, these managers arguably played a major role in allowing the managers of our public corporations to exploit the advantages of their own agency, not only in executive compensation, perquisites, and mergers and acquisitions, but even in accepting the "financial engineering" that has come to permeate corporate financial statements, endorsed—at least tacitly—by their public accountants.

But the failures of our institutional investors go beyond governance issues to the very practice of their trade. These agents have also failed to provide the due diligence that our citizen/investors have every reason to expect of the investment professionals to whom they have entrusted their money. How could so many highly skilled, highly paid securities analysts and researchers have failed to question the toxic-filled lever-aged balance sheets of Citicorp and other leading banks and investment banks and, lest we forget, AIG, as well as the ethics-skirting sales tactics of Countrywide Financial?* Even earlier, what were these professionals thinking when they ignored the shenanigans of "special-purpose entities" at Enron and "cooking the books" at WorldCom?

---

*I'm speaking here of the buy-side analysts employed directly by these managers. The conflicts of interest facing Wall Street's sell-side analysts were exposed by the investigations of New York Attorney General Spitzer in 2002–2003.

The Role of Institutional Managers

But the failure of our newly empowered agents to exercise their responsibilities to ownership is but a part of the problem we face. The field of institutional investment management—the field in which I've now plied my trade for more than 58 years—also played a major, if often overlooked, role. As a group, we veered off-course almost 180 degrees from stewardship to salesmanship, in which our focus turned away from prudent management and toward product marketing. We moved from a focus on long-term investment to a focus on short-term speculation. The driving dream of our adviser/agents was to gather ever-increasing assets under management, the better to build their advisory fees and profits, even as these policies came at the direct expense of the investor/principals whom, under traditional standards of trusteeship and fiduciary duty, they were duty-bound to serve.

Conflicts of interest are pervasive throughout the field of money management, albeit different in each sector. Private pension plans face one set of conflicts (i.e., minimizing plan contributions helps maximize a corporation's earnings), public pension plans another (i.e., political pressure to invest in pet projects of legislators). And labor union plans face yet another (i.e., pressure to employ money managers who are willing to "pay to play"). But it is in the mutual fund industry where the conflict between fiduciary duty to fund shareholder/clients often directly conflicts with the business interests of the fund manager.

Perhaps we shouldn't be surprised that our money managers act first in their own behalf. Indeed, as Vice Chancellor Leo E. Strine, Jr., of the Delaware Court of Chancery has observed, "It would be passing strange if . . . professional money managers would, as a class, be less likely to exploit their agency than the managers of the corporations that make products and deliver services."* In the fund industry—the largest of all financial intermediaries—that failure to serve the interests of fund shareholders has wide ramifications. Ironically, the failure has

---

*Leo E. Strine, "Toward Common Sense and Common Ground? Reflections on the Shared Interests of Managers and Labor in a More Rational System of Corporate Governance," *Journal of Corporation Law* (Fall 2007): 7.

occurred despite the clear language of the Investment Company Act of 1940, which demands that "mutual funds should be organized, managed and operated in the best interests of their shareholders, rather than in the interests of [their] advisers."*

The Triumph of Speculation over Investment

As control over corporate America moved from owners to agents, our institutional money managers seemed to forget their duty to act solely in the interest of their own principals, those whose savings were entrusted to mutual funds and whose retirement security was entrusted to pension plans. These new investor/agents not only forgot the interests of their *principals*, but also seemed to forget their own investment *principles*. The predominant focus of institutional investment strategy turned from the wisdom of long-term investing, based on the enduring creation of intrinsic corporate values, to the folly of short-term speculation, focused on the ephemeral prices of corporate stocks. The own-a-stock strategy of yore became the rent-a-stock strategy of today.

In what I've called "the happy conspiracy" between corporate managers, directors, accountants, investment bankers, and institutional owners and renters of stocks, all kinds of bizarre financial engineering took place. Management became the master of its own numbers, and our public accountants too often went along. Loose accounting standards made it possible to create, often out of thin air, what passes for earnings, even under GAAP standards. One good example—which is already sowing the seeds of yet another financial crisis that is now emerging—is hyping the assumed future returns earned by pension plans, even as rational expectations for future returns deteriorated.

Here, again, we can't say that we hadn't been warned well in advance. Speaking before the 1958 Convention of the National Federation of Financial Analysts Societies, Benjamin Graham, legendary investor and author of the classic *The Intelligent Investor*,† described "some contrasting relationships between the present and the past in

---

The Vanguard Group, Inc., 47 S.E.C. 450 (1981).
†Benjamin Graham, *The Intelligent Investor*, rev. ed. (New York: HarperBusiness, 2003).

our underlying attitudes toward investment and speculation in common stocks." He further commented:

> In the past, the speculative elements of a common stock resided almost exclusively in the company itself; they were due to uncertainties, or fluctuating elements, or downright weaknesses in the industry, or the corporation's individual setup. . . . But in recent years a new and major element of speculation has been introduced into the common-stock arena from outside the companies. It comes from the attitude and viewpoint of the stock-buying public and their advisers—chiefly us security analysts. This attitude may be described in a phrase: primary emphasis upon future expectations. . . . The concept of future prospects, and particularly of continued growth in the future, invites the application of formulas out of higher mathematics to establish the present value of the favored issues. But the combination of precise formulas with highly imprecise assumptions can be used to establish, or rather to justify, practically any value one wished, however high. . . . Given the three ingredients of a) optimistic assumptions as to the rate of earnings growth, b) a sufficiently long projection of this growth into the future, and c) the miraculous workings of compound interest—lo! the security analyst is supplied with a new kind of philosopher's stone which can produce or justify any desired valuation for a really "good stock." Mathematics is ordinarily considered as producing precise and dependable results; but in the stock market the more elaborate and abstruse the mathematics the more uncertain and speculative are the conclusions we draw there from. . . . Whenever calculus is brought in, or higher algebra, you could take it as a warning signal that the operator was trying to substitute theory for experience, and usually also to give to speculation the deceptive guise of investment. . . . Have not investors and security analysts eaten of the tree of knowledge of good and evil prospects? By so doing have they not permanently expelled themselves from that Eden where promising common stocks at reasonable prices could be plucked off the bushes?*

---

*Ibid., 563–572.

This obvious reference to Original Sin reflected Graham's deep concern about quantifying the unquantifiable (and doing so with false precision). The implications of that bite into the apple of quantitative investing were barely visible when Graham spoke in 1958. But by the late 1990s, this new form of investment behavior had become a dominant force that continues to be a major driver of the speculation that has overwhelmed our financial markets.

Consider with me now how the erosion in the conduct, values, and ethics of business that I have described has been fostered by the profound—and largely unnoticed—change that has taken place in the nature of our financial markets. That change reflects two radically different views of what investing is all about, two distinct markets, if you will. One is the *real* market of intrinsic business value. The other is the *expectations* market of momentary stock prices. The British economist John Maynard Keynes described this dichotomy as the distinction between *enterprise*—"forecasting the prospective yield of the asset over its whole life"—and *speculation*—"forecasting the psychology of the markets" (p. 155). Just as Keynes forecast, speculation came to overwhelm enterprise, the old ownership society became today's agency society, and the values of capitalism were seriously eroded.*

It is little short of amazing how long ago these prescient warnings were issued. Justice Stone warned us in 1934. John Maynard Keynes warned us in 1936. Benjamin Graham warned us in 1958. Isn't it high time for us to heed the warnings of those three far-sighted intellectual giants? Isn't it high time we stand on their shoulders and shape national policy away from the moral relativism of peer conduct and greed and short-term speculation—gambling on expectations about stock prices? Isn't it high time to return to the moral absolutism of fiduciary duty, to return to our traditional ethic of long-term investment focused on building the intrinsic value of our corporations—prudence, due diligence, and active participation in corporate governance?

Yes, now *is* the time for reform. Today's agency society has ill-served the public interest. The failure of our money manager agents represents

---

*John Maynard Keynes, *The General Theory of Employment, Interest, and Money* (New York: Macmillan, 1936; Harcourt, Brace, 1964).

not only a failure of modern-day capitalism, but a failure of modern-day capitalists. As Lord Keynes warned us, "[W]hen enterprise becomes a mere bubble on a whirlpool of speculation, the job of capitalism will be ill-done" (p. 159). That is where we are today, and the consequences have not been pretty.

In all, our now-dominant money management sector has turned its focus away from the enduring nature of the intrinsic value of the goods and services created, produced, and distributed by our corporate businesses, and toward the ephemeral price of the corporation's stock—the triumph of perception over reality. We live in a world in which it is far easier to hype the price of a company's stock than it is to build the intrinsic value of the corporation itself. And we seem to have forgotten Benjamin Graham's implicit caution about the transience of short-term perception, compared to the durability of long-term reality: "In the short run, the stock market is a voting machine; in the long run it is a weighing machine."*

The Mutual Fund Industry

My strong statements regarding the failure of modern-day capitalism are manifested in grossly excessive executive compensation; financial engineering; earnings "guidance," with massive declines in valuations if it fails to be delivered; enormous, casino-like trading among institutional investors; staggering political influence, borne of huge campaign contributions; and, in the financial arena, bestowal of wealth to traders and managers that is totally disproportionate to the value they add to investors' wealth. Indeed, the financial sector actually subtracts value from our society.

Finance is what is known to economists as a rent-seeking enterprise, one in which our intermediaries—money managers, brokers, investment bankers—act as agents for parties on both sides of each transaction. Our intermediaries pit one party against another, so what would otherwise be a zero-sum game becomes a loser's game, simply because of

---

*Benjamin Graham and David Dodd, *Security Analysis* (1934, 1940; New York: McGraw-Hill, 2008).

the intermediation costs extracted by the various croupiers. (Other examples of rent-seekers include casinos, the legal system, and government. Think about it!)

I know something about how the financial system works, for I've been part of it for my entire 58-year career. The mutual fund industry—in which I've spent my entire career—is the paradigm of what's gone wrong with capitalism. Here are just a few examples of how far so many fund managers have departed from the basic fiduciary principle that "no man can serve two masters," despite the fact that the 1940 Act demands that the principal master must be the mutual fund shareholder:

1. The domination of fund boards by chairmen and chief executives who also serve as senior executives of the management companies that control the funds, an obvious conflict of interest and an abrogation of the fiduciary standard.

2. Focusing on short-term speculation over long-term investment, the ultimate triumph of expectations investing over enterprise investing, resulting in great financial benefits to fund managers and brokers, and commensurately great costs to fund investors.

3. Failure to exercise adequate due diligence in the research and analysis of the securities selected for fund portfolios, enabling corporate managers to engage in various forms of earnings management and speculative behavior, largely unchecked by the professional investment community.

4. Failure to exercise the rights and assume the responsibilities of corporate ownership, generally ignoring issues of corporate governance and allowing corporate managers to place their own financial interests ahead of the interests of their shareowners.

5. Soaring fund expenses. As fund assets soared during the 1980s and 1990s, fund fees grew even faster, reflecting higher fee rates, as well as the failure of managers to adequately share the enormous economies of scale in managing money with fund shareholders. For example, the average expense ratio of the 10 largest funds of 1960 rose from 0.51 percent to 0.96 percent in 2008, an increase of 88 percent. (Wellington Fund was the only fund whose expense ratio declined; excluding Wellington, the increase was 104%.)

6. Charging fees to the mutual funds that managers control that are far higher than the fees charged in the competitive field of pension fund management. Three of the largest advisers, for example, charge an average fee rate of 0.08 percent of assets to their pension clients and 0.61 percent to their funds, resulting in annual fees of just $600,000 for the pension fund and $*56 million* for the comparable mutual fund, and presumably holding the same stocks in both portfolios.*

7. Diluting the value of fund shares held by long-term investors, by allowing hedge fund managers to engage in "time zone" trading. This vast, near-industry-wide scandal came to light in 2003. It involved some 23 fund managers, including many of the largest firms in the field—in effect, a conspiracy between mutual fund managers and hedge fund managers to defraud regular fund shareholders.

8. Pay-to-play distribution agreements with brokers, in which fund advisers use *fund* brokerage commissions ("soft" dollars) to finance share distribution, which primarily benefits the *adviser*.

9. Spending enormous amounts on advertising—almost a half-billion dollars in the past two years alone—to bring in new fund investors, using money obtained from existing fund shareholders. Much of this spending was to promote exotic and untested "products" that have proved to have far more ephemeral marketing appeal than enduring investment integrity.

10. Lending securities that are the property of the *fund* portfolios, but siphoning off a portion of the profits from lending to the *adviser*.

Given such failures as these, doesn't Justice Stone's warning that I cited at the outset seem even *more* prescient? Let me repeat the key phrases: "The separation of ownership from management, . . . corporate structures that . . . vest in small groups control over the resources of great numbers of small and uninformed investors, . . . corporate officers and directors who award to themselves huge bonuses[,] . . . financial

---

*These figures are based on 2002 data. In a March 2010 decision in the *Jones v. Harris Associates* case, the U.S. Supreme Court found that the effectiveness of the process by which mutual fund managers set the fee rates that they charge to the funds under their control needed improvement. I had provided an *amicus curiae* brief in favor of sterner measures than the Court ultimately suggested.

institutions which consider only last, if at all, the interests of those whose funds they command." Just as we ignored the fiduciary principle all those years ago, we have clearly continued to ignore it in the recent era. The result in both cases, using Justice Stone's words, is: "The loss and suffering inflicted on individuals, the harm done to a social order founded upon business and dependent upon its integrity, are incalculable." Today, as you know, much of that harm can be calculated all too easily, amounting to several trillions of dollars. So, this time around, let's pay attention, and demand a return to fiduciary principles.

A Piece of History

While the overwhelming majority of financial institutions operate primarily in the interests of their agents and at the expense of their principals, not quite all do. So I now draw on my personal experiences in the mutual fund industry to give you one example of my own encounter with this issue. As far back as 38 years ago, I expressed profound concern about the nature and structure of the fund industry. Only three years later, my convictions led to action, and 35 years ago this September, I founded a firm designed, to the best of my ability, to honor the principles of fiduciary duty.

I expressed these principles when doing so was distinctly counter to my own self-interest. Speaking to my partners at Wellington in September 1971—*1971!*—I cited the very same words of Justice Stone with which I opened my remarks this evening. I then added:

> I endorse that view, and at the same time reveal an ancient prejudice of mine: All things considered, absent a demonstration that the enterprise has substantial capital requirements that cannot be otherwise fulfilled, it is undesirable for professional enterprises to have public stockholders. This constraint is as applicable to money managers as it is to doctors, or lawyers, or accountants, or architects. In their cases, as in ours, it is hard to see what unique contribution public investors bring to the enterprise. They do not, as a rule, add capital; they do not add expertise; they do not contribute to the well-being of our clients. Indeed, it is possible to envision circumstances in

which the pressure for earnings and earnings growth engendered by public ownership is antithetical to the responsible operation of a professional organization. Even though the field of money management has elements of both, there are, after all, differences between a business and a profession. . . . [So we must ask ourselves this question]: if it is a burden to our fund and counsel clients to be served by a public enterprise, should this burden exist in perpetuity?

My candor may well have played a supporting role in my dismissal as chief executive of Wellington Management Company in January 1974. While it's a saga too complex to detail in this article, my being fired gave me the chance of a lifetime—the opportunity to create a new fiduciary-focused structure for our funds. I proposed just such a structure to the directors of the Wellington funds.* Wellington Management Company, of course, vigorously opposed my efforts.

Nonetheless, after months of study, the directors of the funds accepted my recommendation that we separate the activities of the funds themselves from their adviser and distributor, so that the funds could operate solely in the interests of our fund shareholders. Our new structure involved the creation of a new firm, The Vanguard Group of Investment Companies, owned by the funds, employing their own officers and staff, and operated on an at-cost basis, a truly *mutual* mutual fund firm.

While Vanguard began with a limited mandate—to provide only administrative services to the funds—I realized that, if we were to control our own destiny, we would also have to provide both investment advisory and marketing services to our funds. So, almost immediately after Vanguard's operations commenced in May 1975, we began our move to gain substantial control over these two essential functions.

---

* The lecture at Columbia University, on which this article is based, is essentially the third part of a trilogy that chronicles the development of the fund industry and of Vanguard itself. The first two parts of the trilogy were presented in Chapter 12 and Chapter 13, "Re-Mutualizing the Mutual Fund Industry—The Alpha and the Omega" and "A New Order of Things: Bringing Mutuality to the 'Mutual' Fund."

By year's end, we had created the world's first index mutual fund, run by Vanguard.

Then, early in 1977, we abandoned the supply-driven broker-dealer distribution system that had been operated by Wellington since 1928 in favor of a buyer-driven "no-load" approach under our own direction. Later that year, we created the first-ever series of defined-maturity bond funds, segmented into short-, intermediate-, and long-term maturities, all focused on high investment quality. In 1981, Vanguard assumed responsibility for providing the investment advisory services to our new fixed-income funds as well as our established money market funds. (As you can imagine, none of these moves was without controversy!)

Since our formation in 1974, the assets of the Vanguard funds have grown from more than $1 billion to some $1 *trillion* currently, now the nation's largest manager of stock and bond mutual funds. Some 82 percent of that $1 trillion—$820 billion—is represented by passively managed index funds and "virtual" index funds tightly linked to various sectors of the fixed-income market. Some 25 external investment advisers serve our remaining (largely actively managed equity) funds, with Wellington Management advising by far the largest portion of those assets. Most of these funds have multiple advisers, the better to spread the risk of underperformance relative to their peers.

More than parenthetically, that long string of business decisions was made in a situation in which Vanguard's very existence was in doubt, because the Securities and Exchange Commission had initially refused to approve Vanguard's assumption of marketing and distribution responsibilities. But after a struggle lasting six (interminable!) years, the SEC reversed itself in February 1981. By unanimous vote, the Commission declared that

> [t]he Vanguard plan is consistent with the provisions, policies, and purposes of the [Investment Company Act of 1940]. It actually furthers the Act's objectives . . . enhances the funds' independence . . . benefits each fund within a reasonable range of fairness . . . [provides] substantial savings from advisory fee reductions [and] economies of scale . . . and promotes a healthy and viable mutual fund complex in which each fund can better prosper.*

---

* *The Vanguard Group, Inc.*, 47 S.E.C. 450 (1981).

A Prescient SEC?

The SEC's words now seem prescient. With few exceptions, the Vanguard funds—and their shareholders—have prospered. Measured by Morningstar's peer-based rating system (comparing each fund with other funds having distinctly comparable policies and objectives), Vanguard ranked first in performance among the 50 largest fund complexes.

Vanguard has also provided shareholders with substantial savings from advisory fee reductions and economies of scale, in fact, the lowest costs in the field. Last year, over all, our funds' aggregate operating expense ratio came to 0.20 percent of average assets, compared to 1.30 percent for the average mutual fund. That 1.1 percentage-point saving, applied to $1 trillion of assets, now produces savings for our shareholders of some $11 billion annually. And, as the world of investing is at last beginning to understand, low costs are the single most reliable predictor of superior fund performance. As we read in Homer's *The Odyssey*, "fair dealing yields more profit in the end."

If you are willing to accept—based on these data—that Vanguard has achieved both *commercial* success (asset growth and market share) and *artistic* success (superior performance and low costs), you must wonder why, after 35 years of existence, *no* other firm has elected to emulate our shareholder-oriented structure. (A particularly ironic outcome, as I chose the name Vanguard in part because of its conventional definition as *"leader* in a new trend.") The answer, I think, can be expressed succinctly: Under our at-cost structure, all of the profits go to the fund shareholders, not to the managers, resolving the transcendent conflict of interest of the mutual fund industry. In any event, the leader, as it were, has yet to find its first follower.

Vanguard represented my best effort to align the interests of fund investors and fund managers under established principles of fiduciary duty. I leave it to wiser—and surely more objective—heads than mine to evaluate whether or not I overstate or hyperbolize what we have accomplished. But I freely acknowledge that we owe our accomplishments to the three simple principles: the firm is (1) *structurally* correct (because we are owned by our fund investors); (2) *mathematically* correct (because it is a tautology that the lower the costs incurred in investing, the higher the returns); and (3) *ethically* correct (because we exist only by earning far greater trust and loyalty from our shareholders than any of our peers). Measured by repeated evaluations of loyalty by independent research firms, there has been no close rival for our #1 position. Please be appropriately skeptical of that self-serving claim, but look at the data. In a 2007 survey, one such group concluded, "Vanguard Group generates far more loyalty than any other company."*

To Build the Financial World Anew

Creating and restructuring Vanguard was no easy task. Without determination, expertise, luck, timing, and the key roles played by just a handful of individuals, it never could have happened. So when I suggest that we must now go beyond restructuring the nature and values of a single firm to restructuring the nature and values of the entire money management business—to build the financial world anew—I am well aware of how difficult it will be to accomplish that sweeping task.

And yet we dare not stand still.

> For we meet at a time when, as never before in the history of the country, our most cherished ideals and traditions are being subjected to searching criticism. The towering edifice of business and industry, which had become the dominating feature of the American social structure, has been shaken to its foundations by forces, the full significance of which we still can see but dimly. What had seemed the impregnable fortress of a boasted civilization has developed unsuspected weaknesses, and in consequence we are now engaged in the altogether wholesome task of critical re-examination of what our hands have reared.

As you may have suspected, I've once again cited a section of Justice Stone's 1934 speech, and it's high time we take it seriously. For the fact is that there has been a radical change in our investment system from the ownership society of a half-century ago—which is gone,

---

*Murray Coleman, "Few Firms Earn Loyalty of the Wealthy: Well-Heeled Investors Search for Consistency; Vanguard Rates Highest," *Wall Street Journal*, March 15, 2007, C13. Figures are based on data from Cogent Research. The Vanguard loyalty score (percentage of strong supporters minus strong detractors) was a positive 44. The fund industry scored a pathetic negative 12.

never to return—to our agency society of today—in which our agents have failed to serve their principals—mutual fund shareholders, pension beneficiaries, and long-term investors. Rather, the new system has served the agents themselves—our institutional managers.

Further, by their forbearance on governance issues, our money managers have also served the managers of corporate America. To make matters even worse, by turning to short-term speculation at the expense of long-term investment, the industry has also damaged the interests of the greater society, just as Lord Keynes warned.

Yet despite the extraordinary (and largely unrecognized) shift in the very nature of corporate ownership, we have failed to change the rules of the game. Indeed, in the financial sector we have rolled back most of the historic rules regulating our securities issuers, our exchanges, and our investment advisers. While we should have been improving regulatory oversight and administering existing regulations with increasing toughness, both have been relaxed, ignoring the new environment, and therefore bear much of the responsibility for today's crisis.

Of course American society is in a constant state of flux. It always has been, and it always will be. I've often pointed out that our nation began as an agricultural economy, became largely a manufacturing economy, then largely a service economy, and most recently an economy in which the financial services sector had become the dominant element. Such secular changes are not new, but they are always different, so enlightened responses are never easy to come by. Justice Stone, once again, recognized that new forces demand new responses:

> It was in 1809 when Jefferson wrote: "We are a rural farming people; we have little business and few manufactures among us, and I pray God it will be a long time before we have much of either." Profound changes have come into American life since that sentence was penned. [These] inexorable economic forces, [create] public problems [that] involve an understanding of the new and complex economic forces we have created, their relationship to the lives of individuals in widely separated communities engaged in widely differing activities, and the adaptation to those forces of old conceptions developed in a different environment to meet different needs.

To deal with the new and complex economic forces our failed agency society has created, of course we need a new paradigm: a fiduciary society in which the interest of investors comes first, and ethical behavior by our business and financial leaders represents the highest value.

Building a Fiduciary Society

While the challenges of today are inevitably different from those of the past, the principles are age-old. Consider this warning from Adam Smith way back in the 18th century: "Managers of other people's money [rarely] watch over it with the same anxious vigilance with which . . . they watch over their own. . . . [T]hey very easily give themselves a dispensation. Negligence and profusion must always prevail."* And so in the recent era, negligence and profusion have prevailed among our money manager/agents, even to the point of an almost complete disregard of their duty and responsibility to their principals. Too few managers seem to display the "anxious vigilance" over other people's money that once defined the conduct of investment professionals.

So what we must do is develop a new *fiduciary* society to guarantee that our last-line owners—those mutual fund shareholders and pension fund beneficiaries whose savings are at stake—have their rights as investment principals protected. These rights must include:

1. The right to have money manager/agents act solely in their principals' behalf. The client, in short, must be king.
2. The right to rely on due diligence and high professional standards on the part of money managers and securities analysts who appraise securities for principals' portfolios.†

---

*In those days, *profusion* was defined as a "lavish or wasteful expenditure or excess bestowal of money, substance, etc., squandering, waste" (*Oxford English Dictionary*, 2nd ed., vol. XII, 1989, p. 584).
†Peter Fisher, widely respected BlackRock executive and former Treasury Department official, recently told the *Wall Street Journal* ("Principles for Change," March 29, 2009) that he believes we should force institutional investors to do a better job of analysis, and establish demanding minimum standards of competence.

3. The assurance that agents will act as responsible corporate citizens, restoring to their principals the neglected rights of ownership of stocks, and demanding that corporate directors and managers meet their fiduciary duty to their own shareholders.
4. The right to demand some sort of discipline and integrity in the mutual funds and financial products that they offer.
5. The establishment of advisory fee structures that meet a "reasonableness" standard based not only on *rates* but *dollar amounts*, and their relationship to the fees and structures available to other clients of the manager.
6. The elimination of all conflicts of interest that could preclude the achievement of these goals.

More than parenthetically, I should note that this final provision would seem to preclude the ownership of money management firms by financial conglomerates, now the dominant form of organization in the mutual fund industry. Among today's 40 largest fund complexes, only 6 remain privately held. The remaining 34 include 13 firms whose shares are held directly by the public, and an astonishing total of 21 fund managers are owned or controlled by U.S. and international financial conglomerates—including Goldman Sachs, Bank of America, Deutsche Bank, ING, John Hancock, and Sun Life of Canada. Painful as such a separation might be, conglomerate ownership of money managers is the single most blatant violation of the principle that "no man can serve two masters."

Of course it will take federal government action to foster the creation of this new fiduciary society that I envision. Above all else, it must be unmistakable that government intends, and is capable of enforcing, standards of trusteeship and fiduciary duty under which money managers operate with the *sole* purpose and in the *exclusive* benefit of the interests of their beneficiaries—largely the owners of mutual fund shares and the beneficiaries of our pension plans. As corporate reformer Robert Monks accurately points out, "capitalism without owners will fail."

While government action is essential, however, the new system should be developed in concert with the private investment sector, an Alexander Hamilton–like sharing of the responsibilities in which the Congress establishes the fiduciary principle, and private enterprise establishes the practices that are required to observe it. This task of returning capitalism to its ultimate owners will take time, true enough. But the new reality—increasingly visible with each passing day—is that the concept of fiduciary duty is no longer merely an ideal to be debated. It is a vital necessity to be practiced.

So a lot is at stake in reforming the very nature of our financial system itself, which in turn is designed to force reform in our failed system of governance of our business corporations. The ideas I've passionately advocated in this article, however, are hardly widely shared among my colleagues and peers in the financial sector. But soon, perhaps, many others will ultimately see the light; for example, in March 2009, the idea of governance reform received encouraging support from Professor Andrew W. Lo of the Massachusetts Institute of Technology, one of today's most respected financial economists:

> [T]he single most important implication of the financial crisis is about the current state of corporate governance . . . a major wake-up call that we need to change [the rules]. There's something fundamentally wrong with current corporate governance structures, [and] the kinds of risks that typical corporations face today.*

In sum, the change in the rules that I advocate—applying to institutional money managers a federal standard of fiduciary duty to their clients—would be designed in turn to force money managers to use their own ownership position to demand that the managers and directors of the business corporations in whose shares they invest also honor their own fiduciary duty to the holders of their shares. Finally, it is these two groups that share the responsibility for the prudent stewardship over both corporate assets and investment securities that have been entrusted to their care, not only reforming today's flawed and conflict-ridden model, but developing a new model that, at best, will restore traditional ethical mores.

---

*Andrew W. Lo, "Business Insight (A Special Report): Executive Briefing—Understanding Our Blind Spots: Financial Crisis Underscores Need to Transform Our View of Risk," *Wall Street Journal*, March 23, 2009.

And so I await—with no great patience!—the return of the standard so beautifully described by Justice Cardozo all those years ago, excerpts from his words cited earlier in my remarks:

> Those bound by fiduciary ties . . . [are] held to something stricter than the morals of the marketplace . . . a tradition unbending and inveterate . . . not honesty alone but the punctilio of an honor the most sensitive . . . a level of conduct . . . higher than that trodden by the crowd.

In his profound 1934 speech that has been the inspiration for this article, Justice Harlan Fiske Stone made one further prescient point on serving the common good:

> In seeking solutions for our social and economic maladjustments, we are too ready to place our reliance on what (the policeman's nightstick of) the state may command, rather than on what may be given to it as the free offering of good citizenship. . . . Yet we know that unless the urge to individual advantage has other curbs, and unless the more influential elements in society conduct themselves with a disposition to promote the common good, society cannot function . . . especially a society which has largely measured its rewards in terms of material gains. . . . We must [square] our own ethical conceptions with the traditional ethics and ideals of the community at large. [There is] nothing more vital to our own day than that those who act as fiduciaries in the strategic positions of our business civilization, should be held to those standards of scrupulous fidelity which [our] society has the right to demand.

The 75th anniversary of Justice Stone's landmark speech reminds all of us engaged in the profession of investment management how far we have departed from those standards of scrupulous fidelity, and gives us yet one more opportunity to strengthen our resolve to meet that test, and build a better financial world.

Chapter 15

Mutual Funds at the Millennium: Fund Directors and Fund Myths*

A s I was doing the research for my Princeton thesis on the mutual fund industry in 1950, a mere half-century ago, I discovered a report from the Securities and Exchange Commission that described mutual funds as "the most important financial development in the U.S. during the past 50 years." Just how the SEC reached this powerful conclusion about an industry that had but $2.5 billion of assets and represented only 1.5 percent of the financial assets of American families was not at all clear to me. But, by golly, they were right! Since then, the fund industry has lived up to that early promise—and then some. Today, with assets totaling $7.2 trillion, and accounting for a stunning 90 percent of the net additions to family liquid savings over

---

*Based on a speech delivered to The 1940 Act Institute of PLI (The Practicing Law Institute), New York City, on May 15, 2000.

the past five years, mutual funds have become the largest aggregation of financial assets in the land.

But this industry has lost its way. A half-century ago, it was far more an *investment* business than a *marketing* business. Today, the reverse is true. Measured not only by the fund industry's very nature and focus, but by its relative expenditures on each function, the industry is primarily a marketing business. Then, funds were long-term investments, fund managers were long-term investors, and fund shareholders held their shares for an average of 15 years. Today funds come and go at a remarkable pace: Each business day, three new mutual funds are born and one existing fund dies, its performance usually poor, its purpose passé. Fifty years ago, fund costs were well within the ambit of fairness. Now, despite the industry's quantum 2,900-fold increase in assets, *unit* expenses of funds have risen by one-third, giving rise to a far larger 4,300-fold(!) increase in the dollar amount of direct fund operating expenses—from $15 million in 1950 to $*65 billion* in 1999.

Today I'm going to present to you graphic evidence of these trends, which, I fear, bode ill for this industry, and for the financial markets as well. While I have been speaking out on these trends for more than a decade now, they've only gotten worse. On the other hand, confession being good for the soul, I acknowledge that there is little evidence of their baneful effects on the stock market—so far at least.

Protecting the Interests of Those Whose Funds They Command

Nonetheless, these trends—the focus on marketing, the soaring levels of fund investment activity, and the huge increase in fund expenses—could combine to engender, a year or two or three down the road, the kind of statement made in 1934 by Justice Harlan Fiske Stone as he reviewed the events that led to the Great Crash of 1929 and the Great Depression that followed.*

---

*H. F. Stone, address to the University of Michigan School of Law on June 15, 1934, reprinted in the *Harvard Law Review* (1934).

When the history of the financial era which has just drawn to a close comes to be written, most of the mistakes and its major faults will be ascribed to the failure to observe the fiduciary principle, the precept as old as holy writ, that 'a man cannot serve two masters'. . . .

The development of the corporate structure so as to ves in small groups control over the resources of great numbers of small and uninformed investors, make imperative a fresh and active devotion to that principle if the modern world of business is to perform its proper function.

Yet those who serve nominally as trustees, but relieved, by clever legal devices, from the obligation to protect whose interests they purport to represent . . . consider only last the interests of those whose funds they command, suggest how far we have ignored the necessary implications of that principle.*

In this industry, then as now, small groups "control the resources of great numbers of investors," and it is fund managers who must accept the lion's share of the responsibilities for the baneful trends I will discuss today. But fund directors—"those who serve nominally as trustees"—must bear their share as well, given the responsibilities they are assigned under federal and state law. And it is a heavy burden, given not only what they have done but what they have failed to do. Whether affiliated with the fund management company or *not*, they are serving two masters—the management company and the fund shareholders—and that is the root cause of the problem. Yes, we need entrepreneurs to start fund organizations, and, yes, they have a right to make a profit. After all, that's the American way. But when that profit is excessive, it creates an unacceptable burden on the returns earned by fund shareholders, who are, after all, the owners of the fund.

---

*I last used that quotation in my "State of the Firm" address to the officers of Wellington Management Company in 1971, more than three years before I founded Vanguard. I was reflecting on the harm the fund industry inflicted on investors during the "Go-Go Era" of the 1960s, the precursor of the devastating 50 percent market crash of 1973–1974.

I am not prepared to argue that today's fund directors have been, as were the trustees of Justice Stone's era, "relieved of their trusteeship obligation by clever legal devices." Indeed, their trusteeship obligation clearly exists; the problem is that it is given short shrift. There is compelling evidence that the interests of the managers/marketers *are* being placed first. To the extent that is true, it suggests that fund directors today "consider only last the interests of those whose funds they command . . . and whose interests they purport to represent."

I'm going to develop my analysis of recent industry trends by demythologizing, if you will, the traditional attributes ascribed to mutual funds—attributes that it would be impossible for anyone to seriously argue prevail today. I'll deal with five of them:

Myth 1: That mutual *funds* are long-term *investments*.
Myth 2: That mutual fund *managers* are long-term *investors*.
Myth 3: That mutual fund *shareholders* are long-term *owners*.
Myth 4: That mutual fund *costs* are declining.
Myth 5: That mutual fund *returns* are meeting the reasonable expectations of investors.

I'll challenge these myths by presenting the realities of how radically this industry has changed over the years, especially in what we might consider the "modern era" of funds, beginning in the mid-1980s, when fund assets first crossed the $500 billion mark. Then, lest I leave you with all problems and no solutions, I'll conclude with a Golden Rule and Ten Commandments for directors that would help to begin the arduous process of putting the fund shareholders back where they belong: in the driver's seat of this critically important financial machine.

Myth #1: Mutual Funds Are Long-Term Investments

Once, mutual funds were considered investments for a lifetime. The idea was to buy a mutual fund as a complete, diversified investment program and hold it, well, *forever*—Warren Buffett's favorite holding period for a stock—much as wealthy families use trust companies and private trustees. But over the years this industry has moved from a focus on sound investment management to the marketing of what have come to be known as "financial products" (I don't care for the choice of words, but the phrase surely hits the nail on the head!). This trend means, as I recall one firm putting it, "we're in the ice cream business. We prefer vanilla and chocolate, but if the customers want pistachio-maple-walnut, we'll give it to them."

This change in strategy does much to explain the creation of the go-go funds of the 1960s, those lamentable "government-plus" funds and the global short-term income funds of the 1980s (all of which came and now are gone), and of the Internet, technology, and so-called focus (20-stock limit) funds of the turn of the century. During the past five years, more than 2,000 new equity funds have been formed, most of them designed to capitalize on the public appetite to duplicate in the future the fabulous returns captured in the past by stocks in this so-called New Economy of technology, telecommunications, and science. If history is any guide, few of these funds will be with us a decade hence.

During the more quiescent years of the 1960s, just 28 funds out of but 200 didn't survive the decade, an acceptable fund failure rate of 14 percent for the decade. During the 1970s, in the inevitable hangover that followed the wild spree of the earlier decade, 297 funds, including most of the go-go funds, gave up the ghost, and the failure rate soared to an astonishing 62 percent. Thus cleansed, the industry was more sedate during the 1980s, and the rate receded to 21 percent. But despite the Great Bull Market, fund failures accelerated during the 1990s, to a surprising 55 percent for the decade. In the past two years alone, an estimated 450 funds have disappeared.

Clearly, too many funds have been formed with the principal purpose of being sold to investors. Often lacking durable investment principles and doomed to performance failure, they were born simply to die. If in the first decade of this century the failure rate of the last decade of the previous century holds, more than 2,300 of today's 4,500 funds won't be around in 2010. Mutual fund directors, whether or not they are aware of what is happening or aware of their fiduciary duties, have presided over this change in the very nature of the mutual fund—from being a sound, long-term investment to a product offering a short-term marketing opportunity; from providing stewardship for a lifetime to the participating in the momentum of the marketplace (see Figure 15.1).

FIGURE 15.1   MYTH #1: MUTUAL FUNDS ARE LONG-TERM INVESTMENTS

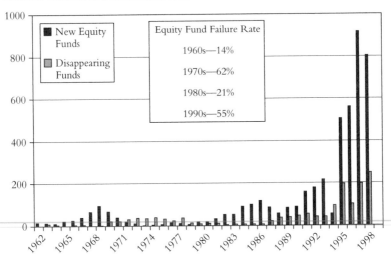

SOURCE: 1962–1995, Carhart; 1996–1999, Vanguard estimate.

Myth #2: Mutual Fund Managers Are Long-Term Investors

Equally depressing, at least to me, is the baneful change in focus of mutual fund managers. I mince no words: *Fund managers, once long-term investors, have become short-term speculators.* From the time I wrote my Princeton thesis until the mid-1960s, average fund portfolio turnover normally ran in the 15 percent–20 percent range, a putative holding period of five to seven years for the average stock fund. In recent years, turnover has consistently run over 80 percent, and was 90 percent last year. Alas, in this era of day traders—one-day traders—fund managers can be accurately described as "406-day traders." If "speculator" is too strong a word for the typical fund manager, it's surely infinitely closer to the mark than "long-term investor."

Their high turnover rate, interestingly, is remarkably pervasive. It ranges from an average of 146 percent for mid-cap growth funds to 62 percent for small-cap value funds. And even the *median* large-cap fund turns its portfolio over at 63 percent (excluding stock index funds, which turn over at only about 9%). High turnover is not a statistical aberration; it is almost as prevalent as the air we breathe.

Again, this industry's shift to a marketing ethos bears an important share of the responsibility for soaring portfolio turnover. Only a few decades ago, it was the *investment committee* that managed the fund and focused on the long-term, but today it is the *portfolio manager* that is in charge. Portfolio managers, focusing on the short-term, can be "hot," and when there is heat, huge capital inflows are not far behind. And larger assets mean larger fees. So, ever since the mid-1960s, we've lionized our hot portfolio managers; they became our stars, glamorous and glittering. "A star is born" has become the watchword. Alas, as we now know, most *stars* have proved to be *comets*, illuminating the financial firmament for but a few moments in time and then burning out, their ashes gently descending to earth (see Figure 15.2).

Unlike those staid old committees, the new breed of manager was lighting-quick on the trigger. The portfolio managers just can't seem to sit still for very long, echoing Pascal's maxim: "All human evil comes from this, from man's inability to sit quietly in a room." What is more, the managers don't hold their jobs for very long, and considerable *portfolio* turnover arises simply from portfolio *manager* turnover. The average manager of an equity fund with at least five years of operations is but six short years, and when he or she moves on—a failure, or such an ostensible success that the hedge fund sirens beckon, or simply a

FIGURE 15.2 MYTH #2: MUTUAL FUND MANAGERS ARE LONG-TERM INVESTORS

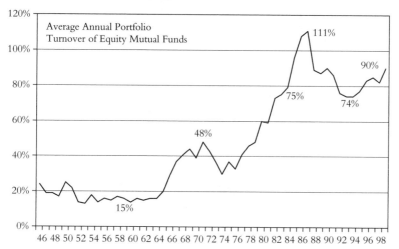

reorganization of the investment department—the broom of the new manager sweeps the portfolio clean.

What's so evil about this turnover frenzy? First, it cannot possibly serve fund investors as a group, because as much as half of all turnover—perhaps even more—takes place among mutual funds themselves. Second, it costs money to trade securities—commissions, spreads, and market impact costs—conservatively estimated at one-half to one percentage point per year of return. Third, its tax impact is, well, devastating. Capital gains, about one-third of which are realized on a short-term basis and thus taxed as ordinary income—have resulted in a hit to fund returns of almost three full percentage points of return each year during this bull market.

Yes, as some naive defenders of the present ethos argue, some 40 percent of equity fund assets are held in tax-deferred accounts, so taxes don't matter. *But there is no evidence whatsoever that all of this flailing around enhances returns.* Thus, the high turnover that is radically diminishing the returns of 60 percent of fund shareholders does nothing that benefits the remaining 40 percent. The shift from long-term investing to short-term speculation, then, is hurting the very shareholders that fund directors are duty-bound to serve.

Myth #3: Mutual Fund Shareholders Are Long-Term Owners

Like the "ILOVEYOU" virus, the virus that has so adversely infected the duration of the lives of *mutual funds* and the duration of the horizons of fund *portfolio managers* seems to be wildly contagious. Mutual fund shareholders are now suffering from the same malady—a game of "follow the leader" that is, I am confident, utterly unproductive. When I wrote my thesis, and for 20 years thereafter, share redemptions by fund shareholders averaged about 7 percent per year, suggesting an average holding period of slightly over 14 years. (The reciprocal of the redemption rate is a crude, but reasonably accurate, indicator of the holding period.) This figure gradually drifted upward to the 15 percent range by the mid-1980s, a 7-year holding period.

But in the late 1970s, another source of shareholder activity began. As the concept of the fund family took hold, the *exchange privilege* came into wide use. Investors could redeem shares in, say, the family's value fund and buy its growth fund or, for that matter, its money market fund—still clearly a redemption, but not "counted," as it were, in the official data, understating the true redemption rate of fund investors by more than half. From the mid-1980s through 1997, regular redemptions of equity funds averaged some 17 percent of assets. But exchange redemptions ran at an even higher 19 percent rate, bringing the typical year's all-in redemption rate to 36 percent, a holding period of less than three years for the average shareholder, fully 80 percent shorter than the 14-year average of the 1950–1975 era.

In 1987, with the short-lived market crash and its aftermath, there was a rare departure from this norm. Redemptions jumped to 20 percent of assets and exchange redemptions (largely into money market funds) leaped to 42 percent, a combined redemption rate of 62 percent. In October alone, the annualized rate soared to 120 percent. (That's right, a rate that, had it persisted for a year, would have been larger than the entire equity fund asset base!) That rate may well be a harbinger of what lies ahead if stock market conditions move from unsettled, as they are today, to bearish. In any event, the upward trend seems to be accelerating. The all-in redemption rate rose to nearly 40 percent in 1999, and in the first three months of 2000 has soared to 50 percent, reflecting an abandonment of value funds, a surge in technology funds, and, to a small degree, a flight to money market funds.

This sea change in the character of fund owners, from long term to short term, violates the most fundamental principle of investment success: *Invest for the long pull.* I am confident that this frequent switching causes investors to relinquish far more investment return than can be explained by the high out-of-pocket transaction costs and taxes they incur. Rapidly jumping from one fund to another is *not* a formula for investment success. Yet these appalling figures of aggregate redemptions are, as far as I know, almost *never* presented to fund directors, who remain unaware of the shifting nature of their constituency and the added risks and costs to which the funds they serve are exposed (see Figure 15.3).

**FIGURE 15.3   MYTH #3: MUTUAL FUND INVESTORS
HOLD SHARES FOR THE LONG TERM**

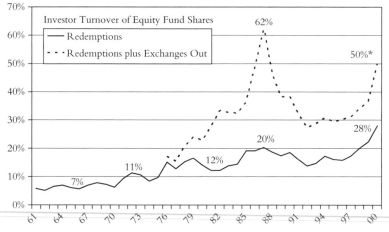

*2000—1Q annualized.

Myth #4: Mutual Fund Costs Are Declining

Back in 1950, when I was writing my thesis, the expense ratio of the
average equity fund was 0.77 percent. It has been rising ever since, hit-
ting 0.96 percent in 1980, 1.20 percent in 1987, leveling off at about
1.40 percent through 1995, and then, with the rapid formation of
new—and higher-cost, *always* higher-cost—funds, rising to 1.58 percent last year. In all, the expense ratio of the average equity fund has
risen by more than 100 percent—a doubling of unit costs.

Yet, sparked by heavily publicized industry data, a myth that fund
costs are actually declining has developed. Specifically, one industry study says, using a thoroughly inaccurate formulation, the "costs
of fund *ownership*" are declining. What it *meant to say* is that the costs of
purchasing funds is declining. The industry study concedes that the
average *unit* cost of equity funds is now 1.93 percent (*35% higher* than
even my 1.58% figure). But it alleges that the average cost of *purchasing* equity funds—when weighted by each fund's sales volume—has
declined from 2.26 percent in 1980 to 1.35 percent in 1998.

The study leaves, dare I say, much to be desired. Loading the dice
by making sales volume the basis of cost measurement, the study merely
captures the remarkable shift in investor choice from high-cost funds

**FIGURE 15.4   MYTH #4: MUTUAL FUND COSTS
ARE DECLINING**

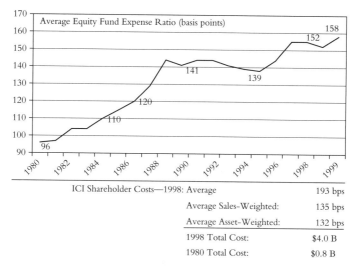

ICI Shareholder Costs—1998: Average	193 bps
Average Sales-Weighted:	135 bps
Average Asset-Weighted:	132 bps
1998 Total Cost:	$4.0 B
1980 Total Cost:	$0.8 B

to a relative handful of no-load funds, low-expense-ratio funds, and minimal-cost index funds. *But price competition is defined, not by the actions of consumers, but by the actions of producers.* So the trend that this tortuous methodology measures is hardly evidence of what is described as "vigorous price competition" in the fund industry. Indeed, since few, if any, fund groups have slashed their fees to take on the low-cost funds in the marketplace, price competition is hardly intense; it is barely alive.

And the study has still *more* weaknesses. It completely ignores a *huge* cost of fund ownership, *fund portfolio turnover.* That would add 0.50–1.00 percent-plus to the putative 1.35 percent total. It amortizes sales loads based on 25-year-old data, ignoring today's infinitely shorter (and therefore far costlier) holding period. It ignores the *opportunity cost* that funds incur by their failure to be fully invested in stocks—another 0.60 percent cost. And it no longer even *reports* the fact, buried deep in the first of its two studies, that the average expense ratio of the lowest cost decile of funds has actually *risen* by 27 percent since 1980—from 0.71 percent to 0.90 percent in 1997—perhaps up 35–40 percent if Vanguard were excluded. Even the lowest-cost funds will not be denied their fee increases. Since fund costs have soared from $800 million to $65 billion over the past two decades—increasing at an annual rate of 25 percent—it is clearer that declining costs are just one more myth (see Figures 15.4 and 15.5).

FIGURE 15.5   MYTH #4: MUTUAL FUND COSTS
ARE DECLINING

ICI Position:
• Ownership cost of equity funds down 40 percent.
• 1980—231 bps; 1998—135 bps (Load 200 bps, No-load 83 bps).

Specific Flaws:
1. Weighted by sales volume. Unweighted expense ratio up 64 percent—96 to 158 bps.
2. Lowest cost decile up 27 percent from 71 bps to 90 bps (1997).
3. Ignores hidden cost of portfolio turnover (50 to 125 bps).
4. Ignores opportunity cost (60 bps).
5. Ignores fees on "wrap accounts."
6. Amortization of sales loads based on 25-year-old data. If updated, 1998 cost up by 50 bps, to 185 bps (estimated).

Fundamental Flaw:
Price competition is (correctly) defined by the actions of producers, not the actions of consumers. Thus price competition is not "intense" in fund industry; it is barely alive.

Myth #5: Mutual Funds Are Meeting the Reasonable Expectations of Investors

Given the high fees and operating costs, the short-term investment horizons, and the substantial transaction and tax costs that go hand-in-hand with this rise in investment activity, it is small wonder that mutual fund returns have lagged so far behind the substantial returns generated by U.S. stocks during this greatest of all bull markets. Assuming only that the expectation of most fund investors is at least to enjoy a fair participation in the long-term returns generated by common stocks—and that seems a minimal assumption indeed—the idea that mutual funds have met the reasonable expectations of investors proves to be yet another myth.

I am speaking not only of the failure of the average fund to match the returns of the Standard & Poor's 500 Stock Index. While that large-cap index is not a *bad* comparison—after all, it represents 75 percent of the stock market, and its return has been *identical* to that of the total stock market over the past 30 years—it is a *crude* comparison, given that nearly one-half of all equity funds today focus principally on mid-cap and small-cap stocks. The net result is that the performance of the average fund was somewhat *better* than it appeared during the surge in large-cap stocks from 1994 through 1998, even as it was *worse* than it appeared during the small-cap outperformance of 1990–1993 and in the past 16 months.

But more sophisticated comparisons are readily available. For example, we can compare *large*-cap funds with a *large*-cap index (the S&P 500 is fair enough), and compare mid- and small-cap funds with indexes of mid- and small-cap stocks. Result: On a pre-tax basis, over the past 15 years, large-cap funds have lagged their benchmark by 2.9 percentage points per year, mid-cap funds by 4.7 points, and small-cap funds by 2.0 points. (Given the high failure rate of funds, I've tried to adjust conservatively for survivor bias, using an average of 1.2%, but— generously!—ignored sales charges.*) On an after-tax basis, as you might expect, the lags increase substantially, to 4.5, 6.2, and 3.0 points, respectively. The brute fact: All-in fund costs have consumed about one-third of the *annual* investment returns earned by their bogeys, *even after the benchmarks are adjusted for estimated index fund expenses and taxes.*

Alas for the fund shareholder, that's the least of it. Even as we have the famously accretive *magic of compounding* of investment returns, so we have the subtly decretive *tyranny of compounding* investment costs. Result: The *cumulative* investment returns earned by mutual funds over the past 15 years have been a pale shadow of the cumulative returns by comparable market indexes. Large-cap funds have provided 51 percent of the cumulative after-tax profit generated by the S&P 500 index. Mid-cap funds have provided 37 percent of the profit generated by the S&P 400 Mid-Cap Index. Small-cap funds have provided 56 percent of return generated by the Russell 2000 Small Cap Index. That's just not good enough (see Figure 15.6).

It is as hard to imagine fund directors basking in the glory of this record of their stewardship as it is easy to imagine their general concern, even their embarrassment, although there is no evidence of either. So it is easiest of all to imagine that the fund directors unaffiliated with fund management are completely unaware of these facts. (To be sure, their affiliated director counterparts must be all too aware of them.) Yes, I'm reasonably confident that nearly all directors receive presentations showing returns on an annual basis and a cumulative annualized basis, but I wonder how many boards are exposed to cumulative after-tax returns on a comprehensive comparative basis.

---

*I believe my adjustment for survivor bias is extremely conservative. Princeton's Burton Malkiel calculated survivor bias during 1976–1991 at 4.2 percent per year.

FIGURE 15.6 MYTH #5: MUTUAL FUNDS ARE MEETING THE REASONABLE EXPECTATIONS OF INVESTORS

15-Year Returns on $10,000 Investment—Blend Funds vs. Index Funds

Fund Type	Annual Return Pre-Tax	After-Tax	Final Value Pre-Tax	After-Tax	The Cost of Cost*
Large-cap	15.0%	12.2%	$81,400	$56,200	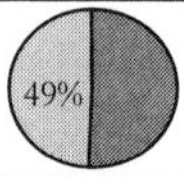
S&P 500	17.9	16.7	118,200	101,700	49%
Mid-cap	12.8%	9.8%	$60,900	$40,600	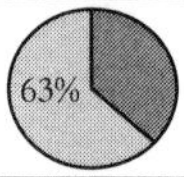
S&P 400	17.5	16.0	112,300	92,700	63%
Small-cap	10.2%	7.5%	$42,900	$29,600	
Russell 2000	12.2	10.5	56,200	44,700	44%

*Appreciation of active fund investment as % of index fund.
Fund returns adjusted for survivor bias of 0.3, 1.2, and 2.0 percent, respectively.
Benchmarks adjusted for index fund expenses and estimated taxes.

Yet despite what the data shows, we have virtually no examples of the termination of contracts of fund managers primarily by reason of consistent inferior performance. That strongly suggests that directors either don't know, or don't care, or don't think it is their role to take action. If they don't know, they are derelict in their duty. If they don't care, they are financially illiterate. And if they don't think their role is to take action, who else do they think will fulfill that role?

Where Do We Go from Here?

Taken together, the shift of industry focus from management to marketing; the rising rate of fund failures; the incredibly short horizons of portfolio managers; the increasing use of funds as vehicles for trading, not investment; and the soaring costs and tax bills have combined to ill-serve fund shareholders and create a clear record of performance inadequacy. What's to be done? I suggest that independent directors have a major role to play in the resolution of these seemingly intractable problems. After all, who but fund directors are in a position to bring funds into compliance with the clear mandate of the Investment Company Act of 1940:

> The national public interest and the interest of investors are adversely affected . . . when investment companies are organized, operated and managed in the interest of investment advisers, rather than in the interest of shareholders . . . or when investment companies are not subjected to adequate independent scrutiny.

This Act's preamble clearly makes two demands: (1) that it is shareholders who come first, with funds organized, operated, and managed with *their* interests the highest priority; and (2) that it is independent directors who have the responsibility for the careful scrutiny that assures the primacy of those interests.

The Ten Commandments

You don't have to tell me how tough a job it will be for this industry to reach that worthy goal. I've been doing my best, even in the years before "The Vanguard Experiment" began, but the tangible results are disappointingly few. Vanguard began its thousand-mile journey with a single step in 1974, and lots more steps have followed. (Few of you know how arduous and demanding each of those steps have been, and continue to be.) But let me suggest some further steps along the way to meeting the clear—and wholly desirable—mandate of the 1940 Act. While I wish we could take a giant step—establishing a federal standard of fiduciary for fund directors would be my choice—the fact is that a series of small but deliberate steps is more realistic. So I would propose that we begin by setting down these Ten Commandments for independent directors:

1. **Thou Shalt Retain Thine Own Independent Counsel.** Recommended by the Securities and Exchange Commission, this step seems so obvious and so essential that it is hard to imagine why it hasn't been mandatory ever since this industry began in

1924. Just imagine, in any other business, the anomaly of a firm being represented, not by its own counsel, but by counsel for its largest supplier of services, who depends on it for its very existence. Yes, I read all the arguments against independent counsel—there aren't enough lawyers; they won't be as experienced; they won't be the best; they won't have enough financial incentives; and believe it or not, in the face of the failings I've described, the industry "is not aware of any problems that have arisen as a result of current practices." Although I have no doubt that the present proposal can be sharpened, these make-weight arguments must be disregarded, and the independent counsel proposal implemented.

2. **Thou Shalt Elect an Independent Director as Thy Fund Chairman.** The present fund chairman, by and large, is chairman or president of the fund's management company. But it must be clear that the management company is a business corporation, and the primary responsibility of its chairman is to keep the business running soundly and to earn the largest possible profit for its owners. The *fund* chairman's primary responsibility is, in a sense, precisely the same . . . *but for a completely different constituency*: to keep the *fund* running soundly and to earn the largest possible profit for *its* owners. The two responsibilities directly conflict: The more the manager charges in fees, the less remains for fund shareholders. Only by separating these two distinct responsibilities can we possibly begin the process of bringing management fees and profit margins under control. After all, when the *fund* chairman negotiates fees with the *management company* chairman, and they are the same person, we can hardly expect shareholders to come first. Warren Buffett put it perfectly: "Negotiating with oneself rarely produces a barroom brawl."

3. **Thou Shalt Get the Facts about Performance.** Demand full, fair comparisons. Consider risks, peers, and appropriate market indexes. Look at *cumulative* returns over extended periods, and don't forget *after-tax* returns.

4. **Thou Shalt Get the Facts about Costs.** For each fund you serve as a director, "follow the money." Review the adviser's profit-and-loss statement. How much did the fund pay? How much was spent on investment management? How much on marketing, and on

administration? (Press hard on exactly how those expenditures on advertising—directly or indirectly, through 12b-1 plans—benefit the shareholder.) What was the manager's pre-tax profit margin—before and after marketing costs—on each fund you serve? On all funds in the complex? This information should be readily accessible. Indeed, 30 years ago, we regularly provided such information to the directors of the mutual funds managed by Wellington Management Company. *You can't intelligently consider fund fees without knowing where the money goes.* And, while I'm on the subject of costs, let me reiterate my call for the Securities and Exchange Commission to undertake a comprehensive economic study of the mutual fund industry, first determining and then publishing industry-wide data on where $65 billion of fees and expenses paid by fund shareholders went last year. Examining sources and uses is the only way to follow the money.

5. **Thou Shalt Compare the *Dollar* Fees Thy Fund Pays with Those of Competitors.** This industry has done a *marvelous* job at one thing: placing public focus on fee *rates* rather than fee *dollars*. It brags that the cost of mutual fund ownership has fallen from 2.26 percent to 1.35 percent of assets since 1980. When the total dollar costs paid by all funds (excluding sales charges) have soared from $800 million in 1980 to $65 billion in 1999, it takes some kind of brass to make that argument. Expense *ratio* comparisons are fine as far as they go, but they don't go far enough. It is *dollars* that fund shareholders pay and *dollars* that the managers extract. A 1.00 percent expense ratio may *look* low—indeed is *almost* universally acclaimed as low—but on a $25 billion fund, it produces $250 million for the manager every year, $1 billion over four years. Make sure you know how the *dollars* your fund spends compares with the dollars spent by its peers.

6. **Thou Shalt Challenge Thy Fee Consultants.** Many fund managers retain fund consultants to provide comparative data to the Board. But like executive compensation consultants, fund consultants know what their job is: to justify existing compensation (fee) levels, and to provide a basis for compensation (fee) increases. "Heaven forbid," they suggest, "that your [*sic*] fund should be in the bottom quartile in expense ratio." But let me assure you that when you're down

there, it's really *good* for shareholders. Honest! So demand that the consultants calculate dollar fees as well as fee rates. While you're about it, demand that they include data for index funds, and data for funds run by differently structured (low-cost) fund organizations. I'm told that some consultants ignore such funds and firms on the grounds that they're "different," and somehow unworthy of inclusion. Yes, index funds and mutual organizations are "different," but only if you see the figures can you be the judge of whether or not *different* is *better*.

7. **Thou Shalt Keep an Eagle Eye on Portfolio Turnover.** Consider the level of fund turnover, and demand to see the attendant costs of brokerage commissions and market impact, the amount of gains realized, the extent of short-term gains, and the dollars-and-cents burden in unnecessary federal, state, and local taxes borne by shareholders. Find out how turnover affected performance: Did it help? Did it hurt? By how much? Ask for a simple examination of the results of the portfolio held at the year's outset, assuming that no changes have been made all year. ("Static Portfolio Analysis.") Ask for an explanation of the frequent rotation of portfolio managers, and demand to know the extent and cost of anticipated portfolio changes when a new manager is appointed.

8. **Thou Shalt Not Disdain Incentive Fees.** We all—fund officers, directors, managers, shareholders—expect, or at least hope for, outstanding performance. It is a consummation devoutly to be wished, but, on the record, all too rarely achieved. *Don't pay for expectations or hopes.* Pay for achievement, a standard easily accomplished by adopting a fee schedule that awards premium fees for performance that exceeds agreed-upon benchmarks, and assesses penalty fees for performance that falls short. While the equity of such a system seems self-evident, incentive fees have almost vanished from the mutual fund scene.

9. **Thou Shalt Consider Redemption Fees.** One of the easiest, and fairest, ways to mitigate the use of mutual funds as speculative vehicles for short-term gains, and to return them to their traditional use as investment vehicles for long-term accumulation, is the imposition of reasonable redemption fees. Today, equity fund redemptions are running at an astonishing 50 percent annualized rate. Yet largely as the result of a redemption fee of 2 percent in

the first year and 1 percent for the next four years, the funds in the industry's first tax-managed series, now in their sixth year, have an annual redemption rate running at just 5 percent. Surely there are lessons to be learned from this potential 90 percent reduction in redemption activity. (Alas, even as it effectively excludes short-term investors, the redemption fee retards marketing. So you serve the shareholders at the expense of the manager.)

10. **Thou Shalt Evaluate Thy Fund as If It Were Thine Own Money.** Bring this attitude to your work as a director: Is this the way *my* money should be run? Is my performance satisfactory? How about my tax-efficiency? How about continuity of my portfolio management? How much would *I* be willing to pay for this service? When performance lags, how patient would *I* be? When would *I* terminate my own fiduciary relationship and move to another? In all, behave as if you *were* a large shareholder, and assume that the assets were important to you. Better yet, actually *own* shares of the funds you serve as trustee. The investment of a significant portion of your own assets in the funds you serve is the single most meaningful step you can take in demonstrating both your commitment and your independence.

These are hardly radical steps, and most require no new laws or regulations. A statement of these principles by the Investment Company Institute, or by the new Mutual Fund Directors Education Council, or by the SEC—or even a speech by a senior SEC official— would start the ball rolling, and it would not soon stop. It's high time we begin the process.

The Golden Rule

There are 80 million mutual fund shareholders out there. They need the support and commitment of independent directors to make those five old myths about mutual funds into five new realities—realities that recognize mutual funds as long-term investments, with managers who are long-term investors and shareholders who own their shares for an investment lifetime; operated at reasonable—and therefore far lower—levels of cost and far higher levels of tax-efficiency; providing shareholders with returns that meet, and even exceed, their expectations for a fair share of market returns.

So, before history repeats itself, and Justice Stone's words come to describe the developments of *this* era and their causes, and the myths surrounding mutual fund management, let's make our philosophical anchor the preamble of the Investment Company Act of 1940 that has served this industry well in so many other arenas. Remember the Golden Rule of the 1940 Act: *Put fund shareholders first.* If fund directors will take seriously the Ten Commandments I've laid down today, and guide managers toward their own enlightened self-interest in serving investors "honestly, efficiently, and economically"—the very words I used in my Princeton thesis a half-century ago—we can avoid onerous and contentious regulation and legislation—and, for that matter, litigation—and we'll have come a long, long, way toward finding our way back to our roots. It's only common sense.

Chapter 16

"High Standards of Commercial Honor . . . Just and Equitable Principles of Trade . . . Fair Dealing with Investors"*

For something like two full decades during the 1960s and 1970s, I maintained an active involvement with NASD regulation as a member and then chairman of the Investment Companies Committee, and as a member of the Long-Range Planning Committee. While I have had little experience with regulators for the New York

---

*Based on an address in Washington, D.C., on October 15, 2007, to the Financial Industry Regulatory Authority (FINRA), at its first joint enforcement meeting following the combination of the enforcement divisions of the New York Stock Exchange and the National Association of Securities Dealers.

Stock Exchange, I believe the consolidation of these two enforcement groups will significantly enhance investor protection.

In the mid-1970s, long-range planning for the securities industry was no mean challenge. The long era of (high) fixed commissions on brokerage transactions had ended in 1974, replaced by today's system of (minuscule) negotiated commissions. Financial technology was just being introduced, and it was clear that the slow, old order (and its glacial pace of change) hath changeth to be replaced by a new order operating at a millisecond pace. And securities regulations were beginning to change and litigation to grow. In the phrase that I used then, "*competition, communications*, and the *courts* will reshape the securities industry." In some ways these changes were easily foreseen (I've reviewed the ancient minutes of our committee meetings) and in some ways totally unforeseen. But the securities industry survived and thrived, and is wallowing in prosperity today.

I reveled in those years of working on industry issues with a classy, integrity-laden group of financial leaders and regulators, dedicated to the public interest. While I haven't participated in NASD affairs for a long time, it occurs to me that the basic mission remains unchanged. As Mary Schapiro, your chief executive, pointed out recently, "investor protection and market integrity remain FINRA's overarching objectives." So I'm glad to be back, though I note with some vague concern that among your 50 workshops, none discusses mutual funds. I hope that the reflections and policy recommendations that follow will fill that gap.

I'll focus on investor protection in the mutual fund industry, discussing what can be done to assure that fund investors get a fair shake, or, as I wrote in my senior thesis at Princeton University almost 57 years ago, that "mutual funds must be operated in the most efficient, economical, and honest way possible." It was that thesis that opened the door to my first job in this industry, and I've been with the same firm ever since, although it has changed greatly.* That was a pretty

---

*I joined Wellington Management Company in 1951, assumed the position of CEO in 1965, and was fired in January 1974. The creation of Vanguard in September 1974 involved the firm's assumption of the responsibilities for the operations of the then–Wellington Funds. In 2000, I formed the Bogle Financial Markets Research Center, which remains a unit of Vanguard.

good characterization of how the industry worked in 1951. But it is with regret that I report to you that the ethos of today's mutual fund industry—with some, but not nearly enough, exceptions—has moved away from those principles. I am a tough critic of today's fund industry, but acknowledge that my views are not widely shared by my industry colleagues. Indeed, one veteran industry leader has stated that "Mr. Bogle's view of ethics may be somewhat outside the mainstream." He was, of course, quite right.

Commercial Honor, Equitable Principles, Fair Dealing

To set the stage for my remarks, I've chosen as my title the three central standards of the NASD Rules of Fair Practice: "A member, in the conduct of its business, shall observe high standards of commercial honor and just and equitable principles of trade," and shall engage in "fair dealing with investors." With these principles in mind, let me discuss how they relate to the mutual fund industry, which has changed in so many fundamental ways.

- **A new mission.** We've moved our central mission from steward-ship to salesmanship, and our core value from *managing* assets to *gathering* assets. We have become far less of a management industry and far more of a marketing industry, engaging in a furious orgy of "product proliferation" that has ill-served our investors. Once an industry that "sold what we made," our new motto has become "If we can sell it, we will make it." For example, right at the peak of the late, great bull market, we created 494 new "aggressive growth" funds, investing largely in technology and telecommunication stocks. The consequences for our investors were devastating.
- **Our funds, once broadly diversified, became largely special-ized.** In 1951, almost 80 percent of all stock funds (60 of 75) were broadly diversified among investment-grade "blue-chip" stocks, pretty much tracking the movements of the stock market itself, and lagging its returns only by the amount of their then-modest operating costs. Today, our total of 512 "large-cap blend funds" account for only 11 percent of all stock funds. These "market

beta" funds are now vastly outnumbered by 4,200 more special-ized funds—3,100 U.S. equity funds diversified in other styles; 400 funds narrowly diversified in various market sectors; and 700 funds investing in international equities, some broadly diversi-fied, some investing in specific countries. The challenge in pick-ing funds, dare I say, has become roughly akin to the challenge in picking individual stocks. I don't regard that change as progress.

- **The wisdom of long-term investing has given way to the folly of short-term speculation.** In 1951, a mutual fund held the average stock in its portfolio for about six years—*investing*. Today, the average holding period for a stock in an equity fund portfolio is just over one year—*speculation*. Neither is that change progress.

- **We've discouraged long-term investors.** With the substan-tial differences in short-term returns that inevitably occur among these different fund styles, investors have come to chase past per-formance. In 1951, most fund investors just *picked* funds and *held* them—on average, for about 16 years. Today, investors *trade* their funds, now holding the typical fund in their portfolios for a period of only about four years—a negative reversal with unfortunate consequences for our clients.

- **The ethos of fund managers has changed.** Once dominated entirely by small, *privately owned firms* and operated by *professional investors*, the industry is now dominated by giant, publicly owned firms, largely operated by businessmen bereft of investment experi-ence. Today, 41 of the 50 largest fund managers are publicly held, including 35 owned by giant U.S. and international financial con-glomerates. Small wonder that these firms are all too eager to focus on maximizing the return on *their own capital* invested in the fund management companies they own, rather than focusing on maximiz-ing the return on *the capital they are investing for fund shareholders*—another compelling negative for our clients.

All of these departures from our traditional role as fiduciaries have ill-served fund investors. Think about it. With all due respect, the motivations of the businessman in financial services, who must gather assets in order to prosper and who must constantly *sell* something, week after week, differs, not only in degree but in kind, from the motivations of the trustee, a member of a profession with high standards of conduct and a duty to serve client before self.

The drive for asset gathering is importantly responsible for our product proliferation. We must always have a "product" that will sell. But it also has another negative aspect. We allow—and indeed encourage—our successful funds to grow too large to maintain the investment flexibility that produced the attractive returns that drew the attention—and the dollars—of investors in the first place. Too rarely is the marketing spigot turned off.

Crowd-like behavior is another obvious cause of the changes I've described. I remember an industry in which "there are some things that one simply doesn't do." But today what I see is, "When everyone else is doing it, I can do it, too." (I concede that the mutual fund industry is hardly alone in manifesting this debasement in values.)

Finally, greed rears its ugly head. Of course we don't think of ourselves as greedy. (Perhaps no one does.) But the enormous management compensation now generated by this giant industry can easily blind us to our underlying motives. Paraphrasing Upton Sinclair: "It's amazing how difficult it is for a man to understand something if he's paid a small fortune not to understand it." The lack of introspection by industry leaders, then, has been just one more negative force. (Ironically, the amount of dollars and cents paid to fund executives is kept secret from the shareholders who own our funds, the *only* publicly held U.S. corporations with a blanket exemption from such disclosure.)

I've been asked this fundamental question: "Are fund managers now less ethical than they once were?" I'd have to answer, "I doubt it." With a handful of truly horrifying exceptions (tact, not usually my strong point, precludes my naming them), the industry leaders I've known have been men and women of high character, impressive integrity, and substantial intelligence. But they are part of a system in which traditional values have eroded, operating in a new "bottom-line society" that worships a bottom line so easily measured in dollars and cents, rather than in qualities not susceptible to measurement—for example, character, and integrity, and trust.

How else to explain the disgraceful conduct of so many of the oldest, largest, and once most respected management companies in this industry—now representing *$2 trillion* of fund assets, almost 30 percent of the total—in aiding and abetting illicit market-timing schemes.

Or the number of leading brokerage firms engaged in "breakpoint" frauds in which excessive sales loads were imposed on investors. Or having one of the bluest of the industry's blue-chip firms—one of the three largest firms in our field—violate NASD rules by allocating brokerage commissions as a *quid pro quo* to brokers that sold the shares of its funds. What's more, according to the NASD decision, the firm's executives were duplicitous on the witness stand. (The actual word was "disingenuous.") While the examiner recommended a $100 million fine, it was reduced to $5 million on the grounds that the illicit practice was rife in the industry (i.e., "Everyone else was doing it, so I can too").

Together, this disgraceful conduct represents a sorry chapter in this industry's history. But I know of no easy way to regulate or legislate a return to our industry's traditional values. Competition, in fact, is driving us in quite the opposite direction. As long as our industry participants— our fund managers and marketers, our brokerage firm account executives, and our financial advisers—have more information at hand than their clients possibly could—the economists call this *information asymmetry*— a largely unaware investment public will be inadequately informed. Regulations calling for more complete disclosure would be a huge help in protecting investors from their own naiveté and lack of information.

So I'll now focus on three major problem areas. By doing so in some depth and detail, I hope to convey not only the nature of the problems, but the change—for the worse—in the industry environment, and the historical context in which they have arisen. I think you'll be amazed at what you'll see. The three areas are:

1. The importance of investment income.
2. Fund returns versus shareholder returns.
3. Measuring shareholder satisfaction.

The Importance of Investment Income

One of the great unexplained curiosities of the mutual fund industry is its unwillingness to call attention to the vital role of investment income in shaping the returns on equities. Theory tells us, and experience confirms, that dividend yields play a crucial role in shaping stock market returns. In fact, the dividend yield on stocks has accounted for almost *one-half* of their total long-term return. Of the 9.6 percent nominal *total* return earned by stocks over the past century, fully 9.5 percent has been contributed by *investment* return—4.5 percent by dividend yields and 5 percent from earnings growth. (The remaining 0.1% resulted from an 80% increase in the price-earnings ratio, from 10 at the start of the century to 18 at the end, amortized over the long period. I describe changes in the p/e ratio as *speculative* return.)

When we take inflation into account, the importance of dividend income is magnified even further. During the past century, the average rate of inflation was 3.3 percent per year reducing the *nominal* 5 percent earnings growth rate to a *real* growth rate of just 1.7 percent.* Thus, the inflation-adjusted return on stocks was not 9.6 percent, but 6.3 percent. In real terms, then, dividend income has accounted for almost 75 percent of the annual investment return on stocks.

But while dividend income has accounted for nearly 50 percent of the long-term *nominal* annual return on stocks and 75 percent of the *real* annual return, even these figures dramatically *understate* the *cumulative* role played by dividends. Consider this: An investment of $10,000 in the S&P 500 index† at its 1926 inception (Figure 16.1) with all dividends reinvested, would by the end of September 2007 have grown to $33,100,000 (10.4% compounded). If dividends had *not* been reinvested, the value of that investment would have been $1,200,000 (6.1% compounded)—an amazing gap of $32 million. Over the past 81 years, then, reinvested dividend income accounted for approximately 95 percent of the compounded long-term return earned by the companies in the S&P 500.

These stunning figures would seem to demand that mutual funds highlight the importance of dividend income. But in this era of "total return," income is virtually ignored. Why? Because dividend income plays a remarkably *small* role in equity fund returns. Today, in fact, the average domestic stock fund is offering a dividend yield of just 0.4 percent. Where did all the income go? It was slashed by fund expenses.

---

* Some analysts believe that the real earnings rate is even less, about 1 percent per year. William J. Bernstein and Robert D. Arnott, "Earnings Growth: The Two Percent Dilution," *Financial Analysts Journal* (September/October 2003).

† The Standard & Poor's 500 Stock Index came into being just 50 years ago, in 1957. For the earlier years, I have linked the returns of the S&P 90 Stock Index.

FIGURE 16.1   THE IMPORTANCE OF DIVIDENDS

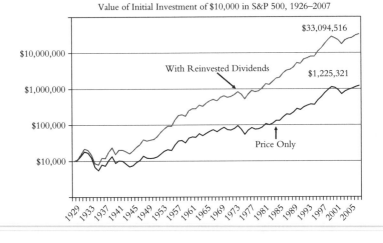

Value of Initial Investment of $10,000 in S&P 500, 1926–2007

The expense ratio of domestic stock funds averages 1.4 percent, reducing the funds' gross dividend yield of 1.8 percent to 0.4 percent. Unsurprisingly, then, it appears that the average stock fund earns the stock market's present dividend yield of 1.8 percent and then consumes fully 80 percent of that yield in fees and expenses.

It didn't need to be that way. When I began my research on this industry in 1950 for my Princeton University thesis, an interesting fact came to my attention. The first mutual fund—Massachusetts Investors Trust, founded in 1924—calculated its expenses, not on the basis of a percentage of *assets*, but as a percentage of its investment *income*. During its first 25 years, MIT charged investors the then-standard trustee fee of 5 percent of income.

Throughout that quarter-century, MIT was the nation's largest mutual fund, and its growth was substantial. By 1950, its assets had grown to $362 million. The dividend income on its investments grew commensurately, and the 5 percent charge against income was soon producing far too much money for the fund's trustees to accept. (Imagine *that*!) So they promptly reduced the annual fee to 2.9 percent of income.* Since dividend yields were then relatively high (MIT's stocks

---

* They did this by capping the number of shares on which the fee would be levied at 6 million.

were yielding about 5.5%), the net dividend yield received by MIT's shareholders was 5.3 percent. (For the record, measured against fund assets, MIT's expense ratio was 0.33%.)

For reasons lost in history, few of the mutual funds organized in the years after MIT began followed the pioneer's precedent. Instead they chose to set their management fees as a percentage of net assets rather than as a percentage of investment income. The typical annual charge was set at 0.5 percent of assets, typically scaled down to ⅜ of 1 percent on fund assets in excess of $100 million.* Modest fee structures, then, for an industry then managing modest amounts of assets.

A 1950 snapshot of that tiny mutual fund industry (Table 16.1) shows both management fees and total expenses at a reasonably low level, along with a recognition by fund managers that, as their funds grew large (then, "large" meant more than $100 million in assets!), fund investors were entitled to share in the substantial economies of

TABLE 16.1   MANAGEMENT FEE RATES AND AMOUNTS, 1950

	Assets (million)	Management Fee Rate	Other Expenses	Expense Ratio	Management Fee
Affiliated Fund*	$116	0.41%	0.31%	0.72%	$476k
Dividend Shares*	82	0.50	0.24	0.74	410k
Fidelity Fund	43	0.50	0.16	0.66	215k
Incorporated Investors*	97	0.50	0.05	0.55	485k
Mass. Inv. Trust	362	0.33	0	0.33	1,200k
Wellington Fund*	154	0.40	0.20	0.60	616k
Average	$142	0.44%	0.16%	0.60%	$566k

*Now, respectively, Lord Abbett Affiliated, Alliance Bernstein Growth & Income, Putnam Investors, and Vanguard Wellington.

---

* One partial exception was the George Putnam Fund, with a fee of 4 percent of income plus 0.4 percent of assets, both scaled down on assets above $25 million.

scale that accompany asset growth (i.e., that it cost little more to manage $200 million in assets than it did to manage $100 million).

But a funny thing happened on the way to 2006. Those old values seemed to vanish. Remarkably, each of those six industry pioneers still exists, but, with a single exception, the idea of sharing substantial economies of scale with shareholders has gone up in smoke. (By 1969, alas, even MIT had abandoned its dividend-based fee rate in favor of the conventional asset-based fee rate. Its expense ratio subsequently more than tripled, from 0.33% to 1.09%.) Amazingly, despite the truly staggering growth in total fund assets, expenses have grown at an even faster rate, resulting in expense ratios that have actually *increased*.

For five of these six funds, more and more of that priceless component of investment return known as dividend income was consumed by costs (Table 16.2) from 10 percent of income in 1950 to nearly 60 percent in 2006. Even as assets have increased nearly 60 times over, from $770 million to $42 billion, their expenses have increased even faster—more than 100 times over, from $3.4 million to $395 million. Result: Expense ratios have nearly doubled, from 0.57 percent to 1.0 percent. This evidence totally contradicts the consistent stand of the industry, articulated over and over again at the annual membership meetings of the Investment Company Institute, that "the interests of mutual fund managers are directly aligned with the interests of mutual fund shareholders." It's just not so.

TABLE 16.2   GROWTH IN ASSETS AND EXPENSES, 1950–2006

	Assets (million)		Expenses (million)		Expense Ratio		Percent of Dividend Income	
	1950	2006	1950	2006	1950	2006	1950	2006
Affiliated Fund	$116	$21,200	$0.8	$191	0.72%	0.90%	12%	44%
Dividend Shares	82	4,600	0.6	61	0.74	1.32	13	63
Fidelity Fund	43	7,700	0.3	42	0.66	0.55	10	39
Incorporated Inv.	97	4,100	0.5	48	0.55	1.16	10	82
Mass. Inv. Trust	362	4,900	1.2	53	0.33	1.09	6	58
Average	$140	$ 8,500	$0.7	$ 79	0.60%	1.00%	10%	57%
Wellington Fund	$154	$45,700	$0.9	$114	0.60%	0.25%	12%	8%

But there is a case—just one, and one with which I am well-familiar—in which the ICI was right. That fund's assets also soared—from $154 million to $46 billion. But while its expenses leaped from $924,000 to $114 million, the expense ratio actually *declined* by 60 percent, from 0.60 percent of assets to 0.25 percent. Most importantly, after absorbing 12.5 percent of income in 1951, Wellington Fund's costs actually absorbed even less of the fund's income—8.0 percent—in 2006. I attribute this obvious success largely to the facts that (1) the Fund is a unit of Vanguard, a unique *mutual* mutual fund group owned by its fund shareholders, and is operated on an "at-cost" basis; and (2) in the 1980s and 1990s, we vigorously renegotiated the advisory fee scale with our external adviser, demanding that our fund's owners share in the economies of scale. (Today, the annual advisory fee we pay to Wellington Management Company comes to just $3/100$ of 1% of assets—a measly three basis points.)

And now, a dream: Suppose now that industry practice had followed MIT's early lead, pegging management fees to 5 percent of investment income rather than to fund assets. Further suppose that *no* economies of scale—none—were shared with fund shareholders, and that the 5 percent fee remained unchanged. On that basis, equity fund expenses last year would have totaled just $5.7 billion, compared to the actual total of $56 billion, a huge potential annual "dividend" of $50.3 billion to fund shareholders. Well, I can dream can't I? But in any event, it's high time that we require mutual funds to disclose to investors and prospective investors the amount of their dividend income that is consumed by costs, and its impact on the fund's long-term returns.

Bond Funds

Now a brief word about bond fund expenses. While in bond funds the consumption of income by expenses is lower, the impact on long-term returns is higher (Table 16.3). The average bond fund is presently earning a gross yield of about 5 percent, but after the average expense ratio of 1.0 percent, the net yield averages 4.0 percent. In all, bond fund expense ratios, on average, are consuming about 20 percent of the interest payments the funds receive. (Here, I've ignored the impact of sales loads and transaction costs.)

TABLE 16.3   BOND FUNDS: CURRENT YIELDS AND EXPENSES

	Gross Yield	Expense Ratio	Net Yield
IT Corporate	5.4%	1.1%	4.3%
IT Government	5.2%	1.0%	4.2%
IT Municipal	4.6%	1.0%	3.6%

TABLE 16.4   CURRENT YIELD AND FUTURE RETURNS

	Year-End 1996 Yield	10-Year Annual Return Through 2006
Intermediate-Term		
Corporate	6.2%	5.2%
Municipal	4.7	4.3
Treasury	6.2	4.9
Long-Term		
Corporate	6.9%	6.1%
Municipal	5.1	4.4
Treasury	6.1	6.9

NOTE: Yields and returns exclude impact of sales charges.

But income takes on a special importance in the case of bonds. Why? Because the income yield on a bond fund at the point of purchase establishes the parameters of its future return.* Said straight out, today's yield on a bond fund is an excellent proxy for its total return in the subsequent decade. For example, the initial interest rate on a 10-year U.S. Treasury bond has had a correlation of a mere 0.91 with its returns over the subsequent 10 years (1.00 is perfect correlation).

This cause-and-effect proposition among bond mutual funds is demonstrable. Table 16.4 compares the yield of various types of bond funds as of December 31, 1996, with their returns during the following decade, ended December 31, 2006. On average, the actual yield of 5.9 percent a decade ago resulted in a total annual return averaging

---

* I've always thought that this issue should be explored by academics. It has rarely, if ever, been discussed.

TABLE 16.5 RELATIONSHIP BETWEEN EXPENSES AND RETURNS

	IT Corporate Bond Funds		
	10 Cheapest	10 Most Expensive	Low–Cost Advantage
Initial Yield	6.6%	5.9%	+11%
Expense Ratio	0.2%	1.9%	(89%)
10-Year Annual Return	6.1%	4.5%	+35%
Profit on $10,000	$8,100	$5,500	+47%

5.2 percent per year. (That gap reflects those other bond fund costs coming into play.)

If investors were more aware of this relationship, surely they'd seek out the lowest-cost—and, therefore, generally highest-yielding—bond funds. For example, Table 16.5 shows the returns earned by today's 10 lowest-cost intermediate-term corporate bond funds—expense ratios averaging 20 basis points—and the 10 highest-cost funds—expense ratios averaging an amazing 190 basis points—their yields a decade ago, and their returns over the subsequent 10 years. The low-cost group provided an enhancement of fully 35 percent to the investor's annual return, and a compounded enhancement of almost 50 percent, with zero increase in risk.

Investors are largely unaware of these clear relationships between bond fund costs and yields, and between today's net yield and tomorrow's total return. Expenses are the principal determinant of relative yields, and yields are highly predictive of future returns. But as a group, bond fund managers are unwilling to reduce their fees to enhance the returns earned by their shareholders. Since I don't see how regulation can solve this problem, it's high time that bond funds, too, be required to put their prospective investors on notice by disclosing these relationships. As in the case of stock fund costs, failure to disclose could hardly be said to represent "fair dealing with investors."

Fund Returns versus Shareholder Returns

I now turn to the issue of the returns actually earned by fund shareholders. When we were an industry that *sold what we made*, those returns closely paralleled the returns reported by the funds themselves.

But when we became an industry that focused on *making what would sell*, those two returns sharply diverged, with great detriment to fund shareholders. This departure began in the "Go-Go" era of the mid-1960s, when we created scores of risky funds, seeking high returns by rapid trading, investing in small and often risky companies, and following new "investment concepts."

Many of these funds reported past returns that were achieved by dubious means, including buying "letter stocks" from insiders at substantial price discounts and marking up their prices to the higher market price. The investment records of many of these "incubation funds" that were later taken public were little short of fraudulent. These funds were "hot," the money flowed in, and then they turned cold. Fund investors paid a high price for our folly.

In the recent era, while the conditions were different, the outcome was the same. In the late 1990s, fund investors again paid a high price for our focus on the promise of the technology-driven Information Age, and on the promised land of the Great Bull Market. The price they paid can be measured by the errors that fund investors made in the *timing* of their fund purchases and the *selection* of the funds they chose.

The next two figures reflect those destructive patterns. The *timing* penalty (Figure 16.2) was evidenced by the fact that fund investors placed little money into equity funds during the cheap markets of the late 1980s and early 1990s (less than $10 billion per year), but invested more than $500 billion at the peak market levels of 1998–2000.

The *selection* penalty (Figure 16.3) made a bad situation worse. Investors poured the lion's share of that $500 billion into those "New Economy" growth funds, technology funds, telecommunication funds, and even Internet funds. It was these funds that led the market upward, and then led the market downward, with late-to-the-party fund investors paying an awful price. Ironically, at the height of the bubble, investors were actually liquidating their stodgy old value funds, which would provide excellent downside protection during the bear market that followed.

We are only now beginning to calculate the devastation that these two patterns dealt to the wealth of mutual fund investors. But the data showing investor returns—resisted by the industry ever since I first mentioned it in a speech to the financial writers in Chicago 11 years

**FIGURE 16.2   TIMING PENALTY: EQUITY FUND CASH FLOW
FOLLOWS STOCK MARKET RETURNS**

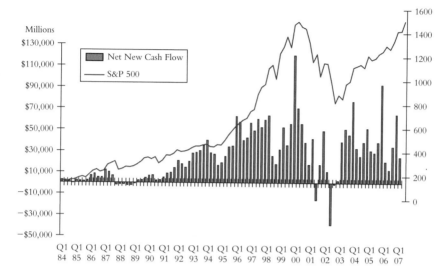

**FIGURE 16.3   SELECTION PENALTY: EQUITY FUND SECTOR
SELECTION FOLLOWS SECTOR RETURNS**

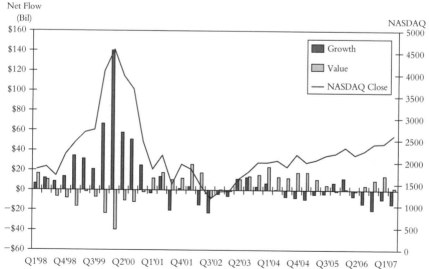

SOURCE: Strategic Insight.

ago—can no longer be hidden. We can now readily compare the returns earned by the *fund* itself—as reported in its shareholder reports and prospectus—to the returns actually earned by its *investors*. The technical distinction is between *time*-weighted and *dollar*-weighted (or *asset*-weighted) returns. The results are not pretty.

Begin with the fact that during the 25-year period 1980–2005, when the S&P 500 index rose at a 12.3 percent annual rate, the return of the average fund averaged 10.0 percent annually, or 2.3 percentage points less. But the returns earned by fund investors fell far short of that 10.0 percent return. We can't be sure of exactly how far short, but an analysis of the past decade suggests that the gap was huge (Figure 16.4). For example, the 200 funds with the largest cash inflows during the 5-year period 1996–2000—essentially the duration of late, great bull market—reported an average return of 8.9 percent for the 10 years 1996–2005. But the *dollar-weighted* returns of those 200 funds—the returns actually earned by their *shareholders*—was just 2.4 percent, only 25 percent of the annual return reported by the fund themselves.

FIGURE 16.4   GAP BETWEEN ANNUAL TIME-WEIGHTED AND DOLLAR-WEIGHTED RETURNS, 1996–2005

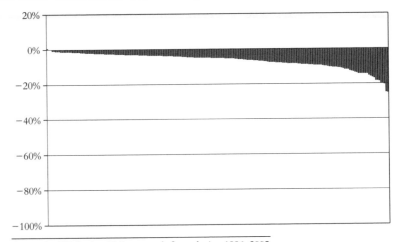

Covers the 200 funds with largest cash flows during 1996–2005.

The consistency of this pattern is remarkable. Among those 200 funds, the shareholders of 198 funds actually earned *less* money than the funds reported. In only two cases did the shareholders do better: in the best case, by just 0.5 percent per year (50 basis points); in the other case, by a minuscule five basis points per year. When we compound these shortfalls, the results are little short of astounding (Figure 16.5). For fully 76 of the 200 funds, that cumulative shortfall ranged from *minus 50* to *minus 95* percentage points(!).

Unsurprisingly, given the marketing ethos of today's mutual fund business, the funds that reported the highest returns during the bull market experienced the largest gap between fund returns and shareholder returns, and vice versa. The chart in Table 16.6, showing the relationship between the various quartiles of *reported* performance and the actual *shareholder* performance, makes it clear that the higher the performance quartile in the bull market, the lower the returns earned by investors. As it might be said in Biblical terms, "and the first (in reported returns) shall be the last (in shareholder returns)."

The fund industry, naturally, argues that it bears little responsibility for this state of affairs. Rather, it is the foolishness of the investing public that is to blame for these disastrous results. But the industry surely

FIGURE 16.5   AMAZING GAP BETWEEN CUMULATIVE TIME-WEIGHTED AND DOLLAR-WEIGHTED RETURNS, 1996–2005

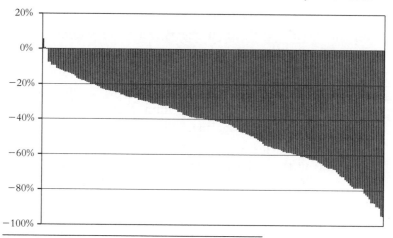

Covers the 200 funds with largest cash flows during 1996–2005.

**TABLE 16.6   HIGH FUND PERFORMANCE PRODUCES
LOW SHAREHOLDER RETURNS**

	Cumulative Returns				
	Time-Weighted Returns			Dollar-Weighted	Dollar-Weighted
	1996 to 2000	2001 to 2005	1996 to 2005	1996 to 2005	Minus Time-Weighted
Q1	149%	−8.5%	50.8%	0.03%	−50.7%
Q2	106%	−5.8%	39.3%	0.05%	−39.3%
Q3	92%	2.5%	40.3%	0.18%	−40.1%
Q4	70%	2.3%	31.6%	0.13%	−31.5%
Average	103%	−2.4%	40.4%	0.10%	−40.3%

bears a heavy responsibility—I would argue, the largest share—for the harm that has been done. Consider these facts:

- It was we in the fund industry who created those new funds that were to create such havoc for investors. As the market soared ever higher, we introduced those 494 brand-new "New Economy" funds. Only a precious few of the major fund marketers had the courage to stand firm against the market madness, and forbear from creating and offering such funds.

- When we had funds whose performance turned "hot," we marketed them aggressively. Our public relations departments were willing co-conspirators with the press in establishing interviews with our "star" portfolio managers, many of whom, inevitably, turned out to be comets.

- The higher a fund's performance soared, the more we advertised our returns. Example: In March 2000, the month the market hit its high, there were 44 equity funds that advertised their performance in *Money* magazine. The average advertised annual return was +86 percent. Imagine! (During the next three years, these funds were to plummet by 39 percent.) Unsurprisingly, after the fall, in the October 2002 issue of *Money* there were only four funds that did so.

I believe that the mandatory and prominent disclosure of *shareholder* returns alongside *fund* returns would alert fund investors to the true returns that managers have actually achieved for their shareholders. Such disclosure, I suspect, would also discourage fund managers—and brokers and financial advisers, too—from following the "fund-of-the-week" syndrome, remind them of the perils of aggressive marketing, and give them some self-discipline regarding the creation and promotion of high-risk funds.

Measuring Shareholder Satisfaction— The Redemption Rate

In the early years of my career at Wellington Management Company, as I recall, I was asked to prepare a brochure, to be entitled "The Wellington Story," designed to persuade both potential investors and the stockbrokers who in those days sold the fund's shares that Wellington Fund was a creditable investment. Of course, I included sections about the fund's remarkable growth; its conservative objectives (it was a *balanced* fund, investing in both stocks and bonds); its past investment record; and its management depth.

I also created what I called "an index of shareholder satisfaction," simply calculated by presenting the ratio of the annual dollar amount of the shares of the Fund redeemed to the Fund's total net assets. The Wellington Fund redemption rate was then less than 4 percent—about half of the industry rate—suggesting an average holding period of 25 years for its shareholders. We believed that we were the industry leader in shareholder satisfaction, and we were determined to emphasize our bragging rights.

In those days (Figure 16.6), industry redemption rates were far below today's levels. Note that the 7 to 8 percent rates that persisted through the 1950s and 1960s didn't reach 20 percent until the 1980s. Rates soared to 62 percent in the 1987 bear market but then settled down to the 30–40 percent range through 2004, suggesting a remarkably short average holding period of 2.5 to 3 years by fund shareholders.

But it turns out that much of that soaring leap in redemption rates was less about plummeting shareholder satisfaction than about a fraud that was being inflicted on the long-term shareholders of mutual funds.

FIGURE 16.6   EQUITY MUTUAL FUND REDEMPTION RATES

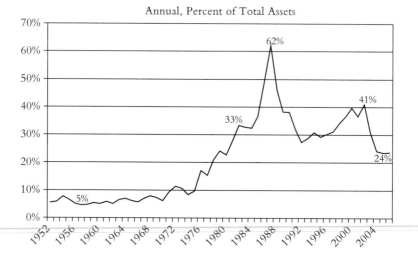

Annual, Percent of Total Assets

Much of that increase in redemptions, in fact, reflected the growing use of mutual fund shares in "market-timing" programs, largely by substantial investors and hedge funds.

As the years passed, more and more investors became aware of how easy it was to make purchases (or redemptions) of funds *after* the local markets for the stocks they held had closed. The funds priced their foreign stocks at the closing prices in local markets, which had closed long before the New York Stock Exchange closed at 4 P.M. eastern time. Periodically, opportunities arose to, as it would later be alleged by Attorney General Spitzer, "bet on the horses after the race was over." The betting, as it were, was widespread. The SEC later identified some 400(!) hedge funds that described their strategy as "mutual fund market timing."

International funds, of course, were the prime victims of what became known as "time-zone trading." As the chart in Figure 16.7 shows, the problem goes back at least to the late 1990s, when redemption rates on international funds leaped above the industry-wide rate of 30 to 40 percent. But by 1998, as more investors became aware of the, well, opportunity to engage in this essentially risk-free arbitrage, the international fund redemption rate began to steadily increase.

FIGURE 16.7   INTERNATIONAL FUND REDEMPTION RATES

Monthly Annualized, Percent of Total Assets

It crossed 60 percent in December 1997, 70 percent in September 1998, 90 percent in March 1999, 100 percent (a one-year holding period) in March 2000, and 110 percent in July 2000, reaching an all-time peak of 128 percent in October 2001 and again in October 2002.

Finally, *after* the Spitzer revelations in the fall of 2003, the time-zone trading practice began to abate, with redemption rates falling below 30 percent by January 2004. It's remained in the 25 percent range (with a few upward thrusts) through July 2007, a four-year holding period that, although it seems to me absurdly short, suggests that time-zone trading has been substantially eliminated.

The remarkable fact is that the data showing these extraordinary redemption patterns was not hidden. The amount of redemptions in international funds was published by the industry's trade association, the Investment Company Institute, in every single one of the 212 months shown in Figure 16.7. All that remained was to compare those redemptions with the fund's assets and calculate the rate. Is it possible that the industry and its leaders weren't aware of what was going on? Only out of inexcusable ignorance of what the business had become, or because it was a good idea, in the interest of building assets in international funds, to turn a blind eye to the disservice it clearly represented to the long-term shareholders of these funds.

But if it was ignorance, it should have been exorcised with the publication of an article in the *Financial Analysts Journal* of July/August 2003. Written by four NYU professors, it was titled "Stale Prices and Strategies for Trading Mutual Funds." The authors demonstrated how easy—and how profitable—it was for investors to develop winning strategies. It concluded: "Should mutual funds even worry about trying to prevent these strategies? Because the gains are offset by losses to the other [long-term] shareholders in the funds, the funds have a fiduciary duty to take preventative action. . . . Why [don't they]? . . . because short-term trading increases assets under management and [increases] management compensation . . . and managers may have the perception that [blocking these strategies] puts the fund at a competitive disadvantage." In short, taking action to limit trading would hurt fund marketing.

Rather than being alerted to the problem, the industry ignored it. Worse, the only published response to the article came from a senior executive of an industry leader, who condemned the *Journal* for publishing the article: "Your article raises serious questions about the policies, oversight, and judgment in selecting articles. Publishing [it] is a bad idea in the best of times but is abhorrent in a period when investor confidence is shaken by corporate greed and fraud, bad accounting, and a bear market overall." That response is a classic "shoot the messenger" reaction. (It was about this time that his firm finally added redemption fees for its international funds, at last curtailing the trading.)

But it wasn't only managers of international funds who participated in this scandalous conduct. One example: In its 2002 annual report, a U.S. growth fund with assets of $530 million reported, as all funds must, its sales and redemptions: share sales for the year, $3,509,527,000; redemptions, $3,604,272,000. Redemption rate (calculated but not published), 679.2 percent. Average holding period, *seven weeks.* Is it *possible* that market timing was going on? You tell me. Tell me, too, where the fund directors were, or for that matter, where the SEC examiners were, or even where the press was.

A sad anecdote: In the spring of 2006, I spoke at the Union League Club of New York, afterward signing copies of my new book, *The Battle for the Soul of Capitalism.* One person who asked me to sign his book requested that I endorse it to him. When he told me his name, I recognized him as the man who was in charge of the administration of the fund I just described. He told me that he'd only recently been released from prison for allowing the rapid-fire trading to take place, and then trying to hide the evidence. He said he knew it was wrong, but the firm had always done it, and he felt compelled to go along. "Everyone else is doing it" strikes again. There's a telling message there.

While most of the abuses in market-timing and time-zone trading seem to have been eliminated by the exposure of the practices, by legal actions, and even by the fairly modest financial penalties imposed (and at least that one jail sentence), I conclude that funds should be required to prominently disclose not only the amount of their annual redemptions (as they must today), but their redemption rate as well. Investors would be alerted by high rates—suggesting some combination of shareholder dissatisfaction and excessive market timing—and perhaps encouraged by low rates—suggesting a high level of shareholder satisfaction and a long-term focus among existing fund owners. When I listed Wellington Fund's modest redemption rates in *The Wellington Story* all those years ago, that's precisely what I was trying to accomplish.

What's to Be Done?

Without full disclosure, it's hard to imagine that brokers and advisers can measure up to the high standards of commercial honor, equitable principles of trade, and fair dealing with their clients that are demanded by regulatory principles. I've already described, in great detail, three of the disclosures that should be mandatory:

1. The amount of investment income consumed by their fees and expenses.
2. The returns actually earned by their shareholders.
3. The annual rates at which their shareholders are redeeming their shares.

But that's only the beginning: I believe funds should also be required to disclose:

4. Historical returns, not only in *nominal* terms, but also in *real* terms, adjusted for rates of inflation. After all, investors saving for retirement ought to be on notice that the kinds of compound returns

funds show are not always what they seem. (For the record, a 9% nominal return increases capital by 762% over a quarter-century; at a real rate of 6%, the increase is only 329%—barely 40% of the putative capital accumulation.)

5. The actual dollar amounts of expenses paid by each fund share-holder each year. This need be neither complicated nor precise. Simply calculate the fund's expense ratio for the year just ended, and multiply it by the dollar value of the shareholder's investment at year-end. The actual dollars they spend, I believe, are more meaningful than ratios to investors.

6. The *total* annual costs incurred by fund investors. Not merely the fund's expense ratio, but its estimated costs of portfolio turn-over, and the annual impact of the initial sales charge. While the industry leaves the self-serving impression that a fund's expense ratio represents the total cost of owning a fund, that is far from the truth. The fact is that often there is sort of a three-legged stool of costs that drag down fund returns. The expense ratio of the aver-age equity fund is 1.4 percent; the average (hidden) cost of port-folio turnover probably runs between 0.5 percent and 1.0 percent; and, for funds with sales changes, the amortized cost of the typical 5 percent load runs to more than 1.0 percent per year. (The aver-age holding period is now about 4.5 years.) So average total all-in costs may reach as much as 3 percent a year or more. Such costs, to state the obvious, constitute a powerful drag on net returns earned by fund investors, magnified manyfold over the long term.

7. I'd also like to see reforms in advertising regulations. Since only funds with exceptional records advertise them (and then only until they turn negative), I've come to the conclusion that advertising fund performance is inherently misleading. It should simply not be allowed. (I'd also bar endorsements. Just what could it possibly matter to an investor that Lance Armstrong or Paul McCartney, presumably in return for a healthy fee, is plugging a particular fund family?)

8. We also ought to disallow the publication of records of incubation funds and funds with hypothetical past returns. Full-page ads brag-ging about back-tested, cost-free, and entirely theoretical returns that allegedly were earned by funds following today's "fundamental

indexing" fad—now appearing in all their full-page glory—are simply improper, inappropriate, and materially misleading. The practice must be stopped.

The "Statement of Policy"

Time does not permit me to go into more detail with my litany of reforms designed to assure that fund investors get the straightforward information to which they are entitled, and are protected from deceptive information that can only mislead them. So let me conclude with a constructive suggestion: my recommendation that FINRA adopt a new "Statement of Policy" regarding the sales and sales literature published by fund sponsors, stockbrokers, and financial advisers.

Hardly anyone in this business today remembers (although I do!) that from 1950 until 1969, mutual funds operated under a fairly rigorous code of standards for advertising and sales literature. It was called the "Statement of Policy," and was administered by the NASD. Under the SOP, it was deemed "materially misleading" to, among other things, combine into a single figure dividends for investment income and distributions from any other source; to present charts showing results of initial investments that include dividend reinvestments; to present charts or tables that do not provide adequate and accurate disclosure of material facts; to make extravagant claims regarding management ability or competency; or to compare a fund's record with any other fund or market index without pointing out the material differences or similarities between the subjects of the comparison.

The SOP, however, proved unduly restrictive, prohibiting, for example, the publication of a fund's total annual return. (Ironically, total return has become the universal metric for today's industry.) It also required levels of detail that obscured the clear presentation of returns that included dividend reinvestment. Nonetheless, if we are to protect investors without burdensome regulation, we must educate them in the sunlight of full disclosure. Exactly how to do this, I do not know, for it involves shareholder reports, sales literature, and prospectuses, each of which operates in a different regulatory framework. But if there is a will, I'm sure there'll be a way.

But don't count on support from the mutual fund industry or the brokerage industry, nor likely from most financial advisers. Should the strong message of these remarks reach the press and public, I can already hear the Investment Company Institute saying, "More disclosure? It will just confuse investors. They already have too much information." There is, of course, some truth in that allegation. Most investors don't know about, or don't use—or perhaps don't even understand—the abundant information they have today. But publishing the important data to which I urge giving attention today—even on each fund's web site—would cost essentially nothing. And even if only a single investor were to benefit—and I believe that ultimately millions of investors will benefit—the cost-benefit ratio would be, well, infinite.

A Retrospective View, and a Look Ahead

What's more, as I noted at the outset, the past half-century has been one in which a beautifully simple concept—owning a broadly diversified list of investment-grade stocks (and/or bonds) at low cost, investing for the long-term rather than speculating for the short-term, designed for fund investors who buy and hold for the long-term—has become a complex, expensive, confusing exercise in, to a greater or lesser degree, speculation, giving rise to a huge depletion of wealth for the 100 million American families who own mutual funds.

In that half-century period, we—at least, too many of us—have tried lots of clever, faddish ways to gather more assets from the investing public: option-income funds, "government-plus" funds, short-term global funds, adjustable-rate preferred-stock funds, to say nothing of funds investing in "sin" stocks, and so on. Nearly all of them have come and gone, and fund failures have now risen to an annual rate of about 5 percent. Not bad? Only until you realize that at that rate, a decade hence, fully one-half of today's 4,700 equity funds will be *gone*—consigned to the dustbin of history.

Yet, I regret to say, the trend toward specialization in mutual funds is not abating. It is actually increasing. In most industries, innovation is an unvarnished asset, but in the fund industry it has proved to be an asset to fund managers but a liability to fund investors. (Remember those sadly deficient returns that fund investors have earned over the past decade.)

Some innovation, of course, has been positive. I think few would disagree that the Vanguard experiment in mutual fund governance; our creation of the first index mutual fund, the first series of defined-maturity bond funds, and the first series of tax-managed funds; our focus on low costs—not only in expense ratios, but also in eliminating sales charges, and minimizing portfolio turnover costs—have created substantial shareholder value. And surely target-date retirement funds and asset-allocation funds, properly used, also offer substantial potential benefits to investors.

But the new wave of innovation is something else again. I've long made my position clear that exchange-traded funds (ETFs)—index funds that one can trade "all day long, in real time" (as the advertisement says), and overwhelmingly focused on narrow, even minuscule, sectors of the market—are likely to do investors more harm than good. The stolid, simple, classic old index funds—that have, in fact, worked brilliantly—are also being challenged by new funds purporting to be "better" index funds, but in fact are pursuing active investment strategies.

Variable annuities are another problem. The original TIAA-CREF annuity was a truly great creation, and with costs that are so low as to barely be believed, deservedly leads the field to this day. But, with rare exceptions, its successors have piled on costs that are totally unacceptable (to investors, although hardly to salesmen). Equity-linked annuities, where downside protection is provided—at a grossly excessive cost—are but one more way to escape NASD regulations on the technicality that they are actually (exempt) insured products, not securities subject to federal oversight. A *BusinessWeek* article describes them as "a sucker's game dressed up to look like a free lunch." I hope the SEC will demand the investor protection and disclosure that is clearly required.

What's more, we now have 130/30 funds (or 120/20 funds), whose respective ratios speak to the fund's long and short positions, our sad attempt to challenge the hedge fund industry. When I see these kinds of innovations, I say, "Watch out!" Also on the drawing board are funds that make automatic monthly payouts directly from capital—which I pray will include a "worst-case" disclosure—and funds offering "growth and guaranteed income." Where this innovation will end, knows God. But my long experience tells me that many, perhaps even all, of today's innovations will end badly for investors.

For we know that complexity is usually associated with higher— and often hidden—costs, and with higher—and usually undisclosed—risks. As these "new products" (as we are wont to call them) proliferate, the new Statement of Policy I propose must have the flexibility to deal with them. Again to be clear, not by regulating them (though I'm not at all sure that might not be a good idea), but by requiring the full and fair disclosure of all relevant information, and with "CAVEAT EMPTOR" written on every page.

All of this will require sensitive, objective handling by our regulators, I hope relying on the concept of "principles-based" regulation. Given the unforeseen nature of what may come along, that reliance on judgment is every bit as important as the process we put in place to require full and fair disclosure. So, to you at FINRA, I say, using the principle I regularly commended to our crew when I ran Vanguard, "Let's always keep FINRA a place where judgment has at least a fighting chance to triumph over process."

I close by expressing again my admiration for our industry's regulators and enforcement officers. You are doing the Lord's work, and I heartily endorse, yet again, your mission of investor protection, buttressed by the need for investor education that I've emphasized today. Much of your work involves crooks and charlatans. But there are few, if any, of either in the fund business today. Our problem is more subtle: We believe unfailingly in our mission, in our competence, and in our integrity, without ever standing back and asking exactly what have we wrought in changing our traditional values of stewardship into a new set of values focused on asset gathering and marketing. That's the vital issue that I've put on the table today.

This dichotomy poses a major challenge to our system of regulation and enforcement. In my *Battle* book, I quote James Madison: "If men were angels, no government would be necessary." Using a similar formulation, I'd suggest that "If fund managers, and stockbrokers, and financial advisers were angels, no regulators would be necessary."

As far as I know, however, this industry has no angels. So we need our regulators—who have served us so well ever since the enactments of the Securities Acts of 1933 and 1934—to demand the kind of full disclosure I've described, helping to assure that mutual fund and fund distributors operate under "high standards of commercial honor, just and equitable principles of trade, and fair dealing" with the investors of America.

Part Four

WHAT'S RIGHT
WITH INDEXING

Despite the manifest shortcomings that characterize the modern-day mutual fund industry, some mutual funds still offer intelligent investment strategies and policies that allow investors to avoid the pitfalls described in Part Three. My clear choice among these soundly managed funds is the *index fund*—traditionally based on the Standard & Poor's 500 Stock Index or the Dow Jones Total Stock Market Index. The index fund is one way—and almost always the best way—for investors to capture their fair share of the returns generated by American business. In Part Four, I expand on the reasons for this certainty.

The role of minimal advisory and management fees is vital. The three other crucial factors are having the broadest possible diversification, the lowest possible portfolio turnover, and the highest possible tax-efficiency that the best index funds offer. It must be obvious that the optimal means of capturing whatever returns the stock market generates is to work in a structure in which the interests of fund shareholders take precedence over the interests of fund managers. (The same principles apply to capturing the returns of the bond market.) Thus, the *Alpha* structure, previously described in Chapter 12, offers the optimal opportunity for investment success.

I alluded to the idea of a shareholder-friendly structure and its almost-inevitable twin, the index fund, way back in 1951 in my Princeton University thesis. In 2000, I filled in those ideas with considerable detail in "Success in Investment Management: What Can We Learn from Indexing?" (Chapter 17). In it, I lay out the case for passive indexing in some detail and describe the profound impact it will have on the practice of active investment management, though that impact will, sadly, be gradual. (Ironically, one of the two sponsors of the report on which my response was based was brokerage firm Merrill Lynch.) Given the role of costs in creating "negative Alpha" (the margin by which managers lose to the index), I explain why active managers must ultimately adopt strategies focused on lower advisory fees; reduced operating and marketing costs; lower portfolio turnover, leading to minimal transaction costs and maximum tax-efficiency; and the minimization of cash holdings in an equity portfolio, with its accompanying opportunity cost.

In Chapter 18, "As the Index Fund Moves from Heresy to Dogma . . . ," I describe the growing importance of index mutual funds, and present the intellectual basis for indexing. Years before the market crash of 2007–2009 caused much debate about the validity of the EMH (*Efficient Markets Hypothesis*), I had the common sense to dismiss it as the explanation of why indexing worked. (Sometimes markets are efficient; sometimes they are not.) In place of the EMH, I offered the CMH (*Cost Matters Hypothesis*) as mathematical proof that an index of the entire market must and will outperform market participants as a group by the difference in costs. Whether or not markets are efficient, the explanatory power of the CMH holds, at all times and under all circumstances.

Always thinking about profound metaphors to describe my values, I cite the Bible as the source of the title and theme of Chapter 19, "The Chief Cornerstone," inspired by this sentence from Psalm 118: *And the stone that the builders rejected became the chief cornerstone.* And so it was with the index fund—from odd outlier to the accepted standard for the measurement of investment returns. I also build on the alliterative "Four *E*'s" expressed by Warren Buffett: "The greatest *Enemies* of the *Equity* investor are *Expenses* and *Emotions*." The index fund battles these enemies and emerges victorious. To this day, it remains the chief cornerstone, a monument that, finally, can be neither shaken nor compromised.

While it took time, the original idea of broad stock market indexing caught hold, and index mutual funds grew from $11 million in 1976 (all in that single pioneering fund) to $637 billion in 2004, and would continue to grow to $1.5 trillion in 2010. That 41 percent annual compound growth rate was far higher than any other sector of the fund industry, a commercial success that accompanied its artistic success in terms of superior returns generated for investors. But during the past decade it has been variations on that original theme that have driven the growth of indexing.

This development is described in Chapter 20, which carries an even longer title than the other chapters in this section: "*Convergence! The Great Paradox: Just as Active Fund Management Becomes More and More Like Passive Indexing, So Passive Indexing Becomes More and More Like Active Fund Management.*" The final reference is to the development of exchange-traded funds, index funds that offer the ability to "trade all day long in real time" (as some of their advertisements say) and are dominated by ETFs focused on narrow sectors of the market, often highly speculative in nature. Whether that growth will continue, only time will tell. But while it's easy to see how ETFs serve short-term stock traders, it's difficult to see how they serve long-term investors significantly more effectively than the classic, low-cost regular index mutual fund.

Chapter 17

Success in Investment Management: What Can We Learn from Indexing?*

nless you're the legendary economist Peter Bernstein, it will probably be news to you that the year 2000 marks the 100th anniversary of a truly seminal academic paper. Mr. Bernstein has achieved legendary status in finance, best known through his bi-monthly publication, *Economics and Portfolio Strategy*, and his books, including his marvelous chronicle of risk, *Against the Gods*. But it was in his *Capital Ideas*, published in 1992, that I first learned of Louis Bachelier's 1900 dissertation, *The Theory of Speculation*. In that paper lay the roots of the huge volume of academic research that we now refer to as Modern Portfolio Theory.

---

*Based on a presentation to the Investment Analysts Society of Chicago on October 26, 2000.

Bernstein—perhaps our preeminent expert on capital markets history—credits Bachelier as the father of MPT and of the Efficient Market Hypothesis as well. At its outset, *Capital Ideas* quotes the French academic's key words—"past, present, and even discounted future events are reflected in market price . . . and it is impossible to aspire to mathematical predictions of [price]"—and then moves on in history.

It is a curious paradox, however, that we don't *require* modern portfolio theory—and we surely don't require the efficient market hypothesis—to understand the wisdom of the simple but profound idea that Bachelier presented (and italicized): *"The mathematical expectation of the speculator is zero."* We now understand that to be the central fact of finance.

Probably the first systematic study of the real-world application of the theory came in a 1933 article in *Econometrica*, reporting the findings of the Cowles Commission.* The Commission asked the question: "Can stock market forecasters forecast?" After the study of mountains of evidence, its answer was: "It is doubtful." Fast forward now to the 1950–1985 era, and capital market pioneers such as Harry Markowitz, James Tobin, William Sharpe, John McQuown, Jack Treynor, William Fouse, and Paul Samuelson—a distinguished list of well-known practitioners and academics—make their extraordinary contributions to the study of finance and investment.

The Theory of Transaction Costs

In Bachelier's 70-page dissertation, he makes no reference to the role costs play in speculation and investment. But costs obviously matter. And costs matter not only in financial markets, but in *all* economic transactions. Yet it is only in the past year that much academic attention has been paid to transaction costs. Just a month ago, in a report on e-commerce, the *New York Times* described a paper on transaction costs entitled "The Nature of the Firm," written way back in 1937, which resulted—but not until 1991—in a Nobel Prize in Economics

---

* Alfred Cowles, "Can Stock Market Forecasters Forecast?" *Econometrica* 1, no. 3 (July 1933).

to Professor Ronald Coase of the University of Chicago Law School.* In his paper, he showed that it was transaction costs (then prohibitively high) that should determine whether a company should produce goods or services on its own, or farm them out to suppliers.

Similarly, a recent paper by Professors Maurice Obstfeld of the University of California at Berkley and Kenneth Rogoff of Harvard has gained important attention. An article in *The Economist* noted their finding that economic puzzles regarding international trade, savings and investment, investors' preferences for domestic portfolios, and the lack of relationship between exchange rates and economic activity all prove to have a common denominator: *the cost of trade*. Trade costs money, they argue. And when trading costs reach 25 percent of the cost of goods, expected outcomes don't materialize. And so it is in the financial markets as well.†

Reality Bites Theory

So, while Bachelier was right that the mathematical expectation of the speculator—and, for that matter, the long-term investor—in outpacing the returns earned in any given segment of the financial markets is zero, that expectation implicitly assumes that costs, too, are zero. But *after* the costs of speculation (or investing) are taken into account—after all of the fees, the transaction costs, and the hidden costs of financial intermediation—the mathematical expectation is for a loss precisely equal to those costs. (In the mutual fund field, as it happens, costs appear to approach that apparently critical point—25 percent of the market's returns—a particularly ominous sign.) So it is only to state the obvious when I say—as I do, one way or another, in almost everything that I write—*the financial markets are not for sale, except at a high price*. By excluding investment costs and taxes, data presenting long-term returns in the stock market—whether using the Standard & Poor's 500 Stock Index or CRSP or the Ibbotson data—reflect the entirely theoretical

---

*Ronald H. Coase, "The Nature of the Firm," *Econometrica* 4, no. 16 (1937).
†Maurice Obstfeld and Kenneth Rogoff, "The Six Major Puzzles in International Finance: Is There a Common Cause?" *NBER Macroeconomics Annual* 15 (2000).

possibility of cost-free, tax-free investing. Those stated returns, therefore, grossly distort economic reality. When we consider the inevitable costs of investing, *reality bites theory*. And the reality is self-evident and inescapable: *The net return of all investors as a group must fall short of the gross return of the market by the amount of their costs*. Beating the market is a loser's game.

Now, 100 long years after Bachelier wrote his paper, this reality has finally taken root, *even among financial market participants who are not among the lowest-cost players in the game*. Consider the recent paper prepared by Merrill Lynch and BARRA Strategic Consulting Group entitled "Success in Investment Management: Building and Managing the Complete Firm." Written by senior executives of the two firms—after consultation with as distinguished a list of money managers and powerful fund sponsors as one could possibly imagine*—the study reaches this major conclusion: *Management of Embedded Alpha, the frictional costs of running a portfolio, will emerge as an essential contributor to investment manufacturing quality and performance.*[†]

The Merrill Lynch/BARRA Study

For me—and I think for you as investment professionals—the heart of the ML/BARRA study is not its long series of speculations, however intelligent, about the future development of investment management— the business itself, investment *manufacturing* (their off-putting word); distribution; viable business models; and optimal size. Rather, the heart of the study is its clear articulation of what it calls *Embedded Alpha*, the frictional costs that detract from the return that can be theoretically produced by an investment portfolio in a frictionless securities market.

---

* Among the firms named as providing assistance and perspective for the study: Fidelity, Putnam, Mellon, State Street, Oppenheimer, Citigroup, and Massachusetts Financial Services. I hope that you will pardon me if I wonder how carefully they considered its sweeping implications.

[†] "Success in Investment Management: Building and Managing the Complete Firm," Merrill Lynch & Co., Inc. and BARRA Strategic Consulting Group (June 1, 2000).

In a special appendix, firms are urged to "Manage Embedded Alpha, Cut Those Hidden Costs." The costs are identified in these direct quotations from the study:

1. Tangible Costs . . . management fees and trading commissions. Each dollar given away for, say, management fees is a dollar explicitly detracted from the portfolio net return.
2. Managed Costs . . . unintended risk exposures, tax costs, and Not-Equitized-Cash, an opportunity cost for not keeping funds fully invested.
3. Invisible Cost . . . the adverse market impact of trading and the opportunity cost of delaying trade execution.

Result: "Simply put, every incremental basis point increase in rate of return translates into competitive advantage [by which] a firm improves its absolute performance and its ranking relative to its peers." Thus, what the study calls *the Complete Firm*, the firm that "will lead the way . . . will diligently seek to minimize these performance detractors." Thus spake, I remind you, not Vanguard/BOGLE, but Merrill Lynch/BARRA. Here is their prescription for curing the disease: "Releasing Embedded Alpha."

1. Take a Holistic View [whatever exactly that *is* in this instance]. Appoint a single Embedded Alpha champion with the firm.
2. Take an Alpha Inventory. Develop a coherent policy, and review all work processes.
3. Set Priorities. Widen managerial bandwidth. [Again, I confess my ignorance of the term in this context.]
4. Develop a Strategic Agenda that sets goals by which to measure success.
5. Make It Real on the Shop Floor, communicating the agenda and aligning incentives accordingly.
6. Tell the Market. Make the approach to managing Embedded Alpha credible, then aggressively promote it. . . . This approach can improve the probability of superior returns. [I'm not quite sure how aggressive promotion can relate to superior returns.]

Perhaps surprisingly, the study presents no data whatsoever on the dimension of Embedded Alpha. "Purposely," we're told, "the paper does not focus on data and statistics." But, the dimensions of cost are astonishingly large. Since I'm not an expert on the economics of the investment counsel business, let me now turn to the mutual fund business to give you some idea of just how large they loom. Based on my best estimates of the costs currently incurred by mutual fund investors, here is the picture:

Average Equity Mutual Fund	Percent of Average Assets
1. Advisory Fees	1.1%
2. Other Operating Expenses	0.5
Total Expense Ratio[a]	1.6%
3. Transaction Costs[b]	0.7
4. Opportunity Cost[c]	0.4
5. Sales Charges[d]	0.6
Total	3.3%
6. Taxes[e]	1.6
TOTAL	4.9%

[a]Unweighted mutual fund ratio. The weighted ratio is about 1.1%.
[b]Most studies show far higher transaction costs. But since market impact itself must be a net zero, (i.e., your aggressive sale creates my bargain purchase), my low estimate reflects how much "The Street" charges for its trading services.
[c]Assuming 12% stock return; 6% cash return; 7% of assets in reserves.
[d]5% sales charge, amortized over 10-year holding period.
[e]Assuming 10% fund after-cost return, 1% income, 9% capital; 50% of gains realized annually, two-thirds long-term, one-third short-term; maximum tax bracket.

You don't need me to tell you that 330 basis points—490 basis points if we include even a modest estimate of taxes—is a lot of Embedded Alpha.

Now let me show you how all of this works out in practice. First, to be conservative, I'm going to slash that 330-basis-point charge, first by ignoring the 60 basis points for sales charges (which are ignored in most industry performance data), then by using an expense ratio weighted by fund assets (another 50-basis-point drop), reducing costs to 220 basis points. Let's use that conservative figure as a benchmark for the Embedded Alpha of the average fund. Next, I'm going to assume that funds earn average returns equal to those of the stock market itself. Of course, managers have the opportunity to earn higher returns (or, for that matter, lower returns) than those of the market. While my own data for the past 15 years suggest that, before the deduction of all that Embedded Alpha, the average fund actually outpaced the stock market (Wilshire 5000 Total Market Index) by 50 basis points per year, these data include only the records of funds that survived the period. (And, believe it or not, only about one-half survived.) So a market-matching return seems not only fair, but generous.

Now let's look long term. Despite today's environment of frighteningly short-term investment horizons, most investors start their programs with their first $1,000 in an IRA or 401(k) and will still be investing, not 50, but 70 years hence. I'll use 50 years. What toll would a 220-basis-point cost have taken on the 13.3 percent return earned on the Standard & Poor's 500 Stock Index over the past 50 years? The fund would earn 11.1 percent, or 2.2 percent less. When compounded, $1,000 in the S&P index itself would grow to $514,000; the fund, after costs, would grow to $193,000—a $321,000 loss to the financial intermediaries. When we include taxes in the equation—given the high market returns of the past 50 years, I'll use 240 basis points, a conservative tax rate—the mutual fund annual pre-tax return of 11.1 percent drops to 8.7 percent after taxes, and the compounded value falls *another* $128,000 to $65,000.

But there's more trouble ahead. Each year, intermediation costs and taxes are paid in *current* dollars, while the investor's final capital must be measured in *constant* dollars. During the past half-century, the inflation rate was 4.0 percent. Result: *Real* annual return for the investor, 4.7 percent. The final purchasing power was reduced *another* $55,000 to $10,000. Wow!

Put another way, the mutual fund's real annual return *before* costs was not the 13.3 percent earned by the S&P index, but 9.3 percent, so the 2.2 percent intermediation cost reduced each year's *real* return, not by 16 percent, but by 24 percent. And that 2.4 percent annual tax cost *further* reduced the fund's net return, not by 22 percent, but by 34 percent. When we apply to the annual data that remarkable magnifying glass called *compounding*, we can describe the investment returns earned by the fund—on cost and tax assumptions that I think we can all agree are hardly excessive—as shocking. The investor lost 63 percent of the market's cumulative return to the intermediaries, 66 percent of *that* to taxes, and 85 percent of *that* to inflation, ending up with just 2 percent of the compound market return we calculate from all of those annual return data that the fund industry publishes.

In fairness, an index *fund* modeled on the Standard & Poor's 500 Index would also have fallen well short of the index itself, but still performed quite remarkably relative to the average managed mutual fund. Assuming costs of 20 basis points, the 13.1 percent return would have compounded to $471,000 versus $193,000 for the managed fund; after a 120-basis-point charge for taxes (index funds are typically about twice as tax-efficient as ordinary funds), its net total value would be $276,000 versus $65,000. And the Index fund total would have been cut to $45,000 after inflation, versus $10,000. That, too, may seem like a far cry from $514,000, but it's hardly realistic to eliminate taxes from the real world of investing. The important reality is that the Index fund would have provided 2.4 times the after-cost value of the mutual fund, 4.2 times the fund's after-tax value, and 4.5 times the fund's *real* terminal value. Yes, Embedded Alpha is a powerful destructive force.

What Active Managers Can Learn from Indexing

Paraphrasing the Greek philosopher Horace, I fear that, like the mountains, the financial giants and fund managers who developed the ML/BARRA study have "labored and brought forth a mouse." Had they made their own calculations of annual Embedded Alpha, then compounded the resultant return over the long term, and then considered the reality that costs and taxes are paid in *current* dollars but long-term returns are received in *real* dollars, they would have realized the enormity of the issue. Having done so myself, my recommendations on controlling costs and my strategy for doing so would be less cliché-ridden, more blunt, and surely more difficult for managers to swallow. If you don't accept my thesis, of course, feel free to ignore them:

1. **Remember that the mathematics are immutable.** Explicitly recognize and acknowledge that investment success—not just in the long-run, but every day of every week, and every month of every year—is defined by the apportionment of market returns

between investors on the one hand and financial intermediaries on the other.

2. **Reduce basic advisory fees**, but endeavor to maintain firm revenues by incorporating incentive/penalty fees. These actions will reward the successful firm and penalize the unsuccessful. (They will, of course, reduce the *total* level of industry-wide advisory fees.)

3. **Cut operating and administrative costs.** This may mean less awesome views of America's most magnificent skylines and harbors, less lavish entertainment, fewer client junkets, fewer seminars in Bermuda, less glossy presentations, less first-class travel, and more modest wine cellars . . . *the whole nine yards.*

4. **Reduce marketing expenses to the bare-bones level.** Advertising is expensive! Special note to the mutual fund industry, where some firms' annual marketing budgets exceed $100 million: Those expenses raise serious questions of fiduciary duty, questions about whether the *investment* interests of fund clients are playing second fiddle to the *marketing* interests of the adviser.

5. **Take a hard line on transaction costs.** Even more importantly, *take a hard line on transactions.* Carefully and regularly evaluate whether your transaction activity has enhanced or detracted from the returns you have realized for your clients.

6. **Taxes are the largest single detractor from Embedded Alpha.** If your clients are taxable, *evaluate your managers on after-tax returns* and use after-tax returns as the basis for incentives. If you have both taxable and tax-deferred accounts, offer separate funds for each.

7. **Eliminate opportunity cost.** Cash, to be sure, is fine when raised just before a market decline. But you know as well as I that there's simply no evidence of firms that have been successful at market timing. Thus, the return-*enhancing* characteristic of cash in down markets is inevitably a small fraction of its return-*reducing* characteristic in the rising markets that are far more common.

8. (For mutual funds only) **Get rid of 12b-1 fees**, those sales commissions that are built into expense ratios. They make your reported returns look *terrible*; they usually entail heavier costs to the investors you serve; and simply, by being hidden, they raise serious questions about your candor and integrity.

While together these steps will change the nature of institutional investing, given the influence of Embedded Alpha on long-term returns, I believe it is only a matter of time before clients will demand change. Forewarned is forearmed.

The S&P 500 Index

You'll note that I've used the S&P 500 Index in my market measure for the past 50 years. While it was the only good standard available in 1950, it remains the most widely accepted standard and, most importantly, continues to provide an excellent if imperfect measure of the stock market. You may have heard—and even believed!—the apocryphal story about the bumble bee: After carefully examining its aerodynamics, weight, and size, an expert group of scientists proved beyond doubt that the bumblebee can't fly. Yet fly it does. It occurs to me that a similar fable is applicable to the Standard & Poor's 500 Stock Index. It doesn't look like it should work, but it obviously does. One only has to consider a few anecdotal examples to understand why it can provide outstanding relative performance.

Consider first the S&P 500, 50 years ago, then as now an index of large-cap stocks in a large-cap dominated market. (Well, *not* the S&P *500*; it was the S&P 90 from 1926 through 1957.) In 1950, it represented a highly concentrated tribute to industrial America. Although I don't recall anyone examining the composition of the index with the kind of attention lavished on it today, General Motors, its largest holding, represented 13.6 percent of its weight. Standard Oil of New Jersey was next at 9.3 percent, and the top 10 holdings accounted for 51.3 percent of its weight, making it more than twice as concentrated as the 24 percent weight of the top 10 today. (IBM, which was to be the star performer of the subsequent two decades, didn't join the index until 1957.) Surprisingly, AT&T, with a market capitalization larger than General Motors', was conspicuous by its absence. Despite its initial "Old Economy" base, the S&P index dominated the active fund managers during the era that followed.

Now advance the calendar to 1964. AT&T, now part of the index, had a 9.1 percent weight, followed by General Motors at 7.3 percent,

Standard Oil of New Jersey at 5.0 percent, and IBM at 3.7 percent. The "top 10" then accounted for 39 percent of the index, again far higher than today's top-10 weight of 24 percent. But even this continued reliance on the Old Economy of autos, chemicals, oils, and utilities— together, 52 percent of the index—failed to diminish its sharp advantage over the average mutual fund during the subsequent decade, despite the surge of the "go-go" concept stocks during the middle of the period.

Just one more example: In 1980, with the quantum surge in oil prices and high expectations for the petroleum industry, the energy sector's weight rose to an all-time high of 32 percent. It would have seemed, I suppose, foolish to own such a single-industry-dependent index fund back then, and in fact during 1976–1985, the index didn't, well, fly very impressively. Nonetheless, the long-term record of the S&P 500 over the past half-century, as we have seen, brooks no apologies. Like the bumble bee, the index *can* fly. And on long trips, it can *soar*.

Today, of course, the index has an equally heavy weighting in the New Economy, including an important dependence on technology stocks (32% as year 2000 began, now 27%). I admit that concentration unnerves me a bit. But I'm such a believer in the magic of indexing that I remain unshaken in my conviction that, no matter what the short-term holds, indexing continues to represent the best way to invest for the long term. Finally, broad diversification, low cost, minimal portfolio turnover, and tax-efficiency conquer all.

Is the S&P Really "The Market"?

For all of its well-known idiosyncrasies, the S&P 500 has proven it can be an excellent representation of the stock market itself. Composed solely of large-cap stocks, it represents about three-quarters of the market's total capitalization; its returns have maintained a fairly stationary correlation (R2) of 0.97 with the total market; and its performance has been virtually identical to that of the Wilshire 5000 Total Equity Market Index over the nearly three full decades in which both indexes have been available.

That is not to say the S&P is an easy target for an investor—or even an average index fund manager—to track. Change it does! Indeed in the past 20 years there have been an astonishing 489 changes in the 500 Stock Index. These are not trivial changes; on average during that period, each year has resulted in the addition of stocks accounting for 2.8 percent of the index's capitalization—an aggregate two-decade replacement equal to 58 percent of its value. Typically, these changes are represented by mergers; the few stocks deleted from the index for other reasons typically have very small market caps.

In essence, we have a process in which old stocks are deleted from the index at a rate of about 3 percent per year, meaning that the weightings of each of the other holdings is reduced by about 3 percent per year. I estimate that had the 500 index remained unchanged over the past six years, Microsoft, Cisco, and Intel, for example, would have apparently represented, not the 4.9 percent, 2.8 percent, and 2.3 percent of the index that they represented as 2000 began, but 5.5 percent, 3.2 percent, and 2.5 percent. While these are not to be taken as hard numbers, they do suggest that the structure of the S&P Index may have helped to marginally improve its performance. Active managers may want to take note.

No similar adjustments are required in the Wilshire 5000 Total Stock Market Index, which includes not only the large-cap stocks in the S&P 500, but mid- and small-cap stocks as well. Yet despite modest short-term variations, it has tracked the S&P 500, as I noted, with virtual perfection over the long-term. Stocks normally come into the index when they are very small and there is no reason to remove them when they hit an arbitrary size. And they are held *forever*— or at least until they are merged into another corporation. It is largely for these reasons that I favor the all-market index fund as the best choice for most investors.

"Benchmarking"

The compelling data I've presented show a substantial shortfall in the long-term returns of mutual funds despite cost and tax assumptions that are remarkably conservative. I've also assumed that domestic funds as a group can be fairly compared with the S&P 500 Stock Index, which closely tracks the total U.S. stock market. And fund portfolios, weighted by assets, closely resemble the configuration of the market, with about the same proportions of large- (70 percent), medium- (22 percent), and small-cap (8 percent) stocks as the market itself. Further, over the very long run, the returns of the various investment styles (small-cap vs. large-cap; growth vs. value, etc.) tend to revert to the market mean, with interim variations ironed out over time. I've also assumed that the long-run objective of *any* equity mutual fund, whatever its style, is, at least implicitly, to "beat the market." (Some funds may hold themselves out as endeavoring to provide a higher "risk-adjusted" return, but I'll not deal with that issue here.)

Nonetheless, I can accept, if a bit grudgingly, the current fashion of "benchmarking"—comparing the return of a small-cap growth fund, for example, with the return of an index of small-cap growth stocks. As a short-term tool for ascertaining whether the manager is investing in accordance with his own proscriptions (and, assumedly, those of his clients), benchmarking seems reasonable enough. But over the long run, it seems to me obvious that *the fairest comparison of return is with the all-market index, not the style index.* It is difficult to imagine that a client seeking a particular style—and a manager offering that style as representative of his or her particular area of expertise and comparative advantage—does not make that selection because it is expected to enhance long-term returns. "What gaineth the client," one might say, "if he winneth the style derby, but loseth to the whole stock market."

For all of the scientific computerized data we see presented with grand precision—comparative returns, risk-adjusted returns, Alpha and Beta (with Omega not yet on our horizon), measured over short periods and long, and taken out to two decimal points and sometimes more—I think we in the profession have the duty, simply as a matter of fair and complete disclosure, to present *both* sets of comparisons—the style benchmark and the all-market benchmark—to our clients. Let's let narrow style benchmarking dictate neither our investment decision making nor our standard for appraising long-term accomplishment.

Variations on Long-Term, All-Market Indexing

If the all-market index standard should—finally, must—be the long-term standard for equity accounts of all stripes, what use is served by the scores of index variations on this basic theme over the past decade-plus? I confess that, with the passage of time, I have become increasingly concerned about the utility of these variations, and I owe this audience the professional courtesy to tell you what bothers me and why it does so.

First, confession being good for the soul, it was primarily because of my own drive and conviction that Vanguard became the pioneer in index funds. We formed the first S&P 500 Index fund in 1975, and then in 1987 pioneered the *completion* ("Extended Market") index fund, tracking the small- and mid-cap stocks unrepresented in the S&P 500. The idea: to enable investors to make a commitment to the *entire* stock market, which I consider as the full fruition of the index fund concept. But adjustment of stocks between the two index funds was required as stocks moved in and out of the 500, creating portfolio turnover and potential tax-inefficiencies. So, in 1992 we created the all-in-one Total (U.S.) Stock Market Index Fund. That same year, when Standard & Poor's/BARRA answered my public prayer and developed a growth index and a value index—each regularly adjusted to represent one-half of the weight of the 500—we started our Growth Index and Value Index Funds. I stated then—and reiterate now—my expectation that the long-term *total* returns were unlikely to differ significantly. The idea was to allow more aggressive long-term investors to hold the Growth Index Fund for lower taxable income, higher tax-efficiency, and higher likely volatility. More conservative investors could hold the Value Index Fund (for higher retirement income and lower volatility, at the cost of some tax-efficiency).

Still earlier, in 1989, we converted a tiny actively managed Vanguard small-cap fund into a passive Russell 2000 Index fund, creating the industry's first small-cap index fund. And a few years ago, my successors at Vanguard added three more index funds—mid-cap (S&P 400), small-cap growth (half of the Standard & Poor's 600), and a small-cap value fund (the other half). Over their histories, the segment funds formed before 1992 have done quite respectably—if largely unspectacularly. The newer funds, in even narrower market segments, have not been around long enough to fairly evaluate.

If the longer-run past results of our market-segment index funds are at least respectable—and given the survivor bias that significantly *overstates* the achievements of actively managed small-cap and mid-cap mutual funds, they are doubtless far better than that—what's my concern? First, my instinctive feeling is that the use of segment funds is unlikely to add long-run value to the total market return. Second, I believe too many investors are using these funds to shift among market segments based on past performance, a formula apt to result in failure. Given the market trends that have favored growth stocks during the past five years, for example, the assets of our Large-Cap Growth Index Fund currently total $14 billion, compared to $3.5 billion for its Value Index counterpart. (Surprise!) Third, segment funds carry far higher portfolio turnover: Small-Cap Growth and Small-Cap Value, each about 80 percent last year; Small-Cap (total), 42 percent; Large Value, 41 percent; Large Growth, 33 percent; and even Extended Market, 26 percent.

In fairness, the extraordinary index fund management strategies of Vanguard's skilled director of Quantitative Management, Gus Sauter, have resulted in virtually *zero* net cost for all of these purchases and sales, and each fund has tracked its appointed index with extraordinary precision. But compare those double-digit turnover figures with our S&P 500 Index Fund (6 percent) and our Total Stock Market Fund (3 percent!) and you'll clearly see *what a difference a benchmark makes.* Tax impacts, too, have been nicely constrained. But if our shareholders move their money around rapidly in less generous markets than these, or heavily withdraw substantial assets in a bear market, the roadblocks to maintaining that excellence will be formidable.

Nonetheless, I have not lost all hope for the market-segment index fund, for most of these problems could be solved by the creation of better market-segment *indexes*—indexes with new definitional concepts that offer less sensitivity to stock substitutions, and therefore lower portfolio turnover—and the imposition of redemption fees to reduce short-term trading in these funds. For those investors who cannot resist the urge—which they probably should resist!—to overweight or underweight one market segment or another, such funds may well provide the most sensible approach.

In any event, indexing of all types continues to grow. But much of the growth is coming, not through conventional index funds, but through novel index funds known as ETFs (exchange-traded funds), an acronym that trips from the tongues of almost every industry maven worth his or her reportorial salt, if only of a small subset of market speculators. The assets of these funds, I read in the *New York Times* last Sunday, totaled $53 billion at midyear, and they are aggressively promoted. But—make no mistake about it—few of their holders are long-term investors. This year, the *Spiders* (SPDRs) are being turned over at an annualized rate of 1,415 percent, and the NASDAQ 100 *Qubes* at a rate of 5,974 percent: Respective average holding periods: 26 days, and six days. Why not? They are not only being *used* for short-term goals, but *promoted* as short-term investments. A full-page advertisement for SPDR index shares in *Barron's* magazine dated September 18, 2000, is headlined: "Buy and sell the S&P 500 just as easily as you trade a single stock." (Then adding, "with real time pricing, you can trade your position throughout the trading day.") Yet Sunday's *Times* also reported this statement by a SPDRs executive: "Our customers are *long-term* investors" (italics added). That doesn't seem consistent with either the facts or the ad. So, lest we forget, I reiterate: There is a critical difference between designing a *product* to sell to customers and creating an *investment* to serve its owners.

Indexing: Losing Its Way?

Today, changes are swirling all around those of us in the investment community. The soaring volumes, the volatile markets, the heightened public interest in financial matters, the intense media coverage, a mutual fund industry whose excessive expenses and increasingly short-term focus have combined to create an insuperable Embedded Alpha, and an unsound departure from the proper use of index funds—still the best way I know to fully capture the returns of the financial markets. Have we forgotten that the most productive investing is the most peaceable investing, the lowest-cost investing, the most tax-efficient investing—investing with the most consistent strategies and over longest time horizon? If we have forgotten, it's high time to relearn those basics.

If investors do so, the profession of managing the accounts of substantial (especially, the management of taxable) individual investors holds great opportunity. Mutual fund competitors and ETF competitors are hell-bent down a road that, unless it turns, may even provide a near-monopoly on the management of the accounts of investors of both moderate and substantial means. Investors can learn and profit from their weaknesses. But investors won't get there by ignoring the timeless truth of the financial markets. Whether it is Louis Bachelier speaking, or a group of Nobel Laureates, or Malkiel or even Bogle, now buttressed by the Embedded Alpha paper of Merrill Lynch/ BARRA, *the mathematics of the markets are eternal.* The investment success of investors in the aggregate is defined—not only over the long term but every single day—by the extent to which market returns are consumed by financial intermediaries. So capitalize on the failures of so many other managers that I've described, and learn from the simple reasons behind the success of the index fund. Opportunity beckons!

Chapter 18

As the Index Fund Moves from Heresy to Dogma, What More Do We Need to Know?*

September 2005, a little more than a year from now, will mark the 30th anniversary of the creation of the first index mutual fund. That fund—originally, and proudly, named First Index Investment Trust—is now, as Vanguard 500 Index Fund, the largest mutual fund in the world. But that is only one indication of the success of index investing. For the *heresy* that was indexing—passive portfolio management that invaded a kingdom ruled, indeed populated solely by, active portfolio managers—has now become *dogma*, part of the academic canon, taught almost universally in college finance courses and in business schools, and part of the daily discourse of investors.

The evidence on the triumph of indexing is overwhelming. In the mutual fund industry, total assets of equity index funds, barely $1 billion

---

*Based on a lecture presented as part of the Gary M. Brinson Distinguished Lecture series at Washington State University on April 13, 2004.

in 1990, now total over $550 billion, one-sixth of all equity fund assets. While that first index fund of 1975 wasn't copied until 1984, nearly a decade later, there are now 430 equity index funds, and even 30 bond index funds. In the pension world, where the idea of indexing took hold several years earlier than in the fund field, the indexed assets of corporate and state and local retirement plans, $900 billion in 1990, now total *$3.5 trillion.*

Combined indexed assets—linked to U.S. and international stock and bond indexes—of mutual funds and retirement plans now exceed $4 trillion. Indeed, three of America's 10 largest money managers (State Street Global Advisors, Barclays Global Investors, and Vanguard, all overseeing from $700 billion to $1 trillion in assets) have reached this pinnacle largely on the basis of their emphasis on index strategies.

But the impact of indexing has gone far beyond the trillions of dollars of assets that rely on pure index strategies. "Closet index funds" that closely track the Standard & Poor's 500 Index, for example, are rife, seeking to add value by making relatively modest variations in index stock weightings, all the while engaging in tight "risk control" by maintaining a high correlation with the movements in the market index itself. And rare is the active "buy-side" institutional portfolio manager who, seeking to minimize what has come to be called "benchmark risk," fails to compare the weights of his portfolio holdings with those in the index. The icing on the cake of indexing: Wall Street's "sell-side" analysts no longer recommend "buy, sell, or hold." Today, "over-weight, under-weight and equal-weight" stocks relative to a firm's share of the market's total capitalization have become the profession's words of art, itself a sort of closet indexing approach.

There can be no question that index-matching strategies—simple and broadly diversified, heavily weighted by stocks with large capitalizations, with low fees and low portfolio turnover—have changed the landscape of our financial markets, and set a new standard in the way we both measure and enjoy our investment returns. Yes, our focus has turned away from absolute return and toward relative performance— beating or falling short of the index benchmark. Of course, absolute performance is what investors can actually spend, but, to state the obvious, the fund that has the best *relative* performance is also the *absolute* champion.

The Intellectual Basis for Indexing

While the clear triumph of indexing can hardly have surprised thoughtful observers of the financial scene, few commentators have recognized that two separate and distinct intellectual ideas form the foundation for passive investment strategies. Academics and sophisticated students of the markets rely upon the EMH—the *Efficient Market Hypothesis*—which suggests that by reflecting the informed opinion of the mass of investors, stocks are continuously valued at prices that accurately reflect the totality of investor knowledge, and are thus fairly valued.

But we don't need to accept the EMH to be index believers. For there is a second reason for the triumph of indexing, and it is not only more compelling but unarguably universal. I call it the CMH—the *Cost Matters Hypothesis*—and not only is it all that is needed to explain why indexing must and does work, but it in fact enables us to quantify with some precision *how well* it works. *Whether or not the markets are efficient, the explanatory power of the CMH holds.*

More than a century has passed since Louis Bachelier, in his Ph.D. thesis at the Sorbonne in 1900, wrote: "Past, present, and even discounted future events are (all) reflected in market price." Nearly half a century later, when Nobel Laureate Paul Samuelson discovered the long-forgotten thesis, he confessed that he "oscillated . . . between regarding it as trivially obvious (and almost trivially vacuous), and regarding it as remarkably sweeping." In essence, Bachelier was, as far as he went, *right*: "The mathematical expectation of the speculator is zero." By 1965, University of Chicago Professor Eugene F. Fama had performed enough analysis of the ever-increasing volume of stock price data to validate this "random walk" hypothesis, rechristened as the *efficient market hypothesis*. Today, the intellectual arguments against the general thrust of the EMH religion are few. While it would seem extreme to argue that *all* stocks are efficiently priced *all* of the time, it would seem equally extreme to deny that *most* stocks are efficiently priced *most* of the time.

But whatever the consensus on the EMH, I know of no serious academic, professional money manager, trained security analyst, or intelligent individual investor who would disagree with the thrust of

EMH: *The stock market itself is a demanding taskmaster.* It sets a high hurdle that few investors can leap. While the apostles of the new so-called "behavioral" theory present ample evidence of how often human beings make irrational financial decisions, it remains to be seen whether these decisions lead to predictable errors that create systematic mispricings upon which rational investors can readily (and economically) capitalize.

But while the precise validity of the EMH may be debatable, there can be *no* debate about the validity of the CMH. It posits a conclusion that is also, using Dr. Samuelson's formulation, both "trivially obvious and remarkably sweeping" and it confirms that Bachelier's argument had to be taken one step further. The mathematical expectation of the speculator is not zero; *it is a loss equal to the amount of transaction costs incurred.*

So, too, the mathematical expectation of the long-term investor also is a shortfall to whatever returns our financial markets are generous enough to provide. Indeed the shortfall can be described as precisely equal to the costs of our system of financial intermediation—the sum total of all those advisory fees, marketing expenditures, sales loads, brokerage commissions, transaction costs, custody and legal fees, and securities processing expenses. Intermediation costs in the U.S. equity market may well total as much as $250 billion a year or more. If today's $13 trillion stock market were to provide, say, a 7 percent annual return ($910 billion), costs would consume more than a quarter of it, leaving less than three-quarters of the return for the investors—those who put up 100 percent of the capital. We don't need the EMH to explain the dire odds that investors face in their quest to beat the stock market. We need only the CMH. *Whether markets are efficient or inefficient, investors as a group must fall short of the market return by the amount of the costs they incur.*

Now for the *really* bad news. Investors pay their investment costs each year in nominal *current* dollars, but they measure their long-run investment success in *real* dollars, almost inevitably eroded in value by inflation. The *nominal* long-term returns of about 10 percent on stocks that the financial intermediation system waves before the eyes of the naive investing public turn out to be about 6.5 percent in *real* terms. When we realize that in the mutual fund industry intermediation costs total at least 2.5 percentage points annually, *they confiscate nearly 40 percent of the historical real rate of return on equities, reducing the return to 4 percent.* And when we subtract the cost of taxes (which have been nearly 2% per year) the net after-tax return tumbles to 2 percent, and the confiscation of real return by costs and excessive taxes rises to 70 percent. In a coming era in which returns may well fall below historic norms, we must look at potential investment accumulations in a new and harsh light.

The academic and financial communities have dedicated enormous intellectual and financial resources to studying past returns on stocks, to regression analysis, to modern portfolio theory, to behaviorism, and to the EMH. It's high time we turn more of our attention to the CMH. We need to know just how much our system of financial intermediation has come to cost, to know the extent to which high turnover may pay, and to understand the *real* net returns that managers deliver to investors.

Two Schools of Indexing— Quantitative and Pragmatic

All these years later, the distinctly different intellectual approaches of the EMH and the CMH illuminate the history of indexing. The *Quantitative School*, led by masters of mathematics such as Harry Markowitz, William Fouse, John McQuown, Eugene Fama, and William F. Sharpe, did complex equations and conducted exhaustive research on the financial markets to reach the conclusions that led to the EMH. In essence, the "Modern Portfolio Theory" developed by the Quantitative School showed that a fully diversified, unmanaged equity portfolio was the surest route to investment success, a conclusion that lead to the formation of the first index *pension* account (for the Samsonite Corporation), formed by Wells Fargo Bank in 1971. That tiny $6 million account was invested in an equal-weighted index of New York Stock Exchange equities. Alas, its implementation proved to be a nightmare, and in 1976 it was replaced with the market-capitalization-weighted Standard & Poor's 500 Common Stock Price Index, which remains the principal standard for pension fund indexing to this day.

While the Quantitative School developed its profound theories, what I'll call the *Pragmatic School* simply looked at the evidence. In 1974, the *Journal of Portfolio Management* published an article by Dr. Samuelson entitled "Challenge to Judgment."[*] It noted that academics had been unable to identify any consistently excellent investment managers, challenged those who disagreed to produce "brute evidence to the contrary," and pleaded for someone, somewhere to start an index fund. A year later, in an article entitled *The Loser's Game*,[†] Charles D. Ellis argued that, because of fees and transaction costs, 85 percent of pension accounts had underperformed the stock market. "If you can't beat the market, you should certainly consider joining it," Ellis concluded. "An index fund is one way."[‡]

In mid-1975, I was both blissfully unaware of the work the quants were doing and profoundly inspired by the pragmatism of Samuelson and Ellis. I had just started a tiny company called Vanguard, and was determined to start the first index *mutual* fund. It was then that I pulled out all of my annual *Weisenberger Investment Companies* manuals, calculated by hand the average annual returns earned by equity mutual funds over the previous 30 years, and compared them to the returns of the Standard & Poor's 500 Stock Index: Result: Annual returns, 1945– 1975, S&P Index were 10.1 percent; average equity fund, 8.7 percent.

---

[*] Paul A. Samuelson, "Challenge to Judgment," *Journal of Portfolio Management* 1, no. 1 (Fall 1974).

[†] Charles D. Ellis, "The Loser's Game,"*Financial Analysts Journal* 31, no. 4 (July/ August 1975).

[‡] I should note that one of the earliest calls for indexing came from a book that I did not read until many years later: *A Random Walk Down Wall Street*, by Princeton University Professor Burton S. Malkiel (New York: W. W. Norton, 1973). Dr. Malkiel suggested, "A New Investment Instrument: A no-load, minimum-management-fee mutual fund that simply buys the hundreds of stocks making up the market averages and does no trading (of securities). . . . Fund spokesmen are quick to point out, 'you can't buy the averages.' It's about time the public could." He urged that the New York Stock Exchange sponsor such a fund and run it on a nonprofit basis, but if it "is unwilling to do it, I hope some other institution will." In 1977, four years after he wrote those words, he joined the Board of Directors of First Index Investment Trust and the other Vanguard funds, positions in which he has served with distinction ever since.

As I mused about the reasons for the difference, the obvious occurred to me. The index was cost-free, and its 1.4 percent annual advantage in returns roughly approximated the total costs then incurred by the average fund—the expense ratio plus the hidden costs of portfolio turnover. To illustrate the enormous impact of that seemingly small percentage difference, I calculated that a hypothetical initial investment of $1,000,000 in 1945 would by 1975 have grown to $18,000,000 in the index, versus $12,000,000 in the average fund. In September 1975, using those data and the Samuelson and Ellis articles, I urged a dubious Vanguard board of directors to approve our creation of the first index mutual fund. They agreed.

How Vanguard Came to Start the First Index Mutual Fund

The idea of an index fund was hardly anathema to me. Way back in 1951, the anecdotal evidence that I had assembled in my Princeton University senior thesis on the then-minuscule mutual fund industry led me to warn against the "expectations of miracles from mutual fund management," and shaped my conclusion that funds "can make no claim to superiority to the market averages." When the newly formed Vanguard began operations in May 1975, I had realized my dream of establishing the first truly *mutual* mutual fund complex. The next item at the top of my agenda: an index fund.

Why? Because while the idea of an index fund would have hardly appealed to a high-cost fund manager whose very business depended on the conviction that, whatever his past record, he could outpace the market in the future, indexing would be a natural for us. We were organized as a shareholder-owned, truly *mutual* mutual fund group, with low costs as our mantra. So while our rivals had the same opportunity to create the first index mutual fund, only Vanguard, like the prime suspect in a criminal investigation, had both the opportunity *and* the motive.

Our introduction of First Index Investment Trust was greeted by the investment community with derision. It was dubbed "Bogle's Folly," and described as un-American, inspiring a widely circulated poster showing Uncle Sam calling on the world to "Help Stamp Out Index Funds" (Figure 18.1). Fidelity Chairman Edward C. Johnson led the skeptics, assuring the world that Fidelity had no intention of following Vanguard's lead: "I can't believe that the great mass of investors are going to be satisfied with just receiving average returns. The name of the game is to be the best." (Fidelity now runs some $38 billion in indexed assets.)

The early enthusiasm of the investing public for the novel idea of an unmanaged index fund designed to track the S&P 500 index was as

FIGURE 18.1   BOGLE'S FOLLY?

subdued as the admiration of our detractors. Its initial public offering in the summer of 1976 raised a puny $11 million, and early growth was slow. Assets of First Index didn't top $100 million until six years later, and only because we merged another Vanguard actively managed fund with it. But the coming of the Great Bull Market that began in mid-1982 started the momentum, and the fund's assets crossed the $500 million mark in 1986.

From the outset, I realized that the 500 Index, by owning large-cap stocks that represented 75 to 80 percent of the value of the total U.S. market, would closely parallel, but not precisely match, the stock market's return, since the S&P index excluded mid-cap and small-cap stocks. So in 1987, we started a fund called the Extended Market Fund, indexed to those smaller companies. If used in harness with the 500 Fund, it would provide a *total* market exposure. By year end, combined assets of the two funds were nearly $1 billion. In 1990, we added another "Institutional 500 Fund" designed for pension plans, and in 1991, a Total Stock Market Index Fund, modeled on the Wilshire Total (U.S.) Market Index, bringing total assets of these essentially all-market index funds to $6 billion.

During 1994–1999, as the bull market continued, and as our index funds continued to outpace the overwhelming majority—upwards of 80 percent!—of actively managed funds, asset growth accelerated—$16 billion in 1993, $60 billion in 1996, $227 billion in 1999. Much of this success, as I warned our index shareowners, "should under no circumstances be regarded either as repeatable or sustainable." *It wasn't.* But even in the ensuing bear market, the index funds outpaced more than 50 percent of their actively managed peers, and solid growth continued. Assets of our four "all-market" index funds now total some $200 billion, with our other 33 index funds bringing our total indexed assets to $300 billion today.*

So indexing has enjoyed a considerable commercial success, drawing huge assets to Vanguard, and even larger amounts to other managers and pension funds. It has enjoyed that success, not only because of the

---

* This figure includes our specialty index funds (small-cap, growth, value, Europe, Pacific, etc.) as well as a series of bond index funds and enhanced index funds. Their rationale and development, however, are stories for another day.

sound and pragmatic foundation on which indexing relies, but because it has, over three decades now, worked effectively in providing superior returns. This is to say, indexing has not been merely a *commercial* success. It has been an *artistic* success. *Indexing worked!*

Brute Facts

How *well* did it work? Thirty years ago in "Challenge to Judgment," Dr. Samuelson wrote: "When [respected] investigators look to identify those minority groups endowed with superior investment process, they are quite unable to find them. . . . [Even] a loose version of the 'efficient market' or 'random walk' hypothesis accords with the facts of life . . . any jury that reviews the evidence must at least come out with the Scottish verdict: Superior performance is unproved." And so he issued his challenge: "The ball is in the court of those who doubt the random walk hypothesis. They can dispose of that uncomfortable brute fact in the only way that any fact is disposed of—by producing brute evidence to the contrary."

So today, three decades later, let's examine some brute evidence. Let's go back to the era in which the Samuelson article was published, and see what lessons we can learn by examining the evidence on the ability of mutual fund managers to provide market-beating returns. In 1970, there were 355 equity mutual funds, and we have now had more than three decades over which to measure their success. We're first confronted with an astonishing—and important—revelation: *Only 147 funds survived the period.* Fully 208 of those funds vanished from the scene, an astonishing 60 percent failure rate (Figure 18.2).

Now let's look at the records of the survivors—doubtless the superior funds of the initial group. Yet fully 104 of them fell short of the 11.3 percent average annual return achieved by the unmanaged S&P 500 Index. Just 43 funds exceeded the index return. If, reasonably enough, we describe a return that comes within plus or minus a single percentage point of the market as statistical noise, 52 of the surviving funds provided a return roughly equivalent to that of the market. A total of 72 funds, then, were clear losers (i.e., by more than a percentage point), with only 23 clear winners above that threshold.

**FIGURE 18.2   LOOKING FOR A NEEDLE IN A HAYSTACK:
RETURNS OF SURVIVING MUTUAL FUNDS, 1970–2003**

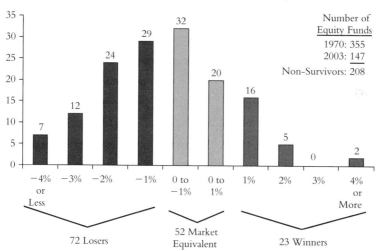

If we widen the "noise" threshold to plus or minus two percentage points, we find that 43 of the 50 funds outside that range were inferior and only 7 superior—a tiny 2 percent of the 355 funds that began the period, and an astonishing piece of the brute evidence that Dr. Samuelson demanded. The verdict, then, is here, and it is clear. The jury has spoken. But its verdict is not "unproved." It is "guilty." Fund managers are systematically guilty of the failure to add shareholder value.

But I believe the evidence actually overrates the long-term achievements of the seven putatively successful funds. Is the obvious creditability of those superior records in fact credible? I'm not so sure. Those winning funds have much in common. First, each was relatively unknown (and relatively unowned by investors) at the start of the period. Their assets were tiny, with the smallest at $1.9 million, the median at $9.8 million, and the largest at $59 million. Second, their best returns were achieved during their first decade, and resulted in enormous asset growth, typically from those little widows' mites at the start of the period to $5 billion or so at the peak, before performance started to deteriorate. (One fund actually peaked at $105 billion!)

Third, despite their glowing early records, most have lagged the market fairly consistently during the past decade, sometimes by a substantial amount (Figure 18.3). The pattern for five of the seven funds is remarkably consistent: a peak in relative return in the early 1990s, followed by annual returns of the next decade that lagged the market's return by about three percentage points per year—roughly, S&P 500 +12 percent, mutual fund +9 percent.

In the field of fund management it seems apparent that "nothing *fails* like success"—the reverse of the threadbare convention that "nothing *succeeds* like success." For the vicious circle of investing—good past performance draws large dollars of inflow, and having large dollars to manage crimps the very ingredients that were largely responsible for the good performance—is almost inevitable in any winning fund. So even if an investor was smart enough or lucky enough to have selected one of the few winning funds at the outset, selecting such funds by hindsight—after their early success—was also largely a loser's game. Whatever the case, the brute evidence of the past three decades makes a powerful case against the quest to find the needle in the haystack. *Investors would clearly be better served by simply owning, through an index fund, the market haystack itself.*

FIGURE 18.3   EXAMINING THE SEVEN 34-YEAR WINNERS

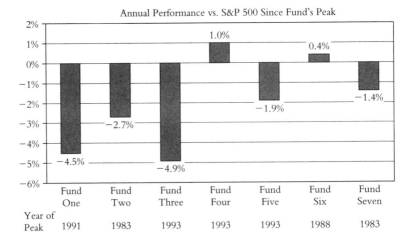

Annual Performance vs. S&P 500 Since Fund's Peak

More Brute Facts

In the field of investment management, relying on past performance simply *has not worked*. The past has *not* been prologue, for there is little persistence in fund performance. A recent study of equity mutual fund risk-adjusted returns during 1983–2003 reflected a randomness in performance that is virtually perfect. A comparison of fund returns in the first half to the second half of the *first* decade, in the first half to the second half of the *second* decade, and in the first full decade to the second full decade makes the point clear. Averaging the three periods shows that 25 percent of the top-quartile funds in the first period found themselves in the top quartile in the second—*precisely* what chance would dictate (Figure 18.4). Almost the same number of top-quartile funds—23 percent—tumbled to the bottom quartile, again a close-to-random outcome. In the bottom quartile, 28 percent of the funds mired there during the first half remained there in the second, while slightly more—29 percent—had actually jumped to the top quartile.

Perfect randomness would distribute the funds in each performance quartile randomly in the succeeding period—16 blocks, each with a 25 percent entry. As the matrix shows, the reality comes close to perfection. In no case was there less than a 20 percent persistence or more

FIGURE 18.4   DOES MUTUAL FUND PERFORMANCE PERSIST? AN EXAMINATION OF RISK-ADJUSTED RETURNS

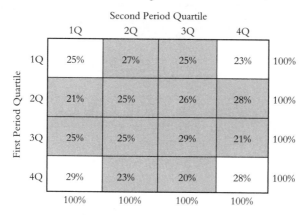

		Second Period Quartile			
		1Q	2Q	3Q	4Q
First Period Quartile	1Q	25%	27%	25%	23%	100%
	2Q	21%	25%	26%	28%	100%
	3Q	25%	25%	29%	21%	100%
	4Q	29%	23%	20%	28%	100%
		100%	100%	100%	100%	

than a 29 percent persistence. Simply picking the top-performing funds of the past fails to be a winning strategy. What is more, even when funds succeed in outpacing their peers, they still have a way to go to match the return of the stock market index itself.

Yet both investors and their brokers and advisers hold to the conviction that they can identify winning fund managers. One popular way is through the *star* system espoused by the Morningstar rating service. Indeed, over the past decade, fully 98 percent(!) of all investment dollars flowing in equity mutual funds in the nine Morningstar "style boxes" was invested in funds awarded five stars or four stars, the firm's two highest ratings. (The ratings are heavily weighted by absolute fund performance, so we can hardly blame—or even credit—Morningstar for primarily being responsible for these huge capital inflows. Stars or not, high returns attract large dollars.)

But as Morningstar is first to acknowledge, its star ratings have little predictive value. The record bears out their caution. Academic studies show that the positive risk-adjusted returns ("Alpha") that distinguish the four- and five-star funds *before* they gain the ratings typically turn negative *afterward*, and by a correlative amount. Data from *Hulbert's Financial Digest* confirm this conclusion. *Following* their selection, the funds in the top-ranked Morningstar categories typically lag the stock market return by a wide margin. Over the past decade, for example, the average return of these "star" funds came to 6.9 percent per year, fully 4.1 percentage points behind the 11.0 percent return on the S&P 500 Index. What is more, that 37 percent shortfall in annual return came hand in hand with a risk (standard deviation) that was 4 percent *higher*. Even for the experts, picking winning mutual funds is hazardous duty.

A Case Study

So the search for "long-term investment excellence" is an elusive one. A fine new book (*Capital*, with the foregoing words in its subtitle) by respected analyst Charles D. Ellis drives this point home.* Mr. Ellis describes a firm of consummate professionals, serious about their trade,

---

*Charles D. Ellis, *Capital* (Hoboken, NJ: John Wiley & Sons, 2004).

with an excellent investment *process*. But for all that obvious excellence, we also are given, perhaps inadvertently, an illustration of the wide gap between manager achievement and shareholder achievement, as well as a warning about casually accepting the assumption that the past is prologue.

The Ellis book is a history of The Capital Group Companies, a Los Angeles firm that may well be the most widely respected investment manager in America. Certainly the accolades, from impartial observers and competitors alike, could hardly be more glowing: "one of the most outstanding investment firms ever created," "one of the best firms in our business," "a premier investment firm," and "people with a passion for long-term investment success." I would hardly disagree with these endorsements. Indeed, I've been singing my own praises of Capital since the early 1960s. (In my previous career at Wellington Management Company, I even explored the possibility of a merger of our firms!)

Yet despite their organizational integrity and investment focus, and despite the fact that the net returns they have delivered to their fund shareholders are clearly superior to those of most of their peers, the returns achieved by Capital can hardly be said to have been extraordinary relative to the stock market itself. The book documents the return of their flagship fund, the Investment Company of America (ICA) during 1973–2003 at +13.2 percent per year, or 1.8 percentage points over the 11.4 percent return on the S&P 500 Index. But, as nearly all fund comparisons do, it ignores the impact of the initial 8.5 percent sales charge paid by investors. For a typical investor, such a cost would reduce that excess return by about 0.8 percent to a single percentage point, although even that small advantage is admirable in an industry that, as we now know, struggles and ultimately fails to match the stock market's return.

But of course, like all comparisons, it is *time dependent*. Other periods give rise to different, and less compelling, results. For example, during the past 25 years (1979–2003), ICA underperformed the market in 16 years. While it outpaced the market by 0.7 percent (14.5% vs. 13.8%) for the period, after adjusting for the sales charge, it fell slightly *behind*, with a *net* annual return of 13.7 percent. Indeed since 1983—two full decades—no matter in which year we choose to begin the comparison, the results of the ICA have pretty much paralleled those of the market itself, with a correlation of a remarkable 95 percent. (To be fair, ICA is less volatile, significantly lagging as the bull market bubble inflated during 1998–1999, and then recouping the ground lost during the ensuing bear market.)

But in an industry that ultimately fails to match the market's return, why not just salute ICA as equal or even preferable to an index fund? First, because despite its long-term focus, it is relatively tax-inefficient. During the past 25 years, for example, federal taxes consumed an estimated 2.5 percentage points of its annual return, reducing it from 13.7 percent to 11.2 percent for taxable investors. While an S&P 500 Index fund is hardly exempt from taxes, its passive market-matching strategy is highly tax-efficient. During the same period, taxes on an index fund would have cost an estimated 0.9 percentage points, reducing its 13.8 percent pre-tax return to 12.9 percent, a net *after-tax* advantage over ICA of 1.7 percentage points per year. Not only do taxable investors pay high costs in fund advisory fees, operating expenses, and sales commissions when they buy active fund management, they also pay a remarkably high tax cost.

A second reason for caution before we salute is that, as our earlier evidence suggests, the past is rarely prologue. And not just because of the "random walk" that characterizes the returns typically achieved by active managers in highly efficient markets. Success—even perceived success—in investment management goes not unrecognized; indeed it is often hyped from the rooftops. It draws money, creating that vicious circle we described earlier. Warren Buffett warns us that "a fat wallet is the enemy of superior returns," and the record clearly confirms his wisdom.

Today ICA's assets total $66 billion, an enormous sum compared to assets of $1.3 billion 25 years ago. That exponential growth hardly makes the job of active management any easier. The number of investments large enough to make a meaningful impact on the portfolio shrinks, even as the difficulty and cost of buying and selling stocks escalate. What is more, the size of ICA is only the tip of the iceberg, for the fund is part of a $500 billion investment complex, and many of its largest holdings are also held by Capital's other funds and pension clients. The organization currently holds, for example, some 11 percent of Target Corp. and GM, and from 7 percent to 10 percent of Altria, FNMA, J. P. Morgan Chase, Eli Lilly, Bristol-Myers, Dow Chemical, Tyco, Texas Instruments, and Fleet Boston. Whether the massive growth in the assets Capital manages will impede the firm's ability to turn its past into prologue, only time will tell.

What Is the Intellectual Foundation for Active Management?

Let me summarize what I see as the intellectual basis for indexing: Even if the EMH is weak, the CMH remains a tautology—all the more important in the mutual fund arena where costs are so confiscatory. The brute evidence on the rarity of superior management goes far beyond the relatively few examples I've cited today. And the vicious circle of superiority generating growth, generating inferior returns— with few managers courageous and disciplined enough to defy it—has become a truism. That the typical fund portfolio manager holds his post for less than five years, furthermore, means that a long-term investor has to identify not only a superior manager, but bet on his longevity. And the astonishing fund failure rate that, at current rates, implies a 50–50 survival rate over the coming decade, is the icing on the cake of the case for indexing.

What, then, is the intellectual foundation for active management? While I've seen some evidence that managers have provided returns that are superior to the returns of the stock market *before costs*, I've *never* seen it argued that managers as a group can outperform the market *after* the costs of their services are deducted, nor that any *class* of manager (e.g., mutual fund managers) can do so. What do the proponents of active management point to? Themselves! "We can do it better." "We have done it better." "Just buy the (inevitably superior performing) funds we that we advertise." It turns out, then, that the big idea that defines active management is that there *is* no big idea. Its proponents offer only a few good anecdotes of the past and promises for the future.

Alas, it turns out that there is in fact one big idea that can be generalized without contradiction. *Cost* is the single statistical construct that is highly correlated with future investment success. The higher the cost, the lower the return. Equity fund expense ratios have a *negative* correlation coefficient of −0.61 with equity fund returns. In the fund business, you get what you don't pay for. *You get what you don't pay for!*

If we simply aggregate funds by quartile, this correlation jumps right out at us. During the decade ended November 30, 2003, the lowest-cost quartile of funds provided an average annual return of 10.7 percent; the second-lowest, 9.8 percent; the second-highest, 9.5 percent; and the highest quartile, 7.7 percent—the difference of fully three percentage points per year between the high and low quartiles, equal to a 30 percent increase in annual return! The same pattern holds irrespective of the time period, and essentially irrespective of manager style or market capitalization. But of course, with index funds carrying by far the lowest costs in the industry, there are few, if any, promotions by active managers of the undeniable relationship between cost and value.

Changing Times and Circumstances

So it is the crystal-clear record of the past, an understanding of the present, and the realization that even the future returns of today's successful managers are unpredictable that together seem to make the search for the Holy Grail of market-beating returns a fruitless quest. It is the recognition of this reality that has carried indexing to its remarkable eminence and growth. But please don't imagine that I am sitting back and reveling in where indexing stands today. I press on in my mission as an apostle of indexing, not only because complacency doesn't seem a very healthy attitude and resting on one's laurels is too often the precursor of failure, but for three other reasons: First, because indexing has not yet adequately fulfilled its promise. Second, because we have subverted the idea of indexing, adding to its role as the consummate vehicle for long-term investing ("basic indexing") a new role as a vehicle for short-term speculation ("peripheral indexing"). And third, because not nearly enough individual investors have yet come to accept the extraordinary value that indexing offers.

The initial promise of indexing was reflected in an article that appeared in *Fortune* magazine in June 1976, smack in the middle of the launch of our First Index Investment Trust. Written by journalist A. F. Ehrbar, it was entitled, "Index Funds—An Idea Whose Time Is Coming," and concluded that "index funds now threaten to reshape the entire world of money management." Yet nearly three decades later, while the influence of indexing has clearly been powerful, it has failed to reshape that world. This failure has been most abject in the mutual fund field, where active managers have largely ignored the lessons they should have learned from the success of indexing.

The reasons for that success are the essence of simplicity: (1) the broadest possible diversification, often subsuming the entire U.S. stock market; (2) a focus on the long-term, with minimal, indeed nominal, portfolio turnover (say, 3% to 5% annually); and (3) rock-bottom cost, with neither advisory fees nor sales loads, and minimal operating expenses. Rather than being inspired to emulate these winning attributes, however, the fund industry has largely turned its back on them.

Consider that only about 500 of the 3,700 equity funds that exist today can be considered highly diversified and oriented to the broad market, bought to be *held*. The remaining 3,200 funds focus on relatively narrow styles, or specialized market sectors, or international markets, or single countries, all too likely bought to be sold on one future day. Portfolio turnover, at what I thought was an astonishingly high 37 percent in 1975 when the first index fund was introduced, now runs in the range of 100 percent, year after year.

While fund costs essentially represent the difference between success and failure for investors who seek to accumulate assets, they have gone *up* as index fees have come *down*. The initial expense ratio of our 500 Index Fund was 0.43 percent, compared to 1.40 percent for the average equity fund. Today, it is 0.18 percent or less, while the ratio for the average equity fund has risen to 1.58 percent. Add in turnover costs and sales commissions and the all-in cost of the average fund is at least 2.5 percent, suggesting a future annual index fund advantage at least 2.3 percent per year.

Pointedly, however, Vanguard's actively managed funds have learned from the success of our index funds. Indeed, with low advisory fees paid to their external managers, relatively low portfolio turnover, and our reasonable, if sometimes erratic, success in selecting managers, these funds, according to a study in the *Journal of Portfolio Management*,* have actually outpaced our index fund since its inception. (However, if after-tax returns had been considered, or if the base date of the study had been 1989 rather than 1976, the index fund would have had the superior record.) While I cannot agree with the authors' suggestion that I should take "more joy" in our active funds than in our index funds, be assured that I take great joy in the application of the principles that underlie the success of our index funds and managed funds alike.

A Great Idea Gone Awry

My second concern is that the original idea of the index fund—own the entire U.S. stock market, own it at low cost, hang onto it forever—has been, to put it bluntly, bastardized (Figure 18.5). The core idea of relying on the wisdom of long-term investing is being eroded by the folly of short-term speculation. And index funds are one of the

FIGURE 18.5   "LOOK WHAT THEY'VE DONE TO MY SONG, MOM!" EQUITY INDEX FUNDS IN 2004

	Bought to Be Held	Bought to Be Sold
Broad-Mkt Index Funds	96 Funds $297 B	13 Funds $90 B
Specialized Index Funds*	21 Funds $17 B	203 Funds $154 B

*Broad international funds on left; sector funds on right.

* Kenneth S. Reinker and Edward Tower, "Index Fundamentalism Revisited," *Journal of Portfolio Management* (Summer 2004).

principal instruments for this erosion. Why? Because the term "index fund," like the term "hedge fund," now means pretty much whatever we want it to mean.

In addition to 109 index funds now linked to a relative handful of *broad* market indexes (S&P 500, Wilshire Total Market, Russell 3000), there are 224 index funds linked to narrow market indexes—small cap-growth stocks, technology stocks, even South Korean stocks— funds that seem to be bought to be sold. (I confess that, for better or worse, I did my share in the creation of market segment index funds— growth, value, and small-cap, for example. But today's segmented index funds are far narrower in scope.)

Much of the expansion of the index fund marketplace has taken the form of "exchange-traded funds" (ETFs), essentially mutual funds that are designed to be traded in the stock market, often day after day, even minute-by-minute. The assets of ETF index funds now total $150 billion, one-fourth of the index mutual fund total of $550 billion. It seems logical, as far as it goes, to actively trade specialty funds, and 118 of them have come in ETF form, with assets of some $60 billion. But, to my amazement and disappointment, the dominant form of ETF is not these narrow segment funds, but the broad market index funds, including the S&P 500 "Spiders" and iShares, the NASDAQ "Qubes," and the Dow-Jones "Diamonds." It is these ETFs that domi- nate the field, representing some $90 billion of assets currently—index funds originally bought to be held, now bought to be sold.

"Bought to be sold" is hardly hyperbole. ETFs turn over at rates I could never have imagined. Each day, about $8 billion(!) of Spiders and Qubes change hands, an annualized portfolio turnover rate of 3,000 percent, representing an average holding period of just 12 days! (Turnover of *regular* mutual funds by their shareholders now runs in the 40 percent range, itself an excessive rate that smacks of speculation.) The extraordinary ETF turnover should hardly be surprising, however. The sponsor of the Spiders regularly advertises this product with these words: "Now, you can trade the S&P 500 Index all day long, in real time." (To which I would ask, "What kind of a nut would do *that*?")

So the rules of the game are changing—for the worse. The simple broad market index fund of yore, which I believe is the greatest medium for *long-term investing* ever designed by the mind of man, has now been engineered for use in *short-term speculation*. What is more, it has also been joined by far less diversified index funds clearly designed for rapid speculation. Please don't mistake me: The ETF *is* an efficient way to speculate, trading opportunistically in the entire market or its segments, and using them for such a purpose is surely more sensible (and less risky) than short-term speculation in individual stocks. But what's the point of speculating—costly, tax-inefficient, and counter-productive as it is—an almost-certain loser's game. Mark me down as one whose absolute conviction is that long-term investing is the consummate winning strategy.

What More Do We Need to Know?

My third concern is that, for all of the inroads made by indexing, it has achieved only a small fraction of the success that its clear investment merits deserve. *If heresy has turned to dogma, why hasn't indexing become an even more important part of the financial scene?* Yes, the assets of index mutual funds now total over $550 billion, representing nearly 15 percent of equity fund assets. Yes, investors have invested $130 billion in index funds over the past three years, some 35 percent of the total cash flowing into equity funds.

But no, American families now hold $8.0 trillion of equities, meaning that nearly *$7.5 trillion* is *not* indexed. Indexing has achieved a far smaller share of individual equity investments than in the pension field. And yet its cost advantage is much larger in the highly priced fund marketplace than in the competitively priced pension marketplace. If we as a nation are going to rely even more heavily on individual retirement and thrift plans than on corporate pension plans and Social Security, the retirement savings of our citizens are going to be far less robust. *What more do we need to know in order to accept the superiority of index funds so that they earn the acceptance they clearly deserve?*

I, for one, don't think we need more information. But the problem will not be easy to solve. The fund industry, like the insurance industry, is a marketing business, and in both cases the high costs of marketing represent a dead weight loss on the net returns that investors receive. The problem faced by low-cost, no-load index funds is that, as I have often observed, "(almost) all the darn money goes to the investor!" The more money that goes to the investor, of course, the less that goes to the manager and marketers, the brokers and advertisers, the marketing system that drives the world of financial intermediation. So we need to work, day after day, to get across the message of indexing to the "serious money" investors who, truth told, need it the most.

Conclusion

There are lots of lessons to be learned from the issues I've discussed today. Broadly, I've suggested that, while innovation cannot be separated from luck, it can't be separated from intellectual discipline and determination, either. I've also suggested that simple ideas can hold their own—or more—with complex concepts. When you get out in the business world, *Occam's Razor*—"when confronted with multiple solutions to a problem, choose the simplest one"—is worth keeping in mind.

I hope you also take note that it is indeed possible to gild to excess a sound innovation—in this case, the lovely lily of all-market indexing—which needs no gilding—as well noting the powerful forces that would like nothing better than to stop indexing in its tracks before it strikes at their wallets. Their only weapon is to use the records of their successful funds during their flowering periods and imply that such success will persist—and you now know how rarely that happens. Most of all, of course, I hope I've explained not only the universal mathematical logic of indexing—*gross return minus intermediation costs equals net return*—but also presented an overwhelming array of brute evidence that ought to persuade even the most skeptical among you of its worth as an investment strategy.

Now think of this in personal terms. What difference would an index fund make in your own retirement plan over, say, 40 years? Well, let's postulate a future long-term annual return of 8 percent on stocks. If we assume that mutual fund costs continue at their present level of at least 2.5 percent a year, an average mutual fund might return 5.5 percent. Extending this tax-deferred compounding out in time on your investment of $3,000 each year over 40 years, an investment in the stock market itself would grow to $840,000, with the market index fund not far behind. Your actively managed mutual fund would produce $430,000 — only a little more than one-half as much.

Looked at from a different perspective, your retirement plan has earned a value of $840,000 before costs, and donated $410,000 of that total to the mutual fund industry. You have kept the remainder— $430,000. *The financial system has consumed 48 percent of the return, and you have achieved but 52 percent of your earning potential.* Yet it was you who provided 100 percent of the initial capital; the industry provided none. Confronted by the issue in this way, would an intelligent investor consider this split to represent a fair shake? Merely to ask the question is to answer it: "No."

So when you begin your careers, begin your own families and begin to save for their future security, and consider the nest-egg you'll need 40 or 50 years from now when you retire, I shamelessly commend to your using an all-market index fund—the lower the cost, the better—as the centerpiece of the savings you allocate to equities. If you do, as Dr. Samuelson has written, you will become "the envy of your suburban neighbors, while at the same time sleeping well in these eventful times."

Finally, a word for those of you who will seek careers in investment management. Please don't be intimidated by the obvious odds against beating the market. Rather, learn, as so few fund managers seem to have done, from the reasons for the success of the index fund. It is long-term focus, broad diversification, and low cost that have been the keys to the kingdom in the past; active managers who learn both from the disciples of EMH and the apostles of CMH will have the best chance of winning the loser's game, or at least providing respectable long-term returns for their clients in the future. So whatever you do in your investment career—indeed whatever you do in *any* endeavor to which you may be called—*never fail to put your client first.* Placing service to others before service to self is not only an essential part of whatever success may be, it is the golden rule for a life well lived.

Chapter 19

"The Chief Cornerstone"*

A
lmost exactly 30 years ago, on December 31, 1975, the first index mutual fund was founded. Proudly known as "First Index Investment Trust" when it began, that original fund, now named Vanguard Index 500, is the largest mutual fund in the world.

Since that first index fund was formed all those years ago, indexing has come of age. Now part of the language of investing, "index fund" no longer needs an elaborate explanation; it has gained almost-universal acceptance in the world of academe; and it has established the standard—"the hurdle rate," if you will—against which the investment performance of active managers is measured.

What is more, indexing has changed the behavior of investors. Rare is the Wall Street research report that uses those archaic terms "buy," "sell," or "hold" to define its recommendations. Today it is "over-weight" or "equal weight," or "underweight" relative to a stock's capitalization in the Standard & Poor's 500 Stock Index, an index-oriented

---

*Based on a speech before the Superbowl of Indexing in Phoenix, Arizona, on December 7, 2005.

approach to investment advice. Indexing has spawned a half-trillion-dollar "enhanced index" (quantitative fund) industry, largely based on computer-driven strategies aiming to hold market risk constant while marginally outpacing the index with small, often nearly invisible, variations in the weights and composition of the index's individual stock components.

Indexing has also forced managers of mutual funds holding portfolios of large-capitalization stocks to minimize their risk of materially departing from the stock market's return, the better to stabilize cash flows from investors—essentially, therefore, a marketing strategy. Of the 100 largest equity funds, fully three-quarters have market correlations of 0.90 or above, including one-fourth at 0.97 to 0.99. (We call these funds "closet index funds.")

Even more important, though almost never mentioned, is that indexing has been instrumental in awakening the investment world—the buyers and sellers of investment services alike—to the vital importance of *costs*. Intermediation costs, it turns out, are the *only* reliable predictors of the future relative returns of mutual funds. (No, past performance doesn't do the job.) At the same time, indexing has at long last required us to open our eyes to the failure of our financial agents to serve, first and foremost, the interests of the principals who have entrusted their hard-earned money to them. It's fair, I think, to say that indexing has changed the way we think about investing.

The Birth of the Index Fund

It is no secret that the first index fund, while easily conceived, had a difficult birth, and that its neo-natal years were hardly punctuated with success. In fact, without the inspiration of Nobel Laureate economist Paul Samuelson, it might have taken many more years for the creation of "First Index." In an article entitled "Challenge to Judgment," published in the *Journal of Portfolio Management* in the autumn of 1974, Dr. Samuelson demanded that those who did not believe that a passive index would outperform the vast majority of active managers produce "brute evidence to the contrary." He pleaded for someone, somewhere to at least establish an in-house portfolio that tracked the S&P index.*

I quickly accepted the challenge, and examined the brute (or brutal!) evidence. Poring over the records of equity mutual funds from 1945 to 1975, I found that they had consistently failed to beat the market. My study convinced the directors of the newly formed Vanguard Group to approve the formation of the index fund. When he received the First Index offering prospectus in the mail, Dr. Samuelson was elated. Writing in his *Newsweek* column in August 1976, he happily declared, "sooner than I dared expect, my explicit prayer has been answered."

But the applause for the new idea was, well, less than universal. The offering of that first index fund, planned for $150 million, produced proceeds of barely $11,320,000. The annual returns of the index itself, after outpacing more than 70 percent of equity funds in 1969–1975, fell to the 22nd percentile in 1977–1979, and cash flows into the new fund were minuscule. Small wonder that the fund was widely referred to as "Bogle's Folly."

Its detractors were voluble, unrelenting, and confident. Fidelity's Edward C. Johnson III couldn't "believe that the great mass of investors are going to be satisfied with receiving average returns." An executive of fund manager National Securities and Research Corporation categorically rejected any thought of settling for the averages, asking, "Who wants to be operated on by an average surgeon?" Another commentator, flaying the indexing concept, urged striving for excellence: "No one ever came up with a handful of dust when he reached for the stars." And a popular poster of the day called index funds "*un*-American" and urged that they be stamped out, the sooner the better.

---

*Other articles that have contributed to my thinking included "The Loser's Game," by Charles D. Ellis, *Financial Analysts Journal* (July/August 1975), and (although I didn't read it until many years later) Burton Malkiel's classic book, *A Random Walk Down Wall Street* (1973). Several years after our index fund was formed, Dr. Malkiel joined Vanguard's board of directors, serving with distinction to this day. In 2001, Mr. Ellis, also with outstanding credentials, joined Vanguard's board.

Today, 30 years later, the jury is in. Mr. Johnson's Fidelity joined the index parade in 1988, and now administers nearly $50 billion in index assets. Eager to compete more successfully, the firm recently slashed its index fund expense ratios to a mere 10 basis points ($^1/_{10}$ of 1%). By 1993, National Securities—whose funds had continued to lag the market averages that they didn't wish to settle for—had ceased to exist. As for whether "reaching for the stars" in investing would preclude failure, 114 of the equity funds that were alive and well when First Index was formed—more than one-third of the 333 funds then in existence—have, well, bitten the dust and gone out of business. And rather than being stamped out, that first index fund has now been joined by 362 others, including such "*all*-American" managers as Merrill Lynch, T. Rowe Price, Dreyfus, Scudder, and Morgan Stanley.

By way of contrast, the steadfast Dr. Samuelson soldiers on. He credits First Index with funding the education of his six children, and remains a vocal advocate. Just three weeks ago, now in his ninety-first year and speaking before an audience of investment professionals in Boston, he declared that the creation of the first index mutual fund all those years ago was the equivalent of the invention of the wheel and the alphabet.

A Slow Start

In the early years, acceptance was painfully slow. But our commitment to indexing never faltered, and our patience was rewarded. As the assets of First Index Investment Trust (renamed Vanguard Index 500 in 1980) crossed the $500 million-mark in 1987 and headed toward $1 billion, we expanded our index ambit, forming a second 500 Index Fund for institutions, a Total Bond Market Index Fund, and an Extended Market Index Fund (enabling investors to own the remaining 20 percent of the U.S. stock market, and, combined with Index 500, to own the *total* market). In 1992, we formed the first Total Stock Market Index Fund. With its creation, assets of these funds—all holding assiduously to the classic all-market mandate—reached $25 billion in 1993, $50 billion in 1997, $100 billion in 1998, and now total $218 billion.

As the concept of all-market indexing burgeoned, we created the industry's first "enhanced" quantitative index fund in 1986. (Defying the odds, Vanguard Quantitative Portfolios—later renamed—has actually outpaced the 500 index itself by an average of some 30 basis points per year since inception.) We also added other funds designed to index major segments of the market—a small-cap index fund in 1989; European and Pacific index funds in 1990 (and later two broad international stock index funds); then in 1992, a growth index fund and a value index fund (each segments of the S&P 500), a balanced index fund, and three defined-maturity bond index funds; and in 1994 a series of three index-based tax-managed funds, followed later by four "life strategy" funds with differing allocations to bond and stock indexes. Most recently, we formed a series of four index-based "target maturity" funds, gradually reducing equities as the investor's retirement date approaches.

Vanguard remains by far the largest manager of index mutual funds, now operating some 42 index funds with $385 billion of assets. However, our indexed assets pale by comparison with the institutional index accounts administered by Barclays Global Investors and State Street Global, each of which administer more than *$1.2 trillion* using indexing strategies. Currently, index managers oversee some $2.2 trillion in U.S. stocks, $900 billion in bonds, $1.1 trillion in international stocks and bonds, along with $500 billion in enhanced indexed strategies. All told, indexed assets now total some *$5.2 trillion,** with the $3.2 trillion in U.S. equities representing the ownership of fully 20 percent of our stock market's capitalization.

The Chief Cornerstone

As much as I value Dr. Samuelson's extraordinarily high appraisal of the creation of the first index mutual fund, I'm not so sure he isn't too generous. But I freely concede that indexing has changed the world of

---

*Including corporate pension and state and local pension funds, which administer perhaps $500 billion in "in-house" index strategies.

investing in all those ways that I enumerated at the outset. My belief is best encapsulated in something I heard while sitting in church some months ago, focused (I *think*) on thoughts far more spiritually uplifting than mere investment strategy. The words were from Psalm 118: *And the stone that the builders rejected has become the chief cornerstone.*

And so it is that "the chief cornerstone" is the title I have chosen, and the foundation of my remarks. I'll first discuss the remarkable achievements of the classic index strategy, and then discuss a strange new direction taken by indexing in the recent investment environment.

Let me begin by carefully defining what I originally meant by the term "index fund": *An index mutual fund is a fund designed to return to investors 100 percent of the returns delivered by the stock market, less a nominal charge for expenses, simply by owning the preponderance of stocks in the market, weighted by the value of their capitalizations.* Thirty years ago, that definition was best reflected in the Standard & Poor's 500 Stock Index, which we chose as the tracking standard for First Index Investment Trust, now Vanguard 500 Index Fund. (The 500 represents about 80% of the value of the U.S. stock market.) Today, the Dow Jones Wilshire Total Stock Market Index constitutes virtually 100 percent of the market, a broader standard, if only marginally more efficient. One day it will likely surpass the 500 as the prime index fund vehicle.

For me, then, indexing still means today just what it meant to me all those yesterdays ago when it was so roundly rejected by the investment community: a fund created and designed simply to track the returns and risks of the stock market itself, as measured by the Standard & Poor's 500 Composite Stock Price Index. Let's call it the *classic* index fund.

The Classic Index Fund

The classic index fund is characterized by:

1. The broadest possible diversification, sustained over
2. The longest possible time horizon, operated at
3. The lowest possible cost, thereby assuring
4. The highest possible share of whatever investment returns our financial markets are generous enough to provide.

The investment concepts reflected in that simple definition of the classic index fund have lived up to their promise.* After those early years of difficulty described previously, the returns achieved by the passively managed Vanguard 500 Index fund have done exactly what we expected them to do—outpace the returns of the average actively managed equity mutual fund by an amount approximating the costs that the typical fund incurs—advisory fees, operating expenses, sales charges, portfolio turnover costs, and the opportunity cost represented by the failure to be fully invested in stocks.

The Triumph of Indexing

How has classic indexing worked? Beautifully. Consider the record for the 25-year period from December 1980 to December 2005. During that quarter-century, Vanguard Index 500 earned a compound annual rate of return of 12.2 percent per year, compared to a rate of just 9.9 percent for the average equity fund.† Assuming a $10,000 initial investment in each, the investment in the index fund grew by $162,500 during that period, compared to growth of just $95,000 by the average equity fund, fully 40 percent less than the index fund accumulation.

That 2.3-percentage-point gap in favor of the passively managed index fund is suspiciously similar to, albeit slightly lower than, the estimated all-in annual costs incurred by the average actively managed equity fund: a total expense ratio of 1.5 percent (including some deferred sales charges), estimated front-end sales charges of 0.4 percent, hidden portfolio turnover costs of at least 0.8 percent, and 0.4 percent in opportunity cost.‡

---

* Pension fund investors get no benefit from the optimal tax-efficiency of classic investing, but it is an enormous benefit for taxable investors.

† *Source:* Lipper. Total reported rate of return for the average equity fund was 10.8 percent, which we reduced by an estimated 0.5 percent to account for sales charges and an estimated 0.4 percent to account for survivor bias, for a net return of 9.9 percent.

‡ Five percent of assets held in cash earning 5 percent vs. stocks that earned 12-plus percent.

Not to beat this now-ailing actively managed fund horse to death, but in the *real* world, the index fund advantage gets even *larger*. While the annual return of each investment drops by the same 3 percentage points per year when adjusted for inflation during the period (active fund real return, 6.9%; index fund real return, 9.2%), when we compound those returns, the gap in favor of indexing reaches staggering proportions. That $10,000 in the index fund grew by $78,000 in real dollars, while that same investment in the active fund grew by just $42,800.

The active fund, then, produced a cumulative real profit that was a mere 55 percent of the profit that lay readily at hand simply by *passively* owning the stock market itself—with the broadest possible diversification, sustained over the longest possible time horizon, operated at the lowest possible cost, thereby assuring the highest possible share of whatever investment returns our financial markets are generous enough to provide. Buying American business and holding it forever, at minimal cost, is what indexing is all about. And it works!

(I should note that the triumph of indexing is not just an equity fund phenomenon. In the other major segments of the mutual fund industry, the triumph has been equally evident. Vanguard Bond Index Fund, now nearly two decades old, has surpassed its peer-group average in 12 of its 19 years. And Vanguard Balanced Index Fund has outpaced its average peer in 10 years of its 12-year history. Yes, indexing works.)

We Are *All* Indexers Now

Small wonder, then, that "the stone that the builders rejected"—that original index fund of 30 years ago—"has become the chief cornerstone" of an intelligent investment strategy today. But I have a vested interest in index funds, so don't take my word for it. Listen to Warren Buffett. Listen to endowment fund superstars from Harvard (Jack Meyer) and Yale (David Swensen). Listen again not only to Paul Samuelson, but to (as far as I know) every other U.S. Nobel Laureate in Economics. Ask what the finance professors with whom you studied recommend, and then ask how they invest their own money. Almost without exception, these investors and academics are committed to the validity of indexing as the core investment strategy. Even managers who don't accept that conclusion measure both their results and the composition of their portfolios against an index. The conclusion is clear: *We are all indexers now.*

But, when you think about it, we all have *always* been indexers! That is, all investors together have always held the market portfolio. There's simply no way around that tautology. The problem, simply put, is that, individually, investors are constantly trading its component stocks back and forth with one another, and fall behind the market's return by the amount of their aggregate costs. The net result of all that shuffling of paper: The market portfolio remains unchanged, but the brokers and dealers who facilitate all those trades are enriched. And when investors don't do all that trading *directly*—and in today's financial system, in which financial intermediaries own 68 percent of all stocks, they *don't*—they do it *indirectly*, largely through agents such as pension trustees and mutual fund managers who engage in the same feverish activity, all the while arrogating yet another layer of costs—and an additional share of the market's returns—to themselves.

We don't know precisely how much these agents take. But based on SEC reports, we can estimate the revenues of broker-dealers last year at some $250 billion; mutual fund advisory fees, operating expenses, and sales charges approximated $75 billion; pension fund fees, $15 billion; hedge fund fees are now estimated at the $40 billion level; financial advisers are paid perhaps $10 billion; variable annuity commissions, maybe $10 billion. Rounding up only the usual suspects—who are by no means the *only* intermediaries in the system—we quickly come up with $400 billion of intermediation costs, more than $1 trillion dollars out of investors' pockets every three years! Playing off the inspired title of a book published a half-century ago—*Where Are the Customers' Yachts?*—we now know why so few of those yachts in the harbor are owned by the customers who play in the stock market casino; they're mostly owned by those who operate the casino. What else is new?

A New Wave in Indexing

And yet, something else *is* new. Even as the share of equity mutual fund assets accounted for by index funds soared from less than 1 percent in 1988 to 5 percent in 1996, to 10 percent in 1999, to 15 percent currently, the character of the index fund is changing. The growth in the assets of classic index funds has come to an abrupt stop, perhaps because they participated fully in the 50 percent market crash of March 2000 to October 2003, as well as in the subsequent modest recovery. No surprise there. The stock market today is slightly below its level at the end of 1999, although when dividends are taken into account its total return is a bare, if positive, 1 percent, hardly enough to make investors who jumped on the index (i.e., market) bandwagon in the late years of the bull market salivate.

That 5 percentage point increase—in fact, a 50 percent gain—in index fund market share is entirely represented by the rise of a new kind of index fund—the exchange-traded fund. The largest ETF remains the *Spiders* (Standard & Poor's Index Depository Receipts), which make it possible to, in the words of their advertisement, "trade the Standard & Poor's 500 Index all day long in real time." The Spiders and similar ETFs, of course, represent substantially the same broad market portfolio as Vanguard Index 500. But these classic index funds have now been joined by a whole panoply of specialized index funds, tracking various market segments—from growth to value and from large-cap to small-cap—industry sectors—real estate, energy, technology, and so forth—and international—diversified, as well as specific country.

But are these *truly* index funds? Well, let's call this new breed of index funds *nouveau*,* and see how they meet the four conditions of that original definition that accounted for the success of the *classic* index fund in the past (see Table 19.1).

If the original paradigm of indexing was long-term *investing*, surely using index funds as trading vehicles can fairly be described as short-term *speculation*. If the original paradigm was the broadest possible diversification, surely holding discrete—even widely diversified—sectors of the market offers far less diversification. (In fairness, diversified international funds could fit either as "broad" or "specialized.") If the original paradigm was minimal cost, it's clear that holding market sector index

---

*I understand that I am credited with coining the term *closet index fund*. Whether the coinages *classic index fund* and *index fund nouveau* will take the similar leap into common parlance, only time will tell.

TABLE 19.1 COMPARING INDEX STRATEGIES

	Classic Index Fund	Index Fund Nouveau	
		Broad Index Trading	Specialized Index
Broadest Possible Diversification	Yes	Yes	No
Longest Time Horizon	Yes	No	Rarely
Lowest Possible Cost	Yes	No*	No*
Highest Possible Share of Market Return	Yes	Unknown	Unknown

* Including trading costs.

funds that are themselves low cost still carries the substantial brokerage commissions, bid–ask spreads, and market impact costs entailed in moving money from one sector to another.

I'm also amused by the idea of the classic ETF as a temporary holding between manager changes. Presumably, the terminated manager has failed to beat the market, so the pension fund will garner the market's return in the interim, before hiring a new manager, who has, of course, beaten the market in the past and is therefore expected to do so in the future. Will it happen? Who knows? But the odds are not good. Surely moving from an index fund, even as a temporary holding, to a new active manager is a classic example of the triumph of hope over experience.

Spiders and Sectors

The amount of trading carried on in the shares of ETFs each day is little short of astonishing. Turnover in the Spiders is now running at about 4,000 percent per year, compared to a minuscule 15 percent for the shares of that original index fund. Turnover in the Qubes is now at 4,700 percent per year. Whereas it's only guesswork, perhaps 20 percent of the assets of Spiders (about $12 billion), are held by investors with longer-term (if not long-term) horizons, with the remainder held by arbitrageurs and market-makers making heavy use of short-selling and hedging strategies. While the turnover of the more specialized funds is much lower—generally running in the range of 200 – 400 percent—it is still many times over the (in my opinion, itself excessive) 30 percent shareholder turnover rate for actively managed equity mutual funds.

Yet recent trends show that the Spider-like ETFs are barely gaining ground, while the specialized ETFs are exploding. Since 2002, broad-based ETFs have drawn but $3 billion of cash flow, while the latter group has drawn $88 billion—$36 billion in international and country funds, $26 billion in style funds, and another $26 billion in sector funds—in each case, of course, flows that are hardly unrelated to the buoyant returns in the respective markets (international $14 billion, Japan $8 billion, energy $4 billion, gold $3.5 billion). "I'm shocked, *shocked* to find that 'performance chasing' is going on here!" (Note, too, the small portion of *non*-ETF index funds now flowing into the classic index model—$21 billion of the $81 billion total. That is *not* a hopeful sign.)

The record is clear that ETFs are used largely for speculation, either through extremely rapid trading of the stock market itself ("in real time") or through moving money from one market sector or style to another, albeit at a slower rate. I have no problem whatsoever in conceding that it is more sensible to speculate in ETFs than in individual stocks. But why speculate at all? Speculation is, finally, a loser's game, in part because our emotions usually lead us in the wrong direction (i.e., looking to the past as prologue to the future performance; it suffers from the fact that it just isn't so).

The Four *E*'s

I also freely concede that, properly used, ETFs have merit. They enable investors to make long-term bets on the total market or given market segments, or to diversify portfolios that are dominated by concentrated holdings of individual stocks. But when "new products" emerge in the marketing-driven mutual fund industry, the reason is far more often that they are introduced to make money for *managers* (i.e., to increase assets under management, thereby increasing advisory fees and commission revenues) rather than to serve *investors*. Even when these new products in fact provide solid returns on a time-weighted basis, however, they are apt to produce *asset*-weighted returns that are pallid, given the tendency of investors to *buy* them (and the tendency of marketers to *sell* them) only *after* high returns have been realized. When a senior executive of one fund firm, eagerly seeking to build an ETF asset base, is quoted as saying, "For most people, sector funds don't make a lot of sense," questioning the *raison d'être* for the boom in ETFs is hardly unreasonable.

The difference between the classic index mutual fund—that stone of all those years ago that the builders of institutional investing rejected; that stone that has become the chief cornerstone—and today's breed of ETF index funds *nouveau* that are used far more by traders, speculators, and investors who think they can successfully select winning market sectors in advance can be put simply: It is the difference between a long-term *investment* strategy and a short-term *trading* strategy. I do not believe that is a plus for investors. And if Warren Buffett is right with what I have come to call the four *E*'s—"The greatest *E*nemies of the *E*quity investor are *E*xpenses and *E*motions"—there is little doubt about the ultimate victor in this schism, dare I say, of competing religions. It *must* be the classic index fund.

For as to the final, quintessential, aspect of the original classic paradigm—assuring, indeed virtually guaranteeing, the achievement of substantially all of the stock market's return—the fact is that an investor who trades ETFs—after all the selection challenges, the timing risks, and the extra costs—has *absolutely no idea* of what relationship his or her investment return will have to the returns earned by the market itself. The ETFs march to a different drummer than the original index fund, yet today they are in the, well, *vanguard* of index investing. I'm left to wonder, "What have they done to my song, Mom?" (Answer, according to the lyrics: "They've tied it up in a plastic bag and turned it upside down.") Yet surely when those awesome apostles of indexing whom I cited earlier proffered their powerful endorsements, it was not this old tune that they sang, but the original song that they hummed and then applauded.

How Do Investors Fare?

There is an important difference between the returns that mutual funds achieve and the returns that their shareholder/owners achieve, for trading among sectors has proven dangerous to the wealth of investors.

Whatever returns each sector ETF *itself* may earn, the *investors* in those very ETFs will likely, if not certainly, fall well behind them. For there is abundant evidence that the most popular sector funds of the day are those that have enjoyed the most spectacular recent performance, and that such "after-the-fact" popularity is a recipe for unsuccessful investing.

I have observed this evidence in the data, and I have observed it first hand. And I confess to my own share of responsibility for the development of style index funds. When we created the industry's first Growth Index and Value Index funds in 1992, I believed that the former would be held by younger investors seeking tax-efficiency and willing to assume larger risks, and the latter held by older investors seeking higher income and happy to reduce their risks. Alas, while the original idea was strong, the ensuing reality was weak. What followed their introduction was as crystal-clear an example of performance-chasing as one could imagine.

The stock market was relatively placid during the 1993–1997 period, and value stocks and growth stocks delivered similar returns. Then growth stocks took off in the "New Economy" bubble, leaving value stocks in their dust, peaking at a 70 percent premium in early 2000. *Après moi, le déluge!* (Figure 19.1). As reversion to the mean took hold, growth stocks plummeted through 2002. Today the cumulative returns of both growth and value index funds for the full period are about the same.

Investor interest in the two fund styles was well-balanced during the relatively placid stock markets of the mid-1990s. But during the bubble that followed, investors poured $11 billion dollars into the soaring Growth Index Fund, four *times* the $2.8 billion invested in the sedate Value Index Fund. Then, in the aftermath, investors switched their loyalty, with net *redemptions* of $1 billion in the growth fund and net *purchases* approaching $1 billion in the value fund (see Figure 19.1).

Since 1993, the two *funds* have achieved returns that were virtually identical on a standard *time-weighted* basis—10.2 percent per year for Growth, 10.7 percent for Value. The *investors* in each index fund, however, by their counterproductive timing and selection, have not come even close. The average *dollar-weighted* return of the investors in the Growth Index Fund was a pathetic 0.7 percent per year. Investors in

FIGURE 19.1 VANGUARD GROWTH INDEX / VALUE INDEX (TOP), NET CASH FLOW (BOTTOM)

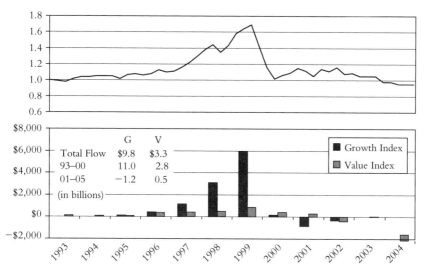

the Value Index fund did better, but their return of 7.1 percent still lagged the Value Index by 3.4 percentage points per year. Compounded since 1993, with both index funds gaining about 220 percent in value on a time-weighted basis, the Growth Index investor earned but 9 percent, and the Value Index investor earned about 130 percent. Despite my best intentions at the outset, our Growth and Value index funds proved to be a paradigm for the ways that investors fool themselves, relinquishing perfectly acceptable long-term returns in the search to find the Holy Grail of extra returns in the short run. *Mea culpa.*

The Chief Cornerstone Remains

Warren Buffett's timeless warning about the toll taken by expenses and emotions is gradually getting out to the world. Given my role in creating the first index mutual fund and my dedication to classic indexing, of course I welcome his strong support. But I *know* I'm on the right track when even the conservative editorial opinion page of the *Wall Street Journal* joins the chorus:

Will fund customers keep supporting the enormous overhead required to sustain ineffectual, unproductive stock picking across an array of thousands of individual funds devoted to every "investing" style and economic sector or regional sub-group that some marketing idiot can dream up? Not likely. A brutal shakeout is coming and one of its revelations will be that stock picking [and sector picking] is a grossly overrated piece of the puzzle, that cost control is what distinguishes a competitive firm from an uncompetitive one.*

For those active investors—and active managers—who are using index funds *nouveau* that are different—not just in degree, but in kind—from that original *classic* index fund of nearly 30 years ago, I do not foresee a favorable long-term outcome. Sooner or later, the job of investment strategy is to deliver to investors their fair share of market returns. Some investment programs designed primarily to meet the marketing objectives of fund managers will, of course, succeed for a time. But if they fail to build client wealth—and I believe that is exactly what will happen—they will ultimately fade away.

Even all these years later, the original index fund design continues to represent the chief cornerstone for investors. If that is true, then by definition every *other* strategy—whether actively managed, passively indexed in sectors or styles, rapid trading, or anything else—represents, at least theoretically, a dilution of that standard. And because the returns of investors in the aggregate fall short of financial market returns by the amount of intermediation and trading costs, the more we pay the intermediaries for those strategies and the more we trade to implement them, the more we lose.

So there's a simple, undeniable fact here: The winning strategy is *long-term investing*; the losing strategy is *short-term trading*. There is too much at stake in providing optimal wealth to the investors who have entrusted their hard-earned dollars to us for investment professionals to allow a Gresham's law to prevail in which bad indexing drives out good indexing. "Good indexing," clearly reflected in the concept of that very first classic index fund, remains the chief cornerstone of investing today. It cannot, finally, be shaken or compromised.

---

*Holman Jenkins, Jr., "Also Stalking the Fund Industry: Obsolescence," *Wall Street Journal*, December 10, 2003.

Chapter 20

Convergence!*

*The Great Paradox: Just as Active Fund Management
Becomes More and More Like Passive Indexing,
So Passive Indexing Becomes More and More
Like Active Fund Management*

I t was almost exactly 30 years ago, on September 24, 1974, when
The Vanguard Group was born. As we celebrated that milestone
last week, it occurred to me that the opportunity to set the keynote
for this gathering today would be a perfect time for a retrospective look
at index investing, and an appraisal of where it stands today. Why?
Because it was the creation of Vanguard, more than any other event,
that led to the formation of the first index mutual fund.

This first strategic decision of our newly born enterprise was
taken, not, I assure you, because we had a superior insight about the
obvious reality that it is impossible for most managers, competing ably
but among themselves, to outpace the returns delivered by the markets.

---

*Based on my speech to "The Art of Indexing" conference in Washington, D.C.,
on September 30, 2004.

409

Surely anyone who had even superficially considered the index fund idea must have realized that. Rather, it fell to Vanguard to create the index fund because it fit perfectly with my goal of creating a firm with a unique mutual structure that would put the shareholder first, and by so doing, become the industry's lowest-cost provider of investment services.

Given the trade-off between manager revenues and shareholder returns, a typical fund management company, seeking to maximize its own revenues, would hate the idea of indexing. But a firm organized under a mutual structure—a management company owned by the shareholders of the funds it serves, and seeking to minimize investor costs—would love it. So whereas every firm in the investment field had the *opportunity* to form the first index fund, Vanguard also had the *motive*. Like the prime suspect in a criminal case, we alone had both opportunity and motive. And so "First Index Investment Trust" (the fund's original name) was born.

Indexing has come a long way since that first index mutual fund was incorporated late in 1975. "Index fund" has become part of the language of investors, has gained almost-universal acceptance in the world of academe, and has established the standard by which the investment performance of active managers is measured. And it has *worked*, providing to investors in properly structured index funds exactly what they were promised: their fair share of financial market returns, no more, no less—not quite 100 percent, but almost.

The Paradigm of the Original Index Fund

What *is* it that has worked? For me, indexing still means today just what it meant all those yesterdays ago when that first fund was created, designed simply to track the returns and risks of the stock market itself, as measured by the Standard & Poor's 500 Stock Composite Price Index:

1. The broadest possible diversification sustained over
2. The longest possible time horizon operated at
3. The lowest possible cost with

4. Optimal tax efficiency thereby assuring
5. The highest possible share of whatever investment returns our financial markets are generous enough to provide.

That definition has held up well, and has been almost entirely responsible for the growth of our original index mutual fund from its $11 million initial underwriting in August 1976 to its present total of almost $100 billion ($140 billion if we include its institutional counterpart), the largest mutual fund in the world. The total of all indexed assets at Vanguard now exceeds $300 billion, by far the dominant part of our industry's $620 billion index fund total. We have witnessed, I believe, the triumph of the index fund.

That first fund's formation and birth were hardly without peril. It was no mean task to persuade a skeptical Vanguard board, only a few short months after we began operations in May 1975, that our first strategic move should be to plow this new and unexplored ground that was to prove so fertile. And it was an even more difficult a task to gather a group of Wall Street investment bankers to handle its initial public offering in the investment environment of the day.

After the great 50 percent stock market crash of 1973–1974, the fund business was dead on its feet. Industry assets, almost entirely in equity funds, had tumbled from $62 billion in 1972 to $38 billion in 1974. With $9 billion of share liquidations for the period, $2 billion larger than the $7 billion in sales of new shares, the fund business was hemorrhaging. The idea of bringing a new equity fund to market—particularly one that, by having the temerity to be unmanaged, broke all precedent—hardly made the task easier. But we had a few potent weapons to begin the battle:

- The five sound underlying precepts of indexing, outlined a moment ago.
- The facts of life, in the form of a statistical study—in those ancient days, I actually did it by hand—showing that from 1945 through the first half of 1975, the 11.1 percent annual return on the Standard & Poor's 500 Stock Index had outpaced by 1.5 percentage points the 9.6 percent annual return of the average equity fund. As a result, an initial investment of $1 million would have

grown to $24.8 million in the 500 index, driven by "the miracle of compounding *returns*," dwarfing the growth to $16.4 million in the average fund, overwhelmed by "the *tyranny* of compounding costs." The advantage: a cool $8.4 million.

- The missionary zeal, infectious enthusiasm, and "press-on" determination of all of us on the new firm's crew, which began with just 28 souls. (That claim may sound—and may be—self-serving. I leave that judgment to you.)

Answering the Prayers of a Nobel Laureate

But we overcame the obstacles we faced, wrote the prospectus of First Index Investment Trust, filed it with the SEC, distributed it, and awaited the public's response. It began on an exhilarating note. When I opened *Newsweek* magazine early in August 1976 and read this endorsement of the fund in Dr. Samuelson's regular column, I almost jumped out of my chair.

"Sooner than I dared expect," he wrote, "my explicit prayer has been answered. There is coming to market, I see from a crisp new prospectus, something called the First Index Investment Trust." He conceded that the fund met only five of his six requirements: (1) availability for investors of modest means; (2) proposing to match the broad-based S&P 500 index; (3) carrying an extremely small annual expense charge of only 0.20 percent; (4) offering extremely low portfolio turnover; and (5) "best of all, giving the broadest diversification needed to maximize mean return with minimum portfolio variance and volatility." His sixth requirement—that it be a no-load fund—had not been met, but, he graciously conceded, "a professor's prayers are rarely answered in full."

(Less than seven months later, we answered the sixth part of Dr. Samuelson's prayer, abandoning the "supply-push" system of dealer distribution that had served the Wellington—now Vanguard—funds for nearly a half-century, and moving to a "demand-pull" no-load system. To state the obvious, I've *never* had cause to regret that decision.)

Even earlier, in June 1976, we had taken heart from a major cover story in *Fortune*: "Index Funds: An Idea Whose Time Is Coming."

It concluded that, "index funds now threaten to reshape the entire world of money management." Together, the endorsement of our ideas in those two articles buttressed our confidence that the $150 million IPO we and our bankers would soon bring to market would mark an exciting major step forward in the affairs of Vanguard, this tiny, barely newborn, organization overseeing less than $2 billion of assets and shrinking, day after day, from capital outflows generated by tiny investor purchases that were overwhelmed by massive share liquidations.

Alas, the disconnection that so often exists between ambitious plans and actual deeds—the slip, if you will, 'twixt cup and lip—again prevailed. When the books on the First Index offering were closed on August 30, 1976, purchase orders totaled not $150 million, but just $11,320,000. Disappointed, the underwriters offered to abort the deal, but we decided to go forward. While we, too, were deeply disappointed by the *figures*, we were elated by the *fact*: The world's first index fund was a reality, started in a beleaguered industry, by a minute upstart that, then less than two years of age, had just begun to toddle.

The Growth of Indexing

Success came with speed that was truly glacial. That first index mutual fund didn't cross the $100-million-asset milestone until 1982, and then only by virtue of $58 million of assets acquired through an opportunistic merger with an actively managed Vanguard equity fund that had outlived its usefulness. Our index fund was not copied until 1984, and the second copy didn't arrive until 1986—a full decade from its founding, hardly a sign, in an industry so prone to quickly copying any good idea, that we were on the right track. These two new index funds, loaded with sales commissions and high expense ratios, were pallid versions of our original index fund, reminding one of Yogi Berra's wisdom: "If you can't imitate us, don't copy us."

But our commitment to indexing never faltered. As the assets of First Index Investment Trust (renamed Vanguard Index Trust 500 in 1980, our first application of the Vanguard name to any of our mutual funds) gradually reached the $500 million mark in 1987 and headed toward $1 billion, we expanded our index ambit, forming our Total

Bond Market Index Fund in 1986, our Extended Market Index Fund in 1987 (enabling investors to own the remaining 20 percent of the U.S. stock market, and, combined with Index 500, to own the *total* market), quickly followed in 1989 by our Small Capitalization Stock Index Fund. As the Eighties ended, we were overseeing four index funds, with assets of more than $2 billion.

As we moved into the Nineties, we continued to expand our index base—European and Pacific Index Funds (which could easily be combined into an EAFE Index Fund) in 1990, Total Stock Market Index, Balanced Index, and Growth Index and Value Index in 1992, with more soon to come. We also developed new variations on the "pure" index theme, with, in 1994 alone, 11 more—the industry's first series of tax-managed funds (all three index-centered); the first bond-market-maturity segment index funds (What imagination! A long-term portfolio, an intermediate-term portfolio, and a short-term portfolio. But sometimes the simplest ideas are the best); an Emerging Markets index fund; and a series of four "LifeStrategy" funds, each with a different level of equity exposure. Nearly two-dozen more index funds, even more specialized, followed. We crossed the magic $100 billion mark in 1997, and our growth barely paused. Today, the $300 billion assets of our 42 index-based funds constitute some 47 percent of the long-term assets under Vanguard's aegis. Indexing is Vanguard's driving force.

In the asset-gathering competition that characterizes the mutual fund industry, of course, our success hardly went unobserved by our rivals. While it took a long time, nearly 100 traditional active managers have now jumped on the index bandwagon, an endorsement of the concept that can scarcely be gainsaid. The fact that such marketing-driven firms as Fidelity, Dreyfus, T. Rowe Price, Scudder, Morgan Stanley, and Merrill Lynch have all put aside their reservations and joined the parade has made it impossible for even the most dyed-in-the-wool zealots who despise indexing to argue that it doesn't, in fact, work.

Assets of equity index funds now total $570 billion, nearly one-sixth of all equity fund assets. The growth of index funds has far surpassed the growth of the fund industry itself, reflected in the steady growth of its share of the three major industry sectors. The incursion into bond and balanced assets has been far smaller, but still healthy—$40 billion on the taxable bond side and $6 billion in balanced funds.

But Vanguard's share of indexing remains dominant—currently 66 percent of all index mutual fund assets. Indexing, in short, has driven our growth.

Commercial Success, Artistic Success

The growth of indexing's share of *assets* of stock and bond funds has been remarkably steady, with index funds now accounting for 15 percent of equity fund assets and 17 percent of bond fund assets.* But its real impact can be seen in the growth of its share of *new cash flows*—purchases of index fund shares, less redemptions. Over the past five years, index funds have accounted for 32 percent of equity fund cash flow and 38 percent of bond fund cash flow. To state the obvious: *Indexing has been a commercial success.*

Why has indexing been such a commercial success? *Because it has also been an artistic success.* Over the past 20 years, for example, a (S&P 500) stock index fund would have outpaced the average equity fund by 2.8 percent per year. A total bond market (Lehman Aggregate) index fund would have outpaced the average bond fund by 1.7 percent per year. An investor who placed $10,000 in a low-cost index fund in each category 20 years ago would have increased his or her wealth by some $43,500 and $15,400 respectively. And on an after-tax basis, given the remarkable tax *inefficiency* of actively managed equity funds, the advantage would be even larger (Table 20.1).

Some idea of the raw power of the index fund advantage can be seen by relating its returns to that initial $10,000 investment. The *extra* return on that investment is astonishing: 435 percent for equity funds and 154 percent for bond funds—a staggering extra return generated

---

*I wish that I could devote more of my commentary to the merits of bond index funds. But since the first index fund was a stock index fund, I've confined my comments largely to that aspect of indexing. However, in a market where the return spreads among active managers are so narrow and the cost advantage of indexing so powerful, the merits of intelligently administered bond index funds are at least as great as in equity index funds.

TABLE 20.1   RETURN ON $10,000 INITIAL INVESTMENT, 1983–2003

	Annual Return		Cumulative Return			Advantage as Percent of Initial Investment
	Managed Funds*	Comparable Index Fund	Managed Funds	Comparable Index Fund	Index Fund Advantage	
Stock Funds	10.0%	12.8%	$67,300	$110,800	$43,500	435%
Bond Funds	7.5	9.2	42,000	57,800	15,400	154

* Stock and bond fund annual returns have been conservatively reduced by 0.8% and 0.3% respectively to reflect "survivorship bias." Index returns have been reduced by 0.2% per year to reflect index fund expenses.

SOURCE: Lipper.

simply by owning those financial markets directly, rather than paying the high costs of intermediation that mutual funds incur.

The powerful incursion of indexing, then, has radically injected change into a fund industry that would have been just as happy to have had it magically vanish into thin air. The appellation given to First Index Investment Trust when it was introduced was "Bogle's Folly." But like William Seward's purchase of Alaska, Robert Fulton's steamboat, and New York Governor DeWitt Clinton's Erie Canal, the index fund turned out to be anything but a folly. Like all radical departures from the conventional wisdom—"You mean that no management whatsoever not only can, but must, and does, provide better returns than the aggregate net returns achieved by experienced, professional active money managers?"—the index fund was at first ridiculed, then tolerated, then grudgingly accepted, then reluctantly endorsed, and finally copied *en masse*. It has changed how we think about investing.

Reverberations

Just consider some of the major changes that indexing has wrought in traditional investing since that first index fund was created in 1975:

- **How investment professionals look at their portfolios.** It is now commonplace for money managers to review their portfolios with a list that shows not only each security held and its portfolio weightings, but its comparable weight in the Standard & Poor's 500 index, as well as the portfolio's diversification in each investment sector (technology, energy, etc.) compared with that of the S&P index. Further, it is hardly without precedent for a portfolio manager's supervisors to also ask for a list of the S&P stocks that are *not* in the portfolio, and even demand reasons *why* they are not held.
- **Benchmarking.** Similarly, almost without exception, returns of managed fund portfolios are regularly (usually quarterly) compared with the returns of the S&P 500, and the discussion that follows is conventionally driven by an analysis of where and why the portfolio differs. For better or worse, we also now often see performance benchmarks by investment style (i.e., large-cap value, small-cap growth, etc). Nonetheless, the ultimate test of the combination of a manager's style and his stock selections is the extent to which the portfolio itself outpaces—or, more likely, falls short of—the stock market itself. (I believe that any evaluation that focuses solely on the *style* benchmark and ignores the *market* benchmark is inappropriate and inherently misleading.)
- **Redefining risk.** As indexing has driven the focus on benchmarking, it has driven a new definition of risk. As we define it today, "risk" has come to have little relevance to what we all know it *really* is—the loss of substantial capital. Rather, risk is defined as the portfolio's volatility relative to the volatility of the benchmark. It takes only a moment of reflection to realize that this change has moved the focus from risk of the *client's* losing his money, to the risk to the *manager's* losing his client, the source of his gainful employment. It's hard to imagine that such a change is not, in the long run, detrimental to our financial markets, to say nothing of detrimental to our clients' wealth.
- **"Closet" index funds.** As benchmarking has become our talisman, and as investment risk has been redefined, we would expect to see the pervasive development of funds whose portfolios are shaped around an attempt to edge out the returns of the market index, all the while striving to maintain its risk characteristics.

Unsurprisingly, we have seen exactly that. "Closet" index funds are commonplace today; an amazing 81 percent of all actively managed funds in Morningstar's comparable "large-cap blend" style box have 90 percent or more of their returns explained simply by the returns of the S&P 500 index.*

- **Anti-benchmarking approach.** The managers most admired and applauded, however—those who buy stocks based on their intrinsic value and their price attractiveness—want nothing of such narrow benchmarking, and, more often than not, seem to have distinguished themselves by an almost *anti*-benchmarking approach—for example, Longleaf's Mason Hawkins; Legg Mason's Bill Miller; Windsor's John Neff; Dodge & Cox's investment committee (of all things); Paramount's Bob Rodriquez; and First Eagle's Jean-Marie Eveillard.

- **Wall Street recommendations.** The influence of indexing has also changed the very terminology used by the "sell-side" security analysts of brokerage and investment banking firms. Not so many years ago, they rated stocks as "buy," "hold," or "sell," though, given the nature of the great Wall Street marketing machine and the pressure not to offend actual and potential investment banking clients (that is, the managements of almost *all* corporations), there were few "sell" recommendations. Now, the near-universal terminology is "overweight," "equal weight," and "underweight," obviously a closet indexing approach.

The Simple Logic of the CMH

Nonetheless, the acceptance of indexing merely accelerated—and benefited from—the benchmarking trend that would have inevitably developed as the equity holdings of the mutual fund industry burgeoned. Let's face it: When the industry holds 1 percent of all U.S.

---

*Included in this total are quantitative funds whose specific policy is to outpace a given market benchmark while rigorously retaining their risk characteristics. Since this policy is publicly described—even bragged about—they are not "in the closet," and are often described as "enhanced" index funds.

stocks, its professional managers theoretically share at least a fighting chance to outpace the market. But when it holds 23 percent of all stocks as it does today (and fully 56 percent when mutual fund holdings are combined with the holdings of the firms' pension management affiliates), the probabilities against success for such a formidable aggregation of assets are staggering.

The fact is that the idea that this awesome mass of accumulated capital could somehow meaningfully outpace the market in total is absurd if we ignore costs, and inconceivable when we take costs into account. Indeed, as my earlier data for 1945–1975 showed, even a much smaller (and far-lower-cost) fund industry failed to do so, a failure that was, if unsurprising, hardly inevitable. But at our industry's present size, what was once unlikely but at least possible has become impossible. What happens is what has always happened, and will continue to happen in the future: Professional managers as a group will inevitably earn the market's return before the costs of financial intermediation, and, equally inevitably, lose to that return by the amount of that cost—now, I believe, in the range of $300 billion per year.

What we are seeing, then, does not require the acceptance of the EMH (Efficient Market Hypothesis, which in my view is largely but not entirely valid) but rather the realization of the reality of the CMH (Cost Matters Hypothesis), that is, that investors in the aggregate will *earn* the gross return of the total stock market *before* costs, but *share* only in the amount of that return that remains *after* costs. It is that elemental fact that explains the inevitable artistic success of the index mutual fund in outpacing active management and assuring its commercial success in the past, even as it assures similar artistic and commercial success in the future.

A Specific Example

Our industry's largest firm presents us with a truly classic case study in the growing importance of indexing and its implications for the future. So let's examine some of the actions and reactions of Fidelity Management and Research Corporation, which now manages an estimated $900 billion of assets, including equities valued at $620 billion, nearly 5 percent of all U.S. stocks.*

When Vanguard's unique index mutual fund was introduced almost three decades ago, Edward C. Johnson III, Fidelity's chairman, publicly scorned the idea: "I can't believe," he told the press, "that the great mass of investors are going to be satisfied with just receiving average returns. The name of the game is to be the best." In those ancient days, Fidelity *was* deemed to be a superior manager, though in retrospect much of its success had been achieved by the aggressive investment strategies it followed during the boom of the "go-go" era during the mid-1960s. Even Mr. Johnson himself managed a hot fund (Fidelity Trend Fund) during that era. But the risks Fidelity's funds assumed came home to roost, as 5 of their 11 funds tumbled by 50 percent or more in 1973–1974, including Fidelity Trend Fund. (By 1965, Mr. Johnson had turned the portfolio over to the first of the six managers to follow him.)

But it is in Fidelity's Magellan Fund that we see the greatest example—indeed the virtual apotheosis—of how the fund industry has changed. Under the aegis of the legendary Peter Lynch, it had a truly sensational run from 1978 to 1983, outpacing the S&P 500 index by an astonishing 26 percentage points *per year!* (See Figure 20.1.) With such success, the fund's assets burgeoned during that period from a mere $22 million to $1.6 billion. While its performance then reverted *toward* the mean, its excess return from 1984 through 1993 remained a healthy four percentage points per year. By then, its assets had grown to a staggering $31 billion.

In 1990, Mr. Lynch retired as portfolio manager, and Magellan's excess returns began to dwindle, losing to the S&P 500 in five of the next seven years. Nice gains came in the next two years, followed by four of five losing years, including the current year-to-date. In all,

---

*Hesitant as I have been to "name names" in my public remarks, this audience can hardly be unaware of the examples I'll present here, and would know the firm I was describing even if I coyly avoided using its name. What's more, the firm recently abandoned similar restraint by specifically mentioning Vanguard in its full-page advertising comparing, of all things, the expense ratios of the respective firms' index funds.

**FIGURE 20.1   FROM ACTIVE MANAGEMENT TO
CLOSET INDEXING**

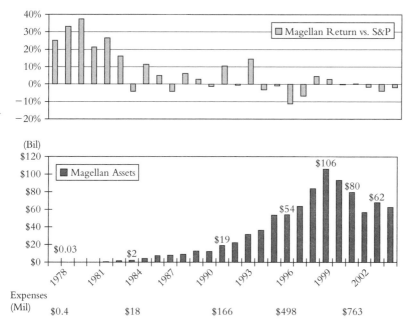

since 1993, the fund has fallen an average of more than two percentage points per year behind the S&P 500 index—a far cry from the success of its earlier years. Yet, in a soaring stock market the growth of the fund's assets persisted, from $31 billion at year-end 1993, to $106 billion at the close of 1999, and even, after the crash, $62 billion today.

Reversion to the Mean

The larger the fund grew, of course, the more it came to resemble an index fund. Reversion to the market mean strikes again! In 1978– 1982, the S&P return explained 82 percent of the return of Magellan, but in 2001–2004 fully 99 percent. I'm *not* arguing that is bad. (After all, I'm an indexer!) But I *am* arguing that cumulative management fees and operating expenses of *$5.5 billion*(!) during a 10-plus-year period when the fund lagged the market by two percentage points per year (largely because of those costs) is, well, absurd—a waste of corporate assets. Absurd, I quickly add, when looked at from the vantage point of the investors who are paying them. From the standpoint of the management that is receiving them, they are the soul of rationality: "We made the fund large, and we deserve to be paid for that accomplishment." Make what you will of that argument.

Magellan Fund today is the prototypical closet index fund. But it is hardly Fidelity's only index-linked fund. Ten of its 15 largest equity funds have correlations with the market of between 0.92 and 100 (even excluding the aforementioned Fidelity Trend Fund, now itself with an eye-popping correlation of 0.99), only one of which succeeded in outpacing the index during the past decade. The reality is that such funds are virtually locked into closely approximating the returns delivered by the stock market itself. *But only before the deduction of the substantial fees, operating expenses, and portfolio turnover costs they incur.* It would take a Herculean leap of faith to believe that, after the deduction of such costs, they could match the returns of an index fund.

Thus, I was surprised to read in a recent *Wall Street Journal* article that, despite Magellan's lag to the S&P 500 since 1998 under his aegis, Robert Stansky, Magellan's portfolio manager, not only expects to *beat* the market, but "to beat the market over time by two to five percentage points annually."* With a 99 percent correlation with the market, and the two (or more)-percentage-point handicap of the fund's all-in costs, that would require a sustained three-to-seven-point margin of advantage, something not a single mutual fund has attained over the past decade. But of course the past may not be prologue, and I wish Mr. Stansky well.

As funds reach boxcar-asset levels, of course, closet indexing is inevitable. After all, because of the high market impact costs of portfolio turnover that tie the funds of large organizations, Gulliver-like, to the market itself, the soaring size of Fidelity's equity position was inevitably accompanied by much more restricted investment decision making. Fidelity's portfolio turnover has plummeted, from 100 percent

---

*John Hechinger, "Magellan's Manager Has Regrets: Stansky Tries to Dispel Perception That He Is Essentially Helming an Index Fund with Higher Fees," *Wall Street Journal*, May 28, 2004.

in 1980 to 50 percent last year. The firm recently faced up to that reality, plunging aggressively into the growing index parade.

"If You Can't Beat 'Em, Join 'Em"

Following the ancient aphorism, "If you can't beat 'em, join 'em," the firm had started its first index fund, modeled on the S&P 500, out of commercial necessity in 1988. But their recent decision to slash, if only temporarily, the expense ratios of their index funds and launch an expensive advertising campaign to catch the public's eye clearly reflects a new strategic commitment to build their indexing business. (It is fair to speculate that both the "loss leader" strategy and the advertising costs are, in effect, subsidized by the fees paid to Fidelity by its actively managed and closet index funds.)

With the clear success of indexing, the debilitating costs of active management, and the straitjacket of massive size, it's hard to imagine they had any other choice. The firm's first move was to temporarily reduce the expense ratios of their index funds to an annualized rate of 10 basis points (from the previous level of 25 basis points), blasting out the news in full-page newspaper broadsides, with the boldface heading: **Perfect 10!*** As one commentator noted, this was a frontal assault on Vanguard's franchise as the low-cost provider of index funds; not "a shot across the bow," but "a shot right at the mast." A price war—uniquely, in my experience, a war to *lower* prices rather than to *raise* them—has broken out.

As few have noted, however, this price war comes at a time when a *really* low-cost stock index fund—part of the $130 billion Federal Employees Thrift Savings Plan—is already operating at a mere seven basis points, and is driving to reduce that cost to five basis points in 2005 and to four in 2006. Since cost is *almost* everything in an index fund, this action will serve to drive out any complacency in the

---

* Clearly, if the firm intended to permanently reduce their index fund fees, they would have submitted a new advisory agreement for the approval of their shareholders. However, such a step would have precluded raising the fees again later, without again requesting approval.

attitude of index managers. Index fund investors will be well served—and active managers and high-cost indexers ill served—by the arrival of this price competition.

It will be interesting to observe Vanguard's response, if any, to this assault on its franchise: to sit tight (after all, Fidelity has waived fees before and then raised them back later); or to throw down the gauntlet with its own (perhaps temporary) waiver. Only time will tell how the marketplace responds, especially how the larger Vanguard index fund investors, who already pay Vanguard just 10 basis points, react. But perhaps the most important reaction to Fidelity's change of heart will be whether investors continue their willingness to pay exorbitant fees for putative actively managed funds that are in fact closet index funds. Surely Fidelity is the textbook example of how active management has converged toward passive indexing in the fund industry.

And it's not only Fidelity. When 656 of 1,873 equity funds in the Morningstar "style boxes" have correlations with the market that exceed 0.90, that convergence is almost palpable. It's hard to imagine that this convergence will not only continue but accelerate in the years ahead, with major implications for the way funds are managed, the strategies they employ, the fees they charge, their portfolio turnover, and the asset levels at which they close their doors to new investors. With thanks to the rise of the index fund, these issues will shape the way the industry operates, and will ultimately help us all to more effectively serve mutual fund shareholders.

The Great Paradox

So now to the other half of the great paradox: As active fund management becomes more and more like passive management, so *passive indexing is becoming more and more like active management*. Nothing could better illustrate that paradox than the title of this conference—"The Art of Indexing"—and its agenda—"the rising tide of . . . new products that will benefit investors"; "the expanding world of ETFs"; "the increasing role of index derivatives"; and so on.

The original index fund, of course, required little, if any, "art." It's hardly an art to own the 500 stocks in the S&P 500 index, own them at low cost, hold them forever, and let the chips fall where they may. But in today's sprawling index fund marketplace, "art" may be a fair enough description, though I warn you that the word "art" means not only "the principles governing a craft," but also "trickery and cunning."

The New Paradigm of Indexing

Consider how "The Art of Indexing" compares with the original paradigm. If investing for the longest possible time horizon was the original paradigm, surely using index funds as trading vehicles can only be described as short-term speculation. If the broadest possible diversification was the original paradigm, surely holding discrete—even widely diversified—sectors of the market offers far less diversification. If the original paradigm was minimal cost, it's clear that holding market sector index funds that are themselves low-cost obviates neither the brokerage commissions entailed in trading them nor the tax burdens entailed if one has the good fortune to do so successfully.

And as to the final, quintessential, aspect of the original paradigm—assuring, indeed virtually guaranteeing, the achievement of the stock market's return—the fact is that an investor who trades ETFs—after all the selection challenges, the timing risks, the extra costs, and the added taxes—has *absolutely no idea* of what relationship his or her investment return will have to the returns earned by the market itself. So the ETFs march to a very different drummer.

The *exchange traded fund*, the imaginative creation of Nate Most* more than a dozen years ago, has become, in recent years, a significant part of the $570 billion index fund asset base—a 28 percent share, up from just 9 percent at the close of 1999, albeit a growth in market penetration that has slowed considerably in recent years. Despite

---

* In 1990, as he developed his ideas for ETFs, Mr. Most visited me in my Valley Forge office to solicit my support. I described several flaws in his concept, but told him, even if he could correct them, Vanguard would not be interested, because we believed that like trading stocks, trading index funds was a losing strategy. As he tells the story, on his train ride back to New York, he fixed the flaws I'd noted. The rest, as they say, is history.

their stark contradiction of the five concepts underlying the original index fund, ETFs have become a force to be reckoned with in the indexing arena.

Assets and Cash Flows

When we look beyond the aggregates, it becomes clear how far ETFs have departed from the norm. As Table 20.2 shows, the diversity of the investment choices available is remarkable.

While the *assets* of ETFs, dominated by the relatively broad market indexes, are small relative to traditional index mutual funds, they have grown at a more rapid rate. In terms of *cash flow*, ETFs have drawn $150 billion of net new money since 1999, even larger than the $114 billion flowing into their traditional cousins. What's more, the flow into style, sector, and foreign funds has overwhelmed the flow into the broad stock market index funds. While in the early ETF years, these broad funds accounted for 100 percent of the total inflow, during 1999–2003 they accounted for less than one-half, and so far this year their $3 billion of cash flow has represented only 12 percent of all ETF flow, with the less-diversified groups adding $22 billion.

But those all-stock-market ETFs are, in my view, the *only* instance in which an ETF can replicate, and possibly even improve on, the five paradigms of the original index fund. *But only when they are bought and held for the long-term.* Their annual expense ratios are usually—but not always—slightly lower than their mutual fund counterparts, although

TABLE 20.2   DIVERSITY OF ETF INVESTMENT CHOICES

Number of Funds	ETF Type	Examples	Total Assets
7	Total Stock Market	Spider/Viper	$64 billion
10	Other Broad Indexes	Qubes, Diamonds, EAFE Intl.	40
32	Market Styles	Growth, Small-Cap	39
61	Market Sectors	Tech, Telecom, Energy	19
25	Foreign Countries	Japan, Brazil	12
5	Bond	—	6
140	Total		$180 billion

commissions on purchases erode, and may even overwhelm, any advantage. While in theory their tax-efficiency should be higher, practice so far has failed to confirm that theory. But the fact is that their use by long-term investors is minimal. The Spiders are, in fact, marketed to day traders. As the advertisements say, "Now you can trade the S&P 500 all day long, in real time."

We know that ETFs are largely used by traders. The turnover of Spider shares is now running at about 2,400 percent per year, compared to 20 percent for the shares of that original index fund. The turnover of the NASDAQ Qubes is even higher, at 3,700 percent(!) per year, and of course the turnover *within* the NASDAQ Index and the Dow Average are themselves substantial. It's only guesswork, but perhaps 20 percent of the assets of these broadly diversified funds are held by long-term investors, or about $12 billion. The remainder of the Spider-type holdings, I presume, represents the activities of arbitrageurs and market-makers making heavy use of short-selling and hedging strategies.

A Vast Departure

Thus $168 billion of the $180 billion ETF base represents a vast departure from the beneficial attributes of the original index fund. Trading in all types of ETFs is high. Specialized ETFs are diversified only in their narrow arenas; owning the semiconductor industry is not diversification in any usual sense, nor is owning the South Korean stock market. While sector ETFs themselves frequently have the lowest expense ratios in their fields, they can run *three to six times* the level of the lowest-cost all-market index funds. What is more, they not only carry the costs of trading, but are often sold as parts of actively managed portfolios with adviser fees of 1 percent or more, or in wrap accounts with annual fees of 1.5 to 2.0 percent or more. While the *portfolios themselves* display far lower turnover than that of their actively managed counterparts, their *investors* typically turn over their shares at a remarkable average of some 3,000 percent per year.

The net result of these differences is that sector ETFs are virtually certain to provide, as a group, returns that fall well short of the returns delivered by the stock market itself. Perhaps 1 to 3 percent a year is a

428 WHAT'S RIGHT WITH INDEXING

fair estimate of these all-in costs, many times the 10- to 20-basis-point cost of the best index funds. It is not a trivial difference. For no matter how often derided or ignored, the tautology remains that sector investors must and will earn a net return equal to the gross return of that sector, less intermediation costs.*

But only to the extent they buy and hold them. For whatever returns each sector ETF *itself* may earn, the *investors* in those very ETFs will likely, if not certainly, fall well behind them. For there is abundant evidence that the most popular sector funds of the day are those that have recently enjoyed the most spectacular recent performance, and that such "after-the-fact" popularity is a recipe for unsuccessful investing.

Let's Look at the Record

The record of regular mutual funds investing in market sectors sends up a red flag that warns of a serious storm in prospect. The 25 most popular sector funds of the recent era, for example, earned a *positive* average annual return of 5.5 percent during the up-and-down-and-up period of 1998–2003, in fact, slightly ahead of the stock market's return of 3.8 percent per year. But, the average sector fund *investor* actually lost money, with a negative (dollar-weighted) return of minus 8.3 percent, an astonishing 13.8 percentage points less. By way of contrast, the comparable figures for the 25 largest diversified equity funds were: fund return 3.7 percent, investor return 1.3 percent, a negative gap of only 2.4 percentage points, a small fraction of the deficit incurred by the remarkably counterproductive timing of sector investors.

----

* I confess to my own share of responsibility for the development of style index funds. When we created the industry's first Growth Index and Value Index funds in 1992, I believed that the former would be used by younger investors seeking tax-efficiency and willing to assume larger risks, and the latter by older investors seeking higher income and happy to reduce their risks. Alas, while the original idea was strong, the ensuing reality was weak. While investor interest in the two funds was well-balanced during the relatively placid stock markets of the mid-1990s, during the bubble that followed investors poured $11 billion dollars into the soaring Growth Index Fund, five times the $1.8 billion invested in the Value Index Fund. *Mea culpa.*

Compounded for the full six-year period, the loss of capital in sector funds was staggering. While the cumulative return was a positive 43 percent, the cumulative return of the average sector fund averaged a capital *loss* of minus 26 percent, an astonishing 69-point negative differential. (In the worst case, the differential was minus 190 percentage points!) While the average diversified fund itself gained 26 percent cumulatively, its investors gained an 11 percent appreciation, admittedly modest, but a solid 37 percentage points of return ahead of their sector cousins. Given these data, it is almost impossible to deny that, for the overwhelming majority of investors, sector fund investing is playing with fire (Figure 20.2).

Those fund managers who offer sector ETFs must be aware of this counterproductive pattern, if not of these exact figures. For it is commonplace that when investors act on the eternal stock market emotions of hope, greed, and fear, they make the wrong choices. They seek out sectors that have led the market, and then shun those sectors when they lag. Whereas the duration of that pattern of reversion to the mean is not predictable, the pattern itself is as sure a phenomenon as can be witnessed in the stock market. The *economics* of owning the U.S. stock market has yet to fail to create long-term value for its

FIGURE 20.2   SPREAD BETWEEN CUMULATIVE FUND RETURN AND INVESTOR RETURN, 1997–2003

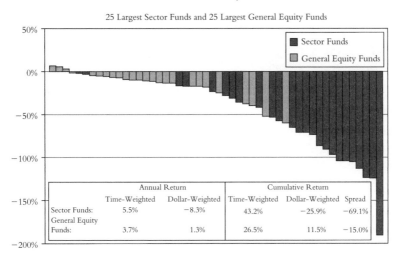

	Annual Return		Cumulative Return		
	Time-Weighted	Dollar-Weighted	Time-Weighted	Dollar-Weighted	Spread
Sector Funds:	5.5%	−8.3%	43.2%	−25.9%	−69.1%
General Equity Funds:	3.7%	1.3%	26.5%	11.5%	−15.0%

participants; the *emotions* of trying to outguess it by positive selection or market timing has devastated investor wealth.

"Don't Just Stand There—Do Something"

Yet we live in a world where "Don't just stand there—do something" is the watchword. Ignore the fact, please, that the stock market is essentially a closed system in which when you buy a stock, someone else sells it to you, and vice versa. And when you *exit* the stock market, someone else *enters* it. But when money changes hands in the market, it is not a zero-sum transaction, it is a loser's game, with the croupiers of our system of financial intermediation enriched not only by being the middlemen for each transaction, but by charging the management and advisory fees involved in supervising and maintaining the accounts of those who are doing the transactions.

So we are inevitably left with a certain melancholy about the objectives of those who provide these intermediation services. They must be well aware that most investors will be best served by the kind of all-market index strategy that I outlined at the outset. Indeed, as he relinquished the reins of Magellan in 1990, even Fidelity's remarkable Peter Lynch declared, "Most investors would be better off in an index fund." He was right! But we all have businesses to run, and, however unfortunately, we feel great pressure to give the customer whatever he or she wants—a fact of life that, for better or worse, rules at least as strongly in financial services as it does in automobiles, perfume, toothpaste, and jewelry.

All of this shuffling of financial paper, of course, represents a cost that ill-serves investors. As Benjamin Graham pointed out way back in September 1976—coincidentally, only moments after the first index fund was launched—"The stock market resembles a huge laundry in which investors take in large blocks of each other's washing, nowadays to the tune of 30 million shares a day."* (He could not have imagined today's volume: *3 billion* shares a day.)

---

*Benjamin Graham, "A Conversation with Benjamin Graham," *Financial Analysts Journal* 32, no. 5 (Sept./Oct. 1976).

"Don't Do Something—Just Stand There"

Alas, the reverse proposition, "Don't do something—just stand there," *while the inevitable strategy of all investors as a group*—think about that, please—is not only counterintuitive to the emotions that play on the minds of virtually all individual investors, but also counterproductive to the wealth of those who market securities and manage securities portfolios. While it is easy to argue that investors should ignore indexing because they have different objectives and requirements, Ben Graham had an opinion on that, too: "only a convenient cliché or alibi to justify the mediocre record of the past."

Let me freely concede that there are sound uses for ETFs. Buying Spiders and Vipers and holding them for life is a winning strategy. The employee of Microsoft is hardly a fool to own all market sectors except for technology. The wisdom of the owner of a portfolio of highly appreciated large-cap stocks who purchases and holds a small-cap ETF can hardly be faulted. But so far at least, there is little evidence that it is such transactions that are driving the growth of ETF index funds.

Rather it is trading in broad-market ETFs and the rise of sector ETFs that are in today's driver's seat. While trading sector ETFs may well be cheaper and more efficient than doing the same in individual stocks (or, for that matter, in regular mutual funds), all of that vigorous activity inevitably constitutes a reduction in returns earned by investors as a group, and can slash the potential returns of the individuals who try it. Put another way, while sector ETFs may well represent a better way to speculate, place me firmly in the camp of those who believe that *any* speculation in stocks is the ultimate loser's game.

In addition to their growing use by individual investors, investment advisers, and brokers as a more efficient way of implementing active investment strategies, ETFs are increasingly used as a tool for active managers, "trading on downticks, used in hedging strategies, and useful for increasing or decreasing investment exposure to a sector or in shifting asset allocations . . . [quickly] acting without picking specific stocks and then replacing the ETF with individual names when you have more time for research," according to Byron Wien, Morgan Stanley's highly respected market strategist. As a result, he predicts, "within five years . . . their use will be common in the field of active portfolio management."* No comment could better illustrate the clear convergence of passive indexing and active management.

Wrapping Up

How will it all turn out? How will this great paradox—active management becoming more and more like passive indexing even as passive indexing becomes more and more like active management—be resolved? Let me close with a few ideas.

First, so long as the managers of today's giant fund complexes maintain, let alone increase, the massive equity fund assets they now oversee, there will be less and less escaping the high market correlations that accompany giant size. As active management continues to morph into passive indexing—already approaching the commonplace in the large-cap fund category—managers will have to reduce their fees commensurately. After all, a correlation of 99 comes close to meaning that 99 percent of the portfolio is effectively indexed. A 1.5 percent expense ratio on the remaining 1 percent of the portfolio, therefore, represents an annual fee of 150 percent(!) on the actively managed assets. Clearly, something has to give. I believe it will be the fee.

Even if investors are willing to tolerate that cost at the moment, it is only a matter of time until they realize that their ongoing deficit to the stock market's return is a reflection of the simple fact that they effectively own an index fund, but at a cost that is grossly excessive. "If it looks like a duck, waddles like a duck, and quacks like a duck, in all likelihood it *is* a duck." But a duck, if you will, with none of the advantages of the kind of broad-market, long-term, low-cost, tax-efficient index fund that was first designed nearly three decades ago. So, I expect that original passive index strategy will continue to expand its dominance over traditional mutual funds in the years ahead.

---

*Byron Wien, "Exchange-Traded Funds Are in Your Future," Morgan Stanley U.S. Strategy Research Report, June 14, 2004.

With respect to the opposite trend—the metamorphosis of passive indexing into active management—my conviction is that there are only limited prospects for that trend to markedly expand. But despite the fact that to "just stand there" remains the winning strategy, the unwillingness of investors to do so, and the need of financial intermediaries to justify their existence, means that trading in ETFs won't soon go away. Indeed, the apparent coming of leveraged ETFs, currency ETFs, commodity ETFs, and even actively managed ETFs suggests that the peak has not yet been reached. But while investors, acting on their emotions, will continue to jump on the ETF bandwagon for a time, they will not ignore their own economic interests forever.

That message is gradually getting out to the world. Coming from me, it may sound radical. But even the conservative editorial opinion page of the *Wall Street Journal* has joined the chorus:

> Will fund customers keep supporting the enormous overhead required to sustain ineffectual, unproductive stock picking across an array of thousands of individual funds devoted to every "investing" style and economic sector or regional subgroup that some marketing idiot can dream up? Not likely. A brutal shakeout is coming and one of its revelations will be that stock picking is a grossly overrated piece of the puzzle, that cost control is what distinguishes a competitive firm from an uncompetitive one.*

For those active investors—and active managers—who are using index funds that are different—not just in degree, but in kind—from that original fund of nearly 30 years ago, I do not foresee a favorable long-term outcome. Sooner or later, the job of investment strategy is to deliver to investors their fair share of market returns. Investment programs designed to build businesses will, of course, succeed for a time. But if they fail to build client wealth, they will ultimately fade away.

---

*Holman Jenkins, Jr., "Also Stalking the Fund Industry: Obsolescence," *Wall Street Journal*, December 10, 2003.

Lead into Gold?

So mark me down as an index fundamentalist, a passionate believer that the original index fund design, even all these years later, continues to represent the Gold Standard for investors. If that is true, then by definition every *other* strategy—whether managed, indexed, sector- or style-specific, trading, or anything else—represents, at least theoretically, a dilution of that standard. Yet even as the alchemists of ancient days vainly sought to change lead into gold, so, too, do many of today's financial intermediaries seek to provide a similar alchemy in the financial markets. I do not deny that some small number will surely do just that. But I struggle to develop any methodology (other than relative costs!) for identifying winning strategies or winning funds in advance, and for successfully predicting how long those winning strategies will persist and how long those portfolio managers will continue to manage the funds that have delivered those superior returns.

I believe it is up to those who believe they can do so to provide not only the *statistical* support, but the *intellectual* support, for their position, as well as to affirm how long those managers expect to continue to serve the funds under their aegis. Absent such support, active management will continue to converge with passive indexing, and passive indexing will return to its historical roots.

Part Five

ENTREPRENEURSHIP AND INNOVATION

I've done much thinking, research, and writing on entrepreneurship and innovation, the subjects of the next four chapters. These subjects also find their way into my talks on idealism and capitalism. I accept Joseph Schumpeter's thesis that entrepreneurship is the moving force in creating economic growth. But while I salute entrepreneurship that provides better and better goods and services to more and more citizens, more efficiently and at lower cost—all of which add value to our society—I deplore entrepreneurship that involves financial buccaneering and speculation—which subtracts value from our society.

Chapter 21 contrasts the 18th-century community-centered values of entrepreneurship—so beautifully exemplified by Benjamin Franklin—with today's more self-centered values. While I make no claim to being a paradigm of entrepreneurship, I describe in some detail the values that led to the creation of Vanguard, values that arguably were visible in the idealistic bent of my Princeton thesis. I also examine (with, I hope, some humility) how remarkably similar my values are to those of Franklin. The chapter concludes with a striking comparison of my own principles for saving and building wealth with those expressed by Franklin all those years ago.

The title of Chapter 22 is accurate but somewhat tongue-in-cheek: "Seventeen Rules of Entrepreneurship." The essay lays out a sort of roadmap showing the challenges that I faced in the quest to build something new in finance, something designed to serve not just our firm, but also society. This chapter also relies heavily on the values expressed in my ancient Princeton thesis. It describes how—despite the years of struggle; a deeply skeptical board of directors; the opprobrium of our peers; the failure of investors to accept our creation during the early years; and the initial opposition of the U.S. Securities and Exchange Commission—Vanguard came into existence. Yes, the road less traveled by is a rough road, but the challenges of entrepreneurship are a joy.

"Vanguard: Saga of Heroes" (Chapter 23) presents a very different interpretation than you might expect from its title. This chapter is based on a lecture I presented to Pepperdine University (CA) students, at the request of Professor Elliot McGucken, as part of his course, "Artistic Entrepreneurship and Technology 101." "Dr. E" relies heavily upon such classics as Homer's *The Odyssey* and Dante's *Inferno*, and honors me by including with these classics my own *The Battle for the Soul of Capitalism*. This essay focuses on Vanguard's odyssey, a voyage punctuated with challenges, narrow escapes, and ultimate fulfillment. I conclude by urging introspection upon our financial leaders, an idea that failed to gain much traction back in 2007 when it might have helped. But these leaders were simply making too much money, taking too much risk, and showing too little concern about the crisis then building.

The subject of Chapter 24 is entrepreneurship's cousin, innovation. Here I ask the question, "When Does Innovation Go Too Far?" If the idea of innovation is to create "new products and processes, and organic changes that create wealth or social welfare," there can be no such thing as too much innovation. But in the financial sphere, that sort of innovation is rare. Rather, it too often takes the form of "financial engineering," with the creation of complex, risky products designed to increase the wealth of the financial innovators, which almost inevitably end up depleting the wealth of their clients. "First comes the innovator," as Warren Buffett points out, "then the imitator, and finally the idiot."

In retrospect, this final chapter of Part Five now seems an almost prescient warning about the highly complex and inordinately risky derivative securities that played a major role in the stock market crash and economic collapse of 2008–2009. The chapter closes with a warning: "It is time to face up to these realities." But it was too late. The seeds of the crisis were already beginning to sprout; and only after the fall did market participants and public policymakers finally face up to those realities. The legislation that was signed into law by President Obama in July 2010 represents the necessary first step—fraught with compromise, political pressure, and lobbying—to reform the financial system. Only time will tell the extent to which these reforms will preclude or mitigate future financial crises.

Chapter 21

Capitalism, Entrepreneurship, and Investing: The 18th Century versus the 21st Century*

L ast summer, I at last got around to reading a book that the late Neil Postman—prolific author, social critic, and professor at New York University—had autographed and given me in 1999. The central message of *Building a Bridge to the Eighteenth Century* is encapsulated in its opening epigram:

> Soon we shall know everything the 18th century didn't know, and nothing it did, and it will be hard to live with us.

---

*Based on a speech to the Greater Philadelphia Venture Group in Philadelphia, Pennsylvania, on January 25, 2006.

Postman's book presented an impassioned defense of the old-fashioned liberal humanitarianism that was the hallmark of the Age of Reason. His aim was to restore the balance between mind and machine, and his principal concern was our move away from an era when the values and character of Western Civilization were at the forefront of the minds of our great philosophers and leaders, and when the prevailing view was that anything that's important must have a moral authority.

In the present era of information technology, by way of contrast, numbers and scientific techniques seem to be at the forefront of our values. Metaphorically speaking, *if it can't be counted, it doesn't count.* Surely this change has been clearly reflected in the change in capitalism from a system with values like trusting and being trusted at the fore, to a system relying heavily on numbers, with the profound conviction that financial matters are rational simply because numbers, however dubious their provenance, are definitive.

While Postman made the bold assertion that truth is invulnerable to fashion and the passing of time, I'm not so sure. Indeed I would argue that we've moved away from *truth*—however one might define it—to (with due respect to Steven Colbert) *truthiness*, the presentation of ideas and numbers that convey neither more nor less than what we wish to believe in our own self-interest, and persuade others to believe, too. This change in turn has given us what I describe in my new book, *The Battle for the Soul of Capitalism*, as a "pathological mutation" from owners' capitalism to managers' capitalism in our business and financial systems—in corporate America, investment America, and mutual fund America alike, the three principal targets of my book.

Yet while Vanguard, too, has emerged as a sort of prototypical *21st-century* firm—a virtual organization, enormous in size, heavily reliant on process, on real-time communications and computer technology, and managed largely by the contemporary numeric standards of modern management—its founding values remain intact. At our core, we remain a prototypical *18th-century* firm, thriving on our early entrepreneurship, on our simple investment strategies, on eternal verities such as service to others before service to self, and on putting the interests of shareholders ahead of the interest of managers, doing our best to hold high the belief that ethical principles and moral values must be, finally, the basis for any enterprise worth its salt.

The opportunity to make this contrast between Vanguard and the financial field in which we ply our trade comes at an especially propitious moment, for we recently celebrated the 300th anniversary of the birth of Benjamin Franklin, surely one of the most remarkable Americans of all time. While the tercentenary makes us more aware than ever of Franklin's extraordinary accomplishments as founding father, framer, statesman, diplomat, scientist, philosopher, author, master of the epigram, and fount of earthy wisdom, far less attention has been paid to his strict sense of values, his talents as an entrepreneur and inventor, and his sensible investment wisdom—the prototypical 18th-century man.

I also discuss how Franklin's entrepreneurial values and inventions focused on the common good, and how his investment principles focused on common sense. In both cases, it is easy to imagine those values and those principles as precursors to those of Vanguard. I also contrast his 18th-century values with the very different 21st-century values that now pervade America's corporate and investment system.

Franklin's Entrepreneurship and Invention

Let's begin with Franklin's entrepreneurship. It was not only remarkable for his era; it was remarkable for *any* era. While in today's grandiose era of capitalism the word "entrepreneur" has come to be commonly associated with those who are motivated to create new enterprises largely by the desire for personal wealth or even greed, the fact is that *entrepreneur* simply means "one who undertakes an enterprise," a person who founds and directs an organization.

But at its best, entrepreneurship entails something far more important than mere money. Please do not take my word for it. Heed the words of the great Joseph Schumpeter, the first economist to recognize entrepreneurship as the vital force that drives economic growth. In his *Theory of Economic Development*, written nearly a century ago, Schumpeter dismissed material and monetary gain as the prime mover of the entrepreneur, finding motivations like these to be far more powerful: (1) "The joy of creating, of getting things done, of simply exercising one's energy and ingenuity," and (2) "The will to conquer: the impulse to fight, . . . to succeed for the sake, not of the fruits of success, but of success itself."

There is a difference, then, between an entrepreneur and a capitalist. Had Franklin possessed the soul of a true capitalist, "he would have devoted the time he saved from printing to making money somewhere else."* But he did not. For Franklin, the getting of money was always a means to an end, not an end in itself. The other enterprises he created, as well as his inventions, were designed for the public weal, not for his personal profit. Even today, Dr. Franklin's idealistic 18th-century version of entrepreneurship is inspirational. When he reminded us that "energy and persistence conquer all things," Franklin was likely describing his own motivations to create and to succeed, using Schumpeter's formulation, for the joy of creating, of exercising one's energy and ingenuity, the will to conquer, and the joy of a good battle.

> Franklin's creation of a mutual fund insurance company was the classic example of his community-minded approach to entrepreneurship. In the eighteenth century, fire was a major and ever-present threat to cities. In 1736, when barely 30 years of age, Franklin responded to that threat by founding the Union Fire Company, literally a bucket brigade that protected the homes of its subscribers. In a short time, Philadelphia's fire companies joined in a common cause, making it possible to insure the homes under their aegis against loss by fire. So on April 13, 1752, Franklin joined with his colleagues in founding The Philadelphia Contributionship.
>
> The name of the new enterprise was inspired by the Amicable Contributionship of London, founded in 1696. Its name, in turn, was derived from the contemporary definition of contribution— "that which is given by several hands for a common purpose," an apt name for a mutual company owned by its policyholders. This combination of ownership and service—creating a true mutuality of interest between the owners of a firm and its managers—was

---

*H. W. Brands, *Benjamin Franklin—The First American* (New York: Doubleday, 2000).

not then, nor is it now, the common mode of business organization. But it was an inspired idea for its day and for its purpose. And it has endured. The Philadelphia Contributionship survives today, the oldest property insurance company in the United States. And while Franklin's selfless idea of mutuality has met the test of time, that was only part of his creativity. He also founded a library, an academy and college, a hospital, and a learned society, all for the benefit of his—now *our*—community. Not bad!

Like many entrepreneurs, Franklin was also an inventor. And once again, his goal was to improve the community's quality of life. Among other devices, he created the lightning rod and the Franklin stove (to say nothing of bifocals and swim fins). He made no attempt to patent the lightning rod for his own profit; and he declined the offer by the Governor of the Commonwealth for a patent on his Franklin stove, the "Pennsylvania fireplace" that he invented in 1744, revolutionizing the efficiency of home heating with great benefit to the public at large. Benjamin Franklin believed that "knowledge is not the personal property of its discoverer, but the common property of all. As we enjoy great advantages from the inventions of others," he wrote, "we should be glad of an opportunity to serve others by any invention of ours, and this we should do freely and generously."

Vanguard's Entrepreneurship and Invention

If it crosses your mind that Franklin's concepts of service for the greater good of the community rather than for personal gain, and of creativity and innovation designed to improve the quality of life, are rarer than they should be in today's personal-wealth-driven, often greedy, version of entrepreneurship, you have strong powers of observation. But however rare, examples do exist. I'm very familiar with one example, for the creation of the Vanguard Group in September 1974 reflects the very same values of entrepreneurship and innovation that Franklin held high.

Just as Franklin founded the Philadelphia Contributionship on the rock of true mutuality in 1752, so mutuality was the rock on which I founded Vanguard two centuries later, in 1974. Vanguard, however, did not begin spontaneously; it sprang, Phoenix-like, from a troubled existing enterprise. We trace our lineage to 1928, when another remarkable Philadelphian, financial entrepreneur and fund pioneer Walter L. Morgan, founded Wellington Fund, one of the nation's oldest mutual funds that thrives to this day. His company, Wellington Management Company, operated and managed the fund, building its own profits from the growing advisory and distribution fees the fund generated.

Vanguard changed the operation of Wellington Fund—originally a profit-making entity for its *managers*—to an entity that sought to optimize the returns earned by its *shareholders*. Flying in the face of industry tradition and practice, the fund shareholders, not outside investors, actually owned the new management company, operating it on an "at-cost basis." Under Vanguard's aegis, Wellington Fund and its sister funds took the unprecedented step of becoming a truly *mutual* mutual fund group. When the change was made, the assets of the then-Wellington fund group were $1.4 billion. We knew that this new venture was not without risk, for in the wake of the 1973–1974 market crash, fund assets were being withdrawn by shareholders at a fearsome rate. In fact, we would endure 78 consecutive months of capital outflow that did not end until June 1981. And then the Vanguard era began.

When operations began, we were a tiny company with just 28 *crewmembers* (I never cared for the term *employees*). Today our crewmembers number nearly 12,000, our seven mutual funds (I never cared much for the use of the word *product* to describe a mutual fund, either) now number 130, and our assets exceed $900 billion. The fastest growing firm in our field, we are now one of the two largest fund complexes in the world.

Our true mutuality—and the low costs and "shareholder-first" values that it engendered—has been the single most important factor in the firm's astonishing growth. Why was mutuality so important? Simply because of the central reality of investing: *costs matter.* Since equity mutual funds are simply diversified investment portfolios that invest in the securities traded on America's stock market, as a group they earn *gross* returns on their portfolios that are roughly equal to the returns generated in the stock market. *But only before fund costs are deducted.* The *net* returns that funds actually *deliver* to their investors fall short of those *gross* returns by the amount of their costs—all of those management fees, operating expenses, portfolio transaction costs, and sales commissions that funds incur.

Just as gambling becomes a loser's game after the croupier's rake descends, so beating the market becomes a loser's game after the costs of our financial intermediaries are deducted. The fund business, arguably, is the only business in which "you get what you *don't* pay for." In fact, for fund investors as a group, "you get *precisely* what you don't pay for." (Later, I'll give you a powerful example of the long-term impact of fund costs.)

But while our mutuality has been the central factor in Vanguard's growth, the concept is hardly winning any popularity contests. Part of the reason for my choice of the name *Vanguard* for our new firm was to suggest that our structure would establish a new trend, one in which we would be the *leader*. Alas, despite the passage of more than three decades, our mutualized structure has yet to attract its first *follower*.

The reason that mutuality has so far failed to rule the financial seas, I fear, is that the Schumpeterian *entrepreneurs* who originally created mutual fund enterprises—"for the joy of creating . . . for success itself, *not* for the fruits of success"—are in the ordinary course of events succeeded by *businessmen* who are more susceptible to temptation by the fruits of success for themselves and the greater personal wealth that results from building their empires. And so it has been in the mutual fund field. The small, privately held organizations managed by investment professionals that were the foundation of this industry when I joined it in 1951 have been replaced, largely by giant publicly owned financial conglomerates that are in the business to earn a return on *their* capital, not a return on *yours* (as a mutual fund shareholder). Just as my book points out, mutual funds are the paradigm of the triumph of managers' capitalism over owners' capitalism. Yet the winning strategy ultimately is held by the firm that provides a *community* advantage that serves shareholders and owners, simply by taking the lion's share of those oppressive costs out of the investment equation. It is hard to imagine that Dr. Franklin, reborn in our age, wouldn't have sought to serve, not himself, but the community in exactly the same way.

Our innovative structure and the low costs it engendered in turn were our springboard for a wide range of inventions, largely new funds designed to capitalize—both in concept and in substance—on making the importance of those low costs most meaningful and obvious. The first invention took place only months after we began, when a simple thought, indeed one that had first occurred to me when I wrote my senior thesis at Princeton University in 1949–1951, began nagging at my mind. *If mutual funds as a group fail to deliver stock market returns by the amount of their heavy costs, why not own the entire market at the minimal cost we were prepared to deliver?* Then, investors could capture almost 100 percent of that annual return, rather than the 70–80 percent fraction that would likely be achieved by our peers. This banally obvious insight quickly led to the simple invention that has been the most powerful manifestation of Vanguard's philosophy—the first index mutual fund in history. Today, "Bogle's Folly"—now Vanguard 500 Index Fund—is the largest mutual fund in the world.

It also took no more than the obvious arithmetic in which investment cost plays the critical role in shaping returns to recognize that the implications of indexing go far beyond the simple all-stock-market index fund and the all-bond-market index fund that followed. Result: We developed a second precedent-breaking invention, and then a third. The second came in the bond fund sector, when in 1977 we launched the industry's first *defined-maturity* series of bond funds, including a short-term portfolio, and an intermediate-term portfolio, and a long-term portfolio. It may not seem very imaginative—it wasn't!—but the simple concept revolutionized the bond fund sector, and virtually the entire industry quickly followed suit. The three-tier bond portfolio is now the industry standard.

That same simple arithmetic was the key to a third Vanguard invention that would also be quickly imitated (except, of course, for the low costs). In 1993, recognizing (albeit far later than we should have!) that excessive tax costs incurred by actively managed funds were at least as much of a burden to fund owners as operating costs, management fees, loads, and turnover costs, we created the industry's first series of funds designed to minimize taxes—two equity funds and a balanced fund, all following largely passive index-oriented strategies, all delivering on their promise in the years that followed.

Following Franklin's wonderful precedent, Vanguard placed its inventions in the public domain rather than seeking private profit. We made no attempt to patent the index fund, nor the three-tiered bond fund, nor the tax-managed funds, nor for that matter, did we seek to patent any of our other inventions and innovations. Our idea was to be "in the Vanguard" by giving investors a range of intelligent choices, to provide a *community* advantage, all the while garnering a *competitive* advantage for the firm.

Investment Wisdom—Franklin in the 18th Century; Vanguard in the 20th

The civic virtue that Benjamin Franklin brought to his entrepreneurship and invention has overshadowed the remarkable wisdom of this investment sage. Yet, perhaps because it is so simple that it seems unremarkable, this wisdom goes virtually unheralded among his other grand accomplishments. With his simple precepts, he would have realized that in this new age of investing, we have ignored the crucial lesson: *Simplicity trumps complexity.* All of that shuffling of paper shares of stock that we read about in the press—in the United States, nearly 4 billion shares of stock are traded each day, some *1 trillion* shares a year—is engaged in by speculators attempting to garner competitive advantage, even as it inevitably slashes the returns earned by investors as a community.

While investing in stocks and bonds as we know it today hardly existed in Franklin's era, his sensible advice about savings sets a high standard for today's investment books, most of which provide complex programs that promise to "beat the market," yet inevitably fail to deliver on that promise. In my own books, however, I did my best to focus on the simple principles that define investment success. These investment ideas, it turns out, are eerily similar to Franklin's ideas about savings, set forth largely in his classic, *The Way to Wealth*, first published in 1757. A comparison of the two philosophies suggests that wisdom about sound financial principles goes back at least as far as Franklin's homespun formulations about savings, echoed in Vanguard's founding investment precepts.

Perhaps the best place to begin is with Franklin's acute understanding of the miracle of compound interest. According to *Philadelphia Inquirer* journalist Clark DeLeon,

[I]n 1785, a French mathematician wrote a parody of Franklin's *Poor Richard* called *Fortunate Richard*, in which he mocked the (to him) unbearable spirit of American optimism represented by Franklin. The Frenchman wrote a piece about Fortunate Richard leaving a small sum of money in his will to be used only after it had collected interest for 500 years.*

"Franklin," DeLeon continued, "wrote back to the Frenchman, thanking him for a great idea and telling him that he had decided to leave a bequest to his native Boston and his adopted Philadelphia of 1,000 pounds to each on the condition that it be placed in a fund that would gather interest over a period of 200 years." Franklin assumed that the funds would accrue interest at the annual rate of 5 percent, bringing each original 1,000 pounds to 131,000 pounds ($232,000 at today's exchange rate) after 100 years, and 17,300,000 pounds ($31,000,000) in 200 years.

For a variety of practical financial reasons and complex legal reasons, when Franklin's trusts expired 200 years later in 1994, those totals were not nearly reached. (Boston's funds were worth almost $5 million and Philadelphia's about $2.25 million.) Nonetheless, the results were an impressive display of the massive accumulation of capital that could be achieved when the explosive mix of *rate of return* and *time* are combined. We call that mix "the magic of compounding."

Similarly, for as long as I can remember, compound interest has been at the center of my own investment thinking. The opening words in the very first chapter of my very first book† were:

> *The Magic of Compounding.* "The greatest mathematical discovery of all time" is how Albert Einstein described compound interest . . . the value of $1,000 invested in stocks in 1872 would have grown to $27,710,000 in 1992 [when the book was published, and the historical rate of return on stocks was 8.8 percent.] . . . *the magic of compounding writ large.*

---

*Clark DeLeon, "Divvying Up Ben: Let's Try for 200 More," *Philadelphia Inquirer*, February 7, 1993.

† *Bogle on Mutual Funds* (Irwin Professional Publishing, 1993). In the book, I used a $1 initial investment rather than the $1,000 in this example.

While that 8.8 percent rate of return was higher, and that 120-year period shorter, than Franklin's 200-year horizon, however, both periods seem so long as to be useless in our own personal financial planning. Since a comfortable retirement is the principal objective of nearly all U.S. families, in my new book I use a 65-year time horizon, one that assumes a 45-year working career (to age 65) and a further 20 years of life (to age 85) based on today's actuarial tables: "$1,000 invested at the outset of the period, earning an assumed annual return of, say, 8 percent would have a final value of $148,780—*the magic of compounding returns.*"

But I quickly warned that this total was unlikely to be achieved. Why? Because the obvious *magic of compounding returns* was all too likely to be overwhelmed by the subtle *tyranny of compounding costs*, a concept that, in a simpler age, even the great Franklin failed to contemplate. Here's what happens:

> Assuming an annual intermediation cost (by mutual fund managers) of only 2½ percent, the 8 percent return would be reduced to 5½ percent. At that rate, the same initial $1,000 would have a final value of only $32,465—*the tyranny of compounding costs.* The triumph of tyranny over magic, then, is reflected in a stunning reduction of almost 80 percent in accumulated wealth for the investor . . . consumed . . . by our financial system.

When Wall Street—essentially our money managers, marketers of financial products, investment bankers, and stockbrokers—puts up zero percent of the capital and assumes zero percent of the risk yet receives fully 80 percent of the return, something has gone terribly wrong in our financial system. As I note in the book, "[T]he shift in our system from owners' capitalism to managers' capitalism has been devastating to investors."

So what are investors to do? How do we plan sensibly for our financial futures and strive for a comfortable retirement? Once again, Franklin's ideas prefigure my own. Let me note a handful of his aphorisms, largely taken from *The Way to Wealth*, and compare them to the advice, which I describe as "pillars of wisdom," in my own books.

On saving for the future:

Franklin: If you would be wealthy, think of Saving as well as Getting. Remember that time is money. Lost time is never found again.

Bogle: Not investing is a surefire way to fail to accumulate the wealth necessary to ensure a sound financial future. Compound interest is a miracle. Time is your friend. Give yourself all the time you can.

On the importance of cost control:

Franklin: Beware of little Expenses; a small Leak will sink a great Ship.

Bogle: Basic arithmetic works. Your net return is simply the gross return of your investment portfolio, less the costs you incur. So keep your investment expenses under control.

On taking risks:

Franklin: There are no Gains, without Pains. He that would catch Fish, must venture his Bait.

Bogle: Invest you must. The biggest risk is the long-term risk of not putting your money to work at a generous return, not the short-term—but nonetheless real—risk of market volatility.

On understanding what's important:

Franklin: An investment in knowledge always pays the best interest. Learning is to the Studious, and Riches to the Careful. If a man empties his purse into his head, no man can take it away from him.

Bogle: To be a successful mutual fund investor, *you need information*. If information about the past returns earned by funds—especially short-term returns—is close to meaningless, information about risks and costs is priceless.

On the markets:

Franklin: One man may be more cunning than another, but not more cunning than everybody else.

Bogle: Don't think you know more than the market, nor act on insights that you think are your own but are in fact shared by millions of others.

On safety:

Franklin: Great Estates may venture more, but little Boats should keep near shore.

Bogle: Diversify, diversify, diversify. By owning a broadly diversified portfolio of stocks and bonds, only market risk remains.

On forecasting:

Franklin: 'Tis easy to see, hard to foresee.

Bogle: It takes wisdom to know what we don't know.

On looking after your own interests:

Franklin: If you would have a faithful Servant, serve yourself.

Bogle: Investors must not ignore their own economic interests.

And finally, on steadfastness:

Franklin: Industry, Perseverance, and Frugality make Fortune yield.

Bogle: Stay the course. No matter what happens, stick to your program. Think long term. Patience and consistency are the most valuable assets for the intelligent investor. "Press on, regardless!"

Surely you can learn at least these two things from this litany of sound financial advice shared, despite the nearly three centuries that separate them, by two Philadelphians: (1) 18th-century Franklin had a far better way with words than 21st-century Bogle; and (2) the principles of sensible savings and investing are time-tested, perhaps even eternal. The way to wealth, it turns out, is to avoid the high-cost, high-turnover, opportunistic marketing modalities that characterize today's financial service system. While the interests of the *business* are served by the aphorism "Don't just stand there—do something!," the interests of investors are served by an approach that is its diametrical opposite: "Don't do something—just stand there!"

Virtue

It turns out that the 18th-century version of entrepreneurship, mutuality, and invention have something in common: *virtue*. While *virtue* is a word that tends to embarrass us today, it surely didn't embarrass Dr. Franklin. In 1728, when he was but 22 years of age, he tells us that he "conceived the bold and arduous project of arriving at moral perfection. . . . I knew, or thought I knew, what was right and wrong, and I did not see why I might not *always* do the one or avoid the other." The task, he tells us, was more difficult than he imagined, but he ultimately listed 13 virtues—including *Temperance, Silence, Order, Frugality, Industry, Sincerity,* and *Justice*—even ranking them in order of importance. He began each day with "The Morning Question: What good shall I do this day?," and ended with the "Evening Question: What Good have I done today?" It is hard to imagine a more ethical philosophy.

Even viewed through the lens of 21st-century cynicism rather than 18th-century idealism, I confess a sense of wonder at the young Franklin's moral strength and disciplined self-improvement. While few of us in today's society would have the will to pursue a written agenda of virtue, Franklin had established, in his own words, the "character of Integrity" that would give him so much influence with his fellow citizens in the struggle for American independence. That character was also central to his dedication to the public interest, so easily observable in his entrepreneurship, in the joy he took from his creations, and from exercising his ingenuity, his energy, and his persistence. Echoing the same ideals that Schumpeter would echo more than a century later, he succeeded solely for the sake of success, exercising his talents not with a view toward personal gain and private profit, but toward serving the community. "America's first entrepreneur" may well be our finest one.

I hope you will forgive my boldness in comparing the peerless accomplishments of our nation's first entrepreneur with my own humble entrepreneurship and inventiveness, my own joy in what Providence has led me to create, my own energy and persistence, and my own love of the battle to improve the lot of the American investing public. I confess that I'm proud of my career, but I console myself with Benjamin Franklin's own confession, written when he was about my age:

> In reality, there is, perhaps, no one of our natural passions so hard to subdue as *pride*. Disguise it, struggle with it, beat it down, stifle it, mortify it as much as one pleases, it is still alive, and will every now and then peep out and show itself; you will see it perhaps often in this history; for even if I could conceive that I had completely overcome it, I should probably be proud of my humility.

So if I have allowed my own pride to peep out and show itself this afternoon, I assure you that it is with great humility with which I regale you with this chronicle of Vanguard's formation, our founding values, our inventions, and our investment principles. But I hope that, taken together, they will help you, in your own entrepreneurship and your own creativity and inventiveness, to avoid, using Franklin's timeless words, "life's tragedy—[in which] we get old too soon and wise too late." Let me sum up my hope with this revision of Neil Postman's epigram that I cited at the outset:

> While we now know nearly everything the 18th century didn't know, we still remember what it did know, and it will be easy to live with ourselves.

Chapter 22

Seventeen Rules of Entrepreneurship*

Awonderful series of happy accidents—beginning with my admission to this best old place of all as a member of the great Class of 1951—led to the creation of Vanguard. Today we manage some $720 billion of investor assets, one of the two largest mutual fund complexes in the world. Like all numbers, that number, in and of itself, is not particularly important. What *is* important is that we created a unique corporate structure, a more efficient and economical way to serve investors, and a new way of managing investments that together have begun to reshape the way the financial community thinks about investing.

Of course Vanguard is a story of entrepreneurship, too. But an odd kind of entrepreneurship, involving (1) the conversion of an existing enterprise to a higher use; (2) a business that demands virtually no capital assets; (3) an innovative corporate structure that was unlikely to be—and even 50 years later has yet to be—copied; and (4) an

---

*Based on remarks at the Princeton Entrepreneurs' Network 5th Annual National Conference in Princeton, New Jersey, on May 28, 2004. The original title was "Vanguard—Child of Princeton."

original idea, the index mutual fund, which, simply put, is the "killer app"—an investment strategy that cannot be empirically improved upon. And if that's not enough to make Vanguard atypical, I would add: (5) a firm specifically designed to provide neither equity nor entrepreneurial reward for its creators. (More about that later!) If those five peculiarities undermine my credentials to speak authoritatively on entrepreneurship, so be it. But I'll try, anyway.

Where It All Began

The story begins with the first of the almost-infinite number of breaks I've been given during my long life. It came at Blair Academy, where, thanks to a scholarship and a job, I received a splendid college-preparatory education. That priceless advantage in turn presented me with another break. With the help of another full scholarship and a job waiting on tables in Commons, I entered Princeton University in the late summer of 1947. (It was easier to get admitted then!)

Despite my academic success at Blair, I found the early going at Princeton tough. The low point came in the autumn of 1948, when I struggled with the first edition of Paul Samuelson's *Economics: An Introductory Analysis*. It was not a happy introduction to my major field of study, and I earned a well-deserved 4+ (D+ today) as my mid-term grade. With my other grades scarcely more worthy, my scholarship—and hence my Princeton career, for I had not a *sou* of outside financial support—was in dire jeopardy. But I ended the term with a nice upsurge . . . to a hardly distinguished 3 (today, C) average.

Academic distinction continued to elude me, but a year later fate smiled down on me once again. Determined to write my senior thesis on a subject that no previous thesis had ever tackled, Adam Smith, Karl Marx, and John Maynard Keynes were hardly on my list. But what topic *should* I choose? Perusing *Fortune* magazine in the reading room of the then-brand-new Firestone library in December 1949, I paused on page 116 to read an article about a business which I had never even imagined. And when "Big Money in Boston" described the mutual fund industry as "tiny but contentious," this callow and insecure—but determined—young kid decided that mutual funds should be the topic of his thesis. I entitled it, "The Economic Role of the Investment Company." Thus, the first **Entrepreneurial Lesson** that I'll present today is: **#1: Get lucky.**

A Design for a Business?

I can't tell you that my thesis laid out the design for what Vanguard would become. But there's no question that many of the values I identified then would, 50 years later, prove to lie at the very core of our remarkable growth. "The principal function of mutual funds is the management of their investment portfolios. Everything else is incidental. . . . Future industry growth can be maximized by a reduction of sales loads and management fees," and, with a final rhetorical flourish, funds should operate "in the most efficient, honest, and economical way possible." Sophomoric idealism? A design for the enterprise that would emerge a quarter-century later? I'll leave it to you to decide. But whatever was truly in my mind all those years ago, the thesis clearly put forth the proposition that mutual fund shareholders ought to be given a fair shake.

In any event, the countless hours I spent researching and analyzing the industry in my carrel at Firestone were rewarded with a 1+, and led to a *magna cum laude* diploma—a delightful, if totally unexpected, finale for my academic career at Princeton. And it came with a fine sequel: A half-century later, Dr. Samuelson, by then a Nobel Laureate in Economics, would write the foreword to my first book! (Another turnabout: In 1999, exactly 50 years after *Fortune* introduced me to the industry, that very magazine named me one of the four Investment Giants of the 20th century.) **Entrepreneurial Lesson #2: Turn disaster into triumph.**

Fate smiled on me yet again when a great Princetonian named Walter L. Morgan, Class of 1920 and the founder of Wellington Fund, read my thesis. In his own words: "Largely as a result of his thesis, we have added Mr. Bogle to our Wellington organization." While I agonized over the risks of going into that "tiny but contentious" business, my thesis research had persuaded me that the industry's future would be bright. So I cast my lot with this great man, my good friend until his death at age 100 in 1998, and never looked back. He had given me the opportunity of a lifetime. Bless his soul! **Entrepreneurial Lesson #3: Get a mentor.**

In the Business, Then Out

By 1965, Mr. Morgan had made it clear that I would be his successor. At that time, the Company was lagging its peers, and he told me to "do whatever it takes" to solve our problems. Young and headstrong (I was then but 36 years of age), I put together a merger with a high-flying group of four "whiz kids" who had achieved an extraordinary record of investment performance over the preceding six years. (Such an approach—believing that *past* fund performance has the power to predict *future* performance—is, of course, antithetical to everything I believe today. It was a great lesson!) Together, we five whiz kids whizzed high for a few years. And then we whizzed low. The speculative fever in the stock market during the "Go-Go Era" of the mid-1960s "went-went." Just like the recent "New Economy" bubble, it burst, and was followed by a 50 percent market decline in 1973–1974. The once-happy band of partners had a falling out, and in January 1974 I was deposed as the head of what I had considered *my* company. **Entrepreneurial Lesson #4: Get fired.**

But without both the 1951 hiring, which providentially brought me *into* this industry, and the 1974 firing, which abruptly took me *out* of it, there would be no Vanguard today. Removed from my position at Wellington Management Company, I decided to pursue an unprecedented course of action. The *company* directors who fired me composed only a minority of the board of Wellington Fund itself, so I went to the *fund* board with a novel proposal: Have the Fund, and its then-10 associated funds (today there are 100), declare their independence from their manager, and retain me as their chairman and CEO.

It wasn't *exactly* the Colonies telling King George III to get lost, as it were, in 1776. But *fund independence*—the right of a fund to operate with its own leadership, in the interest of its own shareholders, free of domination by the fund's outside manager—was at the heart of my proposal. *Mirabile dictu!* After a contentious debate lasting seven months, we won the battle to administer the funds on a truly mutual basis, under which they would be operated, at cost, by their own wholly owned subsidiary. **Entrepreneurial Lesson #5: Dare to be bold!**

With only weeks to go before our incorporation, we still had no name for the new firm. Fate, of course, smiled again. In the late summer of 1974, a dealer in antique prints came by my office with some small engravings from the Napoleonic War era, illustrating the military battles of the Duke of Wellington, for whom Mr. Morgan had named his first mutual fund 46 years earlier. When I bought them, he offered me some companion prints of the British naval battles of the same era. Ever enticed by the sea and its timeless mystery, I bought them, too. Delighted, the dealer gave me the book from which they had been removed. Even as I had browsed through *Fortune* in Firestone Library 25 years earlier, I again browsed through the text.

With my usual luck, I happened to turn to the saga of the historic Battle of the Nile, where Lord Nelson sank the French fleet and ended Napoleon's dreams of world conquest. There was Nelson's triumphant dispatch from his flagship, "*Vanguard*, off the mouth of the Nile." Together, the Wellington tie-in, the proud naval tradition embodied in HMS *Vanguard*, and the leading-edge implication of the name *vanguard* were more than I could resist. So on September 24, 1974, nearly 30 years ago, *The Vanguard Group* was born. Consider this syllogism: *No Princeton, no thesis; no thesis, no Morgan; no Morgan, no Wellington; no Wellington, no merger; no merger, no firing; no firing, no Vanguard.* Without Princeton the patriarch, Vanguard the child would never have been born. **Entrepreneurial Lesson #6: Getting lucky multiple times beats getting lucky once.**

A Narrow Mandate

Given the fiery crucible of contention out of which Vanguard was born, the Fund directors decided to allow Vanguard—owned, under its new mutual structure, by the funds themselves—only the narrowest of mandates. Our sole task was to handle the Fund's *administration*. Our crew, numbering only 28 members when we began the long voyage, was responsible only for the Fund's operating, legal, and financial affairs.

But administration comprises but one of the three sides—and arguably the least important side—of the triangle that represents mutual fund activities.

The other two, more critical, sides of the triangle—*investment management* and *share distribution*—were to remain with my rivals at Wellington Management. Yet it didn't take a genius to realize that our destiny would be determined by what kind of funds we created, by whether the funds could attain superior investment returns, and by how—and how effectively—the funds' shares were marketed. When we were prohibited from presiding over these activities, I knew that a rough road lay ahead. **Entrepreneurial Lesson #7: Never get discouraged.**

The fact that investment management was outside of Vanguard's mandate led us, within months, to an unprecedented action that today seems obvious—the fruition of an idea I had toyed with for years. Based on evidence that I had gathered in my Princeton thesis, I had written that mutual funds should "make no claim to superiority over the market averages." Was this thought the precursor of my later interest in simply *matching* the market with an index fund? Honestly, I don't know. But when I wrote those words way back in 1951, that moment may well have been when the seed was planted that germinated into my recommendation to the fund Board of Directors in September 1975: that Vanguard organize and operate the first market index mutual fund in history.

When the board reminded me that investment management was not within Vanguard's mandate, I argued that the index fund wasn't "managed"; it would simply own all 500 stocks in the Standard & Poor's 500 index. Disingenuous or not, this argument narrowly carried the day. When we organized the fund in late 1975, we had made our entry into the *second* side—the investment side—of the fund triangle. First Index Investment Trust (now named Vanguard 500 Index Fund), derided for years as "Bogle's Folly," wasn't even copied until 1984, after nearly a decade had passed. *What a great idea!* But our original index fund is now the world's largest mutual fund. **Entrepreneurial Lesson #8: Emerson was right. Build a better mousetrap and the world *will* beat a path to your door.**

Eliminating a Sales Force

How could we take over the third and final side of the triangle—share distribution? Once again, we devised a novel solution to a seemingly insurmountable challenge: We would abandon the network of brokers that had distributed Wellington shares for the previous half-century, and simply eliminate the *need* for distribution. We would rely, not on sellers to *sell* fund shares, but on buyers to *buy* them. After another divisive board battle, we took that unprecedented step in February 1977, converting overnight from the industry's traditional broker-dealer *supply-push* selling system to a sales-charge-free, no-load, *demand-pull* marketing system. In just 18 months from the day our skeleton enterprise began operations with its narrow mandate, we had become the full-fledged mutual fund firm we are today. **Entrepreneurial Lesson #9: Never give up. Never. Never. Never. Never. Never.**

There was really only one further step in the evolution of Vanguard's central concept. Within six months of our no-load decision we created a series of municipal bond funds with an unprecedented structure. Even as I had come to believe that precious few stock managers could outguess the stock market, so I had come to believe that precious few bond managers could outguess the bond market by accurately forecasting the direction and level of interest rates. Yet our peers, offering "managed" tax-exempt bond funds, were implicitly promising they could do exactly that—a promise that could not be fulfilled. So why not depart from the crowd and form not a *single* tax-exempt bond fund, but a *three-tier* bond fund offering a *long-term* portfolio; a *short-term* portfolio; and—you guessed it—an *intermediate-term* portfolio? It's difficult, in truth, to imagine a more banally simple idea. *But it had never been done before.* It changed, almost overnight, the way investors thought about bond fund investing, and the industry quickly adopted the concept.

Strategy Follows Structure

All of the changes I've just cataloged may seem convoluted and even arcane, so let's think for a moment about what we had done in the design of Vanguard's structure and the determination of Vanguard's strategy.

We had created a unique mutual *structure* in which costs could be reduced to the bare-bones minimum, and a *strategy* that emphasized mutual funds in which the linkage between our costs and our investors' returns would be obvious, indeed almost causal. *Strategy follows structure.* The one great—and largely unrecognized—idea of investing is this: *Costs matter.*

Why do costs matter? Consider the analogy of the stock market as a casino, in which the investor-gamblers swap stocks with one another, a casino in which, inevitably, all investors as a group share the stock market's returns, no more, no less. *But only until the rakes of the croupiers descend.* Then, what was inevitably a *zero-sum* game—a fruitless search by investors to beat the market *before* costs—becomes a negative-sum game *after* the costs of investing are deducted. Beating the market, by definition, is then a loser's game. *Gross market return, minus intermediation costs, equals net investor return*—clearly, a highly complex arithmetic formula. **Entrepreneurial Lesson #10: Be a mathematical genius. (Only kidding!)**

Since playing the mutual fund game carries heavy costs and entails lots of croupiers, each wielding a wide rake, the losers lose lots. Sales commissions when most funds are purchased. Fund management fees and operating costs. Marketing costs, including all those expensive advertisements you see. Transaction costs paid to stockbrokers and market-makers when fund managers buy and sell the stocks in fund portfolios over and over again. The excessive tax costs to which funds unnecessarily subject their shareholders as the result of their incessant, often mindless, turnover. Taken together, these costs, roughly 3.5 to 4 percent of fund assets each year, compounded year after year, have given taxable mutual fund investors but about one-half of the market's return during the past decade and—I'm glad you're sitting down!—only a little more than one-third in the past quarter-century. The average fund investor, who put up 100 percent of the capital and assumed 100 percent of the risk, garnered something like 33 percent of the market's after-tax return. Yes, *costs matter.* **Entrepreneurial Lesson #11: Never underestimate the power of the obvious.**

Given those elementary mathematics of the market, the insight that led into a low-cost structure and an index-oriented, structured-portfolio strategy is not only obvious, but startlingly obvious. It can't have been a mystery to the other firms in our industry. All of our rivals had the same *opportunity* as Vanguard to create such a structure, but, just like the prime suspect in a murder mystery, we alone had the *motive* to act. Because of our mutual *structure*, the finger of guilt, as it were, pointed directly at Vanguard. We sought low costs to maximize the returns for our *fund* shareholders; our rivals, eager to maximize the returns for their *management company* shareholders, sought the highest returns that traffic would bear. **Entrepreneurial Lesson #12: Competition is easier if your competitors won't—and can't—compete on costs.**

Opposition from a Formidable Source

While we had struggled long and hard to establish Vanguard on a firm foundation, however, our enterprise was still built on sand. For we were operating only under a *temporary* SEC order that allowed us to operate under our unique mutual fund structure. Astonishing as it may seem today, in 1980, nearly three years after giving us that temporary approval, the SEC reversed its ruling, leaving us in a no-man's-land that I had never contemplated. Aghast, for I knew we were doing what was right for our shareholders, we mounted a vigorous appeal. Finally, in 1981, after a struggle that had lasted *four long years*, the SEC did an about-face, approving our plan with these powerful words:

> The Vanguard plan actually furthers the objectives [of the Investment Company Act of 1940] by ensuring that the Funds' directors . . . are better able to evaluate the quality of services rendered to the funds. The plan fosters improved disclosure to shareholders . . . promotes savings from economies of scale . . . clearly enhances the Funds' independence . . . provides them with conflict-free control over distribution . . . and promotes a healthy and viable fund complex within which each fund can better prosper.

Wow! The Commission's endorsement—virtually a commercial message on our behalf—made the struggle worthwhile. At last, our foundation was a rock, firmly in place. **Entrepreneurial Lesson #13: "I'm from the government and I'm here to help you."** Sometimes.

Assets Double Every Three Years

The years in which our structure was hanging by a Damoclean thread were a challenge. But when the SEC finally gave us the green light in 1981, the stock market had begun to recover, and our assets had doubled, from $1.4 billion to $3 billion. By 1983, they'd doubled again to $6 billion; by 1985, again to $12 billion; by 1986, again to $24 billion; by 1990, *again*, to $48 billion. Assets doubled yet *again* to nearly $100 billion in 1993, then again to $200 billion in 1996, and *again* to $400 billion in 1998. No one thought that remarkable record could continue. *It didn't.* Nonetheless, despite the tough stock market since the bubble burst in 2000–2002, our assets now total $720 billion.

Our simple group of index funds, structured bond funds, and money market funds—each providing a near-causal relationship between low costs and high returns—constitute the powerful engine that has driven that amazing growth. The assets of these funds now total $520 billion, fully 75 percent of our asset base. What is more, we have also applied the principles on which they are based—an emphasis on rock-bottom operating costs, minimal portfolio turnover, no sales charges, diversified, investment-quality portfolios, and clearly defined objectives and strategies—to substantially all of the remainder of our assets, largely actively managed equity funds. In the marketplace of intelligent long-term investors—individual and institutional alike— whom we have chosen to serve, our strategies are mutually reinforcing. **Entrepreneurial Lesson #14: An internally consistent strategy is one of the keys to business success.**

Now, I recognize that creating a new company out of the framework of an existing company may not quite qualify as entrepreneurship. But I hope you'll consider as entrepreneurial the initiatives I've discussed today: (1) the creation of a new form of governance in the mutual fund industry, a *mutual* structure in which the interests of fund investors take precedence over the interests of fund managers and distributors; (2) forming the world's first index fund, a passive portfolio designed simply to provide the returns provided by the stock market, a challenge that precious few portfolio managers have bettered over time; (3) a new paradigm for bond fund management; (4) abandoning a proven distribution system in favor of a new and untried one; and (5) the sheer energy required to get it all done, in the face of a divided board of directors and the initial opposition of a federal regulatory agency. We marched to our own, different, drummer, and it worked. **Entrepreneurial Lesson #15: Take the road less traveled by. It can make all the difference.**

The Fruits of Success . . . or Success for Its Own Sake?

Let me close by considering the classic definition of the entrepreneur, "one who undertakes an enterprise," and ask *why* does a person undertake an enterprise? In his *Theory of Economic Development,* economist Joseph A. Schumpeter dismissed material and monetary gain as the prime motivation of the entrepreneur, concluding that these motives are far more powerful:

- "The joy of creating, of getting things done, of simply exercising one's energy and ingenuity," and
- "The will to conquer, the impulse to fight . . . to succeed for the sake, not of the fruits of success, but of success itself."

When Schumpeter identified entrepreneurship as a vital moving force in human economic progress, he ascribed it as a combination of those motives. Note that he downplayed *the fruits of success* as a primary motivator. Entrepreneurship, he tells us, is really about success itself, accomplishment, creativity, joy, energy, and the will to fight for one's ideas. *And so it is!*

Long before Schumpeter, a man often described as "America's first entrepreneur" also eschewed personal gain. Like many entrepreneurs, Benjamin Franklin was also an inventor, creating, among other devices, the lightning rod and the Franklin stove. He made no attempt to patent the lightning rod for his own profit, and declined an offer by the governor of the Commonwealth for a patent on his Franklin stove, the "Pennsylvania fireplace" he designed to improve the efficiency of home heating and benefit the public at large. Franklin believed that "knowledge was not the personal property of its discoverer, but the common property of all. As we enjoy great advantages from the inventions of others," he wrote, "we should be glad of an opportunity to serve others by any invention of ours, and this we should do freely and generously."

And there is yet another aspect of entrepreneurship that we should not ignore. While *ideas* are a dime a dozen, even the best of them require *implementation* to bring them to fruition. So let's all be humble enough to suppress our entrepreneurial egos and realize that the care and handling of those human beings who join us in the mission to turn an idea into a reality is an essential prerequisite of success. Helen Keller said it beautifully: "I long to accomplish a great and noble task, but it is my chief duty to accomplish humble tasks as though they were great and noble. The world is moved along, not only by the mighty shoves of its heroes, but also by the aggregate of the tiny pushes of each honest worker." **Entrepreneurial Lesson #16 (after John Donne): "No man is an island, entire of itself."**

Taking the Plunge, and Cashing In

The theme of this conference is "The Building Blocks of Entrepreneurship—From Taking the Plunge to Cashing In," and I've done my best to give you 17 lessons (one of which is still to come) that I hope will serve as building blocks that you can use as a frame of reference for your own entrepreneurship. I've tried to honor the first half of the subtitle by describing not only *the* plunge, but the *many* plunges, I've taken during my long career, at first with failure (that early merger that cost me my job), and later with what I guess passes for success—the mutual structure, the index fund, the three-tier bond fund; the gamble on a new marketing system.

Alas, I have nothing to say about the second half of the subtitle, "cashing in." The concept of a mutual structure that is the rock foundation of Vanguard simply doesn't entail cashing in for the founder, or for any one else. To do so would belie the very core of our existence—that our mutual fund shareholders are the actual owners of our firm, and their annual cost savings, estimated at something like $6 billion *per year*, are in effect an extra dividend on their fund investments.

Yet I'm a long way from sackcloth and ashes, for four major reasons: (1) I've been very well paid in salary and bonus incentives; (2) I prefer to save money rather than spend it; (3) I've been dollar-averaging—in part, in our tax-deferred savings plan—for 53 long years, and I can assure you that it works; and (4) I've been wise enough to follow my own prudent investment advice: lots of stocks in youth and middle age, lots of bonds in my later years, nearly all in our low-cost Vanguard funds with index or index-like strategies. That works, too!

Far more important than the rewards of the pocketbook—more things, more material possessions, more useless extravagance—are the rewards of the soul and spirit that come from trying to serve others rather than oneself. Whatever my entrepreneurial achievements may have been, I believe they have helped those honest-to-God, down-to-earth human beings who have invested with Vanguard in order to avoid the many, often deep, potholes on the long road to investment success, and thus capture their fair share of the returns with which our financial markets have rewarded us, and to enjoy a more comfortable retirement than most of their neighbors, just as Dr. Samuelson wrote in his foreword to my first book. I revel in that outcome. So I conclude with **Entrepreneurial Lesson #17: Our greatest rewards come when we foster economic progress, and help to build a better world.**

So that's my story. Sometimes I wonder what my life would have been like had Princeton, 57 long years ago, not opened its heavenly gates and let me in.

Chapter 23

"Vanguard: Saga of Heroes"*

I t's no mean task to measure up to the high appraisal of my career
that has been so generously expressed by Dr. Elliot McGucken.
That he has, remarkably, placed my 2005 book, *The Battle for the
Soul of Capitalism*, on the same reading list as *The Odyssey*—let alone on
the same planet!—adds even more to my burden in meeting the expectations of those who are aware of this background. Just two weeks ago,
however, an article in the Arts & Leisure section of the Sunday *New
York Times* gave me a unifying theme for my lecture.[†]

The article was about someone with whom many young
Americans will be familiar: Brad McQuaid, creator of "EverQuest," a
3-D fantasy video game operating in the virtual world, with 500,000
players, each paying $15 a month for the privilege. (Not as popular as
the champion, "World of Warcraft," with *5 million* players, but amazing

---

*Based on a lecture before Dr. Elliot McGucken's class, Artistic Entrepreneurship
and Technology 101, Pepperdine University, Malibu, California, on February 27,
2007.
[†]Seth Schiesel, "Game On: Hero Returns to Slay His Dragons," *New York Times*,
February 11, 2007.

in its own right.) Typical of my generation, alas, I am not among those players. But in my constant attempt to understand what appeals to today's young citizens, and my effort—however unlikely to bear fruit—to understand the new virtual world, I did read the *Times* article from start to finish. It was about Mr. McQuaid's new virtual game, "Vanguard: Saga of Heroes."

Of course, the new game has nothing to do with "my" Vanguard, the investment firm that I created way back on September 24, 1974. Nor is the story of our wonderful organization a "saga of heroes," save for the multitude of heroes numbered among our now-12,000-member crew, who deserve so much credit for their steadfast loyalty and commitment. This philosophy is not new to me. Indeed, I've expressed it often over the years in my regular speeches to our crew. Here's what I said in 1994, for example:

> This is a time to celebrate what each of you do to make Vanguard the best enterprise that it can be. . . . It is all of us—working together with our customary enthusiasm, energy, and professional skill—who give Vanguard the strength of character that is our greatest asset and our greatest blessing.

Among them are scores of heroes with whom I've worked directly, often over decades or more, including my loyal staff assistants, our senior officers and managers, and our veteran crewmembers—the heart of my legacy at Vanguard. This core cadre of leaders has helped to bring out the best in me and in our crew, the heroes who have dedicated themselves to serving—"in the most efficient, honest, and economical way possible" (a phrase I've used since 1951)—the now-20-million "honest-to-God, down-to-earth human beings, each with their own hopes and fears and financial goals" (another phrase I've used many times!), who have entrusted Vanguard with the stewardship of their investment assets.

And surely "heroes" must also describe those legions of investors who came aboard the good ship *Vanguard* in the early years of our existence. Often without ever seeing a real person or looking up our credit rating, they sent in their checks to "Valley Forge, PA 19482," first in small amounts, but then in the millions of dollars, and then in the billions. I believe that these early believers in Vanguard's mission are also heroes for giving us their blind trust. In return, they are enjoying their fair share of the returns generated in our financial markets. I'm confident that they would agree that we've measured up to their trust in our vision and our values.

The Odyssey, I hardly need tell you, is the story of a hero's journey, the building of character through overcoming the inevitable reverses of life, and the celebration (in Dr. McGucken's words) of the classic American spirit that bestows on us the right, and demands of us the duty, to take ownership of our own lives. While a different saga, however, the Vanguard story is not without tangential parallels to Homer's timeless classic. So, at many levels, "Vanguard: Saga of Heroes" ties my story together with the study of entrepreneurship and technology in today's society.

A Few Disclaimers

Let me be crystal-clear that I make no claim to being a hero. Nor do I claim any particular qualities of leadership for myself. For as long as I remember, I've tried my best to take responsibility for the things that I have touched along the road of life, and to leave each one better than I found it. Sure, I suppose that I also have some of the qualities that are ascribed to the leader—a vision of the ideal; self-confidence (and at least some self-awareness); a mind that, thanks to a wonderful education, is probably above average; a profound skepticism about the conventional wisdom of the day; and a determination to fight for the greater good, laboring in the interests of society at large, and in particular, the interests of the investors of our land.

While I'm about it, I might as well also disclaim much ability as a manager or businessman. (Although I do hold to what I consider to be the prime attribute of the successful manager: I've always trusted those with whom I worked, and I've always done my best to honor their trust in me.) In fact, I find more that I *don't* admire in the conduct of business today than what I *do* admire. I've loved my active participation in the nonprofit world (notably in my many years of service as chairman of the board of trustees of Blair Academy and of the National

Constitution Center) every bit as much as my now 55-year-plus business career. Truth told, I often wish that some of the values of these public-spirited institutions could be reflected in the values of our business leaders. I've reveled in helping to build a better world, solely because, well, it seems like the right thing to do.

Finally, while Vanguard is said to be a story of entrepreneurship, I'm not sure, either, of my credentials as an entrepreneur. In fact, the creation of the firm resulted in the conversion of an existing firm to a new corporate structure, one that was specifically designed to provide neither equity participation nor entrepreneurial reward for its creator or its staff. Rather, the whole idea was to put service in the interests of our investors, rather than service in the interests of our management, as the firm's highest value, and operating—in our own peculiar way— as a not-for-profit enterprise.

Idealism and Entrepreneurship

But even as I disclaim the credentials of the hero, of the leader, of the business manager, and even of the entrepreneur, I shamelessly proclaim my credentials as an idealist. Even more, I am an idealist who revels in the values of the Enlightenment and holds high his admiration for the brilliance and the character of the great thinkers, great doers, and great adventurers of the 18th century, men (as it happens, in particular our nation's Founding Fathers) who gave birth to our modern world. I confess to being immensely proud of the title of one of the chapters of a biography of me that was published a decade ago: "The 18th Century Man."*

A year ago, in a talk on entrepreneurship that celebrated the 300th birthday of Benjamin Franklin, I reflected on this 18th-century connection with a wonderful quotation: "Soon we shall know everything the 18th century didn't know, and nothing it did, and it will be hard to live with us." These words were the opening epigram of *Building a Bridge to the Eighteenth Century*, by the late Neil Postman—prolific author, social critic, and professor at New York University. Postman's book presented an impassioned defense of the old-fashioned liberal

---

* Robert Slater, *John Bogle and the Vanguard Experiment* (New York: McGraw-Hill, 1996).

humanitarianism that was the hallmark of the Age of Reason. His aim was to restore the balance between mind and machine.

But the balance has gone the other way. In our present era of information technology, numbers and scientific techniques seem to be at the forefront of our values. Metaphorically speaking, *if it can't be counted, it doesn't count.* Surely this change has been clearly reflected in the change in capitalism from a system with values like trusting and being trusted at the fore, to a system relying heavily on numbers. We seem to blindly accept that financial matters are rational simply because numbers, however dubious their provenance, are definitive.

While Postman made the bold assertion that truth is invulnerable to fashion and the passing of time, I'm not so sure. Indeed I would argue that we've moved away from *truth*—however one might define it—to (with due respect to Steven Colbert) *truthiness*, the presentation of ideas and numbers that convey neither more nor less than what we wish to believe in our own self-interest, and persuade others to believe, too. We manage our truths by managing our numbers. That old bromide of the management consultant, "If you can measure it, you can manage it," has done us more harm than good.

As the 21st century begins, then, our values have changed, and it is hard to resist conformity with a new society in which, seemingly, *everything* can be measured. Even Vanguard has emerged as a sort of prototypical 21st-century firm, a virtual organization; enormous in size; heavily reliant on process, real-time communications, and computer technology; and managed largely by the contemporary numeric standards of modern management. But at our core—at least through my idealistic eyes—we remain a prototypical 18th-century firm, thriving on our early entrepreneurship, on our simple investment strategies, and on eternal verities such as service to others before service to self, doing our best to hold high the belief that ethical principles and moral values must be, finally, the basis for any enterprise worth its salt.

America's First Entrepreneur

In today's grandiose era of capitalism, the word "entrepreneur" has come to be commonly associated with those who are motivated to create new enterprises largely by the desire for personal wealth or even greed. But at its best, entrepreneurship entails something far more important than mere money. Heed the words of the great Joseph Schumpeter, the first economist to recognize entrepreneurship as the vital force that drives economic growth. In his *Theory of Economic Development*, written nearly a century ago, Schumpeter dismissed material and monetary gain as the prime mover of the entrepreneur, finding motivations like these to be far more powerful: (1) "The joy of creating, of getting things done, of simply exercising one's energy and ingenuity," and (2) "The will to conquer, the impulse to fight . . . to succeed for the sake, not of the fruits of success, but of success itself."

That's the way it was in 18th-century America, at least in the case of Benjamin Franklin. For Franklin, fairly described as "America's First Entrepreneur," the getting of money was always a means to an end, not an end in itself. The enterprises he created were designed for the public weal, not for his personal profit. Franklin founded a mutual fire insurance company, a library, an academy and college, a hospital, and a learned society, all for the benefit of his community. Not bad! His inventions followed the same philosophy. He made no attempt to patent the lightning rod for his own profit; and he declined the offer for a patent on the "Franklin stove" that revolutionized the efficiency of home heating, with great benefit to the public at large. Benjamin Franklin believed that, "knowledge is not the personal property of its discoverer, but the common property of all. As we enjoy great advantages from the inventions of others," he wrote, "we should be glad of an opportunity to serve others by any invention of ours, and this we should do freely and generously."

Franklin's concepts of service for the greater good of the community and of creativity and innovation designed to improve the quality of life, rather than for personal gain, are rarer than they should be in today's personal-wealth-driven, often greedy, version of entrepreneurship. But, however rare, examples do exist. Truth told, the creation of Vanguard (like Franklin's Philadelphia Contributionship, creating a mutuality of interest between the clients who were the policyholders of the insurance company and the firm's manager) reflects the very same values of entrepreneurship and innovation that Franklin held high.

The Vanguard Odyssey

Now, to the extent that the odyssey of Vanguard is—or at least begins as—my story, let me tell you about it. I do so that you will see that no heroism was involved, that no giant brain drew the design, and that the implementation of our strategy required little in the way of inordinate business skill. Each one of you here tonight, given the opportunities and determination that I have been given, can do the same thing in whatever calling you follow. In our case, simplicity rather than complexity called the tune; the relentless rules of humble arithmetic overwhelmed the need for imponderable statistical proofs; and leaps of faith rather than hard evidence ruled the day. The idea that the shareholder—not the manager—should be king accounts for the lion's share of our growth. (It has been said of me, not kindly, that all I had going for me was "the uncanny ability to recognize the obvious.")

The story begins with the first of the almost-infinite number of breaks I've been given during my long life. It came at Blair Academy, where, thanks to a generous scholarship and a demanding job (first as a waiter, then as the captain of the waiters), I received a splendid college-preparatory education. That priceless advantage in turn presented me with another break. With the help of another full scholarship and a job waiting on tables in Commons (I must have been good at it!) I entered Princeton University in the late summer of 1947. (It was easier to get admitted then!)

Despite my hard-won academic success at Blair, I found the early going at Princeton tough. The low point came in the autumn of 1948, when I struggled with my first exposure to the field of economics. It was not a happy introduction to my major field of study, and my low grades almost cost me my scholarship—and hence my Princeton career, for I had not a *sou* of outside financial support. But I pressed on as best I could, and my grades gradually improved. The crisis passed.

While academic distinction continued to elude me, fate smiled down on me once again a year later. Determined to write my senior thesis on a subject that no previous thesis had ever tackled, Adam Smith, Karl Marx, and John Maynard Keynes were hardly on my list. But what topic *should* I choose? In one of the many fantastic appearances of luck in my life, I was perusing *Fortune* magazine in the reading room of the then-brand-new Firestone library in December 1949; I paused on page 116 and began to read an article about a business that I had never even imagined. And when "Big Money in Boston" described the mutual fund industry as "tiny but contentious," this callow and insecure—but determined—young kid decided that mutual funds would be the topic of his thesis. I entitled it, "The Economic Role of the Investment Company."

A Design for a Business?

There's no question that many of the values I identified in my thesis would, decades later, prove to lie at the very core of our remarkable growth. "The principal function of mutual funds is the management of their investment portfolios. Everything else is incidental. . . . Future industry growth can be maximized by a reduction of sales loads and management fees," and, with a final rhetorical flourish, funds should operate "in the most efficient, honest, and economical way possible" (a phrase you heard earlier in my remarks). Sophomoric idealism? A design for the enterprise that would emerge a quarter-century later? I'll leave it to you to decide. But whatever was truly in my mind all those years ago, the thesis clearly put forth the proposition that mutual fund shareholders ought to be given a fair shake.

I threw myself into the task of writing the thesis with abandon, falling madly in love with my subject. I was convinced that the "tiny" $2 billion industry of yore would become huge . . . and would remain "contentious." I was right on both counts! It is now a *$10 trillion* colossus, the nation's largest financial institution. What's more, the countless hours that I spent researching and analyzing the industry in my carrel at Firestone was rewarded with a 1+, and led to a *magna cum laude* diploma—a delightful, if totally unexpected, finale for my academic career at Princeton. "Turnabout is fair play!"

Fate smiled on me yet again when Walter L. Morgan, Princeton Class of 1920 and the founder of Wellington Fund, read my thesis. In his own words: "Largely as a result of his thesis, we have added Mr. Bogle to our Wellington organization." One more stroke of luck! Although I agonized over the risks of going into this young business, my research had persuaded me that the industry's future would be bright. So I cast my lot with this great man and never looked back. He had given me the opportunity of a lifetime.

By 1965, Mr. Morgan had made it clear that I would be his successor. At that time, the Company was lagging its peers, and he told me to "do whatever it takes" to solve our problems. Young and headstrong, with self-confidence that belied my lack of wisdom and experience (I was then but 35 years of age), I put together a merger with a high-flying group of four "whiz kids" who had achieved an extraordinary record of investment performance over the preceding six years. (Such an approach—believing that *past* fund performance has the power to predict *future* performance—is, of course, antithetical to everything I believe today. It was a great—but expensive—lesson!)

Together, we five whiz kids whizzed high for a few years. And then, of course, we whizzed low. The speculative fever in the stock market during the "Go-Go Era" of the mid-1960s "went-went." Just like the "New Economy" bubble of the late 1990s, it burst, and was followed by a 50 percent market decline in 1973–1974. The once-happy band of partners had a falling out, and in January 1974 I was deposed as the head of what I had considered *my* company. I was heartbroken.

What's in a Name?

But, necessity being the mother of invention, I decided to pursue an unprecedented course of action. The *management company* directors who fired me composed only a minority of the board of Wellington Fund itself, so I went to the *fund* board with a novel proposal: Have the Fund and its then-10 associated funds (today there are more than 100) declare their independence from their manager, and retain me as their chairman and CEO. After a contentious debate lasting seven months, we won the battle to administer the funds on a truly mutual basis, under which they would be operated, at cost, by their own wholly owned subsidiary.

With only weeks to go before our incorporation, we still had no name for the new firm. Fate, of course, smiled again. By happenstance, as the battle for the fund board's approval raged on, I stumbled across a book describing the historic Battle of the Nile, where Lord Nelson sank the French fleet and ended Napoleon's dream of world conquest. There was Nelson's triumphant dispatch from his flagship, HMS *Vanguard*. His words, the proud naval tradition, and the great victory, combined with the leading-edge implication of the name *vanguard*, were more than I could resist. So on September 24, 1974, *The Vanguard Group* was born. Ironically, without both the 1951 hiring, which providentially brought me *into* this industry, and the 1974 firing, which abruptly took me *out* of it, there would be no Vanguard today. I'm fond of saying that I left my old job at Wellington in the same way that I began my new job at Vanguard: "Fired with enthusiasm."

Time does not permit me to describe in detail the Vanguard odyssey that was to follow our fortuitous launch. But its parallels to Homer's *Odyssey*, while hardly exact, are nonetheless there. We've wasted our own time with the Lotus-Eaters. We've been enticed by our own wily Sirens. We've sailed uneasily between Scylla and Charibdis. We've brazenly defied more than one Cyclops. We've been threatened by the wrath of our own Poseidon. And we've been temporarily entranced by some bewitching Calypsos. But we've survived our now-32-year voyage, and returned home, proud and prosperous, for a brief moment of reflection. Of course we know that life is a journey, not a destination, and a new odyssey lies before us.

As you might imagine, it's difficult for me to believe that such a new voyage could have the excitement and challenge of Vanguard's first one. After all, putting a new name on the map, creating a unique new structure, and establishing a new set of ethical values can't recur with regularity. True entrepreneurship or not, (1) we created a new form of governance in the mutual fund industry, a *mutual* structure in which the interests of fund investors take precedence over the interests of fund managers and distributors. (2) We formed the world's first index fund, a passive portfolio designed simply to provide the returns provided by the stock market, a challenge that precious few portfolio managers have measured up to over time. (3) We developed a new paradigm for bond fund management, using an innovative three-tier structure of short-term, long-term, and intermediate-term portfolios that quickly became the industry standard. (4) We abandoned, overnight, a proven broker-dealer, commission-oriented "supply-push" distribution system in favor of a new and untried no-sales-charge, "demand-pull" system for self-motivated investors.

None of these changes that we all take for granted today came easily. To accomplish them required a devil-may-care attitude, a blasé disregard for risk, a profound conviction, without hard evidence, that they would work, and the sheer energy required to get it all done. What's more, they were, well, "contentious." Despite what we regarded as our noble intentions, the completion of our structure was initially opposed by our industry's regulatory agency. The Securities and Exchange Commission rejected our structure, and dawdled over our appeal for four long years. When it finally gave us its unanimous approval, it came with a nice bonus and a snappy salute: "The Vanguard plan actually furthers the [1940] Act's objectives, and promotes a healthy and viable complex in which each fund can better prosper."

And prosper we did. By the time the SEC finally gave us the green light in 1981, seven long years after we began, the stock market had begun to recover, and our assets had doubled, from $1.4 billion to $3 billion. They would double again with remarkable regularity, about every three years. In 1983, to $6 billion; 1985, $12 billion; 1986, $24 billion; 1989, $50 billion; 1992, $100 billion; 1995, $200 billion; and again to $400 billion in 1998. Remarkable! While it took longer—seven more years—for our assets to double yet again, we crossed the $800 billion mark in 2005. Today we oversee *$1.1 trillion* of other people's money.

The mighty engine that has driven that amazing growth was powered largely by our simple group of index funds, structured bond funds, and money market funds—each providing a near-causal relationship between low costs and high returns. The assets of these funds now total nearly $800 billion, more than three-quarters of our asset base. What is more, we have also applied their index-like principles— rock-bottom expenses; minimal portfolio turnover; no sales loads; diversified, investment-quality portfolios; and clearly defined objectives and strategies—to substantially all of the remainder of our assets, largely actively managed equity funds.

Most important, in the marketplace of intelligent long-term investors—individual and institutional alike—our strategies have worked effectively for those we serve. The returns earned by our funds are consistently ranked near the top of our industry, most recently by *Global Investor* as #1. It's fair to say, I think, that Vanguard has represented an *artistic* success for our fund shareholders, and a *commercial* success for our firm. So our odyssey not only has been long and arduous; it has been exhilarating and rewarding.

Liberal Education, Moral Education

When I think of the good fortune that has brought me to where I am today, I give the highest order of credit to a set of strong family values and a faith in God, a fine preparation for college at Blair Academy, and the powerful reinforcement and new awakening I received through a liberal education at Princeton University. A few years ago, former Princeton President Harold Shapiro defined these two aims of a liberal education:

> One is the importance of achieving educational objectives, a better understanding of our cultural inheritance and ourselves, a familiarity with the foundations of mathematics and science, and a clarification of what we mean by virtue.

> The other is the importance of molding a certain type of citizen, [one who is engaged in] the search for truth and new understanding . . . the freeing of the individual from previous ideas, the pursuit of alternative ideas, the development of the integrity and power of reason . . . and the preparation for an independent and responsible life of choice.*

President Shapiro also pointed to the "responsibility of a university offering a *liberal education* to provide its students with a *moral education* . . . helping them to develop values that will enrich their lives as individuals and as members of society." During my four years there, I did my imperfect best to acquire these values, and to manifest them in my actions in the years that followed.

---

* Harold Shapiro, "Liberal Education, Moral Education," *Princeton Alumni Weekly*, January 27, 1999.

As I look back in hindsight through glasses that inevitably have a rosy hue, I can only say that the liberal and moral education that was placed before me at Princeton may well have ignited some deep and unimagined spark that began to influence my life and my career in the mutual fund field. This spark, nurtured by time and experience, has erupted into some sort of flame, one that has permeated my ideas about the proper nature of the mutual fund. The flame will spread one day to the industry and become a blaze, one that will not be easy to extinguish.

It is my prayer that my mission—my crusade, if that is not too lofty a characterization of the course of my career—will help an industry to rethink its values, and accordingly be of greater service to growing millions of American investors. Serving these new owners of American business, who are contributing to the highest values of our system of capital formation even as they strive to take personal responsibility for the security of their own financial futures, has been a marvelously worthwhile life's work. I am infinitely blessed.

Returning Full Circle

It is wonderfully ironic that the very same 1949 issue of *Fortune* that inspired my thesis included a feature essay entitled "The Moral History of U.S. Business." Alas, I have no recollection of reading it at that time. But I read it a few years ago, a half-century later. As I reflect on Vanguard's two guiding principles of prudent investing and personal service, both seem to be related to the kind of moral responsibility of business that was expressed in that ancient *Fortune* essay. It began by noting that the profit motive is hardly the only motive that lies behind the labors of the American businessman. Other motives include "the love of power or prestige, altruism, pugnacity, patriotism, the hope of being remembered through a product or institution." Yes, all of the above.

Even as I freely confess to all of these motives—life is too short to be a hypocrite—I also agree with *Fortune* on the appropriateness of the traditional tendency of American society to ask: "[W]hat are the moral credentials for the social power [the businessman] wields?" The article quotes the words of Quaker businessman John Woolman of New Jersey, who in 1770 wrote that it is "good to advise people to take such things as were most useful, and not costly," and then cites Benjamin Franklin's favorite words—"Industry and Frugality"—as "the [best] means of producing wealth and receiving virtue." Moving to 1844, the essay cites William Parsons, "a merchant of probity," who described the good merchant as "an enterprising man willing to run some risks, yet not willing to risk in hazardous enterprises the property of others entrusted to his keeping, careful to indulge no extravagance and to be simple in his manner and unostentatious in his habits, not merely a merchant, but a man, with a *mind* to improve, a *heart* to cultivate, and a *character* to form."

Those demands, uttered more than 160 years ago, were not only inspiring, but seemed directed right at me. As for the mind, I still strive every day—I really do!—to improve my own mind, reading, reflecting, and challenging even my own deep-seated beliefs. As for the heart, no one—no one!—could possibly revel in the opportunity to cultivate it more than I. Just six days ago, after all, I marked the 11th(!) anniversary of the amazing grace represented by the incredibly successful heart transplant that I received in 1996. And as for character, whatever moral standard I may have developed, I have tried to invest my own soul and spirit in the character of the little firm I founded all those years ago. On a far grander scale than just one human life, these standards of mind, of heart, and of character resonate—as ever, idealistically—in how we seek to manage the billions of dollars entrusted to Vanguard's stewardship, and in how I pray that my company will ever see itself, putting the will and the work of a business enterprise in the service of others.

"The Battle for the Soul of Capitalism"

Perhaps it is obvious that these values eventually inspired me to expand my horizons beyond the narrow confines of the mutual fund industry in which I'd spent my entire career. The result: *The Battle for the Soul of Capitalism*, published by Yale University Press late in 2005. In essence, *Battle* is my *cri de coeur* about the state of American capitalism and the state of American society today. *The Battle* is one idealistic book! Just consider its first words, with the dedication to my 12 grandchildren and the other fine young citizens of their generation. With six of them now in college, you students here tonight are part of that generation, and hence of this dedication:

My generation has left America with much to be set right; you have the opportunity of a lifetime to fix what has been broken. Hold high your idealism and your values. Remember always that even one person can make a difference. And do your part "to begin the world anew."

A single turn of the page takes you to five epigraphs (count 'em, five!), the first of which comes from St. Paul: "If the sound of the trumpet shall be uncertain, who shall prepare himself to the battle?" And in my acknowledgments, I get right to the point in the very first paragraph: "Capitalism has been moving in the wrong direction."

The introduction that follows doesn't let up. I start off with a remarkably light revision of the classic first paragraph of Gibbon's *The Decline and Fall of the Roman Empire*, adapted to the present era. Compare the two first sentences. Gibbon: "In the second century of the Christian Era, the Empire of Rome comprehended the fairest part of the earth and the most civilized portion of mankind." *Battle*: "As the twentieth century of the Christian era ended, the United States of America comprehended the most powerful position on earth and the wealthiest portion of mankind."

So when I add Gibbon's conclusion—"[Yet] the Roman Empire would decline and fall, a revolution which will be ever remembered and is still felt by the nations of the earth"—I'm confident that thoughtful readers do not miss the point. But of course I hammer it home, anyway: "Gibbon's history reminds us that no nation can take its greatness for granted. There are no exceptions." As one of two reviews—both very generous—of *The Battle* that appeared in the *New York Times* noted, "Subtle Mr. Bogle is not."

No, I'm not writing off America. But my certain trumpet is warning that we must put our house in order.

The example of the fall of the Roman Empire ought to be a strong wake-up call to all of those who share my respect and admiration for the vital role that capitalism has played in

America's call to greatness. Thanks to our marvelous economic system, based on private ownership of productive facilities, on prices set in free markets, and on personal freedom, we are the most prosperous society in history, the most powerful nation on the face of the globe, and, most important of all, the highest exemplar of the values that, sooner or later, are shared by the human beings of all nations: the inalienable rights to "life, liberty, and the pursuit of happiness."

Something Went Wrong

But something went wrong. "By the later years of the twentieth century, our business values had eroded to a remarkable extent"—the greed, egoism, materialism, and waste that seem almost endemic in today's version of capitalism; the huge and growing disparity between the "haves" and the "have-nots" of our nation; poverty and lack of education; our misuse of the world's natural resources; the corruption of our political system by corporate money all are manifestations of a system gone awry.

And here's where the soul of capitalism comes in. The book reads, "The human soul, as Thomas Aquinas defined it, is the 'form of the body, the vital power animating, pervading, and shaping an individual from the moment of conception, drawing all the energies of life into a unity.' In our temporal world, the soul of capitalism is the vital power that has animated, pervaded, and shaped our economic system, drawing all of its energies into a unity. In this sense, it is no overstatement to describe the effort we must make to return the system to its proud roots with these words: *the battle to restore the soul of capitalism.*" (One reviewer thought that the title was, well, "inflated." But he liked the book anyway.)

This idealism doesn't let up. The reader doesn't even finish the first page of Chapter 1 ("What Went Wrong in Corporate America?") before reading:

> At the root of the problem, in the broadest sense, was a societal change aptly described by these words from the teacher Joseph Campbell: "In medieval times, as you approached the city, your eye was taken by the Cathedral. Today, it's the towers of

commerce. It's business, business, business." We had become what Campbell called a "bottom-line society." But our society came to measure the *wrong* bottom line: form over substance, prestige over virtue, money over achievement, charisma over character, the ephemeral over the enduring, even mammon over God.

That may seem a harsh indictment, but I don't back away from it. Indeed, as *International Herald Tribune* columnist William Pfaff described it, what went wrong was "a pathological mutation in capitalism." The classic system—*owners'* capitalism—had been based on serving the interests of the corporation's owners, maximizing the return on the capital they had invested and the risk they had assumed. But a new system had developed—*managers'* capitalism—in which, Pfaff wrote, "the corporation came to be run to profit its managers, in complicity if not conspiracy with accountants and the managers of other corporations." Why did it happen? "Because the markets had so diffused corporate ownership *that no responsible owner exists.* This is morally unacceptable, but also a corruption of capitalism itself."*

As you know from reading the book, there were two major reasons for this baneful change: First, the "ownership society"—in which the shares of our corporations were held almost entirely by direct stockholders—gradually lost its heft and its effectiveness. Our old ownership society is now gone, and it is not going to return. Today, financial institutions—acting as agents for (largely) mutual fund shareholders and pension fund beneficiaries—own some 70 percent of all shares of U.S. publicly held companies, a new "agency society" in which financial intermediaries now hold effective control of American business.

Agents versus Principals

But these new *agents* haven't behaved as owners should. Our corporations, pension managers, and mutual fund managers have too often put their own financial interests ahead of the interests of their *principals,*

---

* William Pfaff, "A Pathological Mutation in Capitalism," *International Herald Tribune*, September 9, 2002.

those 100 million families who are the owners of our mutual funds and the beneficiaries of our pension plans. As Adam Smith wisely put it 200-plus years ago, "[M]anagers of other people's money (rarely) watch over it with the same anxious vigilance with which . . . they watch over their own . . . they very easily give themselves a dispensation. Negligence and profusion must always prevail." And so negligence and profusion among our corporate directors and money managers have prevailed in present-day America.

The second reason is that our new investor/agents not only seemed to ignore the interests of their *principals*, but also seemed to forget their own investment *principles*. By the latter part of the 20th century, the predominant focus of institutional investment strategy had turned from the wisdom of long-term investing to the folly of short-term speculation. During the recent era, we entered the age of expectations investing, where projected growth in corporate earnings—especially earnings guidance and its subsequent achievement, by fair means or foul—became the watchword of investors. Never mind that the reported earnings were too often a product of financial engineering that served the short-term interest of both corporate managers and Wall Street security analysts.

When long-term *owners* of stocks become short-term *renters* of stocks, and when the momentary precision of the price of the stock takes precedence over the eternal vagueness of the intrinsic value of the corporation, concern about corporate governance is the first casualty. The single most important job of the corporate director is to assure that management is creating value for shareholders; yet investors seemed not to care when that goal became secondary. If the owners of corporate America don't give a damn about corporate governance, I ask you, who on earth should?

And so in corporate America we have the staggering increases in executive compensation, unjustified by corporate performance and grotesquely disproportionate to the pathetically small increase in real (inflation-adjusted) compensation of the average worker; financial engineering that dishonors the idea of financial statement integrity ("If you can measure it, you can manage it," writ large!); and the failure of the traditional gatekeepers we rely on to oversee corporate management— our auditors, our regulators, our legislators, our directors.

In investment America, the agent-owners who now control corporate America don't seem to care. While our institutional investors now own 68 percent of all stocks, all we hear from these money managers is the sound of silence. Not only because they are more likely to be short-term speculators than long-term investors, but because they are managing the pension and thrift plans of the corporations whose stocks they hold, they are faced with a serious conflict of interest when controversial proxy issues are concerned. As one manager reportedly has said: "There are only two types of clients we don't want to offend: actual and potential."

And in mutual fund America, an industry has lost its way. Once a profession with elements of a business, mutual funds have become a business with elements of a profession—and too few elements at that. Once dominated by small, privately held organizations run by investment professionals, the mutual fund industry is now dominated by giant, publicly held financial conglomerates run by businessmen hell-bent on earning a return on the capital of the firm rather than the return on the capital invested by the *fund shareholders*. Result: Over the past 20 years, the typical mutual fund investor has captured only one-quarter—yes, 27 percent—of the compound real (inflation-adjusted) return on stocks that was there for the taking by simply holding the U.S. stock market portfolio through an index fund. (I'm speaking, of course, of the Vanguard 500 Index Fund.)

Facing Up to the Reality

It must seem obvious that there is an urgent need to face up to these and other failures in the changing world of capitalism. But despite the contentious nature of the issues I've just described—broadly reflecting the triumph of the powerful economic interests of the oligarchs of American business and finance over the interests of our nation's last-line investors—it is remarkable that so little public discourse has been in evidence. In the investment community, I have seen no defense of the inadequate returns delivered by mutual funds to investors, nor of our industry's truly bizarre, counterproductive ownership structure; no attempt by institutions to explain why the rights of ownership that one would think are implicit in holding shares of stock remain largely unexercised; and no serious criticism of the virtually unrecognized turn away from the once-conventional and pervasive investment strategies that relied on the wisdom of long-term investing, toward strategies that increasingly rely on the folly of short-term speculation. If *The Battle* helps to open the door to the introspection—and then corrective action—by our corporate and financial leaders that is so long overdue, perhaps the needed changes will be hastened.

This process, I conclude, must begin with a return to the original values of capitalism, to that virtuous circle of integrity—"trusting and being trusted." When ethical values go out the window and service to those whom we are duty-bound to serve is superseded by service to self, the whole idea of the capitalism that has been a moving force in the creation of our society's abundance is soured. In the era that lies ahead, the trusted businessman, the prudent fiduciary, and the honest steward must again be the paradigms of our great American enterprises. I *know* it won't be easy, but if we all work long enough and hard enough at the task, we can build, out of our long-gone ownership society and our failed agency society, a new "fiduciary society," one in which the citizen-investors of America will at last receive the fair shake they have always deserved from our corporations, our investment system, and our mutual fund industry.

Conclusion

And so ends my saga of entrepreneurship that can still be built by focusing on human values rather than on the accumulation of personal wealth. To reiterate, this saga is at least tangentially related to Homer's *Odyssey* that, happily, still resonates in our literature—the hero's journey through triumph and disaster, over and over again. The odyssey of Vanguard, while different, is nonetheless a throwback to today's misguided bottom-line society as well as a reaffirmation of the inspiring moral values of the 18th century, values that belie today's pervasive retreat from yesterday's solid foundation of capitalism.

At the same time, we seem to have lost our bearings as a nation and as a society, focusing more on the tools of success—what we can see and count, facts and figures, courses about the superficial—and ignoring the truly essential tools of higher learning such as intellectual curiosity, the rule (and role) of reason, moral vision, and even generosity of spirit, open-mindedness, self-denial, and integrity.

So what's to be done? We each must do our part. Each of you here tonight can prove that "even one person can make a difference."* Returning to the theme of "Vanguard: Saga of Heroes," Brad McQuaid reminded us, in the final sentence of that *New York Times* article, that "these games should never be finished." Neither your odyssey nor mine should be finished so long as our minds improve, our hearts beat, and our character strengthens. While life is life and death is death, we must nonetheless "press on, regardless" while we can, and "stay the course" as long as the race continues, two phrases I've repeated *ad infinitum* to my colleagues at Vanguard.

But even as I ask you, as I did my grandchildren in the dedication to *Battle*, to enlist in the mission of building a better world, I remain eager for the excitement of the chase; the idealism of a cause worth betting one's life on; and the joy of honoring the values of the past as the key to a brilliant future. So dream your own dreams, but act on them, too. Action, always action, is required on the ever-dangerous odyssey that each of our lives must follow. Be good human beings. Respect tradition and study the great thinkers of our heritage. And not only listen to my ideas, but reflect on them.

I close now, with some words from Tennyson's *Ulysses* (the Greek Odysseus, rendered in Latin) that may explain to you, far better than could any words of my own, the exciting adventures I've enjoyed, the conflicting emotions I've endured, and the single-minded determination on which I have reflected in this essay, as I await with eager anticipation the still-unwritten final chapters of my long career.

Ulysses begins by reflecting on his odyssey:

> I cannot rest from travel: I will drink
> Life to the lees: All times I have enjoy'd
> Greatly, have suffer'd greatly, both with those

---

* This phrase appears on the plaque awarded to Vanguard crewmembers who win our "Award for Excellence."

> That loved me, and alone.
> I am become a name;
> For always roaming with a hungry heart
> Much have I seen and known; cities of men
> And manners, climates, councils, governments,
> Myself not least, but honour'd of them all;
> And drunk delight of battle with my peers.

Then he considers what may lie ahead:

> I am part of all that I have met.
> How dull it is to pause, to make an end,
> To rust unburnish'd, not to shine in use!
> As tho' to breathe were life! Life piled on life
> Were all too little, and of one to me
> Little remains: But every hour is saved
> From that eternal silence, something more,
> A bringer of new things;
> And this gray spirit yearning in desire
> To follow knowledge like a sinking star,
> Beyond the utmost bound of human thought.
> Old age hath yet his honour and his toil;
> Death closes all: but something ere the end,
> Some work of noble note, may yet be done.

Then, determined to take on one final mission, Ulysses summons his followers:

> So come, my friends
> Tis not too late to seek a newer world.
> Push off, and sitting well in order smite
> The sounding furrows; for my purpose holds
> To sail beyond the sunset, 'til I die.
> Tho' much is taken, much abides; and tho'
> We are not now that strength which in old days
> Moved earth and heaven, that which we are, we are;
> One equal temper of heroic hearts,

Renewed by time and fate, still strong in will
To strive, to seek, to find, and not to yield.*

To each of you, with so much of your own odyssey lying before you, unknown, this chronicle of my own past may well be irrelevant. Our task is to live, not the lives of others, but our own lives. But wherever you are on your own journey, I know it holds the promise of being an exciting and rewarding one, if only you remain "strong in will, to strive, to seek, to find, and not to yield."

---

*Note: Regarding the penultimate line of the poem, Tennyson wrote, "Made weak by time and fate, but strong in will." He could hardly have imagined that a heart could be transplanted from one human being to another, renewing the vigor of the soul.

Chapter 24

When Does Innovation Go Too Far?[*]

I t's hard to argue against "Something New Under the Sun," the title of a special report on innovation published in October 2007 by the London *Economist*. The report defines innovation as "new products, business processes, and organic changes that create wealth or social welfare," that is to say, "fresh thinking that creates value."[†] And surely we all agree that innovation, and her sister, entrepreneurship, are among the major forces that drive the growth of our global economy.

As a result of those forces, we have the Internet and superhighways, ever-soaring skyscrapers, jet aircraft that are ever more fuel-efficient, and automobiles with GPS systems that not only show you how to get where you're going, but actually have a person who *tells* you how. (Or is it just a disembodied computerized voice?) The end of the

---

*Based on my remarks before the Philadelphia Federal Reserve Policy Forum on Innovation and Regulation in the Financial Markets, in Philadelphia, Pennsylvania, on November 30, 2007. I chose this title just before the full force of the collapse in the credit markets fell upon us in mid-2008. While my warning proved to be prophetic, it's probably just luck.
† "Something New Under the Sun," *The Economist*, October 23, 2007.

information revolution is—for better or worse—not yet in sight, but it has brought us the benefits of choice beyond imagination and intense price competition that serves consumers better than ever before.

The financial sector, however, is unique in the role that innovation plays. Why? Because here there exists a sharp dichotomy between the value of innovation to the financial institution itself and the value of innovation to its clients. For it is the role of the providers of financial services to organize the instrumentalities of business and government—let's call them stocks and bonds—into packages and, well, "products" that earn profits for themselves, even as they are also designed to serve the needs of investors. Some of these products are simple and cost-efficient; others, at the extreme, are mind-bogglingly complex and expensive.

And so in this field we are eternally bound by this unarguable equation: Gross returns in the financial markets, minus the costs of financial intermediation, equals the net return actually earned by financial market participants. This is one of the "relentless rules of humble arithmetic" that drives our system. To the extent than innovation adds costs, then, it reduces investor returns.

What's more, our institutions have a large incentive to favor the complex and costly over the simple and cheap—quite the opposite of what most investors want and need. Given recent events in the financial markets in which some of our nation's—and the world's—mightiest financial institutions have collectively already taken some $47 billion (estimated to total $77 billion when all's said and done) of write-downs from their forays into relatively new, untested, and complex financial instruments, there can hardly be a more fitting time to consider whether innovation has again gone too far.

The Financial Sector—Costs and Benefits

Unlike the technology sector, where consumer costs decline as innovation leads to greater efficiency, the costs of our financial sector are soaring. I estimate that the costs of the system—the $100 billion annual expenses borne by mutual fund investors; plus those hundreds of billions of dollars of brokerage commissions and investment banking fees; plus all those staggering fees paid to hedge fund managers (the 25th highest paid of whom earned $130 million last year); and those legal and accounting fees, and all those marketing and advertising costs—came to something like $530 billion last year, up from a mere $100 billion in 1990.

Does this explosion in intermediation costs create an opportunity for money managers? You'd better believe it does! Does it create a problem for investors? You'd better recognize that, too. For as long as our financial system delivers to our investors in the aggregate whatever returns our stock and bond markets are generous enough to deliver, but only *after* the costs of financial intermediation are deducted, these enormous costs seriously undermine the odds in favor of success for our citizens who are accumulating savings for retirement. Alas, the investor feeds at the bottom of the costly food chain of investing.

This is not to say that our financial system creates only costs. It also creates substantial value for our society. It facilitates the optimal allocation of capital among a variety of users; it enables buyers and sellers to meet efficiently; it provides remarkable liquidity; it enhances the ability of investors to capitalize on the discounted value of future cash flows, and of other investors to acquire the right to those cash flows; it creates complex financial instruments that enable investors to divest themselves of risks they prefer not to assume by transferring them to others who are willing to bear them. No, it is not that the system fails to create benefits. The question is whether, on the whole, the costs of our financial sector have reached a level that overwhelms its benefits.

The ongoing crisis we are now facing in two relatively recent innovations—collateralized debt obligations (CDOs, backed by pools of mortgages) and specialized investment vehicles (SIVs, essentially money market funds that borrow short and lend long)—are examples of the complex—and costly—vehicles created by our financial sector. Banks like getting paid large fees for lending money, and when they can quickly get the loans off their own books and into public hands (so-called "securitization"), it can hardly be surprising that they aren't much concerned about the creditworthiness of those families for whose homes they have provided mortgages.

With the endorsement—and, I would argue, the complicity—of our rating agencies, this financial legerdemain created a modern version of alchemy. The *lead*, as it were, was a package of say, 5,000—let's call them B-rated—mortgages, miraculously turned into the *gold*, as it were, of a $100 million CDO with (in one typical case) 75 percent of its bonds rated triple-A, 10 percent rated double-A, 5 percent rated A, and only 10 percent rated double-B. (*Hint:* We now know that, despite the risk-reducing character of such broad diversification, lead is still lead.)

Derivatives

Innovation in the financial sector, of course, has included the development of an enormous market of financial derivatives. Hear Warren Buffett's description:

> Essentially, these financial contracts call for money to change hands at some future date, with the amount to be determined by one or more reference items, such as interest rates, stock prices or currency values. If, for example, you are either long or short an S&P 500 futures contract, you are a party to a very simple derivatives transaction—with your gain or loss *derived* from movements in the index.*

Mr. Buffett picked a good example. In fact, the value of derivatives on the S&P 500 index—futures and options, in essence, speculation on the future price of the S&P index—is now said to total $23 trillion compared to the $13 trillion actual market value of the 500 index itself. The "expectations market," then, is almost double the value of the "real market." However striking that relationship, these derivatives are a mere drop in the bucket of the global total of some *$500 trillion* in financial derivatives of all types; as a point of reference, the gross domestic product (GDP) of the entire world is about $50 trillion, a mere one-tenth of the derivatives total.

Back in 2003, a remarkable debate about derivatives occurred between two men who were likely the two most respected leaders of the entire financial community: Warren Buffett and Alan Greenspan. (Did I overstate their reputations? I don't think so.) Here's roughly how "The Motley Fool" web site reported it:

---

* Warren E. Buffett, Chairman's Letter, Berkshire Hathaway 2002 Annual Report, February 21, 2003.

Warren Buffett and Fed head Alan Greenspan have thrown out some fighting words on derivatives. Buffett called them "financial weapons of mass destruction." Greenspan said, "The benefits of derivatives have far exceeded their costs." Buffett's letter to shareholders devoted a whole section to derivatives, their abuse, and the great financial risk they represent both to the parties using them and to the economy as a whole, saying that derivatives could lead to huge financial turmoil for the markets.

For Buffett, derivatives' hard-to-quantify off-balance sheet presence makes it difficult to figure out a financial institution's true market risk exposure—lurking like a looming iceberg beneath the economy's waters. Greenspan countered directly by saying that most banks manage their risks just fine. Financial institutions use vehicles like swaps and futures to hedge their interest rate and market exposures, pointing out that the prudent use of derivatives has helped banks survive the recession by reducing risk.

Buffett thinks they represent a huge risk to the economy and that some sort of further regulation is needed. Greenspan believes that the market can handle derivative risk, and that more regulation could create a moral hazard, actually encouraging banks to assume more risk instead of less.

Who's right? They both are, in a way. But so far the use of most derivatives goes unnoticed because nothing catastrophic has happened. This is a battle that's likely to go on and on, with both sides holding fast to their positions until proven wrong by another big market event.*

Well, four years later, that "big market event" is upon us. The innovation of derivatives has enriched the financial sector (and the rating agencies) with enormous fees, and these overrated, as it were,

---

* "Greenspan vs. Buffett," The Motley Fool, May 8, 2003, http://www.fool .com/news/take/2003/05/08/greenspan-vs-buffett-take030508.aspx (link no longer active).

CDOs have wreaked havoc on the balance sheets of those who purchased them, including the banks and brokers themselves. They, too, bought them, and in the end, with many of them still on their books, were left holding the bag.

What is more (if we need more!), the SIVs have also created havoc. For it turns out that to sell these instruments, our banks increasingly issued "liquidity puts" to buyers, guaranteeing to repurchase them on demand at face value. Citigroup, it turns out, was not only holding $55 billion of CDOs on its books, but also some $25 billion of SIVs that have been "put" back to the bank, a fact not publicly disclosed by Citi until November 5. Astonishingly, Robert Rubin, chairman of Citi's Executive Committee (and a man, one might say, of not inconsiderable financial acumen) has stated that until last summer *he had never even heard of liquidity puts.* (Not quite as embarrassing as former chairman Charles Prince's earlier comment: "As long as the music is playing you have to keep dancing. We're still dancing.")

Innovation in the Mutual Fund Industry

If innovation has again gone too far in the banking sector, that sector is hardly alone. Innovation has also gone too far in the mutual fund industry. When I entered this industry way back in 1951, it was overwhelmingly dominated by equity funds holding a diversified list of blue-chip stocks; investing for the long-term (15% portfolio turnover); operated at modest expense ratios (averaging about 75 basis points); and pretty much closely tracking (before costs, of course) the returns of the stock market itself. We were an industry that sold what we made, and we valued management over marketing, and stewardship over salesmanship.

And then we decided to innovate. It was the mid-1960s when the mutual fund sector began to stray from its commonsense charter that had served investors with reasonable—if not quite optimal—effectiveness. Innovation in the "Go-Go" era, circa 1965–1968, saw the proliferation of scores of new "aggressive growth" funds, focusing on stock prices rather than business values; buying "concept" stocks and trading them with rapidity; and often holding "letter stocks" bought from corporate principals at discounted prices, only to immediately mark up those prices to market value, illicitly inflating fund performance. Of course such an approach was destined to fail. But with the heady returns these funds reported, investors poured billions of dollars into them before it did so. While fund managers prospered, fund investors were ill-served.

When the Go-Go era "went-went," it was quickly replaced by the "Favorite Fifty" era, where the idea was to hold established growth stocks that (if one could ignore the certain decay that high growth rates inevitably experience) would provide permanent performance success. But of course by the time that eager fund investors had jumped on that bandwagon, the ride was over. The stock market crashed by 50 percent in 1973–1974. While investors were once again impoverished, managers were once again enriched.

In the aftermath of the crash, with equity funds in net redemption, the industry came up with still more innovations. They included "government-plus funds," which provided unrealistically high payouts by claiming that premiums on covered call options were "earnings." Grossly oversold to investors and based on a strategy that could not consistently succeed, these funds raised $30 billion from investors—at one point nearly 10 percent of industry long-term assets—and then quickly collapsed. Within a few years, they had literally vanished from the scene, never to return. Again, investors paid a heavy price.

During the next few years, we dreamed up short-term "global income funds" and "adjustable-rate mortgage funds." (Shades of the recent crisis!) While these funds were hardly identical, they had several common characteristics: They offered income that could not be—and was not—sustained; they jumped on current fads in the marketplace; and they charged premium fees, as well as heavy sales loads. Together they attracted nearly $50 billion of assets, generated huge fees to managers and distributors, and ultimately failed investors. They, too, soon vanished.

New Economy Funds and the Bubble

More recently, in the later 1990s (you must be getting the picture by now), innovation in the mutual fund sector was designed to capitalize on the innovation of the so-called "New Economy" of the Information Age. We created literally hundreds of technology funds, telecommunication funds, Internet funds, and, once again, "aggressive growth" funds whose holdings were dominated by stocks in those sectors. Aided by a soaring market, aggressive advertising and promotion, and, yes, investor greed, nearly a half-trillion dollars poured into these funds during the three-year bubble surrounding the market's peak in March 2000. And then came the Great Bear Market, another 50 percent decline in which the NASDAQ ("New Economy") index dropped nearly 80 percent, and the NYSE ("Old Economy") index fell by 33 percent.

We actually can measure how costly this short-lived bubble was for fund investors. Let's compare the returns reported by the *funds themselves* ("time-weighted" returns) to the returns actually earned by *fund investors* ("dollar-weighted" returns) during the 10 years ended December 31, 2005. The 200 funds that enjoyed the largest cash inflows (about two-thirds of the equity fund total—clearly the better performers in the bull market) *reported* an annual rate of return of 8.8 percent—slightly below the 9.2 percent return on the S&P 500. But the return *actually earned* by the investors in these funds was 2.4 percent, a lag of 6.4 full percentage points per year below the 8.8 percent return the funds reported.

Cumulatively, then, these fund investors experienced but a 27 percent *increase* in their capital over the decade. Yet, simply by buying and holding the market portfolio through an index fund, they would have produced an increase in capital of 141 percent. Thanks to the innovation and creativity of fund sponsors, then, investors lost an astonishing 114 percentage points of return relative to the market itself. So much for the well-being of investors! As to the well-being of managers, we can roughly estimate that the total fees and sales loads (excluded from our calculations, which therefore *understates* the gap) paid to fund managers and distributors (including brokers) totaled in the range of $20 billion. So, yes, to answer the question posed by the title of these remarks, even as in the banking and derivative sectors of our financial economy, innovation has gone too far in the mutual fund sector.

And the Beat Goes On

One might have hoped that the fund industry would have learned from its past history of overreaching innovations. But the evidence goes the other way. In recent years, we've created "130/30" funds, in which managers implicitly suggest that overinvesting the traditional 100 percent long position in stocks by 30 percentage points, offset by a 30 percent short position, will produce higher returns. Maybe yes, maybe no—only time will tell—but the drag of the higher fees on these funds is a certainty. Another innovation is a variety of fixed-payout funds in which specific rates of annual withdrawals are offered, along with a warning that these payouts may, over time, exhaust the investor's capital. (One can only hope that warning is in large, bold-face type.)

Other innovations have included tax-deferred variable annuities that assure continued payouts (as a percentage of a fluctuating asset value), a perfectly good idea—except that the grossly excessive costs, commissions, surrender charges, and so on that burden most of these "products" have proved to erase much of their alleged advantage. And we also see new equity indexed annuities, usually providing only a portion of the stock market's return while guaranteeing a minimal annual return in the 1–3 percent range. Even a rudimentary financial analysis suggests that these modest added values are unjustified by costs (and sales practices) that are anything *but* modest.

Of course the major innovation of the recent era is the exchange-traded fund (ETF). I suppose there's nothing wrong, as such, with an index fund that can be traded (as the advertisements say) "all day long, in real time." But I have to wonder why any serious investor would want to do such a crazy and counterproductive thing as rapid trading. Clearly, frequent trading is the artillery of the speculator, not the investor; what's more, the vast majority of ETFs today—some 675 out of 690—are focused not on the traditional broad market indexes, but on narrow market sectors and individual foreign countries. (There are also some ETFs that claim to beat the market; I'll leave it to wiser heads to wonder about the validity of such claims, and how on earth they can call themselves *index* funds.) But ETFs are a "hot new product," appealing to mutual fund managers who have become primarily mutual fund marketers. ETFs are enriching the coffers of financial entrepreneurs, fund management companies, stockbrokers, and certain investment advisers; it remains to be seen whether they'll enrich the investors who trade them.

But Some Innovation Has Served Investors

To be sure, not all mutual fund innovation has ill-served fund investors. Indeed, among the greatest innovations in our industry's history was the money market fund. The first one gingerly began in 1971. But—simply by giving investors the true money market rate (less costs), rather than the regulation-limited rates offered on bank savings accounts—assets had burgeoned to $58 billion by 1979, reaching $237 billion at the peak in 1981, and accounting for fully 80 percent of mutual fund assets! It was money funds that gave the industry breathing room after the 1973–1974 bear market until stocks began their powerful and sustained recovery after the 1987 market crash.

Money fund assets total $2.8 trillion today, accounting for about 24 percent of industry assets. They remain a major factor in the financial markets and a remarkable service to investors. Yes, money funds have also created huge profits for fund managers. But in a sector in which the linkage between fund costs and fund returns is not only essentially dollar-for-dollar, but also clearly visible on a daily basis (simply by comparing relative yields), investors are heavily opting for the lower-cost funds. Nearly one-half of total money fund assets are invested in funds with expense ratios of less than 40 basis points. (Astonishingly, 68 money funds, including that very first fund, get away with ratios of 100 basis points or more.)*

A Self-Serving Conclusion

There are some mutual fund innovations, however, that have well-served fund investors even as they have created no profits for fund managers. I'll now name six major innovations that meet that standard. (Full disclosure: These comments are self-serving, in that they

---

*I don't have time to discuss in depth another promising fund innovation—"target retirement funds"—in which the investor selects his year of retirement and the fund gradually moves from a heavy equity position to a substantial bond position as retirement nears.

involve my creation of Vanguard, way back in 1974.) The first is the creation of Vanguard itself, an astonishing innovation in the traditional mutual fund structure, an innovation designed to resolve the dilemma that must be patently obvious after the events that I have chronicled this afternoon: *the direct conflict between the interests of fund managers, who make money by gathering assets, no matter what their character or durability; and fund investors, whose interests are ill-served by that strategy.* It is a simple truism that, for the fund industry *in toto*, "the more the managers *take*, the less the investors *make*."

The seminal Vanguard innovation was to reverse that tautology: "The *less* the managers take, the *more* the investors make." And so we created our novel and unique structure. Rather than having the mutual funds run under contract by the investment manager (the industry's traditional structure), in business to earn a profit on *its own* capital, at Vanguard the mutual funds would actually *own* their management company operating to serve solely the interests of its fund investors, offering its services on an "at-cost" basis, and in business to earn a profit on *their* capital.

This structure may not be—and is not—entirely conflict-free. But the proof of the pudding is in the eating: Vanguard today operates at a weighted expense ratio of about 21 basis points, compared to about 95 basis points for the fund industry. Applying this differential of 74 basis points to our present asset total of *$1.3 trillion*—up from *$1.4 billion* when we began—means savings of nearly $10 billion dollars *per year* to our fund investors. That's enough savings to keep our money market and bond funds consistently in the 95th (or higher) percentile among their peers, and to place our equity funds fairly consistently in the top quartile of their peers in the returns that we generate for our shareholder/owners.

It is that innovation—based on the commonsense observation that *costs matter*, and that funds should be, well, "of the shareholder, by the shareholder, and for the shareholder"—that has engendered the other major innovations that we have been responsible for over the years. By far the most important of these was our second strategic innovation. Immediately after Vanguard began operations in May 1975, we created the world's first market index mutual fund, simply tracking the returns of the S&P 500 Stock Index.

To do its job, the basic index fund takes diversification to the nth degree. It owns the lion's share of the entire U.S. market, and thus assures that its investors are guaranteed to capture the gross return of the stock market (or the bond market, or any discrete segment of each). But if this diversification assures that the index fund *earns* the market's return, it is rock-bottom costs that assure that it *delivers* to its investors nearly 100 percent of whatever returns the market may provide. (With its passive strategy, it also virtually eliminates portfolio trading costs, and also provides commensurate tax-efficiency.) As Warren Buffett says, "When the dumb investor realizes how dumb he is and buys a low-cost index fund, he becomes smarter than the smartest investors."

Our third major innovation was a *reverse* innovation. Early in 1977, shortly after the index fund began operations, we made the unprecedented decision to eliminate the sales loads on all Vanguard funds, moving from a *supply-driven* broker-dealer selling system to a *demand-driven* system dependent on investors' buying decisions. That change was designed in part to eliminate any incentive to create those fad-and-fashion funds that so devastated the returns of investors in the earlier eras I've described.

Our fourth innovation, also precedent-breaking, came in the bond fund sector. Up until 1977, bond funds were just that: "managed" portfolios of bonds whose maturities could be extended or reduced depending on the portfolio manager's outlook for interest rates. But skeptical that bond managers had—or ever *could* have—such prescience, we again did the obvious. We launched the industry's first defined-maturity series of bond funds, including a long-term portfolio, a short-term portfolio, and (I'm sure you know what's next!) an intermediate-term portfolio, all operated at rock-bottom cost. The idea was to hold broadly diversified portfolios of top-quality bonds (first tax-exempt municipals, later taxables), and maintain essentially constant maturities in each category. That simple concept of defined-maturity segments revolutionized the bond fund sector, and the three-tier bond portfolio quickly became the industry standard.

Our fifth major innovation came in 1992, when we determined to share the obvious economies of scale generated by our largest shareholders. It began with the creation of Vanguard's "Admiral" funds, which slashed expenses for large shareholders in our newly created series of U.S. Treasury bills, notes, and bonds, a concept that would later spread to similar Admiral share classes in most of our other funds, to the benefit of these key owners.

The sixth major Vanguard innovation—my final example today—is one that, like our bond innovation, would quickly be widely imitated (except, of course, for the low costs): our creation, in 1993, of the industry's first series of tax-managed funds. Unnecessary taxes are this industry's Achilles Heel, and we determined to create three funds that would serve the industry's taxable investors, incorporating both minimal costs and maximum tax-efficiency. This series of funds is one more innovation that has sprung from our unique organizational structure. But despite the power of our early innovation, the unremitting growth in our market share, and the growth in Vanguard assets to $1.3 trillion, that structure has yet to be emulated by a single one of our competitors. (Think about why that might be.)

Wrapping Up

Whether in banking or mutual funds, innovation has always been—and remains—a two-edged sword. I am not alone in this view. Consider these prophetic words of the eminent financier Henry Kaufman, from his fine book, *On Money and Markets*, published in 2001.

> When financial buccaneers and negligent executives step over the line, the damage is inflicted on all market participants . . . and the notion of financial trusteeship is too frequently lost in the shuffle. . . . Only by improving the balance between entrepreneurial innovation and more traditional values—prudence, stability, safety, and soundness—can we improve the ratio of benefits to costs in our financial system.

So yes, our financial system surely provides ample "fresh thinking that creates value," just as that *Economist* article on innovation that I mentioned at the outset suggested. But while financial innovations nearly always *create value* for those who devise, construct, promote, and market them, far too many of these innovations have *subtracted value* from investors who have trusted their creators and sponsors and invested in them, with damage that has now gone even further, into our society at large. It is time to face up to these realities.

Part Six

IDEALISM AND THE NEW GENERATION

O ne of the great treats of my long life has been the opportunity to express my values to young men and women, almost always in an educational setting. My goal is to encourage our next generation of national leaders to understand the blessings, rights, and responsibilities of citizenship, and the foundation of idealism that undergirds a worthy life. During this recent era of decadence among so many leaders of our business, commercial, and financial enterprises, this message is especially important. Most of all, I want to assure the new generation not only that idealism still lives, but that it must play an important role in their own careers.

In one of my previous books, *John Bogle on Investing: The First 50 Years*, published in 2001, there were five chapters based on my commencement speeches. I've enjoyed rereading those talks that I delivered at colleges—including Princeton University, University of Delaware, and Vanderbilt University—all those years ago. But my favorite is the short talk I gave to the graduating class at Pennsylvania's Haverford School, entitled "The Things by Which One Measures One's Life." (Don't be misled by the title. My message emphasized that "things" are the wrong way to measure one's life.)

The seven short chapters that follow continue that theme of idealism in many of the speeches that I've delivered during the past decade to members of the coming generation from which America's next leaders will emerge. Chapter 25, "Business as a Calling," was delivered to graduates of the William E. Simon School of Business at the

University of Rochester in 2000. There, citing the great economists Adam Smith, Joseph Schumpeter, and John Maynard Keynes, I call on these newly minted MBAs to, among other things, "put the grandeur and dignity of our own characters first, and only then consider our own self-interest."

The same themes resonate in Chapter 26, a talk given in May 2004 to graduates of the Smeal College of Business Administration at Pennsylvania State University. Here, I focus on the many meanings of "success," pointing out flaws in today's system of capitalism, and urging the new graduates to focus, not on conventional measures of success, defined by wealth, fame, and power, but on the right kind of success—success that contributes value to our society. These themes reemerge in Chapter 27, " 'This Above All: To Thine Own Self Be True,' " delivered in December 2004 to a younger audience, the upper school of Episcopal Academy in Pennsylvania, where my grandson, Christopher Bogle Webb St. John, introduced me to his schoolmates.

" 'Enough,' " the title of Chapter 28, was really fun to deliver, and includes (as you'll see) a wonderful story about what is enough in our lives. This 2007 talk was so well received by the audience of Georgetown MBAs that I decided to expand it into a short book, *Enough: True Measures of Money, Business and Life*. In its first printing in 2008, *Enough* made the *New York Times* bestseller list. In June 2010, it was republished in paperback form with some updated material, a wonderful prologue by Tom Peters (of *In Search of Excellence* fame), and a generous foreword by former president William Jefferson Clinton.

Chapter 29 was inspired by Rudyard Kipling's classic poem, "If." Delivering "If You Can Trust Yourself . . ." was a special delight. Another grandson and my namesake, John C. Bogle, III, was listening as I urged an attentive audience at Roxbury Latin School in Massachusetts to "fill the unforgiving minute . . . with sixty seconds' worth of distance run." In Chapter 30, in a 2010 commencement speech at Trinity (CT) College, I turn from Kipling to Churchill, stressing "The Fifth 'Never' " in Sir Winston Churchill's famous (if perhaps apocryphal) injunction, "Never give up. Never. Never. Never. Never. Never."

In my concluding chapter of Part Six I focus on an American giant, U.S. (and Princeton University) president Woodrow Wilson. Inspired by his essay, "When a Man Comes to Himself," I salute the 2009 graduates of Pennsylvania's Williamson Free School of Mechanical Trades. These young men, about to enter the world of work, will have careers that render services to our society in ways that the world of trade and the world of finance do not and cannot accomplish. The old English saying on pages 551 to 552 makes this point with crystal clarity. In the final words of this chapter, I wish these promising young tradesmen "the power, the stamina, the determination, the wisdom, the spirit of sharing and building, and the passion to leave everything that you touch better than you found it, the sheer pride in a job well done." That's good advice, I think, for all of us.

Chapter 25

Business as a Calling*

O n this glorious occasion, congratulations on earning the advanced business degree you will shortly receive. It is hardly a secret that you are entering a world of unparalleled prosperity in America. Business is booming; salaries to professional school graduates are generous almost beyond imagination; the stock market remains at a level undreamed of as little as a decade ago; our world is spinning in lightning-quick revolutions. The Information Revolution has become the analogue, as some would have it, of the Industrial Revolution of 100 years ago and the Agricultural Revolution 1,000 years before that.

Hyperactivity and speed—perhaps nicely captured by today's acronymic society (ATM, B2B, B2C, DSL, MP3, NASDAQ, to cite just a few)—seem to be the watchwords of these feverish times. We truly live in a New Era, offering exciting opportunities not only in new ventures, but in established firms eager to join the fray. But I want to talk to you about an element of business that I believe is even more important than the whirlwind of change circling around us today: *business as a calling.*

---

*Based on remarks delivered upon receiving the Honorary Doctor of Laws Degree from The University of Rochester William E. Simon Graduate School of Business Administration on June 11, 2000.

My First Break

Here's how the dictionary defines a "calling": A strong impulse toward a particular and higher course of action; the right thing to do; a career to which one is called by the courses of nature and fortune. But I confess that when I graduated from Princeton and went right to work—I didn't have the benefit of a business school education—I hardly considered business as my calling. My only objective, as far as I can recall, was to move on with my life, to do the best I could, and to earn a good living. But in an extraordinary stroke of luck, I had written my undergraduate thesis on the then "tiny but contentious" mutual fund industry. Because of the thesis, Walter L. Morgan, the founder of one of the industry's finest fund managers, gave me my first break, hiring me and then becoming my mentor. That was a half-century ago, but as I reread my thesis preparatory to its publication in my forthcoming book I realized that even then I had a powerful sense of idealism that even a half-century of experience has been unable to diminish. Indeed, I have little doubt that my idealism today is stronger than it's ever been.

Even back in 1951, I urged that the role of mutual funds was *to serve*—"to serve the needs of both individual and institutional investors," to serve them "in the most efficient, honest, and economical way possible . . . with a reduction in sales loads and management fees . . . minimizing investor misconceptions . . . and claiming no superiority over the stock market averages." As it has turned out, in those broad brushstrokes lay the core idea of the firm I would found in 1974: *The soundest way to participate in the long-term growth of our nation is simply to own the stocks of all of the businesses in America, to own them at rock-bottom agency costs, and to hold them forever.* (We apply that same concept to *all* segments of the financial markets.)

This investment strategy, at once innovative and counterintuitive, in turn depends on our unique corporate structure. We are a mutual enterprise owned, not by the fund *managers*, but by the fund *owners*, an enterprise in which service to shareholders and stewardship are our highest priorities. With that combination of investment ideas and human values, we have striven to become one of those all-too-rare enterprises: *a company that stands for something.* We stand for the primacy of the fund shareholder. And it works! Vanguard's growth is, to me at least, living proof that *enlightened idealism is sound economics.*

Business: An Honorable Career

Over the past half-century, business has come to be my personal calling. But I'm not here to talk about *my* life and career. I'm here to urge you to think about *your* calling as you go out into the wide, wide world of business, whether it be commerce or industry, finance or technology. I urge you to fulfill your own personal destiny, to gain a sense of contributing something wonderful—perhaps unique—to society, something that you're good at, something that you enjoy, something that without you would simply not exist.

Make no mistake: Business is an honorable career. Adam Smith told us why: "The pleasures of wealth and greatness strike the imagination as something grand and beautiful and noble, well worth the toil and anxiety . . . [they] keep in continual motion the industry of mankind, to build houses; to found cities and commonwealths, to invent and improve all the sciences and arts, which ennoble and embellish human life; which have entirely changed the whole face of the globe, and [have paved] the great high road of communication to the different nations of the earth."* *He wrote those words 240 years ago.* Could it be better said today?

Yet as I survey America at the millennium, I see our nation's business values eroding. Yes, I see marvelous entrepreneurship, brilliant technology, and creativity beyond imagination. But I see far too much greed, materialism, and waste to please my critical eye. I also see an economy too focused on the "haves" and not focused enough on the "have-nots," underinvesting in education, especially among those who need it most, not merely to *prosper*, but to *survive*. I see shocking misuse of the world's natural resources, as if they were ours to waste, rather than ours to preserve as a sacred trust for future generations, and I see

---

*Adam Smith, *The Theory of Moral Sentiments* (1759; Cambridge, England: Cambridge University Press, 2002).

a political system corrupted by a staggering infusion of money that, I assure you, is rarely given by disinterested corporations that expect no return on their investment.

Markets and Economics

But I also see hope. Everywhere I go I see hope in our youth— you!—and a spirit of idealism, too. Yes, business is about creativity and productivity, and goods and services and jobs and benefits, and success and wealth and greatness—all of these. But business must also be about ideals, about making the world a better place. You've spent two years here studying business, and have been inculcated in the belief that markets work. *They do!* And that economics is, finally, the language of business. *It is!* But without virtue, business is a hollow pursuit. In his remarkable book, *Business as a Calling*, the inspiration for the title of my remarks today, theologian Michael Novak catalogues three cardinal virtues of business:*

- The virtue of creativity . . . the inclination to notice what other people don't yet see, to act on insight . . . to foresee the needs of others and satisfy those needs . . . intellectual capital is the chief source of wealth.
- The virtue of building community . . . the wealth of *all* nations . . . more than ever, work toward a common goal is *work with others and work for others* . . . requiring fidelity, reliability, diligence, industriousness, and especially courage.
- The virtue of practical realism . . . common sense . . . paying your dues by getting your hands dirty and facing day-to-day frustrations . . . a strong sense of how the world really works, from the bottom up, gives you confidence in your ideas, no matter how unrealistic others may think them.

Yes, as Dr. Novak notes, we live in a society where *realism* seems a bit threadbare and outmoded, where what is said to be important is

---

* Michael Novak, *Business as a Calling* (New York: Free Press, 1996).

perception, and who knows whose perceptions are "true"? That notion does not please him, nor, most certainly, does it please me. Ever since I started Vanguard more than a quarter-century ago, my mantra has been: "If there is a gap between perception and reality, it is only a matter of time until reality takes over."

The Worldly Economists

Please realize that the ideal of business as a calling was hardly anathema to the worldly economists of the ages. Years *before* he wrote *The Wealth of Nations*, extolling the virtues of the invisible hand of competition and the essential nature of personal advantage and self-love in making the world's economic system work, Adam Smith wrote *The Theory of Moral Sentiments*. You may be surprised to learn that in that remarkable book he called for "reason, principle, conscience, the inhabitant of the breast, the great judge and arbiter of our conduct, who shows us the real littleness of ourselves, the propriety of generosity, of reining in the greatest interests of our own for yet the greater interests of others, the love of what is honorable and noble, the grandeur and dignity of our own characters."[*] Adam Smith again, here the apostle of virtue.

Joseph Schumpeter saw a similar spirit. Fully 90 years ago, he described for us the motives of the successful entrepreneur: "The joy of creating, of getting things done, of simply exercising one's energy and ingenuity . . . the will to conquer, the impulse to fight, to succeed, not for the fruits of success, but for success itself."[†] In my own calling, those passions continue to excite me, even as I speak to you this very morning.

And John Maynard Keynes followed suit, reinforcing my view that all of these gigabillions of numbers that fly around us are only numbers, quantities on a scoreboard that are only one measure—and, truth told, hardly the best measure—of an enterprise. Keynes emphasized

---

[*] Adam Smith, *The Theory of Moral Sentiments* (1759; Cambridge, England: Cambridge University Press, 2002).
[†] Joseph Schumpeter, *The Theory of Economic Development* (Cambridge, MA: Harvard University Press, 1934).

that it was the merest pretense to suggest that an enterprise is "mainly actuated by the statements in its own prospectus, however candid and sincere . . . based on an exact calculation of benefits to come." Rather, the key to success is *animal spirits*—"a spontaneous urge to action rather than inaction," warning that "if animal spirits are dimmed and the spontaneous optimism falters, leaving us to depend on nothing but a mathematical expectation, enterprise will fade and die."*

Meet Some Great Need . . . Perform Some Great Deed

These three economists—the greatest in modern history—are all sending us the same message. Let's follow their advice. Let's put animal spirits first, and gigabillions second; the joy of creating and the will to conquer first, and the mindless conformity of greed last; and the greater interest of others, the love of what is honorable and noble and the grandeur and dignity of our own characters first, and only then consider our own self-interest. Strive to meet some great need or perform some great deed, not for yourself, but for others. Enter into business with idealism and enthusiasm and energy. Enter into the battle for ideas, a battle for which you've been so well prepared in your studies here, with determination and joy.

Business has been my calling for a half-century. It's been wonderful, and each one of you can be as blessed in your lives and careers as I have been in mine, for today the opportunities are infinite. Go out and make business *your* calling. Help to build a better world.

Just go out and do it!

---

*John Maynard Keynes, *The General Theory of Employment, Interest, and Money* (New York: Macmillan, 1936; Harcourt, Brace, 1964).

Chapter 26

The Right Kind
of Success*

Congratulations to each one of you for having the brains, the guts, and the determination to earn your bachelor's degree from this great American university. You have earned the right to at least a few moments of pride, and I know that your families, here supporting you today, are proud as well. They should be!

Doubtless most of you will soon be entering the world of business, seeking success in whatever careers you find your calling. So I'd like to spend a few brief moments musing on what we mean by *success*, and how we measure it. To tip my hand, I think that achieving the *right* kind of success is a far loftier goal than would be suggested by its conventional definition.

When I graduated from college 53 years ago, I had no thought of going on to business school. Without outside resources but with the help of generous scholarship aid, I'd worked my way through

---

*Based on remarks delivered upon receiving the Honorary Degree of Doctor of Humane Letters at Pennsylvania State University, The Mary Jean and Frank P. Smeal College of Business Administration, State College, Pennsylvania, on May 15, 2004.

Princeton University, and it was, simply put, time to go to work—just as it now is for you—time, at long last, to begin my career. Of course I sought "success," and its going-definition then—"wealth, fame, and power"—seemed reasonable enough to me. And the dictionary still confirms that: "the prosperous achievement of something attempted, the attainment of an object, usually wealth or position, according to one's desire."

While a half-century-plus has passed since then, I see little reason to believe that wealth, fame, and power do not remain the three main attributes of success: *but not in the conventional way in which I defined them all those years ago.* I have come to realize that *wealth* is ill-measured by using mere dollars; that *fame* is ill-measured by public notoriety; and that *power* is ill-measured solely by control over others.

Financial wealth, in fact, is a shallow measure of success. If we accept dollars as our standard, then "money is the measure of the man," and what could be more foolish than that? So how should wealth be measured? What about a life well-lived? What about a family closely bound by love? Who could be wealthier than a man or woman whose calling provides benefits to mankind, or to fellow citizens, or even to a community or neighborhood?

It is not that money doesn't matter. Who among us would not seek resources sufficient to fully enjoy our life and liberty? The security of freedom from want, the ability to pursue our chosen careers, the wherewithal to educate our children. But how much wealth does *that* require? Indeed, we ought to wonder whether the super-wealth we observe at the highest reaches of our society—the ability to acquire an infinite number of the "things" of life—is not more bane than blessing.

Fame, too, is a flawed measure of success. Today, we think especially of the famous imperial chief executives of our corporations, our institutions, and our governments, whose public images seem to give them immunity from the checks and balances of gatekeepers like directors or regulators or courts, or even from their shareowners, who have been conspicuously absent from the governance scene. Too often, though, these CEOs are conceited enough to believe that "I did it all myself"; arrogant enough to view themselves as creators when they are so often merely bureaucratic caretakers; and greedy enough to believe they deserve to be paid, not on the creation of economic value, but on the basis of how much other CEOs are paid—*peer* pay rather than *performance* pay. Such undeserved fame ought to embarrass our society.

Fame, of course, is the great ego-builder of our age. But from what source, and to what avail? The momentary fame of our sports heroes and the glittering fame of our entertainers give us the joy of seeing human beings at the very peak of their potential, but in the fast-paced world of today, much of that glow rarely lasts more than the metaphorical 15 minutes that Andy Warhol promised each one of us. Fame for real accomplishment is one thing; fame based on self-aggrandization, fame that is ill-deserved, and fame that is used for base purposes are quite different things. And please never forget that many—indeed most—of those who make the greatest contributions to the daily working of our society never experience even a moment of fame.

And that brings us to *power*. Sure, power to run an enterprise is a thrill, and power over the *person* and power over the corporate *purse* are fun. (I know!) But when power is used capriciously and arbitrarily, when power is reflected in grossly excessive perquisites, and when power is employed to create ego-building (and compensation-enhancing!) mergers and unwise capital expenditures that are more likely to detract from corporate value than to increase it, not only the shareholders of the corporation but its loyal employees—indeed society as a whole—are the losers.

What we ought to respect is power for a worthy purpose—the power of the intellect, the power of morality, the power to enable the people with whom we work to grow in skill and spirit alike; power that assures respect for the humblest to the highest souls who dedicate themselves to an enterprise; power to help one's fellow man. Power that is, using Adam Smith's ancient words, "something grand and beautiful and noble, well worth the toil and anxiety, to keep in motion the industry of mankind, to invest and improve the sciences and arts, and to ennoble and embellish human life." Now *that's* power worth seeking.

So what are we to make of all of these mixed measures of success? Perhaps the famed economist Joseph Schumpeter can help. Ambitious people are driven, he suggested, by "the joy of creating, of getting things done, of simply exercising one's energy and ingenuity; and by the will to conquer, the impulse to fight, to succeed for the sake, not of the fruits of success" (i.e., wealth, fame, and power), "but of success itself."

Such success cannot be measured in monetary terms, nor in terms of the amount of power one may exercise over others, nor in the illusory fame of inevitably transitory public notice. But it *can* be measured in our contributions to building a better world, in helping our fellow man, in siring—or bearing—children who themselves become loving human beings and good citizens.

In this quest, those of us who select business as our calling carry a special burden. For in our society today it is in business and finance that the most people make the most money, hold the most power, and enjoy an astonishing level of fame. So, as you go out into the competitive dog-eat-dog arena of commerce, earn the *right* kind of success, maintaining your values, your ethics, your bearings, and your integrity.

In today's business world, I fear, our leaders have sought the *wrong* kind of success, and indeed have too often engaged in overreaching that is unethical and often illegal. If our generation has taken business and finance down the wrong track—*and we have*—it is a betrayal of the values of capitalism that have created the greatest global propriety and well-being in all human history.

For your generation, the failure of my generation is your opportunity—the opportunity of a lifetime to restore integrity to capitalism, to replace egotism with idealism. We're all in the human race together, and those of us who are lucky enough to earn a good living through our business careers must, as we run the long race of a life well-lived, do our best to serve our fellow man.

For half a century plus, business has been my calling. As I continue that long journey, I strive to define success by the *right* kinds of wealth, fame, and power. In the coming era in which the opportunities are infinite, I hope for each of you those same kinds of success. Go out and make business your calling; go out and seek *the right kind of success.* Especially, in these troubled times, you can help to build a better world.

Chapter 27

"This Above All: To Thine Own Self Be True"*

While I'm proud of my reputation, as expressed in that lovely introduction by Christopher Bogle Webb St. John, my wonderful grandson, I confess to you all—this may surprise you—that I'm a bit intimidated to stand here before you today. While many of your parents may know a bit about me and Vanguard, you are probably wondering just what this ancient soul can possibly say that would even vaguely interest you. Why would I think that? Because I was actually your age once, trying to find my way in life, in school, and with my family and friends.

My hesitancy is illustrated by this story that I heard last year in a sermon by a Scottish preacher: A father is rapping on his son's door, trying to wake him up to go to school.

---

* Based on a speech delivered at the Episcopal Academy, Overbrook, Pennsylvania, on December 2, 2004.

Through the closed door, the son shouts:

"I'm not going to get up, and I'll give you three reasons why.
"One, I hate school.
"Two, the children tease me.
"Three, because education is boring."

The father shouts right back:

"You must get up, and I'll give *you* three reasons why.
"One, it's your duty.
"Two, because you're 45 years old.
"And three, because you're the headmaster."

Well, despite my concern about "relating" to you young people of my grandchildren's generation, I promised Chris that I'd be here, so here I am. But unlike that apocryphal headmaster, I join you with anticipation and delight.

A Word about Vanguard and Simplicity

I don't want to say too much about my career. Creating Vanguard, and then running the firm during most of the years from its tiny inception in 1974 with but $1 billion of assets, to becoming, 30 years later, one of the largest financial institutions in the world, managing $750 billion of other people's money is, well, whatever it is. But helping 16 million investors to accumulate wealth to help provide for their retirement savings, the homes they buy, their children's college educations—and, for that matter, their children's independent school educations—delights me. Rare is the day that passes without my hearing from, or talking to, at least one of these human beings whom Vanguard has pledged to serve with a sense of trusteeship, duty, and honor, which I understand is your chapel theme of this season.

What makes us unique? The first secret of whatever success Vanguard has enjoyed is that the less the money manager *takes*, the more the fund investor *makes*. Remarkable! So we hold our expenses to rock-bottom levels and manage our mutual funds primarily in the interests of their owners rather than the interests of their managers.

The second secret is that we offer investment programs characterized by utter simplicity. Our foundation is the "index" fund, a fund that simply buys shares in every stock in the stock market and holds them forever, an idea that, when we pioneered it nearly 30 years ago, was heresy. But of course it worked.

I've been described, and not kindly, as a poor guy whose only asset is "the uncanny ability to recognize the obvious." Paradoxical as it may seem, that's probably true. Although important ideas are said to go from *controversial* to *celebrated*, the ideas underlying Vanguard's creation have actually gone from *contemptible* to *commonplace*. "The earth is round!" someone says, and the world's first response is "You're mad!" And then, after someone takes measurements, "Of course it's round! Who didn't know that?"*

Bumps along the Road of Life

But enough about success, whatever exactly that may be. Far more important, you should know that my life and career have not been without challenges. There are lots of bumps along the road of life— many of you have already had some—and all of you—yes, *all* of you—will one day face challenges that will demand that you draw on resources such as honor, courage, character, and determination that you may not even know you possess. Perhaps you can learn something from just four of the challenges that I've dealt with in my own life, each of which, however painful at the time, played a major role in whatever it is that I've been able to accomplish.

First, I grew up in a family of extremely modest means. Ever since I was about eight, whatever I needed or wanted, I had to earn the money myself. I've delivered papers; I've waited on tables—I did it in the summer and the winter; I did it at Blair Academy; and I did it at Princeton, too. (I obviously had a talent for waiting on tables!) I've clerked in two post-offices, been a runner for a brokerage firm, and an

---

* This formulation was put forth in the *New Yorker*, April 1, 2002, regarding the ideas of philosopher Karl Popper.

intern reporter for a newspaper. I've managed a ticket office, served as a camp counselor, surveyed consumers, and shipped gift packages. Whatever it took, I did it. While most of you—certainly not all of you—are growing up with far more material advantages than I even dreamed of as a child, having to work never bothered me. It was simply my lot in life. (You could say it still is!)

But as I've told my own children, "I feel badly that you didn't grow up with all the advantages I had." Not disadvantages, *advantages!* Having to take responsibility, to be self-reliant, to follow orders, to deal with adversity, to work with people from all walks of life, to develop the determination required to overcome the challenges of life—all proved to be priceless blessings. So here's **Lesson #1** of four: Whatever your own circumstances, "make the most of your life." *Yes, you can do it, too!*

Second, I nearly flunked out of college. Working my way through Princeton with those time-consuming jobs, and not the most intellectually gifted of souls, I stumbled badly in my sophomore year, especially over my economics textbook, written by a young economist at Massachusetts Institute of Technology named Paul Samuelson. My D+ average at midterm, if it persisted, would have cost me my scholarship, and with it my Princeton career, for no one was going to pay my tuition for me. But I pressed on, recovered slightly, and ended the term with a not-entirely-snappy C average.

Never Give Up, Never, Etc.

But after stumbling so badly that my college education was at risk, my grades, magically, began to improve. To my astonishment, when I graduated, I was awarded high honors. Even more amazing, 50 years after *his* book had almost done me in, Dr. Samuelson, by then a Nobel Laureate in Economics, wrote the foreword to *my* first book. **Lesson #2:** Never give up. Never. Never. Never. Never. Never! *Don't you ever give up, either!*

A third anecdote: In 1965, I became the head of the mutual fund firm I had joined after Princeton. Headstrong, overly self-confident, ambitious, and immature—probably even stupid!—I put together an unwise merger with another firm. By the early 1970s, it backfired, and in January 1974 the new partners with whom I shared ownership banded together and fired me. I had made a huge error, and I had paid an enormous price for it. Who said life isn't fair?

Being fired isn't fun. But getting fired proved to be an opportunity in disguise, if very deep disguise. For it was that firing that gave me the opportunity to create Vanguard, and I leaped at the prospect. You could say that I left my old job the same way I started my new one: "Fired with enthusiasm." (Think about that double entendre.) And that unique rebel firm that broke all the rules—a firm that might otherwise *never have existed*—has changed the world of investing for the better. **Lesson #3:** When a door closes (mine slammed), a window opens. *You will find that, too!*

My fourth and final anecdote has to do with physical disabilities (I should probably use today's politically correct lingo, describing them as "issues" or "challenges"). In 1960, barely 31 years old, I suffered the first of many heart attacks that would follow. I was told that I would never work again, and that I was unlikely to reach age 40. But, thick-skinned and congenitally focused on just doing the day's labors, I kept on going. My flawed heart continued to deteriorate, and by 1994, only half of it was still working.

In October 1995, at death's door, I entered Hahnemann Hospital in Philadelphia to await a heart transplant. I was connected to tubes that bubbled life-sustaining medicine into me for 128 days before my new heart arrived on February 21, 1996. I'm now enjoying the ninth year of my miraculous "second chance at life," playing squash and biking again, climbing (small) mountains, working away, writing my fifth book, reveling in my family, and counting my infinite blessings. So, **Lesson #4** is my family's longtime motto: "Press on, regardless." *And you, too, must press on, regardless!*

The Principles of Character

When I talk about some of the principles of character that have helped me along the hard road of life—make the most of your advantages; never give up; when doors close, windows open; press on regardless—please understand that I'm not merely talking about my own experience, but the principles of character that you will need if you are to deal successfully with the inevitable bumps on the uncertain road that each of you will march down, too.

No generation ever has it easy. Life has a way of creating new challenges, and the wealth of American life today has created its own challenges—a feeling of entitlement, of economic power, and of military might that has earned for our nation the admiration, the envy, and, yes, the hatred of much of mankind. The world in which you are growing up is more demanding than the more innocent world of six long decades ago, when I was about your age. I'm counting on you to help America to measure up to that challenge.

Competition is in the air, and healthy competition is what has driven our American society and our economy to world preeminence. But it is unhealthy competition that is, I fear, beginning to take hold. Competing to do your personal best is one thing; competing to gain, by fair means or foul, an edge over a classmate or a rival is something entirely different. A recent article in the *Princeton Alumni Weekly* described this as "The Age of Angst" for our young people. Your parents struggle to motivate you to do your homework and excel—in studies, in sports, and in social and extracurricular activities—often to get into one of the so-called "best" colleges. That's fine, as far as it goes. But competition for what? For test scores rather than learning? For form rather than substance? For prestige rather than virtue? For certainty rather than ambiguity? For following their stars rather than your own?

I don't mean to knock parents. After all, the fifth commandment says, "Honor thy father and mother." So always remember, as the old song goes, "Be kind to your parents; remember that grownups are at a difficult stage in life." But at least the older among you are at an age where it's time to take much of the responsibility for your development to yourself. Most of you—even from the humblest of backgrounds—have grown up with entitlements—loving families, food and shelter, a peaceful community—that would be the envy of 99 percent of the world's six billion citizens. With those blessings, you are indeed a royal generation. But not if you lack honor and character.

What Kind of Character?

In a recent *New York Times* essay, David Brooks put it well: "Highly educated young people are tutored, taught, and monitored in all aspects of their lives, except the most important, which is character-building. But without character and courage, nothing else lasts."* What kind of character is it that you will need? The Old Testament describes it well:

> What is man that you are mindful of him, the son of man that you care for him?
> You made him a little lower than the heavenly beings and crowned him with glory and honor . . .
> The fear of the Lord teaches a man wisdom, and humility comes before honor . . .
> Humility and the fear of the Lord bring wealth and honor and life . . .
> He who pursues righteousness and love finds life, prosperity and honor.

The affluent world in which you exist doesn't easily create the ability to build your own character. Often building character requires failure; it requires adversity; it requires contemplation; it requires determination and steadfastness; it requires finding your own space as an individual. And it surely requires honor.

While as I grew up I had the advantage of having to earn whatever I got, most of you have the disadvantage of wealth. So, understand St. Paul's warning: "They that will be rich fall into temptation and a snare and into many foolish and hurtful lusts, which drown men in destruction and perdition. For the love of money is the root of all evil." But you needn't love money to have money, so don't forget, as you heard earlier, St. Luke's demand: "For unto whomsoever much is given, of him much shall be required. . . . And to whom men have committed much, of them they will ask the more." And so the world will ask even more of you.

---

*David Brooks, " 'Moral Suicide,' a la Wolfe," *New York Times*, November 16, 2004.

Be True to Yourself

It's up to you to decide just who it is you are, to establish the right expectations among those with whom you have walked, and will walk, along the road of life—parents, siblings, friends, teachers, spiritual advisers. How to do it? Shakespeare gave the best advice of all:

> This above all, to thine own self be true,
> And it must follow as the night the day,
> Thou canst not then be false to any man.

So be true to yourself. *Be yourself!* And if you're not the kind of person you know you should be—the kind of person you want to be and can be—make yourself a *better* person. You can do it! For each one of us has within our own selves and our own souls the ability to be the exemplar of the dictionary definition of *honor*: "High in character, nobility of mind, scorn of meanness, magnanimity, a fine sense of what is right, and a respect for the dignity of virtue."

Why seek honor? For the very reason that Shakespeare set down in *Richard II*:

> Mine honor is my life, both grow in one.
> Take honor from me and my life is done.

I've loved delivering this message. Unlike that headmaster whom I described at the onset, I'm glad I got up early, and I'm glad I came to school.

Chapter 28

"Enough"*

H ere's how I recall the wonderful story that sets the theme
for my remarks today: At a party given by a billionaire on
Shelter Island, the late Kurt Vonnegut informs his pal, the
author Joseph Heller, that their host, a hedge fund manager, had made
more money in a single day than Heller had earned from his wildly
popular novel, *Catch-22*, over its whole history. Heller responds, "Yes,
but I have something he will never have—*enough*."

Enough. I was stunned by its simple eloquence, to say nothing of its
relevance to some of the vital issues arising in American society today.
Many of them revolve around money—yes, *money*—increasingly, in our
"bottom-line" society, the Great God of prestige, the Great Measure
of the Man (and Woman). So this morning I have the temerity to ask
you soon-to-be-minted MBA graduates, most of whom will enter the
world of commerce, to consider with me the role of "enough" in business and entrepreneurship in our society, "enough" in the dominant
role of the financial system in our economy, and "enough" in the values you will bring to the fields you choose for your careers.

---

*Based on the commencement address to MBA graduates upon receiving the
Honorary Degree of Doctor of Humane Letters from Georgetown University,
May 18, 2007.

Kurt Vonnegut loved to speak to college students. He believed, if I may paraphrase here, that "we should catch young people before they become CEOs, investment bankers, consultants, and money managers (and especially hedge fund managers), and do our best to poison their minds with humanity." And in my remarks this morning, I'll try to poison your minds with a little bit of that humanity.

The Costs of the Financial Sector

Over the past two centuries, our nation has moved from being an agricultural economy, to a manufacturing economy, to a service economy, and now to a predominantly financial economy.

But our financial economy, by definition, subtracts from the value created by our productive businesses. Think about it: While the owners of business enjoy the dividend yields and earnings growth that our capitalistic system creates, those who play in the financial markets capture those investment gains only *after* the costs of financial intermediation are deducted. Thus, while investing in American business is a *winner's* game, beating the stock market before those costs is a *zero-sum* game. But after intermediation costs are deducted, beating the market—for all of us as a group—becomes a *loser's game*.

Yes, the more that our financial system *takes*, the less our investors *make*. Yet the financial field is where the money is made in modern-day America, the breeding ground for the wealthiest of our citizens. (If you made less than $140 million last year, you didn't make *enough* to rank among the 25 highest-paid hedge fund managers.) When we add up all those hedge fund fees, all those mutual fund management fees and operating expenses; all those commissions to brokerage firms and fees to financial advisors; investment banking and legal fees for all those mergers and IPOs; and the enormous marketing and advertising expenses entailed in the distribution of financial products, we're talking about some $500 billion dollars *per year*. That sum, extracted from whatever returns the stock and bond markets are generous enough to deliver to investors, is surely *enough*, if you will, to seriously undermine the odds in favor of success for our citizens who are accumulating savings for retirement.

Yet the fact is that the finance sector has become by far our nation's largest generator of corporate profits, larger even than the *combined* profits of our huge energy and health-care sectors, and almost three *times* as much as either manufacturing or information technology.* Twenty-five years ago, financials accounted for only about 6 percent of the earnings of the 500 giant corporations that compose the Standard & Poor's 500 Stock Index. Ten years ago, the financial sector share had risen to 20 percent. And last year, the financial sector profits had soared to an all-time high of 27 percent. If we add the earnings of the financial affiliates of our giant manufacturers (think General Electric Capital, for example, or the auto-financing arms of General Motors and Ford) to this total, financial earnings now likely exceed 33 percent of the earnings of the S&P 500. While that share may or may not be *enough*, it seems likely to continue to grow, at least for a while.

We're moving, or so it seems, to a world where we're no longer *making* anything in this country; we're merely *trading* pieces of paper, swapping stocks and bonds back and forth with one another, and paying our financial croupiers a veritable fortune. We're also adding even more costs by creating ever more complex financial derivatives in which huge and unfathomable risks are being built into our financial system. "When enterprise becomes a mere bubble on a whirlpool of speculation," as the great British economist John Maynard Keynes warned us 70 years ago, the consequences may be dire. "When the capital development of a country becomes a by-product of the activities of a casino, the job of capitalism is likely to be ill-done."

Once a profession in which business was subservient, the field of money management and Wall Street has become a business in which the profession is subservient. Harvard Business School Professor Rakesh Khurana was right when he defined the conduct of a true professional with these words: "I will create value for society, rather than extract it." And yet money management, by definition, extracts value from

---

*For the record, the 2006 operating earnings of the S&P 500 totaled $787 billion. The earnings of the major sectors (in billions) were: Financials $215; Energy $121; Health Care $79; Manufacturing and Technology each $81.

the returns earned by our business enterprises. Warren Buffett's wise partner, Charlie Munger, lays it on the line:

> Most money-making activity contains profoundly antisocial effects. . . . As high-cost modalities become ever more popular . . . the activity exacerbates the current harmful trend in which ever more of the nation's ethical young brain-power is attracted into lucrative money-management and its attendant modern frictions, as distinguished from work providing much more value to others.*

Standards for a Professional Career

But I'm not telling you *not* to go into the highly profitable field of managing money. Rather, I present three standards for you to consider.

One, if you do enter this field, do so with your eyes wide open, recognizing that any endeavor that extracts value from its clients may, in times more troubled than these, find that it has been hoist by its own petard. It is said on Wall Street, correctly, that "money has no conscience," but don't allow that truism to let you ignore your own conscience, nor to alter your own conduct and character.

Two, when you begin to invest so that you will have enough for your own retirement many decades hence, do so in a way that minimizes the extraction by the financial community of the returns generated by business. This is, yes, a sort of self-serving† recommendation to invest in low-cost all-U.S.—and global—stock market index funds, the only way to guarantee your fair share of whatever returns our financial markets are generous enough to provide.

Three, no matter what career you choose, do your best to hold high its traditional professional values, now swiftly eroding, in which serving the client is *always* the highest priority. And don't ignore the greater good of your community, your nation, and your world. After William Penn, "We pass through this world but once, so do now any

---

* Charles Munger, speech before the Foundation Financial Officers Group, Santa Monica, California, on October 14, 1998.
† Self-serving because I created, in 1975, the world's first index mutual fund.

good you can do, and show now any kindness you can show, for we shall not pass this way again."

Most commencement speakers like to sum up by citing some eminent philosopher to endorse his message. I'm no exception. So I now offer to you new Masters of Business Administration these words from Socrates, spoken 2,500 years ago, as he challenged the citizens of Athens.

I honor and love you: but why do you who are citizens of this great and mighty nation care so much about laying up the greatest amount of money and honor and reputation, and so little about wisdom and truth and the greatest improvement of the soul. Are you not ashamed of this? . . . I do nothing but go about persuading you all, not to take thought for your persons and your properties, but first and chiefly to care about the greatest improvement of the soul. I tell you that virtue is not given by money, but that from virtue comes money and every other good of man.

I close by returning to Kurt Vonnegut's story, which, when I finally tracked it down, turned out to be a poem. It's delightful; even better, it's only 92 words long:

True story, Word of Honor:
Joseph Heller, an important and funny writer
now dead,
and I were at a party given by a billionaire
on Shelter Island.
I said, "Joe, how does it make you feel
to know that our host only yesterday
may have made more money
than your novel 'Catch-22'
has earned in its entire history?"
And Joe said, "I've got something he can never have."
And I said, "What on earth could that be, Joe?"
And Joe said, "The knowledge that I've got enough."
Not bad! Rest in Peace!*

---

*Kurt Vonnegut, "Joe Heller," *New Yorker*, May 16, 2005.

But it's not time for any of *you* to rest in peace, or to rest in any other way. Bright futures lie before you. There's the world's work to be done, and there are never enough citizens with determined hearts, courageous character, intelligent minds, and idealistic souls to do it. Yes, our world already has quite enough guns, political platitudes, arrogance, disingenuousness, self-interest, snobbishness, superficiality, war, and the certainty that God is on our side. But it *never* has enough conscience, nor enough tolerance, idealism, justice, compassion, wisdom, humility, self-sacrifice for the greater good, integrity, courtesy, poetry, laughter, and generosity of substance and spirit. It is these elements that I urge you to carry into your careers, and remember that the great game of life is not about money; it is about doing your best to build the world anew.

And that's *enough* . . . at least for today.

Chapter 29

If You Can
Trust Yourself . . .*

I t's a special honor for me to have the opportunity to speak to you
young gentlemen of Roxbury Latin School. I hardly need tell
you that your school is widely considered to be among the best
schools—some say *the* best—in America. I'm particularly proud to
have your schoolmate, my grandson, and my namesake, John Bogle, III,
here in the audience.

Believe it or not, gentlemen, we have a lot in common. I was once
your age—yes, once a seventh-grader, and finally a twelfth grader, and
there is much about those years that I carry in my mind to this day—
memories of my classmates and especially of my teachers, whom I've
come to describe as "characters who had character." They demanded
of us boys not only that we study and learn, but that we held high
values and developed in ourselves the kind of character to which we
were witness every day. I have no doubt that you are finding the same
experience right here.

---

*Based on an address to the student body at the Roxbury Latin School, Roxbury,
Massachusetts, on March 30, 2009.

What's more, like Roxbury Latin, Blair Academy, the superb school in New Jersey where I spent my final two school years, was an all-boys' school. And so, for that matter, was Princeton University (I guess I should say, "all-*men's* school"), where I spent the following four years. I loved those years, and while both Blair and Princeton are now coeducational, I hope that all-boys' and all-girls' schools will remain as options for our youth for as far ahead as we can see.

In any event, speaking at an all-boys' school gives me the opportunity to quote from one of my favorite poems, which is about becoming a man. My theme is taken from a single phrase of that poem: "If you can trust yourself. . . ." *If you can trust yourself.* Now, trusting what is in your own heart and soul is a truly big idea. But I didn't think much about it until I was perhaps 15 years of age, and my father read me this poem that I have never forgotten. Written 100 years ago by the British poet, Rudyard Kipling, it was entitled "IF. . ."

Many of you may already know it, but since it is a fairly short poem, I'd like to read it to you.

IF . . .

IF you can keep your head when all about you
Are losing theirs and blaming it on you,
If you can trust yourself when all men doubt you,
But make allowance for their doubting too;
If you can wait and not be tired by waiting,
Or being lied about, don't deal in lies,
Or being hated, don't give way to hating,
And yet don't look too good, nor talk too wise:

If you can dream—and not make dreams your master;
If you can think—and not make thoughts your aim;
If you can meet with Triumph and Disaster
And treat those two impostors just the same;
If you can bear to hear the truth you've spoken
Twisted by knaves to make a trap for fools,
Or watch the things you gave your life to, broken,
And stoop and build 'em up with worn-out tools.

If you can make one heap of all your winnings
And risk it on one turn of pitch-and-toss,
And lose, and start again at your beginnings
And never breathe a word about your loss;
If you can force your heart and nerve and sinew
To serve your turn long after they are gone,
And so hold on when there is nothing in you
Except the Will which says to them: "Hold on!"

If you can talk with crowds and keep your virtue,
Or walk with Kings—nor lose the common touch,
If neither foes nor loving friends can hurt you,
If all men count with you, but none too much;
If you can fill the unforgiving minute
With sixty seconds' worth of distance run,
Yours is the Earth and everything that's in it,
And—which is more—you'll be a Man, my son!

Many years ago, I read this poem to my own two sons—including John's father—and, lest they forget its message, had copies of it framed for them. When the time comes, I'm hoping that *my* son in turn will read it to *his* son, your classmate. And if any of you would like to read it, well, just Google it. Better yet, stay with Google long enough to hear Kipling himself reading it, happily captured for eternity on film before his death in 1926. If you're into tennis, go to YouTube and hear the poem recited by Roger Federer and Rafael Nadal, with some of their great action shots showing behind them. (Yes, even at my ancient age, I Google, and I visit YouTube. You can even find *me* there!)

Of course a lot happens in 100 years, and the world has changed dramatically since "IF . . ." was written. But the ideas expressed by Kipling are eternal. So what I'll try to do this morning is relate just a few of those phrases from "IF . . ." to my own life and career, and to their relevance to dealing with the global financial and economic crisis that we citizens face today, the worst since the Great Depression of the early 1930s.

Reflections on My Career

As much as I appreciate the generous introduction by your headmaster, I feel the obligation to bring my own life and career down to earth. I'm a pretty ordinary human being, blessed with a decent intelligence, extraordinary good luck, teachers and mentors who saw some potential in me and demanded that I live up to it, and (with apologies for bragging) a powerful determination to get ahead in the world.

Part of that luck, of course, was being "Born in the USA." (Yes, I'm a fan both of the Boss and of the United States of America.) Another part—this may surprise you—was being born into a family whose wealth had vanished during the Great Depression. For when one is required at a young age to work for what he gets, you learn to take responsibility, to follow orders, and to work with people from all walks of life—"to talk with crowds" in Kipling's words, "nor lose the common touch," a truly priceless blessing as we move from school to college to career.

When I attended Blair and then Princeton, I was given full scholarships that covered my tuition, and earned the money for my room and board by working at demanding, time-consuming jobs. The greatest break of my academic life came in December 1949, when I happened upon an article in *Fortune* magazine that described the then-tiny mutual fund industry. That piece of luck changed my life, for I immediately decided that mutual funds would be the subject of my senior thesis, which set the stage for my now-near-58-year career in the fund industry.

Put simply, my 125-page thesis evaluated the fund industry and found it wanting. Idealistic to a fault, I demanded that mutual funds be operated solely in the interests of their shareholders, in "the most honest, efficient, and economical way possible." I also warned that mutual funds "could make no claim to superiority over the market averages" (i.e., that stock fund managers as a group could not beat the stock market).

The thesis led me right into the fund industry. After I graduated in 1951, Walter Morgan, my greatest mentor, liked the thesis enough to offer me a job at his budding Wellington Management Company. By 1965, at the tender (and in fact, for me, rather immature) age of 35, I was running the firm. But I impetuously entered into an unwise merger, and in 1974 my new partners joined together and fired me from what I had considered "my" company. It was not a pleasant experience. But, yes, I learned something about how to "meet with Disaster," and quickly realized that I should treat my own disaster, using Kipling's word, as an "imposter," just one more obstacle that it was up to me to overcome.

So I used the heavily disguised opportunity created by my being fired to found a new firm built on those idealistic principles that I expressed in my thesis. (As it is said, "If you're given a lemon, make lemonade." No, that's *not* Kipling.) I named the firm Vanguard, and ran it for the next 22 years. Our policies were based on *honest* disclosure, *efficient* management, and—above all—on *economical* operations. (Remember those words—"honest, efficient, and economical"—from my thesis?) We chose a unique and untested, truly *mutual* structure in which we eliminated conflicts of interest by having the fund shareholders own our management company; and we held our costs to the bare-bones minimum, by far the lowest in the field, saving them tens of billions of dollars over the years. And if our managed-fund peers couldn't beat the market, well, we would—and did—create a "market fund" that would beat our managed-fund peers. Of course it did just that, and that first *index* mutual fund that we created is now essentially the largest fund on the face of the globe.

It would be easy to describe as a "Triumph" Vanguard's remarkable ascent to becoming the industry's unarguable leader in the superior investment returns we've earned for our shareholders, in the minuscule costs that they bear, and in the overwhelming trust that our shareholders have placed in us. But I couldn't forget Kipling's implicit warning, "if you can meet both Triumph and Disaster, and treat those two imposters just the same." After my earlier brush with Disaster in my career, it was easy for me to understand that Triumph, too, is an imposter. Far better than preening over the past, please realize that it is focusing on the challenges that lie in the future that must be the order of the day.

Creating a new kind of fund company defied the conventional wisdom. So did creating a new kind of fund that would not trade stocks in the market, but simply buy *all* of the stocks in the stock market—owning corporate America, and holding it, well, forever. The world doubted that this tiny new firm called Vanguard would make a go of it. In fact, our index fund was called "Bogle's Folly" for years. (But no longer!) So, yes, "when all men doubt you," as Kipling put it, simply "trust yourself." And when opportunity knocks, don't forget to answer the door!

Reflections on Today's Crisis

In our present financial and economic crisis, Vanguard's simple strategies have paid off in spades. In a fund industry now deeply troubled by its aggressive marketing of investment fads, its speculative policies, its excessive costs, and its periodic scandals, our firm remains vibrant, healthy, and pristine. In fact, much of today's crisis finds its roots in the very failures of our financial sector that I described in my ancient thesis, and, most recently, in my seventh book, published last November.

In *Enough: True Measures of Money, Business, and Life*, I warn of too much cost and not enough value; too much speculation and not enough investment; too much complexity and not enough simplicity; too much counting and not enough trust; too much salesmanship and not enough stewardship; and so on; even too many 21st-century values and not enough 18th-century values—those values exemplified by the great philosophers of The Age of Reason—men such as Rousseau and Hume and Burke, and Adam Smith, and Tom Paine—who in turn helped shape the minds of our Founding Fathers—especially Washington, Jefferson, Madison, Franklin, and Hamilton. And all of these men in turn stood on the shoulders of earlier giants such as Socrates, Plato, and Aristotle. (Some of them are likely quoted in the halls you walk here each day. Read their words! Think about them! Emulate their wisdom!)

It is the values of these giants of Western Civilization that have inspired me—yes, as you well know, *the dead teach the living**—to speak out on the ethical failings of so many of the leaders of our corporations and our money managers, our regulators and our legislators. What we refer to as Wall Street has become a casino, one in which enormous—but

---

* The translation of the motto on Roxbury Latin's crest, *mortui vivos docent*.

momentary—changes in short-term stock prices are treated as intrinsic reality, rather than ephemeral perception. Think about it. All of today's frenetic trading simply pits one speculator against another, with the only winners being the croupiers—the traders, the brokers, the investment bankers, and the money managers who facilitate those trades. If that undeniable reality reminds you of gambling in Las Vegas, or going to the racetrack, or hoping to hit the jackpot in the state lottery, well, you see where I'm coming from.

The stock market casino has become a giant—and costly—distraction to the serious business of investing. Greed, recklessness, and self-interest ride in the saddle of today's capitalism, and it is high time we undertake the necessary reform, with federal laws that demand the return of fiduciary duty and stewardship to their traditional role in the trusteeship of other people's money. That is my dream. But in this case, I confess, I've failed Kipling, for that dream may indeed have become my master. (I don't apologize for that! After all, almost every rule has its exceptions.)

But while the crisis was created largely by Wall Street, it is Main Street that is paying the price. And I'm sure that many of you students have a father or a mother who has been stung by the stock market crash or by the severe recession we are enduring. It won't be easy, but I hope that they have the strength, after Kipling, to "force their heart and nerve and sinew to serve their turn," and "hold on" until the crisis at last abates and our country again moves forward—*which we will.* And when in your own lives you "watch the things you gave your life to, broken"—which will surely happen to some of you and your families—remember to "stoop and build 'em up with worn-out tools."

Wrapping Up

Let me conclude with a final lesson for you, expressed in the last few lines of Kipling's poem. Recall them with me:

> If you can fill the unforgiving minute
> With sixty seconds' worth of distance run,
> Yours is the Earth and everything that's in it,
> And—which is more—you'll be a Man, my son!

Today, the Earth, as it were, needs leaders with the insight and wisdom that you have the opportunity to develop right here at your extraordinary school, and with determination and virtue that, perhaps without your even realizing it, you are already beginning to develop at Roxbury Latin as you grow to maturity. You *can* help—you *must* help—to make our world a better place. So do your best, every day, to develop the will that says to you, "Hold on." Hold onto your values, and live a full and active life. And do what's right for your family, your school, your community, your nation.

Although none of you is my son—and only one of you is even my grandson—let me pretend for a moment that you are all my sons. So it is that I close by taking the liberty to urge each of you to live your own life, and to give it your best shot over those many exciting decades that lie before you. Run your own distance, at your own pace, with your own values, with your own brains and your own character. *Trust yourself.* Trust yourself, and be worthy of the trust of others. Live a life of honor. Then, I assure you, young gentlemen of Roxbury Latin, that "yours will be the Earth, and everything that's in it," and, which is more, you'll all be men, my sons.

Chapter 30

The Fifth "Never"*

T here is a wonderful story—which is, I fear, apocryphal†—that sets the stage for my remarks this morning to Trinity's great Class of 2010, your proud college's 184th graduation. It is the story of a visit to Harrow School during the early 1960s by Sir Winston Churchill, that lion of the British Empire, returning to the scene of his graduation in 1893.

As the story goes, Churchill was well into his eighties—frail, wizened, and bent over—when he returned to Harrow for the opening of school, a formal affair with the students and their teachers in white tie. At the conclusion of the dinner, Churchill was asked if he'd say a few words. He rose, paused, and then spoke. "Never give up. Never. Never. Never. Never. Never." Then he sat down, to thunderous applause.

That is the simple message I deliver to you today as you enter the tough real world that recent generations have given you: *Never give up.*

---

*Based on a commencement address delivered at Trinity College on May 23, 2010.
†Churchill's biographers cite a 1941 speech at Harrow entitled "Never Give In." Whether he returned 20 years later, as the legend goes, has never been confirmed. But it's a wonderful story anyway.

I've especially loved the fifth "never" in that sequence, not because of the number itself, but because that fifth "never" is a wonderful metaphor for the numerous times in the lives of so many of us when, faced with defeat, we have had to draw on our deepest resources to fight back and defend our lives, our careers, our principles, our honor, and our character.

Churchill's entire life was a battle, and his "nevers" surely must total in the scores. He fought in India, in the Sudan, and in the Boer War, where he was captured and then escaped. He was ousted as Lord of the Admiralty after the disastrous Gallipoli campaign in World War I. In and out of Parliamentary office for decades, he became Prime Minister in 1940. His determination, spirit, and never-say-die leadership rallied Britain in World War II, finally leading the Allies to victory in 1945. Rejected by the voters later that year, he never gave up, returning as Prime Minister in 1951, and writing the six-volume *The Second World War*, and the four-volume *History of the English-Speaking Peoples*.

In 1953, he won the Nobel Prize in Literature. Surely Winston Churchill was the paradigm of his words at Harrow. This great man never gave up.

American history, too, is studded with heroes who spent their lives overcoming defeat and adversity. Think about my favorite Founding Father, Alexander Hamilton, born in Nevis in the West Indies and described by John Adams as "the bastard brat of a Scottish peddler." But he rose to become George Washington's right-hand man; a hero in our final victory of the Revolutionary War at Yorktown; and our first Secretary of the Treasury. Alas for our country, Hamilton died at the age of 49, slain by Aaron Burr in a duel. But while he did not survive to fight again, most of his remarkable ideas have survived. The man may be gone, but his ideas have endured for the ages.

Hartford's local hero—and justly so!—Mark Twain also faced frequent reversals. But he, too, never gave up. His younger brother was killed in an explosion on Twain's steamboat, and the early deaths of his wife and two of his three daughters left him devastated. He squandered the earnings from his books on inventions that failed, and his ventures in publishing also came to naught, even though his publication of the memoirs of General Ulysses S. Grant (talk about a man who never gave up!) was a critical and commercial success. But despite these personal and professional setbacks, Mark Twain kept his sense of humor, kept on writing, and, yes, never gave up.

Like those giants of history, even those of us with far more humble accomplishments have confronted adversity and defeat and never gave up. What accounts for that spirit? I think that in my case it began with my beloved mother reading to her little boys—over and over again—*The Little Engine that Could*: "I think I can [get over that mountain]; I think I can; I think I can." And then, "I knew I could; I knew I could; I knew I could." That spirit gave me strength during my early academic struggles—perhaps some of you can relate to them—at Blair Academy (a 40 on my first Algebra exam) and then at Princeton University, when an early D in Economics threatened my scholarship and thus my continuing there. But I never gave up, earned ever better grades, and graduated with distinction.

That same spirit bolstered my ability to face a lifetime of health challenges. When doctors told this then-31-year-old man, suffering from congenital heart failure, that he was unlikely to reach his 40th birthday, there was little choice but to fight on. Despite another seven or eight heart attacks, I fought my way through the four decades that followed. (Take that, you predictors of my early demise!) But by then, half of my heart had stopped pumping. The only hope was a heart transplant.

After waiting 128 days in the hospital, suffused with life-sustaining intravenous drugs, the strong spirit and the frail body never gave up, and the new heart arrived on February 21, 1996. Such a second chance in life is something of a miracle, though the past few years have presented their own health challenges. (After all, I'm now almost as old as Churchill was when he delivered that powerful peroration at Harrow.) But my reaction is simple: If you've been given 14 additional years of life, it doesn't seem to be a good idea to go around bitching. (Forgive me, please for my crude choice of words, but "complaining" simply doesn't do the job!)

During all those decades of health challenges, I faced major challenges in my career. It's no fun to be fired—some of you, I'm sorry to say, will also have to learn that—but that's exactly what happened to me in January 1974, eight years after I made a foolish—even stupid—decision to merge the firm I then headed. Corporate power politics, alas, trumped common sense; the merger blew up, and I found myself out of work. But—as you may now suspect—I wasn't the giving-up type. By September 1974, I'd started a new firm, named it Vanguard, and went back to work. I tell people that I took on my new job just the way I left my old one—*fired with enthusiasm.* (Think about that one!)

Most of the ideas and values that I invested in Vanguard were themselves greeted with skepticism, opprobrium, and even antagonism. But the "never give up" attitude carried the day. Our unique mutual structure, in which we operate our funds at cost, is now saving our investor/owners billions of dollars each year. We created the world's first index mutual fund (simply holding all of the stocks in the Standard & Poor's 500 Stock Index); pioneered the marketing of funds directly to investors (eliminating those hefty 8% sales commissions); and designed revolutionary new investment strategies for bond fund management and for tax-efficient investing.

Like all radical new ideas, these concepts endured the usual responses: First, "It'll never work." Second, "Yes, it works, but it's all luck, and it won't meet the test of time." And third, "Of course it works; I always knew it would." But together, these ideas have, for better or worse, enabled our firm to become the largest mutual fund manager in the world. So yes, even the most ordinary souls among us, favored by extraordinary circumstances and powerful determination, can help to build a better world. But only if we refuse to give up.

What does all this mean to you men and women of Trinity College Class of 2010? First of all, I have little doubt that just about every one of you have already faced defeat during your young lives and haven't given up, storing up character for the years ahead. In the world you are about to enter, beyond these cloistered walls of The Long Walk, the challenges will likely be far larger. Our economy has yet to return to its previous strength; unemployment remains at a record high for the modern era, and finding jobs is tough (you doubtless know that!); the underpinning of our global financial system is fragile, encumbered by grotesquely excessive debt. Our nation's political process is deeply flawed, with lobbyists paying the piper and too often calling the tune.

In our financial markets, the folly of short-term speculation has gained ascendance over the wisdom of long-term investment. (Why can't we heed Mark Twain's warning? "There are two times when you shouldn't speculate. When you can afford to, and when you can't.") So I continue to fight for financial reform, to channel the rewards of investing to those Main Street shareholders who put up their capital, rather than those Wall Street money changers who, more often than not, greedily gobble up enormous rewards, by fair means or, as is now clear, foul. So I continue the battle to build a better financial system, even in these late years of my long life.

Your careers, your challenges, and your battles will inevitably be different from those I've faced, but I know you'll measure up. Your generation is our nation's hope for years to come. There is much work to be done, and you have the great opportunity to fix what has been so badly broken in our society. Whatever path you pursue, you have a duty to help build a better world. But no matter what you decide—and wherever time and tide may take you—be sure to be a good citizen, and raise good citizens to follow in your footsteps. And when reverses come, as they surely will, *Never give up. Never. Never. Never. Never. Never.*

Don't forget that fifth "never." Someday you may need it.

Chapter 31

"When a Man Comes to Himself"[*]

First of all, hearty congratulations to each one of you on graduation from this wonderful school. I imagine that Isaiah Vansant Williamson, the man of Scots heritage who founded your school some 120 years ago, is looking down on you from above on this bright afternoon, quietly reveling as 61 of those whom he called "his boys" are handed the diplomas that recognize that you have stayed the course; you have completed it successfully; you now begin a new course in your life.

You are no longer boys; you have become men. And somewhere along the long road of life that will follow, each of you will "come to yourself," an expression that, sadly, has fallen out of use. That is my theme today, inspired by an essay entitled, "When a Man Comes to Himself," written in 1901 by Woodrow Wilson, shortly before he became president of my own alma mater, Princeton University.[†] In 1912, Wilson would become the 28th president of the United States of America.

---

[*] Based on a commencement address at The Williamson Free School of Mechanical Trades, Media, Pennsylvania, on May 28, 2009.
[†] Woodrow Wilson, *When a Man Comes to Himself* (New York: Harper & Brothers, 1901).

When does a man come to himself? When do you learn who you are? When do you find your place in society? There is no fixed time; we come to ourselves on our own schedule. Some of you may have gotten there already; most of you will get there before too many more years have passed; some all at once, others imperceptibly, by degrees; and, as Wilson knew, "some men never come to themselves at all," perhaps the sadness of never finding one's place in the world, perhaps the tragedy of a life cut short. But given the remarkable skills you have acquired right here on this magnificent campus, the dedicated teachers and mentors who have given of themselves to you, and your inculcation into the Isaiah Williamson Free School philosophy of service to society, I have no doubt that the world you seek will be yours.

Wilson recognized that coming to yourself is not determined by the passage of time, but by the passage of the spirit. Using Wilson's ageless words:

> It is in real truth that common life of mutual helpfulness, stimulation, and contest which gives leave and opportunity to the individual life makes coming to yourself possible, makes it full and complete. . . . In discovering your own place and force, if you seek intelligently and with eyes that see, you find more than ease of spirit and scope for your mind. You find yourself, as if mists had cleared away about you and you know at last your neighborhood among men and tasks.*

Likely it is that Isaiah Williamson came to himself well before he reached manhood, for he was a remarkable youth. According to his biographer, John Wanamaker (yes, the Philadelphia merchant prince), young Isaiah was "an apt, enthusiastic scholar, a boy who did a man's work; never tired, never absent, never idle; a lad of manly ways, of merit, integrity and industry; a lad who threw himself into the whirl of work and life." Wanamaker then goes even further, describing Williamson's "fairness, good temper, Quaker thrift and industry,

---

* Throughout these quotations, I have taken the liberty of substituting "you" and "your" for Wilson's "he" and "his."

modesty, and absolute trustworthiness."* Could there possibly be a better set of standards for a man who has come to himself than those eternal standards exemplified by your legendary founder?

Work . . . Trade . . . Finance

I have always been a huge admirer of the craftsman who works with his hands as well as his mind, the consummate professional who enhances our daily existence by his talents and his skills. You and your peers—those who came through these halls before you and those who shall follow you, those who study and learn their trades—add great value to our society. Indeed, you constitute the very backbone of our nation, and you should be rightfully proud of learning the trades you will soon practice. Those of us in finance are of a rather different status, for it is no longer any secret that our financial sector subtracts value from our society.

How can that be? Of course credit is central to our economy. Liquidity—enabling one person to acquire the stream of future income generated in a business, by using his capital to purchase shares from another person who wishes to withdraw his capital and relinquish his claim—is vital. And the efficient pricing of shares traded in our financial markets is essential to their functioning. But the principal function of the financial sector is to act as the middleman in a trade between a buyer and a seller, a trade that pits one investor against another, a trade that inevitably constitutes a *zero-sum* game (one side wins, the other side loses). But once the costs of the middlemen—the brokers, the bankers, the money managers, all those croupiers of finance—are extracted, speculation in stocks becomes a *loser's* game, a subtractor from social value.

An old English saying puts it well:[†]

> Some men wrest a living from nature and with their hands; this is called work.
> Some men wrest a living from those who wrest a living from nature and with their hands; this is called trade.

---

[*] John Wanamaker, *The Life of Isaiah V. Williamson* (Philadelphia: J. B. Lippincott, 1928).
[†] I've added the phrase "with their hands" to the original quotation, the source of which is unknown.

Some men wrest a living from those who wrest a living from those who wrest a living from nature and with their hands; this is called finance.

So, yes, I confess to you who will actually *do* the world's work, making your living "from the earth and with your hands," that your commencement speaker has earned his own living, not in that kind of real work, but in finance. But I'm embarrassed about the field in which I ply my trade. All too many of its leaders bear a heavy responsibility for running our economy into the ground, even as they made personal fortunes by playing fast and loose with the system and taking absurd risks, not with their own money (of course!) but with other people's money; even successfully lobbying for the rollback of regulations that had well-served investors for decades.

Taking on the System

But I've marched to a different drummer. I've challenged the financial system and done my best to improve it—to build a better world for investors. Vanguard, the company that I founded almost 35 years ago, was built on a firm foundation of service to our investors rather than service to ourselves, in a unique *mutual* mutual fund structure in which our fund shareholders actually *own* the funds' management company. Vanguard operates on an "at-cost" basis, and our structure and fiscal discipline have resulted in cumulative savings to our shareowners of nearly $100 billion so far, subtracting less value from society than any financial firm on the face of the globe. In short, our rise to dominance in the financial field has come simply because we are (1) structurally correct; (2) mathematically correct; and (3) strategically correct.

Our core investment strategy is the index fund—a fund that, at its best, simply owns the entire stock market (or the entire bond market). Operated at rock-bottom cost, this strategy guarantees that our shareholders receive no more and no less than their fair share of whatever long-term returns on investment that our stock and bond markets are generous enough to provide—or, on occasion, mean-spirited enough to take away. The index fund, arguably, is an exercise in the very kind of plain and simple engineering that your own careers will demand.

Think about it. In the 2005 book, *Power, Speed and Form: Engineers and the Making of the Twentieth Century*,* the best engineering is described as embodying "efficiency, economy, and elegance"†—the very kind of ingenious simplicity and effectiveness that characterize the index fund. It is the antithesis of the discredited "financial engineering," the excessive costs, the product complexity, and the rampant speculation that created the global financial crisis that Wall Street has inflicted on Main Street. And it is now arguably the largest mutual fund in the world.‡

Yet the Vanguard model has yet to be copied, and we remain a renegade in our field. We prefer to be noted for our stewardship rather than our salesmanship; for our management rather than our marketing; for our focus on long-term *investment* rather than short-term *speculation*. In this sense we parallel the career of Isaiah Williamson, who made his fortune in trade by his own efforts and straight business dealing, not by speculation.

Labor and Capital

When capital is used for speculation rather than investment, the relationship between capital and labor in our society is distorted. Of course, as Abraham Lincoln reminded us, capital has its rights, worthy of protection; and property is the fruit of labor, a positive good in the world. This philosophy resonated with Theodore Roosevelt, who in 1910 cited Lincoln's words and added:

> [We must] equalize opportunity, destroy privilege, and give to the life and citizenship of every individual the highest value both to himself and the commonwealth . . . the highest service

---

*David P. Billington and David P. Billington Jr. (Oxford University Press, 2005).
† In fact, in my 1951 thesis at Princeton University, I urged that mutual funds be operated "in the most efficient, economical, and honest way possible." If honesty is understood to represent a certain kind of elegance, the ideas are identical.
‡ Assets of our 500 Index funds total $125 billion; assets of our Total Stock Market Index Funds total $95 billion, a combined total of $220 billion.

of which he is capable. . . . We should permit fortunes to be gained only so long as the gaining represents benefit to the community . . . for every dollar received should represent a dollar's worth of service rendered—not gambling in stocks but in service rendered.*

"Not gambling in stocks but in service rendered" is a worthy standard. Yet when I look at our society today, I am appalled by our tendency to overvalue the managers of our financial sector and to undervalue those who are engaged in work and trade. A recent book entitled *The Craftsman*[†] makes the case for the kind of valuable work that you have been trained to do: "[M]*aking is thinking* . . . for the work of the hand can inform the work of the mind . . . learning to work well enables people . . . to govern themselves so as to become good citizens."[‡] You newly minted Williamson graduates must already understand some of these essentials of useful knowledge cited by the author:

How to negotiate between autonomy and authority (as one must in any workshop); how to work not against resistant forces but with them; how to complete their tasks using "minimum force"; and how to meet people and things with sympathetic imagination; and above all how to play.

And so—whether in your machine shop here, or in your masonry shop or your carpentry or paint shops, or your power plant, or even in your garden—you young craftsmen have already learned so much of what is important not only in work, but in life. And as you come to yourself, you will have learned even more.

---

* Theodore Roosevelt, "The New Nationalism," speech delivered in Osawatomie, Kansas, on August 31, 1910.
[†] Richard Sennett, *The Craftsman* (New Haven, CT: Yale University Press, 2008).
[‡] By curious coincidence, the same theme was echoed in an article in the *New York Times Magazine* only five days ago. (Google it!) In "The Case for Working with Your Hands," Matthew B. Crawford makes the point that for the craftsman, "the intrinsic satisfactions of work count—not least in the exercise of your own powers of reason."

When he wrote his essay all those years ago, Woodrow Wilson recognized the special moment that this commencement celebration represents for you graduates:

> To most men, coming to oneself is a slow process of experience, a little at each stage of life. A college man feels the first shock of it at graduation, when the boy's life has been lived out and the man's life begins. You have measured yourself with boys . . . but what the world expects of you, you have yet to find out, and it works, when you discover it, a veritable revolution in your ways of thought and action[;] your training was not for ornament or personal gratification, but to use yourself (for the greater good) and to develop faculties worth using. The man who receives and verifies the perfect secret of right living, the secret of social and of individual well-being, has discovered not only the best and only way to serve the world, but also the one happy way to satisfy himself. Then, indeed, have you come to yourself.

> Surely you have come to yourself only when you have found the best that is in you, and you have satisfied your heart with the highest achievement you are fit for. It is only then that you know of what you are capable and what your heart demands. . . . No thoughtful person ever came to the end of their life, and had time and a little space of calm from which to look back upon it, who did not know and acknowledge that it was what you had done unselfishly and for others, and nothing else, that satisfied you in the retrospect, and made you feel that you had played yourself as a human being.

So as your lives as men begin today, I wish each of you the power, the stamina, the determination, the wisdom, the spirit of sharing and building. And the passion to leave everything you touch better than you found it, the sheer pride in a job well done. And while you're about it, try also to leave every person whose life you touch a better person. Then, you will have come to yourself. *Then you will have come to yourself.* More than that I cannot wish you.

Part Seven

HEROES AND MENTORS

Whatever one is fortunate enough to accomplish during a lifetime, it is never accomplished alone. In this final section of *Don't Count on It!*, I pay special tribute to the myriad mentors who have inspired me, who have helped set my standards and values, and who have helped me along the road of life. In the chapters that follow, I've described four special heroes:

- My greatest mentor, Walter Morgan, who founded Wellington Fund in 1928, hired me in 1951, and entrusted me with the leadership of his company in 1967. (Chapter 32)
- Nobel Laureate in Economics Paul Samuelson, acclaimed as the foremost economist of the 20th century. Our first encounter, as it were, dates back to 1948, and the index mutual fund would become the core of our symbiotic relationship. (Chapter 33)
- Economist Peter Bernstein, investment strategist, prolific author, and one of the intellectual giants of the financial field. (Chapter 34)
- Bernard Lown, MD, the paradigm of the healing physician, creative, innovative, and world-renowned cardiologist. His care carried me through the crucial middle years of my 34-year struggle with heart disease. (Chapter 35)

These men helped me to become a better human being than I might otherwise have become. In each case, they gave me strength to carry on in my career, in my crusade for the index fund, in my lifelong quest to improve my intellect, and in my fragile life itself. But had they not been pillars of personal integrity and seekers of the truths of their

557

callings, they would hardly be standing in my pantheon. (They were all fun to be with, too.) Surely their long and productive lives—ranging from age 89 (and still going strong) to 100—represent some form of poetic justice.

More Heroes

The world in which I have plied my career, sad to say, is not overpopulated with heroes. But there have been enough heroes over my long career to influence my character for the better—men whom I have been privileged to work with and to know.[*] That I have not known most of them as well as Mr. Morgan, Dr. Samuelson, Mr. Bernstein, and Dr. Lown is my loss. While the accomplishments of these heroes came in a wide range of activities, they share a common identity in high character and unimpeachable integrity that I have done my best to emulate.

First Mentors

James P. Harrington (Princeton 1949) and Philip W. Bell (Princeton 1946): Jim was really my first mentor, hiring me as his successor as director of the Athletic Association Ticket Office, where I worked for three years. His integrity, native intelligence, and kindness left marks on me that remain to this day. Dr. Bell guided me through the process of writing my senior thesis, and went on to become a distinguished economist, with a global social consciousness that was extraordinary for its time.

Early Standard-Setters

Joseph E. Welch and Andrew B. Young (respectively president and chief operating officer, and general counsel at Wellington when I joined the firm in 1951): These two mentors trusted me, nurtured me, and educated me in the ways of business and law, inspiring me with their human decency and impeccable integrity. Equally important in my career was Charles D. Root, Jr., who joined the Wellington Fund

---

[*]In Chapter 23 I mentioned many heroes from Vanguard. But when one creates a firm out of thin air, there are, by definition, few mentors to be found there.

Board in 1960 and served as chairman of the fund's independent directors from 1970 until he retired in 1989. He played a critical role in the restructuring that led to Vanguard's creation; indeed, without Chuck Root's leadership, Vanguard might never have come into existence. His rule of conduct: "Never compromise on matters of principle."

Investment Professionals

Warren Buffett and Charlie Munger of Berkshire Hathaway (both of whom kindly endorsed not only many of my ideas but, even better, many of my books): I admire them for their acute investment wisdom, as well as a talent that is extraordinary in the financial field: a nice way with words. I also delight in the friendship, firm and enduring, with heroes such as Windsor Fund's John B. Neff; Paul F. Miller, Jr., and John J. F. Sherrerd, founders of Miller, Anderson, and Sherrerd; Ted Aronson of Aronson + Johnson + Ortiz; and hedge fund managers Steve Galbraith of Maverick Capital and Cliff Asness of AQR Capital Management: These are all men of high integrity, intelligent fundamental investors who added (and often are still adding) luster to their profession.

Wall Street

William H. Donaldson, John C. Whitehead, and Paul A. Volcker: Bill Donaldson, a truly remarkable entrepreneur, is co-founder of the institutional research and brokerage firm Donaldson, Lufkin & Jenrette, and founder of the Yale School of Management; he has served as chairman of Aetna, chairman of the New York Stock Exchange, and chairman of the U.S. Securities and Exchange Commission. (What a list!) John Whitehead, a sailor who landed our infantry at Normandy on D-Day in 1946, spent most of his career at Goldman Sachs, including nearly a decade as co-chairman. In 1984, he began a career in public service that continues to this day—a paragon of quiet leadership. Paul Volcker's experience (including making bold, tough decisions that well-served our nation as head of the Federal Reserve Board, and now serving as economic adviser to President Obama), brilliance, wisdom, and blunt honesty have combined to make him among America's most trusted financial leaders. Based on the ethical business standards and high character they stood for, these three men represent the best of Wall Street leadership. To our nation's detriment, many of the leaders who have followed them would stray far from the high standards that they established.

The Non-Profit World

T. Chandler Hardwick, Joseph M. Torsella, and Richard Stengel: Beyond my investment career, I've tried to serve the community, and reveled in my near-two-decade service as chairman of the trustees of Blair Academy, largely with headmaster Chan Hardwick and his wife Monie. I hired the then–36-year-old Chan in 1989; he is now the second-longest-serving headmaster in Blair's history. I also served for seven demanding and thrilling years as chairman of the National Constitution Center with presidents Joe and Rick. (Both were Rhodes Scholars; Rick is now managing editor of *Time* magazine.) The rebuilding of Blair Academy and the building of the Constitution Center (which opened on July 4, 2003) allowed me to manifest my conviction that we all have an obligation to leave the things that we touch in our lives better than we found them. It's been an extraordinary privilege to work with these three intelligent, committed, and farsighted leaders, whose talents are every bit the equal of—maybe even superior to—those with whom I've been involved in the world of business.

Authors

Three authors whom I've known for decades also stand out as heroes, not only because of their extraordinary writing skills but because of their deeply held values, their intelligence, and their editorial integrity. William Bernstein, neurologist and investment adviser, has written such wide-ranging classics as *The Four Pillars of Investing*, *The Birth of Plenty*, *A Splendid Exchange*, and *The Investor's Manifesto*. Burton Malkiel, professor of Economics at Princeton (and a former Vanguard director) is best known for *A Random Walk Down Wall Street*, first published in 1972 and now in its ninth edition. James Grant, editor of *Grant's Interest Rate Observer*, has applied his wide-ranging and powerful mind, his respect for history, and his exceptionally graceful prose in six fine books, including *Money of the Mind, The Trouble with Prosperity*, and two biographies, *Bernard Baruch* and *John Adams: Party of One*. Along with Peter Bernstein, these writers put my own meager prose in its proper place, even as I aspire to emulate their gifts.

And a Few More . . .

My final group of heroes includes two leaders with whom I served at the Investment Company Institute, and the originator of the "Boglehead" community. Robert L. Augenblick was the president of the ICI when I served as chairman during the early 1970s. He was a brilliant lawyer and a smart tactician with unshakeable integrity, who led the ICI for a decade. Our working relationship was among the best of my career. D. George Sullivan, former president of Fidelity, was chairman when I joined the ICI's board in the early 1960s. He was smart, energetic, warm, and welcoming. He trusted this new, young industry leader-to-be, and gave a great boost to my modest reserve of self-confidence.

I close my list with a true hero in every way: Taylor Larimore, a member of the Greatest Generation who served as a solider in the Battle of the Bulge in World War II. When he retired from private industry years ago, he became the moving force in forming and leading the Bogleheads of the Internet, a group of investors whose goal is to help one another make sound financial decisions. They follow the kinds of fundamental investment ideas and simple human values that I've espoused over the years. I first met Taylor in 1999, and continue to enjoy spending time with him at the annual Bogleheads forums, face-to-face meetings of some 150 investors that have been held since 2001. Taylor is the paradigm of the gentleman-scholar, selflessly helping others with his wisdom, balance, and integrity.

A Charmed Life

We are all born with our own traits and talents, but their development as we come to be ourselves depends heavily on the impact of those whom we meet and who decide to work with us and help us in ways large and small along our journey. John Donne was right: "No man is an island, entire of itself." We live and we learn, and if we are blessed, our support comes from those who can and do foster our intelligence, our wisdom, and our character—the better angels of our nature. As we read in *The Prophet*, "It is when we give of ourselves that we truly give." The 29 heroes listed in this part of the book have truly given of themselves. I have been a major beneficiary of their gifts.

In my first book, *Bogle on Mutual Funds: New Perspectives for the Intelligent Investor*, the very first sentence reads: "If we stand on the shoulders of giants, we may see further than the giants themselves." I hope that this book, likely my last, reflecting ideals and values that have been fortified by the giants who are my heroes, stands in witness to that objective.

I have been infinitely blessed.

Chapter 32

Walter L. Morgan*

New York Times, **September 4, 1998**

W. L. Morgan, Finance Pioneer, Dies at 100

Walter L. Morgan, a pioneer of finance who founded an early mutual fund that sailed through the booms and busts of seven decades, died on Wednesday at Bryn Mawr Hospital in Pennsylvania. He was 100 and lived in Bryn Mawr.

Mr. Morgan headed the Wellington Fund for 42 years until he retired in 1970. The fund, which later became a mainstay of the Vanguard Group, started with $100,000 pooled by a handful of Morgan relatives and Pennsylvania business people, and it grew into one of the nation's biggest mutual funds, with $23 billion in assets and 900,000 shareholders.

As a young accountant in the boom years before the 1929 stock market crash, Mr. Morgan put together an assortment of stocks, bonds and government securities that he thought would be less risky than competing funds that were borrowing money and concentrating on stocks at wildly inflated prices.

---

*Based in part on my eulogy at his memorial service on September 5, 1998.

"There was so much speculation, and stocks were just too high" before the 1929 break in prices, he recalled in an interview. . . . Mr. Morgan's fund, originally called the Industrial and Power Securities Company, sold United States Steel at $258 a share and watched the stock plummet to $24 as the Depression set in, he recalled. He renamed the fund in 1935 for the Duke of Wellington, the 19th-century British general who defeated Napoleon. "Words like 'industrial' and 'power' sort of fell out of favor with investors after the crash," he said. . . .

Rare is the man for whom the Lord acts as a shepherd for a full century on this earth. Walter Morgan was a deeply religious man who loved the Holy Bible, and often commended the 23rd Psalm to those who were troubled or in ill health. At his passing, he lieth down in green pastures, beside the still waters, his soul restored to eternal life.

Walter Morgan used to say to me, "I don't know why the Lord would keep me alive for so many years." To which I would reply, "Because the Lord knows how much I need you to be with me." His spirit sustains me to this day. This grand and gentle man must have been the most active, vigorous man of his age, whatever his age, all through his life. And during the last half of his life—the nearly 50 years (a half-century!) I have known him—he was remarkably wise, sharp of wit and mind, interested in everything around him, reading the papers, following the financial markets, recalling the past, all with a thirst for the details of names, dates, and numbers.

Before he began his business career, he was a proud member of Princeton's Class of 1920, and he became its last surviving member. Princeton was a big part of his long life, and I was proud to be a fellow Princetonian with Walter Morgan as my role model sharing that common heritage and becoming *eternal* Tigers (as, if you'll forgive me, only Princetonians understand.)

Wellington and Vanguard

Surely he was a tiger in business. His ambition and entrepreneurship led him to found Wellington Fund and to become the dean among industry pioneers. Wellington was the precursor of Vanguard—its *sine qua non*—and he is the real hero of the dramatic history that took both firms to eminence—proud, lustrous names that are recognized all across the land. As he got used to the idea of Wellington and Vanguard together, he loved the historical Napoleonic War era association of the Iron Duke and Lord Nelson, permanently linked in word and picture as part of our joint corporate history.

Walter Morgan retired five years before Vanguard began. While he fully supported this new venture, he was saddened that the new structure required a new name. He didn't much care for the name "Vanguard" when he first heard it, and thought that the index fund was a "wild and crazy idea." But his support for the new road less traveled by for the firm he had created in 1928 was unremitting and unequivocal. I did my best to assure that Wellington Fund would survive and prosper, as it has. Our linked service as chairmen of the Fund's Board of Directors from 1948 to 2000 (including my four years as senior chairman), constitutes a 72-year total that may be unmatched in the annals of America's corporations.

Mr. Morgan inculcated in his young protégé many of the principles that governed his enterprise, where I worked for 23 years, principles that remain at the very core of Vanguard's character today:

- Investment balance—stocks and bonds, working together.
- Conservative investing—quality, quality above all.
- Long-term focus—for the goals of our funds, and for the horizons of our shareholders.
- Fair-dealing with clients—particularly by full disclosure and complete candor, and by keeping costs low.
- Equitable and honorable relationships with the human beings within our two primary constituencies—those shareholders (whom we now call *clients*) and employees (whom we now call *crewmembers*).

Given my eternal love and respect for Walter Morgan and my enduring loyalty to him, I dedicated the first edition of my 1999 book—*Common Sense on Mutual Funds: New Imperatives for the Intelligent Investor*—to him. Providentially, I framed a pre-publication cover and the dedication, and presented them to him on his 100th birthday, only months before his long journey ended. Here's what I wrote:

> Dedicated to Walter L. Morgan, founder of Wellington Fund, Dean of the Mutual Fund Industry, fellow Princetonian, mentor, friend. He gave me my first break. He remained loyal through thick and thin. He gives me strength to carry on.

I shall never forget how he inspired me and challenged me to do my best. When I lacked confidence in myself, he exuded confidence in me. In many respects, he was a father to me—demanding, giving, shaping, loving. After his death, I was told that he considered me the son he never had. His high values—especially his unyielding integrity and uncompromising honesty—reinforced my own values, and made me a better person. I, along with so many others, didn't *dare* let him down.

Remembering Who Gave Me My First Break

Four decades ago, a wonderful public service ad, sponsored by United Technologies, appeared in the *Wall Street Journal*. It was entitled "Do You Remember Who Gave You Your First Break?" Here is part of what it said:

> Someone saw something in you once. That's partly why you are what you are today. It could have been a thoughtful parent, a perceptive teacher, a demanding drill sergeant, an appreciative employer. . . . Whoever it was who had the kindness and foresight—two beautiful qualities—to bet on your future. In the next 24 hours, take 10 minutes to write a grateful note to the person who helped you. . . . Matter of fact, take another 10 minutes to give somebody else a break . . .

Well, I did take those recommended 10 minutes to write that grateful note to Walter Morgan. And I hope that I am not exaggerating when I say that his longstanding kindness and trust helped me to initiate—in a time almost infinitely surpassing that second 10 minutes— what I fervently hope has now become a Vanguard tradition: the idea that people should be given a break, should be encouraged, and should be respected. That is the central basis for our philosophy that "even one person can make a difference," embodied in the Awards for Excellence that we have been awarding to Vanguard crewmembers since 1978.

Walter Morgan cared about people. He was a real, honest-to-God, down-to-earth human being. In contrast to so many business executives, he was not full of himself. A humble man, he was not impressed with the trappings of wealth and power. He loved human beings, not for *who* they were, but for *what* they were. An exceptionally generous man, he reveled in sharing his blessings with others.

I could not begin to do justice to all of Walter Morgan's fine qualities—intelligence, grace, integrity, ambition, generosity, competitive spirit, breadth of vision, range of interests—the list is too long. But, for me, a special quality stands out: his interest in young people, his confidence in their abilities, his willingness to cede to them substantial responsibility if he thought they could handle it ("pile it on them" might be more accurate). He was unsurpassed as my mentor, and it is fair to say that his decision to hire me made a difference, for the better I hope, in the future development of the Wellington organization, and in the founding and creation of Vanguard.

Time, like an ever-rolling stream, has now borne another of her sons away. But he does not fly forgotten, as a dream, dying at the opening day. Walter Morgan lives on, in our hearts and our minds and our souls, not only for those fortunate enough to be close to him, but also for those many others who knew him solely by the glory of his deeds, the strength of his reputation, the high character of his honorable life. As the Psalmist assured us over all those years—and reassures those of us who must carry on in his absence—he will dwell in the house of the Lord forever.

Chapter 33

Paul A. Samuelson

New York Times, **December 14, 2009**

Paul A. Samuelson, Economist, Dies at 94

Paul A. Samuelson, the first American Nobel Laureate in economics and the foremost academic economist of the 20th century, died Sunday at his home in Belmont, Mass. He was 94.

His death was announced by the Massachusetts Institute of Technology, which Mr. Samuelson helped build into one of the world's great centers of graduate education in economics.

In receiving the Nobel Prize in 1970, Mr. Samuelson was credited with transforming his discipline from one that ruminates about economic issues to one that solves problems, answering questions about cause and effect with mathematical rigor and clarity. . . .

Mr. Samuelson wrote one of the most widely used college textbooks in the history of American education. The book, *Economics,* first published in 1948, was the nation's best-selling textbook for nearly 30 years. Translated into 20 languages, it was selling 50,000 copies a year a half century after

it first appeared. "I don't care who writes a nation's laws—
or crafts its advanced treatises—if I can write its economics
textbooks," Mr. Samuelson said. . . .

My first encounter, as it were, with Paul Samuelson came in
September 1948. At the beginning of my sophomore year at Princeton
University, I took my first course in economics; our textbook was the
first edition of Dr. Samuelson's *Economics: An Introductory Analysis*. (My
marked-up copy still graces the shelves of my library.) Truth told, I
found the book tough going, and fared poorly in my first stab at this
new (to me) subject. I received a grade of 4+ (D+ in today's lexicon)
at midterm. Since I was required to maintain an average of at least 3−
(C−) to maintain the full scholarship that Princeton had provided me,
if I did not improve by the end of the semester, my college career
would be over.

I struggled, but I made the grade I needed by semester's end,
gaining the coveted (but marginal to a fault) 3. My grades continued
to improve, and—thanks largely to the 1+ that I earned on my
senior thesis on the mutual fund industry—"The Economic Role
of the Investment Company" (a long way from the macroeconomics of Dr. Samuelson's book!)—I graduated *magna cum laude* in
Economics.

Priceless Endorsements

From its lowly beginning in 1948, my association with Paul Samuelson
had a wonderful turnaround. Some 45 years later, in 1993, I asked
him to endorse my first book—*Bogle on Mutual Funds*. He demurred,
but to my utter astonishment he told me that he would prefer to write
the foreword. Some excerpts:

> The same surgeon general who required cigarette packages to
> say: "Warning, this product may be dangerous to your health"
> ought to require that 99 out of 100 books written on per-
> sonal finance carry that same label. The exceptions are rare.
> Benjamin Graham's *The Intelligent Investor* is one. Now it is high

praise when I endorse *Bogle on Mutual Funds* as another. . . .
I have no association with The Vanguard Group of funds other
than as a charter member investor, along with numerous children and innumerable grandchildren. So, as a disinterested
witness in the court of opinion, perhaps my seconding his
suggestions will carry some weight. John Bogle has changed
a basic industry in the optimal direction. Of very few can this
be said.

Five years after that—a half-century after our initial encounter—
he wrote a wonderful endorsement of the first edition of *Common
Sense on Mutual Funds: New Imperatives for the Intelligent Investor,* and a
decade later offered this lovely endorsement in its 10th anniversary edition published late in 2009, shortly before his long journey through
life came to an end: "The only thing better than Bogle's original book
is its improved revision. Bon appetit!"

But I've gotten way ahead of myself. Paul Samuelson and I finally
met in the mid-1980s in his office on the MIT campus in Cambridge,
Massachusetts, a meeting inspired by the common cause we came to
share: the need for an "index fund" that would own stocks of the
largest 500 corporations in America, providing the broadest possible
diversification, paying no investment advisory fees, with virtually no
portfolio turnover, adding great cost efficiency and remarkable tax
efficiency.

While I had hinted at the merit of an index fund in my Princeton
thesis (mutual funds "can make no claim to superiority over the market averages"), I ignored that important finding for years. But in mid-
1975, I decided that the time was ripe for the world's first index fund,
importantly because of Paul Samuelson's inspiration.

Challenge to Judgment

Then inspiration came when I read "Challenge to Judgment," his lead
essay in the inaugural edition of the *Journal of Portfolio Management* (Fall
1974). In his essay, he pleaded "that, at the least, some large foundation set up an in-house portfolio that tracks the S&P 500 Index—if

only for the purpose of setting up a naïve model against which their in-house gunslingers can measure their prowess. . . . The American Economic Association might contemplate setting up for its members a no-load, no-management-fee, virtually no-transaction-turnover fund," noting, however, the perhaps insurmountable difficulty that "there may be less supernumerary wealth to be found among 20,000 economists than among 20,000 chiropractors."

Paul Samuelson concluded his "challenge to judgment" by explicitly calling for those who disagreed that a passive index would outperform most active managers to dispose of "that uncomfortable brute fact"—that it is virtually impossible for academics with access to public records to identify any consistently excellent performers—"in the only way that any fact is disposed of—by producing brute evidence to the contrary." There is no record that anyone tried to produce such brute evidence, nor is it likely that it could have been produced. But Paul Samuelson had laid down an express challenge for *somebody, somewhere* to start an index fund.

Confronted with that demand, I couldn't stand back any longer. It now seemed clear that the newly formed Vanguard Group (then only a few months old) ought to be "in the vanguard" of this new logical concept, so strongly supported by data on past fund performance, so well known in academia but acknowledged by few in the industry. It was the opportunity of a lifetime: to at once prove that the basic principles enunciated in the JPM article could be put into practice and work effectively, and to mark this upstart of a firm as a pioneer in a new wave of industry development. With luck and hard work, the idea that had begun to germinate in my mind in my ancient senior thesis could finally become a reality.

The *Newsweek* Column

The initial press reception to the underwriting had been reasonably good, but bereft of a single hint that the index fund represented the beginning of a new era for the mutual fund industry. The most enthusiastic comments came from Professor Samuelson himself. Writing in his *Newsweek* column in August 1976, he expressed delight that there had finally been a response to his earlier challenge: "As yet there exists no convenient fund that apes the whole market, requires no load, and keeps commissions, turnover and management fees to the feasible minimum."

Now such a fund lay in prospect. "Sooner than I dared expect," he wrote, "my explicit prayer has been answered. There is coming to market, I see from a crisp new prospectus, something called the First Index Investment Trust" (the original name of what is now Vanguard 500 Index Fund). He conceded that the fund met only five of his six requirements: (1) availability for investors of modest means; (2) proposing to match the broad-based S&P 500 index; (3) carrying an extremely small annual expense charge of only 0.20 percent; (4) offering extremely low portfolio turnover; and (5) "best of all, giving the broadest diversification needed to maximize mean return with minimum portfolio variance and volatility." His sixth requirement—that it be a no-load fund—had not been met but, he graciously conceded, "a professor's prayers are rarely answered in full."

As it was to happen, Dr. Samuelson's prayer would be answered in full within six months. Until then, given our obvious need to enlist broker support for an underwriting, the Trust carried an initial sales charge (low by mutual fund standards in those days—6 percent on smaller investments, tapered down to 1 percent on investments of $1 million or more). However, Vanguard was soon to change its distribution strategy. In February 1977, the Vanguard funds eliminated all sales charges and made an unprecedented conversion to a "no-load" distribution system.

Mutual Admiration

Paul Samuelson and I met face-to-face only perhaps a half-dozen times during our (arguably) 61-year relationship, but he often sent me notes, and must have made at least a score of telephone calls to me in my office. When he called, I'd quickly grab a yellow legal pad and pen, for I knew he'd be giving me a range of rapid-fire ideas to improve that first index mutual fund, in ways large and small. At first I was intimidated (of course!), but as time went on I appreciated not only his brilliance, but his warmth, his friendly sense of humor,* and his patience with a mind far smaller than his own.

---

*Taking on the fallacy that maximizing return is that ultimate goal of investors— we shouldn't ignore risk—he emphasized the simplicity of his point by writing a refutation entirely in words of but one syllable. "No need to say more. I've made my point," *Journal of Banking and Finance*, 3, no. 4 (1979).

One brief handwritten note comes to mind: Late in June 2005 (dated "mid-summer day") he wrote: "Any small influence on you has been more than offset by what Vanguard has done for my 6 children and 15 grandchildren. May Darwin bless you!" Our mutual admiration culminated in the dedication of my 2007 book—*The Little Book of Common Sense Investing: The Only Way to Guarantee Your Fair Share of Stock Market Returns*—to Paul A. Samuelson. The final words: "Now in his 92nd year, he remains my mentor, my inspiration, my shining light."

Surely his highest accolade for my modest accomplishments came in Paul Samuelson's speech at the Boston Security Analysts Society on November 15, 2005: "I rank this Bogle invention along with the invention of the wheel, wine and cheese, the alphabet, and Gutenberg printing: a mutual fund that never made Bogle rich but elevated the long-term returns of the mutual-fund owners. Something new under the sun." Those words from a giant—"the foremost academic economist of the 20th century"—mean much to me, but it is the intellectual challenge, the friendship, and the unfailing support of this fine human being that I shall miss most profoundly.

Chapter 34

Peter L. Bernstein

New York Times, June 8, 2009

Peter L. Bernstein, Explainer of Risks of Stocks, Dies at 90

Peter L. Bernstein, an economic historian and a widely read popularizer of the efficient market theory, which changed trading behavior on Wall Street, died Friday at New York–Presbyterian / Weill Cornell hospital. He was 90 and lived in Manhattan. . . .

Mr. Bernstein published most of his best-known books in the last 20 years of his life, including the best-selling *Against the Gods: The Remarkable Story of Risk* (John Wiley & Sons) in 1996 and *Capital Ideas: The Improbable Origins of Modern Wall Street* (Free Press) in 1991.

In these books and in earlier work, he embraced and explained an investment strategy that came to be known as efficient market theory. Rather than just picking stocks because they seemed to be good bets, investors increasingly diversified their portfolios, using sophisticated mathematical equations, developed in academia, with the goal of measuring and managing risk. . . .

Mr. Bernstein was the founder, in 1973, of Peter L. Bernstein Inc., which published his newsletter and also had as clients wealthy families and foundations, helping them manage their wealth. A year later, he founded the *Journal of Portfolio Management*, a scholarly journal that brought traders and academics into communication with each other as they developed efficient market theory. . . .

[Peter Bernstein graduated] from Harvard magna cum laude, and . . . spent World War II as an officer in the Office of Strategic Services, the C.I.A.'s predecessor, in London. . . .

The financial sector of our American society is hardly overpopulated with Renaissance men—human beings of great intellect, prodigious works, wide-ranging vision, scholarly wisdom, multidisciplinary focus, entrepreneurial spirit, and a commitment to raising our standards of professional conduct. With the death of Peter Bernstein, that microscopic portion of the financial field has been measurably diminished. While I see few today in a position to replace him, I hope and pray we shall see his like again.

That I've been reading his regular "Economics and Portfolio Strategy" essays for as long as I can remember may not be surprising—I'm often told that my reading list is ridiculously long (and I'd be hard-pressed to disagree). But of all of the publications I read, his is the *only* one of which I've saved every copy. I've also read—and have in my library—all of his books, including *Capital Ideas, The Power of Gold, Against the Gods, Wedding of the Waters*, and all the rest, a remarkable output in and of itself, even more remarkable in the range of its subject matter (the Erie Canal, for heaven's sake!). It is hard to imagine the volume of research he must have invested in each one of his books.

Replete though the record of his works may be, the man behind all of those words was a warm, witty, and wise human being. I've known Peter for some three decades, worked with him at industry events, discussed with him the issues of the day, and even had the temerity to challenge his thinking and debate these issues with him.

Nonetheless, when in 2003 he declared that "Policy Portfolios Are Obsolete"—favoring instead a policy of short-term opportunism using many unconventional asset classes—I fear that my elbows may have been a bit sharp, and I fired back. In a speech before The Investment Analysts of Chicago, I described his new position as "wide of the mark, even ill-begotten," words that may have overstated my convictions in this field where uncertainty is the watchword.

Peter handled my criticism with equanimity and respect, but his kind response did little to ease my feelings of guilt (not about my convictions themselves, but about how I expressed them). So I offered a peace-pipe of sorts and sported Peter and Barbara, his wonderful wife and omnipresent partner, to a delightful luncheon. (He chose the tony Hotel Pierre. I winced when the check arrived, but felt good about paying the bill!) When we parted company, we were better friends than ever.

Generous Grace

But for me, the substance of Peter was much more than his incredible range of accomplishments. The descriptive phrase that best describes him is *generous grace*. How many writers of essays, and studies, and papers, and books in our profession did Peter inspire with his endorsements, his compliments, his encouragement—and even his use of a keen editorial pen? Scores of us were the beneficiaries of his comments, public and private, and I was surely among the most favored. As author and journalist James Grant (*Grant's Interest Rate Observer*) wrote, "Bernstein's books were remarkable achievements. Better still, to their recipients, were the notes of friendship, encouragement and praise that he dashed off whenever his generous spirit moved him. He must have written a million of them."*

When I wrote my first book (*Bogle on Mutual Funds*) in 1993, Peter's back-cover endorsement read, "This book sets the standard for all how-to-invest books . . . even over Benjamin Graham's *The Intelligent Investor*." (Peter, bless his soul, was not above hyperbole!) And in endorsing my 2008 book, *Enough*, he created his own new title, *Never Enough of Jack Bogle*. (Ditto on the hyperbole.)

---

*James Grant, "Life Begins at 65," *Grant's Interest Rate Observer*, June 12, 2009.

But it was more than a generous and encouraging sprit that Peter offered in his accolades. He also offered a remarkable perspective, seeing things that others (including we authors ourselves) may have missed. These excerpts from his foreword to my *Common Sense on Mutual Funds* (1999) set the stage for a profound insight into the growing structural problems that would be faced by the mutual fund industry.

> Why this book is unique: Jack Bogle has written a book on investing unlike any investment book that I have ever encountered, because he discusses sensitive matters that other authors ignore. I hesitate to speculate on why these topics receive such short shrift elsewhere, but I suspect that other experts have horizons that are more limited than Bogle's, or they have less concern for their readers' best interests. . . .

> Despite all the high-minded talk we hear from the corporate spinmasters, conflict of interest between seller and buyer is inherent in our economic system. Jack Bogle's goal was to build a business whose primary objective was to make money for his customers by minimizing the elements of that conflict of interest. . . . That has been no easy task. The complexity of the job that Bogle set out for himself, however, has enabled him to look at the competition with a very special kind of eye. One of the loud and clear messages in this book is that he is less than pleased with what that eye sees.

> We must look at the investment management industry (yes, it is an industry even more than it is a profession) as a business and within the framework of the economic system as a whole. . . . Bogle's skill in dispensing uncommon wisdom about how to invest and how to understand the capital markets would be reason enough to read these pages. But the big message in this book is that *what happens to the wealth of individual investors cannot be separated from the structure of the industry that manages those assets.*

On the Shoulders of a Giant

We *all* need strength to carry on. Peter Bernstein's generous grace gave those of us who write and think about investing the strength not only to keep going, but to keep going in the direction of truth and reason. That is, for me, his greatest legacy, even greater than his own preeminent intellectual standing and his prodigious outpouring of words and ideas, all impeccably organized and articulated with precision. (He would have it no other way.)

When we stand on the shoulders of Peter Bernstein, as do many of us in the world of finance—practitioners, academics, essayists, authors—we stand on the shoulders of a true investment giant of our era. While those shoulders are no longer there for us in physical form, they remain in spiritual form, ever available to support us, and to provide perspective, wisdom, and inspiration for generations yet to come.

Chapter 35

Bernard Lown, MD

New York Times, **October 12, 1985**

Nobel Peace Prize Given to Doctors Opposed to War

The 1985 Nobel Peace Prize was awarded today to the International Physicians for the Prevention of Nuclear War, a five-year-old Boston-based group that was jointly founded by American and Soviet doctors.

The physicians group has a membership of 135,000 people in 41 countries. . . . After learning of the award today, Dr. Bernard Lown, the American co-founder of the group, immediately urged President Reagan to stop all nuclear testing. . . . Its [other] co-founder, Dr. Yevgeny I. Chazov, has been the personal physician of the top Soviet leadership. . . .

The Norwegian Nobel Committee, in announcing the choice of the physicians group, said it had "performed a considerable service to mankind by spreading authoritative information and by creating an awareness of the catastrophic consequences of atomic warfare. . . ."

Dr. Lown, 64 years old, is considered a pioneer in research on sudden cardiac death. He is a professor of cardiology at the

Harvard University School of Public Health and a physician at Brigham and Women's Hospital in Boston. He invented the defibrillator, which shocks a damaged heart into beating regularly again. . . . "He's brilliant, mercurial and indefatigable," said cardiologist Sidney Alexander. "The man has an incredible amount of energy and a keen intellect. . . ."

Bernard Lown is surely among the most unforgettable characters whose paths have crossed with mine during my long life. He is truly a man who has made a difference to our planet. In his inspiring 2008 book, *Prescription for Survival*, Bernard cites one of my favorite passages from Shakespeare's *Henry IV, Part I*. There Glendower boasts, "I can summon spirits from the vasty deep." To which Hotspur replies, "Why so can I, or so can any man. But when you summon them, will they come?"

Through Hotspur, the Bard is making the point that while many of us have the audacity to summon the spirits, precious few of us have the power to make them come. Bernard Lown, of course, is among that precious few. He has summoned the spirits of the world—let's call them the public opinion of the citizens of the globe—to take arms against nuclear madness, and the spirits came. And Bernard Lown, as much as any human being, has made our world a little better.

My relationship with this remarkable cardiologist was focused less on his *macro*-accomplishments in the name of mankind than on his *micro*-accomplishments: summoning the spirits of his patients and making them come. By dint of his powerful character and brilliant mind, Dr. Lown has lengthened and enriched the lives of countless patients—thousands of human beings hungry for care, seeking solutions to their complex heart malfunctions, searching not only for reassurance, but for a chance to live full, productive, satisfying, contributing lives.

While I'm but one of Dr. Lown's grateful patients, I can surely speak with authority, for I owe my life to him. Following the first manifestation of my heart disease in 1960, I was struck with a long and ever more serious series of ventricular arrhythmias of unknown origin. In 1967, searching for answers, I was sent to the Cleveland Clinic.

A new invention called the pacemaker, I was told, would solve my ills, and so this rather large box was duly implanted in my chest. Happily, I survived the operation—but only barely. Worse, the presence of several titanium bolts in my heart muscle seemed to encourage rather than rebuff the ventricular attacks. Determined to find help, I asked several local physicians to help me seek out the nation's leading cardiologist.

Enter Superman

Voilà! Enter Superman, albeit not the caped crusader of the comics. Rather, the white-coated master of medicine, an overpowering *human being*. I still marvel at Dr. Lown's earliest visits, interns and fellows in tow, to my room at the old Brigham Hospital in Boston. The warm hands on the torso, the command for deep breaths, the tapping on the chest, the touch of the stethoscope, the probing eyes, the compassionate visage, the soft but firm voice, the confident words. But most of all, this knowledge certain: When Dr. Lown sat at my bedside, there was not a single thought in his mind beyond me, my heart, and my well-being. If there is any single message about surviving a life-threatening illness, it is this: *Find a physician to whom you can completely entrust your heart and soul.*

Recently Dr. Lown described my history: "When we first met, John was afflicted with a bizarre electrical derangement of the heartbeat, threatening catastrophic cardiac arrest—a guillotine about to drop. I gave him the brutal verdict and he was undaunted. He lived his life intently and with exuberant energy. A sense of humor lightened the morbid reality, and he joked that playing squash with a portable defibrillator close by unnerved every opponent." Without Bernard Lown's encouragement that I get on with my life, I can't imagine that I could have stayed the arduous course.

His care and compassion kept me going, but the inevitable downward spiral of my heart disease continued. Cardiac arrests and paddles on my chest. Physical activity fades away. The right side of the heart no longer pumps. Death's shadow draws near. That's *good* news!

At last I was eligible for a heart transplant! I received my new heart on February 21, 1996. Fourteen years later, my new heart still thumps away, minute after minute, like the beat of a jungle drum. Providence has given me something offered to an infinitely small number of human beings—*a second chance at life*. So it is a privilege to remain here on earth to honor Bernard Lown, to thank him, and to reaffirm his high values, values that I have tried to bring to my own profession.

Medicine and Finance

What values, you must wonder, could the field of medicine have in common with the field of finance? At their best, both involve the sanctity of the relationship between the professional and the client. Dr. Lown dispenses care to the patient's body and soul; I attend to the client's financial well-being. And we're both concerned with the deterioration of ethics in our professions. In *Common Sense on Mutual Funds* I use the context of his words about his life's work to discuss mine.

> Medicine (read, the stewardship of financial assets) is a calling—at its core, a moral enterprise grounded in a covenant of trust between the doctor and the patient (read, the fiduciary and the client), in which the primary mission is to promote the patient's (client's) well-being. Central to this relationship is the expectation that the doctor (the fiduciary) will put the needs of the patient (the client) first, over and above the interests of any third party.

Dr. Lown found common cause with my career: "I have long believed that in all worthy activity, one finds a moral core," and generously credits me with "teasing out the central ethical kernel in the accumulation of wealth. Blessed with a new heart John Bogle can continue to teach enduring lessons about courage, dignity, and the meaning of integrity." Those are the very lessons that Bernard Lown has exemplified for me. How, indeed, could I dare to face my dear and respected physician without striving to live up to his lofty standards, applied to my own life's work?

A Magnificent Writer

In addition to his remarkable talents as a humanitarian, a cardiologist, a researcher, an inventor, and a healing physician, Dr. Lown, now 89, is a truly magnificent writer. Perhaps a young man who immigrated to the United States from Lithuania at age 13 had a special gift for the prolific and artful pen, or perhaps starting a few steps behind his American-born peers demanded a special excellence. Three of his books have been published, to wide acclaim: *The Lost Art of Healing* (1966), *Practicing the Art While Mastering the Science* (1995), and *Prescription for Survival* (2008).

The letters he has written to me over the years reflect the— almost—lost art of correspondence (especially in these days when the uncapitalized, unpunctuated slang of e-mail and instant messaging dominates written interactions). His gifts as a writer—and his reflections on our wonderful relationship of more than a half-century's duration—are well summarized in these words about his career:

> In my 50 year romance with patients, I learned much of what I know from them. Few embody more fully what we attempted than John Bogle. We first met more than 40 years ago, when John's days were tenuous and numbered. Early on I realized that he was not a sprinter, but a long distance runner. His continued firm hold on life derived from an unflappable belief that every day lived is a victory to be celebrated. Over all these decades serious illness never constrained his indomitable will, nor diminished his exuberant energy, nor sapped his sharply targeted creativity. My medical objective was to nurture hope by stretching his optimistic mind to the limits of his abundant imagination. . . . In all my years of clinical practice, I have not encountered a person like John Bogle who projected a Marcus Aurelius–like stoicism, and captured the essential of our brief lives, namely the urgency to live without fear and embrace with wonder and affirmation every heartbeat.*

---

*From personal correspondence between Lown and Bogle.

I close this tribute with a daring leap from Shakespeare to the Beatles, paraphrasing the words of my favorite Beatles' song. If you'll think "Ber-nard" rather than "Hey, Jude," you'll get the picture. With a little imagination for the music of that familiar chorus, away we go:

> Ber-nard, you've made it good
> You took a sad song and made it better
> You remembered to let the world get under your skin
> Then you began . . . to make it better.
> Better, better, better, better, better, *oh*
> *Na, na na na na na na*
> *Na na na na*, Ber-nard

And again:

> Then you began . . . to make it better.
> Better, better, better, better, better, *oh*
> *Na, na na na na na na*
> *Na na na na*, Ber-nard.

Speaking for the world, for his patients, and for myself, Bernard Lown made things better for us all.

Index